THE ORDER OF CANADA

Its Origins, History, and Development

THE ORDER OF CANADA

Its Origins, History, and Development

Christopher McCreery

Desiderantes Meliorem Patriam

UNIVERSITY OF TORONTO PRESS
Toronto Buffalo London

© University of Toronto Press Incorporated 2005
Toronto Buffalo London
Printed in Canada

ISBN 0-8020-3940-5

Printed on acid-free paper

Library and Archives Canada Cataloguing in Publication

McCreery, Christopher
    The Order of Canada : its origins, history, and
development / Christopher McCreery.

    Includes bibliographical references and index.
    ISBN 0-8020-3940-5

    1. Order of Canada – History.   2. Decorations of honor – Canada –
History.   I. Title.

    CR6257.M323 2005   929.8'171   C2005-900955-1

This book was published with the help of a grant from the Jackman Foundation.

University of Toronto Press acknowledges the financial assistance to its publishing program of the Canada Council for the Arts and the Ontario Arts Council.

University of Toronto Press acknowledges the financial support for its publishing activities of the Government of Canada through the Book Publishing Industry Development Program (BPIDP).

This book has been published with the help of a grant from the Canadian Federation for the Humanities and Social Sciences, through the Aid to Scholarly Publications Programme, using funds provided by the Social Sciences and Humanities Research Council of Canada.

To my parents Paul and Sharon

The subject of honours is hydra headed. It should be kept submerged ...
and hopefully in that way it will be gotten rid of.

J.W. Pickersgill, 30 September 1950

Contents

Illustrations follow page 172

BUCKINGHAM PALACE

In 1943 my father, King George VI, established the Canada
Medal which, although never bestowed, in many ways served as
the first step towards the creation of the Order of Canada.

Since the Centennial Year in 1967, many distinguished
Canadians have been appointed to the Order, reflecting a wide
range of achievement and representing the rich diversity of the
nation's life.

For nearly forty years, the Order has stood at the centre of the
Canadian honours system, giving due recognition to those who
have excelled on the local, national and international stages.
The stylized snowflake has come to be widely recognized as a
mark of particular distinction and merit.

As Sovereign of the Order of Canada, I am pleased that this
book recounts the history of the Order and portrays the
development of modern Canada through the lives and
attainments of a great many remarkable men and women.

Elizabeth R

Preface

Early in March 1966, there commenced a thirteen-month-long project to create a national institution that is now familiar to Canadians from sea to sea. The spirit that encapsulates the Order of Canada – one of inclusion and democracy – is one that bears the memories of Canada's earlier experience with honours. From early distrust and misunderstanding to the awakening of a national identity, the development of the order has reflected the relationship Canadians have with their country, their government, their culture and their heroes.

The order itself is a product of national identity, politics and history, and it has become imbued with the significance of its recipients' accomplishments. Indeed, the order's history is as fascinating as the more than 4,000 Canadians who have been appointed to it. This book celebrates the spirit behind the order, explaining the provenance of its design (the unique and Canadian snowflake pattern as well as the ribbon) and its various early incarnations. Today, those who are members of the order wear it with pride; those who see it recognize it as a symbol of exemplary service.

This book is the first history of the Order of Canada, and also the first major work on Canadian honours. As such, I have attempted to provide both a history of the order's beginnings and a more general overview of trends in Canadian honours. The Canadians and others who have been involved in developing the Canadian honours system provide personality and intrigue to the debate: from explanations of Mackenzie King's phobia of honours, the oft-misunderstood Nickle Resolution, and R.B. Bennett's use of honours to recognize volunteers and community service, to the active lobbying of Lester Pearson and Vincent Massey, this book pays tribute to the individuals who felt the need for a Canadian system of recognition for its citizens.

Acknowledgments

For me this project began three years ago; but for our country the journey towards a 'Canadian Honour' began, like so many of our national and provincial institutions, with Confederation in that famed year of 1867. At that time Victoria was our Queen and Viscount Monck our Governor General. Monck was keen to build upon the idea of a Canadian nation and proposed the founding of a Canadian honour with the designation 'The Most Exalted Order of St. Lawrence.' Alas, his forward thinking was thwarted by a stuffy and controlling Colonial Office, but the idea for the establishment of a Canadian Honour would persist. We owe much more to Monck than most realize.

To many – myself included on occasion – it seems odd that I undertook this history while simultaneously working on my doctoral thesis. The explanation is found in the fact that this project has served as a refuge for my sanity, a tangible lifeboat in the proverbial sea of abstract theory that has flooded the discipline of history.

I am grateful to Her Majesty the Queen, Sovereign of the Order of Canada, for providing a message at the beginning of this book. Her more than fifty years of service to our country exemplify the motto of the order that she heads.

This project would not have progressed beyond the stage of rough idea had the Reverend Dr. Peter Galloway not befriended me. His constant encouragement and advice have dragged me from the depths of despair on a number of occasions. His contributions to the study of British honours are extensive; if I have a fraction of the impact that he has had I will be contented.

As with all historical research a debt of gratitude is always owed to the archivists. In particular George Henderson helped me through hundreds of reels of microfilm and the William Lyon Mackenzie King Diaries. Similarly Paul Banfield, also of the Queen's University Archives – Canada's other national archives – provided me with endless patience; be it complex photocopy orders or requests for obscure documents, Paul never failed. At the National Archives of Canada, Maureen Hoogenraad helped me find hitherto sealed and obscure documents. Ruth Gardiner LVO, OBE, of the British Cabinet Office provided me with a variety of documents previously unseen by Canadian eyes and provided a unique synopsis of the British perspective. Corinna Pike of Garrard & Company, the Crown Jewellers, provided me with great detail about the cost and manufacture of the first insignia of the Order of Canada. Similarly, Stephen Hart of Rideau Ltée and Alan Trammell of Pressed Metal Products provided important information about the manufacture of the Order of Canada insignia. Mr. and Mrs. John

Evans, who devoted nearly twenty years to photographing Order of Canada investiture ceremonies, were most kind and helpful in locating photos and granting permission for their reproduction.

At the Chancellery of Canadian Honours thanks is owed to Darrel Kennedy, Assiniboine Herald, and Marie-Paule Thorn. Lieutenant General James Gervais, CMM, CD, Deputy Secretary, Chancellery and Deputy Herald Chancellor, also showed a regular interest in my work and provided me with information otherwise unobtainable.

Two friends in particular helped hone this text into a coherent work: Captain Carl Gauthier of the Directorate of History and Heritage at the Department of National Defence and Bruce Patterson, Saguenay Herald at the Chancellery. Each provided me with regular advice and editing assistance. All of this was undertaken outside of their normal office duties – purely out of an interest in the subject of honours in Canada.

Through this project I have come into contact with many of the people involved in the creation and growth of the Order. At all times they have both inspired and encouraged me to continue on, and write this history. I could go on for pages with anecdotes related to our various conversations, but they are the sorts of things relevant only to the parties concerned: The Honourable Gordon Robertson, PC, CC; Georgina Butler; Joan Halstead; Bruce Beatty, CM, CD; Professor John Meisel, CC; Sir Conrad Swan, KCVO; Yves Chevrier, CM, RVM, CD.

I owe much to John R. Matheson, OC, CD, one of the key contributors to the creation of the Order of Canada. While recovering from a stroke Matheson and I spent countless hours talking about many topics, and I am forever grateful for those afternoons together.

My good friend Joyce Bryant, CM, BEM (the illusive Ms Turpin) unflinchingly pushed me to complete this project. Other friends who supported me throughout were Stephen Pallas, CD; Melodie Massey; Geoffrey Pearson, OC; Senator Serge Joyal, PC, OC; Mr and Mrs A.G. Nickle; Jacques Monet, SJ; Vince MacNeil; John Sheardown, CM; Zena Sheardown, CM; John Fraser, CM, Master of Massey College; General John de Chastelain, OC, CMM, CD, CH; The Queen's Canadian Secretary, Major General Gus Cloutier, CMM, CVO, CD; John Aimers; and my employer, Senator Michael Kirby.

It is curious how one's non-academic friends are invariably drawn into projects such as this. In particular this is true of Sean Morency and Lindsay Maynard. Whether while holidaying at my parents' cottage or on one of my visits, they have always taken a keen interest in my work. I can scarcely think of two people who have endured more pithy anecdotes about Canadian Honours than Sean and Lindsay.

Professor Ian McKay of Queen's University has always proven a persistent supporter. Ironically this project was completed almost entirely without his knowledge. Nevertheless his constant challenging of my ideas and conceptions of Canadian history has served to broaden my provincial Upper Canadian outlook into something more complete.

Lastly I am indebted to my family: Paul and Sharon, my parents, and Jonathan my brother. Words cannot express what their support has meant to me. While many families would have thought a project of this size too large for a twenty-seven-year-old attempting to complete his doctorate, they offered nothing but encouragement and love.

Abbreviations

Honours Post-nominial Initials, 1867–1997

Senior British Valour Decorations
VC   Victoria Cross
GC   George Cross

British Orders of Chivalry and Knighthood
KG/LG   Knight of the Garter/Lady of the Order of the Garter
KT/LT   Knight of the Thistle/Lady of the Order of the Thistle
KP   Knight of the Order of St Patrick
OM   Order of Merit
CH   Companions of Honour
GCB   Knight Grand Cross of the Order of the Bath
KCB   Knight Commander of the Order of the Bath
CB   Commander of the Order of the Bath
GCMG   Knight Grand Cross of the Order of St Michael and St George
KCMG   Knight Commander of the Order of St Michael and St George
CMG   Commander of the Order of St Michael and St George
GCSI   Knight Grand Commander of the Order of the Star of India
KCSI   Knight Commander of the Order of the Star of India
CSI   Commander of the Order of the Star of India
GCVO   Knight Grand Cross of the Royal Victorian Order
KCVO   Knight Commander of the Royal Victorian Order
CVO   Commander of the Royal Victorian Order
LVO   Lieutenant of the Royal Victorian Order
MVO   Member of the Royal Victorian Order
GCIE   Grand Commander of the Order of the Indian Empire
KCIE   Knight Commander of the Order of the Indian Empire
CIE   Commander of the Order of the Indian Empire
GBE   Knight/Dame Grand Cross of the Order of the British Empire
KBE   Knight Commander of the Order of the British Empire
CBE   Commander of the Order of the British Empire
OBE   Officer of the Order of the British Empire

MBE   Member of the Order of the British Empire
EGM   Empire Gallantry Medal (converted to the George Cross)
BEM   British Empire Medal

ISO   Imperial Service Order
CI   Order of the Crown of India
Bt   Baronet
Kt   Knight Bachelor (also sometimes listed as KB)

British Bravery Decorations
AM   Albert Medal
GM   George Medal
DSO   Distinguished Service Order
DSC   Distinguished Service Cross
MC   Military Cross
DFC   Distinguished Flying Cross
AFC   Air Force Cross
DCM   Distinguished Conduct Medal
DSM   Distinguished Service Medal
MM   Military Medal
DFM   Distinguished Flying Medal
AFM   Air Force Medal

British Long Service Decorations
ED   *Efficiency Decoration*
TD   Territorial Decoration
RD   Reserve Decoration
VD   Volunteer Decoration

Senior Canadian Valour Decorations
VC   Victoria Cross
CV   Cross of Valour

Canadian Orders
CC   Companion of the Order of Canada
OC   Officer of the Order of Canada
CM*   Member of the Order of Canada (from 1967 to 1972 this was used for the
        Medal of Courage, which was never awarded, and from 1943 to 1967 this
        designation was used for the Canada Medal, which was never awarded)
SM   Medal of Service of the Order of Canada (became Officer of the Order
        of Canada in 1972)
CMM   Commander of the Order of Military Merit
OMM   Officer of the Order of Military Merit
MMM   Member of the Order of Military Merit
COM   Commander of the Order of Merit of the Police Forces
OOM   Officer of the Order of Merit of the Police Forces

MOM   Member of the Order of Merit of the Police Forces
CVO   Commander of the Royal Victorian Order
LVO   Lieutenant of the Royal Victorian Order
MVO   Member of the Royal Victorian Order
RVM   Royal Victorian Medal
Ost.J   Order of St John of Jerusalem

Canadian Bravery Decorations
SC   Star of Courage
MB   Medal of Bravery
SMV   Star of Military Valour
MMV   Medal of Military Valour

Canadian Distinguished Service Decorations
MSC   Meritorious Service Cross
MSM   Meritorious Service Medal

Canadian Long Service Decoration
CD   Canadian Forces Decoration

Other
PC   Privy Councillor

* Note: When the term 'members' is used in relationship to the Order of Canada it refers to all those who have been appointed to the Order; Companions, Officers and Members. When 'Members' is used it refers to just those appointed to the Member level of the Order of Canada.

THE ORDER OF CANADA

False Starts and Honours in Canada, 1867–1917: The Creation of a Canadian Policy

The Crown is the fount of all honour.[1]

Arthur Berridale Keith

At a number of times in Canadian history and for a complex variety of reasons, the fount of honour has been turned off. The history of honours in Canada is as complex as our development as a nation. Indeed, in many respects the development of honours and honours policy in Canada has mirrored the growth of Canadian autonomy and independence – growth that ultimately led to the emergence of a Canadian identity. This national identity has realized its full potential with the creation of the Order of Canada. The Order of Canada is a fellowship of service that embodies more than an institution; it is also a perpetual project of recognition and renewal that contributes to the national well-being and that acknowledges those who have – through their service – expressed a desire for a better country. The Order of Canada is not an ancient institution; it takes elements from what John Buchan, Lord Tweedsmuir – Canada's eleventh Governor General – called the Canadian Mosaic, and it embodies a truly Canadian entity. Far from being a stagnant institution to which the cobwebs of history cling, the Order of Canada is a vibrant and central element of what it means to be a Canadian. Those who are recognized by the order embody our very best: they are not merely individuals whom the Crown wishes to recognize, they are also citizens who have made a significant contribution – locally, nationally, or internationally – to our country and its culture.

Humanity and Honour

The concept of honour is as old as civilization itself. Honours – that is, bestowals of recognition – are not quite as ancient, but the two concepts remain tightly linked. Honour and honours take many forms. Honour involves adhering to what is right: high respect and good reputation are gained through persistent good deeds. Honours are official marks of recognition, be they conferred through proclamations, titles, grants of arms, or insignia. One can be honourable yet never receive official recognition in the form of an honour. Conversely, a person can receive an honour yet be entirely lacking honour. Every society defines honour and establishes honours in accordance with its own social values.

The Canadian system of honours is derived primarily from two of Canada's founding peoples, the British and the French. However, no nation can claim to have invented honours. Modern history has given rise to a myriad of systems, and states and regimes have devised and used awards as essential apparatuses. At times these systems have been displaced by both evolution and revolution, yet always a new system has emerged that is roughly patterned on its predecessor. Today all but two states have adopted a national system of honours.[2] All systems have certain common elements such as meritorious service awards, bravery awards, and long service awards. The tradition of presenting an insignia or badge is also universal; it can be traced back to 290 BC and the gold button given by King Alexander to a high priest for bravery demonstrated in battle. Honour has also been recognized through the bestowal of land and titles: for instance, in Hellenic Greece a complex system of crowns was devised to reward public and military service. The beauty and intricacy of the crown and the materials used in it were dictated by the level of service and achievement. In the Indian state of Pudukkottai, there was an ancient tradition whereby the Raja presented gifts and honours to loyal subjects. This ritual served as a mechanism for recognition; it was also a source of political power, one that ensured stability within the existing order.[3] And few are unfamiliar with legend of King Arthur and his Knights of the Round Table. This ideal of chivalry and honours gradually replaced the granting of land with a title. Thus, insignia were common in the Middle Ages.[4]

The pursuit of honours continues today and is patterned according to class, gender, ethnic, and other hierarchies. Pierre Bourdieu argues that this pursuit is part of a much larger socio-cultural 'game' in which agents pursue strategies to increase their store of 'symbolic capital,' while never allowing themselves to be seen as doing so. To pursue honour is to pursue that to which one is entitled, according to 'a disposition inculcated in the earliest years of life and constantly reinforced by calls to order from the group, that is to say, from the aggregate of individuals endowed with the same disposition, to whom each is linked by his dispositions and interests.'[5] Because of its cultural ubiquity, scholars have found questions about honour to be of profound analytical importance.

'Honours have served the vanities and verities'[6] of human civilization for centuries. Admittedly, this assessment may sound too harshly analytical as well as overly academic. In every society, there are citizens who perform extraordinary deeds for no other reason than to benefit their fellow humans. A selfless devotion that seeks no impressive title or glittering insignia of gold and enamels does exist; it offers the satisfaction of having made a meaningful contribution, and it is not necessarily part of a socio-cultural 'game.'

In Canada, parliamentary debates in 1917–19 resulted in the adoption of the Nickle Resolution and the Report of the Special Committee on Honours and Titles. Any discussion of honours in Canada cannot be separated from these two ordinances, which effectively ended the practice of bestowing British honours in Canada. The intensity of the debate over honours in Canada during this time (an intensity almost matched in the debate from 1942 to 1945) suggests that Canadians have long found the question of honours troublesome, which accounts for the lack of a specifically *Canadian* Order for the first hundred years of our nation's existence. The history of

Canada's policy on this question has conventionally been seen as the story of a new Dominion casting away honours in favour of a more open, 'liberal' society.[7] But this is oversimplifying a complicated past, during which the Dominion set out to wrest control over the distribution of honours from the Colonial Office and to extinguish any notion of hereditary right. Thus, the evolution of Canadian honours policy can be quite straightforwardly integrated into the story of how the Dominion acquired autonomy within the Empire. In this sense, the Nickle Resolution was the first major test of Resolution IX of the Imperial War Conference of 1917, a miniature Statute of Westminster in the field of honours.[8]

Even after Canada gained control over the distribution of honours, the issue remained contentious. The Dominion–Commonwealth honours system was hampered by the intermittent and ineffective use of British awards, which fell far short of what the nation required. The result was a virtual honours vacuum after both the First World War and the Second World War. Politicians from all parties were reluctant to make forays into the forest of honours, which had entangled so many of their predecessors. It took a prime minister who had lived through the Nickle Debates of 1917–19 – and who had been part of the broader system of honours – to push the issue back onto the Cabinet table. Even then, it was a combined effort, one that brought together a group of Canadians who in various ways had contributed much to Canada's maturity and independence over the previous half-century.

It is valuable to examine briefly the history of honours in Canada from the earliest times, for that history – of the debates and of the decisions that arose from them – still resonates today. The character of the debates surrounding honours in Canada profoundly shaped Canada's present-day honours system, in particular the Order of Canada. The order in fact possesses unique Canadian characteristics, especially with regard to methods of selection. Yet, it would be misguided to suggest that our collective honours experience was formed solely within the political confines of modern Canada.

Canada's First Nations and Honours

Canada's Native people have a strong concept of honour and greatly value service to the community. However, at the time the Europeans arrived, they recognized such service not by bestowing gold medals but rather by according respect to the individual and by offering him the title of chief. Chieftainships could be hereditary or non-hereditary.

This system was strenghtened after the Europeans arrived in the sixteenth century. Native people had never awarded insignia or medals, but they learned quickly how to utilize the European system. The newcomers incorporated Chief's Medals into elaborate gift-exchange ceremonies that Native people had always conducted: 'Indians had as much a penchant for honours and prestige as Europeans.'[9] The Mi'kmaq were especially adept at using such occasions to extract better terms out of the Europeans, and the medals became symbols of 'allegiance and authority bestowed on Indians.'[10] Both the French and the British adopted the practice of awarding Indian Chief Medals; invariably, these showed the Sovereign on the obverse and the chief's name on the reverse. These medals, which became an important part of

First Nations hierarchies, were usually distributed to chiefs after a treaty had been negotiated. So potent were these medals as symbols of authority that some communities – such as the Potawatomi – forbade their receipt or possession. Thus, opposition to honours and titles in what is now Canada can be found long before the Nickle Resolution.[11] Indian Chief Medals continue to be awarded by the Crown to Canadian chiefs.

The First Europeans

The Vikings had a distinctive concept of honour that they certainly brought with them to Newfoundland around AD 1000. In Viking society, 'valiant men who exert a good influence [were] called *drengs*.'[12] The Christian ideal of self-sacrifice had merged with the notions implicit in *drengskapr*; the result was a Norse kind of chivalry. The emphasis was on being honourable and on being recognized as such; the idea of presenting an insignia or symbol of honour did not become common until after the decline of the Vikings in Europe.

Honours in Royal France

The Kingdom of France possessed one of the most extensive honours systems in the world. At the top of the social and political hierarchy were the nobility. From time to time the French King elevated subjects to the nobility in recognition of their services to the Crown. Frenchmen could be appointed dukes, marquises, counts, and barons. After the arrival in New France of Louis de Buade, Comte de Frontenac, in 1672, it became customary for Governors General to hold a noble title.

   The most senior honour in France was the Ordre de la Sainte-Ampoule (Order of the Holy Vial), founded in AD 439 by Clovis I; it was reserved for members of the noble classes. The Ordre du Saint-Esprit (Order of the Holy Spirit) served as the 'national honour' and was awarded more often than the Ordre de la Sainte-Ampoule. Founded by Henry III in 1578, it was limited to one hundred knights. Awarded to those who 'hold the Roman Catholic Religion and maintain the dignity of the nobility,'[13] it was also reserved for the nobility. The Ordre de Notre-Dame du Mont-Carmel et de Saint-Lazare de Jérusalem was founded in France by Henry V in 1607. A civil and military award, it was united in 1608 with the Order of Saint-Lazarus, originally founded in 1060 in Palestine, and was awarded for military and civil services rendered to the state. It too came in only one class, and was one of the few French awards of the period for which commoners were eligible. In 1469, Louis XI founded the Ordre de Saint-Michel, to be awarded to those who 'brought credit to the State'[14] through the sciences, discoveries, or art. Limited to one hundred knights, it was open to all levels of French society. The Ordre Royal et Militaire de Saint-Louis was founded by Louis XIV in 1693. Consisting of three levels – Chevalier, Commandeur, and Grand-Croix – it was awarded for military services to the French Crown. For French Protestants who rendered similarly outstanding military service, there was the Ordre du Mérite Militaire, founded in 1759 by Louis XV. Unlike the Order of Saint-Louis, the Ordre du Mérite Militaire came in one class only: Chevalier. Also part of the honours system of the Kingdom of France was the Ordre de Saint-Hubert de Lorraine et du

Barrois. Founded in 1416 by Louis I, Duke of Bar, it was restricted to members of the nobility who had performed philanthropic acts and was limited to one level. It is likely that this order was the first ever created solely to recognize charitable acts. All of these orders were abolished in 1791 during the French Revolution, although many were revived after the monarchy was restored, only to be abolished again in 1848.

In New France, honours were bestowed by the Governor on behalf of the King. Before awarding an honour, the Governor General of New France had to receive permission from the French Sovereign. The advice of the Governor General regarding awards seems to have been followed, although on occasion, the King would bestow an honour without having received a nomination from the Governor.[15] France's honours system was extensive but mainly limited to the noble classes. Indeed, in New France only one title of nobility was ever bestowed on a 'Canadian,' when Charles Le Moyne, 'Seigneur of Longueuil,' was made Baron de Longueuil. Having successfully concluded the Franco–Iroquois peace negotiations in 1694, Chief Teganissorens declared that the Five Nations had adopted Charles Le Moyne de Longueuil and his brother Paul Le Moyne as their children. On hearing this, Governor Frontenac petitioned King Louis XIV to elevate Le Moyne de Longueuil's seigneury to a barony. On 26 January 1700, Louis XIV signed Letters Patent creating Charles Le Moyne and his successors Barons of Longueuil.[16] Le Moyne de Longueuil went on to serve as the Governor of Montreal and Trois-Rivières and later as administrator of New France. Le Moyne de Longueuil was also later appointed a Chevalier of the Order of St Louis. The Barony of Longueuil still exists; the British guaranteed it under the Treaty of Paris of 1763. Ennoblement in France and New France came to a virtual end in the early eighteenth century.[17]

In New France, it was the Ordre Royal et Militaire de Saint-Louis (the Royal and Military Order of St Louis) that was most widely awarded and most coveted.[18] In all, nearly 300 honours of all three classes were bestowed for services to the colony or to France's North American empire. This honour was often bestowed in France, but much less often in New France. This maintained the prestige and status of the Order even after the honour had become common in France.

The most famous Canadian holder of the Order of St Louis, aside from Charles Le Moyne, Baron de Longueuil, was François Coulon de Villiers. Born in Verchères, New France, in 1712, Coulon de Villiers went on to serve in the French Colonial Army with great distinction. In 1754, François's brother Joseph Coulon de Villiers de Jumonville was killed by a detachment of the Virginia Militia led by George Washington.[19] In retaliation, François captured Fort Granville (near Lewiston, Maine), and on 3 July 1754, François Coulon de Villiers laid siege to Fort Necessity. After a day, on 4 July 1754, George Washington and Captain James Mackay signed the articles of surrender. This made Coulon de Villiers the only man to ever have defeated Washington in battle.

Honours Prior to Confederation

In the century between the fall of New France and the year of Confederation, few British honours were bestowed on residents of British North America. In 1820, Lord Bathurst, the Secretary of State for War and the Colonies, attempted to create a

Canadian order based on the Order of the Bath. However, George IV did not favour the idea.[20] On the whole, British officials were content to keep Canada tied to the broader Imperial honours system, and did not establish local awards. An examination of the unsuccessful proposals reveals that there was no real difference between the proposed Canadian order and those which already existed in the British system. In all, only five Baronetcies – hereditary knighthoods – and ten knighthoods were awarded to British North Americans.[21] There was no policy of requesting the consent of a colonial ministry before bestowing an award on a resident of a colony. Decisions with regard to honours were made by the Colonial Office, with input from the Governor; members of the various colonial executive councils were seldom consulted. The system was quite simple: the Governor or Governor General would suggest to the Colonial Secretary that a particular person be recognized. If the Colonial Secretary approved, the award would go forward for the approval of the Sovereign.[22] Recommendations did not have to originate with the Governor or the Governor General; in theory, they could have originated from any member of the general public. In practice, however, it was unlikely that the Colonial Secretary would have acted on the recommendation of Mr McKay of Mimico, Canada West.[23] Similarly, the Colonial Secretary could suggest that a particular person in a colony be recognized, and of course the Governor of the colony in question – the local authority on that colony's circumstances – would always be consulted. The idea of responsible government had not yet been extended to all parts of the royal prerogative, and would not be until the turn of the last century.

Honours in Post-Confederation Canada: The Three Epochs

Since Confederation, Canada's honours system has passed through three distinct epochs: the British Imperial honours system, heavily influenced by patronage and external controls and closely related to feudal notions of bloodlines and lineages; the Dominion–Commonwealth honours system, peripherally patronage-based, but more broadly representative of Canadian society and focused on the achievements of Canadians as Canadians rather than as British subjects; and, finally, the modern Canadian honours system, which is free of the patronage links once so essential to honours in Canada, which combines nation-building with multiculturalism, and which links honours to the concept of citizenship in a system unique to Canada.

Sir Charles Stanley, PC, GCMG, fourth Viscount Monck, arrived in Canada during one of the most tumultuous times in our history. From 1861 to 1868 he served as the Queen's representative in Canada, first as Captain General and Governor-in-Chief for the Province of Canada,[24] later as the first Governor General of the Dominion of Canada. At a time in Canadian history when the Governor actively participated in making government policy, Monck's duties combined those of the Sovereign's representative with those of representative of the British government.[25] Shortly after taking office, he was faced with the Trent Affair, during which war with the United States seemed imminent. Relations between Britain and the United States had deteriorated following the beginning of the American Civil War. After that war ended, British North America faced yet another crisis with the Fenian Raids into Upper Canada and New Brunswick. On top of all this, Monck faced the challenge of administering and advising a colonial government that was often divided along linguistic, regional, and religious lines.[26]

In these extraordinarily difficult circumstances, Monck actively promoted the talks that led to Confederation. According to C.P. Stacey, Monck fought for 'union with a determination which no Canadian politician could have surpassed.'[27] This is perhaps too generous, but it should be remembered that besides dealing with Canadian politicians, Monck had to deal with an Imperial government that had shown little interest in uniting British North America.[28] So it is unfortunate that Monck has not been recognized as a Father of Confederation.[29] He took a keen interest in the development of Canadian institutions and a Canadian identity. Of course he did so in the context of existing Imperial institutions; even so, he was anxious to see Canada become more than simply a British appendage.

Monck wanted the new Dominion to establish a local honour. On 7 September 1866, he wrote to the British Colonial Secretary, Lord Carnarvon. In this letter he addressed a variety of issues, ranging from the name of the soon to be united British North American colonies to proposed titles for members of the Canadian Senate. Among Monck's proposals was to 'institute an order of Knighthood for the B.N.A., on the model of the Order of the Star of India, to be called "the Order of St. Lawrence."'[30] The Most Exalted Order of the Star of India had been founded in 1861 as a means of 'binding them [senior members of Indian society] together in a confraternity and attaching them by a personal tie to the Sovereign.'[31] By the time Monck wrote to Carnarvon in 1866, the Order of the Star of India had three levels. The first class was Knight Grand Commander (GCSI); the second, Knight Commander (KCSI); the third, Companion of the Order of the Star of India (CSI).[32] The patron saint of the order would undoubtedly have been St Lawrence, although one is hard pressed to figure out which Canadian cathedral – Catholic or Protestant – would have been home to the order's chapel! Only the first two classes of the Indian order conferred knighthood, and membership was restricted to a certain number of living members at any one time.[33] Thus, the order that Monck was proposing would likely have taken the name 'The Most Eminent Order of St Lawrence,' and would likely have consisted of the three standard levels: Knight Grand Cross of the Most Eminent Order of St Lawrence (GCSL), Knight Commander of the Most Eminent Order of St Lawrence (KCSL), and Companion of the Most Eminent Order of St Lawrence (CSL).[34]

Monck's reasoning had two branches. He wanted to create an important Canadian institution that would be similar in style and composition to those of the mother country. At the same time, he was concerned that if a Canadian honour were not created, the British Order of the Bath – the only order for which residents of Canada were eligible – would become diluted. He argued that the absence of a local honour would have 'one of two inconvenient results ... either it [the Order of the Bath] must be conferred so sparingly as to omit a large number who would be fairly entitled to some mark of public favour, or if it be given in sufficient quantity to embrace all these it will become so common as to diminish its value as an Imperial mark of distinction.'[35] As always, Monck was walking 'inevitably on the razor edge,'[36] trying to balance Imperial and Canadian concerns with a solution that he thought would alleviate possible tensions between the Imperial and Dominion governments. Monck closed his letter to Carnarvon: 'I have now exhausted all the suggestions which I desire to bring before your Lordship's mind in connection with the "new departure" which this community is about to take in its national life.'[37] Having shrewdly realized that the new entity was not just a collection of British colonies, Monck was articulating that Canada was a community attaining a national life of its own.

The Colonial Office, however, rejected his idea as too unconventional; thus, Canada was deprived of its own order.[38] At the time, allowing Canada to have a local honours system would have been 'almost tantamount to an admission that Confederation had raised Canada's status in the eyes of the Imperial authorities.'[39] Had such a system, separate from other Imperial honours, been conceded, Canadians might have been more favourably disposed in the early twentieth century to recognize their fellow citizens with titular honours.

Even so, the suggestion that a local honour be created for Canada did not go completely unheeded, and a partial solution was devised. But it was not one that applied to Canada alone. Over the following half-century, the Most Distinguished Order of St Michael and St George served as the chief mechanism through which eminent politicians and public servants were recognized, not only in Canada but throughout the British Empire.

Founded in 1818 by the Prince Regent (later George IV), the Order of St Michael and St George was initially intended to reward citizens of the Ionian Islands; later, it was extended to citizens of Malta.[40] For nearly fifty years, the Order of St Michael and St George served as a means of recognizing loyal Ionians and Maltese; much of this purpose was lost, however, when Britain ceded the Ionian Islands to Greece in 1864. With the transfer of the islands to Greece, the order 'had become in effect limited mostly to the people of Malta or for service in Malta; this was a waste of a perfectly good Order.'[41] Within the British Empire, there was a desperate need for another order, or for the existing ones to be enlarged. The Order of the Bath, which had long been the primary mechanism for recognizing imperial and colonial officials, was filled to capacity. The Duke of Buckingham wrote to Queen Victoria in 1868: 'The Order of the Bath is now so full that it is not possible to obtain even a recommendation for each of the larger colonies and ... the Duke submits the suggestion for enlarging the Order of St. Michael and St. George already existing – so as to make it an Order for the reward of services connected with the colonies.'[42] This was done, and the Statutes of the Order of St Michael and St George were reconstituted to make the order the principal method through which imperial and colonial officials were to be recognized for services in or to the colonies or in the field of foreign affairs:

> The Queen has had occasion to observe that the constant progress of the British Empire in population, wealth and enterprise and the increased opportunities thus happily afforded to Her Majesty's subjects of rendering effective services to their sovereign and their country, have in some respects outgrown Her Majesty's means of recognizing those services in a fitting manner ... The Queen is confident that this measure will be received by Her subjects as an evidence of the importance which Her Majesty attaches to Her colonial dominions as integral parts of the British Empire, of Her constant interest in their progress and of Her desire that services of which they are the scene, or the occasion may not pass without adequate and appropriate recognition.[43]

Following this, successive Canadian prime ministers and chief justices, as well as some premiers and other servants of the Crown in Canada, were made Knights Grand Cross, Knights Commander, or Companions of the Order of St Michael and St George.[44] Rather appropriately, the first appointment made after the order was reconstituted was that of Viscount Monck, recently retired and returned from Canada.[45]

Not surprisingly, Monck did not consult any of the Fathers of Confederation about the creation of a Canadian honour. Perhaps this was because they were already dealing with so many other issues, and because the matter was so delicate. The position of the Governor General in the period immediately preceding and following Confederation was such that affairs relating to the royal prerogative were not entrusted to politicians, as they were in the United Kingdom.[46] For much of his career after becoming prime minister, Sir John A. Macdonald was preoccupied with honours, and had he lived longer he would have been made a peer.[47] Confederation had brought him honour, and Macdonald was quite keen on establishing a 'system of graduated classes, like that of England.'[48] Macdonald and the Earl of Dunraven corresponded on the topic of having Canadian peers appointed to the British House of Lords, where they could join their Irish and Scottish counterparts.[49] Macdonald failed to achieve this goal, although some Fathers of Confederation had hoped the Canadian Senate would emulate the British House of Lords.

One wonders why the Fathers of Confederation – in particular Macdonald, a staunch upholder of British tradition – did not propose a Canadian order of chivalry similar to the one proposed by Viscount Monck. With regard to Macdonald, it is likely that as a staunch Imperialist, he saw no need to develop a Canadian honour. From his perspective, the British honours system worked quite well. Acceptance of British honours was not universal among Canadians, however. The most prominent dissenter was George Brown, editor of the Toronto *Globe* and himself a Father of Confederation. On a number of occasions following Confederation, Brown refused a knighthood.[50] He preferred to remain aloof from such worldly devices, and was content to remain 'Brown of the Globe.'[51]

Monck's attempt to create a *Canadian* order was the last until 1942. Not until 1967 would a home-grown Canadian order be founded. Between 1867 and 1967, Canadians were sometimes eligible for British honours. However, Canadians became increasingly sceptical of the effectiveness of even the British system. This will be discussed further after we examine the structure and use of British honours in Canada.

After Confederation, Queen Victoria approved the creation of the 1867 Confederation Medal.[52] Although not an honour per se like the various British orders of chivalry, it was 'awarded for service or merit, open to anyone [and] approved by the government at the highest level.'[53] The medals were struck in gold, silver, and bronze. The sole gold medal was presented to Queen Victoria; it is known that silver and bronze medals were presented to various Fathers of Confederation. These medals were not intended to be worn, being quite large (76 mm in diameter); they were intended more for display. Although more closely resembling commemorative medals such as the 2002 Queen Elizabeth II Golden Jubilee Medal, the 1867 Confederation Medal was awarded for a variety of services to Canada. Some of these services would have warranted a Jubilee Medal; others would be recognized today through the Order of Canada. In some ways the Confederation Medal was the Dominion's first effort to create a government-sanctioned award.

British Imperial Honours in Canada

By the time of Confederation, the British honours system had 'acquired a Byzantine complexity, with literally dozens of different kinds of honours, decorations and titles.'[54] Each of these honours had a specific place within the Table of Precedence. They could only be awarded in a certain order, and the insignia associated with them could only be worn in accordance with strict regulations.

A map of this complex system must begin with the Peerage of the United Kingdom, which comprised various levels of nobility: Dukes, Marquesses, Earls, Viscounts, and Barons. Eleven peerages and one title have been bestowed on Canadians over the span of Canadian history.[55] Among these, five are considered to be Canadian peerages – that is, they were awarded after consultation with the Canadian government.[56] Seven peerages have been conferred since Confederation by the British government on persons born in Canada but for services not rendered in or to Canada.[57] Sir William Pirrie was head of the famous shipbuilding firm Harland and Wolff, which built the RMS *Titanic*. He was made a baron in 1906 and later elevated to a viscountcy in 1921. Born in Quebec, Pirrie was also the only Canadian to be a Knight of the Most Illustrious Order of St Patrick. Although not technically born in Canada, Sir Edward Patrick Morris was the first and only Newfoundlander to be appointed to the peerage, as the First Baron Morris of St John's and Waterford. R.B. Bennett was elevated to a viscountcy in 1941, and Roy Herbert Thomson was made Baron Thomson of Fleet in 1964. The most recent Canadian to be summoned to the House of Lords was the Honourable Conrad Black, PC, OC. In 2001, Black was made a life peer with the title Lord Black of Crossharbour. Between 1867 and 1935, the first appointment of a Canadian to the peerage with the knowledge of a Canadian prime minister was that of Sir George Stephen, who became Baron on 26 June 1891. Stephen, like two other Canadian peers, was president of the Canadian Pacific Railway (CPR). It is not unlikely that he owed his appointment to 'help' he gave the ruling Conservatives in the 1891 campaign.[58] This connection between the CPR and the awarding of titles strengthened opposition to hereditary honours among some in the Liberal Party, who connected the procedure to the operations of patronage and party financing in the Canadian political system. The second Canadian (and sole Canadian woman) appointed to the peerage was Lady Susan Macdonald, who became Baroness Macdonald of Earnscliffe on 14 August 1891. However, she was not entitled to sit in the House of Lords, and in the absence of extensive documentation, it seems safe to conclude that she was honoured in memory of her late husband, Canada's first prime minister. The next appointment to the peerage resumed the theme of the CPR. Sir Donald Smith, the line's former president, was appointed in his capacity as Canadian High Commissioner to London. He became First Baron Strathcona and Mount Royal on 26 June 1900, and continued as Canadian High Commissioner until his death in 1914.[59] Sir Thomas Shaughnessy, the principal catalyst for the 1902 Report of the Privy Council on honours and titles, and like Strathcona and Stephen also a president of the CPR, was elevated to the peerage on 19 February 1916.[60] The last Canadian to be elevated to the peerage after consultation with the Canadian government was the president of the *Montreal Star*, Sir Hugh Graham, whose name figured so prominently in the 1917–19 debate on honours.[61] This appointment was by far the most controversial of the lot, in that Graham was remembered vividly for his somewhat questionable fund-raising activities on behalf of the Conservatives, and for his violently pro-imperial editorials in the *Star* at the time of the Anglo-Boer War.[62] This appointment, made over Prime Minister Borden's objections and politically ill-timed, may well have been the turning point in rendering Canadian peers a politically unpalatable prospect.[63]

Passing now to those Canadians who were awarded hereditary knighthoods, we find the Baronets. These were founded in England by James I in 1611 and extended to Ireland in 1619; Scotland had its own Baronets, founded in 1625 as part of William Alexander's scheme for settling Nova Scotia and preventing it from falling into French hands.[64] The Scottish Baronets, known as the Baronets of Nova Scotia, were established by Charles I of England and Scotland. This was the first honour created specifically for Canada.[65] Although an effective tool for raising money and selling titles, the scheme was not entirely successful in enticing the newly knighted to travel across the sea to protect the British colony from the French.[66] Baronetcies were later amalgamated under the title 'Baronets of the United Kingdom.' In order of precedence in the United Kingdom, Baronets rank just below Barons and one level above Knights of the Order of the Garter.[67] In total, seven Baronetcies were awarded on the recommendation of the Canadian government: three were awarded to politicians and four to businessmen. Baronetcies were in fact highly coveted in Canada; even national politicians battled for them publicly. It is suggestive that less than five days into the first session of the first Parliament of Canada, the question of honours was the subject of a stormy debate, on the vexed question of Sir John A. Macdonald's having bettered George-Étienne Cartier on the field of honours. Macdonald had been made a Knight Commander of the Order of the Bath (KCB), whereas Cartier had been made only a Companion of the Order, an 'insult to himself and the nation he represents.'[68] On 23 March 1868, a motion was introduced championing Cartier's claims to a KCB; less than a month later, Macdonald announced to a cheering House that Cartier had been made a Baronet, and hence had been awarded an honour even more substantial than that given Macdonald himself.[69]

Having examined the British orders of knighthood with Canadian significance,[70] we arrive at the Most Honourable Order of the Bath (variously designated, according to rank, GCB, KCB, and CB), which is thought to have been established in 1128 and which is probably the oldest order of knighthood in the world.[71] This order initially had one class, Knight of the Bath, and consisted of the Sovereign, a Prince of Royal Blood, a Great Master, and thirty-five Knights. It was later reorganized into three levels and two divisions, civil and military, in order to provide awards to officers who had served in the Napoleonic Wars.[72] One of the first awards made after the 1815 reorganization was that of a KCB conferred on Lieutenant General Gordon Drummond of the British Army, born in Quebec City. Eleven awards of the Knight Grand Cross and Knight Commander of the Order of the Bath were bestowed on Canadians between 1867 and 1935. Sir John A. Macdonald became the first in 1867, when he was made a KCB, civil division; he was later elevated to a GCB in 1884 – the first and only colonial politician ever to receive this most senior accolade.[73] The redoubtable Sam Hughes, Minister of Militia and Defence, acquired the other Canadian civil KCB in 1915; his award could hardly have made the distinction shimmer more brightly in the eyes of opponents of conscription and the Conservative government. Six KCBs went to military men; one honoured a member of the RCMP.[74] Proceeding down to the most junior grade of the Order of the Bath, to that of Companion, we find that 166 Canadians have attained this distinction since Confederation.[75]

It can be said that from Confederation until the Nickle Resolution of 1918, the Order of St Michael and St George served as the Order of Canada for the period; it was the premier award available to Canadian politicians, judges, and civil servants. This was partly because of a change in the rules in 1868,[76] which tipped the scales away from the Order of the Bath and toward the Order of St Michael and St George. The order initially consisted of the Sovereign, Grand Master, seven Knights Grand Cross, twelve Knights Commander, and twenty-four Knights Companion. In 1832, the lowest class became non-titular and was renamed Companion of the Order of St Michael and St George. The order was enlarged in 1868, 1877, and 1902 to allow for a maximum of one hundred Grand Crosses of the Order of St Michael and St George (GCMG), three hundred Knights Commander of the Order of St Michael and St George (KCMG), and six hundred Companions of the Order of St Michael and St George (CMG). For Canadians, the order was intended to honour 'high political or official services as distinct from judicial, literary, scientific or artistic eminence.'[77]

The GCMG was reserved for Governors General, prime ministers, and chief justices. Between 1867 and 1935, fourteen of these were awarded to Canadians, most of them politicians, including three Canadian prime ministers: Tupper, Laurier, and Borden. Many other Canadians keenly sought to become a Knight Commander of the Order of St Michael and St George, partly because it was the most accessible honour – it was within the reach of eminent senior civil servants, senators, cabinet ministers, provincial premiers, and even plain party supporters – and perhaps also because of the splendid regalia involved.[78] Seventy-four Canadians succeeded in being appointed to the senior levels of the Order of St Michael and St George: 48 per cent of them were active politicians, and 21 per cent were serving or retired Lieutenant-Governors – most of whom came up through the party system. The remainder went to people in a variety of occupations, from university administrator to engineer. One rung below the KCMG was the Companion of the Order of St Michael and St George, which was awarded to 382 Canadians.[79] Even Mackenzie King, who as we will learn was no great admirer of the British honours system, was awarded this distinction – although it is telling that as prime minister, he never wore the insignia of the order.[80] Of a somewhat different nature is the Royal Victorian Order, founded by Queen Victoria in 1896 with an unlimited number of awards, but which by tradition was awarded with the Sovereign's greatest degree of care and discretion. Four Canadians have been awarded the top two titular levels of the award – Knight Grand Cross (GCVO) and Knight Commander (KCVO); the other levels continue to be awarded to Canadians for services to the Crown in Canada. This order remains an integral part of the Canadian honours system to this day. As was the case with other awards, the Royal Victorian Order in Canada was firmly associated in the early twentieth century with railway executives. Edward VII, known to be somewhat prone to bestow knighthoods on unsuspecting friends and visitors,[81] was also clearly impressed by the claims of railway men: Lord Mount Stephen was made a GCVO in 1905 and Lord Strathcona in 1908; Lord Shaughnessy won the only Canadian KCVO in 1907. Edward VII was also responsible for the creation, in 1902, of the Royal Victorian Chain, which afforded the recipient no titular distinction and was not an order of knighthood, but which was nonetheless considered the most exclusive award available from the Crown and a special mark of the Sovereign's esteem and affection.[82] The award was given to five Governors General of Canada: Prince Arthur Duke of Connaught in 1906, Lord Lansdowne in 1906, Lord Athlone in 1935, Vincent Massey in 1960, and Roland Michener in 1974.[83] A more common award was that of the Most Excellent Order of the British Empire, which consisted of five classes and had military and civil divisions. The highest level was the Knight/Dame Grand Cross (GBE); the second class was the Knight/Dame Commander (KBE/DBE); lower levels included Commander (CBE), Officer (OBE), and Member (MBE), as well as the British Empire Medal (BEM). Because this order was founded in 1917, and the Nickle Resolution came into effect in 1918, the titular levels were available to Canadians for only the periods between 1917–19 and 1933–5. Canadians received two GBEs and eight KBEs; of these, two were awarded to businessmen, three to civil servants, two to individuals for services in medicine and science – here we find Sir Frederick Banting, codiscover of insulin – and one to a Canadian for philanthropic deeds. The lower levels of the order were to come into prominence during the Second World War, with the last award being made in 1964.[84]

Unlike those who receive Orders of Knighthood, a Knight of the United Kingdom – also known as a Knight Bachelor because of the title's non-hereditary character – is presented with a simple insignia and allowed to prefix his name with the title 'Sir.'[85] A knighthood is a title conferred by the Sovereign; Knights Bachelor are not connected with any order. They are members of the ancient concept of knighthood and chivalry, and become such when the Sovereign rests the blade of his or her sword on the shoulder of a kneeling subject. All of those who are made a Knight of the Order of the Garter, the Order of the Thistle, the Order of St Patrick, or Knight Grand Cross/ Commander or Knight Commander of the Order of the Bath, the Order of St Michael and St George, the Order of the Star of India, the Order of the Indian Empire, the Royal Victorian Order, or the Order of the British Empire, are first dubbed as Knights Bachelor and then presented with the insignia of the order into which they have been inducted. Most Canadians who were knighted became Knights Bachelor; 107 received this honour for services rendered in and to Canada. The award was limited but was not always confined to 'the Bench and men of literary or scientific note.'[86] Pressure to award it to the politically connected came from Canada. Most often it was provincial, puisne, and chief justices who were given the honour (39 per cent); politicians received 17 per cent, and businessmen 14 per cent. One should finally mention the Most Venerable Order of the Hospital of St John of Jerusalem, traceable to the crusading knights of the Middle Ages and incorporated by Royal Charter in 1888, which continues to be part of the Canadian honours system. It is awarded to people who 'have performed or are prepared to perform good service for the order.'[87] Many Canadians have been appointed to this order and continue to be. It remains one of the oldest elements of our national honours system.

Such was the complex world of honours in Canada from 1867 to 1935 – a veritable forest of orders, titles, rules, qualifications, signs, favours, and traditions, some of them stretching back to the most distant years far before Confederation, long before the European settlement of North America. Honour was not merely bestowed; once attained, it could be plainly seen, and in ways that differentiated the recipients precisely.[88] Depending on one's perspective, the astonishing complexity of the system, with its bewildering titles and intricate rules of hierarchy, was either a humbling and inspiring embodiment of the ancient and noble Empire or a blatant example of medieval hocus pocus placed at the service of modern snobbery, class distinctions, and partisan politics.[89]

This thick forest of symbols perhaps suggested to Canadians how tightly they were bonded to the Empire. Or perhaps it told them that as colonials and incipient democrats, they could never feel at home within it. Perhaps it was best seen as a system that awarded human excellence and the best virtues, or perhaps as a further reward for the masters of patronage and railway speculation. There was no unanimity in the discourse on how to structure a Canadian system of honours; and as we shall see when we turn to the system's evolution from 1867 to 1935, this debate, far from being simply over 'honorifics,' was in fact close to the heart of Canadian politics.

Considering how comprehensive the honours system was, it is important to ask why Canada did not continue to use British honours. The answers to this question are complex, but to start with, the mood of national independence was growing, and so was Canadians' suspicion of honours. The Dominion's autonomy in the granting of honours mirrored and in some respects anticipated the gradual evolution of its general autonomy under the British North America Act. Indeed, to some degree, Canadian independence was forged out of the honours debate.

Prior to 1935, honours were usually awarded in the following way. During peacetime, honours lists were issued twice a year. One such list was called the New Year's Honours List, the other the King's or Queen's Birthday Honours List. For occasions such as the Sovereign's coronation or anniversary of ascension to the throne, a special list would be drawn up.[90] This would be printed in the *London Gazette*. When a Canadian was recognized, this would often (but not always) also be noted in the *Canada Gazette*.[91] Honours to the military were generally 'gazetted' on the same day as civilian awards. (During a war, these latter honours were awarded as necessary, without being restricted to the New Year's and Birthday Honour Lists.) The Canadian Secretary of State for External Affairs was responsible for ensuring that Canadian awards were printed in the *Canada Gazette*, under the heading 'Despatches: Secretary of State for External Affairs.'

The Crown was (and remains) the fount of all honour, and the bestowal of titles and awards was considered a central part of the Royal Prerogative.[92] Although this prerogative was officially exercised by the Sovereign, years of constitutional advances in the United Kingdom had left the monarch with surprisingly little direct authority; the doctrine of ministerial responsibility had reduced much of the Sovereign's power.[93] So advanced was the British government's control over Royal honours by 1902 that the only honours the King could bestow without consulting the British Prime Minister were the Royal Victorian Order and Order of Merit.[94] Bestowing all other orders – even awards to fellow members of the Royal Family – required the monarch to act on the formal advice of the prime minister.[95] Honours, like other Royal powers, had increasingly become concentrated in the hands of elected politicians.[96] The Sovereign had the right to protest appointments but rarely exercised this right.[97] As honours and titles became valuable political tools for politicians, the role of the Sovereign was further diminished.

In the United Kingdom, all titular honours and non-military honours in general fell under the principle of ministerial responsibility. Thus, most appointments had to be approved by the British prime minister.[98] With regard to the Order of St Michael and St George, they had to be approved by the Secretary of State for the Colonies.[99] The Secretary of State for the Colonies did not always consult the British prime minister about awards, which meant that the Colonial Secretary held effective control over all Canadian appointments. In Canada, the Governor General could not unilaterally confer an honour or perform an act of investiture without special permission from the Crown.[100] The Colonial Office had to approve all honours awarded to Canadians, save for the Royal Victorian Order.[101] In order for an investiture to take place at the hands of someone other than the Sovereign, a Dispensation Warrant had to be issued. For those unable to travel to London, a special Royal Warrant would be issued to allow the Governor General to present the award. Between 1877 and 1902, the Canadian prime minister was always consulted when the civil honours lists were put together. However, the Governor General was not bound to follow the advice of his prime minister; honours were considered quite separate from other parts of the Royal Prerogative.

With Confederation, a new policy emerged. The Dominion's prime minister was consulted regularly, but his advice was not always followed. Nor was he at all times advised of forthcoming awards. Indeed, during Macdonald's first administration (1867–72), even the convention of consultation was only weakly developed. Alexander Mackenzie, in contrast, would be steadfast in asserting his right to advise the Governor General on such questions.

So in the early years of Confederation, the Dominion of Canada was integrated into the British system of honours, but with a host of complications. Because the Colonial Office refused to allow a colonial order of knighthood, the new Dominion was compelled to use a British system that was controlled mainly from London.[102] Prior to the 1902 Report of the Privy Council relating to honours, the role played by the Canadian prime minister in the selection of candidates was completely at the discretion of the Governor General, who could in theory proceed without consulting the Canadian prime minister (although in practice such moments were rare). As the Colonial Secretary, Joseph Chamberlain, explained to Lord Minto in 1902: 'I think you are entitled to claim that recommendations for honours, are, and must continue to be, made on your own responsibility. At the same time you are glad to have suggestions or criticisms from the Prime Minister. You are not called upon to recognize anyone else in the matter.'[103] Chamberlain was basically saying that the Governor General should listen to the prime minister, but if his protests over an appointment (or lack of one) seemed motivated strictly by party considerations, his advice should be treated with some suspicion.[104]

This informal policy of consultation changed in 1902. The Canadian public had expressed little opposition to knighthoods and British awards up until that year, when one particular award enraged many. The Anglo-Boer War had already demonstrated that the interests of the Canadian and Imperial governments were conflicting more and more, and honours would prove to be yet another flashpoint in Dominion–Imperial relations. It should surprise no one that Canada's first imbroglio over honours involved the railway that united the country from sea to sea. Sir Wilfrid Laurier was the first prime minister to try to gain Canadian control over British awards bestowed on Canadians, and his actions in this were closely watched by leaders in other parts of the British Empire.[105] Laurier himself was a knight, and in 1902 he came within a hair of being made Baron Laurier of St Lin by Edward VII.[106] The controversy over honours erupted during the visit of Their Royal Highnesses the Duke and Duchess of Cornwall and York (later George V and Queen Mary). The visit itself was a huge success, one that brought all the splendour, pomp, and pageantry of the monarchy to Canada. Accompanying all the gold braid, court uniforms, and clinking medals of the Royal Visit was a knighthood for Thomas Shaughnessy, the strongly detested president of the Canadian Pacific Railway. The ensuing disagreement between the Canadian prime minister, the Colonial Office, and the Governor General brought the topic of honours to the attention of the federal Cabinet and also came to preoccupy the press.

To the Duke, conferring a knighthood on Shaughnessy must have seemed an eminently sensible move that was fully in line with precedent. Canada had a long tradition of recognizing its railway tycoons with knighthoods; one had even received in an exceptional case a peerage.[107] Although the CPR's president, Shaughnessy was without any sort of title. Worth noting perhaps is that the Duke and Duchess were travelling for free on the CPR.[108]

These considerations would not have deeply impressed Laurier, with whom Shaughnessy was not on friendly terms. Furthermore, Laurier had annoyed Chamberlain by submitting his recommendations for honours at the last minute and without careful consideration and discussion. In addition, Laurier had gone to see Lord Minto with no list prepared and had insisted that Minto suggest names. Laurier refused to permit a knighthood to go to William Mulock or to Frederick Borden,[109] and when Shaughnessy's name came up for a knighthood he 'was not cordial as to Shaughnessy tho' he did not actually object to him.'[110] Minto was furious with Laurier's indifference toward honours and wrote to Chamberlain to denounce the Canadian prime minister: 'He cannot & will not decide for himself & every time he leaves me.'[111]

Minto wrote Laurier to express his view that the CPR's unpopularity was not reason enough that it should 'entitle me to pass over the President of the company on the present occasion.'[112] Laurier was relatively unconcerned with Shaughnessy's impending knighthood; he was more agitated by the possibility that Mulock and Borden might be knighted during the Royal Visit.[113] Minto was not aware of the precarious public position of Shaughnessy and the CPR,[114] but Laurier's seeming indifference toward the awards and his preoccupation with the cases of Borden and Mulock led Minto to tell the Colonial Office that Shaughnessy's knighthood could proceed. Laurier was informed of this on 10 September 1901. A week later, on 17 September, only three days before the press was to be informed of Shaughnessy's knighthood, Laurier bypassed Minto and cabled the Colonial Office, asking that Shaughnessy's award be withdrawn.[115] The Duke and Duchess of York and Cornwall had arrived on 16 September and had already seen the list of those who were to be honoured during their trip. The Duke was so excited that he was prepared to make available an extra KCMG[116] – an offer that Minto did not accept, having had enough trouble coming to an agreement with Laurier over the other awards.[117]

Laurier saw Minto on 18 September and told him to withdraw Shaughnessy's award. Minto was still not satisfied that Laurier, who had made no mention of his correspondence with the Colonial Office, was right. Later the same day, Minto received a cable from Chamberlain at the Colonial Office regarding the award. In the hope of presenting Minto with a *fait accompli*, Laurier had cabled the Colonial Office before meeting to discuss the matter with Minto. This breech of protocol annoyed both Chamberlain and Minto. Chamberlain's telegram to Laurier, which was copied to Minto, asserted that the 'responsibility for the recommendation of honours rests entirely with the Governor General, & is not in the slightest degree at the disposition of his Ministers.'[118] Shortly after receiving Chamberlain's cable, Minto sent the names to the press for publication on 20 September 1901. The matter was now entirely beyond Laurier's control. Minto avoided Laurier during the fireworks on the evening of 19 September, not wanting to discuss the matter. Minto then wrote Laurier to inform him that Shaughnessy's award was to proceed and that the press had been informed: 'I sincerely regret differing with you in opinion – but I am absolutely convinced of the advisability of the bestowal of honour on Mr. Shaughnessy.'[119] Minto's letter would have arrived with the morning dispatches. The morning newspapers on 20 September 1901 were full of news relating to the awards, and Shaughnessy's name was at the top of the list. Unfortunately, not much is known about Laurier's morning routine, so we will never know whether he first read news of Shaughnessy's knighthood in the paper or learned of it from Minto's letter. From this time forward, Laurier took a keen interest in the Honours List, and set out to concentrate the power to write it in his own hands.

The *Gazette* of Montreal looked favourably on Shaughnessy's impending knighthood and the award of a CMG to Principal William Peterson of McGill. The *Toronto Star*, however, was outraged.[120] The *Star* pilloried Shaughnessy and the CPR over freight rates and the handling of the recent CPR strike. It wondered out loud if Shaughnessy was being knighted 'because the CPR charges more and higher rates on Canadian freight than the the the [*sic*] US?'[121]

The press was thus informed about Shaughnessy's knighthood, but it was not until 21 October that he was actually dubbed. The *London Gazette* did not report the award until 31 October 1901 – one of the few instances in Canadian history in which the award was made prior to being gazetted.

Laurier's Cabinet was already under attack for its handling of Canada's involvement in the Anglo-Boer War, and demanded that Laurier raise the 'contentious issue of responsibility for Canadian honours recommendations'[122] with the Imperial government. Laurier quickly set about drafting a new policy in the form of an order-in-council, which the Imperial government chose officially to ignore. In practice, however, from that time on it consistently followed the advice of the Canadian prime minister.

After 1902

The 1902 order-in-council was an attempt to formalize the processes of consultation between the Governor General and prime minister. It argued 'that the great development of Canada, and the high position which she has now obtained, render it advisable that upon this subject as upon all others the exercise of the Royal Prerogative shall conform to the well understood principles of Ministerial responsibility.'[123] It concluded that the Canadian prime minister must enjoy the same rights and privileges as the British prime minister with respect to recommending honours. The report noted that the Canadian prime minister should generally be consulted, but that this was not yet a settled principle. It added that 'the Parliament at Westminster rightfully advises His Majesty with respect to persons who have rendered services of an Imperial Character,' whereas those awards made for the colonies were made on the advice of the Secretary of State for the Colonies and not of the colonial Parliament concerned.[124] The report asked that in order for honours recommendations to be in 'harmony with the principles of our constitutional system,' the Canadian government be given the same powers with respect to recommendations for civilian honours as the government of the United Kingdom.[125] The report cited quasi-constitutional reasons for this request; it also emphasized that His Majesty's ministers in Canada were well acquainted with the standing in the community of those being proposed for honours, and of the character of the services for which such honours were the reward.[126] Essentially, it asked that the Canadian prime minister be given a veto over all civilian honours, citing the principle of ministerial responsibility. The report was sent to the Governor General for transition to the Colonial Office.

The response of the Colonial Office arrived on 23 April 1902. It emphasized the time-honoured theme that the 'Crown is the source of all honours,'[127] and then proceeded to explain that since the Order of St Michael and St George in particular was an Imperial Order and not limited to Canadians, the ultimate responsibility for it resided with His Majesty's government in the United Kingdom: 'If service is of a political or administrative character, rendered solely in the sphere for which the Ministers of the Crown in Canada are responsible, who are constitutionally the proper authorities for making the recommendations.'[128] However, with regard to 'persons whose purely Imperial, Provincial or Municipal services or public services of a charitable, literary or scientific character, are held to merit recognition, I consider that the proper course would be for you [the Governor General] to transmit a list of such persons to your Prime Minister inviting his observations on the same, and such list with the remarks of the Prime Minister should be submitted to me [the Colonial Secretary].'[129]

Chamberlain was giving the prime minister power over political and administrative awards while retaining control over all others. This was perhaps a slight concession to the Dominion's demands. The key provision was the one that afforded the prime minister legitimate scope to make a list of 'remarks' to accompany an Honours List. Up to this point, it had been the Governor General's responsibility to condense and evaluate the prime minister's concerns. After 1902 the Governor General would still have the power to recommend people for honours, but the prime minister's evaluation would be sent directly to the Colonial Office and would be subject no longer to the Governor General's interpretation. This development was clearly a response to Minto's actions during the 1901 Royal Visit.

Laurier had not gained complete control over honours, but he had succeeded in formalizing the process. The Colonial Office still controlled the number of awards to be given and ultimately who was to be recognized, but it could no longer recognize civil servants or politicians without the advice of the Canadian prime minister. The 1902 policy as enunciated by Chamberlain in the letter of 23 April 1902 remained in place until the Nickle Resolution, introduced in March 1918.

The 1902 policy did not still all controversy over such questions. In July 1908, Laurier again became embroiled in a discussion about honours. In early 1908, Austin Deakin, the Australian prime minister, requested roughly the same deal Laurier had negotiated in 1902.[130] Deakin corresponded with Laurier throughout 1908[131] regarding this topic, and later that same year, he was granted the same rights that the Canadian prime minister held with respect to honours.[132]

For all his apparent reluctance to be knighted, and in spite of his 1918 platform, which would become known as his 'democracy first' argument, Laurier – like his Conservative predecessors – enthusiastically integrated honours into his formidable patronage machine.[133] It is of course difficult to say with certainty how many knighthoods Laurier awarded in order to secure new friends for the Liberal Party or to reward old party warhorses. Indeed, during the 1918 Nickle Debates, Laurier's enemies were delighted to remind the House of his use of patronage as a means of securing political advantage. Much of this political innuendo defies exploration today; however, there is some evidence that on at least one occasion Laurier's critics were substantially correct. The paper trail in this case can be followed from the Colonial Office to two Governors General, the prime minister, and the person to receive the 'favour.' In this instance, Sir Wilfrid Laurier, the 'reluctant knight,' was by no means reluctant to use a knighthood to increase his support base in Ontario and the Senate.[134] Only the watchful eye of the Colonial Office undermined the prime minister's schemes.

Senator James Robert Gowan, Liberal-Conservative Senator for Ontario, was eighty-nine years old when he was awarded a KCMG in November 1905, making him one of the oldest Canadians to have been knighted. Gowan had been made a Companion of the Order of St Michael and St George in 1893 and had long hoped to be elevated to a KCMG, which according to him had been promised him years before by Sir John Thompson. Alas for Gowan, Thompson died before making the recommendation.[135] Gowan went so far as to write to the Governor General with the Thompson story, including in his letter a list of his services to the Crown and a glowing declaration of his loyalty.[136] Usually when a Governor General received such a letter, it was filed and given no more attention; but Minto, possibly taking pity on an aging senator with a somewhat plausible case, sent the letter on to Laurier.[137] He expressed the hope that Laurier would see fit to recommend Gowan for a knighthood the following year. New Year's 1900 came and went, and poor Gowan was not mentioned on the honours list.

Laurier told the justice minister, David Mills, about Gowan's plight. At this time the Liberals needed to increase their presence in the Conservative-dominated Senate, and the eighty-five-year-old Conservative in search of a knighthood swam into their sights as the Tories' weak link in the Senate. Late in 1900, Mills approached Gowan and made a deal. On 22 December 1900, Mills wrote to Sir Wilfrid Laurier: 'I have his [Gowan's] resignation in my hands, addressed to the Governor General, which I am authorized to submit to His Excellency, whenever he is knighted, which if not done, I am to return to him. I trust the arrangements will be carried out without any difficulty and the old man will not be disappointed. His place [in the Senate] is of great consequence to us at the present time. I have no doubt his resignation will facilitate the arrangement for bringing Dr. Landerkin, Mr. Wood from Hamilton, and someone else in place of Senator Reesor. If this is done, it will strengthen our position in the Senate at the opening of session.'[138]

Mills hoped to have Laurier persuade Lord Minto to add Gowan to the New Year's honours list. With only a few days' notice, it was unlikely to happen. Laurier went to see Lord Minto the day after Christmas,[139] but neither Laurier nor Lord Minto mentioned Gowan's quest for a knighthood. Laurier did not mention Gowan's KCMG to Minto, and Gowan's resignation was never submitted. Apparently, Laurier was not as concerned as his justice minister with his party's situation in the Senate.

For some time, Lord Minto had supported Gowan's application for a knighthood,[140] but he had been unable to receive permission from Laurier to forward the recommendation to the King. In May 1904, Laurier changed his mind and asked Minto to recommend Gowan and Senator George Cox for the KCMG. Senator Cox was a prominent Ontario Liberal. Laurier told Minto that if Cox and Gowan could not both be recognized with a knighthood, then neither should receive one. Laurier knew that Minto desired to see Gowan knighted, and he calculated that if he added a Liberal appointment to counterbalance that of Gowan, Minto would capitulate. Minto sent a request to the Colonial Office, which was denied, the supply of KCMGs never being sufficient to meet the demand.[141] Had Minto submitted a personal request for one knighthood to be awarded, the Colonial Office would likely have made allowances, but asking for two extra awards was excessive. Minto was certain that Gowan would be elevated to a KCMG.[142] Although Laurier likely forgot about the matter – there is no further mention of a knighthood for Gowan in the Laurier Papers – the Colonial Office, that paragon of efficiency, did not. Over the protests of the new Governor General, Lord Grey, Gowan was made a KCMG on 9 November 1905. Lord Grey wrote to Laurier: 'In spite of my protest His Majesty has been graciously pleased to confer a KCMG on Hector [sic] Gowan.'[143]

Gowan retained his seat in the Senate until 1907 and died in 1909. Laurier's attempt to use a KCMG to get Gowan to resign had failed, and so had his attempt to couple the award of a KCMG for Gowan with one for Liberal Senator Cox. Minto was a supporter of Gowan's claims and was in a position to squeeze an extra two KCMGs out of the Colonial Office, so he must have structured his response to Laurier. Had he been strictly bound by the 1902 order-in-council regarding honours, Minto would have been unable to ignore Laurier's advice that both men and not just Senator Gowan be recognized. In this case, Laurier's attempt to use honours for narrow political advantage backfired; even so, one senses that a tactic which misfired in this case was probably used to better effect in others. Dominion autonomy did not necessarily mean Dominion rectitude.

The use of knighthoods in Canada as blatant tools of political patronage was not common, but the Gowan example shows that it did occur. The situation in the United Kingdom was no different; in fact, there was an actual trade in honours and peerages. Ultimately, events relating to a Canadian living in the United Kingdom brought the honours debate to the fore once again. The result was a virtual end to the award of knighthoods to Canadians, and a periodic prohibition on Canadians receiving any British honour or award. The taint of patronage and corruption would play a significant role in the downfall of the British Imperial honours system in Canada.

Controversy and Discontent, 1917–1935: The Decline and Brief Revival of British Honours in Canada

My resolution would strike at the very root of the iniquity, because I have no sympathy at all with titular distinctions given to men in civil life ... When it comes to granting distinctions to men in civil life for the services they have rendered their state, for great munificence, or for outstanding ability in their profession or business, it is a procedure with which I have no sympathy ...

William Folger Nickle, 8 April 1918

The Great War served as a catalyst for profound change in Canada and for the evolution from colony to nation.[1] As reflected in the display of military valour at Vimy Ridge and in the adoption of Resolution IX of the Imperial War Conference,[2] Canada was coming of age both in action and in law. Among these defining events we must include the Nickle Resolution, which essentially ended the practice of Canadians being knighted, and which also restricted the bestowal of British honours on Canadian residents. Unfortunately, the Nickle Resolution was only a half-measure; although it sought to restrict the bestowal of knighthoods and to prohibit the creation of peerages, it failed to propose some other form of honour that could be used for citizens who warranted national recognition.

The Canadian polity had become increasingly critical of the honours system, which had come to be identified with eastern domination, party corruption, out-of-date habits of deference, and a servile relationship with the United Kingdom. Long before the Nickle Resolution, honours had become a fiercely contested issue in Canada. Sir Robert Borden, by nature a progressive reformer and systematizer more than a reactionary, clearly felt the need for cautious change. He argued consistently for heightened Dominion involvement in recommendations for knighthoods.[3]

After extended debate, the House of Commons adopted the Nickle Resolution in April 1918. This resolution requested the King to cease bestowing titular honours such as peerages and baronetcies on Canadians. It also ensured that control over knighthoods and other honours would be in the hands of the Canadian prime minister. Thus, although the Nickle Resolution did not remove British honours from Canada, it did end further awards of hereditary honours to Canadians. The public accepted the resolution as a virtual ban on all awards; even so, parliamentarians were unsatisfied with it. Thus, a little over a year later a special committee was struck to examine further the issue of honours in Canada. The Report of the Special Committee on Honours and Titles called for a complete end to civilian honours in Canada. Military bravery awards were exempted from the proposed prohibition, but the report was complete in its condemnation of all other honours. Some members of the committee went as far as to suggest that even titles already bestowed on Canadian residents be revoked; had this suggestion been heeded, Sir Wilfrid Laurier would have reverted to plain old Wilfrid Laurier. These provisions were ultimately rejected, as they would have required an Act of the Imperial Parliament; instead, the House of Commons passed a motion of concurrence with the special report. Although it would be regularly cited for the following half-century, this report had no legal power. It was simply a reflection of the House of Commons' views on the issue in 1919.

Sir Robert Borden, Canada's prime minister during the Great War, helped transform Canada's achievements on the battlefields of Europe into greater autonomy for the Dominion. Borden was by no means temperamentally opposed to honours systems. He happily accepted rewards from other countries, and his private diary indicates that he was delighted when he was awarded a GCMG in 1914. But the same diary also suggests that Borden was cautious about awards. Indeed, he took the unprecedented step of consulting his Cabinet in June 1914, before accepting the honour.[4]

Borden's caution was probably born out of a sense that the issue had the potential to generate strong controversy in Canada. On 5 February 1914, John H. Burnham, Conservative MP for Peterborough West, introduced a bill to 'abolish titles of honour in Canada.'[5] Burnham defined 'titles of honour' as all knighthoods and peerages held by Canadians. At the time, there was little support for his bill. Predictably, most of his own party did not favour so drastically egalitarian a move; perhaps still more revealing is that even the 'democratic' Liberals were unsupportive. Laurier declared that he could not support the measure because, since it was in the form of a bill and not a request to the Sovereign, it went against the Royal Prerogative.[6] Echoes of Burnham's gesture, which seemed so futile at the time, would be heard in the far different 1918 debate, which revealed how much could change in four short years.

This transformation was very much related to the war and to heightened patriotism among Canadians. The wartime controversy over honours did not begin with Burnham's bill, but rather with the controversial and unpopular award of a Knight Commander of the Order of the Bath (KCB) to Sam Hughes in 1915. This in itself would not have mattered much had it not been followed swiftly by three further awards. The first was the one given to Max Aitken, a Canadian businessman living in Britain, soon to be known as 'the Beaver.' Aitken would be the object of much bitter attack in the 1918 debate. In May 1916, Andrew Bonar Law – the only Canadian ever to become British prime minister – asked Borden to allow Aitken to be made a Baronet of the United Kingdom. Aitken was residing and working in the United Kingdom, and thus his baronetcy was considered a British matter. Nonetheless, Bonar Law, worried that the baronetcy 'would be regarded as having been conferred through his personal friendship for Sir W.M. Aitken,'[7] wanted the award listed in the *Canada Gazette* as a Canadian award. Borden, standing by his right to prior consultation, refused the request and asked the Governor General to do the same. Devonshire concurred. Aitken's baronetcy was duly listed as a British award in the *London Gazette*.

From one perspective, the entire affair could be interpreted as a quiet triumph for the system of consultation developed by Laurier and Borden. But that was not how this event was perceived. The general public was relatively indifferent as to whether the award was technically British or Canadian; it saw only that a man associated with cement mergers and utility monopolies had been awarded a knighthood. This perception persisted. In January 1917, Aitken was elevated to the peerage and made Lord Beaverbrook. Although this was a British appointment to a British resident, the public saw it as another Canadian being awarded a hereditary title. The Beaverbrook imbroglio was followed by the award of a baronetcy to Sir Vincent Meredith, president of the Bank of Montreal, in December 1916. Meredith was 'under continuous attack in the press as drawing profits from the business in which he was engaged.'[8] A further press uproar followed his receipt of a baronetcy.

The fourth and most damaging episode was the elevation of Sir Hugh Graham, owner of the *Montreal Star* and one of the Conservative Party's premier fund-raisers, to the peerage as Lord Atholstan, in part through the machinations of Lord Northcliffe and Lord Beaverbrook. The controversy centred on Graham's intimate links to Borden's own party. In addition, Graham had a reputation as a unconventional Conservative fund-raiser and was widely rumoured to have taken part in large-scale bribery.[9] Furthermore, Graham ardently supported right-wing causes at a time of rising social unrest and labour militancy. But by far the most serious impediment to his elevation arose from the fact that the appointment had been made against the wishes of the Governor General and the Canadian prime minister. As Sir Robert Borden would remind the Duke of Devonshire in 1918, here was a man who was ordinarily resident in Canada, receiving an honour or titular distinction 'not only without the approval, but against the expressed wish of Your Excellency and of myself.'[10] This was certainly the only instance in post-Confederation history when the advice of both the Canadian prime minister and Canadian Governor General was completely ignored by the Imperial government. In light of such opposition, one must ask why Graham was elevated to the peerage. The answer has much to do with events in the United Kingdom. David Lloyd George had become British prime minister in 1916 with the help of two Canadians, Andrew Bonar Law and Lord Beaverbrook. It is worth pointing out that Beaverbrook and Graham were friends.

There is no solid evidence that Graham purchased his peerage. However, Graham and Beaverbrook were friends, Graham was very wealthy, and there was strong opposition to Graham's award from both the Canadian prime minister and the Governor General. These facts together indicate clearly that there was more to the story than a disagreement between the Canadian and British governments. When one also takes into account that Beaverbrook would later try to purchase a knighthood for Andrew Holt,[11] son of Sir Herbert Holt, president of the Royal Bank of Canada, it becomes highly plausible that Beaverbrook acted as an intermediary between Sir Hugh Graham and Lloyd George's Liberal Party, and ultimately purchased a peerage for Graham. This would explain why Graham, who had rendered relatively little service to either Canada or the Empire during the First World War, was recognized with such a high award. It would also explain why the Canadian prime minister and the Governor General were so outraged at his appointment. In the context of increasing suspicion about honours, this controversy led to a public outcry and served as the catalyst for change.

The sale of honours in the United Kingdom was not uncommon and had an old connection to Canada. The Baronets of Nova Scotia had been founded specifically in order to raise money to colonize Nova Scotia, but this honour had not been bestowed in more than two hundred years.[12] By the twentieth century, honours were no longer being sold for the purpose of expanding the British Empire; rather they were being sold for the more sordid end of raising funds for political parties.[13] David Lloyd George had perfected this less than honourable fund-raising technique, to the point that a general price schedule had developed: a loyal subject and Lloyd George supporter could be made a peer for £100,000[14] (approximately C$6,000,000 today); a knighthood could be purchased for a bargain price of £10,000[15] (approximately C$600,000).[16]

While Beaverbrook's receipt of a baronetcy and elevation to the peerage had been greeted with suspicion, scepticism, and some anger in Canada (even George V was upset with his elevation[17]), Graham's was furiously denounced throughout the Canadian press except, of course, that part of which he himself happened to own. This was the moment when Laurier's compromise inherited by Borden collapsed. The British government had treated advice from both the Governor General and the prime minister with blatant disregard. Borden now had an excuse to reform the appointment process, knowing full well that public opinion would be behind him.

In August 1917, following the elevation of Sir Hugh Graham to the House of Lords, a seventeen-page pamphlet called 'Titles in Canada 1917' appeared. It listed no publisher or price, and it is difficult to ascertain how many copies were circulated, but its appearance in the papers of Borden, Bennett, Meighen, Laurier, and White suggests that it was widely circulated. It contained excerpts from thirty-five English-Canadian newspapers.[18] Although none of the parliamentarians who spoke in 1918 referred directly to 'Titles in Canada,' the speeches of some bore a close resemblance to it.[19]

It is probable that this pamphlet strongly influenced the Nickle Debates; it was in its way a masterful piece of propaganda. Whether or not Lord Beaverbrook's appointment was desired by the Canadian government, and whether or not the British consulted the Canadians on it, one could always dwell on the fear that Lord Beaverbrook or Lord Althostan might return to Canada, progeny in tow, the nucleus of a new hereditary caste. The *Brantford Expositor* described as 'unexplained and unexplainable' the reasons that must have been behind the recent raising of 'Baron Graham.'[20] The pamphlet, which echoed scores of editorials in the Dominion's press, suggested that many people were venting their frustrations on those who had been awarded knighthoods and peerages, and that recent episodes had roused old and bitter memories.

Against these negative images, 'Titles in Canada' counterpoised positive examples of selfless Canadians who had just said no to honours. The pamphlet focused on the case of John Ross Robertson, proprietor of the *Evening Telegram* in Toronto, who on being offered a knighthood and a Senate seat – both on the same day – summoned the nerve to turn both appointments down. Why? Because, although a prominent and prosperous Conservative, he was also a 'true Democrat.'[21] The case of Robertson proved that if knighthoods were 'really a reward of merit, John Ross Robertson would have been knighted years ago.'[22] Of course, it was not just Conservatives who were cast in such a heroic light. Resistance to corruption and honours was constructed as a deep part of the Liberal legacy as well. 'The immediate struggle of Liberalism will be against hereditary legislative authority, and all the caste and class privileges with which it is associated,' the *Toronto Globe* pronounced on 16 February 1917[23] in words reminiscent of George Brown – words that were happily endorsed in many different ways by 'Titles in Canada.' There was much confusion in the pamphlet over the difference between a hereditary title and a knighthood; a number of contributors made statements that all knighthoods were hereditary. Overall, however, its tone was sharply in favour of abolishing all hereditary titles and carefully re-examining the system by which knighthoods were distributed.

With the telling exception of the *Montreal Star*, Graham's flagship paper, it would seem that most of the Canadian press agreed that 'hereditary titles ... are altogether objectionable in this country.'[24] Even former prime minister Sir Mackenzie Bowell's old paper, the *Belleville Intelligencer*, disrespectfully referred to honours and peerages as 'Tin Pot Titles.'[25] The balance of opinion was less clear-cut on the question of knighthoods. Even critics of the system depicted the Canadian people as proud to 'see our Canadians honoured by our beloved Sovereign.'[26] A few voices on the other side attempted to build on this sentiment by depicting the attack on knighthoods as a symptom of rampant Americanization and as a nefarious attempt to introduce republicanism into the Dominion.[27] There was a widespread desire not to interpret an attack on hereditary titles as an attack on Britain. Rather, newspaper commentary focused on the abuse of titles within the patronage system. The prospect of thorough constitutional change was rarely aired, let alone championed.

To the vexing episodes that had sparked public debate was added a further problem: the proposal for a new order, to be called the Order of the British Empire. As announced in a Foreign Office circular report of 25 December 1916, the new order was intended to honour those who had rendered (or were about to render) extraordinary service in the Great War. By 1 November 1917, Borden had been sent a list of Canada's allotment. Only the first two levels were to confer knighthood, so the likelihood that Canada would soon be flooded with three hundred knighthoods – as reported in the press – was fantastically far-fetched. Even so, the new order was attacked in major newspapers across the country.[28] Borden began to receive mail from sources as disparate as the Baptist Men's Union of Toronto, the National Labour Council of Ontario, the National Council of Women in Canada, and even the British Imperial Association, condemning hereditary titles, which were often incorrectly associated with the new 'British Empire Order.'[29] It should be noted that rejection of the Order of the British Empire was far from universal. Many Canadians wrote to Borden to recommend worthy recipients of the new honour. The Lieutenant-Governor of New Brunswick went so far as to submit the names of sixty-two women whom he felt were qualified for this recognition; the Lieutenant-Governor of Prince Edward Island, in contrast, refused to make any recommendations.[30]

The 1918 Order of the British Empire list was never submitted. Although one Grand Cross of the Order of the British Empire (GBE) and three Knight Commanders of the Order of the British Empire (KBE) were awarded to Canadians in 1918, these were not included on the list. For political reasons, appointments to the order were postponed. Borden himself, in a gesture of personal sacrifice, turned down the award of a KBE in February 1919.[31] Accepting such an award at this highly charged moment would have ignited a second debate over titles and honours.

The public's perception that honours were conferred only on rich industrialists, newspaper owners, railway tycoons, and emissaries of the political machines of the Liberal-Conservative and Liberal parties was not incorrect. Of the 183 knighthoods awarded to Canadians between 1867 and 1918, 64 per cent went to prominent members of the country's two main political parties. More than 37 per cent went to serving politicians, 20 per cent to judges, 15 per cent to businessmen, and 10 per cent to civil servants.[32] French Canadians, Roman Catholics, Methodists, and Baptists were significantly underrepresented relative to their share of the population.[33] Given these results, it is not surprising that most knighthoods went to residents of Ontario's and Quebec's major cities. In Canada, women were totally excluded from the senior levels of British orders. A would-be knight was well positioned if he was a Conservative businessman from Montreal or Toronto and had connections in both Ottawa and London. The field of official honours was hardly representative of any portion of Canadian society aside from the Albany Club of Toronto or Montreal's no less exclusive Mount Royal Club. Peripheral regions, the socially marginalized, women, Native people, and those of non-European stock were generally excluded.

This was the general historical context of the Report of the Special Committee on Honours and Titles, which, misleadingly, has come to be known as the Nickle Resolution. There is a more particular history, one that also has a bearing on this moment, and it is that of William Folger Nickle himself. What drove this man to assume a position of leadership on this question, and to push even his own party leader into a premature and somewhat embarrassing debate?

Enter W.F. Nickle

The man whose name has been attached to the debates and resolution deserves some mention. Born on 31 December 1869 to Scottish Presbyterian parents who could afford to give their son a comfortable childhood, William Folger Nickle attended Kingston Collegiate and Vocational Institute, received his Bachelor of Arts from Queen's University, and studied at Osgoode Hall. He was called to the bar in 1895, became a Queen's Counsel in 1898, and enjoyed a busy legal practice in Kingston. He was a long-time member of the Conservative Party and would serve at various times as a municipal politician, federal Member of Parliament for Kingston, and Attorney General for Ontario. Nickle was a maverick – a rogue Tory, one might say – and his personality and personal wealth allowed him to take an independent stand on issues about which he had deep convictions.[34] Nickle's interest in honours has often been associated with his relationship to the principal of Queen's University, Daniel Miner Gordon, his father-in-law. Gordon had been denied a knighthood on a number of occasions, and some have postulated that Nickle was keen to see both his father-in-law and his alma mater recognized with a knighthood; when no honour came, he turned against the system.[35] Nickle was a strong-willed and independent Tory who believed that although born into great wealth, he had a duty to help those less fortunate than himself. Although his wealth freed him to pursue any variety of interests, Nickle seems to have often associated himself more with those in need of a voice than with powerful business groups or the party machine. In later life he would go on to assist M.J. Coldwell with legal issues relating to the CCF; he would even personally advise Canadian Communist Party leader Tim Buck on legal matters. [36]

In some quarters, Nickle has been portrayed as a man ambitious for honour and high office.[37] Actually, he was much more comfortable running things from the background, outside the public view.[38] He had no ambitions for a knighthood, but was under some pressure at home to see that his father-in-law and Queen's University be recognized. Through his father-in-law, Nickle experienced first-hand the partisan and unbalanced nature of honours in Canada under the British Imperial honours system. Nickle observed influential industrialists and those in positions of extreme wealth profiting both monetarily and in terms of honour from the Great War, while the average Canadian was slogging in the trenches of France. Sir Hugh Graham's elevation to the peerage as Lord Atholstan had roused the Canadian public's interest in honours; Nickle's desire to see hereditary titles abolished and knighthoods and other honours more fairly bestowed did much to establish the foundation for the balanced honours system that Canada possesses today.

As someone heavily involved with Queen's University and interested in its administration, Nickle would have been sensitive to the particular way the system of honours intersected with the fate of Canadian universities. In one sense, there was a very limited connection; out of all the knighthoods awarded to Canadians, only five (2.2 per cent of them) were bestowed on serving university administrators.[39] In another sense, titles played a pivotal role in the university system. Knights added an air of respectability and cultural depth to a university community. A university was generally delighted to have a sitting president, principal, or chancellor knighted; if it was unable to obtain a knight by this route, it could always go shopping for a knight to serve in its administration. By Nickle's time, fourteen Canadian knights had been appointed to governing bodies of Canadian universities,[40] and fourteen other Canadian knights were university professors.[41]

In a society acutely conscious of status, universities were ranked no less sharply than individuals. The University of Toronto and McGill University were the most prestigious English-language schools; Queen's was generally considered the poor cousin and naturally tended to resent being treated as such by its wealthier and more established rivals. This situation had become especially acute by 1918. The University of Toronto was clearly winning the competition for high-profile administrators; there, Sir Edmund Walker was board chairman, Sir W.R. Meredith was chancellor, Sir Robert Falconer was president, and Sir Edmund Osler and Sir Joseph Flavelle sat on the board of governors. At McGill, Principal Sir William Peterson was a KCMG.[42] Before and after 1918, Queen's sought to copy its rivals' successes in acquiring the knighted.[43]

Lord Minto and other Governors General were keenly aware of the rivalries among Canadian universities with regard to men holding honours.[44] When the University of Toronto was omitted from the awards made in 1901 during the Royal Visit of the Duke and Duchess of Cornwall and York, it did not go unnoticed. Laurier received an angry letter from J.P. Sheraton, principal of Wycliffe College at the university, protesting this 'great indignity ... done to the University of Toronto in the recent distribution of Royal favours ... Why honour should have been bestowed upon Lavalle [sic], McGill and Queen's, and Toronto passed over in this way, we cannot understand it. Every graduate feels it and resents it.'[45] Sheraton concluded by threatening Laurier: the university's supporters would enter politics to oppose the Liberals. When Robert Ramsay Wright, an eminent zoologist at the University of Toronto, was nominated for a knighthood in 1912, Prince Arthur, Duke of Connaught, as Governor General, remarked that 'there might be heartburning both at Toronto University and McGill, whose heads have not yet received that Honour.'[46] The problem at Toronto would have been that of having Sir Robert serving as a mere professor under a non-titled president. The principal of rank was not confined to political life.

The year 1915 was good to Queen's University, as it had been to so many other Canadians, and the 1915 Honours List saw more Canadians knighted than in any previous year.[47] Daniel Miner Gordon, Nickle's father-in-law, was made a Companion of the Order of St Michael and St George (CMG).[48] His recognition came after thirteen years of service at Queen's. In 1915, Gordon was not yet in a position to be awarded a KCMG. Because of the long-standing rule which held that a person had to work his way through the ranks of the Order of St Michael and St George, a person could not initially be appointed above the bottom rank. Borden could have recommended Gordon for a Knight Bachelorship (Kt), but this probably would not have succeeded for two reasons. First, the award of a KCMG to McGill and the more junior Knight Bachelorship to Queen's would have been interpreted as a slight against the latter university. Second, knighthoods were in high demand because of war work; all of the KCMGs awarded in 1915, except for the one awarded to William Peterson, principal of McGill, were for war-related efforts. Honours, both titular and non-titular, were being reserved for those taking a prominent part in causes related to the war. It seems entirely likely that Gordon received his CMG in 1915 because the Governor General and Borden were concerned that difficulties might arise if Queen's was not recognized alongside McGill.[49]

Gordon received many congratulatory letters, a few of which addressed him as 'Sir Daniel' – further evidence of Canadians' confusion over the difference between titular and non-titular awards.[50] His health was poor, and his time as principal was limited; an elevation to a KCMG was unlikely.[51] With the death on 22 July 1915 of Sir Sanford Fleming, the renowned engineer who had served as chancellor, the university had lost its last remaining titled administrator. Nickle identified with his university; he was connected to Gordon by his marriage to Gordon's daughter Katherine. In 1917, to the chagrin of Queen's men, the university was once again passed over, and the King's Birthday Honours List instead featured Sir Robert Falconer, president of the University of Toronto.

By all accounts, Nickle was in his own mind a true 'democrat' who identified strongly with his American mother's strong sense of liberty.[52] Nickle was firmly opposed to peerages and baronetcies because of their hereditary nature, but he was not opposed to knighthoods and other British honours, provided they were bestowed fairly and with the consent of the Canadian prime minister. Motivations are often unreadable; it is highly likely that Nickle was influenced by the broad currents of his day and had the political instincts and the maverick impulses to make the most of them. But it also seems likely that his frustrated ambitions for Queen's and the university's humbling at the hands of McGill and Toronto played a role in his resentment of the honours system – as well as in his interest in broadening his attack to encompass all honours rather than just hereditary ones. Certainly, some of Nickle's contemporaries thought that his connections to Queen's explained the fiery words of this unlikely cultural revolutionary. In his memoir, Sir Robert Borden referred to Nickle as the 'agitator' and remembered that he was 'resentful of the titles conferred upon the President of the University of Toronto and the President of McGill, while the President [sic] of Queen's University had not been included.'[53] Borden here was drawing inferences from the evidence; the snubbing of Queen's University certainly did drive Nickle, but it was not all that drove him. Borden had little use for Nickle, but after the resolution was brought to the House of Commons and the debate was engaged, he had little choice but to deal with him.

Borden's exasperation with Nickle must have been all the more intense because, in the wake of all the difficulties caused by honours over the preceding two years, and unknown to most Members of Parliament, the prime minister had taken precautions against just such a recurrence of unpleasantness and confusion. He had established a Privy Council Committee charged with developing an honours policy that would avoid further embarrassment. The first draft of this committee's order-in-council was completed on 9 March 1918, and a copy was sent to the Governor General, the Duke of Devonshire. By the time it finally emerged from the bureaucracy and was approved by the Governor General, the report declared that

1. No honour or titular distinction (saving those granted in recognition of military service during the present war or ordinarily bestowed by the Sovereign *proprio motu*) shall be conferred upon a subject of His Majesty ordinarily resident in Canada except with the approval or upon the advice of the Prime Minister of Canada.
2. The Government of the United Kingdom shall exercise the same authority as heretofore in determining the character and number of titles or honours to be allocated to Canada from time to time.
3. No hereditary titles of honour shall hereafter be conferred upon a subject of His Majesty ordinarily resident in Canada.
4. Appropriate action shall be taken, whether by legislation or otherwise, to provide that after a prescribed period no title of honour held by a subject of His Majesty now or hereafter ordinarily resident in Canada shall be recognized as having a hereditary effect.[54]

Borden had had to overcome strenuous objections to arrive at this formula. The Duke of Devonshire, who was favourably disposed to the intent of the first two paragraphs, and who was quite in sympathy with Borden's assessment of hereditary titles – 'I believe there is a strong feeling against creating such in Canada' – offered no comment on the proposal to extinguish the heritable quality of peerages held by Canadians. Borden worried that Parliament might demand a more precise enunciation of these conditions.[55] Sir Joseph Pope, Under-Secretary of State for External Affairs, was a great deal more critical: 'The first thing that strikes me on reading this

Minute,' he wrote with a certain sense of shock, 'is the sweeping character of its provisions.'[56] He warned that the government was laying down a broad line of policy that would have an impact on future generations; he also warned that the proposed attack on the hereditary principle might be 'resented in high – in the highest – quarters' – an unmistakable hint that the King himself would be offended.[57] Borden set about making minor adjustments to the Privy Council report; for example, he provided scope for those serving in the war to be knighted without the prime minister's permission. As 25 March 1918, the Governor General approved the Report of the Committee of the Privy Council, which became Order-in-Council 1918-668. Two days later, on 27 March, the proceedings for the coming week in Parliament were published. Among them was notice that one W.F. Nickle was going to introduce a motion regarding honours. Borden immediately began preparing for the debate, requesting that the Governor General obtain permission from the Colonial Office to make public the 1902 Privy Council report in which Laurier had requested greater control over honours bestowed on Canadian residents.[58] Borden, nursing a fragile Unionist government in a war-divided country, found himself facing precisely the parliamentary drama that he had been working to avoid.

The Nickle Debates

You call them toys; know that by these toys people are led.

Napoleon Bonaparte[59]

In Ottawa on 8 April 1918, the political atmosphere was charged; the war was placing unprecedented demands on Canadian society. Conscription, war profiteering, the proposed income tax, and the enforcement of labour discipline were the leading issues of the day. There was a sense of urgency in the air, and the Union government – which was specifically a war government, the first ever to govern Canada – had a full and pressing agenda.

Into this situation walked forty-eight-year-old William Folger Nickle, KC, a relatively obscure Conservative-Unionist MP from Kingston. He did not cut an imposing figure; one historian describes him as 'a small spare man, with an abrupt and caustic manner and domineering disposition.'[60] After a career in municipal and provincial politics, Nickle had been elected to the House of Commons in 1911, part of the general wave of Conservatives replacing Liberals in Ontario. He was a difficult, unpredictable, and irascible man who could not be counted on to follow the party line. In 1914 he had opposed legislation that would have continued to guarantee the bonds of the Canadian Northern Railway and thereby save it from bankruptcy. Years later, the bitterness of his attack on his own government's proposal would be remembered, and not fondly, by fellow Conservatives.[61] Later, he would figure as a resolute foe of Ontario's Conservative government on the question of the enforcement of the Ontario Temperance Act.[62] He was 'not a good Tory,' it would later be said.[63] His non-partisanship was perhaps best demonstrated during the Parliament Hill fire of 1916, when he rescued a portrait of Sir Wilfrid Laurier from the flames.[64]

On the question of honours and titles, Nickle had passionate convictions, which dove him to steal the march on his own leader Sir Robert Borden, who had hoped to deal with the issue circumspectly and without a public parliamentary debate. Nickle stood as a private member to introduce a resolution from the House of Commons to His Majesty on the question of hereditary titles:

> We, Your Majesty's most dutiful and loyal subjects, the House of Commons of Canada in Parliament assembled, humbly approach Your Majesty praying that your Majesty hereafter may be graciously pleased to refrain from conferring any hereditary titles upon Your subjects domiciled or living in Canada, or any title or honour that will be held or can be used by, or which will confer any title or honour upon any person other than the person in recognition of whose services the honour or title has been conferred. All of which we humbly pray Your Majesty to take into Your favorable and gracious consideration.[65]

Nickle began his speech by noting that a colleague of his, John Burnham of Peterborough, had introduced the subject to the House in 1914 but did not feel that now was the time to do so again, given the emergency conditions of war. Nickle disagreed, arguing that wartime was precisely the time to do so. After the war, Nickle pointed out, 'you are likely to have the greatest crop, if I may use that term, of decorations and recognitions that are from time to time seen.' Moreover, it was a time of an experimental Union government, 'a Government that is supposed to have within its ranks representatives of the two great political parties in Canada, as well as representatives of Labour.' Hereditary titles should not exist in Canada, and women 'should not bask ... in the reflected glory of their husband's distinction.'[66] Warming to his subject, Nickle proclaimed:

> My resolution would strike at the very root of the iniquity, because I have no sympathy at all with titular distinctions given to men in civil life. I am quite prepared to admit the correctness of men in military life being given rank and distinction, because if the system is to prevail there must be distinctions by which those of higher rank have recognition and priority over those of lower rank; but when it comes to *granting* distinctions to men in civil life for the services they have rendered their state, for great munificence, or for outstanding ability in their profession or business, it is a procedure with which I have no sympathy.

What was iniquitous about ranks and distinctions in civil life? In the first place, they were outdated legacies from England; they constituted an attempt to apply measures designed for an official aristocracy – one that was an essential part of the British government – to an independent Dominion of a completely different complexion. Nickle continued:

> Titles to-day in England are really only the picturesque effect of the days of feudalism. They are distinctions without the responsibilities of service. In the old feudal days in England and on the continent the granting of a title was a recognition, but it carried a duty. It was the giving of a privilege, but it carried an obligation, and, as a rule, titles were granted in respect of territorial possession ... Many of the members of this House

have, like myself, been in England. I do not know whether I am a deeper dyed democrat than they are, but there was one thing that always grated upon me, and that was when a man rose to address an assemblage of Englishmen, an assemblage of Britishers, he began his address by, 'My lords and gentlemen ...' My lords and gentlemen may be all right for England, or Britain, but from my point of view it is not all right for Canada.[67]

The honours system perpetuated an unjust sense of caste and exclusion, and it flattered the inept and the useless with a false sense of their own distinction. Nickle postulated that with time, if titles continued to be awarded to Canadians, class privilege and inequality would entrench themselves. Why follow this path in a land of immigrants, a land made by those who had realized, like Nickle's own father, 'that the Old Country did not offer ... the opportunity ... to advance? Now, Sir,' Nickle declared, 'as I said at the beginning, I am a democrat.' And to these words, Sir Wilfrid Laurier, the Liberal leader and former prime minister, added his own: 'Hear, hear.'[68]

Pioneers – these were the true 'makers of Canada.' But what – asked Nickle – of their legacy in 1918? It was imperilled by the emergence of a very different society:

> No man who has lived in this country within the last ten years can think of Canada's development prior to the war without being shocked by realizing how far we were getting away from the simplicity of our ancestors. We have had in Canada tremendous national and industrial expansion. People grew rich; if a man wanted to make money it was almost impossible for him not to grow rich, if he made money his ideal. A new standard was developing prior to 1914 in the matter of how a man was to be measured. We were beginning to value a man by what he was worth – the size of his house, the number of his motor-cars, and the elegance of their equipment, and the extent of his wife's dinner parties, and the number of gowns she had was beginning to determine what a man's family station was.[69]

The war had made Canadians look twice at this emergent social stratification. It had brought so many sufferings on Canadians, but it had also brought them one great blessing: it had inspired them to value their fellow Canadians not by what they possessed but by their characters. This was in some ways a socialist message, and Nickle did not flinch from that term:

> Some people call me a Socialist. I should like to define my Socialism. Socialism is a very general term; you may regard it as synonymous with anarchy, or you may define it as the recognition of the right that every man is entitled to a fair chance. I am a Socialist, if by that term you mean that there should be a reasonable equality of opportunity; if you lay down as a fundamental principle that every man should get a due amount of this world's goods for the services that he renders; that no group, no class, no individual should be crippled just because of lack of money to get a fair start in life. I have run, not one, but five or six elections, parliamentary and municipal, in the city from which I come, and if there is one thing that has wrung my heart it has been to find, among the households of people whom I call my constituents, especially bright boys or girls who were obliged to leave school because the factory age had come and the family could not

afford to keep the child at school because of the necessity of their earning to assist the other members of the family. I am a Socialist, to the extent of my belief that the child is entitled to a chance. It has been strongly borne in upon me that 'slow rises worth by poverty oppressed.' My views are to this extent socialistic: that unbearable burdens of this kind should be lifted from the masses of the people.[70]

Nickle predicted that a great avalanche of hereditary titles was about to land on Canada – specifically, bestowals of the new Order of the British Empire, with regard to which the Canadian prime minister would have little say as to the recipients. (Here, Borden twice interrupted Nickle to tell him that his impression on this score was erroneous, both with respect to the prime minister's advisory role and with respect to the nature of the awards, which were to be non-hereditary.[71])

After descending briefly into the minutiae of a recent conference of the premiers of the overseas Dominions, which had dealt with this issue, Nickle returned to the 'philosophy of titles' – and considered the motives of those who vied for them. Why did people want titles at all? 'As far as I can find out, and as far as I can think it out, I suppose we must admit that there is vanity in most people. Human beings desire recognition, and the people at large are pleased when such recognition is justly given. Besides, there is in the world a certain class of people who will do more if they are going to get something for it; in other words, if you recognize them. They like it to be known by the world in general and by people with whom they mix that other people recognize their abilities, and that they have a handle to their name as evidence of their virtue and their character.'[72]

But the problem, Nickle added, was that any such recognition was prone to caprice and tended to escape any rationally defensible process. The result was a system that encouraged jealousy and division: 'Instead of stimulating a nation to united effort as the result of recognition of only those who are outstanding, the majority of the people are indifferent, and there is a tendency to think that nothing need be done because nothing will be heard of what has been done.'[73] The position of women was especially contradictory, in that they tended to see themselves reflected in the titles attained by their husbands:

A cynic in this country once said that a man measured his worth by his intellectual capacity and the money he could make, and a woman by her social status, and I have been shocked at the social superiority that some women attempted to assume, simply because their husbands had been singularly successful in making money, and had shown great tact in the method they had adopted in giving donations to certain objects. I think a woman's status entitles her to recognition as of her own right, and I believe if there were no reflective titles, you would have less seeking after them, and you would have greater equality in society, and for these reasons, briefly put, I think there should be no such thing as a woman being given the title of a 'lady,' by virtue of the fact that her husband is called 'Sir.'[74]

Nickle's position was not overtly antifeminist; he believed, so he said, that women's equality with men was inevitable and desirable. But this goal would never be achieved as long as the system perpetuated the belief that women could bask in the honour and glory of their titled husbands. No less dated was the assumption that the awarding of honours should follow the rule of primogeniture, which likewise ran roughshod over the fundamental principle that a man ought to be honoured only for that which God, and not the accident of birth, had bestowed on him.[75]

The enunciation of this curiously left-wing Unionist 'philosophy of titles' was followed by a detailed exploration of the history of titles, which drew on such sources as the recent biography of Lord Sydenham by Adam Shortt, and on Bryce's *American Commonwealth*, not to mention recent criticisms of hereditary titles pulled from the *Ottawa Journal-Press*, the *Hamilton Herald*, the *Edmonton Journal*, and even the *Westminster Gazette* of England. This last-named publication had argued that 'honours do create and intensify class divisions, they encourage snobbism, and stamp inequality, but we cannot do without them because without these things you could not finance political parties nor could you reward political services.' In this extract, Nickle saw evidence that the British system of honours fed the worst kind of 'flunkeyism.'[76] For him the risks of the present moment were great. Paraphrasing Asquith, he concluded. 'We are establishing a class in this country who are sincere "in the tranquil consciousness of effortless superiority." I do not want that class in this country ... it is pregnant with possibilities of irretrievable injury to this country, and will militate against the establishment of a wholesome democracy for which we crave and pray.'[77]

This was a strong speech. Nickle's rhetoric forcefully summoned the image of a democracy at war for ideals – ideals that the titles conferred by the Crown on Canadians would irretrievably damage. Other members responded warmly to Nickle's words. According to A.R. McMaster, Liberal MP from Brome, Nickle had spoken to a motion he himself had meant to place on the order paper, one that would have declared hereditary titles undesirable for Canadians on Canadian soil. 'I do not believe,' McMaster added,

> that, if you questioned a hundred men, you would find one that was in favour of that principle. If you went to the metropolis of Canada, the city of Montreal, and placed yourself on St. James Street, unless by chance you found some financial magnate who had already received a hereditary title, I feel satisfied the result would be the same. In Toronto I am inclined to believe that not two people out of a hundred would be in favour of hereditary titles. As you went westward, I believe it would be well for you to be accompanied by the Sergeant-at-Arms and the Mace, because, if you asked that question of the stalwart democrats of the West, I am afraid you might be in danger of personal violence; they would not tolerate being even asked such a question.[78]

Snobbery was the inevitable consequence of an honours-perpetuated caste system. 'Snobbishness is not one of the lesser evils,' McMaster continued. 'It is one of the greater evils ... Snobbishness often means extravagance. Snobbishness means contempt for and disrespect of parents. It means very often delay in marriage until the young folks can start where the old folks left off, and delay in marriage produces all sorts of social evils.'[79] In effect, McMaster was saying that the Imperial honours system led to prostitution.

The three francophone voices in the debate were those of Sir Wilfrid Laurier, Ernest Lapointe, and Rodolphe Lemieux. Laurier declared himself in agreement with 'every syllable' that Nickle had uttered. He allied himself especially with the democratic sentiments in the speech, and he contrasted the principles of democracy with those of aristocracy.

> Democracy and aristocracy are not compatible institutions, and as democracy advances aristocracy must recede ... I am a Liberal of the old school of England. I would have been a Whig if I had been in England. I wish, for my part, that the British aristocracy had continued to do as they did in the past. But they do not understand the times in which we live. Whether the British aristocracy like it or not, or whether men generally like it or not, at the present time England is on the eve of a revolution ... The days of aristocracy are over; a new force is now entering into the Government of Great Britain, that is to say, the great masses of the nation. Whether it be for woe or for weal the future will show.[80]

Laurier sensed unanimity in the House against the very idea of creating peers in Canada; he also broached the possibility of going even further and abolishing the bestowal of titles of any kind: 'Everybody will, I believe, agree that in Canada badges, titles, honours and trappings will never take root. We are a democratic country; we have been made so by circumstances.' Perhaps aware that he might be accused of hypocrisy, he noted that he himself had accepted a title, but then continued flamboyantly: 'I see here a little class of titled people, knights commanders of this order or that order. If they will make a bargain with me, I am quite prepared, if we can do it without any disrespect to the Crown of England, to bring our titles to the marketplace and make a bonfire of them.'[81]

Ernest Lapointe, the Liberal MP from Kamouraska (and eventually to become Mackenzie King's French-Canadian lieutenant), was also inclined to prohibit those titles which were not hereditary. From his perspective, the British government itself had brought honours into disrepute and had unwittingly democratized Canadian public life.

> We must be grateful to the Government, or whoever are responsible for the condition of things which exists to-day, because by distributing titles by the bushel in this country they have aroused a public opinion and have created a feeling of resentment which will cause the disappearance of a threatening evil for Canada. We have been assured that the Crown was giving those titles of its own grace; but everybody realizes in this country that the appointments are ordinarily made on the recommendations of the Government ... We have come to the point where citizens in every quarter of Canada are enquiring why certain gentlemen have had titles conferred upon them, and where, on the other hand, many titled citizens prefer that the people should not enquire why they have received their titles. ... In this country [in comparison with the United States or France] we have titles of all kinds, flavours and descriptions. I say that this is a condition of things which must be done away with, and that blue plague of aristocracy, or muck [mock?] aristocracy, must be driven from our shores ... There is no place in the public life of this country for hereditary leaders or rulers. Brains, honesty and work should be the only qualifications for leadership in a democratic country like ours. This contagious disease, this thirst for titles, is not new. It has been so for centuries. It is a remnant of the

Middle Ages, and in these modern days the people are getting sick of it ... The institution itself is vicious and productive of evil.[82]

Rodolphe Lemieux, the Liberal MP for Maisonneuve, agreed that the resolution might be broadened to include abolition of the entire institution of honours. He responded to Oliver Goldsmith's 'The Deserted Village' by citing the words of a French-Canadian poet:

Sur cette terre sauvage
Où les titres sont inconnus,
La noblesse est dans le courage
Dans les talents, dans les vertus.[83]

Unlike most speakers in the debate, Lemieux took aim at a recent notorious case: the awarding of a title to Lord Beaverbrook, 'a Canadian far more famous for his cement merger than for his accomplishments on behalf of the Empire. I am sorry the name of Canada is to-day being branded in England on account of the bestowal of titles on such an individual. Sir, I cannot forget that during many months before the last election that individual libeled and slandered the province to which I belong, the faith which I profess, and the race from which I come.'[84] Over the repeated interruptions of Sir Sam Hughes, who leapt to the defence of the new Lord Beaverbrook, Lemieux underlined the anti–French-Canadian sentiments he had found in Aitken's *Epitome of the War* and in his writings in the *Daily Express*. Lemieux also reinterpreted the history of Quebec, which, he argued, had once been characterized by a nobility, but which never had a feudal system. He then returned to more recent controversies. The recent honouring of journalists had 'poisoned' the wells of public opinion, and there was still an acute danger that a revival of 'blatant jingoism, acute imperialism and haughty militarism, the curse of every land,' could mean the revival of titles in Canada. He then surreptitiously returned to the subject of Lord Beaverbrook: 'When a journalist has acquired a large fortune in this Canadian commonwealth, if he tastes the wine of imperialism and of jingoism, if perchance he goes across and meets lords and dukes, he suddenly asks himself: "Why should I not get a title?" That is the psychological moment when he forgets his Canadian citizenship and adopts flunkeyism. He then is ready to sacrifice the independence of his paper, to sell his pen and that of his editors in order to parade as Sir So-and-So, or Lord So-and-So.'[85]

This was too much for the irascible and ultra-Imperialist Sir Sam Hughes, who would brook no criticism of Lord Beaverbrook, 'a gentleman of whom every honest Canadian may be proud.' He sought to turn the tables on the Unionist movers of the resolution and on its Liberal supporters. The 'inflation of honours' had become epidemic under Laurier himself, Hughes pointed out, and Lemieux's hostility to the system could be traced to his own unusual failure to

get a knighthood when nearly every Liberal in the Cabinet of the Right Hon. gentleman who sits at his left (Sir Wilfrid Laurier) was plastered with titles, hereditary and others, obtained from the British Government ... Why did not the leader of the Opposition recommend for a knighthood the Hon. member from Maisonneuve? Nearly every man in his Cabinet got one. Canada was dosed with them as never before, and if there is a revulsion of feeling against titles coming from Great Britain now it is partly due to the fact that the leader of the Opposition accepted a title himself after declaring on every platform that he was a democrat to the hilt, and then labeling his own followers for sixteen years until titles got to be common.[86]

Sir Sam was far from done. As for Lemieux's accusations against Beaverbrook, his own record was known across the country: the 'dirtiest transaction in which Lord Beaverbrook was ever concerned was clean in comparison with the best I have heard of you.'[87] As for Sir Wilfrid Laurier,

the spirit shown by the right hon. leader of the Opposition in his little braggadocio was amusing to me. Imagine for an instant, if you can, the right hon. Sir Wilfrid Laurier sliding over to the market square to deposit his insignia of office in a pile. Why, wild horses would not drag him there. Talk about autocracy and democracy, there is not a democratic act I have known of that the right hon. the leader of the Opposition has ever practiced. In the past he has taken the most autocratic position, and as a member of the old Liberal party he always did that. He ruled his following then and rules them now more firmly than the Kaiser ever ruled Germany.[88]

Hughes, who considered himself a far more committed democrat than Laurier, took time to praise the British aristocracy, a 'race of men who have so solidly stood for the cause of democracy and have again and again intervened between the tyranny of the Crown on the one hand and the tyranny of the mob on the other.' In fact, the aristocracy had *always* been on the side of *true* democracy, to a greater extent than even the Sovereign himself. The exception that proved the rule – and here, Hughes was surely engaged in a piece of Catholic-baiting, was William, Prince of Orange. Hughes then took aim at the other perceived enemy of honours and titles, the trade unions, whose 'autocracy' posed the greatest threat to the country. Bolshevism was an attempt 'to raise a nation from labour unions,' an experiment undertaken by those who, unlike Hughes, merely 'pose as democrats.' Hughes commented: 'Until these labour unions are put in their place, until the country sees that these organizations have no right to limit the production of commodities in our factories, until labour unions abrogate the right to hold themselves as a separate and distinct body in the nation – a nation within a nation, – we will never have democratic government, we will have government by the most irresponsible and autocratic element in any land.'[89] A debate that had inspired one member to discuss prostitution thus led another to an analysis of the labour movement and its Bolsheviks.

The emotive energy Hughes generated in the House was missing from Borden's ultimately decisive contribution, which, because it reflected his own detailed preparation of the Report of the Privy Council – which had been 'scooped' by Nickle – was by far the most detailed and pragmatic contribution to the debate. He began by extending his congratulations to the mover and seconder of the resolution for their eloquence, even if (he implied) much of this eloquence had been beside the point. Whatever the merits of the case for egalitarianism, the mere abolition of hereditary titles – or even all titles – would not do away with plutocracy. True, there were class distinctions in Britain and an order of precedence at social and other functions, but evaluations of a man's worth there did not in fact generally proceed on the basis of whether or not he held a seat in the House of Lords. He also disputed Nickle's contention that there had been 'a very great grasping for titular distinctions in the country,' queried his preoccupation with women basking in the titles of their husbands, questioned the likelihood of the principle of primogeniture ever being re-established in Canada, and wondered if Nickle's arguments did not lead to the *reductio ad absurdum* of a refusal of *all* titles, no matter how harmless, such as the title 'Honourable,' claimed by cabinet ministers and premiers in provincial legislatures.

On the question of the relative authority of the Canadian and Imperial governments with respect to the granting of titles and honours, Borden drew on the recent scholarship of Arthur Berridale Keith in his *Responsible Government in the Dominions* (1912) and *Imperial Unity and the Dominions* (1916). Keith sustained the conclusion that "the Governor has a delegation of so much of the royal prerogative as is required for the conduct of the executive government of the Dominion or State of which he is Governor, and time and good sense have united to make it clear that this necessary delegation includes practically all the prerogatives of the Crown in the United Kingdom."[90] With respect to the bestowal of honours, the practice in the United Kingdom was that the prerogative of the Crown was almost invariably exercised on the advice of some minister.[91] Borden concluded from this that, given Canada's emergent status as a self-governing Dominion, there was 'no reason why the Government of this country, represented by its Prime Minister from time to time, should not have the same right and the same responsibility in respect of the bestowal of honours upon persons domiciled in Canada as that which is employed by the Prime Minister of the United Kingdom in respect of the bestowal of honours upon persons domiciled in the British Islands.'[92] This conformed to Borden's reading of a Canadian order-in-council of 19 February 1902, which argued that honours should conform to the rule of responsible government, and to Order-in-Council 668 of 25 March 1918, which held that 'no honour or titular distinction shall hereafter be conferred upon any subject of His Majesty ordinarily resident in Canada except upon the direct advice and responsibility of His Majesty's Canadian Government.'[93] Borden pointed out that in a sense, his order-in-council actually went beyond Nickle's resolution, because it would prohibit holders of hereditary honours who came to reside in Canada from perpetuating their titles. In Borden's view, no title of honour held by any person resident in Canada should continue 'to have the heritable quality.'[94]

This was a landmark debate. The Nickle Resolution continues to be cited, incorrectly so, as a blanket prohibition against Canadians accepting British peerages and knighthoods.[95] The debate itself is a rich and telling document because it reveals – contrary to much conventional wisdom – that the question of honours has never been a minor issue in Canadian history. Consider that in the very depths of a war crisis, with a massive strike movement threatening war production, with serious French/English disturbances brewing on the question of conscription, and with a novel coalition government of Liberals and Conservatives struggling for survival and compelled to undertake far-reaching experiments in public borrowing and state planning, the House of Commons debated the question of honours for six acrimonious hours. Everyone in the debate was a self-professed 'democrat,' but there were wide divergences of perspective. French Canadians resented slights to their 'national' honour and attacked the honours bestowed on the perceived enemies of their race; Imperialists resented attacks on their Imperial identity and defended the honours bestowed on the stalwarts of the war effort. There were at least two subgroups among the defenders of honours: the dyed-in-the-wool Imperialists, headed by Hughes, and the more moderate Imperialists, including Borden and W.S. Fielding, who wanted to reform the system by removing hereditary titles and by placing control over recommendations for awards in the hands of Canadian authorities, most specifically the prime minister. There were at least two subgroups on the other side as well. There were the 'abolitionists,' who wanted an end to *all* honours and titles, not just hereditary ones. This group included Ernest Lapointe and – as unlikely as Hughes rightly made it appear – Sir Wilfrid Laurier himself, who spoke to a widespread sense of public revulsion against these distinctions. To the abolition of honours and titles was attached the notion that the war in Europe was leading Canada into an 'age of democracy,' a meritocratic epoch in which brains, honesty, and work would be a leader's primary qualifications. According to this view, knighthoods and titles were feudal holdovers often acquired by disreputable means. There were also the 'extreme abolitionists,' who supported the abolition of all hereditary titles, knighthoods, titles held by members of the Privy Council and Imperial Privy Council (such as Honourable and Right Honourable), and even, on occasion, military ranks. As expressed by Levi Thomson, the spokesman for this tiny group, 'titles of any kind are absolutely useless.'[96]

There was much emotion in this debate, but apart from Borden's lawyer-like presentation, little subtlety or detail. Over and over, criticism of Canadians developing their own made-in-Canada system of hereditary honours (a system defended by no one, and a political liability everywhere) was broadened into criticism of Canadians being allowed to accept non-hereditary honours in the United Kingdom – a far more complex issue. The Nickle Resolution, which survives to this day as a focus of public debate, revealed but did not itself resolve the complexities of honours in the Canadian polity; that said, the part it played in restricting the bestowal of British honours on Canadian residents was a key factor in the development of Canada's present-day honours system. The overwhelming desire of the politicians and civil servants who followed Nickle to avoid a lopsided and patronage-riddled awards system played no small role in the creation of the Order of Canada, perhaps the fairest system this country has ever known.

The Nickle Resolution and Report of the Special Committee on Honours and Titles

It has often happened in Canadian history that events in other parts of the world have caused a re-examination of circumstances at home. With regard to honours, controversy in Canada led to a sea change in government policy toward them, and once again Canada pre-empted Britain and the entire Empire in rectifying the problem.

The parliamentary debate over British honours – the debate that enshrined the name of W.F. Nickle in Canadian constitutional history – began on 8 April 1918. Herein lies a substantial irony. There is little doubt that Nickle knew rather little about the topic his resolution addressed. To compound the irony, Nickle himself did not vote for the amended resolution that today carries his name; this bore in fact much more the imprint of his critic and principal de facto opponent, Sir Robert Borden.

As a consequence of the so-called Nickle Resolution, Canadians were prohibited from accepting peerages, whereas knighthoods – provided they were bestowed in accordance with the advice of the Prime Minister of Canada, were permitted to continue. Subsequently, in 1919, Nickle introduced another resolution related to honours, one that was amended to form a committee. The Special Committee on Honours and Titles, chaired by Nickle himself, released a report approved by the House of Commons. It requested that the King cease awarding knighthoods and peerages to persons ordinarily resident in Canada, and that all hereditary titles in Canada be extinguished on the death of the current holder. Essentially, the special committee was recommending that no further titles or honours be awarded, whether titular or non-titular. Even the practice of addressing the holder of a knighthood with the appellation 'Sir' was to be discontinued. Parliament later passed a motion of concurrence with this report, but it has rarely been adhered to in any aspect. This report is often referred to as the Nickle Resolution, although it was really the Report of the Special Committee on Honours and Titles. Thus there are four entities – Order-in-Council 1918-668, Nickle's original resolution, Nickle's resolution as amended, and the Report of the Special Committee – confusingly bound up with what is today remembered as the Nickle Resolution. This explains much of the confusion and amnesia that surround honours in Canada.

The Nickle Resolution, 1918

The Nickle Resolution underwent a metamorphosis after being introduced to Parliament, and its final outcome was far different from the radical reforms Nickle intended. His original resolution was amended and reclaimed by Borden, who in all fairness was probably the person from whom Nickle had borrowed the idea in the first place.[97] Borden's extremely well-prepared and measured interventions were the result of his having extensively consulted the authorities with regard to Order-in-Council 1918-668, which was distributed to members during the debate. With Nickle's blessing, the original Nickle Resolution was later amended by Robert L. Richardson, a radical MP, who proposed to have the King 'refrain from conferring any titles upon ... subjects domiciled or living in Canada' – a substantial radicalization of Nickle's original motion, which had targeted hereditary titles. Debate then resumed on 21 May 1918, with Nickle suspecting that Borden had his own amendment up his sleeve.[98] He was quite correct. Borden took the floor and once again attacked the motion as amended as too broad. He then executed his *coup de grâce* by introducing an amendment of his own. He replaced Richardson's amendment and Nickle's motion with the four clauses contained in Order-in-Council 1918-668. To this, Borden added a promise to make public the reasons why a person could be knighted prior to their dubbing.[99] There was still widespread concern – expressed eloquently by Laurier – that the prime minister would still be able to recommend awards. Nickle remained confident that history was on his side, and in his closing remarks congratulated Parliament on its decision to abolish all titles, which was clearly not a sensible reading of the resolution at hand. Sensing danger, Borden declared that 'if the House does not propose to accept the course which I have asked them frankly and with much respect to take, I should consider that I am relieved from my duty of carrying on any longer the Government of this country.'[100] Borden would later write of the honours question that it was at most a minor matter,[101] and historians have tended to agree with him; but his blunt warning that, if crossed on the question of honours, he would resign, is evidence that in 1918 he thought otherwise. Few members were prepared to plunge the country into another wartime election or to risk a constitutional crisis. Richardson's amendment to Borden's amendment failed, while Borden's four clauses as set out in Order-in-Council 1918-668 passed, 104 votes to 71.[102] No further hereditary honours or titles were to be awarded Canadians. The prime minister was to have control over recommendations for knighthoods. The hereditary quality of peerages awarded to Canadian residents was to be extinguished by legislation. Only one Unionist MP voted against the amended resolution; his name, not surprisingly, was W.F. Nickle.

Report of the Special Committee on Honours and Titles, 1919

The British government accepted the first and second clauses of the Nickle Resolution – namely, Order-in-Council 1918-668. It was also agreed that the King would no longer confer hereditary titles on residents of Canada 'save on the formal recommendation of the Prime Minister of Canada.'[103] This signalled an end to Canadian residents accepting peerages. The fourth proposal, regarding the hereditary effect of peerages awarded to residents of Canada, 'presented many difficulties, and would require very grave consideration.'[104] This was because extinguishing the hereditary quality of peerages would have required an act of the Imperial Parliament.[105] Through Devonshire, the Colonial Office asked Borden to allow this part of the resolution to 'remain in abeyance.'[106] Canada had finally gained control over civilian awards and done away with the practice of having Canadian residents appointed to the peerage. Borden had achieved a major advance in gaining Dominion control over vital aspects of the Royal Prerogative, although complete control would not follow until passage of the Statute of Westminster in 1931.

The 1919 British New Year's Honour List was so full of appointments to the various orders of knighthoods in recognition of services rendered during the First World War that the *London Gazette* had to print a number of special supplementary issues. Borden, having spent Christmas 1918 in Britain dealing with matters of state, cabled the acting prime minister, Sir Thomas White, in early January 1919. Borden had decided temporarily to cease recommending or approving honours and knighthoods for Canadians,[107] and suggested that at some later date a committee be founded to deal with the issue.[108] Sir Thomas White concurred, and Cabinet, not wanting to reopen a difficult issue, agreed.[109] Borden calculated that if for the moment no further awards were made, the issue would solve itself.

Borden was well aware of the delicacy of the moment. After passage of the Nickle Resolution, only eleven knighthoods were awarded, and seven of these were to military officers and effectively beyond the control of the prime minister. Of the civilian knighthoods, all but one were gazetted on 6 July 1918. The recommendations for these awards would have been submitted at least two months earlier, prior to the passage of the Nickle Resolution.[110] Parliament did not object to the military awards; it had been previously agreed that officers serving in the war could be awarded honours without the consent of the Canadian government. Curiously, the appointment of Ernest Lapointe did not cause a stir either.

After the 1918 debate, events in Britain helped bring honours and titles back into the public realm. With the passage of the Nickle Resolution, it seemed as though the issue had been solved. However, an ongoing scandal in Britain did much to reopen the topic for discussion in Canada. In December 1918, Lloyd George's coalition government had won a landslide victory. In contravention of a 1917 resolution of the House of Lords, Lloyd George began selling peerages and baronetcies on an unprecedented scale. Upwards of £2,900,000 was collected 'by devious means to finance [the] Lloyd George Liberals.'[111] This generated outrage in Britain and fuelled suspicion of all honours and titles in Canada.

Throughout late 1918 and most of 1919, the British press was full of reports about House of Lords hopefuls such as Sir John Robinson. During the scandal, the King agreed to withdraw a peerage that was to have been awarded to Robinson. A messenger went over to deliver the message to Robinson at the National Liberal Club; on hearing that his peerage had been revoked, he reached for his chequebook and asked, 'How much more?'[112] Even officials in the British government were admitting that 'everyone knows that not only the present [British] Government but all Governments give honours and take money for political funds.'[113] Canadians assumed that if the system worked that way in Britain, it must work in a similar manner in this country.

The honours issue reared its head again as the result of increasing worry that many Canadians might soon be awarded the Order of the British Empire. In Britain, honours lists of gargantuan length were being printed. Peerages were being bestowed on successful military leaders such as Field Marshal Sir Douglas Haig, and many of those involved in war-related work at senior levels of government and business were being knighted.[114] Nickle was not one to be daunted by setbacks: on 14 April 1919, almost a year to the week after introducing his original resolution, he introduced a second one. Alarmed by reports that there would be a 'large list of Empire Day Honours which [the] Government desires to have approved,'[115] he again sought parliamentary approval for a motion proposing that 'Your Majesty hereafter be graciously pleased to refrain from conferring any titles upon your subjects domiciled or living in Canada, it being always understood that this humble prayer has no reference to professional or vocational appellations conferred in respect to commissions issued by Your Majesty to persons in Military or Naval Services of Canada or to persons engaged in the administration of Justice of the Dominion of Canada.'[116]

This time, Nickle was arguing against titles in general, not just peerages. He contended that knighthoods were an integral part of the aristocracy, and compared the development of the aristocracy in Canada with that of the autocracy in Germany, which had 'such an awful hold on the people.'[117] Parliament was reluctant to deal with the topic again, but Nickle pushed the issue forward. Conveniently for him, Borden at the time was attending the Paris Peace Conference.

Once more, Nickle related this seemingly particular issue to the greatest – indeed, cosmic – issues facing humanity in the war's aftermath:

For the past four years Canada, with the rest of the world has been engaged in a great struggle to determine what class of citizenship should predominate through the world ... There is a fundamental difference that lies between a democracy and an autocracy. An autocracy proceeds on the assumption that the chosen few have the right to govern and that to them is given, almost by way of divine right, the right to enjoy what is commonly called the good things of life; that the many submit to the government of the few, because they must, not because they are willing ... We have been fighting for democracy, and if we were sincere in what we spoke from the platforms and in what we said in this House, then I say now that the war is over and the fighting has been won, let us be consistent and legislate a little for democracy, and let the first legislation that this House undertakes be legislation that will do away as far as possible with class distinctions.[118]

Charles Sheard, a fellow Conservative from Toronto, wanted to go even farther down the road to social reform; he argued that the people wanted not only to abolish titles, but also to do away with the Senate.[119] The redoubtable R.L. Richardson proposed an amendment seeking to extinguish the heritable quality of peerages held by residents of Canada.[120] In the absence of Sir Robert Borden, only a few cautionary voices were raised. One belonged to the acting prime minister, Sir Thomas White. He explained to the House that the resolution would disadvantage Canadians, who would be denied the opportunity to receive distinctions open to other Imperial subjects. White recounted the achievements of Canadians who had been awarded knighthoods. He then proposed an amendment to Richardson's amendment to Nickle's resolution. White called for all but the first three lines of Nickle's motion to be replaced with a proposal for a special committee: 'That the subject matter of the said motion is amended together with the questions of conferring honours, titular distinctions and decorations upon the subjects of His Majesty ordinarily resident in Canada including those who have performed overseas, in Canada or elsewhere, naval, military or civilian services in connection with the war be referred for consideration and report to a Special Committee.'[121] White's amendment passed, 71 votes to 64, and a committee headed by Nickle was struck.

After the Parliament Hill fire of 1916, the legislature had been moved to the Victoria Memorial Building in Ottawa. Many documents were lost in 1920, during the move to the new Parliament building. Among these were the proceedings and minutes of the Special Committee on Honours and Titles. The committee's first meeting was held on 24 April 1919 and quickly dealt with the subject of hereditary titles; all members were opposed to their continuance.[122] The committee also discussed extinguishing hereditary titles and made further recommendations with regard to knighthoods; for example, it called for the removal of the titular value of knighthoods already held by Canadians. It also considered whether titles such as 'Right Honourable' and 'Honourable' should be abolished. The subject of foreign honours was also examined.

On 22 May 1919, the report was submitted for the approval of the House of Commons. The debates of April and May 1918, and those of April 1919, now replayed themselves, but with a greater emphasis on Parliament's obligation to act against these arbitrary social divisions. The report asked the King to cease conferring all honours and titular distinctions save military ranks and vocational and professional titles on residents of Canada, despite the British government's refusal to allow this request.[123] The report also recommended that action be taken to extinguish the heritable quality of peerages and baronetcies. The committee approved of the continuance of naval and military decorations such as the Victoria Cross, the Military Cross, and other decorations for valour and for devotion to duty. The final part of the report underscored the committee's desire to ensure that no resident of Canada would be able to accept a title of honour or titular distinction from a foreign government.

During the debate on the report, Nickle questioned the honour of honours in an era when those with enough money could simply purchase them. To hammer home his point, he alluded to the ongoing British scandal over the sale of honours. Drawing from the list of recent peers and knights printed in the 3 May 1919 edition of London's *Spectator*, he concluded that of the four new barons, twenty-three baronets, and forty-nine new knights, most had 'gained their dignities, titles and promotions not by virtue of any great national service that they had rendered, but by virtue of the fact that they had been instrumental in the maintaining of a certain Government in power.'[124]

Before Parliament accepted the report, George B. Nicholson, with the support of William Cockshutt, introduced an amendment that would entitle the prime minister to continue to recommend Canadians for knighthoods. This introduced a new perspective on the honours debate. Cockshutt noted that there were relatively few links between Canada and Britain and that knighthoods were one 'slender thread'[125] that continued to bind Canada to the mother country. Cockshutt attacked supporters of the committee report as the same people who wanted to abolish appeals to the Judicial Committee of the Privy Council and to end the office of Governor General. The amendment was not well received by the weary House. Nicholson's amendment failed, 43 votes to 96. Parliament then voted on the motion of concurrence with the Report of the Special Committee on Honours and Titles. Borden allowed his members to 'vote as they see fit'[126] – an indication that unlike in 1918, Borden was not willing to risk the government's stability on the issue of honours and titles. The fragile Union government was in a state of constant leadership crisis; and by allowing a free vote, Borden was avoiding further division as 'unionism lurched towards its inevitable doom.'[127] The motion of concurrence was accepted, and the report was engrossed. Nickle introduced a further motion that an address be forwarded to His Excellency the Governor General for transmission to the King.[128] This motion was agreed to. Fittingly, the last word on the issue went to the irascible Sir Sam Hughes, who requested that his name not be included on the report.

Borden was well aware that the British government would advise the King to temporarily cease awarding knighthoods to Canadians. The British government informed the prime minister that he could at any time resume making recommendations for knighthoods; at the same time, it held to its position that altering the heritable quality of peerages would 'lead to a difficult situation between the Parliament of the United Kingdom and the Parliament of Canada.'[129] Borden had been advised of this within weeks of drafting Order-in-Council 1918-668, in March 1918. Inclusion of this issue in the report was for public consumption only.

Overall, the report had a somewhat vague, 'unreal' quality. It mentioned certain military decorations but not others, which brings into question its underlying seriousness of intent. To this day, Canadians still sometimes receive appointments to both the titular and non-titular levels of the various British orders of chivalry. So it seems that the report has been implemented with little consistency. In practice, the report has simply been an extension of the Nickle Resolution, as restructured in the light of Borden's original Order-in-Council 1918-668.

According to Borden's deputy justice minister, all awards except those mentioned in the report would 'fall within the general prohibition.'[130] But this was clearly not the case. As we shall see, Prime Minister R.B. Bennett would later recommend that eighteen knighthoods be awarded to Canadian residents and that numerous appointments be made to the non-titular level of the Order of the British Empire. Similarly, during the Second World War, Mackenzie King allowed for the awarding of the non-titular levels of the Order of the Bath, the Order of St Michael and St George, and the Order of the British Empire. The report's exemption of 'professional or vocational appellations conferred in respect to commissions issued by Your Majesty to persons in the Military or Naval Services of Canada, or to persons engaged in the administration of Justice in the Dominion,' was a rather large loophole. Is a title that accompanies a peerage not a vocational appellation granted by Royal Warrant? Clearly, the report was too vague as to the type of awards that Canadian residents were entitled to receive. This report was never strictly enforced, although its impact as a statement of Parliament's opinion endures to this day.

By this time, Canada was playing a leadership role in the Commonwealth. Two years after the Canadian report on honours and titles, the British Parliament established a full-blown Royal Commission.[131] Not coincidentally, this commission's vice chairman was the Duke of Devonshire, past Governor General of Canada, who had been in office during both the Sir Hugh Graham affair and the Nickle Resolution debates. After the report of the Royal Commission on Honours was released, the British Parliament took action, and in 1925 the Prevention of Abuses Act was passed.[132] This act outlawed the sale of peerages, knighthoods, and honours in general. When the Irish Free State was established in 1922, one of the first acts undertaken by Ireland's new government was to prohibit its citizens from receiving British peerages, knighthoods, or honours. In 1925, the Union of South Africa followed suit, forbidding its citizens to accept knighthoods.[133] In both South Africa and Ireland, allowances were made for Governors General to be knighted on taking office. Newfoundland, in contrast, made no attempt to follow Canada's lead. In fact, the number of Newfoundlanders awarded civil honours actually increased, making Newfoundland the most knighted colony in the British Empire![134] Australia and New Zealand would continue to embrace the British honours system until the late twentieth century.

British Honours in Canada after the Nickle Resolution, 1918–1935

An outside observer would have thought that with the Nickle Resolution and the Report of the Special Committee on Honours and Titles, the issue of honours in Canada had been dealt with fully. But this was true only up to a point. The prohibition on Canadian residents receiving most British awards had created a vacuum.

Canadian public servants, politicians, and philanthropists had been left with no formal recognition beyond 'great work, wonderful job.' The Canadian identity was not yet sufficiently developed to allow for the creation of a truly Canadian honour or, at the very least, one that avoided the problems inherent in the British system.

During Arthur Meighen's brief tenure in office, no awards were made. An attempt within Cabinet to reintroduce the practice of recommending Canadian residents for knighthoods failed to gain acceptance.[135] Meighen's second term as prime minister, in 1926, did not yield any new Canadian knights either. Even the Canadian Bar Association defeated a resolution in favour of resuming the award of knighthoods.[136] Thus, no recommendations were made. Clearly, the issue remained contentious.

Meighen's time as prime minister was brief. He was succeeded by William Lyon Mackenzie King, who would guide Canada for eighteen of the next twenty-four years. Mackenzie King was not unfamiliar with honours. As the young Deputy Minister of Labour, he had been made a Companion of the Order of St Michael and St George, having been nominated by his mentor, Sir Wilfrid Laurier. In 1910, Laurier offered Mackenzie King a knighthood,[137] but he declined it, no doubt believing it would hinder his progress in politics. Being knighted so young would have brought him many problems. Again in 1935, he was offered a knighthood in the form of a GCMG – the most senior chivalric award a resident of the British Dominions could receive. Again he declined the offer, although not without some thought.[138] In terms of honours, Mackenzie King faired quite well; by the end of his life he had been appointed to the Order of Merit, the most senior and exclusive non-titular British order, joining the ranks of Florence Nightingale, Sir Winston Churchill, and Jan Christian Smuts. Strangely, Mackenzie King petitioned the Chancellery of the Order of St Michael and St George for permission to cease wearing his CMG insignia; his concern was that the public would assume he had a knighthood![139]

In many respects, Mackenzie King was the father of modern Canada; he took the autonomy won by Borden at the Imperial War Conference and converted it into virtual independence. Mackenzie King was not the most loved Canadian prime minister, but he was the most durable: 'Mackenzie King was the rock upon which many broke but upon which modern Canada was built.'[140] He would bring Canada close to creating a Canadian honour, but he ultimately shied away from the task, believing it too contentious an issue for even him to deal with. As we shall see, he developed a complex attitude toward honours, one that allowed him to practically ban political honours, while permitting the occasional award of military valour and exemplary service awards.

By the time he became prime minister, he wanted nothing to do with honours or titles, and the Nickle Resolution provided him with the perfect excuse to avoid the issue. When Sir William Mulock asked him to recommend Colonel Alexander Fraser, Archivist of Ontario and aide-de-camp to the Lieutenant-Governor of Ontario, as a Companion of the Order of St Michael and St George, Mackenzie King replied: 'I fear ... that the resolution of the House of Commons respecting the receipt by Canadians of titles and decorations makes it impossible for any recognition of the kind being granted.'[141] Here, he was cleverly using the Nickle Resolution to avoid the issue of honours. That resolution empowered him as prime minister to make such recommendations, but he chose not to do so, and he used the resolution as a convenient shield.

Yet he well knew the Report of the Special Committee on Honours and Titles was non-applicable, as would be demonstrated during the Second World War, when Canadians again resumed receiving honours, albeit non-titular ones.

Mackenzie King was against residents of Canada being awarded knighthoods, yet he had no objection to people born in Canada but living elsewhere receiving knighthoods and honours from the British government for services to the United Kingdom or other parts of the Empire. The most thoroughly documented case of this loophole is the example of Dr George Washington Badgerow. Badgerow was born and educated in Canada but left for Britain in his early twenties. He quickly became the most renowned otolaryngologist in Britain. Badgerow was also the personal physician to His Royal Highness, Prince Arthur, Duke of Connaught. Prince Arthur wanted to have Badgerow knighted in 1923 for his services to British medicine, but ran up against a genuine British reluctance to agitate Canadian authorities. The Colonial Office was aware of how contentious the issue of honours was in Canada, and asked Peter Larkin, the Canadian High Commissioner, if the Canadian government would have any objection to the award being made. Larkin cabled Mackenzie King for a decision. Mackenzie King cabled back: 'In view of the fact that the House of Commons Honour resolution apparently relates only to persons domiciled or ordinarily resident in Canada, it would be for Dr. Badgerow to determine whether he considers himself as coming under that category.'[142]

Clearly, Mackenzie King saw Badgerow's award as falling outside the scope of the Nickle Resolution. Unfortunately for Badgerow, this information was not relayed to the British government, and the award was not made for some years. Mackenzie King wrote to Larkin in November 1924 asking why Badgerow had not been included on the New Year Honour's List; once again, he stated that 'the resolution of the Canadian House of Commons could not possibly be construed as applicable to him [Badgerow].'[143] He even added that he had specifically mentioned Badgerow's immunity from both the Nickle Resolution and the report of the Special Committee to Prime Minister Stanley Baldwin; the Duke of Devonshire; Prince Arthur, Duke of Connaught; and the Secretary of State for the Colonies. He was certainly adamant that Badgerow could receive a knighthood, yet it was not until the New Year's Honours List of 1928 that Dr George Washington Badgerow, CMG, CVO, was gazetted as a Knight Bachelor. The Badgerow case demonstrates that Mackenzie King understood the Nickle Resolution and the report of the Special Committee. By allowing Badgerow to accept a knighthood, Mackenzie King was setting a precedent whereby Canadians living in the United Kingdom would be permitted to accept peerages and knighthoods.[144]

In early February 1929, Charles H. Cahan, Conservative Member of Parliament for St Lawrence–St Georges (Quebec), introduced a motion in the House proposing the creation of a special committee to examine the honours system.[145] Mackenzie King was in favour of the committee, but his party was not. During the debates, Mackenzie King refused to divulge his opinion on the subject. Other Liberal MPs attacked the proposal, declaring that the Nickle Resolution had dealt with the matter. Even some Conservatives were reluctant to create a new committee: 'I have heard no person ... express a desire to return to medieval times,' proclaimed one member.[146] The motion failed, 114 votes to 60. Mackenzie King had voted in favour of forming the committee.

An election was on the horizon, and he was not to remain in office much longer; the country's economic woes and soaring unemployment would bring about his electoral defeat.[147]

In 1930, with economic crisis and social strife gripping the country, Mackenzie King was replaced by R.B. Bennett. Bennett was of New Brunswick Loyalist stock and the son of a sea captain; he had risen from a very modest background to become one of the wealthiest men in Canada. As a child, he told his schoolmates he intended to become prime minister of Canada and then sit in the Imperial Parliament.[148] Staunchly pro-British and a Tory, Bennett would clash with Mackenzie King on almost every issue ever presented to Parliament. It is not surprising that the two men would disagree on the topic of honours and awards in Canada.

The Brief Revival of British Honours in Canada

R.B. Bennett's nascent Canadian nationalism extended to more than just helping frame the Statute of Westminster and create such institutions as the Bank of Canada and Canadian Broadcasting Corporation. As prime minister, he was keenly aware of the importance of national symbols, from flags to honours. His vision of Canada was of a nation closely tied to Britain and the Commonwealth, but he was not the imperialist dinosaur that many have portrayed him to be.[149] Throughout his tenure as prime minister, he worked toward the adoption of a new Canadian flag and other Canadian symbols.[150] His interest in honours was sparked in part by a personal desire to eventually sit as a peer in the House of Lords, but it was also rooted in the belief that many Canadians deserved to be recognized for their public service.

To Bennett, the British Imperial honours system was a valuable – albeit imperfect – mechanism for recognizing worthy subjects of the Crown who had performed exemplary service. This need for recognition was only enhanced by the sufferings caused by the Great Depression. Those who were working to alleviate the social and economic hardships experienced by so many Canadians provided Bennett with a perfect pool of people on whom to confer honours. There was still strong opposition to titular honours and even honours in general, but few disputed the appointment of social workers, women, and philanthropists to the various British orders of chivalry. The Canadians awarded honours between 1932 and 1935 served as a transitional group of honoured citizens. Bennett eased Canada away from the Imperial honours system toward what I have termed the Dominion–Commonwealth honours system – that is, a British system controlled by Canadian officials and used to serve Canadian interests.[151] Bennett used honours stratigically, to move the country away from a system dominated by central Canada and rife with partisan appointments toward one that recognized exemplary acts of loyal subjects. The appointments had to be balanced, and they could not follow the traditional pattern; otherwise, his initiative would be discredited by opposition in the press, Parliament, and even his own party. For honours to continue to be part of the Canadian symbolic landscape, they would have to be made palatable for the public.

Lord Bessborough, Canada's Governor General from 1930 to 1935, remarked to George V: 'My own view is that Bennett is a man of excellent patriotic intentions and not self-seeking and has courage to successfully shoulder the entire responsibility for resumptions of Honours.'[152] After 1933, Bennett reinstituted the practice of recommending Canadians for British honours, including knighthoods. Canada still lacked a home-grown honours system, and since 1918 there had been a prohibition on the bestowal of British honours.

Only 18 knighthoods and 189 non-titular honours were awarded to Canadians during Bennett's tenure; even so, from these one can gather a general idea of how the Canadian honours system would have developed had it been allowed to grow within the Empire. Awards made during the Bennett administration were highly representative of the Canadian population; they were also overwhelmingly non-partisan, especially considering the fact that until 1918, knighthoods in particular had been notorious as tools of patronage and political coercion.[153] Those whom Bennett recommended for honours were in many ways similar to those recognized today through the Canadian honours system (i.e., the Order of Canada and Meritorious Service Decorations). Canadian politicians and judges had often been rewarded with honours; under Bennett – for the first time in this country's history – philanthropists, community leaders, eminent scientists, and those involved in cultural pursuits were also recognized. This was in stark contrast to the highly politicized awards made from 1867 to 1918, when party membership and donations were of key importance.

Since passage of the Nickle Resolution in March 1918, no Canadian prime minister had submitted an Honours List to the King. In 1929 the House of Commons considered establishing another committee to examine a revival of honours in Canada, but this idea was swiftly rejected. It was not until 1932, well into the Bennett administration, that a Canadian Honours List was again submitted.

Bennett's Revival of Honours

Knighthoods were under intense public scrutiny, so Bennett had to make it clear that he had purged the system of its politics and that he was rewarding only the worthiest of individuals. There is no question that the knighthoods awarded from 1933 to 1935 went to some of the most deserving Canadians: Sir Frederick Banting, the codiscoverer of insulin; Sir Ernest MacMillan, the noted composer and conductor; Sir Edmund Wyly Grier, the famous portrait painter and president of the Royal Canadian Academy; Sir Charles Saunders, the Dominion cerialist, who revolutionized Canadian agriculture with the Marquis, Ruby, Reward, and Garnet wheat hybrids; and Sir Thomas Chapais, the eminent historian.[154] The breadth of these appointments set them apart from those of earlier times. Bennett wanted to use honours as a tool of national recognition, not as a political device.[155]

By the time Bennett submitted a Canadian Honours List in December 1932, Canada's legal status had changed profoundly. Although the country remained the 'Dominion of Canada,' the Statute of Westminster in 1931 effectively made the country independent of the United Kingdom.[156] Resolution IX of the 1917 Imperial War Conference had affirmed a Dominion's rights, but it was the Statute of Westminster that formalized them and that granted real independence to the Dominions.

In terms of Canadian recommendations for honours, the Report of the Special Committee on Honours and Titles was an attempt to make it impossible for Canadians to be recommended for titular honours such as peerages and knighthoods. The

Nickle Resolution and Order-in-Council 1918-668 were given precedence over the Report of the Special Committee. Yet the Nickle Resolution was just what the name implied – a resolution, not an act of Parliament – which meant it could be ignored.[157] After all, a resolution simply expresses the feelings of Parliament at any given time. Its status as an order-in-council could similarly be overridden with ease. R.B. Bennett chose not to override it – in fact, he followed it to the letter. It just happened that he was the first Canadian prime minister to submit an Honours List since the resolution's passage.

In November 1932, Bennett asked the Governor General to enquire about what allotment of honours Canada would be afforded by the Dominions Office. Bennett was given no firm numbers, but was told that Canadian recommendations would be treated in the same way as recommendations from Australia and New Zealand. Several months before the Honours List was published, the Governor General, having taken advice from the prime minister, was to ask the Secretary of State for the Dominions how many honours would be available to Canada.[158] On receipt of this information, the Governor General would inform the prime minister, who would then submit a list of recommendations through the Governor General to the Secretary of State for the Dominions.[159] These recommendations would then be forwarded to the Secretary of State for the Dominions or to the British prime minister, depending on the award.[160] The approval of the Secretary of State for the Dominions and the British prime minister was a mere formality, one that reflected the role of various Whitehall departments in administering British orders. That the memorandum containing this information came from Buckingham Palace and not the Secretary of State for the Dominions or the British Prime Minister's Office was of central importance. It signified that effective control over honours was now in the hands of the Canadian prime minister, who was in effect dealing directly with the Sovereign. The lists would have to be submitted to the Secretary of State for the Dominions and the British prime minister because it was they who administered the various British orders, but they would not be at liberty to question the decisions of the Canadian prime minister. In their capacity as Ministers of the Crown, they could register an objection with the King; of course, this would place His Majesty in the precarious position of having to decide whether to follow the advice of British ministers or the Canadian ones.

An agreement was reached with the Canadians long before such a situation could arise. The Dominions Office and the British prime minister were to set out the number of awards that Canadians could receive. This figure soon became standardized (as they already were for Australia and New Zealand), so that a prime minister could expect to have a certain number of awards at his disposal from year to year. Basically, the Canadian prime minister submitted an Honours List, which was transmitted to the King unaltered, restricted only by the number of awards allotted to Canada. This was the Nickle Resolution in action. The British government, fearing that it might again be drawn into the honours controversy, decided to examine the legal status of the Nickle Resolution and Report of the Special Committee on Honours and Titles. Ultimately it was decided that 'the Resolution and Address of the Canadian House of Commons has no effect in law and can not limit the King's prerogative.'[161] Although the British government understood this, the legal advisor to the Dominions Office, H.G. Bushe, insisted that Bennett make a statement to this effect, which was done in due course. The King did not want to be dragged into the Canadian honours debate. The resumption of awards was seen as doing much more than simply recognizing worthy citizens. In a telephone conversation between Sir Clive Wigram (the King's private secretary) and the Governor General, it was postulated that the bestowal of honours 'is considered a counter to the influence of the United States' and would 'be welcomed by the mass of the Canadian people.'[162] Bennett's project was welcomed by British officials and especially by George V.

Bennett decided to test the waters first, and recommended only one appointment. On 4 February 1933,[163] the *Canada Gazette* announced that Sir George H. Perley, KCMG, was to be elevated to a GCMG. Although Perley was a member of the government, he was regarded more as an elder statesman than as a party hack. Perley had been knighted in 1915, and the 1933 award would be simply an elevation; it would not alter his title, except that his post-nominal initials would be changed from PC, KCMG, to PC, GCMG. Vincent Massey, the Canadian High Commissioner in London, slightly overstated the situation, declaring that 'the recent honour conferred upon Sir George Perley has met with universal approval.'[164] Mackenzie King did not approve of the award and throughout 1933 voiced his protest. Yet it was not until 14 March 1934 that the Liberals took action. Humphrey Mitchell moved 'that in the opinion of this house, the Prime Minister should refrain from recommending to His Majesty the King the granting of titles, honours and awards to British subjects resident in Canada.'[165] After a short day of debate and a restatement of the same arguments used in the 1918 and 1919 debates, the motion was lost on division, 93 votes to 113. A similar motion was introduced to the House of Commons by Ernest Lapointe on 28 January 1935. The key difference with this motion was that it only asked the prime minister to cease making recommendations for 'any barony or knighthood,'[166] and made no mention of non-titular awards such as the Imperial Service Order and non-titular levels of the Order of the British Empire and the Order of St Michael and St George. Although this motion also failed upon division, the fact that non-titular awards would have been permitted to persist signalled an important change in Liberal policy. The party was no longer opposed to all awards – only to those which conferred a titular distinction. As we shall see, this was the policy that Mackenzie King's Liberals would pursue during the Second World War.

Regardless of these attempts to derail Bennett's recommendations, 17 more knighthoods and 189 appointments to the non-titular levels of the Order of the Bath, the Order of St Michael and St George, the Order of the British Empire, and the Imperial Service Order were made between 1932 and 1935.

When we compare the awards made during Bennett's tenure as prime minister with those of his predecessors, it is obvious that the recipients were the most carefully selected and non-political appointments ever recommended by a Canadian prime minister. Indeed, Bennett was not using knighthoods as tools of patronage. However, despite his good intentions, public reaction to the awards was mixed. The Liberals claimed that Bennett was contravening the Nickle Resolution and thwarting Parliament's resolve to end all titular honours. Yet Mackenzie King knew that the Nickle Resolution could not be used to deny Canadians honours from the Crown,[167] if the prime minister asked the King to use that part of the Royal Prerogative. Mackenzie King was so concerned about the reintroduction of honours that he contacted the spirit of his father on 13 May 1934. He was told by his father's spirit that William Herridge, H.J. Cory, Vincent Massey, and Herbert Marler were to receive knighthoods in the Dominion Day Honours List.[168] However, the 1934 Honours List saw only Banting and Saunders knighted.

The resumption of Canadian appointments to the British orders of knighthood was greeted with great satisfaction by George V. He, like many in Britain, had never fully understood why the Canadian government had stopped making recommendations in 1919.[169] The Sovereign's role in the appointments made during the Bennett administration should not be underestimated. The King was even prepared to make extra awards available to accommodate Canada.[170]

A variety of honours were bestowed on Canadians, ranging from Knight of the United Kingdom (Kt), to one of the various levels of the Order of the Bath (Knight Grand Cross, Knight Commander, Companion), to one of the various levels of the Order of St Michael and St George (Knight Grand Cross, Knight Commander, Companion), to one of the levels of the Order of the British Empire (Knight Grand Cross, Knight Commander, Commander, Officer, Member, and Medal of the Order of the British Empire). Of these awards, the Order of the British Empire was most freely awarded. At the time, it was also the only British Order of Chivalry for which women were eligible.[171]

Bennett's most significant contribution related to the recognition of women. Although 27 per cent of the total awards made during Bennett's prime ministership were to women, they were restricted to the various levels of the Order of the British Empire. Indeed, Bennett went out of his way to ensure a balance in the awarding of the Order of the British Empire.[172] During his tenure, 77 of the 165 awards given (47 per cent) went to women.

It is important to note that although women were fairly well represented on the scale of awards for which they were eligible, 75 of the 77 awards made to women were for services in 'traditional' fields such as health, education, and community service. The two women recognized for non-traditional contributions were rather exemplary individuals: Lucy Maud Montgomery was made an Officer of the Order of the British Empire for her literary contributions, and Mary Winifred Kydd was made a Commander of the Order of the British Empire for her service as president of the National Council of Women. Even so, this was an important change, and one that the founders of the Order of Canada would take into account when developing the domestic honours system in 1966.

Bennett took great interest in his award recipients and personally selected most of them (except for the military awards).[173] He went so far as to write all the letters, personally informing the recipients that they had been nominated. No form letters can be found in Bennett's archives, only highly personalized letters of thanks for their services to the Crown and to Canada.

No one could claim that Bennett was totally egalitarian in his dispersal of honours; that said, he certainly did revolutionize the British honours system in Canada. He expanded the breadth of awards to more than just men, politicians, and friends of the party; he recognized contributions to art, culture, and what we would today call volunteerism. Neither women nor Native Canadians received high awards during his tenure. However, his use of non-titular awards to recognize women was unique and demonstrated a significant shift in Canadian government policy toward honours. Over the two years during which Bennett submitted honours lists to the King, more awards were made to women than during the whole of the Second World War.[174] In many ways, Bennett was the father of the modern Canadian honours system. This statement relates not so much to its structure as to its propensity to recognize a wide variety of services rendered to citizens and the state alike. His successor would have many opportunities to supplement the British honours system – not supplant it – by creating a Canadian order. However, Mackenzie King would choose to continue with a hybrid version of the British honours system, and would take little interest in who was recognized and who was not, as long as the choices did not cause controversy in Cabinet or in the country.

Bennett's government was crippled by the Depression. 'Bennett buggies' were filling the streets, and editorialists were mocking everything from his manner of dress[175] to his reinstitution of honours in Canada.[176] He lost the 1935 election to Mackenzie King. In 1938, after three years in opposition, he retired to Britain, never to return to Canada.[177] He purchased a country estate next door to his childhood friend, Max Aitken, Lord Beaverbrook, and in 1941 was summoned to the peerage as Viscount Bennett of Mickleham, Calgary, and Hopewell. He had realized his dream of serving both the Canadian and British Parliaments.

Bennett's honours policy was eventually discarded, and no further knighthoods were awarded on the recommendation of the Canadian government. As we shall see in the next chapter, some of the non-titular British Imperial honours would be reinstituted for the duration of the Second World War. Bennett was the last Canadian to make full use of the British Imperial honours system; he was also the first to recognize non-traditional endeavours, as well as groups that had previously gone unrecognized.

The change in Canadian attitudes toward honours crystallized towards the end of the Great War. Canadian public scepticism about honours would endure well into the late twentieth century. Key elements of the debate over honours related to Canada's relationship with Britain, the tainted image of civilian honours as easily bought and sold, and the absence of any discussion about creating a Canadian honour devoid of this stigma. The Nickle Resolution and the practical prohibition on honours in Canada from 1919 to 1932 provided a respite from the heated controversy of 1917–18, and allowed the reintroduction of a 'clean' honours system.

The Dominion–Commonwealth system attempted – within the same British Imperial honours system – to recognize exemplary citizenship through philanthropy, public service, and contributions to the community. Imperial achievements and party patronage were no longer emphasized. The transition from aristocratic privilege to democratic egalitarianism was far from complete. Nonetheless, there was a general realization that honours could be used for the greater public good and not just to reward the wealthy. This ethos would help shape the criteria devised by the Order of Canada more than a quarter-century later.

CHAPTER THREE

The Honours Quagmire, 1935–1948:
The Ubiquitous Canada Medal

For reasons of governmental policy, no awards of this Medal have as yet been approved.[1]
W.R. Wright, executive assistant to the prime minister, 1949

When William Lyon Mackenzie King returned to power in 1935, there was little reason to believe that honours of any type would be reintroduced or continued in Canada, yet during his wartime tenure the country came within centimetres of creating a national order. This brush with creating a Canadian order was largely precipitated by the Second World War.

The history of attempts to create a Canadian honours system and Canadian order is not dominated entirely by well-meaning civil servants; a large role was also played by soldiers eager to see their comrades – and themselves – recognized. Wars always generate a demand for honours, and in times of armed conflict the connections between chivalry, violence, and honour are not difficult to discern. During the Second World War, members of the Canadian Armed Forces became ever more keenly aware of their 'honours handicap' relative to their Commonwealth and American peers. This served as a catalyst for the Department of National Defence to offer a number of proposals for establishing a Canadian order and honours system. These proposals did not stop flowing after peace was won in August 1945; they would continue through the 1950s and 1960s and play an important role in the creation of the Order of Canada. The underlying influence of the military must not be ignored or discounted.

With the return of Mackenzie King to office in 1935, hopes of a continued revival of British honours were dashed. The prospects for creating a 'Canadian' honour were equally unrealistic. Mackenzie King had very specific views on honours; in general, he wanted nothing to do with them. He had already indicated this through his policies during his earlier terms as prime minister, 1921–6 and 1926–30. His hostility to honours, which verged on a phobia, was further demonstrated by the fact that he twice turned down a knighthood. Quite simply, this was an issue he did not want to deal with, and the Nickle Resolution provided the perfect excuse for him to avoid it.

During the Bennett administration, Mackenzie King's Liberals and the CCF had been opposed to honours, and Mackenzie King would continue this opposition in peacetime. Other members of the Liberal Party were compelled to support the leader, but many did not agree completely with his stand. Governor General Lord Bessborough, in a letter to George V, wrote that a number of Liberals 'have actually made, in private, direct or indirect advances to have their own names, or those of their friends added in list of recommendations for honours.'[2] A cynic might take this as a sign of Liberal duplicity; it is better to say, this was an indication that the country desperately needed a mechanism for recognizing loyalty and exemplary service. There was no consensus with regard to honours – not in Parliament, and not within the Liberal Party. This lack of consensus, which was so obvious in the debates over the Nickle Resolution, would cause Mackenzie King to constantly shelve attempts to create a Canadian honour, notwithstanding the Cabinet's desire to press ahead.

After Mackenzie King visited Rideau Hall yet again to take up the post of prime minister, he had no reason to expect that the honours question would return to cause him any worry. His opposition to titular honours such as peerages and knighthoods was well known, although there is little indication that he opposed non-titular honours. From Mackenzie King's perspective, every time the King or Governor General opened a presentation case to award an honour, he found himself staring into a Pandora's box, from which controversy and division threatened to fly out. He had no desire to deal with either, and preferred the safe political course when he could possibly find one.

Within weeks of taking office, he was besieged by R.B. Bennett, who insisted that he should be able to submit one last Honours List, as was the tradition in the United Kingdom for a defeated ministry. As one would expect, Mackenzie King refused this 'last request' and settled into his prime ministerial routine. Lord Bessborough, with whom Mackenzie King had never been very friendly, knew better than to bring up the topic of honours, and thus the issue faded into the scenery. Everything was proceeding like clockwork for Mackenzie King, who had returned to office with a strong majority and was ready to tackle the problems of the Great Depression. He had no reason to worry about awards. Only a few civil servants, party loyalists, and military officers merited recognition, and the country was hardly going to collapse if their desires for 'baubles' went unfulfilled.

November 1935 brought Canada a new Governor General, the renowned author John Buchan, recently raised to the peerage as Lord Tweedsmuir. Tweedsmuir took an interest in the founding of a Canadian order and the use of honours to promote public service. On his arrival in Quebec City, surrounded by court uniforms and all the splendour of Quebec's provincial legislature, he was sworn in as Canada's twelfth Governor General. Fresh off the boat, he mentioned the prospect of an honours list for the coming New Year. The prime minister replied politely that this was not an option, but Tweedsmuir insisted that they discuss the matter later.[3] Tweedsmuir wrote to the King's private secretary, Lord Wigram: 'My Prime Minister will welcome an offer of CMGs, CBE etc. But might jib at any K.'[4] He had much to learn about his politically determined prime minister.

If the story of Canadian honours were one of John Buchan's novels, the next chapter would be titled 'Enter Faithful Massey,' since Massey would work hard and long to establish what would become the Order of Canada. Massey is often remembered as 'the Imperial Canadian.' From 1935 until his death in 1967, he would covet an honour – even Mackenzie King expected him to be knighted in the 1935 Honours List – but that honour never came.[5] Massey wanted Canada to remain within the existing British honours system, but he also wanted this country to establish its own unique honour. He had already discussed this concept several times with his old friend John Buchan, and on 3 November 1935 they discussed it again.[6] Massey hoped that Canada would adopt a three-level order similar to the Order of the Star of India, which conferred a knighthood on the top two levels. He was familiar with accounts of Viscount Monck's efforts to found the Order of St Lawrence in 1867 and now he introduced Tweedsmuir to the topic. Like a good Imperial statesman, Tweedsmuir latched onto the idea as an 'important bond with the Crown, and a recognition of public work: not to be associated with snobbery, but with service to the State.'[7] At his first formal meeting with Mackenzie King, Tweedsmuir opened a discussion about the merits of an honours system, and how Canada 'might have something in the nature of the Order of St. Lawrence.'[8] Mackenzie King was horrified that the Governor General had an interest in the topic, and was equally perplexed as to where His Excellency could have acquired such an extensive knowledge of the situation in Canada. So furious was Mackenzie King at Tweedsmuir's honours agenda that he threatened to introduce an act that was 'certain to be passed doing away with all existing titles.'[9] Such an act would have been a parliamentary first. Actually, it is highly doubtful that Mackenzie King would have gone to such an extreme.[10]

The prime minister collected himself, replied politely that he did not think it was 'advisable to enter into any discussion of the matter,'[11] and steered the discussion toward more important concerns. This left the prime minister with a bad taste in his mouth: 'I confess I felt a little annoyed at being confronted with the title business as the first matter of state between the Governor and myself.'[12] Mackenzie King knew who was behind these backroom viceregal manoeuvrings – the culprit was obvious. In his diary, he wrote: 'I have not the slightest doubt that when Massey was with the Governor on Sunday he may have talked over the questions of titles and even made mention of the Canadian Order. I know how desirous above all else he is for this kind or recognition and at one time he spoke to me of a Canadian honour.'[13]

Having experienced one constitutional crisis with a Governor General, Mackenzie King feared that Tweedsmuir would overstep his constitutional authority and take the matter of honours into his own hands. He wasted no time in writing to Tweedsmuir to express his view of the situation. On 11 December 1935, in an unusually ingratiating letter, he told His Excellency: 'I know I have been able to rely with confidence upon Your Excellencies [sic] confidence.' He skirted the issue at hand but left an underlying message that the Governor General must always consult his prime minister. Tweedsmuir responded on 13 December 1935, merely stating that 'you have written me a most extraordinarily kind letter,' with no mention of the honours problem. Tweedsmuir was taking his own advice in 'walking the razor's edge' – something that all Governors General must do.[14] The only other time that Tweedsmuir would introduce the topic of honours prior to the outbreak of the Second World War was in 1939, while travelling with George VI and Queen Elizabeth across the country during their historic Royal Visit. At this time, Tweedsmuir and Mackenzie King had a friendly but brief discussion about Tweedsmuir's recent appointment as a Knight Grand Cross of the Royal Victorian Order (GCVO).[15] Mackenzie King had been present in the Royal Train when Tweedsmuir was knighted – the first time in Canada a person had ever been knighted by a reigning Sovereign, and also the first instance in Canada when a person was knighted in a moving train![16]

Relations between Mackenzie King and Lord Tweedsmuir were cordial, and only ended with the latter's untimely death.[17] To Mackenzie King's delight, Tweedsmuir never reopened the honours question. The prime minister could curtail the Governor General's influence over such matters in peacetime, when the necessity for honours and decorations was relatively light; this would change with the war's outbreak.

Outbreak of War

With the Nazi invasion of Poland in September 1939 and Canada's declaration of war, the High Commission in London, Canada House, became a hub of activity. Cablegrams were exchanged between London and Ottawa at an unprecedented rate. Many of these were written by a young diplomat, Lester Pearson, and then approved by Vincent Massey, the High Commissioner. So it should be no surprise that although Canada's wartime policy toward honours was formulated mainly in Ottawa, it was invariably in response to questions asked by the High Commissioner, Massey.

With the declaration of war on 10 September, the Royal Canadian Navy (RCN), Canadian Army, and Royal Canadian Air Force (RCAF) were mobilized.[18] The issue of honours and awards was of little concern to Mackenzie King and his Cabinet at a time when they were facing unrelenting pressure to prepare an ill-equipped and undersupported military for the conflict ahead. The Canadian government seemed to be taking no interest in the question of honours and awards for its servicemen and women; in contrast, the British government cared deeply, and wanted very much to avoid a situation where Canadians would be prevented from receiving recognition for bravery or meritorious service. As a natural reaction to the state of war, the British government immediately set up a 'Committee on the Grant of Honours, Decorations and Medals in Time of War,' commonly remembered as the Wilson Committee.[19] This committee began dealing with questions relating to the awarding of gallantry decorations and meritorious service awards. In theory, the committee was creating a policy for the entire British Commonwealth; however, on the third page of its first report it acknowledged the peculiar situation in Canada and South Africa, where government policies toward honours contrasted greatly with those of the British government.

In Canada, the contentious issue of honours was left largely in the hands of O.D. Skelton, Under-Secretary of State for External Affairs, and E.H. Coleman, Under-Secretary of State. Mackenzie King had little interest in the controversial topic; he wrote in his diary: 'When I saw honours and awards still on the agenda, I said quite frankly it annoyed me every time.'[20] In Ottawa, the British High Commissioner, Sir Gerald Campbell, found time to write to Skelton. Campbell was concerned that the Nickle Resolution and Canadian policy in general would cause a disparity of honours between Canadians and serving men and women from other parts of the Commonwealth.[21] Skelton replied that all gallantry awards and any others for service would have to be approved by the Canadian government.[22] Here he was stating the obvious, and reflecting a convention developed by Laurier back in 1902. The fact that he was reiterating a well-known process indicates that the Canadian government was concerned that the British government was once again going to meddle in the Canadian honours question. Skelton sounded calm and collected in his correspondence with the British High Commissioner; he was much more frantic in his letters to the Minister of National Defence, Norman Rogers. The same day he wrote the British High Commissioner his note about maintaining the convention of Canadian consultation and approval, he sent a letter to Norman Rogers stating that the question of honours and awards was 'most urgent.'[23] There was in fact no formal written process for recommending and approving awards for Canadian servicemen. Perhaps the sense of urgency had been precipitated by the fact that the second part of the Canadian Army's First Division had sailed from Halifax to Britain that very morning.[24] To most Canadians, the conflict was rapidly escalating. It was expected that the Canadian Army would soon enter into combat with the German Wehrmacht.

The Interdepartmental Committee

To deal with the immediate problem of honours and awards, the Minister of National Defence created a committee to examine the question of gallantry awards and honours.[25] Eventually, in 1942, the Special Committee on Honours and Awards, or Interdepartmental Committee, would evolve into the Awards Coordination Committee.[26] The Interdepartmental Committee was responsible for interpreting existing government policy toward honours and for proposing changes.[27] It drafted the various orders-in-council that pertained to honours and awards. At first, the committee had five members: the Judge Advocate General, Brigadier R.J. Orde, Captain C.R.G. Taylor, Brigadier F. Logie Armstrong, and Group Captain H. Edwards, with John Read, a civilian, acting as chairman. Read would go on to distinguish himself as a jurist for the International Court of Justice at The Hague, and would be one of the first recipients of the Order of Canada in 1967.[28] The committee would grow to include E.H. Coleman, Under-Secretary of State; Sir Shuldham Redfern, Secretary to the Governor General; Frederick L.C. Pereira, Deputy Secretary to the Governor General; and J.F. Delaute, an employee of the Department of External Affairs. The military members of the committee changed over the course of the war. By 1941 there were a few new members: Brigadier Perry, representing the Army; Wing Commander MacLean and Flying Officer Mee, representing the RCAF; and Captain Houghton, representing the RCN.

On 8 February 1940, the committee submitted a report to the Minister of National Defence that summarized existing government policy and necessary changes. Read had drafted an order-in-council to establish a new policy that would entitle Canadian service personnel to receive gallantry decorations 'in operations against the enemy.' On 9 April 1940, this was ratified as Order-in-Council 1430. No provision was made for the award of British orders of chivalry to Canadians. 'Periodical' and 'operational' awards would have to be approved by the Governor-in-Council; immediate awards were to remain under the 'control of Commanders in the field.'[29] Given that the bulk of awards were periodic and operational, this meant the prime minister intended to keep a tight control on honours. This temporary solution seems to have worked, although the bulk of the work did not fall on the prime minister but rather on his overworked Under-Secretary of State, E.H. Coleman.[30]

Norman Rogers's Visit to the United Kingdom

The pressures of war compelled Norman Rogers, Canada's defence minister, to visit London with increasing frequency. Constantly frustrated with the Canadian government's policy toward honours, Massey arranged a meeting between Rogers and George VI. Coincidentally, Rogers held the very same parliamentary seat that W.F. Nickle once represented (Kingston). The two men were actually acquainted: Nickle was a member of the Board of Trustees at Queen's University while Rogers was professor of political science there. A veteran of the Great War, Rogers had been educated at Acadia University and Oxford. On first being elected in 1935, he was appointed Minister of Labour. He became Minister of National Defence on 18 September 1939, after the war's outbreak.

It is entirely plausible that Rogers would have paid a formal visit to the King regardless of Massey's efforts. That said, Massey's involvement made it inevitable that honours would be discussed. On 24 April 1940, Rogers arrived at Buckingham Palace for his meeting with the Sovereign. At 11:30 in the morning he was ushered into a drawing room and encountered the King dressed in his RAF uniform. The meeting lasted thirty minutes. They talked about the war effort in Canada and the situation in France, but the topic of honours for Canadians dominated the discussion: 'The King then brought up the question of honours, decorations and awards. Evidently there had been previous discussion on this matter with Sir Alexander Hardinge, because I had received a message from Mr. Massey, who said that Hardinge had asked him if I had brought over a submission on this question ... It was quite evident however that the King was interested in this subject.'[31]

Rogers explained to the King that the government felt bound by the terms of the Nickle Resolution, and that with time a new policy toward non-titular honours would be developed. At this point there was no mention of creating a 'Canadian Honour'; the more immediate concern was that Canadians in the services be recognized by the existing British awards. Throughout his reign and especially during the Second World War, George VI took a particular interest in the bestowal of honours, decorations, and medals. Well beyond his constitutional duties as Sovereign and the daily presentation of awards at Buckingham Palace, he always cared deeply about ensuring that bravery and exemplary service were recognized.[32] Rogers was not unsympathetic to the King's concerns and relayed them to Mackenzie King.

But more than Rogers, it was Skelton, the Under-Secretary of State for External Affairs, who formulated Canada's policy for honours and awards. At some point in 1940, Rogers mentioned the idea of creating a Canadian order, but the exact date cannot be pinpointed.[33] Tragically, Rogers was killed in an airplane accident on 10 June 1940, before his idea for a Canadian order could be realized. With the new Minister of National Defence, Colonel James L. Ralston, Skelton attempted to carry on the work of defining Canadian policy toward honours. The process of interpreting a Canadian policy and creating a Canadian honour would be hindered by yet another untimely death, that of Skelton in late January 1941. By then, however, Skelton had cleverly transferred some of this workload to the desk of Ephriam Coleman, Under-Secretary of State and Deputy Registrar General.

Coleman was a native of Ottawa and a lawyer. He served as dean of the Manitoba

Law School from 1929 to 1933. He was lured away from academe by R.B. Bennett, who appointed him Under-Secretary of State in 1933. After Skelton deferred the honours question, Coleman quickly became the resident expert; it would be he who administered much of the government's policy for the duration of the war.

Even from his office at Canada House in Trafalgar Square, Massey remained involved in steps toward the creation of a Canadian honour and Canadian honours policy. After Rogers's audience with the King, Massey grew even more adamant that Canada should create an order. He repeatedly sent telegrams to his friend Mackenzie King, who was no doubt becoming rather annoyed with the issue. During a meeting of the War Committee of the Cabinet on 31 October 1940, the justice minister, Ernest Lapointe, said that he favoured 'the establishment of a purely Canadian Order of merit which would be conferred upon Canadians by the King.'[34] Once again the issue was not discussed any further, the immediate issue of gallantry awards having been dealt with through the order-in-council passed on 9 April 1940.

A Special Canadian Award

The first modern proposal for a Canadian order came in November 1940, from John Read, chairman of the Interdepartmental Committee. Read had discussed the need for a Canadian honour with Norman Rogers prior to his death and had drafted a memorandum based on their discussions. Read outlined the structure and name of the award. In terms of the name, he proposed 'The Royal Elizabethan Order for Distinguished and Meritorious Service.' In the same memorandum, he commented: 'It is possible that an Order linked with the Queen or with the Princess Elizabeth, would meet with Royal approval, and, at the same time, with the approval of the common people of this country.'[35] Read envisioned an order consisting of three levels, with a military and civilian division: Royal Elizabethan Order (REO); Companion of the Royal Elizabethan Order (REC); and Member of the Royal Elizabethan Order (REM). This hastily developed proposal was never formally presented to the Interdepartmental Committee. It was quickly set aside. The issue of how to administer British gallantry awards was far more immediate.

Parliament and Honours

Parliamentarians – specifically, members of the House of Commons – had little interest in questions relating to honours. According to many, the necessary debate had occurred in 1918 and 1919, and the question had been satisfactorily dealt with through the Nickle Resolution and Report of the Special Committee on Honours and Titles. The subject of honours and awards was brought up and debated only twice in the House of Commons during the Second World War.[36] The first suggestion – that Parliament should re-examine honours policy – arose during the 19 November 1940 meeting of the War Committee, at which time it was considered inexpedient to reopen the issue in the House.[37]

The issue was reintroduced to Parliament at the request of Coleman's Interdepartmental Committee.[38] Poor John Read, legal adviser to the Department of External Affairs, had spent much time attempting to interpret the previous government policies toward honours, as well as attempting to help the Interdepartmental Committee introduce new policies. After consulting with the Minister of National Defence for Air, Read (and the Interdepartmental Committee) concluded: 'It is impracticable to make provisions for recognition of conduct and action involving gallantry, courage, meritorious service and devotion to duty without contravening the principles embodied in the Report (1919 Report of the Special Committee on Honours and Titles).'[39] Much of Read's manoeuvring was wasted effort: his statements to the Special Committee on Honours and Decorations later in 1942 demonstrated that there were no impediments to Canadians receiving gallantry awards, so long as the Governor-in-Council was consulted. Read and the Interdepartmental Committee were tired of the extra workload involved in serving as the prime minister's gatekeepers for honours; they wanted Parliament to develop a coherent policy that would be simpler to administer. Also, they worried that any comprehensive policy they arrived at would generate controversy, seeing how honours were such a contentious issue in Canada. The issue was formally introduced to the Cabinet War Committee on 11 October 1941. There, it was decided that 'the subject of honours and awards to Canadians (apart from titles) be referred to a special committee of the House of Commons.'[40]

The first mention of honours and decorations in the House of Commons after the beginning of the Second World War came from the Secretary of State, Norman McLarty. In the hope of avoiding any controversy over this contentious issue, he proposed that the House adopt a motion to 'appoint a committee to consider the application of the principles accepted in 1919 to members of the Canadian Forces.'[41] There was no desire from any quarter to harken back to the 1917–19 debates that had surrounded hereditary titles and knighthoods, and McLarty was adamant that the committee would only examine gallantry and service awards and that there would be 'no question of conferring titles.'[42] After a very brief exchange of words, the motion was entered on the order paper, to be discussed the following day. After yet another short debate, the House of Commons voted in favour of creating 'the Special Committee on Honours and Decorations.' This was followed by an attempt by the CCF leader, M.J. Coldwell, to reopen the debate on titles and pass an act banning the use of such appellations.[43] Coldwell's proposal was rejected. The committee created by the House turned to another pressing issue, one that would not be resolved for many years: the creation of a Canadian flag. The coupling of these two debates is hardly coincidental. The report that would be tabled in the House on 24 June 1942 included, for the first time, a reference to the importance of Parliament sanctioning the creation of a Canadian order. The Special Committee of the House was appointed to

Inquire into and to report upon the expediency: –
(a) of maintaining the principles that form the basis of the recommendations contained in the said Report (of 1919, Special Committee on Honours and Titles), and confining in effect the said recommendations or,
(b) of cancelling, altering, modifying or adding to the said recommendations, in so far as they relate to honours and decorations which do not involve titles, and if so, in what respect to extent.[44]

The Public and Honours

In many ways, it is unfortunate that the subject of honours was not discussed more fully in the public realm; but with the war, rationing, and other pressing problems, the Canadian public could hardly be expected to develop a spontaneous interest in honours. The story of the creation of the Order of Canada revolves mainly around a handful of men in Ottawa; that said, the public did have a marginal interest in the subject. Public interest in honours had been sparked in the latter half of Bennett's administration, and the war had fanned this spark. The *Financial Post* ran a series of opinion pieces under the heading *Should We Set Up Our Own Honours System?*[45] Opinion was split; however, this was largely because the *Financial Post* purposefully chose an equal number of contributors from each side. Arguments against creating a Canadian system revolved around Canada's relationship with Britain and the Empire; those in favour of creating a Canadian system were more perceptive, not wishing to disparage what had come before, but wanting to build a unique Canadian institution. Abbé Maheaux of Quebec City commented: 'Canada is old, prosperous and responsible enough to create and distribute its own honour.' A.B. Dunlop of Neepawa, Manitoba, was sceptical, and feared that a Canadian honour 'would lack much honour and glory involved.' The final comment was left to a law professor – and poet – from McGill: 'Let us through our own procedures build a native tradition of respect for our outstanding leaders and our creative minds and let us place the responsibility in the hands of a representative body free from any political relationship. He who has well served his country deserves this recognition.' A quarter of a century later, F.R. Scott would be one of the first people appointed a Companion of the Order of Canada.[46]

The Special Committee on Honours and Decorations

The Special Committee on Honours and Decorations met eight times between 2 July and 24 July 1942. Chaired by the Honourable Cyrus Macmillan, a veteran of the First World War,[47] the committee comprised fifteen MPs: ten Liberal, three Conservative, one Social Credit, and one CCF. Five of these men had served in the Canadian Army during the last war.[48] Without question, the Honourable Herbert Bruce, a Conservative, knew more about honours than any of the other members. A noted surgeon, he had served as Inspector General of the Canadian Army Medical Corps as well as Lieutenant-Governor of Ontario. On this committee, there was much confusion as to the nature of the Nickle Resolution and 1919 Report of the Special Committee on Honours and Titles. Its members deliberated a number of times on the question of whether or not the Nickle Resolution would allow for the award of the recently created George Cross and George Medal. Many members seemed unable to distinguish between orders of chivalry and gallantry awards.[49]

The committee called six witnesses in all, ranging from the Department of External Affairs' legal adviser, John Read, to Philip Konowal, an employee of Parliament who had the distinction of having been awarded the Victoria Cross during the last war.[50] Vincent Massey corresponded with the committee as an absentee witness. Overall, the committee's proceedings were rather dull, aside from a few comments. On 7 July 1942 the committee's lone CCF member, Perry Ellis Wright, announced: 'I think there should be a distinctive Canadian Order.' To this, John J. Kinley (a leading Liberal member of the committee) retorted: 'I feel that as we proceed as an independent entity of the British Commonwealth of Nations, it may be that we are coming to a stage when that should be considered.' Kinley did not feel that Canada was yet developed enough. The question was not discussed again for over a week, when Read assured the committee there 'is no reason why the King should not establish a Canadian order,'[51] since that there was no legal impediment to such an entity being created.

The committee's minutes contain no further discussion of a Canadian order. However, for the second half of the 21 July session, the committee went in camera, so we can only speculate as to what was discussed at that time. It is likely that the 21 July in camera session revolved at least in part around Bruce's suggestion that 'the committee ask the House to enlarge its Order of Reference, to include all awards of honour and Chivalry.'[52] In essence, this amendment would have reopened the debate over knighthoods and titles. Clearly, the committee was unimpressed with Bruce's attempt to impede the progress already made, being less than a week away from completing its report. The other purpose of the 21 July in camera session was quite simply to draft the report that was going to be issued to Parliament. On 24 July the committee put the final touches on its report to Parliament. Not surprisingly, the report was largely 'edited' by the Under-Secretary of State, E.H. Coleman, since he was one of the leading experts. More to the point, it was Coleman who was administering Canada's honours policy, and it was he who would have to answer to the prime minister if anything went amiss.

The committee's final report[53] was submitted to the House of Commons on 24 July 1942. Seven days later, the House passed a motion of concurrence with the report.[54] One of the shortest documents ever entered into the parliamentary record, it made only two recommendations:

(1) That His Majesty's subjects domiciled or ordinarily resident in Canada be eligible for the award of Honours and Decorations, including awards in the Orders of Chivalry, which do not involve titles.
(2) That His Majesty's Government in Canada consider a submission to His Majesty the King, of proposals for the establishment of an Order limited in number but not involving titles for which His Majesty's subjects domiciled or ordinarily resident in Canada shall alone be eligible.[55]

Essentially, the committee was proposing that Canada adhere to the Nickle Resolution, which allowed for the bestowal of honours only on the advice of the Canadian government; at the same time, it was discarding the proposals of the Special Committee on Honours and Titles, 1919, which sought to end the awarding of all orders of chivalry to Canadian residents. It reaffirmed that Canadians were eligible for gallantry awards and for the non-titular levels of the various British orders of chivalry – the Order of the Bath, the Order of St Michael and St George, and the Order of the British Empire. In this way, a more restricted version of Bennett's Dominion–Commonwealth honours system was adopted. The changes were not entirely cosmetic, given that the report also called for the creation of a Canadian order. Although this was the first time that such a proposal had been entered into the public record, there was little reaction to it.

Shortly after the motion of concurrence was passed, the subject of Canada's National Anthem was discussed. The importance of establishing Canadian institutions was not lost on parliamentarians, although the pressures of war and reluctance to discuss potentially divisive issues would place the creation of a Canadian flag, the establishment of a Canadian order, and the acceptance of a Canadian National Anthem at the bottom of the list for several decades.

After the release of the report of the Special Committee, three members of the Interdepartmental Committee – Read, Orde, and Mee – set off on a fact-finding mission to London. Canadian officials suffered from 'institutional amnesia': no Canadian minister or department had submitted an honours list in more than twenty years. Aside from Coleman, there was no one left who knew how to administer the honours system in Canada. Read, Orde, and Mee consulted various British officials and gathered information about how the honours system worked in Britain. Perhaps the most productive meeting they had was with Sir Robert Knox. A veteran and hero of the Great War, Sir Robert Uchtred Eyre Knox devoted his entire life to the administration of Britain's honours system. As private secretary to the Permanent Secretary of the Treasury Office from 1928 to 1939, and later as secretary to the Political Honours Scrutiny Committee from 1939 until his death in 1965, Knox was unquestionably the honours expert. His interest in the honours system was matched only by that of the King.

At this meeting, Knox explained to the visitors the complete working structure of the British honours system, from honour boards to quotas and civilian honours.[56] A separate meeting was convened on 7 August, between Massey, Read, and Sir Alec Hardinge, the King's private secretary. These three men discussed the possibility of founding a Canadian order, and how such a project might best be executed. They also discussed the King's views with regard to such a development, which were largely favourable.[57]

On the basis of their findings, the Interdepartmental Committee developed a new procedure for awarding honours and awards. As a consequence, Order-in-Council 1430 was abolished on 15 November 1941 and replaced with Order-in-Council 8882.[58] Most of the suggestions embodied in the new order-in-council were proposed by none other than the King himself.[59] This new policy made it possible to award British orders of chivalry to Canadian citizens and service personnel.

On 11 September, Coleman called a meeting of the Interdepartmental Committee[60] in his office in the West Block. This meeting was attended by Read; Sir Shuldham Redfern, Secretary to the Governor General; Paymaster Commander R.A. Pennington, from the Royal Canadian Navy; Brigadier O.M.M. Kay; Wing Commander D.E. MacKell; Flight Lieutenant C.T. Mee; and J.F. Delaute, who acted as secretary.[61] These men reviewed Read's findings and discussed the possibility of creating a formal body to deal specifically with honours and awards.[62] On the subject of creating a Canadian order, it was decided that Massey was the most knowledgeable. Read wrote to Massey: 'In view of the interest you have taken in the subject, it would be of great assistance to me if you could undertake to suggest the outline of a draft.'[63]

At the suggestion of the Interdepartmental Committee that a separate committee be founded, Read set about creating such a body. At first it was given the cumbersome title 'A general policy committee to deal with honours in war in Canada.' Arnold Heeney, Clerk of the Privy Council, abbreviated this title to 'Awards Coordination Committee (ACC)'[64] before submitting it to the prime minister. Mackenzie King was introduced to the proposed ACC on 28 October 1942.[65] The issue went unaddressed for nearly a month. On 26 November, the prime minister reviewed the submission and forwarded it to the Governor General, who was in turn to seek permission from the King to create the ACC. Within a week, Sir Shuldham Redfern wrote Heeney to say that no formal submission to His Majesty was necessary and that the body could be created forthwith.[66]

The ACC came into being on 2 December 1942. In many ways, it was the successor to the Interdepartmental Committee and the predecessor of what would become the Order of Canada Advisory Council in 1967. However, the committee had much more immediate concerns unrelated to gazing into the future. The ACC was mainly 'charged with the responsibility for the maintenance of central records of all honours in war in Canada and with the maintenance of uniformity of standards between Canadian civilian, navy, army and air force authorities, and as between Canadian and other authorities dealing with like matters in other parts of His Majesty's dominions.'[67] Although the committee was endowed with sweeping powers in the realm of honours, its recommendations were subject to the prime minister's approval.

The committee initially had the following members: the Under-Secretary of State (Chairman); the Under-Secretary of State for External Affairs; the Deputy Minister of Labour; the Dominion Archivist; the Secretary of the Naval Board, RCN; the Adjutant-General of the Canadian Army; and the Air Member for personnel, RCAF. Later, a representative of the Governor General would join the committee. Other departments would also sometimes be represented.[68] Essentially, it was the old Interdepartmental Committee, reconstituted with a formal mandate.

Even before the ACC was formally created, E.H. Coleman – who would end up serving as its chair – was developing proposals for the Canadian order: 'We have taken the view that the practice of the proposed Canadian Order should be similar to the Order of the Companions of Honours.'[69] The ACC held its first meeting on 2 December 1942, in the West Block of Parliament.[70] The minutes of that first meeting indicate that it was consumed mainly by administrative matters; only brief mention was made of the creation of a Canadian order.

After the first meeting, E.H Coleman drafted a memorandum to Heeney outlining the proposed Canadian order. At first glance, it would seem that Coleman and the ACC had with one report solved all of Mackenzie King's honours problems and created a new Canadian order, and all within less than a week! Heeney passed the report on to the prime minister, who was asked 'for an expression of your views upon the points dealt with in [Coleman's] memorandum.'[71] Coleman was very much an admirer of the Order of the Companions of Honour, which had been founded by George V in 1917. Consisting of only one level and limited to only fifty members, it was seen as an ideal model, as it did not confer a title.

So detailed were Coleman's initial proposals that he also included a list of prospective honorary recipients, including such luminaries of the period as Winston

Churchill, Field Marshal Smuts, Franklin Roosevelt, 'General Chaing Kai-sheck [sic] and Mr. Stalin as the representative leaders of the two largest powers associated with the British Commonwealth and the United States in the war.'[72] Coleman proposed that the honour be titled either the 'Royal Canadian Order' or the 'Royal Order of Canada,' in an attempt to 'emphasize the connection of the Canadian Order with the Crown.'[73] The insignia was to depict the Arms of Canada. Coleman was well aware of the 'obvious danger that a brand new order of chivalry which does not carry a title might not be considered as high an honour as a title, or might indeed not even attain to the prestige which is attached to the lower grades of the established Orders.'[74] The proposed order would have two levels: Companion and Officer. Membership in the order would be limited to fifteen Companions and fifty Officers.[75] This was only the first of many proposals that would be informally and formally submitted to the prime minister.

The proposal was formally introduced in 2 December but had already been in existence for some time. In a letter dated 1 December 1942, Major General Letson commented to Read 'that we might give serious consideration to extending the proposed Canadian Order to lower grades than G's and K's[76] and would welcome an opportunity to discuss this proposal with you.'[77] Letson continued: 'I note with satisfaction that the General Committee on Honours in War in Canada [the ACC] has been approved.'[78] This was prior to the first meeting of the ACC. Clearly, Letson was undertaking a bit of 'lobbying' on behalf of a more generously distributed honour. Letson wanted a four- or five-levelled honour, similar to the Order of the British Empire or the Legion of Merit,[79] which had been established by the U.S. Congress on 20 July 1942.[80] To this end, he prepared an alternative proposal. The King's Canadian Order was to consist of five levels: Counsellor of the King's Canadian Order (KCO); Seigneur of the King's Canadian Order (SKCO); Companion of the King's Canadian Order (CKCO); Officer of the King's Canadian Order (OKCO); and Member of the King's Canadian Order (MKCO).[81] This proposal was not well received and was quickly discarded; the post-nominals sounded more like the call signal of a CBC radio station than those of a nation's highest order.

When it came to honours, Mackenzie King was uneasy with his position as the chief adviser to the Sovereign. He found vetting the Honours List for New Year's 1943 an especially daunting task. Having rejected the first list, he resorted to approving a much smaller list. Having been greatly impressed by the services rendered to the Dominion by members of the crew of the RCMP cutter St Roch, he insisted that they be awarded the Polar Medal.

The 1943 Honours List was well received by the RCMP, but civilians and members of the military alike were disappointed that there were no awards of the non-titular levels of the Order of the British Empire. Redfern, the Governor General's ever-perceptive secretary, wrote to the Dominions Office in London: 'The Government this year dipped its toes into the waters that flow from this Fountain [of Honours] and found it chilly, so chilly that the only honours that emerged were – not inappropriately – eight Polar Medals.'[82]

Despite the prime minister's reluctance to deal with honours, and to allow many to be awarded, the ACC continued its work. The questions it dealt with covered the spectrum from operational awards to protocol for investiture ceremonies. Early in

1943, Massey was consumed with his work at the Canadian High Commission in London, but he found time to develop a proposal for the ACC. On 9 February, Coleman circulated Massey's proposal to the ACC.[83] Massey was proposing a 'Royal Order of Canada,' to consist of two levels. The senior level, Companion of the Royal Order of Canada, would be limited to fifteen members, while the lower grade, Officer of the Royal Order of Canada, was to be restricted to fifty members. In the Order of Precedence, Companions would rank just after the Companion of Honour; Officers would follow Knights of the Order of the British Empire. Evidently, Massey had developed his 'Royal Order of Canada' some time before the ACC was created. On 18 October 1942, he had had a meeting with Sir Alec Hardinge, the King's private secretary. They began by discussing the problem of naval honours for Canadians, but then they had a 'short talk ... about the proposed new Canadian Order.' Massey found Hardinge 'receptive to my idea on the subject including the suggested name, the Royal Order of Canada.'[84] Later, an outside observer would note: 'The proposed new Canadian Order is very interesting. It is clear there are strong opposing currents on the subject in Canada.'[85]

Major General Letson was shocked by the highly limited nature of the proposed order, and suggested that it consist of five levels rather than two and be renamed 'The King's Canadian Order.'[86] On 9 February the Cabinet War Committee was introduced to the work of the ACC inasmuch as it was told that a proposal for a Canadian order would be forthcoming and that the ACC would need its support. Heeney urged the Cabinet War Committee that 'a decision should now be made ... This matter is of some urgency if the Order is to be established in time for recommendations thereon to be made for inclusion in His Majesty's Birthday List.'[87] Mackenzie King had clearly become annoyed by the prospect of creating a Canadian order; he had enough trouble dealing with the British honours system and had no desire to increase his workload by taking on the additional responsibility of administering a Canadian order. A forlorn Coleman wrote to Vincent Massey on 25 February 1942: 'The government has decided to defer dealing with the proposed Canadian Order for the present.'[88] In a rather cutting letter to the Dominions Office, Sir Shuldham Redfern commented: 'I doubt if we shall hear anything more of it. No tears will be shed except, perhaps, by some of the Canadian generals who see the war slipping by without there being any high decoration to adorn their martial chests.'[89] This would not be the last proposal for establishing a Canadian order – there would be many others – but for the balance of 1943, the ACC would be consumed with developing what would become known as the 'Canada Medal.'

From their distant perspective on events in Canada, certain senior members of the British government were uniquely positioned to assess the prospects for a Canadian order. At all times, British officials kept a quiet interest in the subject, right through until the 1970s. Having shed the mantle of 'Imperial Meddlers,' their interest was purely out of curiosity. In March 1943, Clement Attlee, Secretary of the Dominions Office, wrote to Winston Churchill, then prime minister, outlining 'that the Canadian Government have considered the possibility of instituting a Special Canadian Order of Merit to cover cases which merit high distinction but which cannot be recognized by appointment to knighthoods. This has been found to present considerable difficulties and the proposal has, I understand, been abandoned, at any rate for the time being.'[90] Aware of the disadvantage faced by senior Canadian service personnel – because they were unable to accept knighthood – Atlee proposed to expand the Order of the Companions of Honour to include a set number of subjects from the Dominions. This expansion was also encouraged as it was more favourable than each Dominion creating 'new Orders of their own, limited to citizens of the particular Dominion.'[91] More junior British civil servants took a condescending view of the proposal, referring to it as 'amusing.'[92] However, there was a distinctive hands-off approach.

Expansion of the Order of the Companions of Honour

Events in Australia brought the question of senior Imperial honours being awarded to Canadians back into discussion. A disagreement between the Australian prime minister and one of the state premiers in that Dominion had led the British government to make changes to the prestigious Order of the Companions of Honour. Originally the order had been limited to 50 members at any one time, but a Dominions Office telegram sent out on 19 May 1943 proposed to enlarge the order to 70, allotting seven awards for Canada, five for Australia, two for New Zealand and two for South Africa.[93] The order was awarded on the recommendation of the British prime minister to the King, however the proposal allowed for the various Dominion prime ministers to submit their own lists directly to the King, provided they remained within the allotted quota. Canadian reaction to this proposal was cold, and the South Africans reacted in the same manner. It was felt that 'the number of allocations involved would be entirely inadequate to meet Canadian needs ... the Order would be unsuitable for the highest ranking military officers.'[94] The proposal was rejected outright by Mackenzie King and never sent forward to the ACC. An official telegram sent to the Dominions Office on 6 July 1943 stated that 'it has been decided that the Canadian Government, for their part, should not concur in the proposal to enlarge the Order of the Companions of Honour to include an allocation for Canada.'[95] The decision of Canada and South Africa not to participate in the proposed alterations led the British government to alter its plans, although room for Canadian awards was left open. It was decided to increase the membership from fifty to sixty-five members, as follows: United Kingdom 41; Australia, 7; New Zealand, 2; other commonwealth countries, 11.[96] With the passage of time, the allotment of seven awards began to look much more useful in the absence of a Canadian order. Indeed, between 1945 and 2004, eight Canadians have been made Companions of Honour – a continuing part of our lexicon of honours.[97]

The Canada Medal

The idea of the Canada Medal originated in the Army Council, most likely with Major General Letson. This medal was initially called the 'Canadian Meritorious Award,'[98] but it was soon noted that this designation would be difficult to translate into French; thus the 'Canada Medal' was born. It was introduced at the same time as the proposed Canadian order but was overshadowed at first by the much larger project. However, when the ACC was essentially told there would be no approval for a

Canadian order in the near future, it turned its energies to the Canada Medal. By the time of the ACC's second meeting, on 21 January 1943, Letson had already submitted a proposal. In true bureaucratic fashion, the ACC decided to establish a subcommittee to 'redraft the recommendation to the Council.' The subcommittee consisted of Read and Commander MacTavish. Curiously, this subcommittee was not to report to the ACC but instead directly to the prime minister. In this way, Coleman was making sure he would not have to deal with another rejected honours proposal from Mackenzie King. By 4 February, the subcommittee had submitted its proposal for the Canada Medal to the prime minister and the ACC.[99] This proposal first had to pass through the hands of Arnold Heeney, Clerk of the Privy Council, who was slow in summarizing the committee's submission. This summary did not reach the prime minister's desk until 15 February.[100] Heeney assured Mackenzie King: 'The proposal does not contemplate the establishment of an order, but merely of a medal, primarily a Service medal, to be awarded on the determination of the Minister of National Defence.'[101]

By late May 1943 the ACC had submitted a revised proposal to the Cabinet War Committee.[102] This committee studied it, and by 12 July 1943 Coleman was able to report to the ACC that Cabinet had approved it.[103] Among other important provisions, the proposal set out such things as who was to receive the medal and what it would look like:

1. Designation: The medal shall be designated and styled 'THE CANADA MEDAL.'

2. Description: The medal shall be circular in form and in silver, it shall bear on the obverse the crowned Effigy of the Sovereign and on the reverse the Arms of Canada and the word 'CANADA.' The words 'Merit' (or 'MERITE') shall be inscribed on a bar attached to the mount of the medal.

3. Ribbon: The medal will be worn on the left breast, suspended by a ribbon one and a quarter inches in width of red, white and red equal stripes and will be worn immediately after the British Empire Medal and before War Medals.

5. Precedence: The award of the medal shall not confer any individual precedence but shall entitle the recipient to the addition, after his name, of the letters 'C.M.' in the case of English speaking recipients and (Should they so desire) 'M du C' in the case of French speaking recipients.

6. Eligibility: Personnel eligible to receive the medal shall be:

(a) Citizens of Canada, whether civilians or members of the armed forces or of the Merchant Navy.

(b) Citizens of other countries who have rendered valuable and meritorious services of the nature set forth in the next succeeding paragraph.

7. Service Required: The medal may be awarded to persons named in the preceding paragraph for specially valuable and meritorious service of a high standard, faithful or zealous performance of ordinary duty not being sufficient in itself. There must be either:

(a) special services of a high degree of merit, such as discharge of special duties superior to the person's ordinary work, or

(b) highly meritorious performance of ordinary duties where these have entailed world of a specially trying character, or,

(c) display of a high degree of initiative and forethought.[104]

On 23 July, Mackenzie King signed the draft order-in-council and transmitted it to the King through the Governor General's secretary, Sir Shuldham Redfern.[105] In early August, Redfern received a despatch from Sir Alec Hardinge, the King's private secretary; it indicated that the King would likely approve the creation of the Canada Medal, 'subject to the suggestion that there be added to it, reference to the control and limitation of the quota.'[106] The King did not want the Canada Medal to become a worthless trinket for politicians to use as a patronage tool.

To deal with His Majesty's concerns, the ACC created another subcommittee, this one consisting of Brigadier Noel, Squadron Leader Gillingham, and Sub-Lieutenant Bucke, who were to devise a quota system. This subcommittee reported on 20 August; no objections were raised to its findings. It was agreed that

i) Quotas, to be on a half yearly basis of one per two thousand, instead of one per thousand. Based on present strength, this will limit each half-yearly list of Service awards to approximately 375 instead of 750.

ii) publish CM, list at the same time as Birthday Honours and New Years Honours so that it will 'not then be considered a "consolation" award.'

iii) first list to be issued on 1 January 1944

iv) no more than 50 percent of the total allotment to be awarded to officers.[107]

Finally, on 27 August 1943, Redfern informed the ACC that 'His Majesty the King had approved the establishment of the Canada Medal.'[108]

The Sovereign's approval having been given, the ACC set about dealing with practical considerations, such as ordering the medal. It was decided early on that the ribbon should represent Canada's 'national colours.' Canada had been granted Arms in 1921; at that time, George V had suggested that the national colours of Canada ought to be *gules* and *argent*[109] – in plainer terms, red and white. Canadians were not unfamiliar with these colours; they had first been used for the Canada General Service Medal, sanctioned in 1899 by Queen Victoria. This medal had been awarded for service defending Canada against the Fenian Raids of 1866 and 1870 and also to those who had served in putting down the Red River Rebellion. The ribbon had three equal parts: red, white, and red. The ACC approved this colour combination on 17 September 1943, although Commander McTavish was concerned that 'the similarity between the colours of the Canada Medal ribbon and those of the ribbon of the Riel Rebellion Medal might cause some unfortunate reaction in the minds of some members of the Canadian public.'[110] Perhaps McTavish was being a little too cautious. First of all, the ribbon was not used on the Riel Rebellion Medal (more correctly known as the North West Canada Medal 1885) – only on the Canada General Service Medal, which had been awarded mainly for service against the Fenians.[111] Furthermore, any recipient of the Canada General Service Medal who was still alive would have to be at least in his eighties. Thus the risk that the holder of a Canada General Service Medal was also going to be awarded the Canada Medal was quite remote. The Canadian Armed Forces were short of men, but not so desperate as to enlist veterans approaching their centenary. The ACC did not consider McTavish's concern legitimate.[112]

The ribbon issue decided, linguistic concerns arose. The prime minister's private secretary was concerned about the medal's unilingual nature. Two versions of the medal were to be issued: one in French, the other in English. Turnbull was concerned that anglophones might be sent the French version and francophones the English version. To remedy this problem, he proposed that the Latin term 'MERITUM' replace the French and English.[113] The ACC did not want to change its original submission to the King, so no change was made: there would be two separate issues, one for each linguistic group.

At this point the ACC received word that the Royal Canadian Mint would be able to tool the dies for the medals and have four hundred struck and named by December 1943.[114] Curiously, the committee had yet to approve a design, even though one had been set out in the order-in-council that had been submitted to the King. Thomas Shingles of the Royal Canadian Mint designed the Canada Medal; in October 1943 the design was slightly modified by the RCAF commercial art section.[115]

The entire Canada Medal project was formalized through Order-in-Council 7964, dated 14 October 1943. Canadians were informed of the Canada Medal through a press release issued on 17 October (the first draft of this document was dated 23 September).[116]

Public reaction was muted; the war news was more important to Canadians. Some newspapers expressed concern about the 'new' nature of the medal, postulating that if too many were awarded, it would become quite worthless. The *Toronto Globe* struck a balanced tone, stating that the new medal would 'win the approval both of keen Imperialists and ardent Canadian nationalists,'[117] and emphasizing the 'democratic flavour' of the project. The Canada Medal was seen as a way to blend the British honours system – especially the orders of chivalry – with a distinctive Canadian award. The press in French Canada was even more enthusiastic. *La Presse* in particular endorsed the creation of a Canadian award, but like the *Globe* expressed concern that too many might receive it.

The ACC hoped to make the first awards of the Canada Medal on 11 November 1943. There is some evidence that the first recipients were to include His Majesty the King, Queen Elizabeth, Winston Churchill, Franklin Delano Roosevelt, and the Governor General, the Earl of Athlone. The first full list was to be published on 1 February 1944. However, Cabinet was not prepared to proceed quite so quickly.[118] At the 3 November meeting of Cabinet it was decided that the medal would be awarded for outstanding service and not to those already in the highest positions. Mackenzie King recounted that when Heeney noted that the ACC had already arranged to proceed with awards,

> this got under my skin at once and I said it was the strongest of reasons why we should not proceed any further; that I objected altogether to these matters being forced on the Cabinet; that nothing should be done ... It would have been a scandal to permit this kind of thing to mar the face of the Government with the problems that are being confronting it at this time ... Perhaps the country itself will have little comment on the decision we have made. On the other hand, had we continued with the granting of decorations when there is no time to consider them, we would have a very bitter opposition aroused against us from coast to coast and in Parliament itself.[118]

This was a decidedly inauspicious beginning for the Canada Medal. There was another, more practical consideration: the Royal Canadian Mint had not yet finished engraving the dies for striking the Canada Medal. The ever-eager Minister of National Defence, Colonel Ralston, was disappointed that the project was not proceeding at high speed. He wrote to Heeney, asking him to encourage the prime minister to move faster and to ensure that the New Year's 1944 Honours List would include some awards of the Canada Medal. In this letter, he underscored the importance of official recognition: 'Honours and decorations are exceeding useful in maintaining enthusiasm and service by tangibly demonstrating that such service is appreciated.'[120] But, Heeney was well aware of his boss's views on the matter and had no desire to risk his own standing by pressing the issue.

The Canadian Award of Honour and Canadian Decoration of Honour

The Canada Medal was not the ACC's only project. Besides compiling lists of possible recipients and establishing the protocol for investitures at Government House, it had another task, albeit a lesser one. The committee had been told that it was not yet a favourable time to create a Canadian order; even so, it continued to work on plans for one, although it quickly became a 'poor cousin' to the Canada Medal, which seemed destined for success. On 3 May 1943, the ACC examined a proposal that would expand on Massey's proposal for a 'Royal Order of Canada.' This new Canadian order was to consist of two separate awards: the Canadian Award of Honour and the Canadian Decoration of Honour.[121] The ACC stated that the proposal was based 'upon the assumption that it might be desirable to establish a senior award which would not be an order of chivalry, but which would enable recognition to be given for distinguished and meritorious service to persons whose services can not otherwise be appropriately recognized.' This was a shell game – the ACC felt that if the 'order' was not called an 'order,' yet was in every other respect analogous to an order of chivalry, the prime minister just might be coaxed into accepting the proposal.[122] The preamble of the draft stated: 'It is considered that exceptionally distinguished service by citizens of Canada, whether as civilians or as members of the Naval, Military and Air Forces and of the Merchant Navy, should be recognized by the award of suitable decorations which could also be given to citizens of other countries who may render distinguished services of the same high order.'

Recipients of the Canadian Award of Honour and Canadian Decoration of Honour would have their names published in the *Canada Gazette* and would be entitled to use the post-nominal letters CAH and CDH. The award was to be 'conferred by His Majesty the King, on the recommendation of the Prime Minister of Canada,'[123] although of course the ACC would compile the honours lists for the prime minister. The proposal went so far as to suggest that each award and decoration be a nine-sided badge, 'charged with three maple leaves conjoined on one stem, proper, superimposed on a laurel wreath seeded proper. And underneath, the motto ACER GERENDO in raised letters enameled in red.[124] The whole ensigned with the Royal Crown in gold.' This badge would be worn around the neck from a 1¾ or 1½ inch wide ribbon (the wider ribbon for the award). Each ribbon would be of watered silk in autumnal colours: red, yellow, green, purple, and scarlet. Although the badge was conventional, the ribbon had an unprecedented flare to it. The basis for this unique award was first worked out between Letson and Colonel A. Fortescue Duguid on 23 March 1943. It began life with a variety of names:

Badge		Honour
		Recognition
Jewel		Merit
	of	Distinction
Decoration		Zeal
		Eminence
Legion		Accomplishment
		Service

It is believed that the designs were drawn by Lieutenant Commander Alan Beddoe, the noted heraldic artist, and reviewed by Dr Charles Comfort.[125]

There was some debate about the award's name. The Dominion Archivist, Major Lanctot, suggested that 'Canadian Award of Honour' and 'Canadian Decoration of Honour' were too general. He proposed that the new awards be titled 'the King's Canadian Award' and the 'King's Canadian Decoration.' This was a contentious issue for the ACC, and resulted in one of the few formal votes the committee ever took. Lanctot's proposal failed, and the original designations Canadian Award and Canadian Decoration remained. In terms of precedents, the award and decoration were to be worn after the Victoria Cross and George Cross. Thus, the Canadian Award of Honour was to take the same place as the Order of the Garter held in the rest of the Commonwealth. Even so, the ACC remained adamant that the award and decoration were not 'orders.' Eventually, the ACC approved the proposal and sent it to the prime minister and the Cabinet War Committee. The ACC then left the matter in abeyance until 16 August 1943, when Major General Letson reported to the committee that there was an 'urgent necessity of granting suitable recognition to high ranking officers of the USA and other Allied Nations.'[126] Letson's concern arose from the fact that the United States had created the Legion of Merit in 1942 and was now beginning to award it to Allied servicemen. There was a certain desire to keep up with the Americans. The Canadians were creating a new award in large part so that they would have one to bestow on foreigners. There was an awkwardness to bestowing British honours on foreign citizens on behalf of the Canadian government. The recipient invariably felt as if the award had come from the British and not from the Canadians.

In terms of the Canadian Armed Forces, there was little apparent resistance to the idea of creating a senior Canadian order or decoration. One would have expected some, given that the British orders were universally recognized and accepted. At the same time, the prohibition placed on honours in Canada, and the growing sense of nationhood, played into the desire for a Canadian institution that blended old with new.

Not wishing to be outdone by the Americans, a number of officers wrote Letson and the ACC 'requesting the re-opening of this matter'[127] and hoping that something could be instituted before the 1944 New Years Honours List was printed. The eighteenth meeting of the ACC brought Letson and the other committee members the news they had been awaiting anxiously. John Read delivered this memorandum to the ACC from the Cabinet War Committee.[128] At its 10 November meeting, the War Committee had decided 'that the whole question of honours and awards be revisited, after the war, along with proposals for the establishment of a specifically Canadian Order or award of honour.'[129] Read rephrased this message to the ACC, stating that 'considerations of the Canadian Award of Honour and Canadian Decoration by the Cabinet War Committee have been deferred indefinitely.'[130] In civil service dialect, this meant the proposal was dead and unlikely ever to be resurrected. So it was back to the drawing board to develop a new idea, although at this point the ACC's enthusiasm for creating a senior Canadian award or order had ebbed. The committee would soon be faced with the daunting task of compiling the New Year's 1944 Honours List for submission to the prime minister. The public was informed of the decision not to create a Canadian order through a press release from the Prime Minister's Office: 'An examination of the suggestion would involve considering the respective degree of significance to be attached to distinctive Canadian Orders and decorations in relations to awards in the existing Orders. The government has reached the conclusion, that while the war is in its critical phase, it would be inexpedient to take up these questions.'[131]

The experts on the ACC had in fact come to no such conclusion, which of course had been reached by Mackenzie King and the Cabinet War Committee, who clearly saw no political profit to be made at this stage. The ACC's attention, which had been focused on the Canada Medal, was directed to other matters, none of which related to the Royal Order of Canada, the King's Canadian Decoration, or the Canadian Decoration of Honour. Two comprehensive proposals had been strongly rejected by the prime minister and his colleagues, and the ACC had no desire to expend more energy on this matter – for the moment.

1944 New Year's Honour List

Mackenzie King had decided that there would be no further awards of the various British orders of chivalry to Canadians until the end of the war. Gallantry decorations continued to be awarded, but the great majority of these were bestowed on members of the army, RCN, and RCAF. The British orders of chivalry (Order of St Michael and St George, Order of the British Empire, and Imperial Service Order)[132] were the only means of official recognition available to Canadian civilians. Thus in 1944 there was no New Year's Honours List or King's Birthday Honours List. This deeply disappointed many civilians, who were no doubt expecting some recognition, with the war now entering its fourth year and the Canada Medal having recently been unveiled. The Cabinet War Committee was aware that the ACC had a rough list of civilian recipients; regardless, it decided that 'in the circumstances it would be preferable not to proceed with any extensive civilian recommendations, particularly at a time when the war is approaching a climax.'[133] To an untrained observer, this decision could only be described as ridiculous: if ever there is a time to start handing out awards, it is when the battle is reaching its climax, and the new Canada Medal would have provided the perfect opportunity for bestowing recognition. The seasoned observer would, of course, simply note that what Mackenzie King wanted in Cabinet, he invariably received. The members of the ACC were unhappy with this decision – even though it relieved them of the significant amount of work entailed in compiling an honours list – yet they also felt confident that the Canada Medal would be awarded in the coming year. After all, it was hardly practical for the prime minister to authorize the award of a medal that had yet to be struck.

Developments in 1944

The year 1943 had been highly productive for the ACC: it had submitted two separate proposals for a Canadian order/honour (both rejected), and it had established the Canada Medal. One would have expected 1944 to be another significant year for honours in Canada, with the first awards of the Canada Medal on the horizon. Alas, this was not the case. On 14 April 1944, the ACC was presented with a bill from the Royal Canadian Mint for $150, to cover the cost of the dies for the Canada Medal and clasps. The ACC ordered seven English and seven French medals. It forwarded one of each to the King, the Department of National Defence for Naval Services, the Department of National Defence for Air, and the Department of National Defence, Army. The committee would keep the remaining samples.[134] These fourteen medals would be the only tangible product of its work on the Canada Medal.

The prime minister was being pressured from a variety of directions to sanction the first Canada Medal List. Major General Letson was perhaps more disappointed than anyone with the slow progress of the Canada Medal. On 12 July he presented a memorandum to the ACC 'urging that provision be made for awarding the Canada Medal to members of the Allied Forces.' The committee agreed that steps should be taken to have the medal awarded to Allies in the near future, and to Canadians as well.[135] Fearing the prime minister's wrath, the ACC forwarded the memorandum to each of the three Ministers of National Defence (Navy, Army, and Air), in the hope that they would encourage the prime minister to act. But no action was taken with respect to the Canada Medal, and the proposal began to gather dust.

Throughout 1944 the ACC reviewed lists of proposed 'operational awards,' which were submitted by the three branches of the Canadian Armed Forces and also by the Merchant Marine. The committee also reviewed lists for 'periodic awards' – that is, awards for services not rendered in the field.[136] Besides this, Coleman began soliciting nominations from various government departments for the Canada Medal and the British orders.

In 1945, as in the previous year, no honours lists were submitted. Mackenzie King still felt strongly that the time was not right to inaugurate the Canada Medal or to resume awarding the non-titular levels of the British orders of chivalry. So although awards continued to flow to members of the armed forces, civilians at home and serving abroad were still being left out. This came as no great surprise to Canadians, as the Prime Minister's Office had announced that there would be no further awards of the British orders of chivalry until the end of the war.

While the main body of the ACC worked on compiling the various honours lists, the ACC's senior subcommittee was developing yet another Canadian order. The

King's Canadian Order was to consist of five levels, of which the lowest two grades were actually medals:

- Commander of the King's Canadian Order
- Officer of the King's Canadian Order
- Member of the King's Canadian Order
- The Canada Medal
- The Meritorious Service Medal.[137]

This proposal was quickly scrapped, and replaced in May 1944 by two other proposals, one from the army, the other from the air force. Members representing the navy continued to express the view that the existing British system, if liberalized, would suit Canada quite well. The army's proposal referred to the Order of Canada and consisted of five levels and a separate medal:

- Grand Commander of the Order of Canada GCC
- Grand Officer of the Order of Canada GOC
- Commander of the Order of Canada CC
- Officer of the Order of Canada OC
- Canada Medal CM
- Meritorious Service Star MSS[138]

The Canada Medal was considered part of the order, but the Meritorious Service Star was not, although the proposals were not separate. Perhaps the most unconventional ideas came from the RCAF. The King's Most Honourable Order of Canada was also to consist of five grades, but it was in some ways rooted in the history of New France:

- Grand Seigneur GKC
- Seigneur SKC
- Commander CKC
- Officer OKC
- Member (Canada Medal) MCK[139]

Perhaps the authors of the RCAF proposal were unaware that the term 'seigneur' was in many ways a title and referred to the ownership of land. All of these proposals were discussed by the ACC's senior subcommittee, but none made it to the ACC, let alone to Cabinet. One can only imagine how Mackenzie King would have reacted to an attempt to revive the title of seigneur.

The Final Year of the War, 1945

With the successful Allied landing in Europe in 1944 and advances in the Pacific theatre, 1945 would be the year of victory. The ACC again began examining projects that did not pertain solely to compiling honours lists. There was no immediate prospect for a civilian honours list, although Coleman and the ACC had been well prepared for a great influx of requests. The ACC soon turned its attention to an old familiar project – the quest for a Canadian Order.

The Order of Canada

Having been thwarted in its first two attempts, the ACC had basically given up on the idea of creating a Canadian order. It took some pressure from the Department of National Defence for the committee to look again at the issue. With the war in Europe over and the Pacific campaign drawing to a close, the opportunity to found a Canadian order arose again, especially in light of the fact that the prime minister had made statements to the effect that after the war, the possibility of establishing a Canadian order could be discussed.

The first proposal came from the ACC's senior subcommittee and was a truncated version of the various 1944 proposals. The order was to be styled simply 'the Order of Canada.' Consisting of three levels, it was to have a military division and civil division:

- Commander of the Order of Canada COC
- Officer of the Order of Canada OOC
- Member of the Order of Canada (Canada Medal) MOC[140]

Little effort was invested in this proposal; it quickly faded, and was replaced by a more grandiose plan.

The most significant proposal of 1945 came not from the ACC, but from the Personnel Members Committee (PMC) of the Department of National Defence, on behalf of the Defence Council. The PMC had been heavily involved in the creation of the Canada Medal before the ACC took control of its development. On 8 August, the PMC sent a memorandum to the ACC outlining the need for a Canadian order. It was clear that the military wanted more awards and that with regard to honours, there was a disparity between Canadians and other Commonwealth and Allied servicemen. There was also a certain level of nascent Canadian nationalism that had not been much seen in earlier proposals for a Canadian order. In a confidential memorandum, Major General A.E. Walford, chairman of the PMC, set out his case for the project:

> It has recently become conclusively evident that the establishment of a high-ranking and distinctively Canadian Order is necessary for the following purposes:
> (a) To permit adequate reciprocity in awards with Allied and other Commonwealth Forces.
> (b) To provide a suitable means of recognizing distinguished and meritorious service by Canadian Service personnel not otherwise provided for.[141]

In terms of the first point, during the Second World War more than four hundred foreign (non-British) awards were bestowed on Canadian service personnel, yet Canada had no decoration of its own with which to reciprocate. However, it was the second point that carried the most weight. Given that Canadians were unable to receive knighthoods, those who had rendered the most outstanding service at an international and national levels would only be able to receive a honour like the Commander of the Order of the British Empire, which in the United Kingdom and other Dominions was awarded for less significant service. On top of this, there were only a limited number of awards available for Canadians. Furthermore, because there was no civilian honours list from 1943 to 1945, a great many of the 1945–6 honours were going to be awarded to civilians; thus, the military would be deprived of its rightful quota.

One must ask why the Department of National Defence had suddenly become interested again in the question of a Canadian honour. As with so many events in Canadian history, the answer has to do with American and British actions. Although the PMC had been discussing the Order of Canada since the fall of Germany in May 1945, urgency was added in August once Japan's surrender became imminent. Ottawa and the Canadian Embassy in Washington traded a series of secret cables. The British had prepared an extensive honours list – to include Americans, Britons, and Canadians – for release on VJ Day. The Canadian Embassy had yet to prepare such a list, and considered the situation unsatisfactory. It wanted consideration to be given immediately to awarding a distinctive Canadian order: 'It is realized that the Canadian Order is still under consideration and that even if it is approved it will not be possible to meet the VJ date line. We hold strongly to the view that if Canada does not recognize the services of U.S. personnel that the effect *will not repeat not be favourable* as compared to the British. It would therefore appear imperative to reach a decision on the Canadian Order at the earliest possible date.'[142]

On 18 August, Major General Walford cabled his reply, simply stating that the matter was being considered and that the Canadian government was not going to submit a list of honours for American personnel.[143]

The DND memorandum was well received by the ACC. At its 20 August meeting, the members decided that 'the general scheme of the proposal should be strongly supported.'[144] The ACC sent a memorandum to Cabinet on 1 September outlining a plan to submit a proposal for a Canadian order consisting of five levels.[145] There was no opposition, and the ACC set about revising Walford's proposal.

At the 10 October meeting of the ACC, the complete proposal from Major General Walford was presented and examined. This was the first formal proposal in which the honour was referred to as the Order of Canada, although 'Canadian Merit Order' or 'Canadian Order of Merit' was also considered.[146] The order was to consist of five levels:

- Grand Commander of the Order of Canada GCOC
- Grand Officer of the Order of Canada GOOC
- Commander of the Order of Canada COC
- Officer of the Order of Canada OOC
- Member of the Order of Canada MOC

The proposal called for civilian and military divisions; also, both men and women would be eligible. In structure, the order would essentially be a Canadianized version of the Order of the British Empire or France's *Légion d'honneur*, both of which also have five levels. The Order of Canada was to be worn immediately after the Victoria Cross and George Cross but before all British orders of chivalry. This was incongruous – even the lowest grade of the Order of Canada (Member) would take precedence over a Companion of Honour or a Knight Commander of the Order of the British Empire.

Awards were to be made by the Governor General on behalf of the King. For members of the armed forces, recommendations would be submitted by the Ministers of National Defence; for civilians, recommendations would be made by the Secretary of State. The prime minister was to have a veto over all appointments and was ultimately responsible for submitting the list to the Governor General for approval.[147]

Designed by Dr. Charles Comfort, the badge of the order was to be 'a nine-pointed star, between the points nine symbolic figures associated with Canadian life: Beaver, Pine, Fish, Trillium, Bird, Maple, Wheat, Shovel and Pick, Microscope. In the centre, shield only of the armorial bearing of Canada' surmounted by an Imperial Crown. The ribbon was to be a plain rust-red. The proposed design was a cluttered collection of diverse symbols, but aesthetics were of little importance – getting the prime minister to approve was paramount. Major General Walford was so thorough in his submission that he included a draft order-in-council that would authorize the creation of the new honour. Whether this reflected his confidence that the proposal would be made reality we can only speculate. That the entire package of materials necessary for establishing the order was present indicates that the PMC (and later the ACC) believed the plan would go forward.

There is no doubt that during these discussions, Major General Letson – the man behind the Canada Medal – was asking what was to become of the ACC's earlier work. It was decided that the Canada Medal would remain and eventually become a junior award similar to the British Empire Medal, although it could still be awarded to all ranks.

Only minor changes were made by the ACC, and Coleman received consent to make twenty-five copies of the revised proposal, along with photostats of the design of the order's badge.[148] The structure was quite unlike Massey's earlier proposal for a two-level and highly limited 'Royal Order of Canada,' and much more traditional than Letson's proposal for the 'Canadian Award of Honour and Canadian Decoration of Honour.' Coleman made the necessary changes to the original proposal and forwarded it to Heeney on 7 November, for Cabinet to review.[149] The proposal was not sent forward to the prime minister until 11 December.[150] The Cabinet minutes for that day give no indication that the proposal was discussed.[151]

Massey always wished to be involved in all things related to honours in Canada. On 11 December, from Canada House in London, he wrote to the prime minister expressing his view that Canadian civilians ought to be recognized for their extraordinary services to the Crown and Canada: 'If no further civilian honours are to be awarded, the positions of Canadians (civilians) ... will be in contrast with that of members of the Canadian Armed Forces ... British domiciled civilians, and indeed Americans and other non-British personnel who are eligible, as Canadians are not.'[152] Clearly, there was concern that the prime minister would continue to put off the civilian honours list indefinitely.

On the same day that Massey sent the prime minister his query about civilian honours, the issue was discussed by Cabinet. The discussion did not focus on whether there was going to be a list, but rather on how to compile the list. The ACC was directed to 'get in touch with the Ministers with the view to the preparation of preliminary lists for consideration by the government and eventual submission to London through the Governor General.'[153] The memo exuded a sense of urgency: 'If a satisfactory civilian list is to be prepared for submission to London within the next two or three months, action will have to be initiated in the immediate future.'[154]

As for the proposed Order of Canada, there was some hope that the honours list would include nominations to the new order. Heeney reminded the prime minister: 'Your statement of 1943 makes reference to "a distinctive Canadian Order" as recommended by the Parliamentary Committee.'[155] He went on to mention the time constraints: 'If the Canadian list is to include recommendations to such an Order a submission to the King for its establishment would have to be made very soon and the "Board or Committee" to consider these questions would have to meet almost at once. In this connection a detailed proposal for an "Order of Canada" has recently been submitted through the Awards Coordination Committee.'[156] Heeney seemed to support the idea, but was no doubt fearful of the mountain of work the creation of the Order of Canada would generate. So he wanted to get the project underway.

The 1946 New Year's Honours List

Immediately, Heeney set about drafting a press statement to inform the public that there would be a civilian honours list in 1946, and also of the impending creation of the Order of Canada. In all, five draft press statements were reviewed by the prime minister. The first mentioned that 'the establishment of a Canadian Order will be announced at the time of the announcement of the special Canadian Honours List.'[157] This was reworded to say that the Canadian order would be founded in 'due course.' Other drafts mentioned the Canada Medal, although this too was eventually omitted. On the eve of 1946 the government issued a reworded yet familiar press release:

> It is not the intention to submit recommendations for inclusion of Canadian civilians in the forthcoming New Years Honours List. The permission of His Majesty the King will, however, be sought for the issue, within the next few months, of a special Canadian Honours List in which recognition may be given to the services of the many Canadians, who during the war, in various phases of civilian life, have served their country with distinction.
>
> The Government's intentions with respect to the award of the Canada Medal and the establishment of a distinctive Canadian Order will be announced in due course.[158]

The fact that the Prime Minister's Office did not give an exact date for when the special list would be issued must have caused some suspicion. Also, it was unusual for the government to announce what it planned to ask the King for permission to do before making informal enquiries. At last, there was going to be an honours list for civilians, and this promise was to be realized within months. In fact, two honours were bestowed in the 1946 New Year's Honours List. Frederick Pereira, assistant secretary to the Governor General and twice Deputy Governor General of Canada,[159] was made a Commander of the Royal Victorian Order; his colleague Colonel Henry Willis-O'Connor, aide-de-camp to a succession of Governors General, was also made a CVO. Perierra in particular had worked extensively with the ACC throughout the war years. These were the last Canadian appointments to the Royal Victorian Order until 1972.

The proposal for the Order of Canada was considered by the Cabinet, 'but no final decision has ever been taken.'[160] On 18 January 1946, Cabinet decided 'that, for the present, no action be taken with regard to the Canada Medal and the proposed Canadian Order.'[161] Once again, the ACC had produced a comprehensive and feasible proposal only to have it shunted aside. No reason was given; perhaps Mackenzie King felt that the ACC and Heeney were once again trying to pressure him.

A practical problem that once again proved the necessity of establishing a Canadian order was the fact that the top Canadian military, naval and air force officers were excluded from the more senior levels of the British orders of chivalry. Nowhere was this more obvious than in the cases of Generals Andrew G.L. McNaughton and Henry D. Crerar. During the Second World War, McNaughton served in a variety of capacities, from commander of the First Canadian Infantry Division to Minister of National Defence. In the First World War, McNaughton had been awarded the Distinguished Service Order and made a Companion of the Order of St Michael and St George. In the interwar years, he was made a Companion of the Order of the Bath; thus, he received almost every British order of chivalry open to Canadians. Crerar was in a similar position as Chief of the Canadian General Staff. He had led the First Canada Corps in Italy and later during the invasion of France. Like McNaughton, he had been decorated during the First World War with the Distinguished Service Order and was also a Companion of the Order of the Bath. There were few awards senior enough in rank for either of these men to accept. In June 1945, General (later Field Marshal) Bernard Montgomery had proposed that Crerar be made a Knight Commander of the Order of the Bath, but this was a titular honour and he was unable to accept it.[162] The only senior honour that could be awarded to Crerar was the Order of the Companions of Honour: a Commander of the Order of the British Empire was not seen as senior enough, being that it was normally awarded to colonels and not full generals!

With the approval of Mackenzie King, the British prime minister – after a lengthy discussion with George VI, Lord Alexander, and Lord Montgomery – decided that Crerar should be awarded the Order of the Companions of Honour.[163] This was gazetted on 7 July 1945. Similar action was taken with regard to McNaughton, the feeling being that 'the part played by McNaughton in organizing and training the Canadian army and his command during a good part of the war merit recognition.'[164] Thus the two generals were accorded recognition in the form of an award usually reserved for civilians.

A similar question was raised when Vincent Massey retired as Canadian High Commissioner to London. His more than ten years of service were unprecedented, and his contributions to the Canadian war effort in Britain were of a similar calibre. While visiting London, Mackenzie King was asked by the new British prime minister, Clement Attlee, for permission to have Massey made a Companion of Honour.[165] At first, Mackenzie King refused to allow it, even though the King had arranged for a special investiture.[166] But when he saw how distraught Massey was, Mackenzie King reconsidered. He cabled Louis St Laurent, the Acting Secretary of State for External Affairs, to get Cabinet's opinion on the matter. The tone of the telegram indicates that Mackenzie King was telling Cabinet what to reply rather than asking for its permission: 'Massey has rendered great service over the ten years that he has been here, and now that he is leaving, recognition of this kind would be appropriate ... It might also be remembered that he was our first Minister at Washington and that he has given not only the war years but all but his entire life to public service.'[167] On 22 May, St Laurent cabled the prime minister: 'Cabinet has approved suggestion made by you on telephone this morning.'[168] To this, Mackenzie King replied: 'Your message just received am greatly pleased with its word.'[169] Massey received his honour. On seeing the prime minister, Massey exclaimed: 'Oh Rex this means so much. There is nothing I would rather have than this. I can not tell you how deeply I feel or how grateful I am to you.'[170] The problem of senior awards for outstanding service at a national level had been temporarily solved, and recognition had been accorded where due, although the prime minister himself remained without.

The Special 1946 'Dominion Day' Honours List

Perhaps it was fortuitous that the Order of Canada proposal did not proceed at the end of 1946. The ACC was about to be confronted with its most daunting task – compiling a postwar civilian honours list. Over the previous three years, few honours had been bestowed on civilians, and every department wanted its share. On 18 January, Cabinet decided to proceed with a civilian honours list, and set Dominion Day of 1946 as the date for its publication.[171] On 31 January 1946, Coleman wrote to the new Secretary of State, Paul Martin, outlining the need for direction with regard to selecting civilian recipients for the 1946 list. Martin ably provided an outline of his expectations, proposing that a letter be sent to each member of the government asking for a list of names and a brief description of each nominee's service. Besides this, various lists were 'already on file ... the names of between 400 and 500 persons who have been recommended or suggested for recognition.'[172] The ACC would then review all of the names submitted and make its selections.[173] Departments, ministers, and members of the government were required to submit their lists by the end of March. Cabinet approved of these steps, and members proceeded to send their nominations to Coleman and the ACC.[174] Between April and early June, the ACC sifted through more than six thousand nominations, at the same time developing a complex quota system of awards by department and residence. By June 1946 the ACC had submitted a list for 1,483 awards,[175] which was slightly more than the allotment the British had approved. It was a remarkable job, considering that at its inception, the ACC only met weekly, for a few hours. Having been assigned this massive task, it met almost daily. On 13 June a special meeting of the Cabinet was held, at which the ACC's nominations were examined and approved for submission to the King.[176]

After the 1946 Dominion Day Honours List was published, as the year drew on, various departments received enquiries about the 1947 New Year's Honours List. So many letters were received that a press statement was issued on 22 November 1946, which stated that 'no recommendations are being made for civilian awards to Canadians in the orders of chivalry for New Year's 1947.'[177] The 1946 Dominion Day Honours List would be the last list of civilian honours in Canada until 1967. The ACC could finally take a well-deserved break.

After 1946, the Prime Minister's Office, the Governor General's Office, and the Secretary of State received many enquiries about the prospect of another civilian honours list. Canadians had come to expect that a yearly list would be issued to recognize outstanding service in peacetime as well as in war. A form letter was sent out, explaining that no further awards of the British orders of chivalry were going to be made; 1946 would be the final list. As the years went on, the number of enquiries dwindled.

Lord Alexander's Proposal, 1948

In November 1947, Mackenzie King attended the wedding of Princess Elizabeth and Prince Philip. George VI took this opportunity to award his loyal Canadian first minister the Order of Merit, 'considered by many to be the most coveted distinction in the whole hierarchy of British honours.'[178] Mackenzie King hesitated, but ultimately accepted the honour. In his diary after making his decision, he wrote: 'It will be a remarkable rounding out of the circle which links the reward placed on Mackenzie's head by the Crown with the highest award from the Crown to his grandson who has been carrying on his work.'[179] The Order of Merit was an appropriate reward for a lifetime of service; his wartime counterparts, Sir Winston Churchill and South African prime minister Jan Smuts, had already received it. In Canada, there was nothing but praise for Mackenzie King's new accolade, and congratulations poured in from every corner of the Dominion. Perhaps the perception that Mackenzie King, in accepting the Order of Merit, had softened his stance toward honours is what led the Governor General, Lord Alexander, to raise the subject once again. However, it was no easy matter to broach this contentious issue, which no Canadian Governor General had discussed with a prime minister since 1935. The reason why the subject had long been taboo was well known, but Lord Alexander had his own reasons for restarting discussions about a Canadian order, which was to be called 'The Order of Canada.' In a letter to his prime minister, Lord Alexander wrote: 'Personally I am very much in favour of the institution of an Order of Canada, in possibly five degrees ... this Order could be along the lines of the U.S. Legion of Merit.'[180] Lord Alexander suggested that the Order of Canada consist of five levels:

- Grand Commander of the Order of Canada GCOC
- Grand Officer of the Order of Canada GOOC
- Commander of the Order of Canada COC
- Officer of the Order of Canada OOC
- Member of the Order of Canada MOC.[181]

Clearly, His Excellency had consulted the ACC's 1945 proposal and resubmitted it with minor revisions. The Governor General's proposed order more closely resembled France's *Légion d'honneur*,[182] but it was clear that he had given the idea some thought, to the extent of designing a ribbon for the new order: 'Ribbon – Red White Red ... the ribbon of the Order of Canada would be slightly wider [than that of the Canada Medal].' Lord Alexander was the first to propose that the new order be hung from a ribbon composed of the national colours; he suggested that it be made up of segments ¼ red, ½ white, and ¼ red – the precise dimensions of the ribbon used for the Order of Canada when it was finally created in 1967. Another reason why Alexander raised the matter of a Canadian order was related to his upcoming visit to Brazil. He was to be awarded a promotion in the Brazilian Order of Military Merit, which he had first been awarded at the end of the Second World War. The Governor General wanted something to bestow in return on General Dutra, the Brazilian president. In an effort to mask his own motives, Alexander wrote to Mackenzie King: 'It would seem to me that Canada, as a sovereign nation, should have its own Order, and that this development would now follow logically the recent official recognition of a distinctive Canadian citizenship.'[183] A most perceptive analysis of the situation, but Mackenzie King had no interest in pursuing the matter and politely turned it aside. No formal reply was drafted, although the two men discussed the matter on 26 March. Realizing that he was not going to persuade Mackenzie King to create a Canadian order, Lord Alexander asked if he could award the Canada Medal to the Brazilian president.[184] This never happened. Once again, Mackenzie King had quashed not only the embryonic Order of Canada but also the stillborn Canada Medal.

A ray of hope appeared in April 1948: General Letson received a note from his First World War comrade, the Minister of National Defence, Brooke Claxton.[185] Claxton wrote: 'The PM is in favour of it [the Canada Medal] but doesn't want to do it until after he is replaced. I am not sure what the reasons for this are.'[186] Mackenzie King retired from public life on 15 November 1948. He was the longest-serving prime minister in the history of the British Commonwealth, and the longest-serving democratically elected leader in the history of modern politics. The last word on the issue rightly belongs to the one man who constantly thwarted every attempt to create a Canadian honour, award, or decoration:

I told the Cabinet I had never experienced more pain and anguish over any public matter than I have on anything that had to do with decorations and honours. I said that personally I was against them and upon conviction, for honours that were done one, multitudes were ignored who are more worthy. That, for instance, a man who had escaped injury or death could not be regarded as being more worthy of a decoration than one who had given his life. Parents were really more entitled to be honoured when they had lost their son than some men who had been fortunate enough to perform a noble deed and get credit for it and escape with his life. I did not say anything about service for service sake which comprised readiness to serve without recognition, but I did say that I had made up my mind as to the Canadian Order. While I thought it looked better than the British Orders, I did not wish to have the name of my Ministry of which I had been a member identified with the establishment of an Order or Decoration in Canada. That I would not approve any recourse to that end. Equally I would not favour the Canada Medal until it was known to whom the Medal would be given. That I was not particularly anxious to see any form of that kind of recognition. Some subsequent Minister could introduce these two things but I would not as long as I was at the Council table.[187]

There was no worry that the issue would soon return: Mackenzie King would be dead within two years, and Vincent Massey was returning to Canada after a decade-long absence.

Mackenzie King's Philosophy of Honour

It is worth asking why Mackenzie King on the one hand was opposed to honours and on the other accepted so many during his lifetime. Mackenzie King's liberal ideals conflicted with Bennett's Dominion–Commonwealth system, and more generally with the broader British honours system used in Canada during the Second World War. The continuing reliance on Britain for honours was incongruous with Canada's independent status. The award of knighthoods was similarly unacceptable because they conferred an exalted status beyond the proper recognition of individual merits. And there was still the ability for politicians to manipulate the system and return to the old patronage system under which Mackenzie King himself had been honoured.

Liberal difficulties with honours were justified. Under the British Imperial system, honours were regularly used for tawdry purposes: to bind Canada closer to the Empire and to reward the rich and powerful. Too often, worthy citizens were ignored. Yet honours were necessary during the Second World War, as a means to reward selfless gallantry and to promote the war effort. Mackenzie King was able to justify the reintroduction of honours as a necessary part of the war effort. In honours, as in politics, Mackenzie King 'represented the seemingly safe Liberal middle ground.'[188] When he removed knighthoods from the Dominion–Commonwealth system and instituted a special committee to compile nominations (the ACC), he was using an existing institution to further the goals of the liberal state – the principal goal being to win the war. It would have been too great a departure at the time to create a wholly Canadian honours system. Doing so would probably have polarized Canadians more than they already were. The war had divided Canadians into pro-British, anti-British, and pro-Canadian factions, each of which lined up to take sides on a variety of issues.

Few people were as aware as Mackenzie King of the disconnect between honours and liberalism. This tension gave rise to his policy of 'honours if necessary, but not necessarily honours.' Like his views on many national issues, Mackenzie King's attitude toward honours changed over time. The overtly critical would say he flip-flopped. A more accurate interpretation would be that he developed a more complex personal policy toward honours. In 1906, as the country's first deputy labour minister, he was made a Companion of the Order of St Michael and St George. This was a senior honour for a mere deputy minister, especially one so young. Yet as we have seen, later in life he tried to resign from the order. Just before his retirement, he accepted the Order of Merit and four foreign awards from France, Belgium, Liechtenstein, and the Netherlands. In the end, he was the most honoured prime minister in Canadian history.

He accepted these honours, yet he presided over a government with the most restrictive policy toward honours in Canadian history. During his tenure, only war-time awards were permitted, and very few civilians were recognized, with the bulk of honours going to military personnel. This made it look as if he was preventing others from accepting honours while at the same time collecting as many as he could. This interpretation is at best simplistic and fails to grasp the intricacy of the honours system, the meaning of different honours, and Mackenzie King's subtle and profound grasp of social evolution.

Mackenzie King disliked most honours because they were, in his time, tools of patronage and corruption that had been discredited during the First World War. Also, while a member of Laurier's Cabinet, Mackenzie King had come to see honours as divisive and as destructive to the collegial atmosphere necessary for a smooth-running government. When one minister was recognized and another was not, this gave rise to tensions not only between the two men involved, but between them and the prime minister, who was responsible for compiling the honours list.

Mackenzie King divided honours into three groups: military, political/patronage, and Royal. Shortly after becoming prime minister again in 1935, he wrote to the British Central Chancery to ask that his appointment as a Companion of the Order of St Michael and St George be terminated. Prior to George V's Silver Jubilee celebrations, he refused R.B. Bennett's offer of an elevation to Knight Grand Cross (GCMG), which would have made him Sir William Lyon Mackenzie King.[189] He viewed honours such as the Order of St Michael and St George as political/patronage honours, because they were controlled by the prime minister. These honours were the most pervasive in the public realm, having been widely awarded during the First World War and later during Bennett's brief foray back into the field of honours. Bennett's honours were evenly distributed among the population, yet many Canadians still saw them as baubles for the rich and powerful. The Dominion–Commonwealth honours system had barely any time to take root before Bennett was swept from office and Mackenzie King imposed his ban on honours.

At the beginning of the Second World War, Mackenzie King instituted a more restricted version of Bennett's Dominion–Commonwealth honours system. Throughout the Second World War, he supported the bestowal of gallantry awards for Canadian service personnel; he even allowed meritorious service honours such as the Order of the British Empire to be awarded to the military, as long as a knighthood was not attached. His favourable attitude toward gallantry awards likely grew out of the death of his best friend, Henry Harper, who died while attempting to save two women from drowning in the Ottawa River. He characterized Harper and his act of bravery as 'noble, unselfish [and] idealistic.'[190] When it came to political/patronage awards, even when these were awarded through a quota system under the Dominion–Commonwealth system, his attitude was much cooler. This is why throughout the entire Second World War there was only one civilian honours list, and even this one was not published until 1946.

His apparent stinginess reflected a profound inner doubt about honours. He could award honours to McNaughton because, like Harper, the general had sacrificed himself to a greater good. Massey was in his books as a completely exemplary citizen. The Order of the Companions of Honour was at the time limited to sixty-five members, and the British prime minister usually selected these recipients. In the case of Crerar, Massey, and MacNaughton, all three were nominated and approved by George VI.[191] Mackenzie King had little trouble approving CHs for Crerar and MacNaughton, since both were in the military sphere. But when it came to Massey's CH, Mackenzie

King almost did not approve the award. It was only after he received Cabinet's opinion on the subject and it was explained that Massey had been nominated by the King, not by a British politician, that Massey received his CH. In this context, the CH was a Royal honour, one that flowed directly from the Sovereign and that was above politics.

It was on the basis of this distinction – between Royal and partisan honours – that Mackenzie King accepted the Order of Merit from George VI in 1947, just before the marriage of Princess Elizabeth to Philip Mountbatten. The Order of Merit is by far the most senior non-titular honour in the Commonwealth; it is limited to twenty-four living members at any one time, each selected by the Sovereign for his order 'exceptionally meritorious service.'[192] The order's membership has included such people as Florence Nightingale, Jan Smuts, and T.S. Eliot. It is the penultimate Royal honour, surpassed only by the Order of the Garter – which is a knighthood. The Order of Merit was free of the political taint that had so thoroughly tarnished the British honours system. It was awarded independent of any political advice from a government minister. Yet Mackenzie King did not immediately accept this honour. He vacillated for days and eventually sought advice from Cabinet and from his friends in the spirit world.[193] Cabinet fully endorsed the award. After consulting his dead grandfather, the prime minister concluded: 'It will be a remarkable rounding out of the circle which links the reward placed on Mackenzie's head by the Crown with the highest award from the Crown to his grandson who has been carrying on his work.'[194]

Mackenzie King's diaries and papers contain little mention of his reasons for accepting the highest honours from Belgium, France, Liechtenstein, and the Netherlands. All of these honours emanated directly from the heads of state of various countries, and it is likely that the prime minister viewed these not as honours for himself, but as recognitions of Canada's significant wartime contributions.[195] This was a logical conclusion. Honours cannot be bestowed on nations; only individuals can receive them. George VI had received a myriad of honours after the Second World War. The only way other countries could recognize Canada was by recognizing the prime minister, as it was he – not the Governor General, and not some other official – who had led Canada. This pattern indicates clearly that Mackenzie King was favourably disposed toward military honours and Royal honours, but decidedly against political/patronage honours unless absolutely necessary.

Why, then, did Mackenzie King – as prime minister – not institute a Canadian honours system that would be untainted by political patronage? He was certainly in a position to do so; during his tenure, many proposals were made to him that would have filled the honours gap. A partial answer is that Cabinet had more pressing issues to deal with. While prime minister, Mackenzie King had many opportunities to institute a Canadian honours system or even just a Canadian order – complete proposals with designs and statutes were submitted to him on five separate occasions – but all of these were just Canadian versions of British honours. They were, figuratively, Maple Leafs pasted over Union Jacks and called 'Canadian.' All of the proposals placed power over honours in the hands of the prime minister. Thus, the taint of patronage was sure to remain. It was not until 1951 and the Massey Commission that a formal proposal was tabled calling for a non-political honours board that would be insulated from partisan considerations. The concept of citizen-focused nominations emanating from the grassroots (and not from a party or government department) was too radical a departure to be considered in the 1940s. The one group that might have envisioned such a citizen-focused nomination process – the CCF – was more concerned about social rights than about honours. Even in the realm of national symbols, there were more pressing issues at hand – most notably the flag and adoption of 'O Canada' – which were regularly discussed in Parliament. These, and not honours, were the symbols that most concerned Canadians.

Mackenzie King found it simpler to impose strict oversight on the flawed Dominion–Commonwealth system than to embark on creating a Canadian order that would undoubtedly rile Imperialists and raise suspicion among nationalists and Liberals. During the Second World War, there was little to be gained by creating a new, likely divisive symbol. The British honours system was imperfect, but Canadians were somewhat familiar with it, and it served the purpose of according recognition to those who had rendered valuable services during the war. It was an immediate solution to a wartime requirement, a useful albeit temporary patch. That the limited Dominion–Commonwealth system was not used after the war indicates that it was a wartime solution to a wartime problem. Because civilian honours awarded during peacetime were still viewed as patronage or political awards – despite the advent of the Dominion–Commonwealth system – they were seen as unnecessary and politically dangerous. Few people envisioned a neutral selection process and honours that could be used to reward exemplary citizenship. Did Mackenzie King intuit that the time of exemplary citizenship lay beyond his era? R.B. Bennett certainly saw a broader and non-partisan purpose to honours, yet Mackenzie King never seemed to have fully grasped this concept – beyond the honours he personally received.

CHAPTER FOUR

More False Starts: Massey Presses Forward

This country should have its own Orders ... and that through them the Dominion might confer fitting distinctions and appropriate honours upon those whom it delighted to honour.

Resolution of the Royal Society of Canada, 1951

Few Canadians knew about the many attempts to create a national honour during and immediately after the Second World War. Many knew about the Canada Medal, which had already been announced,[1] yet that award had never been given. In the other British Dominions, there was no discussion of creating honours systems separate from Britain. Australia and New Zealand were comfortable with the British system. By war's end, Canada had essentially removed this vestige of Imperial furniture, and the South Africans were beginning to consider a few national awards.

Strong interest in honours was found only at the most senior levels of the Canadian federal government, both civil and military. The military very much wanted to see a Canadian honours system. The Order of Canada would be created as a mainly civilian honour, yet the strongest institutional support for it came from the DND. That Canada's honours system was in large part a child of the military highlights the ancient and persistent connection between military service and honours.

The departure of Mackenzie King brought still more changes to Canada. One of his last projects was to introduce the Canadian Citizenship Act in 1946; for the first time, a part of the British Commonwealth was officially differentiating its citizens from other British subjects. During the First World War, Canada had won its autonomy from Britain. While 'legal' independence came with the Statute of Westminster in 1931, it was during the Second World War that Canada truly came of age. Canadian citizenship was the most effective demonstration of this. Later that year, in another important step, new Letters Patent defining the office of Governor General were adopted. The Sovereign's representative was henceforth delegated with all of the same powers as the King.[2]

With Mackenzie King safely retired to his Gatineau estate, Kingsmere, the eloquent and judicious Louis St Laurent took up the post of prime minister. St Laurent was less cautious than his predecessor, and his dealings with the British government were much more cordial than his mentor's. He had no 'King-Byng affair' to reflect on, and thus no great suspicion that the British would attempt to bind Canada to the Empire. Indeed, after the war the Empire was quickly transformed into a Commonwealth – a change that St Laurent embraced and promoted. The St Laurent government went on a 'Canadianizing' spree that focused on asserting Canada's independent status.[3] One of his first important legislative projects involved abolishing appeals to the Judicial Committee of the Privy Council; in effect, this made the Supreme Court of Canada the last court of appeal.[4] Another important symbolic change came with the passage of the Royal Style and Titles Act, 1953, which allowed Elizabeth II to be proclaimed Queen of Canada at the Coronation. The Fathers of Confederation – who in 1866 had dreamed that Canada would become a kingdom[5] – would have been pleased that Queen Victoria's great-great-granddaughter had adopted a Canadian title. With these steps toward creating more Canadian institutions came a variety of attempts to create a Canadian order. One of these proposals came very close to being adopted, and would serve as a partial basis for the Order of Canada in 1967.

As so often happens in Canadian history, this part of the story revolved around the interests and aspirations of a few well-placed individuals who wished to see their fellow Canadians recognized. No one was better placed or more interested in the creation of a Canadian order than Vincent Massey. On his return to Canada after more than a decade as High Commissioner to London, Massey was unemployed. Mackenzie King had considered him for the post of Governor General in 1944; however, the post had already been filled by Field Marshal Lord Alexander.[6] In 1946, Massey was offered the post of Lieutenant-Governor of Ontario, but he rejected this. It was obvious to both Massey and others that Mackenzie King's offer was both 'a calculated political move and a personal affront: he could say with great sincerity that he had offered Massey a high office and had been turned down.'[7] In 1947, Massey was appointed chancellor of the University of Toronto, but this did not provide enough of an outlet for his 'crusade for cultural nationalism.'[8] There was some fear that in the absence of a senior government post, he would leave Canada and take up the post of Master of Balliol College, Oxford. Massey's former assistant, Lester Pearson, wrote to Jack Pickersgill, secretary to the prime minister, about arranging a meeting between Massey and St Laurent. There was a concern that if Massey remained in England, Canada would lose him as a 'supporter and ... agent in the carrying out of Liberal policy.'[9] In February 1949, Massey became chairman of the Royal Commission on National Development in the Arts, Letters and Sciences; appropriately, the body would become known as the Massey Commission. It would eventually put forward a proposal for developing more Canadian cultural institutions, many of which are now firmly fixed as part of the Canadian identity. Included in the proposal was an outline for an 'Order of St Lawrence.' Massey had once again hauled out Viscount Monck's idea of a Canadian honour.

The Awards Coordination Committee Continues

The demand for honours had declined after the war's end, yet the ACC continued to meet periodically. The questions it faced were neither pressing nor as abundant as they had been. Ephriam Coleman relinquished his chairmanship of the ACC in 1949, when he was named Canada's ambassador to Cuba. He had already been made a

Companion of the Order of St Michael and St George, in recognition of his pivotal role on the ACC and as a highly effective Under-Secretary of State during the war years. Joseph Charles Stein, a young lawyer from Quebec, became the new Under-Secretary of State. Stein had already served as the assistant deputy justice minister and had worked closely with the then Minister of Justice, Louis St Laurent. Before the 1949 federal election, St Laurent had Stein appointed Under-Secretary of State. Unlike his predecessor, Stein was not enthusiastic about honours, let alone the creation of a Canadian order.

The ACC had little interest in again proposing a Canadian order. By 1949, there were few holdovers from the war years on the committee, although the institutional memory of constant rejection remained. In the ACC's view, the Liberal Party – whoever was at the helm – was never going to allow a Canadian order. Once again, the interest came from the DND. After the war ended, the Canadian Armed Forces found themselves once again restricted with regard to which honours they could receive. No more appointments to the Order of the British Empire were to be permitted, and sailors, soldiers, and airmen were thus left to receive only long-service medals and decorations.[10] There was a glaring absence of awards for meritorious service, beyond those for serving for a fixed period of time. To rectify this, Commodore W.B. Creery of DND's Personnel Members Committee (PMC) submitted a proposal to the ACC in July 1949.[11]

Creery was a veteran of both world wars and would later rise to become the Vice Chief of the Naval Staff. It may seem an innocuous fact that such a seasoned veteran of the RCN had resubmitted the proposal. However, this signalled a change in attitude not only in the DND, but also and most specifically in the hierarchy of the Royal Canadian Navy. The RCN was widely acknowledged as the most 'British' of Canada's armed services.[12] In 1942 there had been an uproar among RCN officers when they were ordered to place a 'CANADA' shoulder flash on their uniforms.[13] Up to that time, the only way to distinguish an officer of the RCN from one of Britain's Royal Navy was to closely examine the buttons on the officer's tunic! That a senior officer of the RCN had ventured to propose introducing an honour that was not steeped in British history was a significant departure.

The proposal was quite literally nothing new; rather, it was a resubmission of the same outline for the Order of Canada submitted by Major General A.E. Walford in 1945, which had already been repeated in part in a proposal developed by Lord Alexander in 1948. Creery was anxious to reintroduce the topic, and asked that further consideration be given to the 'institution of the Order of Canada and authorization for the grant of the Canada Medal.'[14] Creery was an astute observer of recent events; he was encouraging the ACC to consider the proposal not only because of the veritable trickle of British awards made to members of the Canadian Armed Forces, but also and more importantly because the 'position which Canada has attained in the Commonwealth and in world affairs it is considered that the time has now come when she should have decorations of her own. It is therefore desired that the Order of Canada be introduced and authority be granted to issue the Canada Medal in order to provide a Canadian Decoration for Canadians.'[15]

Commodore Creery was insistent that these awards be made available both to service personnel and to civilians. However, Stein was not terribly interested in the resubmission from the PMC. Indeed, not until October 1949 did he consider the proposal. Writing to Norman Robertson, Clerk of the Privy Council, he suggested that a few changes be made to the proposal; then, in a cold, mandarin-like fashion, he dismissed the project: '[I] respectfully suggest that the next move is Cabinet's and that until we obtain from them a decision, at least on the principle involved, the Awards Co-ordination Committee cannot make any very useful contribution to the project.'[16]

Without strong backing from the ACC, the project was a non-starter. Robertson never formally passed the proposal on to the prime minister or Cabinet,[17] and took thirteen months to reply to Stein's initial submission.[18] Even so, Robertson and the prime minister's secretary, Jack Pickersgill, discussed the matter in November 1949. The ACC was not interested in creating the Order of Canada, but the prime minister was: 'He thought we should go ahead and get the Order of Canada, or something similar, established ... Mr. St. Laurent suggested that I talk this over with you and that we consider the advisability of having the whole question referred in the first instance to the Massey Commission.'[19]

It was rather convenient that the secretary to the prime minister was making such a suggestion. It was just the type of small project that Massey had been looking for ... or rather had planted. The PMC had reported to the defence minister, Brooke Claxton, before sending its submission to the ACC. Not coincidentally, Claxton was a great admirer and friend of Massey's.[20] So it is no great surprise that a copy of Creery's letter can be found in the Massey papers. When we reflect on Massey's earlier attempts to see the government create a Canadian order – especially his prepping of Lord Tweedsmuir to speak with Mackenzie King about the issue in 1935 – we can be certain that Massey had, through Claxton, at least in part orchestrated the reappearance of such a proposal.

In March 1949, Cabinet had discussed handing the issue to the Royal Commission, but it had not done so.[21] Creery's proposal to the ACC once again brought the issue to Cabinet, and this time, on 25 April 1950, it was decided to pass the matter on to the Royal Commission.

St Laurent indicated that it was desirable to ask the Royal Commission 'to consider and comment on policy with regard to the granting of honours and awards.'[22] A savvy politician, he did not directly ask Massey to develop a Canadian Order, but instead asked for the commission's view on the existing policy on honours and awards. The request was broad enough to encompass the creation of a Canadian order; if St Laurent was not satisfied with the product, he could retreat to his original position of having asked merely for 'comment on policy.' In June of that same year, Cabinet decided to prohibit Canadians from accepting foreign decorations. Although a circular to this effect was sent out to the various High Commissions and embassies in Ottawa, there was, in the words of the prime minister, 'no need to tell the press.'[23]

The Massey Commission

The Royal Commission consisted of a chairman (Massey) and four other commissioners. To some extent, each represented a part of the country, and all were academics. These four were Father Georges-Henri Lévesque, dean of social sciences at Laval

University; Arthur Surveyer, businessman and noted engineer (co-founder of SNC Lavalin); N.A.M. 'Larry' Mackenzie, president of the University of British Columbia; and Hilda Neatby, acting chair of the Department of History at the University of Saskatchewan. This was a unique group of eminent Canadians, all of whom had made important contributions to the nation's life before joining the Royal Commission. All were well connected to the federal government elite. Only Arthur Surveyor would not live to receive the Order of Canada.[24]

The commission was established to examine the development of the arts, letters, and sciences in postwar Canada. This fit into St Laurent's plans for solidifying a Canadian identity. The country had 'come of age constitutionally, diplomatically and militarily,'[25] yet it still lacked key institutions such as a national library, a well-funded national broadcaster, and a coherent cultural policy. The Massey Commission was a federally sponsored exercise in building 'cultural nationalism ... through public policy.'[26]

The commission as a whole was charged with assessing the need for a Canadian honour and assembling a proposal, but Massey was obviously the driving force. He had been involved in such questions since well before the war; at various times he had formally or informally submitted proposals to the Governor General, the prime minister, and the ACC.

Shortly after receiving word from the Cabinet that he ought to examine honours in Canada, Massey developed a fairly comprehensive proposal. He immediately divided the honours question into two parts. The first dealt with whether it was advisable to continue using British gallantry awards and if so, how they were to be administered. The second opened the question of establishing a Canadian honour. Massey decided it would be best for Canada to continue to use the British gallantry awards such as the Victoria Cross and George Cross, since they were familiar to all Canadians. On the question of a high Canadian honour, he revived the name Viscount Monck had proposed in 1866: the Order of St Lawrence. The new Canadian order was to consist of four levels:

- Grand Cross of the Order of St Lawrence GCSL
- Grand Officer of the Order of St Lawrence GOSL
- Companion of the Order of St Lawrence CSL
- Officer of the Order of St Lawrence OSL

This proposal was framed without the knowledge of the other commissioners, but no one was going to dispute the fact that Massey was the expert on this topic. The proposal was similar to many of those made over the preceding decade, although Massey injected some distinctly 'Canadian' ideals into his proposal that had not previously been considered.

On completing a draft proposal, Massey posted a copy to his old friend, Sir Alan Lascelles, private secretary to King George VI.[27] Lascelles was very familiar with Canada, having served as secretary to the Governor General from 1930 to 1935, and had become a good friend of the Masseys during Vincent's time as High Commissioner in London. If a Canadian order was to be founded, the King's consent would have to be secured, and the most direct route to the King was through his secretary.

Lascelles was in favour of Canada creating its own order: 'My diagnosis would be that the idea is largely due to a purely practical consideration – namely, the Canadian wish to enable the King to honour those of them who merit it by an award whose statutes do not entail the assumption of a title.'[28] Lascelles went on to reflect on the significance of such a step and how it would likely lead to other parts of the Commonwealth following Canada's example. There was an undertone of reluctance on Lascelles's part to see Canada relinquish the tradition of awarding its citizens the British orders of chivalry, but that change would have to be embraced in view of the Crown's evolving role in the Commonwealth.

One point that Lascelles was not afraid to criticize was the structure of the order: 'I don't altogether like your designations for the four grades.' He suggested that the designation 'Companion' be changed to the more militaristic 'Commander,' and that the most senior level of the order be 'Grand Commander': 'If there were a good English word for "Seigneur," that might do.'[29] This change was suggested because in the British honours system, the level Commander ranks above that of Companion. Massey would consider these points and eventually change 'Companion' to 'Commander'; but he realized that 'Seigneur de l'Ordre du St-Laurent' would not be accepted in either French or English Canada. Lascelles's letter was ipso facto a regal endorsement of the project, provided that some changes were made. This was an encouraging start, but Massey had been through all of this before and knew not to become too confident.

Aside from Cabinet's request that the Massey Commission examine the question of honours in Canada, only a few submissions were received pertaining to the creation of a Canadian honour. In a short document, the Royal Society of Canada outlined the brief history of the Canada Medal during the Second World War. Section V of this document anticipated that 'it is right and proper, and in keeping with the status and dignity of Canada as a sovereign state, that this country should have its own orders and decorations, that while these would not confer titles they would be distinctively Canadian, and that through them the Dominion might confer fitting distinctions and appropriate honours upon those whom it delighted to honour in recognition of outstanding services to the community.'[30] It is fitting that this submission was made by Lorne Pierce on behalf of the society. A champion of Canadian cultural development throughout his life, he was active in the Royal Society of Canada, the Canadian Authors' Association, and the Royal Ontario Museum, and served as editor-in-chief of the Ryerson Press from 1920 to 1960. It is also worth noting that Pierce and Massey, although not friends, were well acquainted with each other.

Through the Royal Society's submission, Massey introduced his proposal to the commissioners. They were on the whole receptive, as evidenced by the fact that a highly detailed proposal was submitted. By March 1951, the commission had worked out a complete structure for the Order of St Lawrence, along with a selection process and other relevant details. The proposal was not sent to the prime minister, but rather to the King. This would certainly have infuriated St Laurent, but he was never to know. Writing to Sir Michael Adeane – who later became Queen Elizabeth's private secretary in 1952 and was another of Massey's London friends – Massey asked where the new Canadian order would rank with respect to the British orders, which many

Canadians still held. The King decided that the highest grade of the new order, Grand Commander of the Order of St Lawrence, would rank immediately after the Order of Merit and would be followed by the Order of the Companions of Honour. The other grades of the order would rank immediately after the Order of the British Empire, depending on the grade (Commander of the Order of St Lawrence would rank after a Commander of the Order of the British Empire). Surprisingly, the King seems to have accepted that after a time, in Canada, the new Canadian order would rank ahead of the Order of the British Empire awarded after the creation of the Order of St Lawrence. Provided the noted alterations were made, 'His Majesty ... would be prepared to approve.'[31]

Further amendments were made to Massey's proposal by Sir Robert Knox of the British Treasury Office.[32] Knox pushed the commission to define more clearly the purpose of the order and the background of the existing situation in Canada. All of these suggestions were considered and eventually included. A final draft of the Order of St Lawrence proposal was completed in May 1951. It was now left for Massey and the commission to convince Cabinet of the proposal's merits.

The final copy of the Report of the Royal Commission on National Development in the Arts, Letters and Sciences was tabled in the House of Commons on 1 June 1951. St Laurent had requested that the commission submit its report on honours separately. This move was made in contempt of Parliament, although it would not be until fairly recently that this fact was unearthed. This was an elaborate attempt to keep the proposal out of the press. In making the honours report separate, St Laurent and Massey had willingly falsified the official record. Mention of honours was expunged from 'the Prime Minister's letter as it was reprinted in the report's opening pages.'[33]

Massey wrote St Laurent on 16 July 1951, outlining the necessity for the government to consider the founding of a Canadian order. In closing, he stated: 'Now I am very pleased to be able to present to you our views on this special subject which are subscribed to by all the Commissioners.'[34] So interested in the project was Massey that he personally presented a draft of the proposal to the prime minister on 9 August. St Laurent assured Massey that 'I shall take the earliest opportunity of bringing to the attending of my colleagues the report.'[35] What St Laurent did not know was that Massey had already secured the support of the King, having sent a copy of the revised proposal to His Majesty several months earlier![36] The document was never included in the final report of the Royal Commission. It was marked 'Secret,' and buried in the back of the prime minister's files.[37]

The first section of the Confidential Report on Honours and Awards dismissed the possibility of reintroducing titular honours such as knighthoods in Canada. The second part outlined the need to keep utilizing the existing British gallantry awards, as 'these decorations are enshrined as part of the history of Canada and represent something sacred to countless Canadians; to replace them with new decorations without the prestige and the sanction of tradition would not, in our view be in accordance with public feeling.' The report went on to sanction the existing system of award recommendations, primarily those of the ACC and PMC. The question of founding a Canadian honour took up the bulk of the report. It was recommended that a five-level Order of St Lawrence be founded, consisting of the following:

- Grand Cross of the Order of St Lawrence GCSL
- Grand Officer of the Order of St Lawrence GOSL
- Commander of the Order of St Lawrence CSL
- Officer of the Order of St Lawrence OSL
- Member of the Order of St Lawrence MSL
- Medal of the Order of St Lawrence SLM (M du SL)[38]

The proposal for the Order of St Lawrence appeared to be a mirror copy of the Order of the British Empire, which also consists of five levels and a medal. However, it was the third section of the confidential report that would prove the most revolutionary in the world of honours. The method for making appointments to the order was to be different from the old system, in which each government department submitted a list of names and the prime minister had the authority to include or exclude whomever he wanted before sending the list to the King. The commission proposed that

> a non-political committee, to be known as The Honours Committee, be established: that the chairman and the members of the committee be appointed by the Governor-in-Council: that its membership consist of eleven persons, including the chairman, among whom would be ex-officio the Clerk of the Privy Council, The Secretary to the Governor General, The Under Secretary of State and the Deputy Minister of National Defence: that appointment to the remaining five places be made in each instance for a specified term of years.[39]

Although this 'non-political composition' was quite a departure from other systems, such as those utilized in Britain, France, and the United States, it was the final part of the selection process that signalled a break with the old practice of using honours as patronage tools. It guaranteed 'that the government of the day consider no appointments to the Order, save those which have received the approval of the Honours Committee.' In other words, the prime minister and Cabinet were to be summarily deprived of their ability to have colleagues and supporters honoured. Although the prime minister would retain the authority to block nominations approved by the Honours Committee, it was understood that these occasions would be extraordinary. The Honours Committee, like the Massey Commission itself, was to be a creature of official Ottawa. The committee was to be composed of what Paul Litt has defined as 'the quasi-official academic elite.'[40] This group was well connected with the federal government. If the order was to promote a national idea of Canada, it would have to be broad enough to 'honour the humble for their contributions.'[41] It would also have to be able to select out those contributions which were truly national in scope. There is no mention of where the Honours Committee was going to obtain nominations. One must assume that the committee intended to select names from its own nomination lists – a system similar to the British one. In the Canadian case, a politically neutral honours committee, would draw up the honours list. The idea of consulting the public for nominations was not considered at this stage.

Cabinet and the Order of St Lawrence ... or St Laurent?

The proposal was transferred from Massey directly to the prime minister, who examined it and passed it on to the leaders of the other parties. St Laurent emphasized the need to keep the issue as uncontroversial as possible; he merely stated that 'the government has reached no conclusion whatever on the matter but it will have to be dealt with in some fashion sooner or later.'[42] Cabinet was informed of the proposal through a memorandum circulated on 29 August 1951.[43] St Laurent had lost interest in the subject, having been encouraged to do so by J.W. Pickersgill, who – like his mentor, Mackenzie King – had no interest in honours or medals.[44] Pickersgill was St Laurent's special assistant and would shortly become Clerk of the Privy Council. In 1953 he was elected to the House of Commons and became Secretary of State; in that capacity he would enjoy control over the whole honours question. He would be a persistent opponent to any effort to reinstate the British honours system in Canada or to see a Canadian order established.[45]

The Second World War had ended only seven years earlier, and many Canadians were still comfortable with British honours and wished to see the old practice of regular honours lists resumed. A practical problem with the order was its name. To establish an Order of St Lawrence while St Laurent was prime minister would have been to court political disaster. One can only imagine the possible jokes about the prime minister creating an order named after himself to reward loyal Liberals. The issue of the order was seen as too contentious to introduce. St Laurent was approaching an election and wanted to avoid controversy, especially when it came to existing or proposed national institutions.

Interest in the Order of St Lawrence would persist for a number of years. One of its most interested followers was the Queen. Her private secretary, Sir Michael Adeane, wrote: 'I wonder whether you have made any progress with the Canadian Order ... of which you have told me at different times.'[46] Massey remained positive, insisting that the project was not yet 'dead,' and expressed his wish to push the proposal forward.[47] Regardless of the Queen's interest and Massey's efforts, the project *was* dead. St Laurent wished to close the matter until a later time.

Shortly after St Laurent rejected Massey's proposal, the defence minister, Brooke Claxton, directed the PMC to prepare a proposal for a Canadian order.[48] This proposal was completed by the PMC and submitted to the Defence Council on 17 September 1952. Subsequently, Claxton submitted a memorandum to Cabinet that outlined the need for a Canadian order and for the awarding of the Canada Medal.[49] This memorandum was presented to Cabinet; however, Claxton was unable to sway the prime minister, and nothing further transpired.

The Korean War

With the end of the Second World War and the departure of Ephriam Coleman as the ACC's chairman, malaise engulfed the committee: it would not meet again for nearly two years.[50] The new chairman, Stein, had little interest in honours. On 10 May 1949, he wrote the prime minister with regard to foreign decorations; Cabinet subsequently adopted a directive that effectively ended the practice of Canadians accepting foreign honours.

When the Korean War erupted, the ACC and Cabinet decided to resume awarding the various British decorations for gallantry to Canadian servicemen. In June 1951, Cabinet adopted Directive 25, which permitted the awarding of British gallantry decorations and non-titular orders of chivalry; this directive was transmitted to the King on 29 June 1951. This step amounted to a reversion to Order-in-Council 8882 of 18 November 1941. In a few exceptional cases, awards of the British orders of chivalry were made. These awards were limited to the Order of the British Empire, of which eighty-three appointments in all were made.[51] Civilians were not included in these awards, even though they had been for the Second World War.

Between the beginning of the Korean War and the institution of the Order of Canada in 1967, only two civilian British honours were bestowed on Canadians:[52] the eminent neurosurgeon Dr Wilder Penfield received the Order of Merit from the Queen in 1953, and the recently retired Governor General, Vincent Massey, was awarded the Royal Victorian Chain in 1960. There was no difficulty with Penfield's receipt of the OM. As we will see, Massey was originally intended to receive a different honour, but the Nickle Resolution was brought out of storage to derail these plans.

The Canada Medal Returns

As soon as the last Canadian civilian honours list was issued in 1946, interest in the Canada Medal evaporated. It would be mentioned in the House of Commons on only a few more occasions. In June 1954, George Nowlan, MP for Digby-Annapolis-Kings, lamented the absence of honours in Canada, although he made some disparaging remarks about the Canada Medal.[53] The subject was raised again by George Drew, the Leader of the Opposition, on 12 January 1956,[54] although in his sarcasm he showed little understanding of the Canada Medal or its purpose. The last real debate over the Canada Medal occurred on 4 July 1956.[55] John Pallett, MP for the riding of Peel, expressed his hope that Canada would establish a system of awards to recognize outstanding service to the arts and the state. John Diefenbaker then entered the fray, urging that the Canada Medal be reinstated. He perceived the Canada Medal as a rather senior award, suitable for statesmen, artists, scientists, and authors, when in fact it had originally been intended as a junior award. This confusion would dog the Canada Medal right up to its formal demise in 1967.[56] At best, these brief forays into the subject of honours demonstrated that there was little understanding in the House of either the Canada Medal or the need for a Canadian honours system.

Policy Revision, 1956

After the Korean War ended, Cabinet adopted a new, more liberal policy toward honours and awards. Cabinet Directive 30 outlined a new policy to allow Canadian civilians to receive the George Cross and George Medal for 'acts of bravery performed at the risk of death or serious personal injury.'[57] This change was made with respect to all civilians, but it was understood that it 'would only concern police officers for the most part.'[58] Canadian servicemen were still eligible for the various British gallantry decorations in time of war; however, a clause that mentioned 'military operations' was added, to reflect Canada's increasing role in UN peacekeeping missions.

The same directive allowed for the bestowal of Commonwealth and foreign decorations on Canadians, provided permission was received from the Queen and that the services rendered were in connection with either an act of bravery or services rendered 'in support of any war effort or military operations in which it [the armed forces] may be engaged or participate as an ally of or in association with Canada or under the auspices of the United Nations.' In the case of Canadians holding dual nationality, acceptance of foreign awards would be permitted provided the recipients were not members of the Canadian Armed Forces or employees of the Government of Canada.

The Cabinet directive laid down a more limited version of the Dominion–Commonwealth honours system. R.B. Bennett had established this system, which originally included all British civil and military honours (gallantry and meritorious service) and even knighthoods. During the Second World War, Mackenzie King permitted a more limited version of this system to operate. Thus, Canadians could receive any British honour as long as it did not confer a title. The new directive took into account the suggestions made in the Confidential Report on Honours and Awards, which the Massey Commission had submitted in 1952. Cabinet had agreed to resume utilizing the British awards for gallantry, but it did not touch the issue of either founding a Canadian order or resuming the practice of nominating Canadians for the non-titular levels of the various British orders of chivalry. The directive was adopted on 7 November 1956 and came into effect immediately.

The Abolition of the Awards Coordination Committee

A separate document, Cabinet Directive 31, was directly related to Directive 30. It called for the abolition of the 'interdepartmental committee on honours and awards,'[59] which was in fact the Awards Coordination Committee. The ACC was to be replaced by a Decorations Committee, which would comprise the following:

- The Under-Secretary of State
- The Secretary to the Governor General
- The Under-Secretary of State for External Affairs
- The Deputy Minister of National Defence (Navy)
- The Deputy Minister of National Defence (Army)
- The Deputy Minister of National Defence (Air Force)
- The Deputy Minister of Transport
- The Deputy Minister of Labour
- The Commissioner of the RCMP
- The Dominion Archivist

The Decorations Committee was the ACC in all but name, the only real change being the addition of the RCMP Commissioner. New wine into old bottles provided change, however; once again, Canadian civilians and military personnel were declared eligible for gallantry awards. However, there were to be no more awards of the British orders of chivalry.[60] The first meeting of the Decorations Committee was held on 21 November 1956, in Room 258 of the West Block of Parliament – the very same room where the ACC had conducted much of its business since 1942.

Sir Vincent: Massey Nearly Knighted

Perhaps no one understood better the need for Canada to create its own order than Vincent Massey. Throughout the late 1950s, as Governor General, Massey was constantly butting into the government's restrictive policy toward honours. Ultimately, this impacted on him directly, when he was denied an accolade he had worked toward throughout his entire life. During the war years, Massey had become a close friend of George VI and his wife Queen Elizabeth, as well as their daughter Princess Elizabeth. These friendships continued long after Massey's departure from London.

As the first Canadian-born Governor General since 1763, Massey was charged with the monumental task of maintaining the prestige of the office. He did this with great dignity and panache. Unlike all of his predecessors, Massey held no knighthood or peerage, and in some quarters this was seen as an unfortunate fact of the Canadian political landscape. During a visit of His Royal Highness Prince Philip to Quebec in August 1954, Massey had intended to present the Prince with a new award for long service in the Canadian Armed Forces – the Canadian Forces Decoration, instituted only three years earlier.[61] By virtue of his high position and the fact that he was Colonel-in-Chief of the Royal Canadian Regiment, the Prince was automatically to receive the CD.[62] On the same visit, Prince Philip had a most extraordinary award in store for Massey; he informed the Governor General that the Queen wished him to accept the Garter.[63]

The Most Noble Order of the Garter, believed to have been founded in 1348, is one of the oldest orders of chivalry in the world.[64] It is limited to twenty-four knights and until the mid-twentieth century was reserved mainly for nobles. Past recipients have included the Duke of Wellington, the Earl of Beaconsfield (Benjamin Disraeli), many European monarchs, Sir Winston Churchill, and Viscount Alexander of Tunis – a veritable Who's Who of British and European history. Those who receive the Garter become 'Sir.' By this time, women were being admitted to the Order, chief among them Queen Elizabeth, the Queen Mother (1936). Unlike many of the other British orders of chivalry, the Sovereign alone makes nominations for the Garter. In the United Kingdom, the prime minister cannot request that the Queen make someone a Knight of the Garter in the same way that, within reason, he can have whomever he wants declared a Knight Commander of the Order of the Bath.[65]

Massey was elated at first. 'I would like Her Majesty to know how deeply and profoundly touched I am at what Prince Philip told me ... and how greatly I hope that it may be possible for me to accept the supreme honour she has so graciously offered me.'[66] The prospect of becoming the first Knight of the Garter who was not from the United Kingdom was an extraordinary offer. Had Massey been a resident of Britain, he could have accepted the honour without hesitation, there being no possibility of interference from the Canadian prime minister. However, he was a Canadian, and moreover he was the Governor General. Massey told the Prince he would have to 'discuss the matter with my Prime Minister,' but he seemed hopeful that he would be able to accept the honour 'while I am serving in my present capacity [as Governor General].'[67] The Queen, Prince Philip, and Massey were well aware of the potential difficulties over approval.

Massey discussed the matter with St Laurent in late October of 1954. The first meeting was less than productive, but a second one was held on 25 November. St Laurent did not offer much hope, but he did say that 'he would like to study still further the records on the subject of honours in Canada before having another talk' with Massey.[68] A skilled diplomat, Massey gave the prime minister ample time to consider the issue. More than three months later, while St Laurent was visiting Rideau Hall, Massey again broached the subject. St Laurent's reaction was typical: he 'told me [Massey] quite definitely that, in the light of past decisions, it would, in his view, be politically embarrassing to the Government if I accepted the honour while in office.'[69] A minor setback, as the Queen, through Prince Philip, had made it clear that the award could be held in abeyance until Massey retired. Despite this ray of hope, Massey well knew the difficulties ahead: 'I need not say that I am profoundly disappointed not to be able to accept at present the very great distinction which the Queen has offered me. I do hope Her Majesty knows how deeply touched I am at her thought of me.'[70] Aside from Massey, there was another disappointed person: the Queen.[71] Massey had almost failed to receive the Order of the Companions of Honour because of Mackenzie King's petty attitude; he was certainly not going to give up on St Laurent.

The entire matter was left until 1957. A great political change had occurred: after more than twenty years of Liberal rule, the Progressive Conservatives had come to power. The staunchly pro-British John Diefenbaker was at the helm and this gave Massey great hope. A month after Diefenbaker had come to power, Massey received a telephone call from Sir Michael Adeane. There was some informal discussion regarding Massey approaching the new prime minister about receiving permission to accept the Garter. Massey was hopeful, Adeane was not.[72] Massey's talk with Diefenbaker went exceedingly well: 'He [Diefenbaker] could not have been nicer when I told him about it; in fact his first comment was "Wonderful!"'[73] There was now hope that the Queen would be able to knight Massey during the impending Royal Tour. Once again, the entire matter was left in abeyance for a year.

Diefenbaker consulted a few of his senior ministers on the subject of Massey's Order of the Garter. They feared that 'the honour might be misunderstood as involving a general change in policy.'[74] The issue of titles in Canada was still so potent that politicians remained unwilling to touch the issue. However, Massey remained hopeful, and the Queen was made aware of Diefenbaker's position.[75] By 1959, Massey was approaching retirement, his term as Governor General already having been extended. There was a general expectation that Massey would receive a high honour for his lengthy and meritorious service to Canada. This discussion did not help Massey's cause; one paper 'played up rather sensationally ... that I was likely to receive a peerage on leaving my present post.'[76] On 24 January, the front page of the *Ottawa Citizen* boldly stated: A PEERAGE FOR MR. MASSEY.[77] It went on to explain that Massey was to be ennobled during the upcoming Royal Visit. The article did not oppose this move; however, it speculated that the Diefenbaker government was taking 'the same view as the Bennett administration from 1929–1935 which in 1934 [*sic*] restored titles.'[78] Even in 1959 Canadians remained split on the issue of awarding Canadians knighthoods. The results of a 1959 Gallup poll revealed that while 38 per cent of Canadians were in favour of fellow citizens being awarded 'titles' (knighthoods and peerages), 46 per cent were opposed and 16 per cent were undecided. The percentages reflected an increase in support for knighthoods and peerages over earlier polls undertaken in 1942 and 1953. Liberals and Conservatives were also almost evenly split on the issue.[79]

Not surprisingly, this led to questions in the House of Commons.[80] Diefenbaker was hit with a barrage of questions, the most complex ones coming from J.W. Pickersgill, who grilled the prime minister on the complexities of the Nickle Resolution. Diefenbaker denied that the government had any plan to reintroduce peerages or knighthoods for Canadians, and the question was closed, with one brief and ignominious mention of the Canada Medal.[81]

The prime minister was under strong public pressure, and Massey knew not to press the issue. Diefenbaker again consulted three of his most trusted colleagues: Howard Green, Minister of Public Works; Sidney Smith, Secretary of State for External Affairs; and Donald Fleming, Minister of Finance. Green was opposed to the award, but Smith was in favour (unfortunately, he died in March 1959). Fleming was in favour of the award 'providing that it was made clear that this was the personal prerogative of the Sovereign ... and ... that the award of this honour had no bearing on future Government policy relating to honours and awards.'[82] During the 1959 Royal Tour, Diefenbaker assured the Queen that he would soon have an answer for her about Massey. Her Majesty had hoped to confer the honour on Dominion Day 1959,[83] but that date had passed. She now wished to confer the honour prior to 15 September, the same day Massey was to retire as Governor General.[84] Diefenbaker and Massey had an 'extremely frank talk' on the subject, during which the prime minister was very 'sincere' in his desire to see Massey recognized. However, problems remained getting Cabinet approval.'[85]

Several days before his retirement, the Queen wrote Massey: 'I wish to send you my congratulations and my sincere thanks for the manner in which you have discharged [your] duties. I know that as my personal representative you have always sought to maintain the right relationship between the Crown and the people of Canada. I am grateful to you for this because I regard it as the most important function among the many duties of the appointment which you have held with such distinction.'[86] A more glowing commendation of his services could not have been written. Her gratitude could only be enhanced by the bestowal of a high honour.

Robertson Davies, a close friend of Massey's, was made aware of the government's reluctance to allow Massey to accept the Garter. Not coincidentally, the *Peterborough Examiner* – which Davies edited – ran an editorial encouraging the government to allow Massey to become a Knight of the Garter; after all, Sir William Slim had been allowed to accept the same honour on his retirement as Governor General of Australia.[87] Despite the covert efforts on the part of Massey's close friends, there was no change in government policy.

On the day of Massey's retirement, Diefenbaker visited him and asked his permission to discuss the matter with the opposition leader, Lester Pearson. Massey had already had a chat with his old friend about the matter, and Pearson was on his side.[88] Unfortunately, Pearson had recently set off on a visit to western Canada, and Diefenbaker was unable to speak with him about the matter. Diefenbaker eventually secured Pearson's support, but then insisted on consulting the entire Cabinet.[89] Cabinet was consulted. On 13 June 1960, Massey received a letter from Windsor Castle:

> The Queen has instructed me to let you know in confidence that much as she would like to make you a Knight of the Garter – the first in the Commonwealth overseas – it is not possible for her to do so because ... the Government in Canada ... advised her that this would be inappropriate ... Her Majesty does not wish to bring it to a close without assuring you once again of her great appreciation of your services as her Representative in Canada and of her deep regret that it is not possible for her to make known to you and to her people in Canada her regard for you and gratitude for what you have done by awarding to you the Companionship of the highest Order of Chivalry.[90]

Massey was crushed; it would have made a fitting finale to his service to Queen and country. The Garter that Massey was to receive was offered to Sir William Slim, who promptly accepted it on his retirement as Governor General of Australia. Canada's sister Dominion had no prohibition on the acceptance of knighthoods.

The Queen did not forget Massey and quickly found another high honour to bestow on her most loyal subject. On 22 July 1960, Massey was awarded the Royal Victorian Chain.[91] He was the first Canadian to receive the honour and only the second commoner to receive it.[92] The Royal Victorian Chain does not confer a title but in many ways is more illustrious than the Garter; it has been awarded only 110 times, and only three times to people who were neither nobles nor heads of state.[93] This would not be the last honour Massey would receive; over time, a version of his grand honours project would come into being.

In bureaucratic terms, the results of the Royal Commission were immediate.[94] By 1957, all of the commission's recommendations had been implemented save the ones relating to honours. It would take another ten years for this part of the story of Canadian honours to draw to a successful close and a new beginning. The late 1950s brought Canada a new government; the country was truly coming of age. St Laurent's 'Canadianization' of the Crown had been underway for almost a decade and was beginning to take root. Soon Canada would celebrate its centenary. Politicians knew the importance of this event, and plans for the birthday party were set in motion by the Diefenbaker government in 1959. What was initially envisioned as a modest celebration would evolve into the biggest party the country had ever thrown. Over the coming decade, Canada would obtain a new national flag, hold the most successful world exposition ever (Expo 67), and, at last, establish a Canadian order. The symbolic landscape was about to be dotted with new Canadian institutions.

CHAPTER FIVE

First Successful Steps: Founding the Order of Canada

It is my pleasure to announce that on the recommendation of the government Her Majesty has approved the issue of letters patent constituting the Order of Canada. ... The government believes that these three awards, the Companion of the Order of Canada, the Medal of Courage and the Medal of Service, will help fill a need in our national life and will enable proper recognition to be given by Canada to its own citizens and to others.

Lester Pearson to the House of Commons, April 1967

With the approaching Centennial, the Canadian lexicon of symbols still lacked a key element. The Beaver had been used as a national symbol in 1851 with Sir Sandford Fleming's design for Canada's first postage stamp. In 1921, Canada had obtained a grant of Arms from George V, along with national colours chosen by the Sovereign himself. This was followed in 1965 by the adoption of the Maple Leaf flag. Yet Canada still lacked a national system of honours. Even newly independent countries such as Malawi and Ghana had instituted national honours; yet Canada, the first 'Dominion,' was still without. Although Canada had been a pioneer in responsible government, autonomy, and peaceful independence from Britain, successive Canadian governments from Laurier to Diefenbaker had failed to deal effectively with the honours question.

Only two other countries lacked (and continue to lack) a national order or honour: the Swiss Confederacy and the Republic of Ireland.[1] In many respects, the lack of a Canadian order could be attributed to the manner in which Canada became independent. There had been no glorious revolution or break with monarchical tradition. Instead of making violent revolution, Canada had taken gradual steps toward greater autonomy within the Imperial framework; eventually, the Imperial connection was dissolved and replaced with the Commonwealth. This led to the development of a 'divisible Crown.'[2] This divisible Crown enabled a wide variety of Dominions and former colonies to retain their connections with the Sovereign, while pursuing separate policies and goals that did not necessarily conform to those espoused by the British government. This 'shared' Sovereign became far more than just a British entity; it wore many different national hats. On paper, such a system looks quite impossible; in practice, it has proved to be a key institution for Commonwealth countries around the globe.

For nearly two decades there had been no honours list for Canadian civilians. In the 1960s, many Canadians were still familiar with the British orders of chivalry, but they were under the impression that these were only awarded to military officers. Few remembered the Canada Medal, which still ranked in the Canadian Order of Precedence for the wearing of decorations and medals even though it had yet to be awarded. Among the public, there was no great outcry for a Canadian honour. Nonetheless, some senior civil servants and members of the military believed the country needed some mechanism for recognizing citizens who had made outstanding contributions. Perhaps no group was more acutely aware of the absence of a Canadian honours system than the military. Between 1946 and 1967, Canadians were 'unique in the western world in that they are without the means of readily recognizing deserving personnel,'[3] said the Chief of the Defence Staff. For men and women in the service, ribbons on the chest signified what they had done for their country. So the military pressed harder than any other group for a Canadian order.

The Order of Canada took many years to develop. Seven separate attempts had already been made to create a Canadian order, and all had failed. Even so, they had an impact; the form the order eventually took would reflect all of these earlier proposals. In the end, the successful proposal was spurred not by a formal proposal, but rather by a completely separate project.

The year 1967 was this nation's first large-scale birthday party. The Golden Jubilee of Confederation (1917) had been held off owing to the Great War, and the Seventy-Fifth Anniversary (1942) was similarly interrupted by war. As a sort of replacement for the Fiftieth Anniversary, a low-key affair was held in 1927 to celebrate the Diamond Jubilee of Confederation, but this was not truly national in its magnitude. Realizing the importance of the approaching Centennial, civil servants and politicians alike began to make preparations. In November 1959, the Diefenbaker government invited each of the provinces to appoint representatives to sit on a national planning committee. In September 1961, Parliament adopted the National Centennial Act,[4] which established the Centennial Commission. This body was directed to 'promote interest in, and to plan and implement programmes and projects relating to the Centennial of Confederation in Canada in order that the Centennial year may be observed throughout Canada in a manner keeping with its national and historic significance.'[5] All parties agreed that the coming national birthday was of great importance; it would be a means to unite Canadians and to tell the world about Canada's achievements. The debate surrounding the National Centennial Act was by no means brief, but it was cordial.[6] The act was unanimously consented to – an indication of the unity of feeling among parliamentarians.[7] One of the commission's key goals was to encourage citizen participation in the Centennial at the local level.[8] This ethos of grassroots involvement would be incorporated into the Canadian order that grew out of the Centennial.

The military was aware of the significance of the upcoming birthday. For members of the Canadian Armed Forces, there had been relatively few new ribbons to decorate their chests. Members serving twelve years received the Canadian Forces' Decoration, provided they had 'a good final eight years of claimed service'[9] – colloquially known as requisite years of undetected crime. Besides this, there were a few UN Medals for service in Egypt, Yemen, and the Congo, but that was pretty much it.

Unlike Britain, France, and the United States, Canada had no general service medals for service in specific areas, and aside from the CD, there were no awards for meritorious service. Veterans of the Second World War and the Korean War who continued to serve into the 1960s sometimes received a bar for their CD. Medals may be of trifling importance to civilians, but they are symbols of service and pride to members of the military.

The Personnel Members Committee (PMC) of the Department of National Defence (DND) continued to operate and review gallantry awards for members of the armed forces, with the assistance of a small subcommittee, the Inter-Service Awards Committee (ISAC). Both these committees began discussing the founding of a Canadian order.[10] At the 5 October 1959 meeting of the Defence Council, it was decided that the question of creating a Canadian order should be further investigated.[11] In December 1959, a very rough draft proposal was submitted to the assistant minister of national defence.[12] From here, a more precise proposal was developed, and by mid-February 1960 the ISAC and PMC had together developed a detailed proposal for an Order of Canada. Although the proposal mirrored the one developed in late 1945 – a five-level honour with military and civilian divisions – a fair amount of effort was put into the project. A rough constitution for the order was devised, along with design sketches and other peripheral details.[13]

The 1960 proposal for the Order of Canada was sent on to the Chiefs of Staff Committee. It had the support of General Charles Foulkes, the chairman.[14] The Chiefs of Staff agreed that an Order of Canada was needed and felt that the defence minister should be consulted. All branches of the military were now willing to accept a Canadian order, but this in itself was not enough. When Prime Minister Diefenbaker learned of the plans, the entire project was quickly shelved.[15] It seemed that Diefenbaker was as phobic about honours as Mackenzie King.

Unswayed by this failure, the PMC sent a proposal to Jean Miquelon in November 1962. In his capacity as Under-Secretary of State, the recently appointed Miquelon was the chairman of the Decorations Committee – successor to the ACC. A veteran of the Second World War, Miquelon had served as Deputy Judge Advocate General of the Canadian occupation force in Germany. On his return to Canada in 1947, he resumed legal practice in Montreal; he was appointed Under-Secretary of State in March 1962 – a post he would hold until 1965.

The proposal Miquelon received called for the striking of a commemorative medal to mark the hundredth anniversary of Confederation.[16] Canada had followed the British tradition of awarding medals at the time of coronation of a new sovereign and, similarly, when the King or Queen marked an important jubilee. This had occurred in 1887 and 1897 for Queen Victoria, in 1902 for Edward VII, in 1911 for George V, in 1935 for the King's Silver Jubilee, in 1937 for George VI, and in 1953 for the coronation of Queen Elizabeth. Although Canada had a tradition of awarding Coronation and Jubilee medals, it had never awarded medals for its birthday as a country. This idea most likely came from India and Pakistan.[17] When these two countries attained their independence, the British Government arranged for special commemorative medals to be struck. Similarly, other countries in the Commonwealth had issued Independence medals, so a precedent had already been set. Although no such medal had previously been awarded in Canada, the Decorations

Committee was willing to make an exception.[18] Miquelon felt that the proposal violated the honours policy adopted in 1956 under Cabinet Directive 30. He postulated that the award could be made, but only to members of the armed forces. The Secretary of State, George Halpenny – himself a veteran of the Second World War and not unfamiliar with military matters[19] – suggested that Cabinet should be consulted before the Decorations Committee invested more effort into the project. At an early stage it was agreed that the medal would only be awarded to members of the armed forces, and that the project should be studied further by the Decorations Committee.[20] The project was left dormant for several months; the Decorations Committee then reopened it for discussion. At the 18 April 1963 meeting, Miquelon expressed concern that the medal was only going to be awarded to military personnel. Past commemorative medals had been awarded to civilians and soldiers alike, and there was no reason why this tradition should not be continued. Miquelon realized the contentious nature of the topic and affirmed that Cabinet would have to decide, not the Decorations Committee. The project was again passed back to the PMC, which drew up a more formal submission. On 22 January 1964, Paul Hellyer, the new defence minister, gave his approval for the award of the medal to both military personnel and civilians.[21] In March 1964, the Secretary of State, Maurice Lamontagne, received a letter from the Centennial Commissioner outlining the commission's view that the matter of creating a commemorative medal was for the government to deal with, not the commission.[22] Once again, the issue of honours was being tied up in red tape.

Hellyer was desperate to find something to give members of the armed forces. In December 1963, he had begun developing a proposal to reorganize the Royal Canadian Navy, Canadian Army, and Royal Canadian Air Force. At first, this proposal was well received by the various chiefs of staff,[23] but their attitude soon changed as Hellyer's plan grew. In late March 1964, Hellyer released a white paper on Defence. This document called for the 'integration of the Armed Forces of Canada under a single Chief of Defence Staff and a single Defence Staff ... the first step toward a single unified defence force for Canada.'[24] Alarm bells began to ring among senior members of the various services. Many would eventually warm to the concept of a unified command structure. However, Hellyer planned to take the project beyond even this: the RCN, Canadian Army, and RCAF would cease to exist, and all would be amalgamated into the Canadian Forces (CF), with a triservice structure.[25] All members of the CF would wear the same uniform, and there would be no more distinctive ranks for the navy, army, and air force. Admirals would become generals, group captains would become colonels, and staff sergeants would become warrant officers. Although the idea of integrating the command structure of the various services was accepted, the seemingly less important issue of uniforms, ranks, and tradition caused the government great problems. When Admiral W.M. Landymore learned he was being retired, he expressed his belief that integration had cost millions more than projected and that 'the cost involved in the new single service uniform were high and wasteful, and that unification had demoralized the officer corps.'[26] This infuriated Hellyer, and increased his determination to push his plan forward whatever the cost. He made few friends while implementing his unification policy, and he hoped to smooth things over by issuing a Centennial Medal.

The honours issue was once again being discussed, mainly because of the Centennial Medal. Hellyer and Lamontagne presented a joint memorandum to Cabinet on 11 May 1965. This memorandum outlined the insufficiency of the existing honours policy as embodied in Cabinet Directive 30 of 1956. The conclusion declared that the Centennial Medal would appropriately recognize 'the specially valuable service of many Canadian citizens.'[27] The submission was discussed at the 20 May 1965 Cabinet meeting, although Prime Minister Pearson pushed the project aside. His reasons were related to another project: 'The Prime Minister indicated [at the May 20 meeting] he wished to discuss the proposal further with Mr. Lamontagne. Mr. Pearson was inclined to the view that the institution of the Centennial Medal should be linked to the establishment of the Canada Medal.'[28] The Centennial Medal was temporarily shelved, although it had the immediate impact of turning Pearson's mind to the idea of creating a Canadian honours system. This momentous project had been on Pearson's mind for some time – it was first introduced to him by Massey – and was later pressed on him by fellow MP John Matheson prior to Pearson's election as prime minister. Matheson would contribute a great deal to the creation of the Order of Canada in 1967, along with Esmond Butler, secretary to the Governor General, Michael Pitfield, an official at the Privy Council Office, and John S. Hodgson, Pearson's secretary. Although he died in 1957, W.F. Nickle – he of the the Nickle Resolution – was indirectly involved as well.

In 1962, Matheson had encouraged Pearson to consider creating a Canadian honour.[29] After being elected in a May 1961 by-election, Matheson quickly became a friend and adviser to Pearson, eventually serving as his parliamentary assistant. While in New York visiting the UN with other Members of Parliament, he found himself in the library of the UN headquarters. There he began skimming through a variety of books about flags and honours. It was here that two ideas began to percolate. Having served as a captain in the Royal Canadian Horse Artillery during the Second World War, he was well acquainted with the British system of awards and well realized that Canada lacked a homegrown honours system. During the Italian Campaign he had been seriously wounded and was subsequently returned to Canada. Having already received a BA from Queen's University, he attended Osgoode Hall Law School. In the late 1940s, as a young lawyer, he worked with W.F. Nickle. He discussed honours with Nickle on a number of occasions, and he was greatly influenced by his mentor's views on the subject. Nickle had never wanted to abolish all honours – only those which bestowed a title or were hereditary. Nickle's egalitarian views on the subject would echo through the Order of Canada as it was finally adopted in 1967, especially with regard to the non-partisan nature of the Order.

Pearson's interest in creating a national honour had been sparked by Matheson in early 1962; however, he had other reasons for wanting Canada to have a distinctive system. Pearson had been made an Officer of the Order of the British Empire in 1934, and the story goes that his OBE was delivered to him over a fence while he was playing tennis![30] In a letter to then Prime Minister R.B. Bennett, he expressed thanks for the nomination but asked for a raise in pay: 'I can not feed my family on an OBE alone.'[31] Pearson stayed on at Canada House for the early part of the Second World War; while there, he dealt with many questions about honours. This must have been among his most frustrating tasks. On the one hand, he was working for Vincent Massey, who was constantly promoting a Canadian order; the other side of the equation was Mackenzie King, who vehemently opposed honours. Pearson was truly walking a tightrope. While posted to the Canadian Embassy in Washington, a deserving friend was overlooked in the 1943 honours list. Pearson recalled: 'This is the sort of thing that makes a joke of Honours Lists. There is another defect in the list. Owing to the decision, a right one, not to permit titles, only junior decorations are available to Canadians on the list who, if they were in England, would probably receive the most senior ones ... The only way to avoid this is to establish our own Canadian Order.'[32] An idea he first recorded in 1943 would eventually come to fruition, but not until Canada received a new symbol of nationhood.

A New Flag for Canada

The Liberal Party had long supported the adoption of an 'official' and distinctive Canadian flag, but this project was too inherently divisive to make much progress. Pearson had a long-standing interest in Canada adopting a new flag. During the Suez Crisis, when the Canadian government announced its intention to contribute soldiers, the Egyptian government did not respond warmly. The Canadian flag was too similar to the British one, and even the military uniforms were the same. All of this had made Nasser suspicious.[33] This seems to have convinced Pearson that a new Canadian flag was necessary. His parliamentary secretary, Matheson, agreed with him.

Matheson's visit to the UN library spurred him on in two projects. The first of these was not the creation of a Canadian order, but rather the creation of a new Canadian flag. The two projects were of monumental significance. Furthermore, they were intertwined: the adoption of a new Canadian flag on 15 February 1965 would greatly influence not only the desire to create a Canadian order, but also the very design of that honour.

Without question, the flag debate was one the most acrimonious the country had experienced since the Conscription Crisis of 1942. Successive prime ministers had attempted to deal with the question of creating a distinctive Canadian flag. Mackenzie King had proposed a flag similar to the Red Ensign with a green Maple Leaf in the field; Bennett had proposed a Red Ensign with 'Canada' in the lower fly.[34] Neither prime minister seemed willing to press his proposal. In 1925, Mackenzie King through his Cabinet allowed for the founding of a committee to examine the possibility of adopting a new flag for Canada. The ensuing debate only entrenched his dislike for the subject! He would succeed in avoiding the issue of flags until 1945–6, when Parliament again examined the issue of establishing a distinctive Canadian flag. Again, the issue was shelved at the prime minister's insistence. St Laurent felt that Canada needed a distinctive flag, but he was more concerned with legislative changes to the country than with symbolic ones. Diefenbaker had no intention of adopting a new Canadian flag. His primary contribution was to have the Maple Leafs on the Red Ensign changed from green to red in 1957.[35]

Pearson's Liberals came to power in 1963 having promised to adopt a new Canadian flag within two years. Thousands of designs poured into the Prime Minister's Office. How was the government to choose a design? A parliamentary committee was established and set about doing so, remaining mindful of the complex rules of heraldry. The design that was ultimately chosen remained true to Canada's heraldic traditions: it incorporated the national colours, red and white, as chosen by King George V, as well as a stylized Maple Leaf. The Maple Leaf was a familiar symbol to Canadians, having been used during the First World War on the cap badges of the Canadian Expeditionary Force and on the first coins struck by the Dominion in 1871.[36]

The red-white-red pattern was taken from the flag of the Royal Military College (RMC),[37] which is said to have been based on the ribbon of the 1866–70 Canada General Service Medal – the same ribbon that was used on the Canada Medal. Matheson would recall that while visiting RMC, he had discussed the flag issue with George Stanley, RMC's dean of arts: 'We had just emerged from the college mess and Dr. Stanley remarked, "There, John, is your flag" ... pointing to the Royal Military College flag flapping furiously [in the wind].'[38] The rest of the story is well known. After an exhaustive public and parliamentary debate,[39] the Maple Leaf flag was formally adopted on 15 February 1965. At last Canada had a truly distinctive flag, just in time for the Centennial. Pearson had other projects than this on his mind. He suggested that 'O Canada' should be adopted as the National Anthem and that Canada should establish a national honour. To these musings, one of his colleagues responded: 'O, my God, please don't. Haven't we had enough trouble about emblems? Please don't submit us to this.'[40] The prime minister heeded this advice and returned to the normal legislative program, deciding it best to leave the question of anthems and honours for another day.

Temporarily at least, Pearson was willing to set aside questions about anthems and honours. Indeed, not until 1980 was 'O Canada' designated the National Anthem and 'God Save the Queen' the Royal Anthem. The honours issue would be dealt with much more expeditiously. While individual Canadians could take it on themselves to sing 'O Canada' – different versions all around – there was no way that citizens could initiate an honours system. Such direction had to come from the most senior levels. Pearson did not lose interest in the honours question, and Matheson continued to encourage him. The initial plan was to use the order-in-council that had established the Canada Medal to create a new Canadian award.

The Canada Medal and Another 'Canadian Order'

The Canada Medal returned briefly to parliamentary debate on 6 November 1963, when Progressive Conservative member Marcel-Joseph-Aimé Lambert – former Speaker and Minister of Veterans Affairs – asked the government: 'Have any awards of the Canada Medal been made since its institution in 1943?'[41] To which Jack Pickersgill, the Secretary of State, replied 'no.' It was curious that the recently dethroned Conservatives had suddenly gained an interest in the Canada Medal, after nearly six years in power during which they could have arranged for its award. The Canada Medal was examined one last time in Parliament on 8 April 1965, when Bill C-92 was introduced by Guy Leblanc, MP for Rimouski, Quebec. Leblanc's bill sought to revoke the order-in-council that had created the Canada Medal and to replace it with a statute: 'The purpose of this measure is ... to establish a distinctive Canadian decoration for the recognition of meritorious service by citizens of Canada or of other countries and to revoke the Order-in-Council which created the Canada

Medal, a medal which has not yet been awarded.'[42] This bill received first reading, but died on the order paper when Parliament was dissolved in preparation for the 1965 general election. That election returned the Liberals to power, and Pearson's mind turned to other important national projects. The election had not given him a majority, but it had reinvigorated him, and he set about creating a new Cabinet and planning for the upcoming parliamentary session.[43]

Pearson felt a certain urgency, which led him to create the Royal Commission on Bilingualism and Biculturalism. There was an immediate need to establish Canadian symbols that were not specifically British or French, but reflected instead a multicultural ideal of Canadian citizenship. The Quiet Revolution in Quebec and the rising opposition to federal institutions would have to be addressed if the country was to remain united; a new Canadian flag, recognition of the country as bilingual, and the Centennial celebrations with their emphasis on Canada rather than on specific founding groups were all part of a patchwork plan to smooth over long-standing difficulties between Quebec and Ottawa.

The prime minister made discrete enquiries about the possible structure of a Canadian order. Over the Christmas break, he took out a few books from the Parliamentary Library. Toward the end of January 1966, he contacted his old friend and former boss, Vincent Massey. The two men had a long conversation about honours and the need for some system in Canada. Pearson asked Massey to re-examine the Confidential Report on Honours and Awards submitted by the Royal Commission in 1951.[44] After reading through his old report, Massey suggested a few minor changes relating to the need to create local honours committees to submit nominations to Ottawa. Massey cautioned that many would criticize any attempt to create a Canadian order, and he foresaw that such an institution could be undemocratic. He reminded Pearson that most of the people receiving awards in France and Britain were from 'very modest walks of life. ... and in most countries are "little people."' Massey elucidated that beyond the local level, 'such a system in Canada would make, I think a definite contribution to Canadian unity.' The former Governor General was well aware of the many arguments that could be used to derail such a project, and was quick to prepare Pearson. Notwithstanding the possible roadblocks, Massey's enthusiasm was obvious: 'I shall be glad at any time to talk about this problem with you. For years I have felt that we should do something towards the establishment of an honours system in Canada. I think the matter has very great importance. Please call on me if I can be of any help.'[45] Realizing the complexity of the project and the time it would require, Pearson asked Matheson 'to look into this important matter.'[46]

At almost the same time, the Centennial Commission received a proposal for a 'Canadian Recognition Roll of Honour.' This proposal came from Judge W.J. Lindal of the Canadian Ethnic Press Federation, which presented a brief to Peter Aykroyd and other Centennial Commission officers. Lindal was proposing that a Roll of Honour be established, listing 'one hundred deceased Canadians who have rendered distinguished service; fifty living Canadians who have rendered distinguished service.'[47] The proposal included an annual ceremony to be held each Canada Day, during which new names would be added. This was a strange proposal, in that it sought to recognize past and present greats. It was quickly passed on to Matheson, who had resumed his research of honours around the world. The entire project was carried out under a dense veil of secrecy; neither the Centennial Commission nor the public had any idea that such a proposal was being developed.

Matheson set to work, directing Philip Laundy, Chief of Research for the Parliamentary Library, to compile information on honours. Laundy went even further, briefly outlining a possible structure for the order. He proposed a Canada order based on the British Order of Merit, which consisted of twenty-four members and was the highest non-titular award in the Commonwealth. Besides this, Laundy thought the award's name should be 'styled simply, The Order of Canada, and that members thereof should be styled Companions of the Order of Canada.'[48] This was a most practical suggestion, as both terms would be easy to translate into French. Matheson set about distilling the information.

An anxious Vincent Massey wrote to the prime minister on 2 March, complaining that he had not yet heard from Matheson.[49] At last, on 8 March, Massey received a call from Matheson. Impressed, Massey cabled the prime minister suggesting that Matheson visit him at Batterwood – Massey's estate – for a day or so 'quite soon.'[50] Pearson dispatched Matheson to Batterwood[51] to meet with the one true expert on the subject. On 16 March, Matheson arrived at Batterwood and stayed for just over a day. Massey remained excited – for the first time, a prime minister was taking an active interest in what he considered 'his' subject – and he wrote to the Governor General's secretary, Esmond Butler, that 'we are making progress!'[52] During their meeting, Massey and Matheson focused on the Canada Medal and Massey's 1951 proposal for the Order of St Lawrence.[53] The two men also discussed problems that might arise. It was soon agreed that the order, as yet unnamed (Massey was pushing for 'St Lawrence,' Matheson favoured 'Canada'), would have only one level and have twenty-five members.[54] This was quite similar to the suggestion made by Philip Laundy of the Parliamentary Library. The single level was agreed to because past governments had rejected multilevel orders on the basis that they encouraged a hierarchy. In tandem with this order, the Canada Medal was to be reconfigured and awarded.[55]

When he returned to Ottawa, Matheson reported to the prime minister. That evening, Pearson called on the Governor General, Georges Vanier, to inform him about the project.[56] His Excellency showed strong interest and thought it would be appropriate if Esmond Butler became involved on his behalf. Butler would become key to the order's success; he would administer it for nearly twenty years and guide it through its difficult early stages. After serving as an RCN officer during the Second World War, Butler became a United Press reporter in Geneva. He returned to Canada in 1952 to take up a post in the federal civil service. In 1955, his organizational talents and eye for detail landed him the job of assistant secretary to the Governor General. (This would be interrupted briefly by a year in London as assistant press secretary to the Queen.) Shortly after returning to Canada, he was appointed secretary to the Governor General – a post he would hold for more than twenty-five years. Much of the growth of the Order of Canada after 1967 can be attributed to his unflagging devotion to ensuring its success. It was Butler more than anyone else who transformed an essentially European institution into a truly Canadian one. A close friend of Vincent Massey, he too was excited by the project: 'I would only be too pleased to help in any possible way.'[57]

Massey was impressed with Matheson, and wrote to Pearson that their discussion had been very useful. Massey also warned the prime minister that time was wasting if the project was to be ready for the Centennial. Like Vanier, Massey suggested that Butler become involved. This of course had already been approved.[58]

In his report to the prime minister, Matheson noted: 'I was delighted with this meeting. My attitudes were solely upon research. Mr. Massey's views were based upon widespread experience.'[59] Aware that the creation of a national honour could develop into a contentious issue, he assured Pearson that 'Mr. Massey's sense of harmony and aesthetics is such that we can move with far greater assurance on this matter than on the flag.'[60] The scars of the flag debate were only just healing. Pearson was not afraid of a good fight, but he wanted to be sure he could win.

These developments led the prime minister to create an ad hoc committee charged with overseeing the creation of a Canadian order.[61] This four-member committee consisted of John Matheson, Esmond Butler, John S. (Jack) Hodgson, and Michael Pitfield. These four would-be honours experts began fleshing out Massey's proposals and structuring the Order of Canada.

Jack Hodgson, Pearson's private secretary, was an unlikely civil servant: He was a distinguished scholar with several academic degrees in music. He rose to the rank of commander during the Second World War and went on to serve in a variety of senior civil service posts. Pitfield was a civil servant in the Privy Council Office. A lawyer by profession, he possessed natural political insight and later rose to become Clerk of the Privy Council. Eventually, he was appointed to the Senate. Like Gordon Robertson, he was involved not only in the creation of the Order of Canada, but also – later – in its administration as a member of the Advisory Council.

After meeting with Matheson, and with Pearson's approval, Massey set about drafting a constitution for the new order. First, though, he redesigned the Canada Medal, updating the monarch and using the Latin motto 'Pro Merito' in place of 'Merit' and 'Merite.' He also changed the ribbon to white-red-white, a reversed version of the original. This was so the order could use the ribbon combination red-white-red. He then set about inventing the order. At first he was reluctant to give it a name; that is why all of his proposals from this time have a large blank space, for a prospective designation to be added later. What he developed was a Canadian version of the British Order of Merit: a single-level order consisting of the Sovereign, the Governor General, and twenty-five members. The Chief Justice of the Supreme Court of Canada was to act as Chancellor of the order; the Governor General's secretary was to be Registrar of the order.

Massey seems to have put more thought into the design of the insignia than into the mechanics of the order itself. His proposal followed traditional British lines, with recipients receiving not only an insignia of the order but also a mantle 'of scarlet satin, lined with white silk, on the left side of which mantle shall be embroidered the Badge of the Order.'[62] Nevertheless, this was a significant departure from his earlier proposals for a multilevel Order with as many as five grades.

Massey completed his proposal on 28 March and posted it to Matheson the following day. The order still had no name, the two men having been unable to agree on one. Matheson immediately went to work defining the mechanics of the order. The single-level award was to be styled 'the Order of Canada' and to consist only of Companions. This was seen as the most advantageous name, as it was easiest to translate. Recipients would be entitled to use the post-nominal initials 'OC.' Some thought was also given to entitling recipients to the 'qualifying adjective' – or title – 'Honourable.'[63]

The order was to be established by an order-in-council. Recipients were to be chosen by an Honours Committee, which was to be composed of the Chief Justice of Canada, the Clerk of the Privy Council (as Registrar of the Order), the Under-Secretary of State, the Under-Secretary of State for External Affairs, and the Chief of the Defence Staff. As with all proposals dating back to the 1930s, the prime minister would hold a veto over nominations. Essentially, Matheson had set out all the necessary details that Massey had omitted.

Realizing that he was about to achieve his lifelong goal of bringing a Canadian order into existence, Massey worked furiously behind the scenes. He attempted to arrange a meeting between himself, Butler, and Matheson at Batterwood, where they could discuss the entire proposal.[64] Butler arranged a meeting with Matheson and Pitfield on 5 April to review Massey's proposed order and the new Canada Medal.[65] At this meeting it was decided that the idea of a single-level order – so limited in membership – was too elitist and would fail to gain Cabinet approval. The order was broadened to three levels. However, Pitfield and Matheson could not reach agreement on its actual structure, so two separate proposals were drafted, one each from Pitfield and Matheson.

Pitfield spent most of a week drafting his memorandum to the prime minister. Realizing that honours were contentious, he noted in a cover letter that care should be taken as it 'would be best to have a fully developed case and some supporters to ensure a favourable reception.'[66] His long memorandum first set out 'whether or not Canada is to have its own honours and awards at all ... and to what system they should follow.'[67] At this point there were still plans to continue awarding the British gallantry awards such as the Victoria Cross, Military Cross, and Distinguished Service Medal. Pitfield took pains to demonstrate the need for a Canadian Order, emphasizing that the 'Centennial of Confederation now provides as [sic] unique opportunity to escape the handicap that historical development in this area has cast upon it.'[68] He noted that failure to act would result in further reliance on semiofficial and 'frequently artificial honours' from public and private organizations that 'can never assume to be national expressions of commendations, gratitude or encouragement.'[69] There was also the possibility that the provinces would begin to found their own orders, which might be 'detrimental to national unity.'[70]

Then, with the style of a top-notch trial lawyer, having made the case for a Canadian order, Pitfield outlined a precise system. His proposal clearly reflected the recommendations of the Special Committee on Honours and Decorations as well as the proposal of the Royal Commission on National Development in the Arts, Letters and Science. He emphasized the need for a 'distinctly Canadian' order, one that did not follow the earlier systems of honours, which were associated with religious and chivalrous history. The method of selection was to be made 'secure from partisanship or favouritism.' The Canadian system 'must provide for the recognition of "ordinary" as well as "great" people,' and it must encourage outstanding service. Pitfield hoped to 'link the system into the past, and care should be taken to present it as a proper Centennial initiative and not a gimmick.' Although the Queen was to act as Sovereign, her role was 'not to be emphasized for fear of creating unnecessary hostility in certain parts of the country.' This was clearly a reference to the recent cool reception given to the Queen during Her visit to Quebec in 1964. The prime minister was to hold a veto over nominations. Finally, Pitfield outlined the precise structure of the order. It was to consist of three levels:

- **Companions**, limited to fifty Canadians, with no more than five being bestowed a year. They would be entitled to the appellation 'Honourable' and to the post-nominal initials COC. In addition to this, Companions would receive the Canada Medal (in gold) with jewel and collar.
- **Members**, limited to twenty-five appointments per year, with a membership limited to three hundred. They would receive the Canada Medal (in silver) and jewel (collar badge) and would be entitled to the post-nominal initials MOC.
- **Associates**, limited to one hundred awards per year, with no limit on the overall membership. Associates would receive the Canada Medal (in bronze)[71] and be entitled to the post-nominal initials CM.

Pitfield made provision for admitting honorary members. Besides this, the order was to have five officers: the Sovereign, the Grand Master (the Governor General), the Chancellor (elected every five years by the Companions); the Secretary (the secretary to the Governor General), and the Registrar (the Clerk of the Privy Council). Appointments would be made by the Queen, on the advice of the Governor General and the 'Committee of Honours and Awards.' This committee was to consist of the Chancellor of the Order, the Chief Justice of Canada, the Speaker of the House of Commons, the Speaker of the Senate, the Chairman of the Canada Council, the President of the Royal Society of Canada, the Under-Secretary of State, the Clerk of the Privy Council, and the secretary to the Governor General. When honorary (foreign awards) were proposed, the Under-Secretary of State for External Affairs would join the committee.

Pitfield's memorandum was sent to Pearson on 13 April, after it was cleared by Matheson. Unhappy with Pitfield's memorandum, Matheson attached a four-page cover letter outlining a somewhat different proposal. He let Pearson know that Pitfield's proposal 'does not harmonize with your views nor, upon careful reflection and further research, with my own.'[72]

Matheson's augmentations to Pitfield's memorandum were both aesthetic and practical. The three levels were to be styled Companions, Officers, and Members. Companions would receive a gold neck insignia and be entitled to the post-nominal initials CC. Officers would receive the silver Canada Medal and the post-nominal OC. Members would receive a bronze Canada Medal and the post-nominal Mem.C. In a more practical vein, Matheson removed the position of Grand Master and made changes to the Honours and Awards Committee. Pearson's handwritten notes indicate that he was uncomfortable with the high proportion of civil servants involved in the Honours Committee. Similarly, he was sceptical of the proposed prime ministerial veto, noting that 'this might be an embarrassment sometimes.'[73] Overall, however, he found the proposal satisfactory.[74] Pearson favoured Matheson's revisions to Pitfield's proposal. The project was now in the hands of the prime minister, his advisers having ably placed the case and structure for the Order of Canada before him.

Pearson was not the only senior official involved in the process. The Governor General kept abreast of the proposals, although his failing health prevented him from being more active.[75] Vanier was well aware that his predecessor, Massey, was playing a central role, and it is likely that he felt confident that whatever the outcome, it would be acceptable.[76] When Vanier and Pearson discussed the order on 21 April, Vanier expressed his agreement with the proposal.[77]

Temporarily, however, the project was given a low priority. This did not prevent Matheson from continuing his work. On 25 April he was visited by Dr Conrad Swan, Rouge Dragon Pursuivant of the College of Arms, London. Swan was the first Canadian to hold senior office in the College of Arms; eventually he would be made Garter King of Arms and knighted. His role in the founding of the Order of Canada related mainly to some advisory work – most directly, on the manufacture of the actual award. In confidence, Swan was informed of recent events surrounding the proposed Order of Canada, and he was most encouraging. After the meeting, Matheson wrote to Pearson: 'Dr. Swan is convinced that the Canadian Order would receive immediate international recognition and respect.'[78] Before the first bestowal of the Order of Canada in November 1967, many of the relevant officials worried that the order would be either rejected or ridiculed. Thus, Swan's unofficial encouragement – as a member of the Royal Household – was welcome news to the prime minister. Swan also dissuaded Pearson from establishing the Order of Canada by act of Parliament. Pearson was worried that if the mechanism establishing the order was only an order-in-council, the order might be ignored or easily abolished; an act of Parliament was more permanent. This view was rooted in the fact that the Canada Medal had been established by an order-in-council and had never been awarded. In Pearson's view, an honour established by an order-in-council was far more susceptible to a misuse or neglect than one created by an act of Parliament. However, parliamentary convention dictated that since honours are part of the Royal Prerogative, it would be improper for the Order of Canada to be established through an act of Parliament. Swan, with the help of Edith MacDonald from the Department of Justice, brought Pearson to accept this view.

There was a strong sense among the key players that if the project was to succeed, it would have to be implemented quickly. Esmond Butler coaxed Vanier to discuss the matter further with Pearson: 'I think it will be most useful if you could ask the PM what the situation is concerning honours and awards. If a decision is not taken very shortly it would seem to me that it would be impossible to implement any plans in time for 1967.'[79] No doubt, Butler was also concerned about the increase in workload for his staff at Government House, who were already inundated with work related to the Centennial.[80]

Massey was also fretting about the seeming lack of progress. At Butler's insistence, he wrote Vanier expressing concern about the glacial pace of the proposed order: 'If we lose this opportunity of getting something in the field of honours, it will never occur. Do forgive me for writing to you – I am taking advantage of the fact that you and I are old friends and can talk to each other very frankly.'[81] Rather conveniently, after Vanier received the note from Massey, Esmond Butler and his wife Georgina paid a visit to Massey on the weekend of 20 July. Butler had worked with Massey during the latter's term as Governor General, and after Massey's retirement they became even closer friends. The two men discussed the progress being made, and it was initially agreed that three 'distinguished persons'[82] should be awarded the Canada Medal in the New Year's Honours List. This would be followed by an announcement about the other classes of the order once the details had been completed. The project was still very fluid; the Canada Medal was still perceived as a central part of the new Canadian order.

In response to Massey's constant inquisitions – which perturbed Vanier – unofficial word came from the prime minister. Vanier wrote Massey a personal letter about the project: 'This is a matter which the PM and I have discussed on several occasions. I know that he is, as I am, keenly interested and aware of the danger of delay which you point out. Je crois que nous sommes tous les trois d'accord; and I am hopeful.'[83] This was the first indication from Pearson that the project was in all likelihood going to proceed for the Centennial.

Butler again encouraged Massey to take action and to write directly to the prime minister – an extraordinary step.[84] Massey had been involved in the project from the start; even so, it was unusual for him to be acting, in essence, as the Governor General in relation to this particular issue. By no means was Massey a pawn of Butler; it was just that both men were anxious to see action taken. Massey wrote Pearson on 28 September to point out the urgency of the matter. In that letter he outlined six reasons why Canada should create a national honour. He was in fact preaching to the converted. Massey emphasized that honours were not undemocratic. Moreover, they could help national unity and promote a sense of identity, and they were an excellent means for the state to say 'thank you to a citizen for outstanding achievement.'[85] He also stressed that if the government did not act soon, other organizations – universities, banks, corporations, and so on – would attempt to fill the void. Pearson's response was concise and positive: 'I am really anxious to proceed ... and have taken certain necessary preliminary steps.'[86] The creation of the Canadian Order was set to proceed; the first awards would be announced on Dominion Day in the Centennial Year. The plan had been for the first awards to be announced on 1 January 1967; unfortunately, the dies and insignia for the order could not be produced quickly enough.

The staff of the Parliamentary Library were kept busy with Matheson's requests for information on all honours and awards, national and local, official and unofficial.[87] A large file of over one hundred pages was compiled and would eventually help Matheson define what exactly the order was going to recognize. By this time he had already visited the United Kingdom to look into the logistics of producing the order. Matheson met with various experts, initially with E.C. Joslin of the British medal manufacturers Spink & Son. Himself a noted expert on honours, Joslin impressed Matheson with his knowledge and credentials.[88] It was Joslin who would design the insignia of the order. Previously, all plans had centred on using the old Canada Medal – updated with a new effigy of the Queen – which would be made of gold, silver, or bronze, depending on the grade. Joslin suggested that the Canada Medal was 'ugly' and unsuitable for a national order. Together, Matheson and Joslin hit on the idea of creating a distinctive insignia or jewel for each level of the proposed order. Spink's would later suggest that the order be divided into military and civilian divisions – in the pattern of the Order of the Bath and the Order of the British Empire. This idea would be rejected by Pearson and Matheson.[89]

In mid-September 1966, Pearson visited the United Kingdom for two weeks to attend the Commonwealth Heads of Government Meeting. At this time, an important meeting took place. In attendance were the prime minister; Dr J.S. Hodgson, Pearson's principal secretary; Dr Conrad Swan; D.F. Spink of Spink & Son; and 'others.'[90] Spink was keen to see the proposed order expanded beyond Matheson and Pitfield's three-level proposal. A proposal was submitted that called for the creation of a five-level order, to consist of Grand Companion, Grand Officer, Companion, Officer, and Member. Being that the order was still nameless, two proposals were offered: The Order of Canada and the Canadian Order of Merit. The order was to be designed by Swan and various artists at Spink & Son. Pearson did not favour expanding the order beyond three levels.

The new proposal – which was mainly Swan's[91] – was in Pitfield's view too similar to the existing Order of the British Empire and *Légion d'honneur*. Swan's key contribution was to insist that the Canadian order be created by Letters Patent and not by a statute, since orders and decorations emanated from the Royal Prerogative and not from Parliament. The prime minister was eventually encouraged to discuss the matter with the Queen. These points may seem minor, but they were not. Canadian officials had a very good idea of what composition they wanted the order to have, but they had little expertise with regard to how to actually create it. Here, Swan was of great help; he provided copies of the statutes of various British orders, and he outlined how the order should be brought into effect.

The attitude of Canadian officials toward the structure and statutes of the existing British Orders is reflected clearly in the words of Hodgson: 'I hope that our own documentation will be more laconic and modern.'[92] This desire for a less complex national order led Pearson to 'take his business' elsewhere. Frustrated with Spink's efforts to simply create a British order with a Canadian name, Pearson chose the Crown Jewellers Garrard & Co. to advise him on the Order's design and to produce the first insignia of the Order of Canada.

During a friendly meeting with the Queen's private secretary, Sir Michael Adeane, Pearson asked Adeane to mention the Canadian order to Her Majesty.[93] Adeane was very positive, and most pleased that the prime minister had taken the time to discuss the matter with him. Through Swan, Adeane was aware that such a project was in the works, and he was probably concerned that the Queen might not be consulted until the last moment. Thus, he was relieved to have this first informal notice.

Having taken a keen interest in the development of a Canadian order, Swan continued to send suggestions to Matheson. Swan was in a unique position as the only Canadian member of the Royal Household, and he hoped to be appointed Registrar of the Order.[94] This was not an unreasonable suggestion, but it was quite unlikely to happen, given the strong desire to make the order wholly Canadian, with no connection to officials in Britain other than through the person of the Queen, as Sovereign of the Order. By this time, Edith MacDonald of the Department of Justice, along with Matheson, had prepared two draft constitutions for the order. After many additions and alterations, this would serve as the basis for the order.[95]

It is unclear exactly when Pearson decided to style the new honour the Order of

Canada, but the decision had been made by November 1966. Certainly, it was appropriate: it was easy to translate into French, and unlike the Order of St Lawrence, it had no religious affiliation.

Cabinet and the Order of Canada

Many times in the past, opposition from the prime minister or Cabinet had derailed attempts to create a Canadian order. Regardless of how ill or well planned a proposal was, it could flourish or be crushed according to the will of Cabinet. The main difference in 1966 was that the prime minister was a strong supporter and had carefully consulted on and constructed the proposal. The augmented Pitfield/Matheson proposal that was presented to Cabinet was a stew of ideas dating back to Viscount Monck, with a strong Massey flavour. Yet in spite of this careful planning, the entire plan was nearly lost. Cabinet ultimately decided to alter it.

In May, Cabinet discussed the possibility of founding a series of military awards. A special committee was established to consider this issue, and the proposal it crafted was totally unrelated to the Order of Canada.[96] Cabinet's reaction was on the whole favourable. A confidential memorandum was circulated to Cabinet on 7 November 1966. It outlined the reasons why Canada needed a system of honours and awards, most specifically a national order. The Order of Canada, L'Ordre du Canada, would consist of three grades:

(a) Companions: never to exceed 30 persons; 10 awards to be made in the Centennial year and not more than 5 in every year thereafter.
(b) Officers: never to exceed 100 persons; 25 awards in the Centennial year and not more than 10 in any year thereafter.
(c) Members: 50 awards in any year.[97]

The rest of the proposal was identical to the augmentations Matheson had made to Pitfield's memorandum in April of that year. Pearson carefully omitted the original idea that Companions would receive the appellation 'Honourable,' knowing that there was great opposition to titles, even those normally accorded to members of the Queen's Privy Council for Canada.[98] The selection committee had been retitled the Advisory Council. The subject was added to the agenda of the 29 November Cabinet meeting.

In the weeks leading up to the 29 November meeting, opposition was voiced by Paul Martin, Sr, and Paul Hellyer. Both these men would be absent from the forthcoming meeting, but they made their positions known well before the fateful day. Martin had been against an honours system since Mackenzie King's time. Paul Hellyer was unhappy that there was no separate military division of the order. From Hellyer's perspective, the military was once again being left out.[99]

When Cabinet met to discuss the matter, Pearson began with a brief synopsis of the history of honours in Canada, emphasizing the symbolic importance that such an institution would have. After reviewing the proposed structure, some members raised questions about the advisability of having different 'classes' of honours. There was a fear that Canadians would not look favourably on a system of classed honours of the sort bestowed in European countries. Three voices of opposition were heard: those of Mitchell Sharp, Judy LaMarsh, and Léo-Alphonse-Joseph Cadieux (Associate Minister of National Defence, representing Hellyer). Sharp and LaMarsh opposed the creation of any order as it was 'out of keeping with the egalitarian tradition in Canada.'[100] Cadieux merely rearticulated Hellyer's concern about limited military involvement. It would transpire that Hellyer wanted a much broader honours system and felt somewhat left out of the whole process.[101] Other Cabinet members were unhappy that the Advisory Council consisted solely of federal officials, with no provincial input or involvement from beyond the governmental sphere.[102]

A compromise was eventually reached. Fearing that the entire project might be lost, Pearson agreed to sacrifice the three-level order for a very different entity: 'The Cabinet agreed in principle that an "Order of Canada" of a single grade be established for award to Canadian citizens for merit, and that details respecting its conditions be generally along the lines outlined by the prime minister but subject to further consideration by him or some of the points raised in the course of discussion.'[103] The single grade was agreed on, a multilevel system being seen as too European and elitist. However, a single grade with strong restrictions on membership would serve only to make the order more exclusive and elitist.[104] One civil servant would later reflect: 'This was a clear cut case of elected representatives allowing political interests to dictate compromise in a technical sphere in which few if any of them were knowledgeable.'[105] It was a short-sighted change that would, out of necessity, not last long. At last there was victory: for the first time in Canadian history, Cabinet had agreed to the creation of a Canadian order. All that was left was to decide on the design, officers, and constitution of the fledgling Order of Canada. Of the twenty-two ministers and secretaries present at the 29 November meeting, nine would eventually receive the Order of Canada. Three of the four who had opposed the creation of the order would receive the accolade later in life.

Having received Cabinet's provisional approval, Pearson and his staff were faced with the daunting tasks of drafting a constitution for the order, having the order designed and manufactured, and selecting a first slate of worthy recipients. All of this had to be done in time for Dominion Day 1967 – a short seven months away. The arrangements were made largely by Pearson's quartet of honours experts, whom he affectionately dubbed his 'Honours Team.' Although not an official member of the ad hoc committee, Edith MacDonald would be responsible for ensuring the legal soundness of the order's constitution and Letters Patent.

The Canada Medal was finally abandoned after MacDonald reviewed the proposed constitution of the order. She suggested that the order-in-council creating the medal be revoked and that an entirely new order-in-council be issued to formalize the Letters Patent founding the Order of Canada.[106] Up until this point, previous proposals had been based on the idea of augmenting the original 1943 order-in-council that founded the Canada Medal.

Informing the Queen

The Queen as Canada's Head of State was the only logical choice as Sovereign of the Order, so her permission had to be sought. On 6 January 1967, Butler posted a letter to the Queen's private secretary, his old friend Sir Michael Adeane. The letter included a brief summary of the initial proposals and Matheson's 19 October draft constitution for the order.[107] On receipt, Adeane immediately consulted the Queen and sent this telegram to Butler: 'The Queen gives provisional approval STOP Ltter on its way.'[108] In the letter, Adeane indicated that the Queen wished 'to be consulted about the designs of the ... Insignia.'[109] A more important question not related to design was also raised by the Queen: Was she to be the Sovereign of the Order? The proposed constitution made no mention of her role; it merely stated that the Governor General was to act as Principal Companion and Chancellor. However, with the Governor General acting as Chancellor, the Queen would naturally be Sovereign, and this fact would be added to future drafts of the constitution. In closing, Adeane assured Butler: 'You can depend on everyone here to help as much as we can but I think it will be quite a task to get it all ready by 1st July.'[110] Vanier in particular was delighted with this news.[111] Almost immediately, Butler began arranging a trip to Britain to consult the various experts on honours and to meet with Garrard & Co. about manufacturing the insignia.[112]

In the meantime, another problem had arisen, one that was quite beyond the control of the Canadian or British government. William Summers, the Crown Jeweller, informed Butler that the King of Jordan had recently commissioned Garrard & Co. to produce a new Jordanian order, which happened to have the exact same ribbon as the Order of Canada. Sir Martin Charteris, a member of the Royal Household, intervened on behalf of Canada and instructed Garrard & Co. to encourage the King of Jordan to alter his proposed ribbon by adding a third red stripe.[113] Butler was quite alarmed by the prospect of there being a similar ribbon,[114] although the worry was quite unfounded (there were already a number of foreign orders with a red-white-red ribbon combination).[115] The situation would eventually be resolved when changes were made to the ribbon of the Jordanian order. Once again, the Commonwealth connection had proven invaluable.

Butler was anxious to finalize all of the arrangements in London, and planned a four-day visit. John Hodgson would accompany him. Butler and the Governor General had together decided that even though Matheson was 'very anxious to go ... it would be much better to keep this entirely non-political.'[116] Matheson had been involved in the project from its inception, but from this point on his role would be diminished, mainly because he was a politician and one of the driving forces behind the order was its non-partisan nature. Butler and Hodgson set off for London, where they were to meet Brigadier Colquhoun, Secretary of the Central Chancellery of the Orders of Knighthood, Sir Michael Adeane, and officials at Garrard & Co.[117] The four-day meeting proved useful; Colquhoun made a number of important suggestions relating to the investiture ceremony and asked whether there would be a special insignia of the order for the Sovereign and Chancellor. Up to this point, Canadian officials had been focusing mainly on creating the order, and they were still largely ignorant of many of the smaller but necessary details. Final arrangements were made with Garrard & Co. relating to the manufacture and cost of the award; thus, the order was well on its way to being complete. However, British officials raised concerns that the single level would not be sufficient and would result in 'difficulty with the selection of Companions.'[118]

The Medal of Courage and Medal of Service

Two clever additions were made to the order, although neither returned the order's structure to the original three levels. The first originated from Hodgson, who proposed that a bravery award be added to the order: 'the Gallantry Medal of the Order of Canada.' In part, this change was meant as a means to address Paul Hellyer's concern that the order was not going to recognize the military. In late October 1966, the Defence Council received a memorandum outlining a proposal for bravery and meritorious service awards. The Defence Council's proposal was seen as too elaborate to implement, at least not simultaneously with the Order of Canada. It was assumed that the Order of Canada would fulfil the need for meritorious service awards, but there was still no mention of gallantry awards. In 1966, Pitfield had encouraged the government to continue to use the existing British gallantry awards, since they were widely recognized and universally respected, and Hodgson seems to have taken this into account. The Gallantry Medal of the Order of Canada – or Medal of Courage of the Order of Canada, as it would later become known – was to rank after the Victoria Cross and George Cross but before all other gallantry awards such as the Distinguished Service Cross, Military Cross, and Distinguished Flying Cross.[119] The Medal of Courage was to be 'awarded in connection with the order to any person who, in peace time, as a civilian or a member of an armed force or police force performs an act of conspicuous courage in circumstances of great danger.'[120] At first glance, it might seem odd to include a gallantry award with an order intended to recognize meritorious service, but it had been done before. In 1922, five years after the Order of the British Empire was founded, the Order of the British Empire Medal for Gallantry was added, commonly known as the Empire Gallantry Medal. It would be replaced by the George Cross in 1940; even so, its existence provided a suitable precedent.[121] Unlike the Companions of the Order of Canada, nominations for the Medal of Courage were to be reviewed by the Decorations Committee and not the Order of Canada Advisory Council. This was quite logical: the Decorations Committee was best suited for gauging the level of gallantry and deciding the appropriate award. Esmond Butler was displeased with this development: 'As you know it is my own personal view that it is a pity to include the Gallantry Award within the Order.'[122] Regardless, approval for the addition of the Medal of Courage was given on 3 January 1967, simultaneous with the request from MacDonald to draft the necessary orders-in-council and Letters Patent.

The next development further altering the order came in late February. Esmond Butler met with Gordon Robertson, Clerk of the Privy Council. A Rhodes Scholar, Robertson was born in rural Saskatchewan and would serve under every prime minister from Mackenzie King to Trudeau. Robertson would strongly influence the order's early development; he would serve eight years on its Advisory Council.[123] Butler was only the council's secretary, but his views were always taken into account.

During their meeting, it was agreed that the order's existing structure – Companion and the Medal of Courage – would not achieve the prime minister's objectives. Esmond Butler argued: 'By having only one grade to the Order which can only be awarded to relatively few people, it would obviously not be possible to recognize a very broad cross section of the Canadian population. I know that it has always been the Prime Minister's wish to honour those of more humble station who serve the country in a distinguished way.'[124] Robertson suggested that there might also be a 'Medal of Service.' Pearson accepted this proposal, incrementally getting closer to his goal of a three-tiered order. The Medal of Service of the Order of Canada was to be awarded for 'achievement and merit of a high degree, especially to Canada or to humanity at large.'[125] The Medal of Service would rank after the Medal of Courage.

The Order of Canada now had three awards consisting of two parts: service and gallantry. The service section of the order consisted of the Companions of the Order of Canada and the holders of the Medal of Service of the Order of Canada. A person holding a Medal of Service could be elevated to Companion of the Order of Canada. The gallantry part of the order was in effect an entirely separate award; the recipient of the Medal of Courage could not be promoted within the order to become a Companion. By 17 February 1967 the basic structure and criteria had been worked out by Hodgson and forwarded to MacDonald in the justice department.

The amended version of the order's constitution was submitted to Hodgson on 22 February and reviewed by him and Butler the following day. There was still some fear that Cabinet would not approve the addition of the Medal of Courage or Medal of Service. The completed proposal was sent to Cabinet in a memorandum on 27 February. In that memorandum, Pearson outlined the relevant changes: the single grade of Companion; the clearer definition of the term 'merit' to be recognized as meaning 'especially service to Canada or humanity at large'; the stipulation that honorary awards would be made on the recommendation of the government and not the Advisory Council; and that all recipients would receive the Queen's formal approval. Tacked on at the end was mention of the Medal of Courage and Medal of Service; clearly, Pearson hoped to gain approval of these awards by not including them in the Companion section of the order. The closing section of the memorandum noted: 'Early approval is needed to allow sufficient time for issue of Letters Patent, establishment of the Advisory Council, issue of a call for nominations and study of them, and finally announcement of the initial list on July 1st of the year.'[126] On 2 March, the proposal passed through Cabinet without serious incident.[127] Butler had already written Adeane, warning him that the necessary documents would not be prepared for at least another two weeks.[128] Adeane took the liberty of discussing the matter with the Queen, who was already aware of events in Canada. Writing on 27 February to Governor General Vanier, Adeane noted the Queen's enthusiasm for the Order and how delighted she was to see Canada create this new institution.[129] The following day, the Queen gave approval for the addition of the Medal of Service.[130]

By February 1967 a key change had been made in terms of the new order's relationship with existing British awards. It was decided that the Medal of Courage would be worn ahead of all other gallantry awards save the Victoria Cross and George Cross. The government had decided to discard the original plan for gallantry awards, which would have seen the Medal of Courage blended with the established British gallantry awards. Now one gallantry medal – the Medal of Courage – would serve for all acts of gallantry, replacing more than ten other gallantry decorations.[131]

The Final Constitution

All of the relevant founding documents had by now been drafted by MacDonald (see Appendix 5). As early as 19 October 1966, she had completed a draft order-in-council, draft Letters Patent, and a draft constitution for the order.[132] There was considerable discussion about whether the order should have a constitution and ordinances or statutes and ordinances. In the United Kingdom, it had been the tradition for orders to have statutes, and early proposals for the Order of Canada were usually accompanied by statutes. It was decided that the order would have a constitution, given that the Governor General could only amend the constitution by issuing new Letters Patent. Future amendments could be enacted by the Governor General after they had been 'sought from the Queen.'[133]

The October 1966 constitution changed with the removal of the original three-level proposal. Companions, Officers, and Members were replaced with the Companion of the Order of Canada, the Medal of Courage of the Order of Canada, and the Medal of Service of the Order of Canada. The early constitution stated that Companions of the Order would wear their Order of Canada before all other decorations and awards. In the late February draft of the constitution it was decided that the Companions should wear their order after the Victoria Cross and George Cross; this was similar to the precedent set in other countries, where the most senior gallantry decorations usually preceded the national order. Other significant changes were made with regard to the Advisory Council of the order. In a February 1966 draft, provisions were made for three Companions to sit on the council. These were to be elected after the first investiture of the order by the other Companions of the Order. Each of the three elected Companions would 'hold office as a member of the council for a period of three years.'[134] This idea would be replaced by the addition of the President of the Association of Universities and Colleges of Canada.[135]

The constitution submitted to the Governor General and later the Queen founded an order consisting of three awards:

- *Companions of the Order of Canada*, to be 'made for merit, especially service to Canada or to humanity at large.' For the Centennial year, provision was made for fifty people to be appointed, with a maximum of twenty-five in successive years. Membership in this level was limited to 150 Companions in addition to the Sovereign and Chancellor. Recipients would be entitled to the post-nominal initials 'CC.'
- *Medal of Courage of the Order of Canada*, to be awarded to 'any person who, as a civilian or a member of an armed force or police force performs an act of conspicuous courage in circumstances of great danger.' There was no limit on the number of Medals of Courage that could be awarded. Those who received the Medal of Courage would be entitled to the post-nominal initials 'CM.' Recipients of the Medal of Courage were automatically to become members of the Order; however, an exception was to be made in the case of posthumous awards. Tradition states that a deceased person cannot become a member of an order.
- *Medal of Service of the Order of Canada*, to be awarded 'to any person for merit,

especially service to Canada or humanity at large.' A maximum of one hundred awards would be made during the Centennial year, and fifty in each year thereafter. Recipients would be entitled to the post-nominal initials 'SM.'

Nominations were to be solicited from the general public. Recipients of the Companionship of the Order of Canada and Medal of Service were to be selected by the Advisory Council of the Order. This council would consist of seven members: the Governor General as Chancellor; the Chief Justice (Chairman); the Clerk of the Privy Council; the Under-Secretary of State; the Chairman of the Canada Council; the President of the Royal Society of Canada; and the President of the Association of Universities and Colleges of Canada. In addition to these members, a Secretary for the Order was appointed. By virtue of his office, the Secretary to the Governor General was chosen. Provision was made for the Governor General to appoint additional council members. Although nominations for the Medal of Courage would be accepted from the public, the Decorations Committee was expected to submit the bulk of nominations. Ultimately, it was left to the Decorations Committee to decide on awards of the Medal of Courage; that committee would then submit its provisional list to the Advisory Council. In essence, the Advisory Council was to deal with merit and the Decorations Committee with deeds of bravery.

Formal Approval by the Queen

On 2 March the Governor-in-Council passed Order-in-Council 389, authorizing the submission of the Letters Patent and Constitution of the Order of Canada to the Queen. This would be the last order-in-council signed by Vanier. The documents travelled from desk to desk, starting with Prime Minister Pearson and moving to Gordon Robertson, Clerk of the Privy Council, then to Judy LaMarsh, Secretary of State, on 13 March 1967.[136] Robertson asked LaMarsh to inform him 'of the Queen's approval when it has been obtained.'[137] From her, the documents were sent on to Esmond Butler and the Governor General at Government House. Unfortunately, on 5 March, General Vanier died, and the submission had to be made by the Administrator of the Government of Canada, Chief Justice Robert Taschereau. Finally, on 17 March, the prime minister's submission was forwarded to the Queen.[138] On 21 March, the Queen approved and signed the Letters Patent founding the Order of Canada, to take effect on 1 July 1967.[139]

The Order Is Announced

On 28 March, the relevant documents were returned to Canada and forwarded to LaMarsh. Pearson prepared to announce the creation of the Order to the Canadian public. With Hodgson's help, he wrote his first draft statement to the House of Commons on 22 March. However, he repeatedly revised it: perhaps the more he worked on his speech, the more the importance of the occasion impressed itself on him. By 11 April, a final draft had been completed. On 17 April, Pearson rose in the House of Commons:

Mr Speaker, I would like to announce to the house the establishment of a system of honours and awards for Canada. Practically every sovereign country has such a system which it uses as a means of recognizing merit or gallantry, or distinguished public service. I believe that recognition of this kind can strengthen national pride and the appreciation of national service.

There has been no system of Canadian honours and awards. The Canada Medal was instituted in 1943 as a possible way of filling the gap, but it has never been awarded and is now being replaced. Because Canada has lacked an official system a number of unofficial and semi official honours and awards have developed over the years ... It is my pleasure to announce that on the recommendation of the government Her Majesty has approved the issue of letters patent constituting the Order of Canada ... Any person or organization is invited at any time to suggest names of persons whom they consider worthy of receiving any of these awards ... The government believes that these three awards, the Companion of the Order of Canada, the Medal of Courage and the Medal of Service, will help fill a need in our national life and will enable proper recognition to be given by Canada to its own citizens and to others.[140]

The Leader of the Opposition, John Diefenbaker, then rose and recounted a brief history of honours in Canada. Although he gave a fairly accurate account, he bated his old rival J.W. Pickersgill, stating that 'certainly this ... must cause deep concerns to the Minister of Transport [Pickersgill] because after all he is the testamentary successor to the Right Hon. Mackenzie King. Mr. King did not like decorations, prefixes or suffixes. The only person who has a close link with the past in this regard – a close link with that Prime Minister – is the Minister of Transport.'[141] Diefenbaker then went on to dissect and criticize Mackenzie King's honours policy and correctly pointed out that Canada had taken such a long time to create a system mainly as result of 'Mackenzie King's lengthy period of service as Prime Minister with those who followed him holding similar views [on honours].'[142] He then indicated a fear on his part that, like the Canada Medal, the Order of Canada would never be awarded and would be relegated to the status of 'numismatic curio.' Diefenbaker offered neither criticism nor support for the endeavour. This was due in part to the fact that he had not been extended the traditional courtesy of being informed beforehand of any such important announcement. This failure to inform the leaders of the opposition parties also accounted for the absence of the NDP leader. David Lewis endorsed the Order on behalf of the NDP: 'On behalf of our party ... we greet the announcement of a Canadian order and the fact that it is Canadian.' Lewis pointed out that thousands of Canadians go unrecognized for the contributions they make to their communities, and that the creation of the Order was a good step. In closing, he applauded the method of selection through the Advisory Council and suggested that 'the same attitude and the same process [of fairness] will be applied to a good many other appointments in our society, which I think would do Canada a great deal of good.'[143] Pearson, although unhappy that the order did not have three levels (Companion, Officer, Member), as he had first wished, was pleased that Canada finally had an honour of its own.[144]

Knowledge of the Order of Canada was now in the public domain, the Prime

Minister's Office having simultaneously issued a press release announcing the creation of the order and encouraging people and organizations to submit their nominations, 'which should include particulars of the merits and accomplishments of the person,'[145] to the secretary to the Governor General. As soon as the order-in-council was published in the *Canada Gazette* on 29 April 1967, all of the legal necessities had been performed.[146] Now the hard task of selecting recipients could begin.

One of the more noteworthy aspects of the new order was the method by which recipients were to be selected. The Advisory Council of the Order of Canada had been given the power – hitherto the prime minister's alone – to advise the Sovereign. In effect, a portion of the Royal Prerogative, which had been persistently eroded by successive governments both in Canada and throughout the Commonwealth, had been returned to the Queen. The Advisory Council of the Order of Canada provided the first purely non-partisan method of selecting citizens to receive national honours. No other country had a system this insulated from political influence. Coincidentally, it was Andrew Bonar Law – the only Canadian ever to become British prime minister – who in 1923 suggested that the British honours lists be vetted by a special committee to ensure that political influence had not been used to obtain awards; however, this fell short of a truly non-partisan selection process. The Canadian system took non-partisanship to a whole new level, by totally removing the prime minister and Cabinet from the nomination and approval process. The emphasis on the role of the citizenry in the nomination process was indicative of the grassroots local involvement that the Centennial was attempting to promote; in effect, this role made the legal category of Canadian citizenship a living social and cultural experience. At the same time, the order as an institution fit neatly into another goal of the Centennial, which was to promote an 'official understanding of Canada.'[147] The new order was to promote both Canadian unity and citizenship idealism. In many respects, the method of selection is what gave the order the respectability that other institutions such as the *Légion d'honneur* and Order of the British Empire lacked when they were first founded.[148]

The Death of the Canada Medal

With the creation of the Order of Canada on 17 April 1967 and the issuing of Order-in-Council 388, the Canada Medal ceased to be.[149] Fourteen specimens of the medal had been struck in 1944; these are the only physical evidence that such a medal ever existed. Always promised yet never awarded, it was doomed to fail by its own lack of political will. The Canada Medal had been envisioned as part of a broader Canadian honours system, as a subordinate award to Massey's 1942 proposal for the 'Royal Order of Canada.' Mackenzie King having repeatedly rejected proposals for a Canadian order, the Canada Medal was quickly elevated from junior service award to the pinnacle of national achievement. It was going to be awarded to the King, Winston Churchill, Franklin D. Roosevelt, Joseph Stalin, and many Canadian service men and women. Although the medal was perceived as more egalitarian than an order, it was impractical. Despite their disdain for titles and traditions, the Soviets had an Order of Lenin – not a Medal of Lenin – as one of their senior national decorations.[150] Sparingly awarded, it was fashioned of gold and platinum at great cost – more impressive than the Canada Medal, with its projected cost of $1.25. The Canada Medal was expected to be Canada's Order of the Garter, but it never did achieve such stature. The precedence it was accorded was that of a junior decoration. The Canada Medal had lived for a quarter century, occasionally polished up and hauled out by successive governments as an example of a Canadian honour. But it was always returned to a locked drawer, where it continued to oxidize. No Canadian ever received it; today it can only be found in museums.

The establishment of the Order of Canada in such a short period of time highlights Pearson's perception that the country needed new Canadian institutions that emphasized the role of citizens and the unity of Canada. Although the Order of Canada was developed at the most senior levels, its emphasis on involving the citizenry through grassroots nominations and on opening the honours system to non-traditional groups obviously reflected the politics of the 1960s – specifically, the idealism and nationalism aroused by the Centennial. That Cabinet nonetheless demonstrated a continuing reluctance to accept a Canadian order demonstrates the government's ongoing political reticence when it came to dealing with the perennial question. W.F. Nickle cast a long shadow.

CHAPTER SIX

Selection and Reaction: The First Honours List

Just over one month ago, the Prime Minister announced the establishment of the Order of Canada. We had no staff, no office space or equipment, no precedents to follow, and a Chancellor only a few hours old. – He has aged considerably since then![1]

Esmond Butler, Secretary General of the Order of Canada

Institutions take time to develop and gain acceptance, and this was true of the Order of Canada. The order, established in 1967, has changed in structure over the years. It is difficult today to imagine that at one time the order was not universally recognized in Canada. In 1967 the Canadian public was quite naive when it came to honours systems.[2] The Governor General, the Duke of Devonshire, had observed this in 1917, and it was still true fifty years later.

Parts of the Order of Canada were drawn from the various French and British orders; however, one tradition was not reproduced in Canada: that of suspicion. Napoleon faced opposition to his *Légion d'honneur*, which was lavishly bestowed in the early years of its existence and was seen as a tool for gaining support for the Emperor. The same happened in Britain in 1815 when the Order of the Bath was expanded, and more than a century later when George V sanctioned another new order. When the Order of the British Empire was founded in 1917, it was not well received. It was intended to 'recognize every level of service,'[3] yet some thought that it was distributed too profusely. Indeed, its honours list of January 1918 contained 2,641 names. The Order of the British Empire 'faced an uphill struggle' to gain respect in the broader honours system; the Order of Canada did not encounter quite the same troubles. It was the only national honour that Canada possessed, it was introduced into a near vacuum, and there were few Canadians left who still believed that the British system of honours was sufficient for this country's purposes.[4] Added to this, the Order of Canada was not to be awarded at the behest of any politician, and the number of awards was to be very limited.

Initial Public Reaction, April–May 1967

The Prime Minister's Office kept a close watch on the public's reaction to the new order. Early on, some cynicism was expressed in the House of Commons. On

26 April, C.W. Cowan noted that Canadians were forbidden to accept foreign decorations and that Canada was already well served by the Nickle Resolution. This honourable member, who clearly disagreed with his leader's involvement in founding the Order of Canada, went on to envision a Canada with 'five classes. We shall have the Governor General ... the Companions of the Order of Canada, the holders of the Medal of Courage, the Medal of Service and so on. We shall have five divisions and we shall all be Canadians and free, but we sure won't be equal.'[5] He then pointed out to the House that 'the Companions of the Order of Canada ... [their] initials, in short, are C-O-O-C: pronounced "kook."'[6] At this point the other MPs responded to his disrespect with boos and hisses of disapproval.

Canada's press from coast to coast and in both official languages endorsed the order. One is strained to think of many other occasions when Canadian newspapers were unanimous in their opinion. All of them approved of the new order; however, some editors and papers were confident in what the order would come to symbolize, whereas others feared it would be transformed into a political device.

Enthusiasm and Endorsement

The *Victoria Daily Colonist* declared: 'At long last Canada is to have a meritorious award which it can bestow upon individuals in recognition of bravery or conspicuous national service ... Establishment of this decoration can be commended; it rectifies an omission which suggested lack of maturity, and it enables the nation to honour those who deserve recognition.'[7] The *London Free Press* echoed this: 'Canadians generally will applaud the government's initiative.'[8]

Both of Ottawa's papers, the *Citizen* and *Journal*, took the same tack. From the *Citizen*: 'At last we can honour our own ... The method of selection and the limit set on the number of medals issued meet all reasonable tests.'[9] From the *Journal*: 'The purpose of the Order of Canada is to give new warmth and dignity to life in this country ... The distinction of distinctions must be that one distinguished between the good and the excellent.'[10] The *Toronto Telegram* noted: 'In a Canada in frank transition, one can glory in the many prospects within our country of the wide range of recipients for the new Canadian decoration, The Order of Canada ... this is another example of how the best of Canadianism is being drawn out by the Centennial Year.'[11]

There was a general realization that the order was key to building a Canadian nation. *Le Soleil* and the *Toronto Star* were pleased with the order and saw it as an opportunity for the government to encourage the growth of a Canadian identity. As *Le Soleil* expressed: 'Après le drapeau national, après l'hymne national, 'O Canada,' voici que les Canadiens pourront porter des décorations nationales. Le processus est plus que logique.'[12] The *Star* commented: 'Our honours system should contribute to a sense of national pride and national service. It fits well with our national flag and O Canada as our national anthem.'[13]

Cautious Approval

While many papers were enthusiastic about the new order, some were concerned that it would become corrupted over time. No one wanted to see the Order of Canada evolve into a patronage tool or political party favour. The consensus was that the character of the order would be dictated by those who received it.

The *Winnipeg Tribune* opined that 'Provided that the determination not to make such honours an aspect of political patronage is strictly adhered to, there should be general approval.'[14] This was echoed by the *Calgary Herald,* which hoped for a balanced approach: 'The value of the new honours program will be determined by the way in which it is applied and its course will be watched with interest.'[15] The *Fredericton Daily Gleaner* acknowledged the importance of the new institution, with this caution: 'There is a place in our national life for distinctions to be given for service to the state. But they should be limited to the recognition of such outstanding service that the awards do not and cannot come within the area of controversy.'[16] Similarly, in *Le Devoir*: 'La création par le gouvernement Pearson de l'Ordre du Canada est une de ces initiatives qui, excellente en soi, appelle quand même certaines réserves. Mais des réserves qui ne doivent pas conduire au rejet pur et simple du projet.'[17] The *Montreal Star* simply asked that 'there should be no easy way into this order ... It should not be served by filling quotas.'[18]

Although it did not dispute the need for a Canadian honour, the *Saskatoon Star-Phoenix* wondered about the impact it would have: 'Perhaps many will not acknowledge the establishment of the Order of Canada with more than a shrug of the shoulders. It is something which will probably not raise more than a ripple on the surface of Canadian society.'[19] The *Halifax Chronicle Herald* echoed this sentiment: 'While the federal government's establishment of the Order of Canada has excited no great interest across the country, it has been generally well received, although with the somewhat self-conscious reserve that is typical of most Canadians.'[20]

Honours Speculation

Possibly the most interesting article was written by Peter Newman, the Ottawa editor of the *Toronto Star*. Newman strongly supported the order and published a prospective list of fifty nominees. Thirty-five of these would receive the order within six years of its founding.[21] If anything, this showed that the Advisory Council was closely attuned to Canadians' views about who deserved the honour. Some twelve years later, Newman himself would be made an Officer of the Order.

Mackenzie King's Reaction

Well aware of Mackenzie King's dislike for all things related to honours, the *Globe and Mail* printed a satirical article in which he was contacted through a seance and asked to comment on the new order. Needless to say, his reaction from beyond was less than favourable. When asked why he did not award the Canada Medal, he replied: 'It's the old carrot and donkey principle, which I may say, stood me in good stead all my life. You've got this donkey, see, which is getting tired. So you tie a carrot to a string, and tie the string to a stick, and attach the stick to the donkey's collar so that the carrot is always hanging out in front. No matter how hard he pulls it's still out of reach, until you get the job done – and if you really do use up any carrots, it defeats the whole idea. How else could a man get E.P. Taylor and dozens like him to work in Ottawa for a dollar a year?'[22] This exercise in satire – which was not an inaccurate synopsis of Mackenzie King's policy – was the only article that could be interpreted as opposing the new order.

Aside from a few diehard Imperialists, Canadians accepted the new order. Editorials and letters to the editor expressed near unanimous approval of the order, and even excitement about it. For Canada, with its diverse geography, multiple languages and fractured politics, this was most unusual. Other national symbols, the flag in particular, had not been received nearly as smoothly. And this approval would last. The only opposition came after the following notice was printed in major newspapers from coast to coast:[23]

ORDER OF CANADA
Government House
OTTAWA

His Excellency The Right Honourable Roland Michener, Chancellor of the Order of Canada, announces the establishment of a Secretariat for the Order.

Appointment to the Order will be made solely for outstanding merit in any field or endeavour in Canadian life. Any organization or individual may nominate one or more Canadian citizens for appointment to the Order, which should be submitted, with relevant supporting material if available to:

The Secretary General of the Order of Canada
Government House
Ottawa.
It is intended that the first appointments to the Order will be made during the Centennial Year.

The *Vancouver Sun* disapproved of 'the federal government's decision to advertise for nominations for the new Order of Canada [as it] tarnishes some of the lustre for the order even before the first has been awarded.'[24] The *Sun* believed that the top fifty deserving people were well enough known that this sort of demeaning public solicitation was unnecessary. The *Sun*'s critique focused not so much on the egalitarian method as on the obviousness of the first potential nominees. The government's notice was seen as threatening to rob the honour of its lustre and magic. Pierre Bourdieau, the anthropologist, would probably have agreed with the *Sun*: the open and public method of nomination had in some sense stripped the honour of its mystical qualities.

Secretariat of the Order

A special committee was established to manage the actual workings of the order. Although Esmond Butler called it an 'interim secretariat,'[25] it became a permanent entity. It was created in early May; the public was informed of it through a press release, which was reported by most Canadian newspapers on 18 May. This notice served two purposes: to inform Canadians about the order's administration, and to remind Canadians to submit their nominations to Government House. Initially, re-sources were seconded from the regular staff of Government House. Butler became the secretary general of the order. In early June, Kenneth Foster was made the acting registrar and Robert Blackburn the acting secretary. Tony Smyth also joined the secretariat. Their job was to read through the nomination letters, prepare files on each nominee, and gather additional biographical information on each to ensure that the Advisory Council had enough information to make an informed decision. The Advisory Council and the secretariat had little more than a month to compile the first honours list. From the beginning they were 'frantically trying to meet the July 1st deadline.'[26] Not until 21 August 1967 did the secretariat gain a member whose duties related solely to the Order of Canada. Joyce Bryant (née Turpin) was a long-time employee of Government House; for six years after Vincent Massey's retirement she had worked as his secretary.[27] Bryant was charged with the basic administration at the clerical level, and would work with the order into the 1990s.

The Flow of Nominations

Nomination forms were available from Government House and other government offices. There was a solid response from the advertisements placed in newspapers throughout the country. Butler also sent out a circular to all national organizations, universities, military bases, parliamentarians, and senior civil servants inviting nominations: 'If there is some outstanding Canadian whose name you feel should be considered by the Advisory Council, I should be grateful if you would submit a confidential nomination.'[28] Coupled with this were extensive nomination lists (of just names) from Vincent Massey and a series of informal lists compiled by Butler. For almost a quarter-century, Canada had lacked a yearly honours list, so there was a huge backlog of worthy nominees. It would have been easy to fill the first Order of Canada list with the names of the most prominent Canadians, but the Advisory Council had to remain cognizant of one of its main purposes: to recognize not only those who had contributed to Canadian life in a very public way, but also those who had devoted their lives to their fellow citizens and to humanity at large, even if not in a highly public manner. Pearson wanted the order 'to honour Canadians at all levels of society and in all fields of achievement, including the great research scientist as well as the little old cleaning lady.'[29]

Nomination forms and information about the prospective recipients were kept confidential, which means that completed forms are difficult to find today. Vincent Massey nominated Eric Ross Arthur, the well-respected architect, for 'admission to the Order of Canada, either as a Companion or as a recipient of the Medal of Service'[30] (see appendix 6). Arthur would be made a Companion of the Order in 1968.

How to Distill the Best from the Excellent

The task of selecting recipients of the new order was a momentous one. Nominations had to be sought from both the public and the government and then distilled into an honours list that represented all Canadians. There was no quota system; that said, the

Advisory Council attempted to balance awards across regions and occupations and between men and women.

In 1942, Massey had advised the government that 'the dignity which a new Canadian Order will enjoy will, of course, depend fundamentally on the choice of the persons who are made members of it.'[31] This was well appreciated by Butler and the Advisory Council. Massey's advice was followed to the letter; although not a member of the Advisory Council, he played an important role in composing the first Order of Canada honours list. In July 1966, he and Butler discussed who exactly should be recognized, both in terms of worthy recipients and in terms of those who would underscore the significance of the new institution. To this end, Massey composed a list of twenty-nine worthy recipients.[32] The list contained such notables as Dr Wilder Penfield, Sir Ernest MacMillan, Gabrielle Roy, and Maurice 'the Rocket' Richard. It is revealing that of the twenty-nine men and women named in Massey's list, all except two would receive the Order of Canada within the first four years of its existence. A week after the order's secretariat was established, Butler completed a working paper that outlined some of the mechanics of how the Advisory Council was going to operate.[33]

The First Meeting of the Advisory Council

Under the order's constitution, an Advisory Council was to be established consisting of six ex officio members, namely, the Chief Justice of the Supreme Court of Canada (chairperson), the Clerk of the Privy Council, the Under-Secretary of State, the Chairman of the Canada Council, the President of the Royal Society of Canada, the President of the Canadian Association of Universities and Colleges, and the President of the Canada Council. Respectively, the Council's first members were Robert Taschereau, Gordon Robertson, Granville G.E. Steele, Jean Martineau, Dr Gerhard Herzberg, and Dr Walter H. Johns. Although not a member of the council, Butler, as secretary general of the order, would play an important role in its decisions. Not until after the prime minister announced the creation of the order did most members of the Advisory Council became aware of their new duties. Only Robertson and Steele had prior knowledge. Other members learned through news reports, and not until 12 May were they formally asked to take part.[34]

The composition of the Advisory Council raised problems: no women were on it, and almost all members hailed from the Montreal–Windsor corridor.[35] But in other respects the membership was acceptable: there were two francophones and one foreign-born member, everyone was bilingual, and all members were at the top of their respective fields.

The inaugural meeting of the Advisory Council took place on 13 June at Government House and lasted two days. Taschereau took the chair, and the meeting began promptly at 9:45. First the council dealt with the administrative matter of selecting a recording secretary. Then it briefly discussed what constituted a meeting and the number of members necessary to form a quorum. The council then sanctioned the presence of non-members: the chancellor, the secretary general, and key members of the secretariat including Blackburn, Smyth, and Foster.

There was an immediate sense of 'feeling one's way around a new institution with the realization that precedent was going to be set.'[36] This sentiment was echoed by Butler in his opening remarks: 'My first words must be an appeal for forbearance. Just over one month ago, the Prime Minister announced the establishment of the Order of Canada. We had no staff, no office space or equipment, no precedents to follow, and a Chancellor only a few hours old. – He has aged considerably since then!'[37]

The atmosphere was light-hearted; at the same time, it was well understood how important the occasion was. Discussion turned first to the number of Honours Lists that should be made every year. Some members believed there should be only one list, on 1 July every year. Others felt that a biannual list would be more useful and would give the order the most public exposure. It was agreed that two lists, one on 1 July and one around New Year's, would be issued. There was the additional problem of what to do with the people involved in Expo '67. The exposition was only halfway through its run, and it would be premature to reward those involved. The council decided to delay nominations of these people until the end of the year.

There followed considerable discussion about the inaugural list. Two members of the council wanted it to be made public so that 'older people whom there had not been a chance to recognize earlier were being recognized in the first list.'[38] This drew strong objections from the others on the council, although the desire to recognize the more elderly nominees first was quite warranted. Many worthy recipients were old or in poor health, and there was a certain urgency to recognize those who had gone unrecognized by the state for so many years. In many ways, the council was playing catch-up. However, agreement was reached that no obvious preference would be given to 'older people,' since so many nominees were senior citizens anyway.

Before the meeting, each member of the council submitted a list of suitable nominees. The secretariat then folded these names into the list of those nominated by the general public. After this began the monumental task of compiling biographical information on the two hundred nominees for the CC and SM. A dossier of four hundred pages was sent to each council member, to be read prior to the inaugural meeting. Included with these detailed dossiers were master lists for both the CC and the SM. These ranked the names of the nominees in order of suitability.

Beyond that point, the method of selection was quite simple. First, the council reviewed the names on the master list to ensure that there were no unacceptable nominees. For Companions, each member of the council wrote down the names of the ten 'most obvious appointees.'[39] The secretariat then tabulated the names and told the council which names had unanimous approval. The first five nominees agreed on were Pauline Vanier, Major General George Pearkes, Dr Wilder Penfield, Vincent Massey, and Louis St Laurent. This process was repeated four times until a list of thirty-five had been compiled. The entire list was then reviewed by the Advisory Council. The same process was then repeated for the nominees for the Medal of Service.

Selecting the most outstanding candidates for the order was only part of the Advisory Council's task. Because the Order of Canada essentially had two levels, a distinction had to be made between those suitable for Companion and those worthy of the Medal of Service. The council found it a great challenge to appoint people to the ideal level. At the outset, Butler told the council: 'The first characteristic which should be borne in mind concerning the Medal of Service is that it should definitely not be considered as a consolation prize for candidates who narrowly miss being appointed Companions of the Order. While the criteria for the selection of Companions and Medal holders are essentially similar as set out in the Constitution, each of the awards has and must maintain its own individual worth.'[40] Although originally it had been meant to recognize people at the community level, the Medal of Service ended up being used as a senior national award.[41] This was the result of two factors, the first being the very large pool of worthy recipients. Canada had been without a civilian honours list for more than twenty years. The other factor had to do with the very structure of the order. Cabinet's refusal to allow a three-level system was forcing the Advisory Council to elevate the Medal of Service beyond its original intent.

The council took most of 13 and 14 May to compile the final list for submission to the chancellor. It was assumed that the process for approval by the chancellor would be similar to the one followed in the United Kingdom, where the Sovereign reviews the lists submitted and approves the awards, usually without incident. This is not to suggest that the Queen lacks the power to block a nomination – just that she seldom does so, and never in public. The 'freewheeling'[42] council had worked hard to finalize the lists and to set a precedent for the order. Out of the two hundred nominees, thirty-five companions and fifty-five recipients of the Medal of Service were selected. It was expected that the list would be submitted to the Governor General as chancellor of the order, approved, and forwarded to the Queen. Sir Michael Adeane would then reply, 'I am to say that Her Majesty is pleased to confirm the approval which, as Chancellor of the Order of Canada, you have given to these lists,'[43] or words to that effect.

A second meeting of the Advisory Council was called, this time by the chancellor, Governor General Roland Michener. On 19 June the council met at Government House for lunch; this was followed by a formal meeting of the council with the chancellor.[44] Michener first expressed concern that the distribution of CCs and SMs 'should approach as much as possible the ideal.'[45] He was worried that some fields were underrepresented – namely, politics and agriculture. He raised these concerns in a gentle way, taking pains to emphasize that he was not insisting on any of the points that he was making – he only wished the council to consider them. The second part of his address to the council served as an important touchstone for the order. Michener told the council he would not guarantee to approve everyone the council recommended for appointment to the order, but then added that he would not appoint anyone that the council did not recommend.[46] He was not going to act as a rubber stamp. He did not intend to interfere with the normal workings of the council, but he was prepared to take action if a situation arose. This was one of his rights as outlined in the order's constitution; it was also his duty as chancellor and Principal Companion.

Following Michener's address, the council reviewed its lists. There was some question about moving a number of nominees from the SM list up to the CC list. The two-level system was causing a number of problems, and a third level was clearly needed. The final list of ninety appointees was confirmed by the council and passed on to the Governor General. His Excellency reviewed and approved the lists and forwarded them to the Queen.

The Medal of Courage

Although the government had ordered twenty-four Medals of Courage, none were awarded.[47] At an early stage, it was realized that the process for selecting the first candidates would be even more involved than the one followed for the first recipients of the Companion and the Medal of Service. Nominations could be submitted by the general public; however, section 18 of the constitution required that they first be reviewed by the Decorations Committee. This body, the successor to the Awards Coordination Committee, was responsible for submitting to the Governor General all nominations for bravery awards. In practice, this committee was to submit a list to the Advisory Council, which would in turn approve those recommendations. The Advisory Council was charged with recognizing long service; the Decorations Committee was responsible for all bravery awards.

Initially, the Medal of Courage (CM) was intended to be Canada's premier bravery award, displacing the Victoria Cross and George Cross. This was overturned by Pearson. It was decided that under the Constitution of the Order of Canada, the Medal of Courage would rank after the VC and GC. The government – or Pearson at least – intended to keep making recommendations for Commonwealth bravery awards. Even Pearson was reluctant to make a complete and immediate break from a Dominion–Commonwealth honours system to a Canadian one free from all ties to the British one.

The Victoria Cross was established in 1856 by Queen Victoria to recognize 'most conspicuous bravery or some daring or pre-eminent act of valour or self-sacrifice or extreme devotion to duty in the presence of the enemy.' Ninety-four Canadians or people associated with Canada have been awarded the Victoria Cross. It is without question the most renowned and recognized bravery award in the world. The George Cross, founded in 1940 by George VI, recognizes extreme acts of bravery, but not necessarily in the face of an armed enemy. In many ways it has served as a civilian version of the Victoria Cross. The George Medal is the junior version of the George Cross. Only ten Canadians have received the GC, which is almost as widely recognized as the VC. As of 1967, Canada had not been involved in an armed conflict since the Korean War, so there was no occasion now to make nominations for the Victoria Cross. The Decorations Committee had handled a number of nominations for the George Cross, but invariably the award was downgraded to the George Medal.[48]

The Decorations Committee was unhappy with this, and in a memorandum to the prime minister suggested that the Medal of Courage be awarded for acts of bravery that had in the past been recognized by the Victoria Cross, George Cross, and George Medal.[49] Its intention was to make the Medal of Courage the most senior bravery award in Canada by ceasing awards of the VC, GC, and GM. Pearson was displeased with this and wanted to include the VC and GC as part of the Canadian honours. The purpose of the Medal of Courage was to replace the George Medal as well as other military bravery awards that ranked below the George Cross.[50]

Disagreement between the prime minister and the Decorations Committee over the purpose of the Medal of Courage stalled its development. In a memorandum to the prime minster, Hodgson emphasized: 'It is very important that the first CM's granted meet with universal approval. To achieve this degree of acceptance it might be well to seek out some particularly extraordinary act of courage for the first (Medal of Courage) CM awards.'[51] This was another attempt to displace the VC and GC, as such an extraordinary act of courage would have been more suited for the George Cross than the Medal of Courage. Because the Medal of Courage was creating many difficulties, it was decided that no awards would be made until a later date. To emphasize the importance and prestige of the new bravery award, it was to be presented at a special investiture and not lumped in with the ceremony for the first Companions and recipients of the Medal of Service.[52] By the end of August, the Medal of Courage had been elevated from the same status as the George Medal to that of the Victoria Cross, if not in the actual constitution of the order, then in the level of bravery required to receive it.

Problems with the Medal of Courage were exacerbated by the prime minister and the Decorations Committee. Pearson did not want the Medal of Courage to replace the VC or GC; on top of this, earlier in 1967 the Decorations Committee had received a proposal for two other bravery awards not connected with the Order of Canada.[53] Officials at the Department of National Defence were disappointed that their proposal for two bravery awards had been pre-empted by the Order of Canada.

The First Companion

Appropriately, the first Companion appointed was Roland Michener, Governor General, Chancellor, and Principal Companion of the Order of Canada. On 6 July, shortly before leaving Canada after a week-long Centennial visit, the Queen – as Sovereign of the Order and Queen of Canada – invested Michener with the badge of the Order. A simple yet moving ceremony was held in the Governor General's study at Rideau Hall. The Queen simply placed the ribbon and badge of the Order (officially numbered 001) around Michener's neck and made a few brief comments about the symbolic importance of the occasion and the order itself.

Earlier, on 1 July, the date that the order came into existence, the letters CC were added to the Queen's style and that of Governor General. In a letter to the Under-Secretary of State, Butler noted: 'On July 1st the letters CC will follow the Governor General's name.'[54]

The First Appointments to the Order

At six p.m. on 6 July, the Secretariat of the Order of Canada issued its first honours list, with a release time of eight a.m. the following day.[55] This list contained the names of ninety Canadians. The press release reiterated the non-partisan method of selection. In an effort to avoid controversy over the omission of some prominent and worthy candidates – most of whom would be recognized later – the Advisory Council issued an additional statement:

> In its report to the Chancellor, the Advisory Council stated that it had not considered nominations of active party politicians or members of the Advisory Council itself, believing that the eligibility of Canadians in these two categories should be considered after their present activities have been completed. In expressing its appreciation for the

widespread public support evidenced in the large number of nominations it received, the Advisory Council noted that, although the names of many outstanding Canadians could not be included in a short preliminary list, it was expected that they would appear on future lists.[56]

This was seen as the most effective way to squelch questions about why one person was included and another was not. To avoid such questions in Parliament, the Governor General personally spoke with the Speakers of the Senate and the House of Commons, telling them that 'in his judgment, questions relating to the selection process, people who were considered, specific reasons for selection or omission etc., are not in order.'[57] This followed the precedent set in other Commonwealth countries.

The first Order of Canada appointment list attempted to reflect the diversity of Canada in 1967. However focused on certain geographic regions, it nevertheless recognized some hitherto unrecognized groups and endeavours. Of the ninety awards (thirty-five Companions and fifty-five Medals of Service), the oldest appointee was R.S. McLaughlin, the ninety-six-year-old president of General Motors Canada, and the youngest was Marlene Stewart Streit, the thirty-three-year-old amateur golfer. The average age of those appointed on the first list was 64.5. The predominance of grey-haired recipients can be attributed to the quarter-century backlog. Almost 74 per cent of the awards went to people from Ottawa, Toronto and Montreal, although each province and territory had at least one recipient. Nearly 20 per cent of those appointed were born outside Canada. For the first time, honours were bestowed on Canada's First Nations.[58] With regard to occupation, there was no great bias toward any single group. The list included a number of senior bureaucrats and politicians, but there were many artists, labour leaders, and scientists (see Appendix 7 for a statistical analysis and Appendix 8 for the first list of recipients).

The appointment of women to the Order of Canada suggested certain difficulties along the path to a modern conception of honour. In the first list, only thirteen awards (14 per cent) went to women. One problem here was the small number of nominations; another was that most women were still in traditional roles not usually perceived as 'fields of honour.'[59] The order had been founded to recognize exemplary service in the public realm. It was not designed to recognize the exemplary housewife or caregiver. The need for gender equality would become a regular item on the Advisory Council's agenda.

Pearson's egalitarian goal of recognizing everyone from the great scientist to the cleaning woman was thus not fully realized. Forty-three of the first ninety appointees could be found in the *Canadian Who's Who*. (At the turn of the century, 100 per cent of high honours were awarded to those listed in *Who's Who*.) The strong emphasis on those involved in the arts – nearly one-quarter of all appointees – points to the order's focus on cultural life in Canada. It clearly singled out and honoured endeavours generally supported by the federal state as fostering Canadian culture and unity. Appointments of those involved in the arts and letters tended to be less controversial than awards to retired politicians and businesspeople. In spite of the constant requests from senior DND officials for a Canadian order, only one award was given to a member of the armed forces.[60] Although other appointees held military rank, there were (aside from General Pearkes, the Victoria Cross winner) no other professional

Table 6.1
Recipients of the Order of Canada, July 1967 (inaugural list), divided by discipline

Field	Number of awards	Percentage of total
Arts/music	7	8
Arts/stage	6	7
Arts/visual	4	4
Arts/writing	5	5
Communications	2	2
Education	9	10
Engineering	1	1
Health	7	8
Heritage	3	3
Industry/commerce	3	3
Labour relations	1	1
Law	4	4
Philanthropy	2	2
Politics	4	4
Protective services/military	2	2
Public service	14	16
Science	3	3
Social science	2	2
Social services	4	4
Sports	3	3
Voluntary services	3	3
Other	1	1
Total	90	96

soldiers. Lieutenant Colonel E.A. Baker was recognized not for his war service but rather for his role as founder of the Canadian National Institute for the Blind.

The Advisory Council had tried to recognize those who had traditionally been excluded from such recognition. The emphasis on those involved in cultural pursuits also extended to sports. Hockey greats Maurice 'the Rocket' Richard and David Bauer were awarded the Medal of Service; so was Marlene Streit, the only woman to win the Australian, British, Canadian, and American amateur golf titles. This inclusion of sporting legends familiar to all Canadians was an attempt to engage Canadians who were not necessarily interested in Inuit art or the Stratford Festival.

Included on the first list were social workers such as V.F. McAdam (founder of the Boys and Girls Clubs in Canada); scientists such as neurosurgeon Dr Wilder Penfield; and the respected educator and historian Donald Creighton. Only three awards were given for contributions to industry and commerce. Contributions to the health field were highly regarded, comprising 8 per cent of the total. Public service – mainly through the federal civil service – was the most widely recognized field aside from the arts; Vincent Massey, Pauline Vanier, Norman Robertson, General George Pearkes, Elizabeth MacCallum, K.W. Taylor, and eight other former senior civil servants made up 16 per cent of the list. Only four former politicians were appointed: Louis St Laurent, Jean Drapeau, M.J. Coldwell, and Thérèse Casgrain.

Two appointments stood out as true Canadian firsts. Dr Alje Vennema was awarded the Medal of Service for his work as a doctor treating the wounded in the then-ongoing Vietnam War. Vennema was an outspoken opponent of American involvement in the region and a regular nuisance to the Canadian government. Isaac Phills was a steelworker from Cape Breton. Like Vennema, he had come to Canada as an immigrant and made what the council deemed an 'important contribution,' despite having started life in abject poverty. Phills was the only person of African descent to be recognized in the first list. He was recognized as a Cape Breton steelworker of West Indian origin, who had raised a large family and despite many difficulties given them a good education and start in life. He had thus set a fine example in the community.

These two appointments were perhaps the most revealing of all, as they pointed to a broader and, at the same time less obvious trend throughout the first list. Clearly, Vennema and Phills were examples of role models. They seemingly demonstrated that new Canadians – and poor Canadians – could rise above their lot and make a contribution. Citizens like these proved that the Canadian federal state worked, because within its structure they had succeeded as individuals. Just as revealing is that some groups were absent from the list. Traditional protest groups were included, such as those working for women's rights and social-democratic causes, but there were no radicals such as communists, labour militants, or Quebec separatists. The honours list was limited to those who were working within the federal state, and excluded those who were working against it. This is not surprising. Few honours systems recognize those who are attempting to overthrow the existing order. It is more prudent to honour those who demonstrate that the existing order works. The list, and the order in general, served to build national unity by Canadianizing honour and recognizing people from across the country in a wide variety of fields seen as valuable within the liberal framework. In this official perspective, 'building Canada' ranged from a health care worker's local efforts to the public and national activities of senior public servants.

Public Reaction to the First Honours List

The Canadian public embraced the honours system and those whom it recognized. Newspapers in every major centre listed the names and brief biographies of the new Companions and recipients of the Medal of Service. The *Ottawa Citizen* reported: 'After a century of national self-effacement, Canada has finally reached the point of admitting that some of its citizens are admirable people, with qualities worthy of public recognition.'[61] Up until when the list was publicized, there was still fear that the order was never going to be awarded: 'One likely public reaction will be a feeling of gratification and relief that the government has actually got the much discussed plan under way. After the apparent demise of the Canada Medal ... it is only expected that some Canadians anticipate that the Order of Canada would meet the same fate.'[62]

The *Montreal Star* – the paper once owned by Lord Atholstan, who was largely responsible for the controversy leading to the end of British honours in Canada – called for Canadians to look at those people who had been recognized and acknowledge their significant contributions: 'Most names will be familiar to most Canadians for they have appeared year after year in print and have been heard frequently on the radio and television reports. Some of the less familiar names are fascinating in their own way, for they tell of a quiet breed which, in dedication have been rewarded in the past neither by massive recognition nor acclaim outside their immediate areas.'[63] The importance of this event to national unity was recognized most strongly in Quebec: 'On sait que la création des ces décorations nationales a été annoncée au printemps dernier; elles ont pour but d'affirmer l'unité nationale et d'affirmer la fierté canadienne.'[64]

Despite efforts to block the inevitable questions relating to why certain people had been omitted, the inevitable occurred. The *Globe and Mail* was generally positive about the appointments; however, it questioned the omission of John Diefenbaker, jazz musician Oscar Peterson, former Conservative leader George Drew, and noted photographer Yousuf Karsh.[65] Peterson, Drew, and Karsh would all be appointed to the order within two years. Diefenbaker remained a Member of Parliament until his death and was thus ineligible for appointment. Without question he would have merited a Companion, but it is likely that he would have refused the order, which he once called 'KOOK.'[66]

Investiture Ceremony

The first investiture was held on 24 November 1967 in Ottawa. The actual ceremony took place in the late afternoon at Government House. This was followed in the evening by an official dinner for the recipients. The ceremony was presided over by the Governor General on behalf of the Queen; the dinner was hosted by the acting prime minister on behalf of the Government of Canada. In effect, the ceremony was a thank-you from the people of Canada, whereas the dinner was a gift from the government. This division of ceremonial labour was probably intended to emphasize the non-political nature of the order. But why, then, have the Government of Canada host the dinner? The likeliest answer is rather prosaic: the Governor General's Office did not have funds to pay for the dinner.

The first investiture ceremony for recipients of the Order of Canada was the crowning touch to the Centennial. The convening of almost ninety eminent Canadians who had contributed in varying ways to the nation's life and well-being signalled the true beginning of the Order of Canada. The simplicity of the ceremony did nothing to diminish it; it was a truly Canadian occasion. The affair was formal throughout. The men wore white tie, and the women wore evening dresses.

A rehearsal for the ceremony was held on the morning of 23 November at Government House, with Esmond Butler working out the final details. That afternoon, two special guests arrived at Government House: Vincent Massey and George Pearkes.[67] As the former Governor General, Massey was a regular guest; Pearkes, the First World War hero and holder of the Victoria Cross, was a guest on account of being Lieutenant-Governor of British Columbia. Unfortunately, Government House was not large enough to accommodate the other seventy-four Order of Canada recipients and their spouses.[68] They were accommodated at Ottawa's Sky Line Hotel; each was given a travel voucher for $20.

24 November 1967

The recipients were asked to arrive at Government House by five p.m. Each attendee was each given a cream-coloured program with an embossed version of the Companion's badge on the cover. The program listed, in alphabetical order, the names of the first thirty-five Companions and fifty-five recipients of the Medal of Service. At 5.25 p.m., the recipients and guests were ushered to their assigned places in the ballroom. This was followed by the entrance of the Governor General and his consort. The ceremony was officially opened by Roland Michener, Chancellor of the Order. Each Companion's name was read; the recipient then approached His Excellency and was presented with the insignia of Companion of the Order of Canada. The Governor General said a few brief personal words to each; the recipient then retired to the side of the room to sign the register of the order.[69] All of this was repeated with the Medal of Service recipients. Photographs of each recipient were taken by the Ottawa photographer John Evans, whose wife took meticulous notes as to the dress of each individual in order to prevent confusion as to who was in which picture.[70] Evans would continue photographing recipients of the Order of Canada well into the mid-1980s.

Once all of the recipients had been presented with their insignia or medal, Michener gave a brief address on the significance of the occasion. This was followed by the singing of 'God Save the Queen' and 'O Canada.' Their Excellencies then withdrew from the ballroom. At this point, all were invited to attend a reception in the tent room, before the dinner.

Between 7:00 and 7:30 the recipients and guests were taken by bus to the Confederation Room in the West Block of Parliament. One member of the original Awards Coordination Committee, Gustave Lanctot, was present, having just been awarded the Medal of Service. He must have felt a sense of closure; many of the ACC's meetings during the Second World War had been held in the West Block. That committee's efforts to found a distinctive Canadian order had been realized at last.

Sadly, Lester Pearson was unable to attend either the investiture or dinner; he was on an official visit to the United Kingdom. The acting prime minister, Mitchell Sharp, presided over the dinner on his behalf.[71] Sharp was unsure how best to get the assemblage to take their seats; he was rescued by Father Georges-Henri Lévesque, who said grace.[72]

Sharp had at first been opposed to the creation of the order; however, his views were completely transformed as a result of this first ceremony. He would later write: 'It was a brilliant occasion ... Before us was as distinguished a group of Canadians as had ever been assembled in one place.'[73] In the years ahead, Sharp himself would be appointed an Officer and later Companion of the Order.

The dinner began at eight p.m., and consisted of melon prosciutto, consommé double au sherry, filet de boeuf-bouquetière and pommes parisiennes, followed by bavaroise à l'ananas, petits fours, café, and vins. At the head table sat Madame Vanier, John Diefenbaker, Louis St Laurent, Vincent Massey, M.J. Coldwell, Robert Stanfield, Mr and Mrs Michener, and others ranked in the order of precedence. Among the newly appointed Companions one is strained to find an unrecognizable name. Every recipient had contributed to the progress of Canada and the life of its people. The list of Medal of Service recipients was equally outstanding.

The Governor General gave the toast to the Queen, as per custom. After the liqueurs, Sharp said a few words about the new order and the assembled recipients. According to Michener, Sharp's speech 'gave the occasion the significance which we all hoped for.'[74] His brief words 'gave a great lift to all who had received the honour and to the standing of the Order itself.'[75]

Michener would recall that the investiture ceremony and dinner 'satisfied the highest expectations of the most knowledgeable and fastidious. It was quite impressive and even stirring.'[76] The first major occasion had been a success; even the most sceptical found words to praise the new order. By design or by accident, the understated ceremony had captured Pearson's vision. It had counterbalanced the elitism traditionally associated with awards from the state.

The founders of the Order of Canada wanted it to become a symbol of Canadian identity and unity. This meant it should be neither British nor French, but Canadian. This goal was realized, in part, through bicultural appointments and by means of ceremonies whose very simplicity discouraged association with other, richer national traditions. The bus journey from Rideau Hall to Parliament Hill was the best indication that the order was a Canadian institution. One can scarcely imagine the French, British, or Americans packing their most honoured citizens onto buses for transport to a special dinner hosted by the head of state. The entire affair had the air of a school trip, not the founding event of the nation's premier honour.[77]

Despite – or perhaps because of – this folksy aspect, the first investiture held deep meaning for its participants. The Governor General's Office was so short-staffed that the wives of many Government House officials attended the investiture and banquet to assist with the ceremony. Some would retire to a pub near Parliament to relax and recount the day's extraordinary events. Since then, the ceremony has evolved. The formality of white tie and a formal dinner has been discarded in favour of business attire and a buffet. Sadly, the group bus journey has also disappeared from the ceremony, now that the Governor General's Office has enough money to pay for the dinner.

The order was not exactly what Pearson had envisioned when he launched the project more than a year earlier, but it was a solid start. Aside from minor problems relating to the motto and the post-nominal letters CC, there were no great embarrassments. Many Canadians were unsure what exactly the order was, but they knew that some of the country's most outstanding citizens had been recognized through it, and that alone was reason enough to accord it respect.

Perhaps no one was more delighted with the new order than Vincent Massey. On 22 June, Butler sent him a telegram asking whether he would be willing to become a Companion of the Order if offered the distinction. Massey immediately replied: 'I would be very happy to accept the order if offered.'[78] Massey held a special place in the heart of the nation, and it was most fitting that he was one of the order's first recipients. He was more elated by the creation of the order than by his own inclusion: 'I am very pleased about this, not only for personal reasons, but I also was delighted that the efforts that some of us have made for so long to get a system of honours established in Canada, have been successful at last. We have been very tardy in this matter.'[79] He died a little over a month after his investiture. In some ways, the order would be his greatest legacy. With the creation of the Order of Canada, Massey had finally triumphed over his old boss, the inveterate sceptic, Mackenzie King.

CHAPTER SEVEN

Transition to a Complete Honours System

Unfortunately the Advisory Council on the Order of Canada seems to be regarding the Medal of Service as a consolation prize to persons who might aspire to become Companions but whom the Council does not consider sufficiently worthy of the higher award ... The result of course, is that some recipients of the Medal feel affronted rather than elated.[1]

John Hodgson to Lester Pearson, 8 January 1968

The decade that followed the creation of the Order of Canada and the appointment of its first members saw significant structural changes to the original institution. By 1972, British honours had been designated as Commonwealth awards and no longer considered Canadian. Then, with the addition of bravery awards and a special order for the military, the Canadian honours system came into being, and the Dominion–Commonwealth system came to a complete end. Between 1967 and 1977, the mechanics of the order's administration and structure were formalized. This was part of a broader pattern of change within the new institution to make the order not only more functional and recognizable, but also more widely distributed among Canadians. Although these changes were significant, there was an overarching unity to the official strategy. At all times, the order was attempting to build a Canadian institution with uniquely Canadian attributes. The most noteworthy change related to the order's distinctive nomination process.

When the Order of Canada was founded in 1967, it was only logical for the government to re-examine Canadian policy toward foreign honours. Since 1956 there had been a virtual ban on Canadians accepting foreign awards other than for bravery. With the new Canadian order established – which included provisions for bestowal on non-Canadians – it would have been inconsistent for the government to continue with its near total ban on Canadians accepting foreign awards. Indeed, the lack of a Canadian foreign awards policy was the main reason why a list of honorary appointments had not been included with the inaugural list of July 1967.[2] Pearson directed the Decorations Committee to develop a new, more liberal policy.[3] The work of the Decorations Committee on the question of foreign awards led to the abolition of the Medal of Courage and the creation of three separate bravery awards in 1972.[4]

The first awards of the Order of Canada were well received by the public as well as by the recipients. However, problems began to arise almost immediately after the second Order of Canada honours list was composed. These difficulties were rooted in the structure of the order itself. Although it contained three separate awards, it was in effect a two-level honour, with the first level being Companions and the second level being recipients of the Medal of Service. The Medal of Courage was an entirely separate affair and something of an anomaly. One could be elevated from Medal of Service recipient to Companion; this was not the case with the Medal of Courage.

In practice, the initial structure was highly restrictive. This was not the result of Cabinet wanting to sabotage the entire affair; rather, it was the by-product of a compromise arrived at in haste. Cabinet had repeatedly been told in November 1966 that most other national honours systems had multiple orders, each with three to five levels; those who were opposed to the order's creation resisted giving credence to the systems used in other countries. This attitude toward the new order verged on puerile. Cabinet members who opposed the new honours system knew they could not stop its creation, but they also knew they could make changes for change's sake. Notwithstanding these problems, the most important and novel aspect of the order was not the number of levels, but rather the non-partisan method of selection. Cabinet wanted a patronage-free honours system that bore no structural relation to British and French honours. This is the system that was born on 1 July 1967. Thus, although the non-partisan, patronage-free method of selection was a great success, the structure of the order became increasingly problematic.

The Advisory Council encountered great difficulties, because the Medal of Service had been intended as an award for citizens who had contributed mainly at the local level. The calibre of those awarded the Medal of Service in the first and second honours lists dictated that the award be the nation's second-highest reward for merit; however, the Advisory Council began to view it as something less. This was likely rooted in the fact that although part of the Order of Canada, the Medal of Service was a 'medal' and not regarded with the same reverence as the Companion. There was the additional reality that although attractive, the Medal of Service was also quite plain. A simple and much smaller version of the Companion's insignia, it was more akin to the design of the insignia awarded to Members of the Order of the British Empire – a fairly junior award. The Companion's insignia, in contrast, was fashioned of eighteen-carat gold and beautifully enamelled – a stunning piece of national symbolism.

The second Order of Canada honours list, released in December 1967, included many familiar names. The Companions included the recently retired chief justice and first chairman of the Advisory Council, Robert Taschereau; Sir Leonard Outerbridge, Newfoundland's former lieutenant-governor; and Charles Best, codiscoverer of insulin. Recipients of the Medal of Service ranged from the eminent photographer Yousuf Karsh and Olympic skier Nancy Greene to John Erskine Read, a former judge on the International Court of Justice and one of the early proponents of a Canadian Order. With the second list, the Advisory Council experienced its first protest refusal.[5]

Morley Callaghan was offered the Medal of Service in October 1967 but refused on the grounds that the award was not high enough.[6] Callaghan had published more than ten novels and hundreds of short stories. An outstanding figure in the Canadian literary community, he was internationally recognized. In his letter to Esmond Butler he stated that being appointed an SM would place 'a second class evaluation on his work,'[7] which he considered to be on par with that of Hugh MacLennan and F.R. Scott, both of whom were Companions of the Order. His contributions warranted the Companion, but under the constitution of the order, there was only room for fifteen more Companions to be appointed in 1967.[8] Callaghan's refusal shocked the Advisory Council into taking action.

Pearson learned of the refusal from Gordon Robertson, Clerk of the Privy Council, and then from his secretary John Hodgson. Hodgson warned Pearson: 'Unfortunately the Advisory Council of the Order of Canada seems to be regarding the Medal of Service as a consolation prize to persons who might aspire to become Companions but whom the Council does not consider sufficiently worthy of the higher award ... The result of course, is that some recipients of the Medal feel affronted rather than elated.'[9]

Hodgson suggested that the Advisory Council be instructed by the Governor General not to use the SM as a consolation prize, and that the Letters Patent be augmented to raise the annual quota from fifty to one hundred. The aim of this latter proposal was to make the award available to more people and thereby to clearly distinguish between the highly limited Companions and the more liberally bestowed Medals of Service. The prime minister agreed with Hodgson's first proposal but refused to allow the Medal of Service to be more lavishly awarded.

Another proposal that Hodgson advanced was the addition of a new level, to be placed between the Companions and the Medal of Service recipients: the level of Officer of the Order of Canada, with fifty awards per year. Hodgson had researched the problem and spoken with a number of Advisory Council members. Gordon Robertson felt that the Advisory Council's selection process would be 'greatly simplified by having the two upper awards, plus the Medal.'[10] Pearson refused to entertain this idea, however, and proposed to increase the number of Companions and reduce the number of Medals of Service awarded.

Many shared the perception that the Medal of Service was a more junior award. The Canadian commissioner general of Expo '67 proposed to the prime minister that every commissioner general of the exhibiting countries be 'given the medal in recognition of their work.'[11] This would have entailed awarding more than sixty Medals of Service, more than were awarded in the entire first Order of Canada honours list. There was the additional problem that aside from the Canadian commissioner general, all of the other awards would have been to foreigners, and the government had not yet devised a firm policy regarding honorary appointments to the Order of Canada. Such a large number of awards would have debased the order and made the Medal of Service appear as little more than a commemorative trinket.

One of the first matters Pierre Trudeau faced on taking office was reform of the honours system. Throughout his tenure, Trudeau took a keen interest in the honours system. In a letter to the Governor General in mid-1969, he observed: 'It is clear that there are problems concerned with the people [the Medal of Service] is desired to honour.'[12] Robertson and Pitfield recommended to the prime minister that the name and design of the Medal of Service be changed to reflect the honour's high status.[13] The prime minister wanted these changes completed by the end of 1969.[14] Of course, these changes would take more time to implement; a third level to the Order of Canada was also in the offing.

Foreign Honours Policy

Pearson was not acutely aware of the problems created by the multipurpose Medal of Service, but he was favourable to necessary changes being made, even though the order was scarcely a year old. The Decorations Committee – which had been charged with developing a Canadian policy toward foreign honours – was also aware that a number of problems faced the existing Canadian honours system.

Besides developing a policy towards foreign honours and decorations, the Decorations Committee also attempted to set out a policy for the award of the Medal of Courage to non-Canadians. The committee decided that 'it would be ungracious if Canadian citizens remained under the disability that honours of whatever kind [excluding bravery awards] must be refused from a country, one or more of whose citizens it is desired to honour through the award of the Order of Canada.'[15]

The committee recommended to Pearson that a number of changes be made to Canadian honours policy. With regard to foreign honours, it advised that the total prohibition be lifted and replaced with a much more open policy, although the prohibition on awards that conferred a title was reaffirmed.[16] The report also suggested that no more Canadians be recommended for British honours or decorations – other than for valour – by the Canadian government, because 'it would be ... incongruous if Canadians, who have not been admitted to membership of the Order of Canada, should have their contributions to some important aspect of Canadian life recognized – instead or in the first instance – by a British award. Such an arrangement would operate to the disadvantage ... of the Order of Canada.'[17] An exception was made in the case of four awards that are the personal gift of the Sovereign and that do not grant the recipient a title. Thus, the Order of Merit, the Royal Victorian Chain, and the non-knighthood levels of the Royal Victorian Order and Royal Victorian Medal could be bestowed on Canadians if the Queen desired that such an award be made.

The draft policy was extensively researched by Carl Lochnan, director of the Art and Culture Branch of the Department of the Secretary of State.[18] Lochnan was a career public servant who had served in the Royal Canadian Navy during the Second World War. He would play an important role in the expansion of the Canadian honours system in the early 1970s, eventually serving as the first Director of Honours at Government House.

In early March, the Secretary of State, Judy LaMarsh – who had never been keen on honours – passed the Decorations Committee report on to the prime minister.[19] Pearson fully agreed that the Queen should continue to be allowed to reward Canadians for personal services to the Crown through the four awards that she personally controlled. He also agreed that in future, the Canadian government should not make recommendations for Canadians to receive British honours for services rendered to Canada. Most importantly, Pearson reconsidered the position of the British bravery awards – namely, the Victoria Cross and George Cross – within the post-1967 Canadian honours system. In a discussion with John Hodgson on 19 March 1968, Pearson ordered that 'courage awards through Br govt shd be stopped quietly ... Decorations Ctte may wish to give further thought to the need of a variety of Canadian awards for courage.'[20]

This decision signalled a major change in the field of honours. When the Order of Canada was founded in 1967, the Medal of Courage was meant to be integrated into the exiting British gallantry awards available to Canadians, namely the Victoria Cross, George Cross, and George Medal. Shortly after the establishment of the Order of Canada, it was decided that the Medal of Courage would replace the George Medal, but Canadians were to continue to be eligible for the Victoria Cross and George Cross.[21] Thus, although a Canadian honours system had been established, it was still partially founded on a Dominion–Commonwealth honours system, which was dotted with British awards. By 1968, Pearson was calling for the creation of new Canadian bravery awards to replace the British ones, which were to be 'quietly stopped.'[22] British honours in Canada thus came to a near-silent end, and the Canadian honours system – independent of the Dominion-Commonwealth honours system – came into being for the first time.

Cabinet discussed changing Canadian policy on acceptance of foreign honours and decorations on 10 April, and endorsed the changes on 17 April. Most importantly, Cabinet agreed that recommending Canadians for receipt of British bravery awards 'be discontinued, and that the Government Decorations Committee be instructed to consider how such acts might be recognized when the relevant circumstances were insufficient to justify the award of the Medal of Courage of the Order of Canada.'[23] This decision was made at the last Cabinet meeting prior to the transfer of the prime minister's position to Pierre Trudeau.[24] Pearson was tidying up old business, having achieved more in the field of honours policy than any of his predecessors. The development of a solely Canadian series of bravery awards would be developed by the Decorations Committee in the following years. Other significant changes to the Order of Canada were already underway.

Restructuring the Order

Frustrated with the limited structure of the Order of Canada in comparison with other national orders, the Advisory Council almost immediately began to consider changing the order's structure. By October 1968, the council had heard from the prime minister's secretary, John Hodgson, and was considering adding a new level, to be placed between the Companions and holders of the Medal of Service.[25] It was soon realized that such a change would likely disenfranchise many holders of the Medal of Service; thus, the council decided to replace the Medal of Service with a new, intermediate grade of the order and also add a third level. The new, second level would be the Officers. The Companions and Officers would receive their awards in recognition of their international and national service; appointments to the third level (that of Member) would be in recognition of services to a particular field or locality. This new, three-level order was devised largely by Butler and Robertson.

In theory, a single-level national order is egalitarian and all-inclusive. In practice, it is often neither. Many countries bestow a single-level national honour as the premier national honour – however, most such countries have three or four national honours. Single-level national honours such as the Order of the Garter (United Kingdom), the Order of Glory (Soviet Union), Order of the Liberation (France), and the Order of New Zealand are limited to between six and thirty members, which makes them highly exclusive. There is no modern instance of a single-level national order being widely bestowed. Multilevel honours tend to have thousands of members.

Table 7.1
Single-levelled national honours[26]

Country and Honour	Annual awards	Maximum total living membership
Britain *Order of the Garter*	At most 1	24
Canada *Companion of the Order of Canada*	5	150
Soviet Union *Order of Glory*	Only 6 were ever awarded	Restricted to heads of state and generals
United States *Presidential Medal of Freedom*	At most 10–12	No maximum but has never exceeded 100

Pearson had always wanted a three-level national order, with the top level limited to national and international achievements, the second for national and local achievements, and the third level for purely local contributions. He had resisted five-levelled proposals because he felt that the top two levels of a five-tiered system would be treated as knighthoods and create a separate class of 'super-honours.' A three-level system coupled with a broader membership would recognize a much broader spectrum of exemplary citizenship and contributions to the wider community. In tandem with all this, the Decorations Committee was repeatedly informing the Advisory Council that the single-level Medal of Courage was insufficient and would likely have to be either expanded or completely removed from the Order of Canada.[27] In the end, bravery awards were excised from the Order of Canada with the blessing of the Advisory Council. Even today, few Canadians can tell you the difference between a Companion, an Officer, and a Member of the Order of Canada; all three are simply members of the Order of Canada.[28]

The Advisory Council finalized the restructuring of the order at a special meeting on 13 November 1970. It was agreed that the Medal of Service would be replaced by the level of Officer of the Order of Canada and that a new level, Member, would be added. No changes were made to the maximum number of Companions allowed; however, limits were placed on the total number of awards of the Officer and Member levels that were to be permitted each year. A maximum of forty Officers and eighty Members could be appointed per year. In addition to this, 'OC' was chosen as the post-nominal designation for Officers and 'CM' for Members. The criteria for bestowal of each level were greatly refined; no longer would there be room for confusion about the intent of each level:

Companions: Appointments as Companions and honorary Companions of the Order shall be made for outstanding achievement and merit of the highest degree, especially service to Canada or to humanity at large.

Officers: Appointments as Officers and honorary Officers of the Order shall be made for achievement and merit of a high degree, especially service to Canada or to humanity at large.

Members: Appointments as Members and honorary Members of the Order shall be made for distinguished service in or to a particular locality, group or field of activity.

Other designations were proposed for the various levels of the restructured order. Esmond Butler and Roger Nantel preferred a less conventional name for the top level: either 'Companion of Honour of the Order of Canada' (CHC) or 'Grand Companion of the Order of Canada' (GCC). Both were intended to 'give prestige to the top Canadian award.'[29] Neither of these proposals was adopted by the Advisory Council, which preferred more modest designations and felt that Grand Companion of the Order of Canada was pretentious.

Once the necessary changes were made to the constitution, the transition to a three-level national order was nearly complete. The addition of the Member level – which today is the mainstay of the order – was in retrospect essential to the order's growth, in that it would now include the contributions of Canadians at the local and national levels. Pearson's desire for a mainly local award had been realized.

Expansion of the Advisory Council

The Governor General was always concerned about the composition of the Advisory Council. Michener felt that there was a great risk of an imbalance developing between anglophones and francophones, and that the council was significantly handicapped by the absence of female members. The first appointments were heavily weighted in favour of men; this was in part due to the lack of nominations made for women. Michener felt that including women on the council would alleviate this problem. With the departure of Chief Justice Taschereau in late 1967, the linguistic balance was disturbed. The problem lay in the fact that all members of the Advisory Council were members by virtue of holding some other office. In the case of the Chief Justice of the Supreme Court and to some degree the president of the Royal Society of Canada, there had been a convention of alternating appointments between anglophones and francophones. This meant that as a result of retirements, the council's membership could end up being heavily weighted with either anglophones or francophones.

At a special meeting of the council on 30 October 1968, a number of changes were made to the council's structure. It was agreed that in the event of a 'language imbalance, the Chancellor would have the power to add a member when he saw fit until such times as the linguistic balance was restored.'[30] The council also agreed that it would be acceptable for a society (the Royal Society of Canada and the Association of Universities and Colleges of Canada) to appoint a member in place of its president if it so desired. Despite Michener's encouragement and Robertson's concern, however, the council decided that 'no really useful purpose would be served by adding a lady to the Council.'[31] The issue was discussed further when an early draft of the order's new constitution was brought to the table on 13 November 1970. It was unanimously agreed that a clause should be added allowing for two members to be appointed to the council from the membership of the Order of Canada.

The revised constitution of the order enshrined these decisions in Section 4(g), which sets out that the Governor General may appoint two other members to the council. These additional members are to be present members of the Order of Canada and are to be nominated by the ex officio members of the Advisory Council. A term of two years is set, although there is no prohibition on reappointment.

At the council's 15 September 1972 special meeting, Michener again emphasized that he wanted more women to be included. He wanted both additional members to be women. The criteria for selecting these additional women were indicative of the times: 'A fair degree of women's organizations activities and a good balance of judgment, preferably not in the federal orbit or capital area, and perhaps not from the academic field.'[32] Three names were put forward: Gertrude Laing, Pauline McGibbon, and (as an alternate) Florence Bird. Laing was from Alberta and McGibbon from Toronto; Bird was placed at the bottom of the list because of her association with Ottawa. The Advisory Council was about to become slightly more representative of Canadian society.

Consort of the Governor General

Within the Order of Canada there were originally only two ex officio holders of the Order: the Queen as Sovereign of the Order and the Governor General as Chancellor and Principal Companion. This policy changed shortly after the order was created with the addition of the Governor General's consort.

At an early stage, the Advisory Council considered making allowances for a number of ex officio members, so as to raise the profile of the order. The list of proposed ex officio members included the prime minister, the Chief Justice of the Supreme Court, and lieutenant-governors. Opposition was immediately raised by the chief justice, Joseph H.G. Fauteaux. After consulting his predecessor J.R. Cartwright, he contended that the incumbent of his office should not automatically become a Companion. It was also agreed that making the prime minister an ex officio Companion would only politicize the order and undermine its independence.[33] The idea of appointing lieutenant-governors to the order ex officio would be raised at a number of Advisory Council meetings and meetings of lieutenant-governors, but it has never been implemented. The general approach has been to have a minimal number of ex officio members.

The question of making the consort of the Governor General a Companion of the Order came about as the result of a decision taken by the Advisory Council at its third meeting, on 19 October 1967. To enhance the order's neutrality in making appointments, it was initially decided to preclude active politicians from being considered. This prohibition was later expanded to include lieutenant-governors, judges, and the wife of the Governor General.[34] These exclusions were meant to ensure that the Advisory Council did not appear to be recognizing only those at the centre of power. It made sense to exclude serving judges and politicians; however, the wife of the Governor General was in a unique position. Invariably the wife (husband) of the Governor General discharges many of the same duties as his (her) partner, both official and social. Even in the constitutional sphere, spouses serve indirectly as principal confidants to the Governor General. The exclusion policy was especially unfortunate in the case of Norah Michener, who, after the Centennial, had been nominated for the Order of Canada.[35] Had she been unaware of the policy, the problem would not have been too great, but she was in a position to know of it. It was only natural for her to desire such recognition, not only for her contributions but also as a symbol of her position as consort.

Michener insisted that the Advisory Council re-examine the position of the Governor General's consort. At its fifth meeting, on 13 November 1968, it agreed unanimously that changes should be made to allow for the 'wife of the Governor General to become a Companion of the Order.'[36] The constitution of the order was already under review, and Butler promised that the alterations would be made to make the Governor General's spouse an ex officio Companion. Impatient with the lack of progress, Michener again had the issue placed on the council's agenda.[37] Under direction from Butler, the council agreed that the award should not be made until the new constitution had been adopted and other changes were complete.

The matter became more urgent as the Micheners prepared for their state visit to the Benelux countries in April 1971. Norah Michener was pleased that she was going to receive the Order of Canada, but she wanted to be invested with the insignia immediately so that she could wear it during the state visit.[38] Michener asked the Queen to 'give me the discretion to proceed in either method as may seem more expedient.'[39] There were two viable options: Michener could 'give her the award on her merits,' or he could promulgate the amendment to the order's constitution, thereby making the spouse of the Governor General an ex officio Companion. The decision on which course to take would be made only after consulting the Advisory Council, which had already agreed that the award should be made. However, it was unsure as to whether it should be bestowed before or after the constitution was amended.

The solution was arrived at during the tenth meeting of the Advisory Council, on 1 April 1971. The council agreed that the wife of the Governor General could immediately be made an ex officio Companion in time for the state visit.[40] That same day, a telegram was received from Sir Michael Adeane, saying simply: 'The Queen Approves.'[41] The matter still had to be discussed by Cabinet, but the prime minister had already indicated his support for the move. On 6 April 1971, without incident, Cabinet approved the necessary changes to the constitution to allow for the spouse of the Governor General to be made an ex officio Companion.[42] It was also agreed that the Governor General and his consort would retain Companionship in the order after retiring from office.[43]

The entire affair was settled when the Queen wrote to Michener agreeing that Norah Michener should be appointed to the order as an ex officio Companion.[44] Mrs Michener was pleased with the resolution, although her husband wrote: 'She regrets a bit that she becomes a companion by force of law when her name had been proposed by so many peoples and her qualifications were recognized by the Advisory Council. It is a pity that marriage can disqualify one for anything!'[45]

Norah Michener was invested as an ex officio Companion of the Order of Canada on 8 April 1971 by her husband. This was the only occasion ever that a Governor General has invested his (her) spouse with the order. Since then, they have been invested with the order by the Queen at the same time as the Governor General.

The Governor General amended the order's constitution to state:[46]

12A. (1) Where a Governor General ceases to hold that office, he shall, notwithstanding section 11, continue, by virtue of his having held that office, to be a Companion of the Order.

(2) Notwithstanding section 11, the wife of the Governor General during any period when he holds that office shall be appointed to be a Campanion [*sic*] of the Order and shall not cease to be a Campanion [*sic*] by reason only of his death or retirement.[47]

This change was effected by passage of Order-in-Council 1971-670. A slightly amended version was included in the 1972 revisions of the constitution under Section 13(2). One notable change was the reference to the Governor General's *spouse* and not *wife*, so as to account for the certainty that a woman would one day be appointed Governor General. Since 1971, every Governor General's consort has been made a Companion of the Order of Canada.

Transition: The Medal of Service

With the restructuring, the Medal of Courage and Medal of Service ceased to be awarded. In effect, both were abolished. This was not a problem with regard to the Medal of Courage, since none had been awarded, but the Medal of Service had been awarded to over three hundred Canadians between 1967 and 1972. The Medal of Service had been intended to reward citizens for local service, but in practice, it had been used extensively to recognize national service. Thus, in the restructured order, recipients fell into both the Officer and Member levels. The council did not consider dividing recipients of the Medal of Service into two separate groups, one to receive the Officer level and the other the Member level. Differentiating among recipients of the Medal of Service would have been certain to cause problems and ill-feeling within the order's membership, not to mention in the media.

Almost by default, it was decided to make all holders of the Medal of Service, Officers of the Order of Canada. This decision seems to have been made at the 13 November 1970 special meeting of the council, during which 'Officer' and 'Member' were chosen as the designations for the second and third levels of the order. Since then, members of the council have referred only to Officers of the Order, not to recipients of the Medal of Service. This has been especially evident in discussions surrounding elevations within the order.

In all, 319 Canadians were awarded the Medal of Service. Thirty-five recipients were invested directly as Officers of the Order in 1972. Only 294 of the medals were actually presented, and most of these were exchanged for the Officer of the Order of Canada insignia.[48] In Section 30 of the 1972 constitution, provision was made to allow for this transition:

Every person to whom the Medal of Service of the Order has been awarded is an Officer of the Order and entitled

(a) to have the letters 'O.C.,' in lieu of the letters 'S.M.,' placed after his name on all occasions when the use of such letters is customary; and

(b) upon returning to the Secretary of the Order the insignia prescribed for recipients of the Medal of Service, to wear as a decoration the insignia prescribed in the Ordinances of the Order for Officers.

As late as 1999, a female recipient of the Medal of Service exchanged her SM for the Officer's insignia. The stipulation has always been that a member cannot receive the badge of Officer of the Order of Canada until he or she has returned the Medal of Service, even though the post-nominals officially changed from 'SM' to 'OC' as soon as the 1972 constitution of the order came into effect.

The Impractical Medal of Courage

After Cabinet decided that no further British bravery awards should be bestowed on Canadians, the Medal of Courage suddenly became the only Canadian bravery award.[49] This made the Medal of Courage a wholly impractical award to bestow, because of its necessarily general character. It was entirely nonsensical for one decoration to recognize everything from a flight attendant calming an armed gunman on an Air Canada flight to a firefighter saving a child from a burning building.

Pearson had not originally intended to include a bravery award within the Order of Canada, but it was seen as advantageous to replace the George Medal with a Canadian award. Awards of the Victoria Cross and George Cross were to continue as in the past, but the Medal of Courage was to become the primary award for bravery – both civilian and military – during peacetime. The final award of the George Medal was made in 1964 to Sergeant Joseph Lessard and Lieutenant Colonel Paul Mayer in recognition of the bravery they demonstrated in rescuing a group of missionaries from rebels in the Congo's Kwilu province. Between 1965 and 1972, no further bravery awards were bestowed on Canadians; in those years, the government was reviewing the position of the British bravery awards within the Canadian system. Including the Medal of Courage in the Order of Canada was an act of convenience – and in hindsight a wasted effort.

In the summer of 1968, Butler suggested to the Governor General that the Medal of Courage be divided into three grades within the Order of Canada.[50] Michener was ambivalent about such changes; within the DND and RCMP, there was outright opposition.[51] By October 1968, plans for abolishing the Medal of Courage were being drawn up, and Butler was at last convinced that 'the Order of Canada should be persuaded to leave the field of bravery awards to quite a separate treatment.'[52]

The draft proposal for abolishing the Medal of Courage emanated from a subcommittee of the Decorations Committee – the Working Group on Honours – which proposed three separate bravery awards: a Hero's Cross; a Medal of Courage; and a Canadian life-saving medal. All these would be separate from the Order of Canada.[53] The working group was chaired by the Under-Secretary of State, Jules Léger, with representatives from Government House, the Privy Council Office, the Department of External Affairs, the Department of National Defence, and the Office of the Secretary of State.[54] In the field of bravery, the subcommittee developed proposals for a Cross of Valour, a Star of Courage, and a Medal of Bravery. The precise names of each award would not be devised until late 1971.

The Order of Military Merit

Changes to the structure of the Order of Canada were not made in an institutional vacuum; rather, they were spurred by the development of not only the three new bravery awards, but also the Order of Military Merit. The DND had been one of the original proponents for the Order of Canada in the early 1960s, yet so far, no serving member of the Canadian Forces had been appointed to it. In 1966 the DND developed a proposal for a Forces Meritorious Service Cross and a Forces Meritorious Service Medal to recognize outstanding service.[55] However, this project was shelved as it was being proposed at almost the same time as Cabinet was considering the Order of Canada.[56]

To fill the need for a military service award based on exemplary and not just long service, the working group briefly considered dividing the Order of Canada into military and civilian divisions, as had been done with Britain's Order of the Bath and Order of the British Empire. This idea was not well received.[57] The need for a separate award for the military was accepted, and there was a consensus that the 'recognition of distinguished service has important moral implications.'[58] The solution emerged in a report of the Decorations Committee, issued in January 1970. This report called for the creation of three bravery awards and also for a new three-level award to recognize 'military merit.'[59] By December 1971 this idea had evolved into the Order of Military Merit, to consist of three levels: Commander, Officer, and Member. Members of the committee were unaware that the new award's name could be traced back to the age of the Kingdom of France, during which the Ordre du mérite militaire was awarded to Protestant military officers who had rendered outstanding service to the Crown.[60]

The Decorations Committee suggested that changes to the Order of Canada and the establishment of the Order of Military Merit and bravery awards would constitute the 'family of Canadian honours, bound together by certain common design elements and each composing three grades.' Clearly, a more comprehensive Canadian honours system was underway. The Order of Military Merit, Cross of Valour, Star of Courage, and Medal of Bravery, as well as new insignia for the Order of Canada, were all designed by Bruce Beatty. With the restructuring of the order in 1972, lapel badges finally came into use. Similar lapel insignia were designed for the Order of Military Merit.

Cabinet Debates the Changes

When Cabinet met on 29 June 1971 to discuss the proposed changes to the Order of Canada and the establishment of a broader Canadian honours system, there was little opposition. Indeed, Cabinet was somewhat impatient to see changes made, having already discussed creating new bravery awards in December 1969.[61] Unlike Pearson, Trudeau was not faced with the task of convincing Cabinet that a Canadian honours system was necessary. Trudeau also had the advantage of being much more in control of his Cabinet than Pearson ever was. Pearson had always taken a collegial approach to the Cabinet; Trudeau was much more ready to enforce his will. Cabinet members were also aware that even though the Order of Canada was only five years old, it was, on the whole, a success. There had been no great backlash against its creation and the effective end to British honours in Canada.[62] The order was even fostering national unity.

Cabinet was in possession of two documents: one from the prime minister, the other from the Cabinet Committee on Science, Culture and Information. Each discussed the need for changes to the existing Canadian honours system and explained in detail why certain changes were necessary. The thoroughness of Robertson and Pitfield ensured that there would be little opportunity for questions. There was some brief discussion about moving the administration of the honours system from the Secretary of State to the Office of the Governor General, but this related more to publicity; there was little opposition to the change itself. This was followed by 'considerable discussion'[63] as to the merits of transferring responsibility for honours and awards to Government House. The prime minister commented that in his opinion 'it would be preferable to have the Governor General make these awards rather than himself.'[64] There was a general consensus that appointments to the Order of Canada had to be apolitical.

However, opposition was voiced by the Minister of Consumer and Corporate Affairs, Stanley Basford. He was concerned that members of the advisory committees were not representative enough of the various regions of Canada; they were drawn mainly from Ottawa. Basford also noted that most of the awards of the Order of Canada had been made to people living in Ottawa, and he demanded a list of 'all those who have received awards to see how representative they were of the regions and types of people in Canada.'[65] Secretary of State Gerald Pelletier assured Basford that he would receive statistics relating to the Order of Canada. At this point, a Cabinet member suggested that 'the government cancel its policy of granting honours and awards.'[66] This suggestion was flatly rejected and quickly dropped.

Cabinet then agreed to eleven specific adjustments to the Canadian honours system:

- The Constitution of the Order of Canada was to be revised so as to create a third level and abolish the Medal of Courage.
- An Order of Military Merit was to be created.
- Three bravery decorations (what would become the Cross of Valour, the Star of Courage, and the Medal of Bravery) were to be created.
- The sequence in which Canadian Orders and Decorations are worn was to be revised.
- The new levels of the Order of Canada were to be established as Companion (CC), Officer (OC), and Member (CM), and the levels of the Order of Military Merit as Commander (CMM), Officer (OMM), and Member (MMM). Also, the names for the two most senior bravery) decorations were to be decided (with the third level to be the Medal of Bravery [MB]).
- The Working Group on Honours and Awards was to submit a report to Cabinet showing the regional, professional, and vocational dispersal of the recipients of the Order of Canada.
- The Queen was to be asked to approve a procedure by which awards of all Canadian Orders and decorations would be made in future by the Governor General without submission of candidates for awards for Her Majesty's personal approval. (This change was not made until later.)

- The administration of honours and awards was to be moved from the Department of the Secretary of State to Government House.
- The question of making posthumous awards of the Order of Canada was to be referred to the new committee on honours and awards.
- A vigorous program was to be instituted to publicize the new awards.
- No public announcement was to be made concerning these alterations without the prime minister's specific authority and approval.[67]

Final Changes Approved

Edith MacDonald of the Department of Justice ensured the soundness of the new Letters Patent. These were submitted to the Queen for approval on 1 May 1972, through Order-in-Council 1971-809,[68] and the changes were made effective for 1 July. The Queen reviewed and approved the revised constitution on 10 May (see Appendix 9).[69] Although the order-in-council was not passed until 1 May, Trudeau – wanting to give Her Majesty ample time to review the changes – had taken the liberty of wiring copies of the Letters Patent to the Queen on 27 April.[70] At the same time as she approved these changes to the Order of Canada, the Queen sanctioned the creation of the Order of Military Merit, Cross of Valour, Star of Courage, and Medal of Bravery.

On 31 May, with the new Letters Patent approved, the prime minister announced the changes to Parliament. First, he took the House through the history of the Order of Canada and explained that an honours system was necessary to every country: 'Of those many ingredients which, together, are nationhood, one of the most important is the voluntary desire on the part of citizens to contribute to national life. A grateful nation should be willing to recognize and honour those persons whose contributions are truly outstanding.'[71] He went on to discuss the purpose of the new honours system: 'In this symbolic fashion, the government seeks to create a means of expressing the gratitude of all Canadians to those of their fellows who have contributed to the quality of life in this country through acts of service, excellence and bravery.'[72]

Members of the opposition parties greeted the expansion of the Order of Canada and the creation of a broader Canadian honours system with little suspicion. They were more upset about being given short notice of the changes and their announcement in Parliament. One point that did raise the ire of members of the opposition was the structure of the new bravery decorations. J.A. MacLean raised questions about where the Victoria Cross fit into the new system; Trudeau avoided answering him directly. In the afternoon, Robert Stanfield pressed the prime minister regarding whether or not the Victoria Cross was going to continue being awarded. Again Trudeau avoided the question: 'I would hope that Canadian governments in the future would prefer to give some status to our own system of awards by placing emphasis on it and seeking to reward Canadians through a Canadian system ... I would hope that the Leader of the Opposition would share this position.'[73]

Creation of the Honours Secretariat

Included with the changes made to the Order of Canada was the creation of the Honours Secretariat, which would later become the Chancellery of Canadian Orders and Decorations.[74] This constituted a significant institutional change for the Canadian honours system. The Secretariat of the Order of Canada, established in May 1967, had been responsible only for the Order of Canada, with recommendations for Companions of the Order and the Medal of Service coming directly from the order's Advisory Council. Recommendations for the Medal of Courage were to pass through the Advisory Council, although these decisions were really left to the Decorations Committee, a body that existed at the behest of the Secretary of State's Office. It could be claimed that the Order of Canada was insulated from political influence; bravery awards were not, in that they remained under the partial control of a government department.

The Secretary of State's role in the honours system dates back to the late nineteenth century, a time when the prime minister exercised great control over honours. In a more practical sense, the Secretary of State was responsible for authorizing awards of the Imperial Service Medal – awarded to junior civil servants after twenty-five years' service – and the various British bravery awards, in that the Secretary of State was responsible for the internal affairs of the Dominion. During Bennett's tenure as prime minister and until the creation of the Order of Canada, responsibility for honours was shared between the Secretary of State and the Secretary of State for External Affairs. Honours were listed in the *Canada Gazette* under the 'External Affairs' section, since they originated in Britain. Of course, all of these nominations passed through the Governor General's Office and eventually reached the Sovereign, although practical control rested with the two Secretaries of State. Such control was thus a colonial relic. Although the British authorities were no longer involved, there was still a high political office – that of Secretary of State – directly involved in decisions regarding bravery awards. So it was inconsistent for one part of the Canadian honours system to be independent of the government of the day, while the other was not.

The idea of transferring control over the remainder of the honours system from the Secretary of State to Government House originated with Hodgson and Pitfield. There were many practical advantages to having the entire Canadian honours system administered by a single, politically neutral office. Trudeau was a strong supporter of the transfer for another reason.[75] According to Butler, it fit into his grand design 'to build up the Office of the Governor General and give it added prestige by increasing the duties and responsibilities of the office. The winds of change are strong these days, and although the monarchy and this Office are generally both held in high regard, undoubtedly both will be subject to careful scrutiny in the days ahead when the Constitution comes under discussion.'[76]

Thus the Decorations Committee, Under-Secretary of State Jules Léger, the Governor General, and the prime minister agreed to transfer administration of 'the whole system of honours and awards from the Dept of Sec of State to Government House.'[77] The transfer led to a strange coincidence: as Under-Secretary of State, Jules Léger was largely responsible for honours; a few years later, he would be appointed Governor General and once again involve himself in the honours system.

Between 1967 and 1971, the Advisory Council's job of selecting recipients of the Order of Canada did not require a great deal of research on the part of Butler's staff. However, with the addition of the Member level – intended to recognize local contributions – and an increase in the number of annual awards from approximately 65 to 135, the overall workload was going to increase. With the new bravery awards and the Order of Military Merit added to this, the clerical work faced by the council was about to triple.[78]

Butler, the organizational wizard of the Canadian honours system, was no longer able to administer the entire show on his own. There was a desperate need for more staff and for new senior administrators who had a knowledge of honours. To alleviate the pressure, two new positions were created: Director of Honours and Registrar of Honours. Holders of both positions were also made assistant secretaries to the Governor General. The Director of Honours was charged with administering the new Canadian honours system. This position was filled by Carl Lochnan, who was one of the leading experts on honours – perhaps Canada's only real expert. He had the confidence of both Butler and Pitfield,[79] and although Léger was sad to see him relinquish the position of Director of Arts and Culture, he was confident that the right decision had been made. In his petition to the Treasury Board for funding, Butler pointed out that 'the implementation of the new Honours System will be very complex and demanding, and Mr. Lochnan is one of the few in Canada who has had experience in this field.'[80] The Registrar of Honours was responsible for many of the same duties as the Director of Honours, but in addition was responsible for overseeing francophone nominations and for advising on honours as they affected Francophones.[81] This position was given to Roger Nantel. A naval pilot, Nantel had served as General Vanier's aide-de-camp from 1961 to 1964. Appointed as Registrar of the Order of Canada in November 1967, he was knowledgeable about the Canadian honours system and well suited for the position.

The transfer of authority over honours and awards – except for authority over the Order of Canada, which was already administered at Government House – was set to occur on 1 July 1972, the same day the restructured order and the new Order of Military Merit and bravery awards were to be officially established.[82] Although this was a significant change in Canadian honours policy, no special Letters Patent were passed to effect the change; the concerned departments merely agreed to allow the transfer. Cabinet had approved the changes in June 1971, and as 'no ministerial duty, power or function was being transferred and as long as there was agreement between the Departments concerned and the Treasury Board was aware, nothing further was required.'[83]

With the honours system about to be administered by Government House, new committees were established to deal with the increased workload. Recipients of the bravery awards were to be selected by a Bravery Awards Committee. The Canadian Forces Decorations Committee would submit a list of appointments to the Order of Military Merit to the Governor General in much the same way as the Advisory Council of the Order of Canada. A special Foreign Awards Committee was founded to review receipt of foreign decorations by Canadians as well as the awarding of the Order of Canada to non-Canadians. Here there was more 'politics' than in the rest of the system.

Honorary Appointments

There were constant problems with honorary appointments to the Order of Canada. This issue was introduced briefly in the House of Commons when Robert Stanfield, the leader of the opposition, asked the prime minister to ask the Advisory Council on 'behalf of Parliament and all Canadians, that the Queen's Privy Council for Canada recommend to the Governor General the appointment of Mr. and Mrs. James Cross as honorary Companions of the Order of Canada.'[84] Cross, the British consul in Montreal, had been kidnapped by the FLQ and was held for many weeks – this was the beginning of the October Crisis. Trudeau agreed that some recognition should be accorded Mr and Mrs Cross for their perseverance, but nothing ever became of the proposal. The events of the October Crisis were still highly contentious, and although Trudeau had the ability to make such a recommendation, he wisely left the matter in abeyance. In any case, the Crosses' bravery would have been best recognized with the Medal of Courage. Cross eventually received recognition from the British government when he was appointed a Companion of the Order of St Michael and St George in January 1971.[85] (The matter of honorary appointments to the Order of Canada is of such complexity that I devote a separate chapter to it.) Not until 1981 would the first honorary award be made.

Posthumous Awards

For a brief period in 1970, the Advisory Council considered awarding the Order of Canada posthumously. Introduced by then Under-Secretary of State Jules Léger, this proposal sparked a great deal of discussion, although there was little interest in deciding on the matter until the council informed itself of practices followed in other countries.[86] At the October 1970 meeting of the council, Butler reported that in most countries, orders were not bestowed posthumously, and stated that 'he did not, himself, see how such awards could be fitted into an Order of living persons.'[87] Despite the practical impossibility of appointing deceased people to a living Order, Léger pushed the matter, since, 'the Council felt that the Order of Canada should be able to recognize outstanding men, who undoubtedly would have been appointed to the Order had they not died before awards could be made.'[88] With this in mind, the council recommended that the order's constitution be changed to allow for posthumous awards 'in exceptional cases.'[89] Paradoxically, posthumous recipients were not to be made members; instead, their family members would be presented with the insignia of the Order of Canada. Also, the number of posthumous awards was not to be deducted from the annual quotas for any particular level. The first three posthumous recipients were to be André Laurendeau, Daniel Johnson, and Pierre Laporte. In retrospect, it is clear that the desire to include French Canadians in the wake of the October Crisis was driving the discussion. Cabinet was uneasy with the prospect of appointing deceased people to the Order of Canada, and requested that the entire matter be referred to the Working Group on Honours; there, the proposal quickly died.

New Order of Wear

With the restructuring of the Order of Canada and addition of new bravery and military awards, the Canadian Order of Precedence for wearing insignia was changed. These changes were far from trivial: they signalled the advent of the Canadian honours system and the end to the Dominion–Commonwealth system and British honours in Canada. Although British honours remained listed in the Canadian Order of Precedence – because many Canadians held decorations from the Second World War and it would have been unfair to ask them to cease wearing their awards – Canadian honours were now given precedence. In early June of 1972, the Order for Wearing the Insignia of Canadian Orders and Canadian Decorations was adopted through Order-in-Council 1972-1206.[90] The Victoria Cross retained precedence over all other awards, but after that, a number of contradictory decisions manifested themselves. Britain's Order of Merit was ranked after Officer of the Order of Canada, as was the Order of the Companions of Honour. Perhaps this was because there were only two living holders of the Order of Merit: Dr Wilder Penfield and Lester Pearson. Yet ranking this, the premier non-titular Commonwealth award, after the Officers of the Order of Canada was illogical. In many respects it was a matter of semantics, in that both Canadian holders of the Order of Merit were also Companions of the Order of Canada. Penfield had received the Order of Merit in 1953 and was one of the first to be appointed a Companion of the Order of Canada, in 1967. Pearson was made a Companion of the Order of Canada shortly after his retirement as prime minister – a fitting reward. His reaction on being informed of the appointment was typical of his modesty: 'GOSH, I didn't expect this!'[91] Shortly before his death, Pearson would also be awarded the Order of Merit. He held each award in equal regard: the one an institution he was instrumental in creating, the other the personal gift of his friend, the Queen. But Pearson was proudest of an award not intended for wear – the Nobel Peace Prize, which he received in 1956. At the time the new Order of Wear was adopted, there were no living Canadian recipients of the Order of the Companions of Honour. The first Canadian appointed after the Order of Canada was established was John Diefenbaker in 1976.

Return of the Royal Victorian Order

The Queen took a keen interest in the development of the Canadian honours system and was pleased that the Government of Canada had once again approved the award of the Royal Victorian Order to Canadians. This order is the principal means through which the Sovereign recognizes personal service to the Royal Family.[92]

The most recent award of the Royal Victorian Order had been in 1946, when the assistant secretary to the Governor General, Frederick Lynwood Clinton Pereira, OBE, was made a Commander after an unprecedented fifty years of service at Government House. The Queen had long wished to resume making awards of the Royal Victorian Order to Canadians who rendered her outstanding service. At the top of her list was Esmond Butler: 'He has a considerable record of service to successive Governors-General and both directly and indirectly to the Queen. From Her Majesty's point of view this service has been both competent and distinguished and she has told me that provided there was no obstacle to her doing so, she would like to make Esmond a Commander of the Royal Victorian Order.'[93]

After receiving the support of the Governor General, the prime minister and the secretary of state (who chaired the Decorations Committee), Butler was made a CVO in the 1972 New Year's Honours List. Since 1972 more than one hundred Canadians have received the various non-titular levels of the Royal Victorian Order, which is now integrated into the broader Canadian honours system.

British Reaction

British officials were on the whole supportive and helpful with regard to the creation of the Order of Canada, although initially they had some doubts about its structure, especially the precarious position of the Medal of Service: it was the 'first Order of this kind ... of an overseas member of the Commonwealth and it does not seem to fit into any of the categories that we have at present.'[94] P.S. Milner-Barry was certain that changes to the order would be necessary within a few years, although the general attitude was that the 'Canadians can do as they like.'[95] The Colonial Office mentality had long since dissipated, at least with regard to Canada. When alterations were made in 1972, British officials took notice. In particular, they approved of the decision to limit the overall membership of the top level of the order and to set annual quotas for the Officer and Member levels. This made the Order of Canada significantly different from the Order of the Bath and Order of St Michael and St George, which have an overall membership limit for each level. Milner-Barry suggested that the Order of the Bath and Order of St Michael and St George alter their statutes to allow for annual limits, instead of imposing caps on total membership.[96] This has been viewed favourably as a far more practical system; even so, the British have yet to make this change. In terms of the three new bravery awards, four years after Canada created them, the British established the 'Queen's Gallantry Medal,' which is similar in purpose to the Medal of Bravery.[97] In effect, they have adopted a Canadian-style system; their three main civilian bravery awards – the George Cross, George Medal, and Queen's Gallantry Medal – were similar in structure to the Canadian Cross of Valour, Star of Courage, and Medal of Bravery.

A Complete Honours System

Pearson's original proposal for a three-level Order of Canada had at last been instituted; the order had adopted the structure that it uses to this day. The Medal of Service was such a precarious award to bestow that change was necessary. Misconceptions among the public and also within the Advisory Council left little choice but to expand the Order of Canada to three levels, as initially proposed to Cabinet in 1966. Similarly, the Medal of Courage was recognized as an impractical award for recognizing all acts of bravery. The addition of the Member level was one of the most important changes made to the order, as it brought citizens from local levels into the membership. This was the sort of local involvement and inclusion that Pearson had been so anxious to ensure in 1967, yet he had to wait until 1972 for his original proposal to be adopted. Pearson was not directly involved in restructuring the Order of Canada, but he was pleased with the alterations. He had finally gotten his way.[98]

Reform to the Order of Canada resulted in the establishment of a broader Canadian honours system, one that attempts to recognize all aspects of meritorious service and bravery. These changes were made very soon after the establishment of the order and signalled that Cabinet had at last lost its aversion to dealing with questions relating to honours. Once political control over such awards had ended, Cabinet had no further reason to meddle in such matters; thus the Order of Canada and the Canadian honours system were allowed to take root unhindered by partisan politics. This did much to bring respect to the Canadian honours system at a very early stage.

CHAPTER EIGHT

Enlargement and Acceptance

It is really rather striking that the Canadians, after a relatively brief experience, have decided that they must have a considerably more elaborate system of honours than that which they started in order to recognize varying degrees of merit and responsibility both in civil and military fields.[1]

P.S. Milner-Barry to Sir Martin Charteris, 27 April 1972

As the Order of Canada acquired the patina of age, the Canadian public came to recognize it more, and even those who were initially sceptical began to accept it. In some cases, the sceptical were converted and eventually even received the accolade. An example is the case of Joseph Smallwood, Premier of Newfoundland and the last living Father of Confederation. Smallwood retired as premier in January 1972 and was subsequently nominated by the Advisory Council to be made a Companion. The Governor General approved, and the standard letter of notification was sent out. Smallwood refused the nomination, contending that he deserved a 'higher award.' Clearly, Smallwood was looking for an honour similar to the one awarded to Macdonald or Cartier: a knighthood! This never came, and over time Smallwood's attitude toward the Order softened as the number of eminent Canadians recognized with it grew. Fearing that Smallwood would again reject the honour, the Advisory Council waited thirteen years before again advising the Governor General that he should be made a Companion. Finally, in 1986, Smallwood was appointed a Companion of the Order of Canada and wore the distinction with pride for the remainder of his life: he and Louis St Laurent would be the only Fathers of Confederation to receive the Order of Canada. Even the most ardent supporters of Imperial honours could be converted, given time.

The structure having been revised, and the first lists of backlogged honours having been awarded, the Advisory Council and Honours Secretariat began formalizing the process for appointing nominees to the Order of Canada. There is now no set formula for 'winning' the Order of Canada. Each nomination is examined on a case-by-case basis, exemplary citizenship being difficult to quantify. That said, a process has developed that seeks to make the entire process more scientific and exact – a far cry from the elitist patronage practices of the British–Imperial era. In specific examples of developments in the selection process we can detect general patterns, which together offer a window into the decision-making process.[2]

Central Principles

In the years following the restructuring, precedents continued to be made, and the Order of Canada as an institution continued to evolve. Three central principles were affirmed within six years of the restructuring: the Governor General's right to call worthy candidates to the attention of the Advisory Council; the Governor General's right to alter decisions of the Advisory Council in extraordinary instances; and the order's non-partisan nature and insulation from interference.

In November 1973 the Advisory Council completed its second biannual list and submitted it to the Governor General. Michener felt that one individual nominated to be an Officer should – on account of his youth and limited contribution – be 'put forward as a Member.'[3] The Advisory Council was consulted, and after some reflection agreed to alter the level of this appointment. On 17 December 1973, the candidate in question was appointed a Member of the Order. At this time, the Governor General also suggested that the Advisory Council consider appointing Mr W.M.V. Ash, the Honourable T.A. Crerar, and Henry R. Jackman as Officers.[4] The council concurred on Ash and Jackman but not on Crerar; it believed he should be appointed a Companion, not an Officer. Michener agreed, and the December 1973 list saw Ash and Jackman appointed Officers and Crerar a Companion. Besides these three men, Michener personally nominated Joyce Bryant, the first member of the order's secretariat, to be appointed a Member. Aside from Pearson and Massey, Bryant was the first person closely involved with the order to receive the accolade. The Governor General and members of the Honours Secretariat went to great lengths to prevent Bryant from learning of her own nomination. This was extremely difficult, as Bryant prepared all lists and nomination letters.

In the history of honours in Canada prior to 1918, knighthoods were sometimes used quite blatantly as tools of patronage. The most outrageous example was Laurier's attempt to have Conservative senator Robert Gowan resign his seat for a knighthood so that a Liberal could be appointed in his place. The Order of Canada can boast no similar tales of intrigue or partisan favouritism. The closest it has come to this has involved attempts to delay or expedite an appointment. Significantly, the one attempt to delay an award did not arise from partisanship, but rather from fears that the appointment would harm the order's image. In 1978, Paul Desmarais was nominated by the Advisory Council for Officer of the Order. Around this time, a long and bitter strike at Desmerais's newspaper, *La Presse*, had just ended. A senior official of the federal government wrote the Governor General to suggest that Desmarais's name 'be withheld from the list [as] an appointment now would be very badly received by the Media.'[5] This was not an attempt to derail the appointment – merely to delay it. Apparently, Prime Minister Trudeau feared political fallout from the appointment, in that the media were still not convinced that the order was non-partisan. The Governor General considered the suggestion, and then nevertheless insisted that the appointment proceed as requested by the Advisory Council. The Council was in the business of selecting worthy candidates on the basis of their long-term contributions and not whether or not an individual was popular in the press at any given time. Desmarais was appointed an Officer of the Order on 4 July 1978. This was not well received in the press, yet the incident did no harm to the order's prestige. The only other similar incident occurred in 1998, when the appointment of an Officer of the Order was expedited – although this was related more to federal–provincial relations than to concerns about the media's reaction. With regard to administration, Canada's honours system is far 'cleaner' than those of many other countries.

Evolution of the Selection Process

The nomination and selection process had developed well beyond the system used at the first meeting of the Advisory Council in 1967. This was necessitated by the introduction of the Member level, which is intended to recognize local service and contributions to a particular field. With the increasing number of nominations and the sharpening focus on local contributions, the earlier process was found to be impractical. After 1975, a formalized eleven-step process was established. Essentially the same process is used today. It attempts to make the selection of exemplary citizens more scientific; even so, the system still relies heavily on case-by-case examinations. Given the number of nominations received annually, and given that members of the Honours Secretariat (which would later become the Chancellery) are relied on to complete much of the research relating to nominations, the risk of interference remains largely unavoidable.

On receipt of nominations from the public, the secretariat takes the following eleven steps.

1 A folder is prepared on behalf of the proposed nominee, as well as an index card for record purposes. Biographical material is assembled to document the file for presentation to the Advisory Council.
2 If additional information or supporting data are required, the secretariat may obtain supplementary facts by consulting, in confidence, recipients of the Order, as well as knowledgeable officials from national and regional organizations, and various other local and provincial sources.
3 The officers of the secretariat assist the Advisory Council by screening nominations, rating them as follows:
   – 'A' level nominees: Appropriate for consideration at the Companion and Officer levels.
   – 'B' level nominees: Appropriate for consideration at the Member level.
   – 'C' drop cases: Considered not to meet the minimum criteria for appointment.
   – 'D' cases: Cases requiring more research.
4 At least one month prior to each semiannual meeting, a list of 'A' and 'B' level nominees, together with their respective biographical sketches, is completed, compiled, and forwarded to the Advisory Council for consideration.
5 Prior to each meeting, additional confidential assessments are obtained from consultants in various spheres of endeavour, as a means to assist the Advisory Council in its deliberations.
6 The Advisory Council meets twice yearly, in April and October, to review nominations previously submitted to each member, as well as a list of special cases tabled at the meeting. In addition to its preliminary work, the council studies each individual case. After careful consideration, a short list of 'A' and 'B' level

nominees is tabled, from which the names of proposed appointees are selected for recommendation to the Governor General, Chancellor of the Order. The Chief Justice, as chair of the council, submits to the Chancellor a letter outlining the council's recommendations.

7 If the Chancellor agrees with the recommendations made by the Advisory Council, he (she) submits a list of proposed appointees for approval by Her Majesty the Queen, Sovereign of the Order.

8 Following approval of the list by the Sovereign, an Instrument is drawn up, sealed, and signed by the Governor General.

9 A preliminary letter is sent to the proposed appointees, seeking their acceptance and asking them to provide an up-to-date biographical sketch and photograph.

10 Biographical material in French and English, as well as prints of the photographs are compiled by the secretariat for distribution to the press at the time public announcement is made.

11 Prior to the press release, an official letter signed by the Secretary General is sent to recipients, confirming their appointment to the order and advising them of the forthcoming publication to be made in the *Canada Gazette*. Recipients are also informed that in due course, they will be invited to a ceremony at Government House, at which time they will be invested with the insignia of the order.[6]

Administration of the Order of Canada and the broader Canadian honours system was revised in a number of ways in 1974, following a report from the Bureau of Management Consulting. The problem was that so much of the compiling of information and lists was done by hand. Maintaining an updated list of all recipients of the Order of Canada and other Canadian honours ballooned into a massive task following the 1972 restructuring. For the Order of Canada alone, seven separate lists had to be constantly updated.[7] So in 1976 the system was computerized, with specialized cards containing the following information: gender, province of residence, national origin, marital status, religion, age, citizenship, and field of service. The most complex category – and also the most important – was 'Discipline,' which comprised twenty-three designations.

Officially at least, there is no formal quota system for allotting the Order of Canada, but there is a general principal that ideally, the order should represent the Canadian people. There should be representation from all disciplines and from every area of the country, as well as fair representation of gender. Regional distribution and gender fairness have been the most difficult issues for the Advisory Council and Honours Secretariat. In the early years of the Order of Canada, the council found it especially difficult to gather sufficient nominations for women and from outside Ontario and Quebec. In the first fifteen years of its existence, the allotments were distributed roughly according to the population of each province. Since the mid-1980s there has been an almost dogmatic adherence to a provincial quota system. Some members of the Advisory Council have complained that the unofficial quota system disadvantages people from Ontario while favouring those from Prince Edward Island and the North.

To facilitate the equitable distribution among various groups, twenty-three separate disciplines have been identified. Each nominee is assigned a discipline according to their field of contribution. Some nominees, however, can cross several disciplines. Serge Joyal was made an Officer of the Order of Canada under 'Philanthropy,' for his contributions to Canadian art and heritage and to a variety of civil organizations; he was also a former cabinet minister. Thus it is possible for people to be cross-listed. The twenty-three disciplines are Agriculture, Architecture, Arts/Music, Arts/Stage, Arts/Visual, Arts/Writing, Athletics, Diplomacy, Education, Engineering, Health, Industry and Commerce, Labour Relations, Law, Military, Non-Professional, Philanthropy, Politics, Religion, Science, Social Welfare, Other Professions, and Other. In 1977 the disciplines were changed: Agriculture and Non-Professional were removed, and Aviation, Communications, Heritage, Protective Services (formerly Military), Public Service, Social Science, Social Service (formerly Social Welfare), Sports (formerly Athletics), and Voluntary Services were added.

The Flow of Nominations

Two years after the Centennial, the Advisory Council encountered a problem with the number of nominations it was receiving.[8] At first, with all the publicity accorded the Order of Canada shortly after its founding, it had little difficulty obtaining a suitable number of nominations from all over the country. But the novelty was short-lived. Also, it was easy to gather nominations for the first two years because of the sheer number of appropriate candidates who had not been recognized over the previous twenty. The backlog of worthy candidates meant that the council began its work playing catch-up.

This shortfall in nominations from outside Ontario and Quebec was remedied through a number of mechanisms. By 1972, the council was again replete with nominations. The Chancellery would often bring forward names of people for the council to consider. In addition to this, each recipient of the Order of Canada was sent a letter within a year of being appointed. This letter asked for nominations: 'It was felt by the Council that you, both as a member of the Order and because of your interests, would be aware of Canadians in other fields of endeavour, as well as your own, who might have qualifications for possible appointment to the Order.'[9] Presidents of various national and provincial organizations were also encouraged to submit nominations.

Women remained (and remain) underrepresented. The first honours list for the Order of Canada contained the names of only thirteen women – a mere 14 per cent of the total awards made. The underrepresentation of women sparked a number of lively debates and discussions within the Advisory Council. The council looked for a way to recognize housewives by selecting 'outstanding women in family life,' but it was (revealingly) decided that this issue was too contentious to inject into the honours system.[10] The council had acknowleged a particular social group when it awarded Isaac Phills the Medal of Service.[11]

In compiling a list of recipients for the new Member level of the order, the council somehow had to solicit nominations from the local level. Up to this point, the secretariat and council had focused mainly on achievements at the provincial and national levels; although they did not totally ignore the local level, there were gaps. In particular, the council was receiving too few nominations from the North, the West,

Queen Elizabeth II, founding Sovereign of the Order of Canada, wearing the Sovereign's Insignia of the Order of Canada and the Sovereign's Insignia of the Order of Military Merit.

KEY FIGURES IN CANADIAN HONOURS HISTORY

William Folger Nickle, K.C., holding the Nickle Resolution? The Tory MP largely responsible for Canada discarding the British honours system in 1919. Nickle's philosophy of honours as a tool for recognizing merit as opposed to patronage lives on as the central pillar of Canada's modern honours system. (Francis J. Harby, oil on canvas on pressed board, 1958, 76.2 × 63.7 cm)

The Chamber of the House of Commons in the Victoria Memorial Building, following the Parliamentary fire of 1916. This photograph was taken in March 1918, the same time as the Nickle Debates were occurring.

Sir Robert Borden, P.C., G.C.M.G., K.C., Canada's prime minister during the First World War. Borden saw the honours system as a valuable mechanism for the recognition of merit, but was well aware of its value as a patronage tool. He hoped to reform the use of British honours in Canada, something he never had the opportunity to do, but that R.B. Bennett would eventually succeed in doing.

William Lyon Mackenzie King, P.C., O.M., C.M.G., Canada's prime minister during the Second World War. Mackenzie King was very familiar with the honours system, and despite ending life as the most decorated Canadian prime minister, his complex attitude towards honours served as the main bulwark against the development of a Canadian honours system.

Field Marshal Lord Alexander of Tunis, Canada's 17th governor general. Alexander encouraged Canadian authorities to create a 'Canadian Order' in 1948. A man not unfamiliar with the value of honours, he was supposed to be appointed a Companion of the Order of Canada in recognition of his services to Canada; sadly the appointment was never made. Upon his retirement in 1952 he was awarded the title 'Baron Rideau of Ottawa' with the consent of the Canadian government.

Vincent Massey, P.C., C.H., C.C., C.D., the first Canadian born governor general since the French Regime. Massey began his quest to create a 'Canadian Order' in 1935 and would continue until the establishment of the Order of Canada in 1967. Denied a knighthood by successive Canadian governments, Massey was acutely aware of Canada's handicap when it came to offering recognition to exemplary citizens.

Lester B. Pearson, P.C., O.M., C.C., O.B.E., and Major General George Vanier, P.C., D.S.O., M.C., C.D., two old friends who served together in the Department of External Affairs when it was in its infancy. Vanier's last official act as governor general was to sign the Order-in-Council authorizing the creation of the Order of Canada.

CHANCELLORS OF THE ORDER OF CANADA

The Right Honourable Roland Michener, P.C., C.C, C.M.M., C.D., Q.C., 1967–1974. (Charles Comfort, 125 × 91 cm, oil on canvas. Courtesy of the Crown Collection of the Official Residences of Canada, National Capital Commission, Ottawa, Canada)

The Right Honourable Jules Léger, P.C., C.C., C.M.M., C.D., 1974–1979. (Jean Paul Lemieux, 125 × 180 cm, oil on canvas. Courtesy of the Crown Collection of the Official Residences of Canada, National Capital Commission, Ottawa, Canada)

The Right Honourable Edward Schreyer, P.C., C.C., C.M.M., C.D., 1979–1984. (Irma Coucill, 87 × 62 cm, pastel on board. Courtesy of the Crown Collection of the Official Residences of Canada, National Capital Commission, Ottawa, Canada)

The Right Honourable Jeanne Sauvé, P.C., C.C., C.M.M., C.D., 1984–1990. (Cleve Horne, 156 × 120 cm, oil on canvas. Courtesy of the Crown Collection of the Official Residences of Canada, National Capital Commission, Ottawa, Canada)

The Right Honourable Ramon Hnatyshyn, P.C., C.C., C.M.M., C.D., Q.C., 1990–1995. (Istavan Nikos, 158 × 116 cm, oil on canvas. Courtesy of the Crown Collection of the Official Residences of Canada, National Capital Commission, Ottawa, Canada)

The Right Honourable Roméo LeBlanc, P.C., C.C., C.M.M., C.D., 1995–2000. (Christan Nicholson, 120 × 100 cm, oil on canvas. Courtesy of the Crown Collection of the Official Residences of Canada, National Capital Commission, Ottawa, Canada)

The Right Honourable Adrienne Clarkson, C.C., C.M.M., C.O.M., C.D., 2000–2005.

SECRETARIES GENERAL OF THE ORDER OF CANADA

Esmond Unwin Butler, C.V.O., O.C., 1967–1985.

Leopold Amyot, C.V.O., 1985–1990.

Judith Anne Larocque, C.V.O., 1990–2000.

Barbra Uteck, C.V.O., 2000–.

THE CANADA MEDAL

The Canada Medal,
English obverse.

The Canada Medal,
French obverse.

The Canada Medal,
reverse.

EARLY ORDER OF CANADA INSIGNIA DESIGNS

The Canadian Decoration of Honour. Design by Lt. Cdr. Alan Beddoe, O.C., O.B.E.

The Canadian Award of Honour. Design by Lt. Cdr. Alan Beddoe, O.C., O.B.E.

The Order of Canada 'Cadillac LaSalle Hood Ornament Design,'
Design by Dr. Charles Comfort, O.C., C.D.

The Royal Order of Canada. Strikingly similar to the Royal Victorian Order this diagram was drawn by Vincent Massey's Secretary Joyce Bryant, C.M., B.E.M. (neé Turpin).

The Order of Canada, as designed by an unknown artist working for the Royal Canadian Navy. Inspiration for these designs was heavily influenced by the various Soviet Orders of the period.

THE SOVEREIGN'S INSIGNIA OF THE ORDER OF CANADA

Sovereign's Insignia of the Order of Canada. This insignia was presented to Queen Elizabeth II by Roland Michener on 23 June 1970, following a luncheon at Buckingham Palace celebrating the 300th anniversary of the founding of the Hudson's Bay Company. The insignia is made of 18 karat gold, inlaid with enamels. The maple leaf and annulus are set with rubies pavé, while each arm of the snowflake is divided by a single square diamond. The insignia was designed by Bruce Beatty, C.M., C.D., and manufactured by Garrard and Company, the Crown Jewellers.

THE CHANCELLOR'S CHAIN OF THE ORDER OF CANADA

The Chancellor's Chain of the Order of Canada. The insignia was presented to Governor General Roland Michener by E.F. Brown Acting Master of the Royal Canadian Mint on 22 December 1968. The chain was designed by Bruce Beatty, C.M., C.D., and manufactured of 18 karat gold by Aargo Aarand and Marvin Cook. The Companion's insignia hanging from the chain was manufactured by Garrard and Company.

The reverse of the Chancellor's insignia, bearing no number – just the letter 'C' denoting that it is the Chancellor's Chain.

Roland Michener in the governor general's summer uniform, wearing the Chancellor's Chain. Esmond Butler once commented in jest that 'His Excellency is wearing the chain so much, I fear he is going to wear it out.'

INSIGNIA OF THE ORDER OF CANADA, 1967–1972

Companion of the Order of Canada, obverse.

Companion of the Order of Canada, reverse.

Medal of Courage of the Order of Canada, reverse.

Medal of Courage of the Order of Canada, obverse.

Medal of Service of the Order of Canada, reverse.

Medal of Service of the Order of Canada, obverse.

INSIGNIA OF THE ORDER OF CANADA, 1972–PRESENT

Companion of the Order of Canada, obverse.

Companion's insignia on a bow as often worn by women.

Companion of the Order of Canada, reverse.

Lapel pin worn by Companions of the Order of Canada.

INSIGNIA OF THE ORDER OF CANADA, 1972–PRESENT, *(continued)*.

Officer of the Order of Canada, obverse.

Officer's insignia on a bow as often worn by women.

Officer of the Order of Canada, reverse.

Lapel pin worn by Officers of the Order of Canada.

Member of the Order of Canada, obverse.

Member's insignia on a bow as often worn by women.

Member of the Order of Canada, reverse.

Lapel pin worn by Members of the Order of Canada.

ORDER OF CANADA APPOINTMENT SCROLL

The Chancellor and Principal Companion of the Order of Canada

Le Chancelier et Compagnon principal de l'Ordre du Canada

To Right Honourable Lester B. Pearson, P.C., O.B.E.

Greeting:

Salut:

Whereas, with the approval of Her Majesty Queen Elizabeth the Second, Sovereign of the Order of Canada, We have been pleased to appoint you to be a Companion of the Order of Canada

We do by these Presents appoint you to be a Companion of the said Order and authorize you to hold and enjoy the dignity of such appointment together with membership in the said Order and all privileges thereunto appertaining

Given at Rideau Hall in the City of Ottawa under the Seal of the Order of Canada this twenty-eighth day of June 1968

Attendu que, avec l'assentiment de Sa Majesté la Reine Elizabeth Deux, Souveraine de l'Ordre du Canada, il Nous a plu de vous nommer Compagnon de l'Ordre du Canada

Nous vous nommons par les présentes Compagnon dudit Ordre et Nous vous autorisons à bénéficier et à jouir de la dignité de telle nomination ainsi que du titre de membre dudit Ordre et de tous les privilèges y afférents

Fait à Rideau Hall, dans la ville d'Ottawa, sous le Sceau de l'Ordre du Canada, ce vingt-huitième jour de juin 1968

By the Chancellor's Command,

Roland Michener

Par ordre du Chancelier,

Le Secrétaire général de l'Ordre du Canada

Esmond Butler

Secretary General of the Order of Canada

Order of Canada Appointment Scroll, addressed to Lester B. Pearson, P.C., O.M., C.C., O.B.E. All persons appointed to the order are invested with its insignia and presented with an appointment scroll.

PROTOTYPE FIVE-LEVELLED ORDER OF CANADA

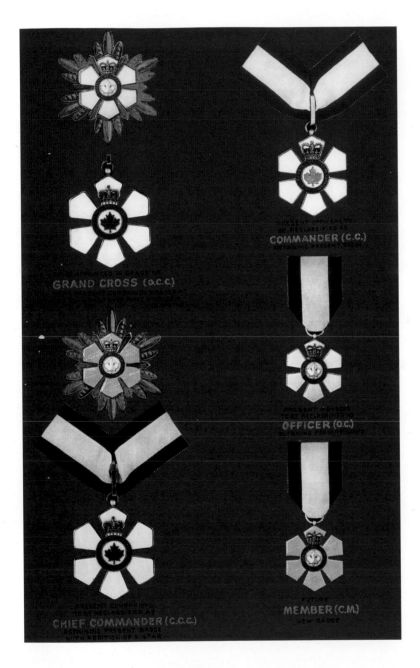

A proposal for a five-levelled Order of Canada, including the addition of breast stars and sashes, as is the custom in Europe. These designs were drawn by Bruce Beatty, shortly after the order was re-organized into three levels in 1972.

THE ORDER OF CANADA IN VARIOUS FORMS

Bronze Order of Canada paperweight. These are usually presented to retiring members of the Advisory Council of the Order. The paperweight is made by the Royal Canadian Mint and is identical to the seal of the order.

Order of Canada china plate. Commissioned in 1977 to celebrate the decennial anniversary of the order, the plates were made by Spode. These plates are only used for the meal following an Order of Canada investiture ceremony.

The stamp issued in 1977 by Canada Post to celebrate the order's tenth anniversary.

The stamps issued in 1992 by Canada Post to celebrate the order's twenty-fifth anniversary, and the life of Roland Michener.

A photo taken during a party held by members of the Order of Canada honours secretariat (today the Chancellery of honours). Joyce Bryant, Esmond Butler, and Bruce Beatty are in the foreground; various other recipients and employees of the Order of Canada secretariat are in the background.

HONOURS WINDOWS AT RIDEAU HALL

The Royal stained-glass window depicting the Royal Arms of Canada. This window was dedicated in 1992 in honour of the fortieth anniversary of the Queen's accession to the throne. The Arms are the first to contain the motto circlet of the Order of Canada. The corners of the window also contain images of the Sovereign's Insignia of the Order of Canada and the Order of Military Merit worn by Queen Elizabeth II.

The Vice-Regal stained glass window, depicting the Vice-Regal Flag and various elements of the Canadian honours system, including the insignia of the Order of Canada. This window was unveiled in 1992 as part of the fortieth anniversary of the appointment of Canadian governors general.

The Royal Arms of Canada, ca. 1957, painted by the noted heraldic expert, Alan Beddoe, O.C., O.B.E.

The Royal Arms of Canada, ca. 1994, as painted by Cathy Bursey-Sabourin, Fraser Herald.
The Queen approved the addition of the motto circlet around the shield on 12 July 1994.

PERSONAL HERALDRY AND THE ORDER OF CANADA

Arms of the Right Honourable Ramon Hnatyshyn, P.C., C.C., C.M.M., C.D., Q.C.

Arms of Mr Israel Asper, O.C., O.Mb.

Arms of Mr Yves Chevrier, C.M., R.V.M., C.D.

Arms of Ms Vera Roberts, C.M.

RECIPIENTS OF THE ORDER OF CANADA

Queen Elizabeth II and Roland Michener, 6 July 1967. This is the first photograph taken of a person wearing the order.

Oscar Peterson, Norah Michener, and Roland Michener, shortly after Peterson was invested as one of the first Officers of the Order of Canada, 11 April 1973. Peterson would later be elevated to a Companion of the Order in 1984. 'With his classical bent and passion for perfection Oscar Peterson is probably today's finest jazz pianist. By virtue of his many world tours he has become Canada's musical ambassador. He is a staunch champion of the equality of our ethnic minorities.'

Jean Béliveau, Roland Michener, Gordie Howe, and Hervé Filion, after being invested with the Medal of Service of the Order of Canada, 29 October 1971. Béliveau and Howe were recognized for their contribution to hockey, Filion, for his success as an internationally renowned jockey and trainer of harness racehorses. Béliveau would be promoted to the Companion level in 1998.

Robertson Davies, after being invested as a Companion of the Order of Canada, 11 April 1973. 'For his many contributions to literature and learning, to the theatre and journalism.'

Roloff Beny, being invested as a Officer of the Order of Canada, 11 April 1976. 'Internationally renowned photographer.'

Sister Alice Gervais, being invested as a Member of the Order of Canada, 11 April 1973. 'In recognition of her fifty years of work for the cause of education, culture and bilingualism in the Prairies.'

Gordon Robertson, being invested as a Companion of the Order of Canada, 7 April 1976. 'For his outstanding service to Canada in many areas of the Public Service, particularly as Clerk of the Privy Council.' Robertson played a key role in the early administration of the Order.

Paul Martin Sr, being invested as a Companion of the Order, 7 April 1976. 'For a lifetime of service to Canada, at home and abroad, as politician and public servant.'

Margaret Laurence, after being invested as a Companion of the Order, 27 June 1972. 'For her contribution to Canadian literature.'

The Iran Hostage Heroes shortly after Zena Sheardown and Patricia Taylor were invested as Members of the Order, 21 October 1981. Mrs. Sheardown was the first person to be appointed to the honorary division of the order. From left to right, unknown, Kenneth Taylor, O.C., John V. Sheardown, C.M., Zena Sheardown, C.M., unknown, Patricia Taylor, C.M., unknown, unknown, Maureen McTeer.

George Stanley and his wife, Ruth, after he was invested as an Officer of the Order of Canada, 20 April 1977. He would later become a Companion of the Order following his retirement as Lieutenant-Governor of New Brunswick. 'An educator and historian whose writings on the Canadian west and military history have won him an eminent place in scholarship.'

David Suzuki and Abe Okpik, after being invested as an Officer and Member of the Order respectively, 20 April 1977. Suzuki as 'A geneticist of international reputation who has succeeded in making science understandable to the layman through his lectures.' Okpik in recognition of 'the important contribution he has made to the preservation of the Inuit way of life, as a broadcaster and interpreter.'

Chief Dan George, after being awarded the Medal of Service of the Order of Canada (which became the O.C. level in 1972), 29 October 1971. 'For services as both an actor and interpreter of his people.'

Solange Chaput-Rolland, being invested as an Officer of the Order of Canada, 15 October 1975. 'Journalist, author, lecturer. For her important contribution to the analysis of current events in Quebec.'

Joyce Bryant (neé Turpin), standing between Elizabeth McAdam and Peggy Bryant, after being invested as a Member of the Order of Canada, 3 April 1974. 'For her dedication through her service at Government House during the tenure of five Governors General.' Bryant worked with every Governor General from Lord Alexander to Ramon Hnatyshyn. She was also the first 'employee' to work for the Order of Canada secretariat.

Rick Hansen, after being invested as a Companion of the Order of Canada, 29 March 1988. 'World-renowned wheelchair athlete, his 44,000 km journey took him to four continents and 33 countries, inspiring people to realize their potential and raising many millions of dollars for spinal cord research.'

Tommy Douglas with his wife Irma, following his investiture as a Companion of the Order of Canada, 21 October 1981. 'Head of the first socialist democratic government in Canada, and former leader of the federal New Democratic Party.'

Jane Mallett, being invested as a Member of the Order, 15 October 1975. 'Actress and script writing. In recognition of her dedication to Canadian Theatre.'

Patricia Messner, being invested as a Member of the Order of Canada, 21 April 1982. 'Women's world champion water-skier, sports broadcaster and orchestra percussionist.'

Kenojuak, being invested as a Companion of the Order of Canada, 20 October 1982. She was also one of the first recipients of the Medal of Service of the Order of Canada. 'Inuit artist of international distinction.'

Blanka Gyulai, being invested as a Member of the Order of Canada, 20 April 1983. 'Tireless worker for civil liberties and an effective advocate of numerous ethnic organizations assisting the adjustment of new Canadians.'

Terry Fox, after being invested as a Companion of the Order of Canada. Fox remains the youngest person to be appointed as a Companion. 'In recognition of his courage in embarking on the Marathon of Hope for the benefit of the Canadian Cancer Society.'

Nelson Mandela, who was invested as an honorary Companion of the Order of Canada on 24 September 1998. 'He is a universal symbol of triumph over oppression who has inspired people everywhere to work peacefully to end intolerance and injustice.'

Paul Desmarais, being invested as a Companion of the Order of Canada, 29 April 1987. Pierre Trudeau had attempted to stall Desmarais's original appointment as an officer in 1978, but the Advisory Council resisted. 'President and CEO of Power Corporation, in recognition of his contribution to Canada's development.'

Peter Lougheed, being invested as a Companion of the Order of Canada, 29 April 1987. 'Former Premier of Alberta, he established the Alberta Heritage Fund and introduced the Alberta Bill of Rights to protect the rights of minorities.'

Eugene Forsey, being invested as a Companion of the Order of Canada, 12 April 1989. Forsey was originally awarded the Medal of Service of the Order of Canada in 1968. 'For his contributions in the fields of labour relations and teaching and his studies on Canadian constitutional matters.'

Sir Christopher Ondaatje, being invested as an Officer of the Order of Canada, 21 April 1993. 'Founder of Canada's first institutional brokerage company, this Toronto financier contributes generously to his community and to his country.' His brother Michael, the noted author, is also an Officer of the Order.

John R. Matheson, being invested as an Officer of the Order of Canada, 16 February 1994. Matheson was one of the architects of the Order of Canada and also one of the designers of the Canadian flag. 'A retired justice of the Ontario Court of Justice, he has distinguished himself in the law, in politics, and as a historian, and as a soldier throughout a career spanning more than fifty years.'

Agnes Benidickson, being invested as a Companion of the Order of Canada, 4 February 1998. 'Former Chancellor of Queen's University, she has continued her record of public service, as an active volunteer helping many causes.' Benidickson was originally appointed an Officer of the Order in 1987.

Karen Kain, being invested as a Companion of the Order of Canada, 30 October 1991. Kain was originally appointed as an Officer of the Order in 1976. 'Principal dancer with the National Ballet of Canada who, by her skill, poise, and effortless grace, has conquered the ballet capitals of the world.'

Etuangat Aksayook, being invested as a Member of the Order of Canada, 16 November 1995. 'He is a living link with the past, whose experience as a whaler and with the old ways of hunting and fishing have been invaluable to the Inuit people.'

Hugh Ungungai, being invested as a Member of the Order of Canada, 8 November 1988. 'He has served in the municipal government, was a founding member of the Inuit Tapirisat of Canada, and owns the first Inuit-owned business in Baker Lake Nunavut.'

Ann Saddlemyer, being invested as a Officer of the Order of Canada, 15 February 1996. 'An authority in the study of Anglo-Irish literature, she has written and published extensively on this subject.'

Frank Shuster, being invested as an Officer of the Order of Canada, 26 February 1997. Shuster along with his comedy partner Johnny Wayne were originally offered the Medal of Service in 1968, but they refused the honour not knowing what it was. 'For tickling the Canadian funny bone with their comedy sketches of the foibles and follies of our society in times of war and peace.'

Jean Goodwill, being invested as a Officer of the Order of Canada, 29 April 1992. 'A native nurse, her life has been dedicated to promoting healthy lifestyles for Canada's indigenous peoples.'

Brian Mulroney, being invested as a Companion of the Order of Canada, 22 October 1998. 'Eighteenth Prime Minister of Canada, he led the country for nine consecutive years. His accomplishments include, the signing of the Free Trade Agreement and the North American Free Trade Agreement, and the Acid Rain Treaty.'

Maurice 'The Rocket' Richard, being invested as a Companion of the Order of Canada, 22 October 1998. Richard was one of the first recipients of the order when he was awarded the Medal of Service of the Order of Canada in 1967. 'A hero in the world of sports, for his contribution to sports, particularly hockey.'

Bruce Beatty, who was appointed as a Member of the Order of Canada on 20 April 1990. Beatty designed the Order of Canada and most of the Canadian honours system. 'His vast knowledge of honours and their history has firmly established him as an authority in the field.'

Wayne Gretzky, being invested as an Officer of the Order of Canada, 28 January 1998. Gretzky waited nearly fourteen years to receive his insignia. 'A superlative athlete who has devoted his life to the sport of hockey, he has rewritten the record book and brought finesse back to the game while earning almost every trophy and award possible.'

Sue Johanson, being invested as a Member of the Order of Canada, 31 May 2001. 'In recognition of her services as a successful advocate for sex education in Canada over the last three decades.'

Edward Broadbent, being invested as a Companion of the Order of Canada. Broadbent was originally appointed as an Officer of the Order in 1993. 'A public servant and educator, he has devoted himself to causes of paramount importance. Former leader of the New Democratic Party, he continues to be active in social and international affairs.'

John Anderson Fraser, being invested as a Member of the Order of Canada, 30 November 2002. 'Award winning journalist, he is always willing to serve his profession and his community and has been a dedicated volunteer on behalf of numerous organizations.'

Lieutenant General Roméo Dallaire, being invested as a Officer of the Order of Canada, 9 May 2003. 'He served with great distinction in the Canadian Forces for over 30 years and continues to be a model of dedication and selflessness. Courageous and caring, he continues his exemplary service to his country and to humanity.'

Margaret Catley-Carlson, being invested as an Officer of the Order of Canada, 21 February 2003. 'A former deputy minister of Health, and deputy executive director of UNICEF and president of DICA, she helped shape and strengthen government aid policies and strategies.'

Irène d'Entremont, being invested as a Member of the Order of Canada, 26 October 2002. 'Founding president of M.I.T. Electronics, she was one of the first women in her region to work in business.'

Catherine Hennessey, being invested as a Member of the Order of Canada, 31 May 2001. 'A tireless advocate for historical preservation in Prince Edward Island, she has raised awareness of the importance of the natural and built heritage in her province.'

Richard Ivey, being invested as a Companion of the Order of Canada, 28 February 2001. Ivey was appointed as a Member in 1988 and an Officer in 1994, making him one of a very few Canadians to have held every level of the Order of Canada. 'One of Canada's quintessential philanthropists, Director of the J.P. Robarts Research Institute, he has served on the boards of many businesses and community organizations.'

Lieutenant General Gilles Turcot, being invested as a Member of the Order of Canada. 'For more than 60 years he has served his country in a dedicated and exemplary manner. Following a successful career in the Canadian Forces he went on to serve as Director General of Service for the Montreal Olympic Games, and has also been a long time volunteer for the Last Post Fund.'

Charles Dutoit, with Adrienne Clarkson. Dutoit was appointed an Honorary Officer of the Order of Canada in October 1997. 'This energetic conductor has directed Orchestre de Montréal with vigour for nearly twenty-five years.'

Her Majesty Queen Elizabeth the Queen Mother, being presented with the Companion's insignia, 31 October 2000. 'In recognition of her near lifelong devotion to Canada, serving as Colonel-in-Chief of a number of Canadian Regiments.' The Queen Mother was originally supposed to be appointed a Companion in 1968, however, government inaction prevented this for more than thirty years.

and the Atlantic provinces. Often, in lieu of formal nominations from the public, the secretariat would undertake research into worthy candidates from each region.

A number of means were considered to increase the number of regional nominations; in the end, it was decided simply to promote public awareness of the order through the media. The council briefly considered creating provincial committees, but feared that over time, these provincial bodies might come to expect an allotment of honours. The order was never meant to be locked into a regional distribution. The council also decided to ask lieutenant-governors informally (by telephone) for nominations and to re-examine past years' 'drop lists' (i.e., lists of those who were nominated for the Medal of Service between 1967 and 1972).[12] One concern raised by Jules Léger – then Under-Secretary of State – was that if the council solicited from too broad a base, it might get too many names for the secretariat to handle.[13] This suggests that the council was not in desperate need of more names; more to the point, it needed more nominations from regions other than Ontario and Quebec. Several months later, in October 1972, the council agreed that members of the order from underrepresented regions of the country should be asked to submit the names of worthy candidates. This went back to Butler's original practice of asking recently appointed members to consider making nominations. The council also considered asking MPs to make nominations. However, Léger warned against such a step.[14] Despite all of these efforts, the issue kept cropping up. Finally, during a special meeting of the council in February 1974, it was unanimously agreed – at the insistence of Pauline McGibbon – that the order should seek to publicize its work in the mass media. This approach had been agreed to in 1969 but only partially executed.[15]

Publicity

The media constitute a double-edged sword; they can both help and hinder. The council directed the secretariat to follow up reports in the press about volunteerism and public service instead of taking out full-page advertisements in newspapers. From 1972 onwards there was an 'increasing number of references to the Order in newspaper articles about individual members.'[16] Gradually, the media began to take more regular notice of the order. After the New Year's Honours List was issued in December 1973, there were 5,508 lines of text printed about the Order of Canada in various newspaper articles. The following April, when the investiture was held, newspapers printed 7,832 lines of text.[17] Past lack of publicity could not be blamed solely on the media. Government House neglected to produce a brochure about the restructured Order of Canada until late 1974; thus in some quarters there was still much confusion about its composition.

Promotions

Promotions within orders are common; indeed, within some orders, recipients must first be appointed at the most junior level and then rise through the ranks. The Order of Canada rejected this sort of strict elevation policy, except that it was set out in 1967 that a recipient of the Medal of Service could be elevated within the order to become a Companion. In November 1970, during a special meeting of the Advisory Council, it was decided 'unless there was something quite unusual, a person would not be considered for promotion from one level to another in less than five years.'[18] The first elevations occurred in 1972, shortly before the order was restructured. Chester Ronning, Colonel Gustave Gingras and Clément Cormier had all been awarded, the Medal of Service in July 1967. These three men were appointed as Companions on 23 June 1972. Cormier, Gingras, and Ronning would be the only recipients of the Order of Canada ever promoted from the Medal of Service to Companion.

The first elevation of a Member to Officer occurred in December 1976. François Mercier, chair of the National Arts Centre's Board of Trustees, had been appointed a Member of the Order in January 1976. Eleven months later, in December 1976, he was raised to Officer. Mercier holds the record for quickest elevation within the order. The five-year rule has generally been adhered to; exceptions have been few. (The statistics relating to this are examined in chapter 10.) Elevations are meant to occur only from Member to Officer or Officer to Companion; so far only one person has been raised from Member directly to Companion.[19]

Citations

In 1977, another important change occurred within the Order of Canada. By that time, citations for each award were always issued in a press release and then read at the investiture. These citations were fairly short – one or two lines. The shortest Order of Canada citation belongs to Pauline Vanier, who was made a Companion in July 1967. Her citation simply reads: 'For her humanitarian work.' Her contributions were widely known; even so, a more extensive citation would have been desirable.

In 1976, one member of the Advisory Council complained that 'the citations read at the last Order of Canada Investiture were too impersonal and the wording could perhaps be improved, avoiding repetition of similar phrases.'[20] It was agreed to make the citations longer and more indicative of the recipient's contributions. Thus the secretariat staff were instructed to include more biographical information. The resulting citations were longer, more personal, and more informative. One of the first long-form citations was released in January 1978, when General Jacques Dextraze was appointed a Companion of the Order: 'Recognized for his courage, initiative and perseverance in Europe, Korea and the Congo. His enlightened leadership as Chief of Staff sensitized the government and his fellow citizens to the important role of the Canadian Armed Forces in our society.'

Since 1978 the citations have grown in length, although shorter citations are still sometimes used. It has long been recognized that the length of the individual citation does not reflect the quality of the recipient; in fact, as with Mme Vanier's citation, brevity can often suggest the overwhelming breadth of service rendered.

Lieutenant-Governors

One group that was anxious to become involved in the nomination process and in the Order as a whole was the lieutenant-governors.[21] At various times in the order's history, consideration has been given to making all lieutenant-governors ex officio Members of the Order.[22] The possibility of appointing each lieutenant-governor a

Deputy Chancellor of the Order has also been considered. Successive Advisory Councils have rejected these proposals, fearing that the order would become diluted if too many ex officio members were appointed. One of the reasons to involve lieutenant-governors in the Order of Canada was to discourage the provinces from creating their own honours. British Columbia had established the Order of the Dogwood in 1957 – a semiofficial award – and concern was growing that each province might in turn create its own local honours with the same goals as the Order of Canada. The federal government had been worried about this as early as 1937.[23] This fear of provincial honours seems to have dissipated; the various provincial orders are now incorporated into the broader Canadian honours system.

The preference has been for the Crown's provincial representatives to have a less overt involvement in the order. Since 1975, lieutenant-governors have regularly been solicited for nominations. By the 1980s, they were in special instances investing citizens with the order on behalf of the Governor General.[24] A sign of the Order of Canada's growing importance since the 1970s is that lieutenant-governors are showing more interest in the biannual appointments.

Influence across the Sea

The establishment of the Order of Canada was of particular interest to Canada's Commonwealth cousins. Specifically, Australia and New Zealand each founded national honours in 1975. Unlike Canada, both countries integrated their new honours into the broader British honours system, placing no prohibition on their citizens accepting peerages or knighthoods. Indeed, Canada, Ireland, and South Africa had been the only countries to impose such a ban.[25]

In Canada's Centennial year, Australia's Leader of the Opposition, Gough Whitlam, asked his prime minister, Harold Holt, in Australia's Parliament:

> He will know that during next week the fiftieth anniversary will occur of the Order of the British Empire, the most prolific and exuberant fount of honours, civil and military, for Australians ... As awards in an order so archaically named cause embarrassment to our diplomats and servicemen in South-East Asia and bewilderment in countries where they serve, I ask the Right Honourable gentleman whether he has noted or considered the system of national honours and awards which Canada has just established during her centennial year and which in accordance with long standing and bipartisan Canadian practice, do not include any titles.[26]

Holt never took up the matter, and neither did his two successors, John Gorton and William McMahon. But then Whitlam became prime minister of Australia in December 1972 and set about establishing the Order of Australia.

The Australian government was strongly aware of developments in Canada, and requested help. To this end, Carl Lochnan, the Director of Honours, visited Australia in March 1974. Australian officials – keen to learn from the Canadian experience – inundated Lochnan with questions about every aspect of the Order of Canada and honours in Canada.[27] In the words of one senior Australian official, Lochnan's counsel made a 'significant contribution'[28] toward the creation of the Order of Australia. In

May, Stephen Wenger, Australian Director of Honours, visited Ottawa to meet with other Canadian officials at Government House. Wenger was very familiar with the British honours system but had little experience with selection processes bereft of political influence.

On 26 January 1975, Australia Day, the Queen signed the Letters Patent founding the Order of Australia. The Governor General of Australia formally announced the new order in late February.[29] This new order had military and civilian divisions, consisting of three levels: Companion, Officer, and Member. Like the Order of Canada, nominations for the Order of Australia were solicited from the public, with recommendations being made to the Governor General of Australia by the Council of the Order of Australia. The Australian council includes one serving politician[30] and thus is not entirely non-partisan. However, this reflects the fact that Australia – like Britain and many other members of the Commonwealth – has a long and uninterrupted history of political involvement in the honours system. The Australian system is still fairly non-partisan relative to the old system, in which the prime minister or state premiers drafted the honours list with little outside advice. Another difference in the composition of the Australian Council is that the States are able to nominate citizens for membership.

Simultaneous with the creation of the Order of Australia, a new series of Australian bravery awards were announced, also modelled on the Canadian system: the Cross of Valour, the Star of Courage, and the Bravery Medal. The Australians had profited greatly from the Canadian experience.

Public reaction in Australia to the founding of the order was far different from Canadians' reaction to the creation of the Order of Canada. In Canada there had been an honours vacuum; in Australia, the British system was well rooted and much more pervasive. Many Australians wanted to continue using the Order of the British Empire as the primary national order; others welcomed the new developments. Partisan divisions were pronounced, with supporters of the Labour Party favouring the new order and Liberals opposing it. In an extraordinary act, four of Australia's states refused to recognize or participate in the new order. Many references were made to Canada, which, in the words of one Australian journalist, 'managed not only to scrap the British honours system but to adopt its own maple leaf flag. Are we such infants in Australia that we are even yet unable to agree on the symbols of our independence?'[31] Despite the animosity and difficulties, over time the Order of Australia gained acceptance. Change within it occurred quickly; within a year, there was a partial return to knighthoods.

Whitlam's Labour government was dismissed by the Governor General in November 1975. The leader of the Liberal Party, Malcolm Fraser, became prime minister and set about making important changes to the order. In May 1976, two additions were made to the Order of Australia: a Medal of the Order, similar to the British Empire Medal, was added and ranked below the level of Member; and a new, senior level, that of Knight or Dame, was added.[32] This top level conferred the title 'Sir' or 'Dame,' just as the British orders of knighthood do. In all, fourteen Knights and Dames were appointed. In 1986, however, this top level was removed from the order.[33] Australians were slow to divest themselves of British honours; the various states – which unlike Canadian provinces had always held the right to submit honours lists directly to the Queen – continued to nominate citizens for the various titular and non-titular levels of the British orders of chivalry. This ended in October 1992, when Paul Keating's Labour government reached an agreement with the Australian states whereby the latter would cease making nominations. Imperial honours came to an end in Australia more than seventy years after they did in Canada. The Queen still appoints Australians as Knights of the Garter, to the Order of Merit, and to the various levels of the Royal Victorian Order.

In New Zealand, the Queen's Service Order was instituted in 1975. It had two levels: Companion of the Queen's Service Order, and the Queen's Service Medal. This system was largely modelled on Britain's Imperial Service Order and Imperial Service Medal. The order was devised by Phillippe O'Shea, who considered developments in Canada.[34] In 1975, New Zealand was not yet ready to establish its own comprehensive honours system. One would develop over the next twenty years: the Order of New Zealand was founded in 1987, and the New Zealand Order of Merit in 1996. The two most senior levels of the New Zealand Order of Merit were originally knighthoods, much like the Order of the British Empire. The various New Zealand orders differ from the Order of Canada in a number of ways (including number of levels and method of selection). That said, New Zealand authorities did make note of the Canadian experience.[35]

Cost

From a financial perspective, it was much cheaper for the Canadian government to work within the old British honours system. There was less to administer in terms of the nomination process, the insignia were less costly, and the entire system was administered by the Department of the Secretary of State. Elements such as award certificates and the maintenance of a register of recipients were all covered by the British government. The Order of Canada cost less than $80,000 to administer in its first year of existence, but its costs grew quickly after that. For the 1969–70 fiscal year, the budget for the honours system was $85,000. By 1977–8, with the addition of the Order of Military Merit and the bravery awards, it had grown to $632,000 – an increase of 744 per cent. As a result of the rising cost of precious metals, even the cost of the insignia was increasing. A Companion that had cost $648 in 1967, by 1975 cost $1,500. Overall, though, the system was still inexpensive, relative to the benefits it yielded.

Decennial Anniversary

Preparations were made to mark the Order of Canada's tenth anniversary. In less than ten years, it had expanded in structure and the Canadian honours system had taken root. So far, there had been only a 3 per cent refusal rate, and only three of the refusals had been for reasons other than modesty. In 1977 there were four hundred new nominations in addition to the reserve lists compiled by the secretariat.[36] In January 1976, Léger broached the topic of undertaking a number of special projects to recognize the order's tenth anniversary. The year had the double-significance in that it was also the Queen's Silver Jubilee. To celebrate that, a Royal Visit to Canada was in the works.

The secretariat lacked the financial resources to 'undertake, for example, a major celebration of the tenth anniversary of the Order'[37]; even so, a variety of special projects were undertaken. Canada Post issued a commemorative stamp, recipients of the order all received a commemorative medallion, and Carl Lochnan, the former Director of Honours, began writing a book about honours in Canada.[38] In addition to all this, the Governor General held a reception in each province for the various recipients of the Order of Canada. Governor General Léger commissioned the noted tapestry artist Micheline Beauchemin to create a tapestry to commemorate the decennial. This modern tapestry depicts the various insignia of the Order of Canada, the Order of Military Merit, and the Canadian bravery decorations, along with Léger's seal,[39] and has been on constant display in a variety of rooms at Rideau Hall since its completion.

On 17 January 1977, a special meeting of the Advisory Council was held at Rideau Hall. Current and former members of the council were invited to attend to review and discuss the purpose and success of the order. The council agreed that, despite chronic understaffing, it was operating well, and that worthy Canadians from every discipline and region were being accorded proper recognition. For some recent members of the council, this was not enough; there was a feeling that the Order of Canada should do more – perhaps take on some social issues.[40] But many – Michael Pitfield in particular – rejected the idea of transforming the order into a group of social activists, since it would inevitably politicize the order. Pitfield reminded the council of Pearson's original intention – 'recognition of outstanding merit as the primary objective' – and dissuaded the council from changing the order in this respect. By day's end, there was agreement that the order's present purpose was sufficient in itself. The council also considered having the Queen preside over an investiture, but it was agreed to put this off. Her Majesty's scheduled visit was already booked solid, and some council members were concerned that those invested by the Queen would be somehow regarded as superior to those invested by the Governor General. This argument was rather weak, in that the Queen had invested fifteen people with the Order of Canada in 1973 – including Léger – and there had not been any perception of favouritism, nor any sense that those fifteen were somehow superior to other members of the Order.[41]

In honour of the tenth anniversary, a special party was held for the staff of the order's secretariat, who had done so much to help establish the order.[42] For this party, Bruce Beatty, the designer of the order, and Joyce Bryant, the first member of the secretariat, wrote a poem:

THE SAGA OF THE ORDER OF CANADA,
or, It's Ten Long Years We've Toiled Away and Lived to Tell the Tale

It's ten long years since first we knew
    An Order we would have,
A 'thank you' to our country's few
    Who served beyond the Call.

Before that fateful April day
   Bruce laboured on designs
But never one word did he say
   To family or friend,

And back and forth to London went
   The Civil Service brass
The die was cast, the badges sent
   The Council set its task.

On April seventeenth last
   The P.M. Gave his speech –
Then Blackburn, Smythe et al worked fast;
   The wheels began to turn.

Alas, some steno slipped one day
   In tying out the Motto –
The Hebrew's verse had gone astray,
   And 'fornication' hovered.

But chaste and virgin now once more,
   We made July the sixth,
When great Canadians (plus fourscore)
   Composed the premier list.

We settled first for grades but two,
   With 'Courage' on one side,
But found too many 'Who's' were 'Who' –
   So added level three.

Now Comps. And Offs. And Members all
   Are 'pinned' within the fold,
And service great and service small
   Is honours with a Badge.

Investitures a score we've seen
   Since that first one was held,
And every discipline has been
   Included in the group.

Lots of laughs, a tear or two
   Has flavoured each event.
But overall, I think it's true –
   We've really had a ball.[43]

After the poem was read, Esmond Butler made a few brief remarks about the order's brief history. Then a special cake was cut by Butler, Bryant, and Beatty.

Changes to the Order

The Advisory Council often found itself divided on the issue of recognizing young Canadians. Canadian athletes were regularly winning medals at international competitions, and the council was looking for a way to recognize them with a national award. This was a problem, since the Order of Canada was usually reserved for outstanding service over a long duration, and many inspiring athletes did not qualify in that regard. This issue had long divided the council. To recognize young Canadians more appropriately, Pitfield suggested that the order's constitution be amended to include a Distinguished Service Award, which 'would recognize the particular contributions of young people such as athletes who had done something quite remarkable.'[44] In the early years, the level of Member was often used to recognize outstanding Olympic athletes. Recently, athletes have been awarded the Meritorious Service Cross instead.

At the 17 January special meeting of the Advisory Council, the matter of making lieutenant-governors 'Dignitaries of the Order' was considered. One proposal called for each lieutenant-governor to wear the insignia of the order and to act as a representative of the Governor General, but not to actually hold membership in the order.[45] It was felt that such a move would only make the lieutenant-governors second-class members and ultimately disenfranchise them. After the special meeting, Butler sent a letter to all lieutenant-governors soliciting their views.[46] Their proposed ex officio designation would be Vice-Chancellor and Principal Officer, and all of them would be admitted at the level of Officer of the Order of Canada. Consensus among the lieutenant-governors and within the Advisory Council was never reached, so no additional ex officio officers were added.

In 1980 came another symbolic change: the Honours Secretariat was renamed the Chancellery of Canadian Orders and Decorations. This was the designation that Butler had originally favoured, although he feared it sounded too grand. It seems that the order had gained sufficient stature that the change was warranted.

The Order in Parliament

As the years passed, the Order of Canada was discussed more and more often in Parliament. MPs would regularly make motions to congratulate recent recipients. This became a concern for the Speaker, and agreement was finally reached so that these congratulations did not become regular events. In November 1977, Erik Nielsen, MP for the Yukon, placed an unusual motion before the House of Commons: 'This House urges the government to consider the award to William Stephenson of an appropriately high Canadian honours, perhaps a Companion of the Order of Canada or honorary membership, in belated recognition of the singular and significant contribution made by this outstanding Canadian to the cause of the Western world during the Second World War.'[47]

The motion did not receive the required unanimous consent and thus it failed. Sir William Stephenson, a noted inventor, had served in the First World War as a pilot and had been awarded the Military Cross and Distinguished Flying Cross. During the Second World War he had been a master spy – chief of British Security Coordination in the Western Hemisphere. Although a Canadian, after the war Stephenson was knighted at the insistence of Winston Churchill. Few actually knew why until 1962, with the publication of *The Quiet Canadian*, an overview of Stephenson's extraordinary service. After the war, Stephenson moved to the West Indies and became influential in that region's development. However, he always kept his Canadian citizenship. His name had been considered during the early 1970s, after the media raised questions about why he had not received the order, but the Advisory Council had always removed his name from the short list. Probably, this was because Stephenson was not a resident of Canada and already possessed a senior honour. Finally, in December 1979, he was appointed a Companion of the Order. Throughout his life a Canadian at heart, he had served with outstanding (albeit silent) distinction during the Second World War.

At various times it was also suggested that John Diefenbaker be made a Companion of the Order. However, he never retired from politics, so he was ineligible for appointment. A suitable award was eventually found; in 1976, at the nomination of Pierre Trudeau, Diefenbaker was appointed a Companion of Honour.[48]

The Queen

One of the last decisions made by Jules Léger before he retired was to stop asking the Queen to approve the Order of Canada appointments list. Since 1967 the practice had been that the Advisory Council submitted its nomination list to the Governor General, who then reviewed it and passed it on to the Queen. In 1971, when the entire honours system was under review, Cabinet had discussed merely having the Governor General affirm the appointments, but the proposal was not implemented at that time. The precise reasons for this change remain unclear, although the decision coincided with the introduction of the Constitutional Amendment Bill (Bill C-60) to the House of Commons.[49] This bill sought to raise the importance of the Governor General. Although the bill failed, it at least inspired discussions about altering the office of Governor General.[50] 'The Queen has instructed me to say that she has no objection to this change but that she would certainly wish to be informed of the awards as they are made,'[51] noted Sir Philip Moore, the Queen's private secretary, who went on to say: 'I think you will be aware that Her Majesty takes a great interest in decorations and the summaries enclosed with the awards provide an admirable way for the Queen to keep in touch with the activities of Canadians who have in various ways played an outstanding part in the life of the country.'[52]

Growth of the Honours System

The question of honorary awards – which had been under review by the Working Group on Honours Policy – remained unresolved. In July 1980 this group submitted its report to the prime minister, but nothing was done with respect to honorary awards. The working group's greatest achievement was to create the Canadian Police Exemplary Service Medal in 1983.

Although scarcely ten years old, the Order of Canada was becoming a recognized national symbol. With the removal of British gallantry awards from the list of Canadian decorations, Canada's long-held Dominion–Commonwealth honours system gave way to a Canadian-grown one. This change was not completed with the creation of the Order of Canada; rather, it was coupled with the restructuring of the order and the introduction of new bravery decorations and the Order of Military Merit. The institutional mechanics of the order began to develop more fully. Increased publicity, the eleven-step nomination/appointment process, and the move of the Honours Secretariat from the Office of the Secretary of State to that of the Governor General all served to further insulate the order – and Canadian honours in general – from partisan politics. The new honours methodology was (or was trying to be) research-based, rigorous, even scientific. Yet precise formulas for bestowing honours remained elusive. The decennial review stated that the central purpose of the order was to reward exemplary service, and that the system was meeting this goal. But improvements were still needed.

CHAPTER NINE

The Logistics of a National Order

The question of Insignia may seem a comparatively trifling one but it is one of those elements which go to contribute to the prestige and attractiveness of an Order.[1]

Vincent Massey, 10 December 1942

The actual mechanics of the Order of Canada had been devised through its constitution; just as great an effort had to be invested in physically creating the order. Problems such as finding a name for the order, what the insignia would look like, who was to make it, and other logistical matters all had to be dealt with quickly. Considering that there were less than seven months between Cabinet's approval of the order and the investiture of the first Companion, it is remarkable how well things turned out. Regarding some elements – the motto, for example – the decisions predated Cabinet's approval. The history of the ribbon of the order can be traced back to the reign of Queen Victoria, nearly seventy-five years prior to its founding. Many of these elements had been incorporated into various proposals submitted to Mackenzie King during the 1940s; it is fairly easy to link pre-1967 designs and elements with the present-day Order of Canada. Two elements that remained constant in every design proposal were the Crown and the Maple Leaf; both were already central elements of Canada's symbolic lexicon.

Nomenclature

The all-important question of what to call the order was one of the first things decided. Viscount Monck's 1866 proposal called for the name to be the Order of St Lawrence. Although this name was also favoured by Vincent Massey, it was unacceptable. Not all Canadians were Christians, so that name would have excluded a large segment of the population. Furthermore, few Canadians knew who St Lawrence was, with the result that many would invariably associate him with the St Lawrence River, which was in turn associated only with eastern Canada and not with the country as a whole. In 1942, Massey had proposed the Royal Order of Canada. The Order of the Maple Leaf was also considered but was rejected as too 'fanciful [and] pretentious.'[2] John Erskine Read, legal adviser to the Department of External Affairs, suggested the Royal Elizabethan Order, in honour of both the wife and the daughter of George VI, but this proposal also failed. Later proposals called for a Canadian Decoration of Honour and Canadian Award of Honour (which later became the King's Canadian Decoration of Honour and the King's Canadian Award of Honour). These proposals were also rejected.

By 1966, when the order was truly beginning to take shape, the most popular choice was the Order of Canada. This had been suggested by E.H. Coleman and Major General Letson in 1943, in 1945 by the Department of National Defence, and again in 1948 by the Governor General, Viscount Alexander. The style 'Order of Canada' was favoured for a number of reasons; mainly, it was short and unpretentious as well as easy to translate. John Matheson favoured this style from the beginning, although he considered lengthening it to the Most Honourable Order of Canada.[3] This would have made it similar to a number of British orders that possessed descriptive prefixes (Most Ancient, Most Noble, Most Excellent, and so on). Pearson, however, did not want a complex name for the order, and 'Most Honourable' was swiftly dropped. Less obvious names continued to float around, ranging from the Order of the Cross of Canada to the Order of the Beaver.[4] The latter suggestion was likely put forward in jest.

As late as 17 August 1966, Pearson was still referring to the order as the Canadian Award or Canadian Order; this suggests that no name had yet been assigned. Pitfield's April 1966 memorandum to Butler and Matheson suggested the Order of Canada on the basis that 'this avoids any religious, chivalrous, or regional connotation.'[5] In the October 1966 drafts of the order's constitution, the award is referred to as the Order of Canada. The final decision came on 16 September 1966, at the Dorchester Hotel in London. Pearson was visiting Britain to work out some of the details relating to the new order, and while there he had meetings with a variety of British officials. Among them was Conrad Swan. In a 28 September letter to Pearson's principal secretary, Swan repeatedly mentioned the Order of Canada. From that time on, all documents referred to the Order of Canada.[6] When the proposal was presented to Cabinet, there was no objection to the name.

The Motto

The motto of the Order of Canada is the oldest component of the order by virtue of its origins in the Bible. It is worth noting that all national orders have some sort of motto. Britain's Order of the Garter has the most notable: *Honi Soit Qui Mal Y Pense* (Evil Be to Him Who Evil Thinks). France's *Légion d'honneur* has simply *Honneur et Patrie* (Honour and Country). Typically, a motto is meant to suggest what the particular Order represents; it is part of the necessary apparatus of honours.

Many of the early proposals for a Canadian order lacked a motto. Vincent Massey had preferred simply to use the motto of Canada – *A Mari usque ad Mare* (From Sea to Sea). Other proposals from the 1940s suggested *Acer Gerendo* (A Productive Maple).[7] However, neither of these provided insight into the people and deeds the order was intended to recognize. Long before the structure of the Order of Canada was defined, Matheson had chosen an appropriate motto. There was no opposition to it; among the successive proposals floated in 1966 and 1967, it was the one part that did not change.

During Matheson's preliminary research at the Library of Parliament, he was confronted with the difficulty of selecting a motto. Philip Laundy, the library's Chief of Research, pointed out the necessity for a motto; his suggestion was 'Our Achievement Is the Nation's Achievement.'[8] Matheson thought this lacked a certain something, and set to work on the problem. A month later, he attended a seminar on international affairs in Ottawa. There, the Reverend Herbert O'Driscoll of Ottawa's St John the Evangelist Anglican Church gave a speech about desiring a better country. O'Driscoll postulated that 'we are seeking to make not our country but all countries fulfil their God-given potential, and thereby of course seeking this for our own country.'[9] He related this specifically to Hebrews 11:16: 'But now they desire a better country that is heavenly; where for God is not ashamed to be called their God for he hath established for them a city.' O'Driscoll distilled great meaning from this simple excerpt, relating it to humanity's movement through history: all of us are immigrants; all of us hold the earth in trust; and all of us are seeking a better country.[10] Matheson immediately latched onto the words 'desire a better country.' To him, the phrase was 'very unusual because it is so non-posturing.'[11] Furthermore, it had strong relevance to Canadians, most of whom came here from somewhere else. He immediately proposed that the Latin translation, *Desiderantes Meliorem Patriam*, become the motto of the Order of Canada.[12] This motto gained early acceptance with the prime minister; by 3 October 1966, it had been confirmed and accepted.[13]

On 17 April, shortly after the order was announced, Matheson wrote O'Driscoll requesting a copy of his 1966 speech that had referred to the motto. Only after the public was informed about the order could Matheson tell O'Driscoll of his role. O'Driscoll was elated that the motto was 'in some sense born from the theme of this address.'[14]

One of the more amusing events in the history of the order occurred on the day it was announced in Parliament. On 17 April, simultaneous with the prime minister's speech, the PMO issued a press release. Unfortunately, that press release stated that the motto, *Desiderantes Meliorem Patriam*, was from Hebrews 12:16. A stenographer had copied the incorrect reference from an early draft of the order's constitution. Hebrews 12:16[15] states: 'Lest there be any fornicator, or profane person, as Esau, who for one morsel of meat sold his birthright.' This was rather comical in light of the Munsinger scandal, which was still fresh in the minds of Canadians, and the claims from the opposition parties that Pearson had sold Canada out by signing the Auto Pact. Hebrews 12:16 was in effect alluding to the political woes of both the Conservatives and the Liberals; the one was being accused of fornicating, the other of selling the country out! The opposition leader, John Diefenbaker, never a fan of the order, commented that 'they can't even quote scripture correctly.'[16] Officials from the PMO quickly apologized for the error.

The Ribbon

The ribbon of the Order of Canada is based on the Canadian flag, which in turn is roughly modelled after the ribbon of the Canada General Service Medal, 1866–1870. This medal was awarded to veterans of the Fenian Raids and the Riel Rebellion of 1870. It was approved by Queen Victoria in 1899. More than 16,000 were issued, and the ribbon's colours soon became familiar to many Canadians. In 1921, George V assigned *gules* and *argent* – red and white – as Canada's national colours. This is the main reason why Canada's flag is red and white, and why the ribbon of the Order of Canada is the same.

It was decided in 1943 that the Canada Medal would utilize the same ribbon as the Canada General Service Medal; however, early proposals for a Canadian Order called for a different ribbon. The 1943 proposal called for a ribbon of watered silk in 'autumnal brown,'[17] red, yellow, green, purple, and scarlet[18] – a rather ghastly combination, even in moiré silk. In 1943, the same ribbon design was suggested for the Canadian Award of Honour and Canadian Decoration of Honour – the non-order awards developed by the Awards Coordination Committee. At this point, the Canadian order and Canada Medal were considered quite independent of each other.

Viscount Alexander of Tunis, during his term as Governor General, was the first to suggest that a Canadian order use a red–white–red ribbon. In March 1948 he wrote to Mackenzie King to suggest that it was time for Canada to have its own national honour. Alexander proposed that the ribbon be 'Red White Red, which was the ribbon of the Canada General Service Medal, 1866–1870. The ribbon of the Order of Canada would be slightly wider.'[19] Later proposals failed to include prospective ribbon designs and focused mainly on the more immediate details of how many levels the order was to have.

Early on in his research into creating a Canadian order, Matheson suggested that the ribbon be 'half red and half white,'[20] similar to the bicolour pattern of Britain's Order of Merit. This was also similar to the ribbon used on the seal of the Royal Proclamation establishing the Canadian Flag in 1965. This would emphasize the symbolic link between the national flag and the national order.

However, Vincent Massey had ideas of his own. Shortly after Matheson's March 1966 visit to Batterwood, Massey devised some rough designs, drawn by his secretary Joyce Turpin.[21] Massey's ribbon had three equal parts, white–red–white.[22] He had decided on this combination so as to prevent confusion between the Order of Canada and the Canada Medal; it would have made little sense for a junior service medal and the national order to share the same ribbon. A few days later, Massey decided that the ribbon should be similar to the new Canadian flag; he promptly changed it to red–white–red[23] and made the ribbon of the Canada Medal white-red-white. He even had Turpin sew a sash so that he could gauge the appearance.[24] Massey included this description in his draft statutes for the Order of Canada, which he sent on to Matheson.

Despite Massey's advice, between March and July 1966 Matheson wobbled between a ribbon of equal parts red and white and one of 'red white red of the flag.'[25] Pearson showed little interest in such trifles as the colours in the ribbon, provided they were red and white. It was during his July 1966 trip to London that Matheson finally made a decision. While visiting the British medal craftsmen Spink & Son, he met with E.C. Joslin, a highly regarded expert on honours and decorations. Joslin suggested 'a ribbon red, white, red in the flag proportions ¼, ½, ¼.'[26] From this point forward, Matheson insisted that the ribbon be identical in proportions to the national flag, and this was ultimately accepted.

The ribbons for the Companions of the Order of Canada, the Medal of Courage, and the Medal of Service were to be of the same design. The Companion ribbon was to be 1.5 inches wide; both the Medal of Courage and the Medal of Service were to be hung from a ribbon 1.25 inches wide. The undress ribbons – those on the uniforms of military personnel – were to be differentiated by small Maple Leaf devices placed in the centre of the ribbon. Companions would wear a red-enamelled Maple Leaf edged in gold; Medal of Courage recipients would receive a plain gold Maple Leaf; Medal of Service recipients would wear a plain silver Maple Leaf. Since the order's inception, the ribbon has been produced by Toye, Kenning & Spenser of England, the oldest manufacturers of order and medal ribbon in the world.

The Design

The design of the insignia of the order was of particular interest to Pearson. He had no desire to open a competition of the sort that had been attempted with the Canadian flag in 1965. Summarizing Canada's symbols in the insignia turned out to be a difficult task: which would be included, and which not?

In August 1966, John Hodgson contacted Flight Sergeant Bruce Beatty from the DND's Directorate of Ceremonial. Beatty was the directorate's chief artist and already well known for his work. One afternoon, Beatty's commanding officer, Lieutenant Colonel N.A. Buckingham, arrived and announced: 'The prime minister wants to see you.' Beatty didn't believe him, and responded, 'Oh sure.' Within an hour, Beatty was standing in front of the prime minister, with no idea why. Pearson soon explained: 'We are going to institute a Canadian Order and you are going to design it.'[27] The prime minister then went on to swear Beatty to secrecy; he was not even to tell his commanding officer. This placed poor Flight Sergeant Beatty in an awkward position; he was being forbidden to tell his commanding officer, a lieutenant colonel, what he was working on. To work on the project, Beatty took extra days of sick leave. Designing the Order of Canada was no easy task: What shape was the insignia to have? What symbols were to be included? Too many symbols would result in a cluttered, ugly design.

There had been a number of past attempts to design a Canadian order. The first formal insignia designs were devised during the Second World War. E.H. Coleman, chair of the Awards Coordination Committee, preferred a simple oval badge with the Royal Arms of Canada in the centre.[28] After Mackenzie King rejected the idea of a Canadian order in 1943, Coleman kept submitting proposals, but he would never again try to design one. Notwithstanding Coleman's 'keep it simple' approach, the ACC opted for heavy use of symbols, as best demonstrated in its 1943 proposal. The insignia of the Order of Canada designed by Dr Charles Comfort for the ACC was a nine-pointed star (symbolizing the nine provinces). In the centre was the shield of the Royal Arms of Canada, surmounted by a Crown. Between each of the points was a separate figure 'associated with Canadian life:'[29] beaver, pine cone, fish, trillium, bird (dove), maple leaf, sheaf of wheat, shovel and pick, and microscope. One wonders why a locomotive was not included; perhaps the ACC felt that the microscope was evidence enough of Canada's status as an industrial nation. Each symbol on its own was appropriate, but the result more resembled the hood ornament on a 1938 Cadillac LaSalle than a national order! Later proposals were much simpler. For the Canadian Award of Honour and Canadian Decoration of Honour, the noted heraldic artist Alan

Beddoe was commissioned to design the insignia. It was to be nine-sided, with 'three maple leaves conjoined on one stem, proper, superimposed on a lauded wreath seeded proper. And, underneath, the motto ACER GERENDO in raised letters enameled in red. The whole ensigned with the Royal Crown in Gold.'[30] The insignia of the more junior Canadian Decoration of Honour was to be identical to that of the Award, although not enamelled.

Successive proposals failed through the 1940s and 1950s. After Matheson's week-end visit to Batterwood, Massey created his own design. It seems that poor Vincent lacked the skill to draw his own proposal, for he assigned the job to his secretary, Joyce Turpin.[31] Although completely unoriginal, it was not unattractive. It was a simple, white, enamelled Maltese cross of eight points 'on an oval centre of gold, within which shall appear a scarlet Maple Leaf, inscribed with the word 'CANADA,' in gold letters, ensigned with the St. Edward's Crown in proper colours.'[32] Except for the Maple Leaf in the centre and the 'CANADA,' this insignia was identical to the Royal Victorian Order.

Matheson knew that the Order of Canada would have to be easily distinguished from the British orders. Early on, he decided that the insignia of Companion of the Order should be made of gold, 'under a Crown a blazing North Star bearing a single red maple leaf and the motto *desiderantes melioram patriam*.'[33] Officers would simply receive the Canada Medal in silver; Members would be awarded a bronze Canada Medal. The suggestion that Officers and Members receive the Canada Medal only in silver or bronze was quickly rejected. Both Swan and Joslin noted that such a system of gold, silver, and bronze, although suitable for the Olympics, was inappropriate for a national order. After July 1966, the Canada Medal was no longer proposed as the insignia to be awarded to the two junior levels of the order. Of course, this part of the discussion was academic, since Cabinet was refusing to adopt the three-level pro-posal (Companion, Officer, and Member) for the Order of Canada.

Apparently everyone involved in the Order of Canada project had an opinion on what its insignia should look like. Joslin of Spink & Son suggested that 'it would be an attractive feature if her [the Queen's] portrait was included.'[34] Matheson for a time considered a simple white oval badge surmounted by a Crown with a red Maple Leaf in the centre and the motto at the base. The oval was similar to the Order of the Companions of Honour. He soon rejected this design as too simplistic.[35] He wanted the order to have an impressive but not too ornate insignia, and maintained that his North Star with red Maple Leaf was the most suitable.

There were a few problems with using the North Star, the first being that Sweden was already using it. The Royal Order of the Northern Star (Kungliga Nordsjärbeirden) had been founded in 1748 by Frederick I. The insignia of the Swedish order is strongly similar to the one Matheson was proposing for the Order of Canada. Matheson was aware of this, but neither he nor any of the other people involved could think of a suitable alternative.

The solution to the order's shape literally fell from the sky – specifically, in the form of Canada's ubiquitous snow. On Friday, 25 November 1966,[36] Beatty left his office for the Sergeants' Mess to relax after a busy week. While walking down Elgin Street in Ottawa, he noticed it was snowing and was at once stuck by the idea of making the Order of Canada look like a snowflake. The following Monday,

28 November, he asked the Parliamentary Library to gather for him some information on snowflakes. Later that same day, Matheson requested information on snowflakes from the same library. Beatty and Matheson had never discussed a snowflake design for the order's insignia.

Matheson had thought of a snowflake because although the creation of the order was supposed to be secret, word about the project was beginning to spread through the government.[37] Since the project did not involve national security, no classification had been formally assigned to it. As parliamentary secretary to the prime minister, Matheson attended a wide variety of government functions and receptions in Ottawa. During a reception at the West German Embassy, Matheson met John Halstead. Halstead was an ardent Canadian nationalist and throughout his life had sought to promote national unity. A foreign service officer with the Department of External Affairs, Halstead would rise to become Canada's Ambassador to NATO and later to West Germany. Somehow, Halstead had learned of Matheson's involvement in founding the Order of Canada. On Monday 21 November, following a meeting with the West German Ambassador,[38] the two men began to discuss possible designs, and Matheson outlined his North Star proposal. Halstead pointed out the possible problems with using a North Star, and then said: 'Have you ever thought of a snowflake?'[39] This suggestion struck Matheson as inappropriate: snowflakes are ornate and fragile; although beautiful, a snowflake would not be suitable for an insignia meant to be worn on the breast or around the neck. But he soon began to like the idea.

Staff at the Parliamentary Library assumed, understandably, that Beatty and Matheson were collaborating. They copied a number of pages about snowflakes and posted them to each man on 12 December. Included in each package were numerous diagrams and sketches of the various snowflake shapes and the processes by which they form. Not until some weeks later did the two men discuss snowflakes; by that time, Beatty had finished the designs. All snow crystals develop in hexagonal symmetry,[40] so the goal was to design a properly proportioned, elegant yet sturdy snowflake. The *Encyclopedia Americana*'s article on snow contained the perfect shape (see page 150, diagram P1b).[41] The diagrams had been taken from Ukichiro Nakaya's *Snow Crystals: Natural and Artificial*. Shortly after receiving the information, Beatty had the Parliamentary Library get Nakaya's book from the National Library. The shape chosen by Beatty was scientifically described as a 'a Plane Crystal; Crystals developed in the basal plane of the hexagonal system of crystallization ... branches in sector form. The branches show the form of tabular sections.'[42] This shape served as the model for the Order of Canada. The plane crystal now replaced the North Star as the design for the Order of Canada.

The symbolism of the snowflake was ideal. It represented the Canadian climate, and furthermore, every snowflake – like every recipient of the order – is unique. Before Christmas 1966, Beatty submitted three separate designs to the prime minister; Pearson then personally chose the design we have come to know today.[43] (He also requested that the Crown be enlarged.) In the coming years, Beatty would also design the Order of Military Merit, the Canadian bravery awards, and many other official insignia and would himself be made a Member of the Order of Canada in recognition of his contributions to the Canadian honours system.

Beatty decided that the Companion insignia would measure 56 mm across and be white enamel with gold edges. In the centre would be a red enamelled Maple Leaf, surrounded by the motto of the order and surmounted by a St Edward's Crown. On the reverse would be the word CANADA and a three-digit number.[44] Made of 18 carat gold, it was a simple yet elegant design. The Medal of Courage and Medal of Service were to be smaller – 34 mm across – but would have the same snowflake shape. The Medal of Courage would be gold in colour, with a simple Maple Leaf in the centre of the insignia surmounted by a Crown. On the reverse would be a circle device containing the word COURAGE. The recipient's name would be engraved on the lower arm of the insignia. The Medal of Service would be sterling silver, the obverse being identical to the Medal of Courage. On the reverse would be a circle device containing the word SERVICE. The recipient's name would be engraved on the lower arm of the insignia. There would be no risk of confusion between the Medal of Courage and the Medal of Service because of the different colour of the insignia. The prime minister and the Governor General approved of the designs; Vanier had examined them shortly before his death. The Queen gave Royal approval to the designs on 21 March 1967.[45] The insignia of the Order was now complete, although no actual insignia had yet been manufactured.

In 1972, with the expansion of the Order of Canada and abolition of the Medal of Courage and Medal of Service, new insignia had to be designed. The Medal of Service was considered austere in appearance, more like a long service award than one of the nation's most senior awards. The Advisory Council, with the help of Beatty, decided that the insignia of the two new levels should be scaled-down versions of the very impressive-looking insignia awarded to Companions of the order. This was in part to promote the view that although the order had three levels, each was a significant part of a broader system of recognition. There had been muffled complaints from some recipients of the Medal of Service that the award looked insignificant when compared with the Companion's insignia.[46]

The Companion's insignia has remained unchanged. The Officer's insignia is nearly identical, except for a few elements to ensure that it can be distinguished from the Companion's. The Officer's insignia is worn from the neck and is also in the shape of a white snowflake. However, it is only 45 mm across. The obverse is enamelled on a sterling gilt frame, and a single gold Maple Leaf is located in its centre, surrounded by the motto of the order and surmounted by a St Edward's Crown. The reverse displays the word CANADA in raised letters with a three-digit number impressed below and silver hallmarks on the lower arm.

The Member's insignia is worn on the breast and measures 35 mm across. It is fashioned from sterling. The obverse is enamelled, with a silver Maple Leaf in the centre, surrounded by the motto of the order and surmounted by a St Edward's Crown. The reverse is identical to that of the Officer's insignia.

The practice of differentiating between the varying levels of an order by using different-sized insignia and different places of wear is rooted deep in the history of honours. The tradition of those holding the two most senior levels of an order wearing their insignia from the neck, whereas recipients of the third level wear theirs on the breast, comes from both France and Great Britain. The Kingdom of France's Ordre royal et militaire de Saint-Louis, which had three levels, was bestowed on many Canadians before the fall of New France. Recipients of the two most senior levels wore part of their insignia around the neck; those made Chevaliers of the order (the most junior level) wore their insignia on the breast. Until 1917, this system was also employed by the British with the Order of the Bath and Order of St Michael and St George.

When presented with the designs for the enlarged Order of Canada, the Chancellor, Ronald Michener, was 'apprehensive that we have not incorporated enough difference between the three levels.'[47] He suggested that different ribbons be employed to remedy this problem. Companions would continue to wear a ribbon of ¼ red, ½ white, ¼ red. He also suggested that Officers use a similar ribbon with a single thin red stripe in the centre, and that Members use the same ribbon again with two red stripes in the centre. These alterations were shelved in favour of retaining the same ribbon for all three levels. This was the practice employed by other national orders. There was no great desire to increase the differentiation between Companions, Officers, and Members. Recipients had all rendered conspicuous service, be it at the local, national, or international level, and emphasizing their various grades beyond the existing changes was not seen as desirable.

With the new insignia came increased costs. All of the order's insignia continued to be made by Garrard's of London. The Companion's insignia, made of 18 carat gold, remained unchanged, which meant so did the cost per unit ($652). The Officers' and Members' insignia were now enamelled, so both cost more to make. Officers now cost $90 each, Members $80 each.[49] This was only part of the more than $300,000 in new expenditures required to restructure the Order of Canada and to establish the new bravery awards and Order of Military Merit.

The Lapel Badge

The practice of wearing a lapel badge or rosette began with France's *Légion d'honneur*. Recipients wore a small swatch of the ribbon or rosette of the order on their lapel. These were typically about one-sixth the size of the actual insignia. When the United States founded its Legion of Merit, provision was made for wearing a miniature version of the badge. Thus Canada was adopting a blend of French and American traditions.

This idea was suggested by Conrad Swan of the College of Arms in London. In September 1966, Swan discussed the matter with Pearson, who found it to be 'highly appropriate and likely to make the Order very acceptable and particularly with French-speaking Canadians.'[50] There was the additional advantage that if recipients regularly wore their lapel badges, members of the general public would learn to recognize the order and its eminent recipients. John Hodgson concurred with all of this, and it was largely at his insistence that the lapel pins were included as part of the order.

Companions were to receive a small version of the insignia with a red Maple Leaf in the centre as their lapel insignia. Recipients of the Medal of Courage were to receive a small gold Maple Leaf lapel pin; those awarded the Medal of Service were to receive a small silver Maple Leaf pin. The exact details were worked out during a special meeting with the Governor General on 23 August 1967. The precise design was then developed by Beatty.[51]

Although sanctioned in 1967, the lapel badges for recipients of the Order of Canada were not manufactured and distributed until after the Order was restructured in 1972.[52] The reason for the long delay was quite simply that the Secretariat of the Order of Canada was too busy dealing with nominations and appointments to be bothered with organizing the logistics of manufacturing and distributing a lapel pin. All recipients of the order now receive a lapel pin shaped like a small snowflake. The various levels are differentiated by the colour of the Maple Leaf: red for Companion, gold for Officer, and silver for Member.

At the time of the order's tenth anniversary, an attempt was made to change the design of the lapel badge, which is possibly the most widely recognized symbol of the Order. Although he always took a sincere interest in the order, Jules Léger was never terribly keen on the insignia. He rarely wore the Chancellor's Chain, and he disliked the lapel badge, which he termed the 'button.'[53] The Governor General hoped to see the lapel badge replaced with a small swatch of ribbon, of the type often used by recipients of France's *Légion d'honneur*. The Advisory Council decided that the lapel badge should be retained, however, as it was more Canadian and was widely recognized: 'We feel that any change at this time might create confusion'[54]

The Sovereign's Insignia and Chancellor's Chain of Office

Generally, the senior officials of an order receive special insignia. Neither the Secretary General nor the Registrar of the Order of Canada received an insignia of office. However, the Queen did as Sovereign of the Order, and so did the Governor General as Chancellor; each now wears a distinctive insignia of office. In the Canadian context, this idea originated with Major General Colquhoun of Britain's Central Chancery of the Order of Knighthood. Colquhoun also suggested to Butler that there be a special insignia for the Secretary of the order. Butler, who was inundated with other important tasks, wrote beside this suggestion: 'Not now anyway!'[55] The prime minister agreed that this was not of immediate importance, so the idea was shelved temporarily. Similarly, the matter of commissioning a special insignia for the Queen was not addressed until 1970.

Once the insignia for the Companions and for recipients of the Medal of Courage and the Medal of Service had been designed, the most immediate physical requirements for the order had been discharged. The Sovereign's insignia and Chancellor's Chain were also designed by Beatty. The Chancellor's Chain was made by the Royal Canadian Mint. Marvin Cook and Argo Aarand made the various parts of the chain from gold, and Aarand enamelled them in a small kiln, which he had in the basement of his home. The chain is made of twenty-three devices linked together by a double-row of small gold links. Twelve of these devices are miniature replicas of the white snowflake. Alternating with these are ten devices, each in the form of a red Maple Leaf on a while background encircled by the red annulet bearing the motto of the order. The chain is completed by a centre device in the form of the shield from the Arms of Canada ensigned by the Royal Crown, each in its proper colours. A Companion's insignia is hung from this device.[56] The chain was presented to Governor General Michener by E.F. Brown, the Acting Master of the Royal Canadian Mint, on

22 December 1968. This part of the project had taken nearly nine months, during which Aarand and Cook spent their lunch hours working on the chain.[57]

The general design for the Sovereign's Badge of the order had been decided upon by August 1967. It was to be 'a reduced version of the white snowflake with a crown to be placed above the snowflake, possibly with full-size jewels and hinged to the snowflake. The entire insignia will be mounted on a ribbon tied in a bow with the crown in the centre of the bow.'[58] By 1970, Beatty had designed a Sovereign's Badge: an 18 carat gold snowflake enamelled white with a large square diamond set between each of the arms. In the centre is a Maple Leaf surrounded by an annulus, both set with calibre-rubies pavé. On the annulus is the motto in pierced gold. Above the cross is a gold St Edward's Crown with the cap of maintenance enamelled red and the ermine enamelled white. The arches are set with twenty-one diamonds, with a larger one in the orb. The base is set with a sapphire, two emeralds, and two rubies. The Sovereign's Badge was manufactured by William Summers of Garrard & Company, the Crown Jewellers. Governor General and Mrs Michener were visiting Britain to attend the Tercentenary of the Hudson's Bay Company. On 23 June 1970, after lunch with the Queen at Buckingham Palace, Michener presented his host with the Sovereign's Badge of the Order of Canada. The Queen is said to have been most impressed with the design and delighted to receive the insignia.

Post-Nominal Initials

All British orders and decorations carry with them post-nominal initials. Since the time of Confederation, use of these post-nominals has become firmly fixed in the Canadian honours landscape, to some degree even more so than in Britain. A prime example of this is that members of the Queen's Privy Council for Canada use the post-nominal initials PC, whereas their British counterparts usually do not. These letters are seen less as status symbols than as symbols of office and as an important part of the Canadian state. The most universally recognized post-nominal remains VC, for the Victoria Cross. This award – and its post-nominals – take precedence over all others.

It was only natural that the Order of Canada would carry with it post-nominal initials. The Canada Medal was intended to allow the recipient to use either CM or M du C, depending on the linguistic preference of the individual. After the Order of Canada was adjusted to consist of three levels – Companion, Officer, Member – the post-nominals were going to be CC, OC, and Mem.C.[59] All three were easily translated into both official languages. It may seem odd that the designation MC was not accorded to the Member level, but those letters were already in use by recipients of the Military Cross. COC, OOC, and MOC, were considered as possible alternatives; however, they were thought to be too long. The last thing the government wanted was confusion among awards because of overlap. This problem would arise, but not until after the order's founding.

When Cabinet agreed to the founding of the Order of Canada with three levels – consisting of the Companions of the Order, Medal of Courage, and Medal of Service – the post-nominals were set as CC (for Companions), CM (for holders of the Medal of

Courage), and SM (for holders of the Medal of Service).[60] MS was unacceptable for the Medal of Service because it was already being used in the medical community to designate Master of Surgery. It was no easy task to devise new post-nominals that would not be confused with existing awards, degrees, or qualifications. This was especially true in the case of the Companions; it was soon discovered that the designation CC was already in use.

In terms of precedence, it was decided that holders of the Victoria Cross and George Cross would continue to take precedence over all others. Members of the Privy Council would rank next, just as they do in other parts of the Commonwealth; they would be followed by Companions of the Order of Canada. Hodgson gave this reason for the decision: 'I believe the CC, should have about the same seniority as the British Knighthoods ... In the UK all of these awards follow after "Privy Council-lors."'[61] The problem of where to rank the CC in relation to the Victoria Cross and privy councillorships was very real, as one prospective recipient, Major General George Pearkes, Lieutenant-Governor of British Columbia, held both distinctions. The Medal of Courage and Medal of Service were to take precedence over other decorations.

Three days after Pearson announced to Parliament the creation of the Order of Canada, Conservative MP Richard A. Bell received a letter from the Ontario Institute of Chartered Cartographers. A past president of the institute, L.M. Baker, pointed out that 'the Ontario Institute of Chartered Cartographers was granted its charter on December 9, 1959 under Ontario Provincial enactment and to its general members the right to use the letters CC, after their names.'[62] By 1967 more than 130 Canadian cartographers were using the letters CC after their name. This was a recipe for confusion between cartographers and Companions. Bell did the gentlemanly thing; instead of bringing the subject up in Parliament, he simply wrote a letter to the prime minister asking his office to clarify the situation with regard to the institute. Pearson set Hodgson to work on devising a solution; the question was in turn referred to Edith MacDonald in the justice department. It was MacDonald who had drafted both the order-in-council and the Constitution of the Order of Canada. Now she examined the Letters Patent founding the Ontario Institute of Chartered Cartographers and found that 'there is nothing in the Letters Patent that give to members of the cartographers' profession the right either to exclusive or limited use of the letters CC. Use of those letters is not referred to in the Letters Patent.' Thus, there was no legal impediment to Companions of the Order of Canada using the post-nominal initials CC. MacDonald went so far as to ask the Registrar of Trade Marks to protect the insignia and initials of the Order of Canada under Section 9(1)(n) of the Trade Marks Act, which protects Royal and Vice Regal Arms and flags as well as the arms, the crest, and the flag of Canada. The registrar 'declined to accept notice.'[63]

MacDonald's report was examined by Butler and Hodgson; however, the final decision was made by the Governor General. Michener felt that 'a letter should go to the cartographers saying that we are sorry that there is a conflict in the usage of these letters, and pointing out the reasons why it is impossible for the Order to make any change, because of the necessity of having letters which are equally satisfactory in English and in French.'[64] The general tone of this letter was apologetic. It pointed out that there would be no cost involved for the institute to make a change. The government expressed the hope that the institute would choose an alternative to avoid confusion. Legally, the Order of Canada was perfectly within its rights, since the institute's authority for using the letters CC was derived from its own by-laws, not their Letters Patent.[65] In due course, the Institute relented and ceased to use CC as its professional designation. One distinguished Companion would later comment that CC 'does sound like something out of chemistry!'[66]

When the order was restructured in 1972, the post-nominal initials had to change. There was little debate about what designation the two new awards should be given. Companions retained the post-nominals CC, the new level of Officer was given the designation OC, and Members were given CM.[67] CM was the original designation given to the Medal of Courage; however, since none had ever been awarded, there was no risk of confusion. It is also worth noting that CM was originally intended to be the post-nominal initials accorded to the defunct Canada Medal instituted in 1943.

Manufacture of the Order

Unfortunately, in 1967 there was no Canadian jeweller or firm capable of manufacturing the insignia for the Order of Canada. This was mainly because the enamelling process required for the Companion's insignia was so complex, and because so many insignia were required so quickly. Initially the London firm of Spink & Son was consulted. Spink's had played a significant role in selecting an appropriate ribbon – and preventing the King of Jordan from using the same – and also in persuading the government to discard the Canada Medal. E.C. Joslin of Spink's had commented that the Canada Medal was 'dated and ugly.'[68] This was a harsh assessment, although there were other reasons why the Officer and Member levels of the Order of Canada could not simply be silver and bronze versions of the Canada Medal. Orders were typically somewhat ornate and enamelled, not simple circular medals. Besides wanting to maintain some continuity with other existing orders, Joslin likely had another motive. The revised Canada Medal would have been struck by the Royal Canadian Mint; a more ornate Order of Canada insignia would have to be made by an outside firm – possibly Spink's.

In fact, Spink & Son were initially chosen to manufacture the insignia for the Order of Canada. Matheson had visited the firm in July 1966 and was certain that 'this is the best firm on which to rely for advice.'[69] Indeed, the Canadian government did follow much of Spink's advice. Until Pearson's visit with various representatives from Spink's – including D.F. Spink and E.C. Joslin – the firm had the complete confidence of the Canadian government. After its 16 September meeting, however, it lost this. Spink's was proposing that the Order of Canada consist of five levels and be modelled on the Order of the British Empire, with military and civilian divisions. The firm had at first supported the three-level system – Companion, Officer, Member – as proposed by Matheson, but it had discarded this by September. This greatly discouraged Pearson, who sought out an alternative.

The alternative was suggested by Major General C.H. Colquhoun, Secretary of the Central Chancery of the Orders of Knighthood, London. Colquhoun was responsible for administering the various British orders of chivalry and was well acquainted with most questions relating to honours. With a few exceptions,[70] all of the British orders of chivalry were manufactured by the Crown Jewellers, Garrard & Company of Regent Street, London. Garrard's was a well-established firm and was famous for the quality of its work. It was considered Britain's premier jeweller and had long been entrusted with maintaining the Crown Jewels. The prime minister was placed in contact with W.H. Summers, the Crown Jeweller himself. Summers assured Pearson that Garrard's could easily handle the contract provided some notice was given.

Garrard's received the diagrams of the Order of Canada in early January 1967, along with a request for an estimate on the cost of fifty Companion insignia.[71] Initially the government enquired about making the insignia out of silver gilt (gold-plated silver). Summers was somewhat appalled at this suggestion: 'In our experience the most Senior award in each country is invariably made in high quality gold ... 22 and 18 carat gold.'[72] As if to engage the Canadian government in a contest of one-upmanship, Summers also pointed out that 'we supply one Order for The Kingdom of Jordan in 18 carat gold and diamonds and two Orders for The Government of Malaysia in 18 carat old, one of which is also set with diamonds.'[73] He then offered the following quote:

> To supply 50 enamel insignias of The Order of Canada, the band of the crown set with precious stones, each insignia numbered on the reverse, all complete in a silk neck ribbon in a leather covered case stamped C.C. lined with silk and velvet.
>   Companions Insignias in Silver Gilt   £105 each
>   Companions Insignias in 14 carat gold   £180 each
>   Companions Insignias in 18 carat gold   £200 each

There was the practical consideration that 18 carat gold provided a much more beautiful finish when contrasted with the white and red enamel of the order. And such a high quality of gold would never tarnish, unlike silver gilt. To someone seeking a bargain, the silver gilt Companion's insignia at half the price of one fashioned of 18 carat gold would have seemed the best deal. But Pearson was not out to cut corners. He directed Butler to arrange for the Companion's insignia to be made of 18 carat gold,[74] with this comment: 'If it looks like gold then it should be gold!'[75] After all, the Order of Canada was Canada's highest award for merit and achievement and of great symbolic importance. On 16 February an order was placed with Garrard's for fifty insignias in 1967 and fifty more in each 1968 and 1969. Summers promised that a sample insignia would be sent to Government House for approval in early May 1966.

Throughout the 1970s and 1980s the price of gold soared, until by 1982 each Companion's insignia cost $6,000.[76] Butler suggested to the prime minister that in future the insignia be made of 14 carat gold to help reduce the cost per unit.[77] Permission was subsequently secured from the prime minister to change the gold content, but this change was never made. Garrard's would continue to manufacture the insignia of the Order of Canada until 1982, when the contract was transferred to a Canadian firm.[78]

Since 1967 the Canadian government had been looking for a Canadian supplier to make the Order of Canada. On several occasions the Royal Canadian Mint tried, but it was not equipped to do the highly complex enamellings. The manufacture of all

Canadian decorations – the Order of Canada, the Order of Military Merit, and the three bravery decorations – was finally brought home in 1982, when the firm Rideau Ltée of St-Laurent, Quebec, began producing the insignia. The Chancellery changed firms again in April 1996 when the current manufacturer, Henry Birks & Son, began producing the insignia.[79] As of November 2004, Rideau Ltée resumed manufacturing the order. The cost of each insignia today – made of sterling silver – ranges from $1,400 for a Companion to $550 for an Officer and $500 for a Member. The Companion insignia continued to be made in 18 carat gold until 1993, when this was changed to gold-plated silver on account of cost.

The cost of manufacturing the Order of Canada has fluctuated with the cost of gold and silver. At the same time, the insignia has acquired a value among collectors of Canadian orders and decorations. Section 26 of the order's constitution states that the insignia is property of the Crown and that on the death of a recipient, it should be returned to the Chancellery. The first public sale of an insignia occurred in May 1981. This caught the attention of parliamentarians, and a motion was subsequently passed: 'That this House deplore the sale of the Order of Canada which was given to the late M.J. Coldwell by the Governor General in recognition of his contributions to Canada, and as such, should not be used for financial gain.'[80] Besides Coldwell's Companion's insignia, Officers' and Members' insignia have also been sold.[81]

The order's constitution prohibits the sale of the insignia, but the Chancellery found this rule virtually impossible to enforce. The Chancellery has since sent a letter to the main Canadian decorations vendors warning them that 'the Chancellery and the Justice Department have agreed that insignia may legitimately come on the market via the estate of a deceased member of an Order (of Canada or Military Merit), but that stolen insignia or insignia sold by the recipient will be confiscated and returned to the Crown.'[82] Families of the recipients are today allowed to retain the insignia; however, recipients are still prohibited (in theory) from selling their insignia. About eight pieces come onto the collectors' market each year.

Certificates and Seal of the Order

The certificates and seal of the Order of Canada were also designed by Bruce Beatty, and were prepared in time for the November 1967 investiture. All certificates depict the Companion's insignia at the top; this is followed by the relevant greeting and information about being made a member of the order. The seal is the same shape as the insignia, with each arm of the snowflake being filled by an element from the shield of the Canadian Coat of Arms.[83] In his letter petitioning the Queen for approval of the seal, Butler boasted that it was 'both attractive and heraldically correct.'[84] Each certificate is signed by the Chancellor and the Secretary General of the order. The seal is impressed in the lower left corner of each certificate.

Officials of the Order

Only four types of officials are designated in the constitution of the order: the Sovereign, the Chancellor (who is also the Governor General), the Secretary General of the order (who is also the Secretary to the Governor General), and members of the

Advisory Council of the order. In other orders, it has been customary to have many officials, including a Grand Master, a Prelate, a Registrar, a King of Arms, and a Gentlemen Usher. The term Grand Master was rejected because it sounded too formal. Similarly, the non-religious nature of the order meant that no Prelate would be appointed. The other positions were also seen as unnecessary vestiges of European hierarchy and not included.[85] A Secretariat was established in May 1967, immediately after it was announced that the order would be created. In terms of official positions, a Registrar and Secretary were added shortly after the Secretariat was founded. In its early years, the order was essentially run by fewer than five people. Administration was left entirely with the Secretary General of the Order, who was for the first eighteen years the ever capable Esmond Butler. As the order grew, so did Butler's staff. Not until 21 August 1967 was a member of the Government House staff employed solely to administer the Order of Canada.[86]

When the Canadian honours system expanded in 1972 with the addition of the Order of Military Merit and the three bravery decorations, a Director of Honours was appointed to oversee the entire system. Like the positions of Secretary General and Registrar, the Director of Honours continues to be an important administrative post in the Canadian honours system.

The Paperweight

Each member of the Advisory Council and official of the order receives a special token of thanks for service rendered. A 'cameo replica of the Order's Seal'[87] – or what has affectionately become known as the 'paperweight' – is presented to members of the Advisory Council after their first meeting, and to officials after one year's service. Made of tombac (copper and zinc), the paperweight is two-and-three-quarter inches in diameter and half an inch thick and is engraved with the name of the recipient. On special occasions, it has also been presented to other people who have rendered exemplary service to the order. When most of the returned Medals of Service were melted down in 1984, the silver was made into two paperweights. One was given to Esmond Butler, and other to Roger Nantel.

Heraldry and the Order

Heraldry and the Order of Canada have been intertwined since the order's creation. Indeed, heraldry is a form of honour much more ancient than the order, although the two have come to be closely associated. John Matheson, one of the key architects of the order, was a noted student of heraldry; so was Bruce Beatty, who designed the insignia. This keen sense of heraldic propriety helped create a well-balanced symbol.

In heraldry it has been the tradition for holders of senior honours to have the insignia of their awards depicted with their arms; this has been the case in most European heraldic traditions.[88] Appropriately, Roland Michener, the first Chancellor and Principal Companion of the Order was also the first person to have the insignia of the order shown with the arms. By Letters Patent dated 10 June 1968, armorial bearings were granted to Michener. Hanging from the shield illustrated on his grant was the insignia of the Order of Canada in dexter and the insignia of the Order of St John of Jerusalem in sinister.

Because Canada was without its own heraldic institution until 1988, the responsibility fell to the College of Arms in London and the Court of the Lord Lyon in Scotland. In 1974 the College of Arms asked the Canadian government if the insignia of the order could be displayed with the arms of any person appointed to the order. This has been the tradition with the various British orders of chivalry. The motto of the most senior order held by an individual would be marshalled (that is, placed) around the shield of the person's arms. The College suggested that for Companions and Officers, the motto be placed around the shield, with a depiction of the particular insignia of the order being suspended from the shield of the armorial ensigns. Members were to be entitled to suspend the insignia from their shield.[89] The College of Arms had thus accepted that the levels of Companion and Officer were equivalent in rank to a knighthood. After the Governor General, the first person to have the insignia incorporated with his arms was Gustave Gingras in 1974. Although he was a Companion of the Order, Gingras's grant did not include the motto of the order. Not until after the Canadian Heraldic Authority was created was the motto shown with the arms.

With the creation of the Canadian Heraldic Authority in 1988, the last element of the Royal Prerogative was patriated. One of the authority's early decisions was to allow all holders of the Order of Canada to use the motto around their shield; this was in recognition of the significance of all recipients of the order, regardless of their level of membership. The Royal Arms of Canada (Canadian Arms) were surrounded by the motto of the Order of Canada on the very first grant made by the Canadian Heraldic Authority. Appropriately, this grant was to Jeanne Sauvé on 7 March 1989.[90] Another early viceregal grant of arms to include the insignia of the Order of Canada was made to David See Chai-Lam, Lieutenant-Governor of British Columbia.[91] On the grant to Bishop's College School, the Sovereign's insignia of the order was depicted below the Royal Arms of Canada. This is the only instance where the Sovereign's badge has been incorporated into a grant.

Beginning in the late 1970s and continuing well into the 1980s, various proposals were made to include the motto circlet of the order in the Royal Arms. Members of the Heraldry Society of Canada – most notably John Williamson, Terry Manuel, and Bruce Hicks – approached various government authorities to encourage the addition of the motto. In particular, Hicks repeatedly lobbied a number of government figures; as the twenty-fifth anniversary of the order approached, he petitioned the Advisory Committee of the Order of Canada to gain support for the change.[92]

The gradual incorporation of the motto circlet into the nation's symbolism was further enhanced when, during the 125th anniversary of Confederation, two stained-glass windows were unveiled at Government House. Both were designed by Christopher Wallis. One depicts the Royal Arms of Canada, with the shield surrounded by the motto. The commemorative medal issued for Canada 125 also depicted the shield from the Canadian coat of arms, surrounded by the ribbon and motto of the order.[93] The augmented arms were drawn by Cathy Bursey-Sabourin, Fraser Herald. The addition of the motto circlet of the Order of Canada to the Royal Arms as used by the Canadian government was approved formally by the Queen on 12 July 1994.

This change to the Royal Arms of Canada went largely unnoticed until MPs remarked that the Coat of Arms printed on reports and some letterhead looked slightly different from what they were accustomed to. Members were long familiar with the Royal Arms from 1957 (which had in turn replaced a depiction created in 1923); the new arms looked slightly different. These hitherto unnoticed changes precipitated sharp debate in Parliament. Many members of the Official Opposition (the Reform Party) expressed concern that the motto and ribbon of the Order of Canada had been added to the Royal Arms without proper public debate. Deborah Grey commented: 'These symbols do not belong to the Liberal government; they belong to the people of the country. If this is real [the augmentation to the Royal Arms] why has Parliament not even discussed it?'[94] The debate was awash with confusion regarding what the actual change was and how arms are augmented in Canada. Many MPs failed to grasp the concept that augmentation to the Royal Arms of Canada was part of the Royal Prerogative and that in Canadian history such armorial augmentations had never been discussed in Parliament. The change to the arms was quite simple: the addition of a motto circlet around the shield of the Royal Arms of Canada. This was a relatively small change, and nothing had been removed or defaced, yet this did not impede further debate. One MP commented: 'Why is the government now sneaking through these changes to the Canadian Coat of Arms and why is it changing the fundamental symbols of the country at a time when we are trying to keep it tied together?'[95]

This sudden interest in heraldry was mainly a function of partisan politics. Opposition MPs did not really care that much about changes to the Royal Arms of Canada. Similarly, the government's answers to questions about the augmentations were dismissive and uninformed.[96] As a result, an otherwise simple change inspired a parliamentary circus. The debate subsided after the Christmas break; since then, the augmented Royal Arms have gradually replaced the version that came into use in 1957.[97]

Included in the 1994 constitution of the order was the addition of a section titled 'Designations, Insignia and Armorial Bearings.' For the first time, heraldry had been incorporated into the governing document of the order. All members were permitted to 'surround their shield of arms with the motto circlet of the order and suspend there from the ribbon and badge of their rank.'[98] In addition, Companions were granted the dignity of being able to have their arms granted with supporters.

The Investiture Ceremony

Little consideration was given to the ceremonial side of the order. Most other national orders involve a great state occasion during which the newly appointed are inducted. At one time, Britain's Order of the Bath included a ceremony where the Sovereign bathed the man being invested.[99] The Canadian government realized that the order would be under close scrutiny, and thus it was suggested that 'the Investiture Ritual should be simple, beautiful and inspirational.'[100] It was also suggested that Dr Healey Willan be commissioned to write music for the ceremony, although this proposal was never acted on. The Royal Anthem and National Anthem were seen as sufficient music for the ceremony.

Vincent Massey had proposed that recipients of the highest level of the order receive a mantle similar to academic robes. This mantle would be worn on important occasions, such as the opening of Parliament. Massey proposed that these robes be made of 'scarlet satin, lined with white silk, fastened with a cordon of white silk, on the left side of which shall be embroidered the Insignia of the Order.'[101] Matheson agreed with this idea and included a similar-style mantle in his early notes. The concept of a mantle was quickly discarded in April 1966, however, when Pitfield insisted that the order be distinctly Canadian and not a mere copy of the British orders of chivalry.[102] The mantle idea did not completely die; Matheson suggested that the Chancellor of the Order – the Governor General – wear a mantle during the investiture ceremonies. This idea, too, was rejected. The Chancellor did eventually receive a Chain of Office.

It was suggested that a sword be forged for Her Majesty to present to the order, and that a banner be commissioned. Neither of these suggestions was acted on; Butler was focusing on other matters. In the end, a Sovereign's Insignia and Chancellor's Chain of Office were commissioned, but no music, banner, or sword.[103] The Advisory Council felt that the new order 'should not depend on procedures and ceremonial associated with the granting of honours in other countries, and that we should make every effort to establish a format which is dignified and simple.'[104] Thus, the first investiture ceremony was quite simple. It took place in the ballroom at Government House. The name of each recipient was announced, followed by the level of award. For example: 'The Right Honourable Louis St Laurent, to be a Companion of the Order of Canada.' The Governor General then simply invested each recipient with the insignia of the order and said a few brief personal words to them. The recipient then walked over to a table and signed the register. Investitures are usually followed by a buffet or banquet.

The investiture ceremony has remained largely unchanged since 1967. Since 1972 the citation that accompanies each appointment to the Order of Canada has been read aloud, and the recipient is then invested with the insignia. In 1973 the Queen invested fifteen people, including Jules Léger, the future Governor General.[105] Ceremonies are typically held in the ballroom at Government House or at La Citadel in Quebec. While Governor General, Jeanne Sauvé held a number of investitures on Parliament Hill in the Senate Chamber.[106] In extraordinary cases the Governor General will travel to the bedside of a recipient; or, if the distance is too great, a lieutenant-governor will be delegated to carry out the investiture.[107] The first bedside investiture took place in November 1969, when Roland Michener travelled to Toronto to invest Sir Ernest MacMillan – the noted Canadian composer – as a Companion of the Order.[108] MacMillan's health was failing and it would have been impossible for him to attend an investiture in Ottawa. Thus one of Canada's greatest musical sons was invested with the insignia in his own house.[109]

Most people appointed to the order are invested with the insignia six months to a year after their award is listed in the *Canada Gazette*. There have been times, however, when the investiture has been delayed for a considerable period. The order is never mailed to a recipient, who is required to attend an investiture or make special arrangements to receive the honour. The record for longest period of time between announcement and investiture belongs to the Honourable W. Bruce Hutchinson, OC, who was awarded the Medal of Service of the Order of Canada in July 1967 but was not invested with the award until 23 April 1990. Professional hockey players seem to have great difficulty finding the time to attend an investiture. Wayne Gretzky waited fourteen years before picking up his OC. Similarly, Phil Esposito was appointed to the Order in 1972, and Bobby Clarke was appointed in 1981, yet neither has yet been invested with his insignia. This problem rarely arises. In 1993, the Advisory Council decided that appointees would not be able to use the post-nominal initials until after their investiture.[110]

Booklets and Publications

Information pamphlets about the order have been a fixture since its creation. The first booklet was completed in May 1967 and sent to members of Parliament, Senators, Canadian Forces Bases, public libraries, and a wide variety of civic-minded organizations. Eighteen pages in length, it included the Statues of the Order, pictures of each of the insignia, and information about the nomination process. This booklet was used until 1972, when the order was restructured. After the reorganization a new booklet, also eighteen pages in length, was printed, and this remained in use until 1977.

The decennial anniversary of the order brought an entirely new booklet, lavishly illustrated, with colour photos of the insignia and containing a brief section on the broader Canadian honours system as well as the constitution of the order.

As a cost-cutting measure, the full-colour booklet was replaced in 1996 by an eleven-page black-and-white pamphlet containing the Statutes of the Order, along with photos of the insignia. A modified version of this pamphlet remains in use.

In terms of studies of the order, relatively little has been written. In 1974, Carl Lochnan, the Director of Honours, began writing a history of honours in Canada. A rough manuscript was completed by 1977, but it was never published. To commemorate the tenth anniversary of the order, the one-thousandth recipient, Maxwell Cohen, wrote a short piece titled 'A Round Table from Sea to Sea.'

The first major publication about the order came in 1991 with the release of *The Register of Canadian Honours*, published by the Canadian Almanac and Directory. It included a very brief section on the history of honours in Canada and focused primarily on listing the recipients of the Order of Canada, Order of Military Merit, and various bravery decorations. Although the original plan had been to publish an update of the register every five years, the project has fallen dormant.

The 125th anniversary of Confederation brought another publication. This one, *125 Companions of the Order of Canada*, contained 125 photos by Harry Palmer. The book was funded as part of the Canada 125 anniversary celebrations.

In 1973, a booklet was published that contained the constitution and the names of all living members of the order. This publication was sent to public institutions and members of the order and was updated annually. Like the full-colour booklet, this publication ceased in the mid-1990s on account of its cost. Today the names and citations of those who have received the order can be found on the Internet at www.gg.ca.

CHAPTER TEN

Unity and Diversity: The Composition of the Order of Canada

I have telegraphed separately to convey the Queen's confirmation of the lists of the Order of Canada. She was glad to find a great many familiar names on them as well as some imaginative new ones.[1]

Sir Michael Adeane to Roland Michener, 12 November 1970

Lester Pearson intended the Order of Canada not only to recognize worthy citizens, but also to bolster the cause of national unity. This unity could only be achieved if people from all regions of the country and all disciplines were recognized equally. Government officials have long claimed that the order is representative of 'Canada's diversity and strengths.'[2] It is easy to look at the list of the more than four thousand Canadians who have received the honour and choose specific examples of out-standing service in a wide variety of fields. A more accurate statistical survey of the order is necessary to discern exactly the kinds of people and activities the state is honouring.

If one chord resounded in the 1918 Nickle debates, it was that there was something dangerously elitist about honours and titles. Speaker after speaker drew a sharp contrast between the pioneer egalitarianism that once supposedly lay at the heart of Canadian values and the degenerate and parasitical growth of a British-style caste system, with its exclusiveness and prejudices. Canada should be – and at its best was – a land of equal opportunity where people of ambition could achieve social standing. Honours and titles came from a land of class privilege and discrimination, one in which social place was dictated by ancestry. A group portrait of men of high principle who refused honours was painted during the 1918 debates. Alexander Mackenzie and Edward Blake in Canada and William Gladstone in England had all rejected tawdry titles for cleaner, more genuinely 'honourable' political lives. Why did such paragons of liberalism reject honours? Because, said the radical critics, each one would 'sooner go down fighting for what he thought to be right than what he thought to be wrong.'[3] Thus there existed a perception that honours were awarded only to the rich and well positioned, and not to the deserving and truly 'honourable.' This debate crystallized Canadians' suspicion about honours to such a degree that British honours in Canada under the Imperial honours system came to an effective end in 1918. Any system that replaced British honours in Canada would have to be free of the stereotypes and inequalities exemplified, for many Canadians, by the British Imperial honours system. From this debate grew the idea that a Canadian honours system would have to be more equally distributed throughout the country, by region and type of contribution. Canadian honours could not simply be parcelled out to Montreal businessmen and Toronto politicians.

The non-partisan and patronage-free nomination/appointment system has allowed for groups not traditionally honoured to be recognized. This system was developed in part to prevent the excesses of the British Imperial honours system. Although military awards were fairly distributed, the dispersal of civil awards was far from egalitarian. From 1867 to 1918 and from 1932 to 1935, 226 knighthoods were awarded to 201 Canadians.[4] The focus was on male politicians and businessmen, most of whom lived in Montreal, Toronto, or Ottawa. In terms of high awards such as knighthoods in the various British orders of chivalry, between 1867 and 1935, 45 per cent of such awards went to members of the Conservative Party and 19 per cent to members of the Liberal Party. With regard to regions, 36 per cent of knighthoods were awarded to residents of Quebec, and 41 per cent to Ontarians; there was certainly no equality among the provinces. In terms of occupations, politicians were more than twice as likely to be awarded a knighthood. There was little recognition of achievements in education, philanthropy, or the arts. An aspiring knight was best advised to join the Conservative Party, enter federal politics, and reside in Ontario.

It is worthwhile to compare those recognized under the British Imperial honours system with those recognized under the Canadian honours system. Canadians are largely unaware of the difference between a Companion and a Member of the Order of Canada. Citizens are appointed as Companions in recognition of a lifetime of service at the national level. So it is reasonable to compare this level with the knighthoods awarded to Canadians from Confederation until the early part of the twentieth century. Such high awards were usually given for service at the national level, although partisan considerations played a highly significant role, and certain fields of endeavour, such as volunteerism and sports, went entirely unrecognized.[5]

Until the Order of Canada was established, there was little formal recognition for contributions to religion, social services, voluntary services, communications, or sport. As Table 10.1 demonstrates, the focus of high awards has since shifted from politicians to the arts, public service, science, and health. Retired politicians still receive a fair number of awards, but they no longer predominate. In many ways, these figures reflect the values and contributions that Canadians hold as important.

Distribution

Officially, the Advisory Council of the Order of Canada uses no formal quota system, although it does try to ensure that recognition is accorded to all disciplines in every region of the country. Nevertheless, a pattern of 'unofficial quotas' has developed, whereby each province and territory receives a proportion of awards that is within 3 to 5 per cent of that province's or territory's proportion of the population. The first formal quotas evolved under the Dominion–Commonwealth honours system. During the 1940s, when honours were administered by the Secretary of State, a complex quota system was devised.[6] This system was rigid, and certain departments – whether

Table 10.1
Knights of the British orders and Companions of the Order of Canada

Field	% of total knighthoods, 1867–1935 (N)		% of total Companions, 1967–2003 (N)	
Politics	38.2	(87)	9.0	(38)
Law	20.4	(46)	10.3	(42)
Business/commerce	14.6	(33)	6.1	(25)
Public service	10.2	(23)	16.0	(65)
Protective services	6.7	(15)	1.2	(5)
Engineering/health/science	4.4	(10)	17.5	(71)
Education	2.2	(5)	7.4	(30)
Arts	1.77	(4)	18.7	(76)
Philanthropy	1.33	(3)	2.2	(9)
Other fields	0	(0)	11.0	(45*)
Total		(226)		(406)

*Only 11 of the 25 fields used by the Order of Canada are listed here. Engineering, health, and science have been combined into one field, as this was the practice followed when Canada worked within the British honours system.

they were deserving or not – were allocated a certain number of obligatory awards. Today the council recognizes twenty-five separate fields of endeavour.[7] During the order's first ten years of existence, special attention was also given to ensure equality of distribution among the various linguistic and religious groups. After the decennial review in 1977, this practice was phased out.[8] It was found that appointments to the Order of Canada were already being well distributed between francophones and anglophones and that people from all religious groups were being included as well. The practice of differentiating between urban and rural was also abolished at this time.

Occupation/Fields

For administrative purposes the Chancellery divides appointees into one of twenty-five fields. These range from architecture to volunteerism. The arts, which are divided into five separate categories, comprised more than 15 per cent of the total appointments made between 1967 and 2002. Volunteerism follows closely at 14.5 per cent, and health at 9 per cent.

Region

As the world's second-largest country, Canada has found it a complicated challenge to ensure that all regions are included in the nation's life. In the early years of the order, few nominations were received from Alberta, Manitoba, and Saskatchewan. In response to this, the Advisory Council sought out eminent people from these provinces for nominations. This practice continues to be followed when there is a shortage

Table 10.2
Ranking of fields recognized

Field	% of total awards, 1967–2002 (N)		Rank
Arts/film	0.62	(29) ⎫	
Arts/music	5.4	(251) ⎪	
Arts/stage	3.1	(144) ⎬	1
Arts/visual	3.4	(157) ⎪	
Arts/writing	2.8	(127) ⎭	
Volunteerism	14.5	(670)	2
Health	9	(418)	3
Industry/commerce	8.6	(396)	4
Education	7.5	(346)	5
Public Service	6.2	(286)	6
Science	5.4	(249)	7
Social Services	4.2	(194)	8
Communications	3.9	(182)	9
Sports	3.7	(172)	10
Law	3.6	(168)	11
Politics	2.9	(136)	12
Philanthropy	2.6	(118)	13
Heritage	2.2	(103)	14
Other	2.2	(100)	15
Engineering	1.8	(84)	16
Religion	1.7	(80)	17
Social Science	1.2	(55)	18
Protective Services	1.0	(48)	19
Labour	0.8	(36)	20
Architecture	0.61	(28)	21
Aviation	0.5	(26)	22
Environment	0.2	(8)	23

of nominations from certain professions or regions. Within a few percentage points, the ratio between appointment and population is very close. In the overall totals of living members of the order, Alberta and Ontario are the most significantly underrepresented.

It is when we compare figures for recipients of the most senior level of the order (Companion) to the population of each province that we see a trend more reflective of the distribution of knighthoods awarded to Canadians between 1867–1918 and 1932–5. Ontario and Quebec are both strongly overrepresented; the West is underrepresented. Part of this uneven distribution of appointments of Companions can be attributed to the fact that most national organizations (including the federal government) are headquartered in Montreal, Ottawa, or Toronto. There is also the reality that although people come from all parts of the nation to serve in the federal government, when they are appointed to the order it is the province that they are resident in at the time of the award (and not birth) that is taken into account for statistical purposes. Thus a Companion such as Gordon Robertson, former Clerk of the Privy Council, who was born and raised in Saskatchewan, is listed under the Ontario section.

Table 10.3
Total living members (Companions, Officers, and Members of the Order of Canada), 2003

Province or territory	% of appointments	% of population (2003)
Alberta	6.8	9.9
British Columbia	11.4	13.0
Manitoba	3.9	3.7
New Brunswick	3.1	2.4
Newfoundland	2.2	1.7
Nova Scotia	3.7	3.0
Ontario	36.8	38.2
Prince Edward Island	1.0	0.45
Québec	26.9	23.8
Saskatchewan	3.4	3.3
Northwest Territories	0.21	0.12
Nunavut	0.21	0.09
Yukon	0.5	0.09

Table 10.4
Companions of the Order, 2003

Province or territory	% of living appointees	% of total appointees (1967–2003)	% of population (2003)
Alberta	0.63	2.3	9.9
British Columbia	7.0	7.9	13.0
Manitoba	3.8	2.3	3.7
New Brunswick	3.8	1.8	2.4
Newfoundland	1.3	1.3	1.7
Nova Scotia	1.3	0.77	3.0
Ontario	48.0	49.5	38.2
Prince Edward Island	0	0.25	0.45
Québec	30.0	31.5	23.8
Saskatchewan	0.63	2.0	3.3
Northwest Territories	0	0.25	0.12
Nunavut	0.63	0	0.09
Yukon	0	0	0.09

The Order's Membership

At the level of Member, we see a closer parity between population and percentage of awards. In many respects the Member level is the most notable in the order, since it is the level that most Canadians are familiar with and the one most often awarded. At this level, every province except Ontario has received a fair percentage of the total awards relative to population.

Overall, then, the statistical distribution of the order reflects Canadian society, except when it comes to gender. Also, it is at the Member level that it most closely reflects Canada's population. Over time, the gender gap will certainly close: in recent years, more and more women have been appointed to the order.

Table 10.5
Members of the Order

Province or territory	% of total appointees (1972–2003)	% of population (2003)
Alberta	7.8	9.9
British Columbia	10.9	13.0
Manitoba	4.8	3.7
New Brunswick	3.7	2.4
Newfoundland	2.9	1.7
Nova Scotia	3.8	3.0
Ontario	33.5	38.2
Prince Edward Island	2.0	0.45
Québec	23.8	23.8
Saskatchewan	4.5	3.3
Northwest Territories	1.0	0.12
Nunavut	0.03	0.09
Yukon	0.8	0.09

Age

Honours typically come after a lifetime of contributions and achievement. The Order of Canada tends to recognize people past middle age; however, young people have not been excluded. The youngest person ever appointed was Anne Ottenbrite, who was made a Member at eighteen after winning a gold medal in swimming at the 1984 Olympic Games. The youngest Companion admitted to the order was Terry Fox, in recognition of his Marathon of Hope to raise funds for cancer research. Fox was made a Companion in September 1980, when he was twenty-two. On the first honours list, the average appointee to the Order of Canada was just over sixty-four; ten years later, the average age had risen to seventy; today, the average age is sixty-one. The person to hold the order for the shortest period of time was John Patrick Savage, former Premier of Nova Scotia. Savage was appointed on 10 May 2003, five days before he died of cancer.

Gender

Attempts to include women more fully in the honours system began with R.B. Bennett's honours lists of 1933 to 1935, when almost half of all non-titular honours were bestowed on Canadian women. After Bennett left office, and throughout the Second World War, women were largely omitted from the honours system.

The Order of Canada was founded at a time when women were beginning to play a greater role in public affairs and entering professions once dominated by men. Yet women comprised only 14 per cent of the first Order of Canada honours list. This number has steadily increased, although it still falls short of the 51 per cent of Canadians who are women.[9] Throughout the early 1970s the Advisory Council struggled to attract more female nominees, and over time the number has increased. In all, 24.5 per cent of appointments since 1967 have been to women. Among national orders, Canada and Australia are leading the way in gender equality. The Order of

Table 10.6
Percentage of living female members of the Order of Canada and the Order of Australia, 2003

Level	Order of Canada (%)	Order of Australia (%)
Companion	27	9
Officer	16	12
Member	33	19
TOTAL	24.5	18

Australia was modelled after the Order of Canada, and in many respects the two countries share similar gender values.

In 1971 the Advisory Council considered establishing a special award for women.[10] This idea was discarded because members of the council felt that such an award would be viewed as inferior to the Order of Canada. At a time when women were fighting for greater equality, it would have been incongruous to create a separate award for them. Few countries have established orders specifically for women and service in the home. Such awards, where they have been established, have tended to be 'stork derbies' rather than means of recognizing women's contributions.[11]

Refusals

Organizations can often be defined on the basis of who would *not* want to be a member. A profile of those who have refused the Order of Canada reveals certain perceptions about both honours and Canada. Few Canadians have refused to accept appointment to the order. Refusals of honours are 'neither common nor unusual, and often motivated by personal factors, whether domestic, religious or ideological.'[12] As of 1997, the percentage of refusals was 1.5 per cent, down from the 3 per cent in the period ending 1976.

The overwhelming reason for declining the order has been modesty. Political ideology has also sometimes influenced a refusal. Very few people have refused simply because they do not believe in honours – which is odd in some ways, given that honours were once so contentious. Of 1,095 appointments offered between 1967 and 1977, 1,064 were accepted. Considering that the order was quite new and in some quarters unknown, this 97 per cent acceptance rate is quite high. The closest comparison with a 'new' order can be made to the Order of the British Empire, which was established in 1917. Between 1917 and 1920 there were around 9,500 awards of the Order of the British Empire, with 761 refusals – a rate of 8 per cent.[13] In the more than eighty years since the establishment of the Order of the British Empire, the refusal rate has dropped to 1.5 per cent.[14]

Unfortunately, the only accurate list of refusals available dates from the period 1967 to 1977. The first refusal came from Claude Ryan, who was offered the Medal of Service in July 1967. Ryan declined the offer because he felt it premature to 'accept such a distinction,'[15] especially since he was contemplating entering politics at the time the offer came. Throughout his public career, he declined a variety of honorary degrees and other distinctions, always for roughly the same reason. Not until after he

Table 10.7
Refusals of the Order of Canada, 1967–76 (n=31)

Reason	Total number	Accepted the Order of Canada	Accepted the Order of Quebec
Modesty/age	14	8	2
Did not agree with honours	6	1	1
Québec nationalist	3	–	1
Wanted a higher honour	3	3	
Did not know what the Order was	2	1	
Other	3	1	

retired from politics did he accept any honours. In 1995, after more than three decades of service to federalism, Ryan was made a Companion. Another prominent refusal came from Glenn Gould. The world-renowned pianist and composer declined appointment as a Companion in 1970 for 'personal reasons,'[16] remarking that he was too young to receive the same award as Sir Ernest MacMillan. Another expression of modesty came from Cecil Meritt, who earned the Victoria Cross during the Second World War. Although he strongly supported the Canadian honours system, he respectfully declined the order on the basis that he had already been given the highest honour he could receive, and there were certainly others more deserving of the order than he. Mordecai Richler refused the Order of Canada twice, but accepted the third time it was offered, in 2000.

There were thirty-one refusals during the order's first ten years of existence. Of these, thirteen accepted the appointment later, when it was offered again.[17]

The most oft-cited reason for refusing the Order of Canada has been modesty. One Olympic athlete felt that she 'should wait until she has accomplished more in her career.'[18] More than half of those who refused for modesty between 1967 to 1977 later accepted. Both Marcel Dubé and Roger Lemelin refused the order under the pretence of modesty but later went on to accept both the Order of Canada and the Ordre national du Québec. Since they accepted both orders, it is unlikely that they initially refused on account of being Quebecers.

Two of the three Quebec nationalists who refused the order did so in a very public manner. Luc-André Godbout turned to the press to vent his frustrations about social conditions and the government of the day.[19] He refused on the basis of being a Quebec nationalist; he did not want to take an award from the Governor General, 'the source of our oppression.'[20] Geneviève Bujold refused in a short letter to *Le Devoir*, which complained of the manner in which the offer of the order was made: via post.[21] Rina Lasnier refused the Order of Canada in 1968 because 'she could not accept the appointment, as she is a French-Canadian citizen.'[22] Lasnier was not philosophically opposed to honours; later, she would become one of the first Quebecers to be made a Grand Officer of the Ordre national du Québec, the most senior level in that order.

Three people refused at first because they felt they deserved a higher level. All three would later accept the order. Joey Smallwood was offered a Companionship in 1973 but refused, demanding that he be knighted. Since the Companion level was the

Table 10.8
Reasons for refusal of the Order of Canada, 1967–1976 (n=31)

Province	Total refusals	Modesty	Did not agree with honours	Québec nationalist	Higher honour	Other*	Later accepted Order of Canada	Later accepted Order of Québec
NF	1				1		1	
NB	1	1					1	
QC	18 (58%)	8	4	4	1	1	8	4
ON	8 (26%)	4	1		1	3	2	
AB	1	1					1	
BC	2		1			1		

*Category includes 'Did not know about Order of Canada.'

highest in existence, this was quite impossible. He finally accepted a Companion in 1986. Morley Callaghan refused the Medal of Service in 1967; he would accept a Companion in 1982. Douglas LePan refused appointment as an Officer in 1974 because he felt that he should be made a Companion. In 1998, LePan accepted his original appointment as an Officer of the Order.

Most refusals emanate from Quebec. That province's profound social and economic transformation has obviously made a difference; so has the marked resistance of some Quebecers to federalism. Many Quebecers distinguished in their own disciplines would not be offered an award. Others would refuse it. On balance, however, it is striking how few Quebecers have refused the award for political reasons. It is interesting that although Quebec has the highest refusal rate, it also has the highest number of refusers who later accepted the Order of Canada. All of those who later accepted the order did so after 1978 – some as recently as 2000. There is a direct correlation between the age of the order and the number of those who refused who later accepted it.

This is related in part to the growing prestige of the order, best demonstrated in the cases of Smallwood and Frank Shuster. Out of the thirty-one refusers only six cited their dislike of honours. Some people have genuinely been misinformed about the order. G.E. Lapalme, a Quebec public servant, refused because he did 'not wish to accept any titles.'[23]

Thus, surprisingly few Canadians refuse the order, especially when compared with the Order of the British Empire, and nearly half of those who initially refused later accepted it. All of this suggests a high level of acceptance for the Canadian honours system. Had most Canadians been emphatically opposed to honours, the refusal rate would have been much higher. Even in the United Kingdom, the refusal rate is nearly three times that of the Order of Canada. The best examples of this willingness to 'try' to get an individual to accept the order have involved Quebec nationalists. It is revealing that Quebecers were awarded 27.3 per cent of the honours between 1967 and 1976 and constituted 58 per cent of the refusals. However, eight of the Quebecers who refused the order later accepted it, thus lowering percentage of refusals to 32 per cent – fairly close to Quebec's share of honours awarded during the first decade.

Promotions

The first elevations occurred in 1972, shortly before the order was restructured. Chester Ronning, Colonel Gustave Gingras, and Clément Cromier had all been awarded the Medal of Service in July 1967. The three men were appointed as Companions on 23 June 1972 – the only recipients of the Order of Canada to be promoted from the Medal of Service to Companion. Moving from Member to Officer or Officer to Companion is not uncommon within the Order of Canada. By convention, the Advisory Council reviews the files of recipients every five years to determine whether promotion is warranted. As of December 2003, 69 Members have been promoted to Officer and 141 Officers to Companion. Only nine people have been appointed to all three levels of the order.[24] An extraordinary case is that of Gretta Chambers, who was appointed a Member in 1994 and then promoted to Companion in April 2000. This promotion was in recognition of her role in the Fourth Global Conference on Aging.

The average promotion from Member to Officer takes eight-and-a-half years; from Officer to Companion takes on average eleven-and-a-half years. The shortest period between promotions is one year. This has occurred with four recipients: Gaétan Boucher, the Olympic speed skater; Ben Heppner, the world-renowned tenor; the noted composer, Victor Bouchard; and François Mercier. Mercier holds the record, having been promoted within eleven months of his initial appointment. The shortest period of time for promotion from Officer to Companion was thirty-five months, for Larkin Kerwin. The longest period of time until a promotion – twenty-seven years – belongs to Doris Anderson. Appointed an Officer in 1974, she was elevated to Companionship in 2002 in recognition of her lifelong service to the cause of women's rights.

Terminations

Like refusals, terminations help us glimpse the 'honour' encapsulated by the honours system. The Order of Canada, like most other national orders, provides for a recipient's membership to be terminated. These terminations are rare even within larger orders. A Knight of the Garter, the oldest honour in the world, can be 'degraded' (that is, have his membership terminated) only if he commits heresy, treason, or cowardice.[25] Being convicted of a felony is not sufficient; there is even one instance of a Knight of the Garter – Lord Somerset in 1606 – committing murder and not being degraded.[26] At the beginning of the First World War, the British and French governments removed the names of enemy aliens from the rolls of their various orders. In other cases, honours have been revoked for more serious reasons, such as treason. The most famous case in this respect is that of Sir Roger Casement, who was made a Companion of the Order of St Michael and St George in 1905 and a Knight Bachelor in 1911. Early in the twentieth century, Casement became a committed Irish Nationalist; in 1914 he travelled to Berlin to seek help from the Germans to overthrow British rule in Ireland. He returned to Ireland in 1916 on a German U-boat and was later caught and found guilty of treason. Just before his execution, his CMG was cancelled and he was 'formally degraded as a knight.'[27] In Canada, few awards have been terminated or revoked. One such occasion was during the First World War, when an apparently shell-shocked lieutenant colonel in the Royal 22nd Regiment had his Distinguished Service Order revoked.[28]

To date, only two appointments to the Order of Canada have been terminated.[29] In 1986, Zena Khan Sheardown's appointment as an honorary Member of the Order was terminated. She was immediately appointed a Member in the general division. This termination was in recognition of her adoption of Canadian citizenship; it was more a transfer than a termination. The second termination occurred after an Officer of the Order was convicted of a felony. Alan Eagleson was a towering figure in Canadian hockey from the 1970s to the 1990s. As founder and executive director of the National Hockey League Player's Association, he was made an Officer of the Order in 1989. Then in 1994 he was charged with defrauding the NHLPA. He pleaded guilty, and almost immediately the media began calling for his removal from the Order of Canada.

Actually, the award was terminated at Eagleson's request. He had resigned from the Order of Canada and returned his insignia and appointment scroll.[30] The Advisory Council issued a press release on 27 February 1998, stating that after reviewing his submission, it had terminated his membership in the order, and that the Governor General had accepted the recommendation.[31] Five other members have been convicted of similar crimes; none has been removed yet. So it seems that in the eyes of the Advisory Council, some crimes are more forgivable than others. Viola MacMillan – the first woman president of the Prospectors and Developers Association of Canada – was made a member of the Order of Canada in 1992, barely a year before her death. Shortly after she was appointed, it was discovered that she had been convicted of stock fraud in the early 1970s. The Advisory Council learned of this in 1995, more than two years after her death.

The Olympic sprinter Ben Johnson was made a Member of the Order in 1985 for his contributions to sports. At the 1988 Seoul Olympics he tested positive for anabolic steroids and was stripped of his gold medal. This was followed by a lengthy enquiry in Canada. Although Johnson was never charged with a crime, his actions disgraced the Canadian Olympic team and at best could be classified as cheating. Nevertheless, there was no cry for Johnson to turn in his Order of Canada.

The most serious criminal offender among the Order of Canada's ranks is Stephen Fonyo, who was made an Officer in 1985 when he was twenty – the youngest Officer ever appointed. Fonyo, an amputee, ran across Canada in 1985 and raised more than six million dollars for cancer research, in an effort that recalled that of Terry Fox. By his late twenties, Fonyo was a cocaine addict. This led to him being convicted of fraud, assault with a deadly weapon, drug-related charges, and a variety of firearms offences. Fonyo avoided going to jail but was given an eighteen-month conditional sentence. Following the ordeal, Fonyo underwent addiction treatment and returned to school. In 1995 the Advisory Council considered terminating his appointment but made no decision on the matter.

The latest and possibly most widely known case of a member of the order being convicted of a serious crime is that of David Ahenakew. In October 2002, Ahenakew made a series of vicious anti-Semitic comments. An RCMP hate crimes investigation was initiated shortly thereafter. Within days there were calls for him to resign not only all of his offices in Saskatchewan's Native community, but also his appointment to the order. He promptly resigned from all his official posts, but kept his Order of Canada, and wore the small white lapel badge during his resignation press conference. In June 2005 Peter C. Newman and other members of the order initiated a campaign in the *National Post* to have Ahenakew removed. At the 29 July 2005 meeting of the Advisory Council it was agreed that Ahenakew's membership should be terminated. Ahenakew was given the option of resigning or having his membership formally revoked; ultimately he chose the latter. On 11 July 2005 Ahenakew was convicted of committing a hate crime.

All of these acts, from embezzlement and stock fraud to cheating and drug use, can be classified as dishonourable. The Advisory Council has been willing to ignore certain dishonourable acts. The MacMillan case is unique in that her crime was committed long before the honour was conferred, and her contributions to women and mining were significant enough to outweigh the stock-fraud charge. Johnson's use of steroids and subsequent disgrace of himself and Canada were serious matters, but the council clearly felt that he had suffered enough. The media has not called for him to be removed from the order. Similarly, the council and the press have ignored Steve Fonyo, who committed the most serious criminal acts. He now serves as an example of rehabilitation and of how a conditional sentence can be more beneficial to an offender than a prison term.

There has been an unwillingness to strip honours from those who have suffered personally or who have made such significant contributions that their crimes are minor in comparison. The lack of action against Johnson is perhaps also related to the scandal that erupted after he was stripped of his gold medal. When it was discovered that his coach and a variety of Canadian Olympic officials had encouraged him to use steroids, the public turned its anger against those who had in some ways 'used' Johnson. There is a similar situation in the Fonyo case. Although he committed a series of very serious offences, he had made a significant contribution, and he has since risen above his own physical disability and drug dependency. His story can thus be cast as a positive one of triumph over adversity. How, then, are the Eagleson and Ahenakew cases different? Eagleson, the hockey manager who helped Canada win the famous 1972 Summit series, angered many fans because he embezzled money from hockey players. David Ahenakew presented a new challenge for the Order of Canada. That Ahenakew was removed from the order, albeit in light of public pressure, has helped preserve the prestige of the order and honours in Canada. It has also sparked debate as to whether or not someone who contributed so significantly to the life of Native Canadians should be stripped of his Order of Canada on account of one incident. Nevertheless, his brutal comments emanate from an evil that saw more than six million people exterminated in the last century, and fall far outside most Canadians' perceptions of permissible speech.

The Advisory Council seems willing to forgive crimes committed by those forced by circumstances into unfortunate situations. Johnson and Fonyo have been allowed to retain their membership in the order because it is easy to sympathize with their plights. Both have given up drugs and made significant efforts to rehabilitate themselves and make further contributions. Eagleson, the wealthy lawyer who stole to make more money, is on the other hand unforgiven. His crimes struck at the heart of the nation's sport and at its sense of honour. Ahenakew has now joined Eagleson, because his comments made Canadians feel ashamed. It is apparent that the order must formulate clearer and more rigorous guidelines for terminating membership – ones that mirror popular ethics to some degree.

The order clearly tries to avoid controversy. Both Eagleson and Ahenakew stimulated a public outcry. Johnson and Fonyo, although widely mentioned in the press, escaped calls for their removal. Responsiveness to public uproar can be viewed in two ways. In one sense, it exemplifies a triumph of the grassroots involvement so desired by Lester Pearson. In another sense, it points to a hypersensitive Advisory Council caving in to public pressure merely to avoid controversy. Obviously, Canadian honours are not supposed to be controversial.

In other countries, highly controversial figures have been appointed to national orders. Dwight Eisenhower accepted the Soviet Order of Victory in 1944, and the Romanian dictator Nicolae Ceaucescu became an august member of Britain's Order of the Bath, which he remained even as his extreme brutality and megalomania became notorious.[32] In the United States, Britain, and most European countries, the public rarely express concern when crimes are committed by someone who holds a national honour. France is one of few countries that regularly suspends and terminates appointments on account of criminal acts. In France, a government official investigates such cases.

The Canadian system – and sense of honour – seems to work in reverse. There is rarely controversy over who is appointed to the Order of Canada, but when holders of the order commit crimes after they have become members, Canadians are much more likely to question their honour. This reflects Canada's more democratic sense of honour. For Canadians, honour is not something one is born with; rather, it reflects an individual's functioning within the social order. The honoured must not take their honours for granted. They are expected to maintain the dignity of the order through continued acts of exemplary citizenship, and if they fail to do so, they may lose their honour.

Automatic Appointments

Aside from the three ex-officio positions of the Sovereign and the Viceregal couple, there are no automatic awards of the Order of Canada.[33] Nevertheless, after retiring from public office, most former prime ministers are made Companions of the Order.[34] Every Chief Justice since the order's creation has been appointed as a Companion shortly after retirement. Long-serving premiers, Clerks of the Privy Council, and Privy Councillors with extended service are also often appointed to the order. Similarly, the presidents of the Royal Society of Canada and the Canadian Association of Universities and Colleges also receive the order after retirement – if they were not previously appointed. Despite these trends, there is no guarantee that a holder of high office will be appointed to the order after retirement. Every case is individually examined and assessed by the Advisory Council.

Group Awards

The question of group appointments was not dealt with until after the order's restructuring in 1972. Following the Canada–Russia hockey series of 1972, both the Governor General and the prime minister received a number of letters nominating the entire Canadian hockey team for the Order of Canada. The Working Group on Honours examined the question, receiving guidance from the prime minister. Trudeau insisted that 'more than one person in a group should be honoured only if each participant, in his own right, meets the criterion of excellence upon which all individual nominations are judged.'[35] There was no room for 'free riders.' Only Phil Esposito was appointed to the order, and this was in recognition of his broader contributions to hockey, not just for the Canada–Russia series. The largest 'group award' was made in 1980–1, when seven staff of the Canadian Embassy in Iran were appointed to the order for sheltering six Americans during the Revolution there. Donald and Joan McBride, husband and wife, were appointed as Members in 1988 for their service with the Salvation Army in building clinics and homes in less developed countries. The McBrides' citations are identical, and they were invested at the same time by the Governor General. Group awards by definition conflict with the values of individualism and independence that the awards are designed to promote. They have been rare because there are so few endeavours in which all participants are equally devoted.

Multiple Honours

Immediately after the Order of Canada was established, it was not uncommon for recipients to already possess a variety of earlier awards.[36] Only over the past twenty years have the provinces instituted their own honours. Today all provinces recognize their outstanding citizens with provincial orders, and often these recipients have already been recognized with the Order of Canada. Most provincial honours are small-scale versions of the order – an indication of the extent to which the transition to the order has been generally accepted.

An examination of the order's composition from 1967 to 1997 indicates that certain of its implicit purposes have changed. The arts and health have remained constant, but there has been a spike in the number of appointments for contributions to industry/commerce and voluntary services. It is revealing that members of the protective services are rarely honoured with the Order of Canada; in part, this can be attributed to the fact that both the Canadian Forces and Canadian police forces possess their own awards.[37] Politicians and public servants are not appointed as often as they were; however, other traditional groups, such as lawyers and judges, continue to make up a sizable number of appointments. Almost as interesting is the way 'disciplines' are categorized. The environment, radical social activism, feminism, and provincial autonomy are not counted as disciplines, yet people from these unrecognized fields have received the order. Peace activists have been included (typically under the 'other' discipline). The disciplines reflect a nuanced system of acceptable contributions that do not necessarily challenge the existing state; rather, they promote public service or contributions to the country in ways that are acceptable to Ottawa.

Without question, there is an unofficial quota in place to ensure that regions other than Ontario and Quebec receive more than their proportion of honours. In this respect, the order serves national unity. It attempts to tie citizens thousands of kilometres away from the centre to the federal state and the Crown, but it does not require them to know one another very well. In terms of refusals, we find that most people refused on account of modesty, not out of disdain for the federal state or honours. Terminations of membership in the order have rarely occurred. The examples of those who have committed crimes yet were allowed to retain the honour demonstrate a certain forgiving nature, and perhaps even a willingness to suspend some moral judgements, in the higher interests of the nation.

The principle of equal representation – and especially the effort to include people from outside Central Canada – emphasizes the underlying Pearsonian philosophy that the order should be used to recognize people in all parts of the country and from all walks of life. They can all be seen as contributors to the federal state and Canadian society. This is why a volunteer social worker in Canada's North is just as likely to be honoured as a philanthropic banker from Montreal or Toronto. This attempt at equal recognition for distinctly different endeavours reflects the liberal state, which increasingly relies on both the banker and the volunteer for its legitimacy. Under this system, honour is recognized as exemplary service over a long period of time, usually in one specific field. Honour stems from contributions that are significant enough to have benefited many more citizens than just the person being recognized. Thus honour in Canada is not a permanent quality that never fades; it can, as the result of a serious criminal act or hateful speech, become null and void. In their pragmatic, state-driven, and judicious ways, the architects of the Canadian honours system have thoroughly transformed the 'hierarchical concept' of honour into something more closely approximating a democratic meritocracy.

CHAPTER ELEVEN

Honorary Membership: The Extended Project

The change reflects the consideration of the Advisory Council of non-Canadians for approval as honorary Officers of the Order of Canada.

Lieutenant General James Gervais, 8 April 1997

From a very early stage, there was a desire to recognize non-Canadian citizens with the Order of Canada. That the first 'honorary' appointment was not made until more than a decade after the order's founding is more a sign of a lethargic bureaucracy than of intentional neglect. In essence, the Order of Canada has two divisions: a general division open to Canadian citizens and an honorary division populated by non-Canadians. This is quite a contrast from other national orders, which usually make no distinction between awards made to citizens and those made to non-citizens.[1] In most British orders of chivalry, honorary awards are bestowed only on foreign heads of states; other foreign citizens are merely admitted to the particular order and presented with a certificate of membership and insignia. Their names are not always added to the main register of recipients, and the award is never deducted from the statutory limit on the number of awards, since they are additional or honorary members.[2] When France's *Légion d'honneur* is bestowed on people from outside the Republic, those recipients too are presented with a certificate and the insignia. Thus, the existence of an entirely separate division for non-Canadian members of the Order of Canada points to our fixation on the importance of citizenship.

Many countries use honours as an extension of foreign policy.[3] Thus, when the president of France visits Brazil, it is customary for the presidents of the two countries to exchange awards. This trading of state symbols is engaged in by about half the world's countries. The origins of this practice can be traced back to nineteenth-century Europe, when various monarchs, who were interrelated through blood or marriage, exchanged awards during Royal weddings, funerals, or state visits. In this sense, they were gifts to members of the extended family. Sometimes, these awards did build relations; other times, jealousy between different Royal houses caused problems. Fortunately, Canada has never engaged in this kind of diplomacy. It does not seem to harm the older, more established orders; newer orders risk being devalued when they are freely distributed to foreign leaders. Because honorary appointments are rarely made to the Order of Canada, such appointments are very significant when they are made.

When the Canada Medal was devised in 1943, it was immediately assumed that it would be awarded to a number of prominent people from outside Canada. It is curious that the Royal Warrant creating the Canada Medal mentioned Canadian citizenship – which did not truly come into effect until 1947 – but did not set out a difference between Canadian and non-Canadian awards. George VI, Queen Elizabeth, and Princess Elizabeth were all to receive the medal as Canadians, and there was a distinguished list of proposed non-Canadian awards: Winston Churchill, Franklin Delano Roosevelt, Joseph Stalin, Jan Smuts, and Chiang Kai-shek.[4]

None of these awards were ever made, the Canada Medal itself never being awarded. However, that such detailed plans existed indicates that the government did consider the positive impact of such gifts. The Canadian government was trying desperately to show the world that Canada was not a British colony but was quite independent, albeit closely allied with Britain. The bestowal of a Canadian medal was seen as one means of demonstrating Canadian independence to world leaders.

The order's 1967 constitution contained provisions for honorary appointments to be made 'for merit, especially service to Canada or humanity at large.'[5] Such appointments were not forwarded to the Governor General and the Queen by the Advisory Council; rather, they had to be made on the advice of the Queen's Privy Council. Thus Cabinet had to be consulted for an award to be made. This provision was included to prevent the Advisory Council from becoming involved in Canada's external affairs, in keeping with the view that honours could be tools of foreign policy. This was the only aspect of the order in which politicians could be actively involved; thus, until relatively recently the order could not truly claim to be totally insulated from political interference.

The question of including honorary appointments to the Order of Canada with the first honours list in July 1967 was set aside on account of the existing government policy toward Canadians accepting foreign awards. Since 1956 the government of Canada has effectively forbidden Canadian citizens from accepting foreign honours other than those for bravery. So it would have been inconsistent for a government that would not allow its own citizens to accept foreign awards to go about bestowing its honours on non-citizens.[6] John Hodgson, Prime Minister Pearson's secretary, advised against rushing into making foreign appointments. To develop a policy, Pearson turned to the Decorations Committee, although this body was focused mainly on creating a new policy with regard to Canadians accepting foreign awards.[7] The new, more liberal policy toward Canadians accepting foreign awards was examined by Cabinet on 10 April 1968 and approved on the 17 April.[8] The more open policy meant there were no remaining barriers to making the first honorary appointments to the Order of Canada.

In February 1968 the Governor General received the first official foreign nomination to the Order of Canada. Major General H.F.G. Letson, who had been involved with the Awards Coordination Committee throughout the Second World War, nominated Lord Alexander, Canada's former Governor General. Besides Alexander, Michener suggested that members of the Royal Family be considered for nomination as well.[9] Pearson had hoped to see Queen Elizabeth the Queen Mother appointed to the order, along with Prince Philip.

The Department of Justice decided that although Alexander had been Governor General of Canada and was a Canadian citizen during his term, he was no longer a

Canadian citizen. Similarly, it was discerned that although the Queen was certainly a Canadian citizen, other members of the Royal Family were 'probably not.'[10] A way was found around this problem for Alexander and members of the Royal Family. On the advice of the Canadian government, the Queen could appoint people as a 'regular [not honorary] Companion "notwithstanding anything in the Constitution [of the Order of Canada]" and to "deem" that this appointment is not within the numerical limit prescribed in the Constitution.'[11] As Sovereign of the Order, the Queen is empowered to make such decisions. This action was not taken, however, since more formalized policy was being developed.[12] It would have been especially fitting for Alexander to be appointed to the order, since he had rendered such distinguished service to Canada, both militarily and as Governor General. Also, it was he, albeit indirectly, who first suggested the design for the ribbon of the Order of Canada in 1948. Alexander died in 1969, having received honours from fourteen countries but only the Canadian Forces Decoration from Canada.

Failed Attempts

The subject of honorary appointments lay dormant until February 1972, when Gordon Robertson, the Clerk of the Privy Council, suggested that guidelines be devised for honorary membership in the order.[13] The Under-Secretary of State, Jules Léger, was also keen to see a policy developed. Esmond Butler set Carl Lochnan to work on the project.[14] Lochnan was still working at the Department of the Secretary of State but would soon be appointed Director of Honours at Government House. Over the next fifteen years, Lochnan would be the expert on honorary awards, producing proposal after proposal to no avail.

   The subject was reintroduced on account of John Grierson, Film Commissioner of the National Film Board during the Second World War and a pioneer in Canadian film. Although he had devoted much of his life to the arts in Canada, Grierson was not a Canadian citizen. Grierson was in failing health, and many in the Canadian arts community were anxious for him to receive recognition from his surrogate native land. The Government Film Commissioner, Sydney Newman, sent an urgent telegram to the prime minister encouraging the government to appoint Grierson to the Order of Canada.[15] This proposal was passed on to the Department of the Secretary of State, which began assembling the necessary documents to have Grierson appointed an honorary Companion. All of this was several months before the Order of Canada was restructured and administrative controls were passed to the Office of the Governor General. There was a great sense of urgency owing to Grierson's rapidly deteriorating health. There was little doubt that Grierson deserved the award; the problem was that no formal policy existed with regard to making honorary appointments. The order's constitution stated that the government of Canada had to approve the award, but there were no guidelines beyond this. Carl Lochnan – an old acquaintance of Grierson[16] – insisted that the Governor General first be approached for his consent; this was to be followed by Cabinet approval. Within a day, Lochnan had secured the Governor General's tentative approval, and – after consultation with Prime Minister Trudeau and Gordon Robertson – had completed a Memorandum to Cabinet seeking approval for the award. The two-page document closed with this recommendation:

'In recognition of his outstanding contributions to the establishment and develop-ment of the National Film Board, his direction of the critically important work on wartime information and his continuing interest and support of the art of film making and film distribution in Canada, it is recommended that the Order of Canada be conferred on John Grierson at the level of Honorary Companion.'[17]

Fate intervened, and on 21 February Grierson died, only one day before Cabinet would surely have approved his appointment. All of the preparations had been made for a telegram to go from the Governor General and prime minister to inform Grierson of his appointment, but poor timing prevented the appointment. In place of the Order of Canada, Grierson's wife Margaret received a personal letter from the prime minister.[18] Lochnan in particular was disappointed at the missed opportunity to 'honour him for what he gave to Canada.'[19]

The New Constitution, 1972

Grierson in fact did make a unique contribution to the order. When the order's constitution was amended to its current structure in 1972 – Companion, Officer, Member – the various provisions were changed with regard to honorary appoint-ments. In place of the Queen's Privy Council for Canada, the Government of Canada was to make the recommendation. This meant that awards could simply be approved by the prime minister and sent on to the Governor General and the Queen.[20] This was in response to the Grierson case, and also out of fears that Cabinet would become embroiled in the honours system again. Robertson and Lochnan wanted to streamline the entire process, not only to prevent excessive administrative formalities, but also to avoid broad political involvement in selecting honorary appointees to the order.[21]

The task of developing a policy for honorary appointments to the Order of Canada was left to the Working Group on Honours.[22] Early on in the process, Léger insisted that the Canadian policy not necessarily be the same as that used by other nations; as a seasoned diplomat, he was apprehensive about Canada entering into the interna-tional game of honours exchange.[23] The Department of External Affairs was invited to involve itself in the process, since so much of the discussion dealt with practices in other countries.[24] The Under-Secretary of State for External Affairs, A.E. Ritchie, was involved early on, in order to ensure that a well-rounded policy was developed.

Almost immediately, the working group began to consider developing a policy that would allow for honorary appointments to the Order of Canada. Besides honor-ary awards, the working group also examined issues such as the expansion of the Canadian honours system, existing difficulties with the 1968 Canadian policy toward foreign awards to Canadians, American awards to Canadian civilians involved in the Vietnam War, the Order of St Lazarus, the Order of Malta, Papal Honours, and the establishment of a Police Long Service Medal.

The Department of External Affairs compiled research for the working group on practices followed in other countries. The question of whether to engage in reciprocal awards was of constant interest to the committee. Lochnan and Butler hoped that non-reciprocal/automatic awards would be made; these were seen as attractive mementos of travel, nothing more. The presentation of a standardized Canadian gift was briefly considered, but no action was taken.[25] The project was further bogged down by discussions of honorary appointments to the new Order of Military Merit.[26] At the December 1973 meeting of the working group, Lochnan presented a paper titled 'Honorary Membership in the Order of Canada.' Consensus was reached that honorary appointments to the Order of Canada should not become like the Nobel Prize; rather, the recipients would be required to have some connection to Canada.[27] The working group reached agreement on the types of service to be recognized by honorary appointments, and expanded greatly on Lochnan's original three briefly described fields:

1. A person who, whether resident in Canada or not, has performed some action, rendered a service or made a discovery of particular benefit to Canada or to the well-being of Canadians
2. A person who has served with distinction outside Canada in the salaried employment of an agency of the Crown.
3. A person, not being in the salaried employment of an agency of the Crown, who has made an important contribution to Canada's external interests.[28]

A more formal report was drafted over the following year. In February 1976, the working group met again to discuss honorary appointments and set limits on the number of awards that could be made in a single year. A maximum of four Honorary Companions, fifteen Honorary Officers, and thirty-five Honorary Members could be appointed per annum.[29] Although Lochnan had retired from Government House in 1975, he remained involved in the process, being the resident expert. In March 1976, Lochnan assembled all of the working group's findings in a draft Memorandum to Cabinet titled 'The Canadian Honours System: Additions and Revisions.' This memorandum set out guidelines for honorary appointments to the Order of Canada and Order of Military Merit, for revisions to the policy on Canadians accepting foreign honours, for the creation of a Commendation for Exemplary Conduct, and for the establishment of a national Police Long Service Medal. Fortunately, the document advised 'against the ritual of exchanging national orders with visiting Heads of State.'[30] The eighteen-page document was approved by the Working Group on Honours (what is today the Honours Policy Committee[31]) and passed on to Prime Minister Trudeau in April 1976. The document was not accepted until 1980, at which time the section on honorary appointments to the Order of Canada was dropped. The chair of the Advisory Council, Bora Laskin, feared that honorary appointments would devalue the order because they were initiated by politicians and were not subject to the approval of the Advisory Council. The entire proposal for honorary appointments thus collapsed.

The First Honorary Appointment

Canadian diplomats have been held in high regard almost from the moment Vincent Massey was appointed Canada's First Minister to Washington. So it is appropriate that the first honorary appointment to the Order of Canada was made to someone who was a Canadian diplomat in all but title. During the 1978–9 Islamic Revolution in Iran, the staff at the Canadian Embassy in Tehran sheltered six members of the U.S.

Embassy's staff. These six were the only people to escape from the U.S. Embassy after its seizure in November 1979.

Members of the embassy's staff sheltered the six American 'house guests' for three months until they could be flown to safety. For almost the entire ordeal, five of the Americans stayed with John and Zena Sheardown. Mr Sheardown, the Canadian Embassy's First Secretary, was heavily burdened by office duties; thus the bulk of the responsibility for looking after the Americans fell to Mrs Sheardown. All Canadian members of the embassy's staff were at great risk – the revolutionaries had little respect for the Vienna Convention on Diplomatic Relations – but one of them was especially vulnerable.[32] Zena Sheardown was a British citizen born in Guyana and was not covered by diplomatic immunity. Had any of the embassy's staff been caught sheltering the Americans, the consequences would have been severe, but even more so for Mrs Sheardown, who was not considered a diplomat. After the Americans escaped, the Canadian Embassy closed in Tehran and the staff returned to Canada.

On their safe return, the story was made public. Almost immediately there were calls for the Canadian diplomats to be rewarded for their bravery. The Advisory Council considered the nominations and subsequently appointed Ken Taylor (the ambassador) an Officer of the Order of Canada. John Sheardown, Mary Catherine O'Flaherty, Roger Lucy, and Laverna Dollimore were all made Members of the Order of Canada on 1 July 1980. But Mrs Sheardown was not appointed to the order, nor was Mrs Taylor – the former because she was not a Canadian citizen, the latter because the council felt that it could not recognize one wife and not the other. Both were weak reasons. John Sheardown considered refusing his award on account of his wife not being included, but was told he could not decline the appointment.[33]

Enquiries were made as to when Mrs Sheardown and Mrs Taylor would be accorded the recognition they deserved, but over the next six months nothing was done. Bora Laskin, chairman of the Advisory Council, was reluctant to see honorary appointments made, because politicians would have to approve them. In January 1981 the Honourable Flora MacDonald – who had served as Minister of External Affairs during the Iran crisis – wrote to Laskin to express her concern regarding the lack of recognition: 'I feel very strongly that both Mrs. Taylor and Mrs. Sheardown are just as deserving of recognition, and I fail to understand why it has not been given.'[34] In a rather tepid response, Laskin pointed out that Mrs Sheardown was not a Canadian citizen and thus could not be nominated by the Advisory Council; he did not mention Mrs Taylor. Laskin did assure MacDonald that both cases would be reviewed in April 1981.[35] Many in the press began to wonder openly whether Mrs Sheardown and Mrs Taylor had been passed over on account of their gender and lack of official status within the diplomatic hierarchy.

Feeling that more had to be done to ensure that the women were recognized, MacDonald introduced a motion to the House of Commons 'strongly supporting the nomination by the Department of External Affairs, that Mrs. Zena Sheardown and Mrs. Pat Taylor receive the Order of Canada for the courageous and indispensable role they played in the rescue of the six Americans from Tehran.'[36] It was highly unusual for such matters to be discussed in Parliament. All parties, however, agreed that there was no partisan aspect to the issue, and the motion passed. Canadians wanted the two women to be rewarded.

Prime Minister Trudeau also wanted both women to receive recognition, although the Advisory Council had made it clear that either both women would be recognized, or neither. Thus, Trudeau had to recommend to the Governor General the honorary appointment of Mrs Sheardown. Never before had the government appointed an honorary member to the order, but 'in your case ... given your expressed intention to become a Canadian citizen and given that you are, except for your citizenship, a full member of Canadian society, we thought it would be appropriate to act.'[37] Following a meeting of Cabinet, an order-in-council was adopted that recommended to the Governor General that Mrs Sheardown be made an honorary Member of the Order of Canada.[38] This was to be the only time that a nomination was sent forward to the Governor General from the government and not the Advisory Council. It is, however, certain that had Mrs Sheardown been a Canadian citizen at the time, she would have been appointed by the usual method. On 27 June 1981, Mrs Sheardown was appointed an honorary Member of the Order, and Mrs Taylor was appointed an ordinary Member.

In October 1985, Mrs Sheardown was finally granted Canadian citizenship after a lengthy battle with the Ministry of National Revenue. The Advisory Council reconsidered her appointment and decided to terminate her honorary membership and simultaneously appoint her to the general division of the order. The reasons for this action were related to various plans being considered by the Honours Policy Committee, which included abolishing the honorary division of the Order of Canada and replacing it with an entirely new Canadian order intended solely for non-Canadians. On 29 December 1986, Governor General Jeanne Sauvé signed 'the Instrument appointing you an Officer of the Order of Canada and, on the same occasion, Her Excellency revoked your appointment as an honorary member.'[39] The letter indicated clearly that Mrs Sheardown had been made an Officer of the Order, yet little more than a month later, after informing family and friends of the promotion, she received another letter from Government House stating that she had been appointed a Member and not an Officer of the Order. This was the result of an unfortunate clerical error: the instrument signed by the Governor General had stated that Mrs Sheardown was being appointed a Member. This was truly an unfortunate episode in the history of the order. Although Mrs Sheardown was moved from the honorary to the general division of the order, she will always remain the first honorary appointee.

The question of further honorary awards would remain dormant until 1986. The Honours Policy Committee – the successor body to the Working Group on Honours – developed a proposal for honours for non-Canadians. Prime Minister Brian Mulroney was keen to see a clear policy developed toward honorary appointments to the Order of Canada. The Honours Policy Committee developed a proposal for an entirely new order, one that would be similar in structure to the Order of Canada but open to non-Canadians only. The three-level order was to be awarded to heads of state and to non-Canadians who had made contributions to Canadian life. This proposal did not shy away from the prospect of Canada engaging in automatic exchange awards. Like so many of the earlier proposals, this one died, although what killed it was the projected cost (more than $300,000 per annum), not fear of creating a new order. There was also the fact that the Order of Canada had provisions for honorary appointments; the only step that really needed to be taken was to develop a more detailed policy for nominations and appointments. The Mulroney government, like its predecessor, did not see an urgent need to make honorary appointments to the order. It seems that an informal agreement had been reached between the Advisory Council and the prime minister to the effect that no honorary appointments would be made until a more non-political process of honorary appointments could be devised. Mrs Sheardown's appointment was allowed to proceed because she was in all but name a Canadian citizen, and because the public was demanding it.[40]

New Appointment Process

The political aspects of honorary appointments were removed in 1997, when new Letters Patent were issued that altered the Constitution of the Order of Canada. Throughout the 1990s the Honours Policy Committee and the Advisory Council repeatedly examined the issue of honorary appointments to the order. More and more worthy non-Canadians were being nominated by the public, and the Advisory Council felt it could no longer ignore the issue. In November 1994 the Honours Policy Committee began to consider a 'more workable policy'[41] toward honorary appointments. A firm proposal, however, was not prepared in time for the 1995 amendment to the order's constitution. It was agreed that the Advisory Council and not the Privy Council would recommend appointments to the Governor General.[42] To ensure that no diplomatic incident could arise from an honorary appointment, the Deputy Minister of Foreign Affairs and International Trade would attend all meetings of the Advisory Council when honorary appointments were being discussed.

Curiously, the new honorary appointment system applied only to honorary Officers. There was a certain sense of urgency to ensure that the amended constitution would be adopted quickly. The Advisory Council had already selected people for appointment. Lieutenant General James Gervais, Deputy Secretary of the Chancellery, who had been influential in seeing the changes made, delivered the revised constitution by hand to the Privy Council Office. Cabinet examined the proposed changes on 8 April and approved them. The Letters Patent amending the order's constitution, issued on 15 April 1997, referred only to 'honorary Officers.'[43] In effect, the levels of honorary Companion and honorary Member had been abolished. One reason given for this change, and for retaining only the honorary Officer level, was that contributions made by most non-Canadians suitable for appointment to the order were at the Officer level. In the long run, this was a short-sighted decision, one that was fuelled by an immediate desire to recognize non-Canadians with the order.

Scarcely two days after the new honorary appointment process had been formalized, the first honorary Officers were appointed. On 17 April 1997, John Kenneth Galbraith and James Hillier were appointed to the order. Galbraith, the world-renowned economist, and Hillier, the co-inventor of the electron microscope, were both born in Canada and retained some connections to this country, although they were no longer Canadian citizens. The appointments were well received. One more honorary appointment was made under the 1997 revised constitution. After twenty-five years of service, Charles Dutoit, director of the Orchestre symphonique de Montréal, was made an Officer of the Order. He would have been appointed much sooner had a more viable mechanism for honorary appointments existed prior to 1997. There is a tradition in most countries to recognize outstanding conductors, so Dutoit's award was long overdue.

The levels of honorary Companion and honorary Member were returned to the order in 1998, when further amendments were made to its constitution. The amended constitution adopted by Order-in-Council 1998-1373 allowed for honorary Companions, Officers, and Members to be appointed to the order.[44] Also, a section was added limiting the number of honorary appointments to five people in any year.

In September 1998, Nelson Mandela was appointed as the first honorary Companion. This was in recognition of his perseverance through decades of incarceration and his eventual triumph over oppression. It was an appropriate award, being that Canada was one of the first countries to condemn apartheid and to impose sanctions on the regime that Mandela had devoted his life to removing.[45] Mandela was subsequently made a honorary Canadian citizen. Because his citizenship is honorary, he has not been moved from the honorary to the general division of the order. In August 2001, on her hundredth birthday, Queen Elizabeth the Queen Mother was appointed the first female honorary Companion of the Order. She had been proposed for nomination as an honorary Companion as far back as 1967, and a number of nominations were on file supporting her appointment. The true impetus, however, came from Adrienne Clarkson, the Governor General. On 31 October, Her Excellency presented Her Majesty with the insignia of the order.[46] After the informal ceremony, the Queen Mother – who was elated with the honour – said: 'It's wonderful. I can't tell you how deeply touched I am to receive this honour and I do thank you very warmly for investing me in it. When I wear it, which I hope I shall, my thoughts and my happiest memories will be with the lovely Canada. Thank you so much.' As the Queen Mother examined the insignia, she turned to show it to those standing around her, remarking: 'That will be very precious indeed. Dear Canada.'

By 2002, appointments to the honorary division of the order had become more regularized. Frank Gehry, the noted architect, became the first non–head of state to be made an honorary Companion. Tanya Moiseiwitsch, whose artistic contributions to the Stratford Festival extended back over fifty years, was made an Officer. More recently, former Czech president Vaclav Havel and former secretary general of the UN Boutros Ghali have been made Honorary Companions. The topic of honorary appointments is now firmly fixed in the minds of Advisory Council members. Thus in the future we are likely to see annual honorary appointments instead of occasional ones.

The Royal Family

From time to time, issues of citizenship have gripped the administrators of the order. In 1967 they hoped to appoint the Queen Mother and former Governor General Lord Alexander as Companions of the Order; the problem was that the Department of Justice felt that neither was a Canadian citizen on paper. Alexander could have claimed citizenship on the basis of having been Governor General and resident in Canada for more than six years – not to mention having been Governor General when the Citizenship Act came into effect. Determining the citizenship of monarchs and former monarchs has long been a difficult question for many countries. Citizenship is typically a status conferred by the state on those meeting certain criteria related to place of birth, parentage, or naturalization. In the case of constitutional monarchies, citizenship – in theory, at least – flows from the Sovereign. As the consort of the King of Canada and herself the mother of Canada's head of state, what citizenship did the Queen Mother possess? No member of the Royal Family travels on a passport. It is simply known who they are. So what is their citizenship? This opens a whole host of questions as to whether a Sovereign can possess citizenship at all. The close relationship between citizenship and subjecthood exacerbates this problem: Can a Queen be a subject of herself?

In 1968 these questions relating to the status of members of the Royal Family and Canada's former Governor General were too sensitive to be dealt with. In nominating Earl Alexander and Prince Philip, Roland Michener observed: 'I am afraid that his nomination [Prince Philip] too, raises certain difficulties.'[47] The prime minister asked the justice department to examine the question of what citizenship members of the Royal Family held. The conclusion was troublingly uncertain: 'Edythe Macdonald is inclined to believe that members of the Royal Family other than the Queen are *probably not* Canadian citizens.'[48] The entire question was set aside for a later date.

The citizenship of members of the Royal Family remains a question of some debate. No federal government has truly investigated this issue, and the 1968 Department of Justice memorandum relating to the topic has not been updated despite changes to the Citizenship Act. Debating the role of the monarchy in Canada has never been a politically advantageous exercise for anyone, be they monarchists or not.[49] It is likely that a similar internal debate arose before the Queen Mother was appointed a honorary Companion of the Order. Anecdotal evidence suggests that the same 1968 Department of Justice memorandum was dusted off and used as the principal reason for the Queen Mother being appointed an honorary (that is, not a general division) Companion of the Order. In one sense, it is surprising that the Queen Mother accepted the honorary appointment; she, like Prince Philip, had been a self-declared Canadian for decades.[50] It is likely that advancing years and a desire to be recognized by Canadians played a role in her acceptance of the order.

It is unfortunate that honorary appointments were not initiated when the order was created in 1967. The list of non-Canadians who devoted their lives to Canada and who made significant contributions is as long as its members are distinguished. With the new honorary appointment system and limits on the number of annual awards, future honorary appointments promise to be interesting. The Advisory Council and the government have sent a clear signal that they have no intention of engaging in the practice of automatically exchanging awards with foreign leaders. Thus the quality of appointments is certain to remain high.

CHAPTER TWELVE

Centrepiece of a Modern Honours System: Recognition from Sea to Sea

The establishment of the Order of Canada required that the Canadian honours system as a whole be expanded. This was understood as early as 1968, and first acted on in 1972 when the order was restructured into a three-level entity, and with the further addition of the Order of Military Merit, the Cross of Valour, the Star of Courage, and the Medal of Bravery.

The broader system has continued to grow, with the addition of the Meritorious Service Cross in 1984, the Meritorious Service Medal in 1991, the return of the Victoria Cross as Canada's pre-eminent military valour decoration in 1993, and the creation of the Star of Military Valour and Medal of Military Valour, also in 1993. In March 2001 the Chancellery announced the creation of the Order of Merit of the Police Forces. This last order recognizes outstanding meritorious service over an extended period of time.[1] It is meant to recognize police officers in much the same manner as the Order of Military Merit recognizes members of the Canadian Armed Forces.

The most recent alterations made to the Order of Canada have included both important structural adjustments and alterations to the number of annual appointments. Successive decennial reviews of the order have found that it is fulfilling its original goal, which is to recognize outstanding Canadians. Suggestions have been made to expand the order to a five-level system similar to the *Légion d'honneur* and Order of the British Empire, but these have been resisted, mainly because the order's structure already functions well. Most of the recent changes were made in the last five years of the twentieth century; these related to the number of people appointed to each level, the method of honorary appointment, and the structure of the Advisory Council. At long last, the federal government has got over its fear of altering and expanding Canada's honours system. This is because honours in Canada are no longer politically contentious.[2]

Enlargement of the Order, 1983

Between 1967 and 1983 the Canadian population grew by 24 per cent, and the Advisory Council was faced with the problem that there were far too many worthy candidates and not enough awards to bestow.[3] Under the order's constitution, fifteen Companions (to a maximum of 150 living), forty Officers, and eighty Members could be appointed each year. To account for population growth, new Letters Patent were issued. The constitution of the order was amended on 17 March 1983 by the Governor General, Edward Schreyer.[4] Annual appointments to the Officer and Member levels were increased to forty-six and ninety-two respectively. Roger Nantel, Registrar of the Order, wanted the Officer level to increase to sixty and the Member level to increase to 120 annual appointments.[5] This proposal was resisted by the Advisory Council, which feared that the order would become cheapened if too many awards were bestowed. Butler also preferred a more cautious expansion, reasoning that such a great increase in the number of awards would necessitate an extra investiture each year.[6] His staff were already overworked, and the prospect of arranging an additional ceremony was not feasible.

Another Anniversary

When the order celebrated its twentieth anniversary, a second decennial report was prepared. It found few problems with the order. The Mulroney government was showing more interest in seeing honorary awards bestowed, and to this end a special report was completed for the Honours Policy Committee. The report called for the creation of an entirely new order that would be open to non-citizens only.[7] This report was subsequently rejected, mainly on the grounds that the Order of Canada was already open to foreigners.

The first formal publication about the broader Canadian honours system was unveiled on 8 July 1991 by Governor General Ramon Hnatyshyn. *The Canadian Register of Honours*, published by the Canadian Almanac and Directory, provided a comprehensive list of all living members of the order at that time; it also outlined the Canadian honour system and its origins. This was the first full-scale publication about the order and yet another step toward broader public recognition.

Growth and Rapid Change

Five years after the order's constitution was amended in 1983, further amendments were already being discussed. The deputy attorney general, Roger Tassé, suggested to the Chief Justice that the prohibition on serving politicians and judges be embedded in the constitution. Similarly, in April 1988 the Honours Policy Committee called for the constitution to be amended to include Tassé's proposal and a section on heraldry as well as to increase the number of annual appointments.[8] With the Canadian population growing, an increase in annual appointments was logical.

The addition of heraldic rules to the order's constitution was related to the creation of another new Canadian institution. In June 1988 the Canadian Heraldic Authority was established; thus the last constitutional power still vested in the British state was patriated. Since the order's founding, it had become custom for those members who were granted arms to have the insignia of the order included in their grant.[9] In the statutes of British orders there is usually a section that deals with what elements of the order can be included in a grant of arms made to a member of a particular order. Since Canada now had its own heraldic agency, it was considered advisable for specific heraldic rules to be included in the Constitution of the Order of Canada. At the fifty-fourth meeting of the Advisory Council, in April 1993, the proposed changes were discussed. The council agreed that the number of Officers and Members appointed annually should be increased to fifty and one hundred respectively. The council discussed but set aside the idea of increasing the number of Companions to 175 living; there was a reluctance to make changes to the order's most senior level.[10] The addition of a small section on heraldry was approved, and the order's 1972 constitution was repealed and replaced. Some parts of the constitution were restructured and reworded, although there were no significant structural or operational changes made besides the ones just noted. The revisions were completed by November 1993, although a series of delays prevented their adoption until 6 December 1994. The Governor General and the prime minister later signed the documents, both having already given verbal approval. The changes were announced in the *Canada Gazette* on 25 March 1995.[11]

Three months after the new Letters Patent were issued and the new constitution was adopted, further amendments were made. To enhance the involvement and experience of the two additional members of the Advisory Council selected from the order's membership, their terms on the council were increased from two years to three years. The council hoped that this extended term would help alleviate the problem of a high turnover rate among council members. In addition, the total number of living Companions was increased from 150 to 165 – again, to account for population growth. Order-in-Council 1995-694 was adopted on 26 April 1995; the amended Letters Patent were signed by the Governor General, Roméo LeBlanc, on 30 June 1995.[12]

Throughout the 1990s the Honours Policy Committee and the Advisory Council wrestled with the question of developing a new policy for honorary appointments. A partial solution was found in 1997, when the order's entire constitution was repealed and replaced by a new document. The new constitution was adopted by Letters Patent signed by the Governor General and prime minister on 26 May 1997.[13] Allowances were made for the Advisory Council to ask the Governor General to appoint non-citizens as honorary Officers of the Order.

A year later, the most comprehensive changes made to the order since 1972 were adopted. To maintain balance with population growth, the numbers of annual Officers and Members appointed were increased to 52 and 106 respectively; there was some discussion of increasing the annual appointments even more.[14] Most significantly, the levels of honorary Companion and Member were returned to the order's structure. It was realized that the level of honorary Officer would be inappropriate for worthy retired heads of state. The new Letters Patent were adopted by an order-in-council on 24 August and signed by the Governor General on 10 September 1998. Little more than a week after passage of the order-in-council, Nelson Mandela was appointed the order's first honorary Companion.

The most recent two amendments to the constitution have increased both the number of annual appointments to the Officer and Member levels and the size of the Advisory Council. To meet increasing demands on the Advisory Council and to recognize more Canadians, the numbers of Officers and Members have been increased to 64 and 136 annually. The prime minister and the Governor General signed the Letters Patent on 1 October 1999.[15] Despite the successive increases in the statutory number of annual appointments to the order, on a per capita basis Canada is still

Table 12.1
Successive Enlargements, 1967–2000

	Companion	Officer	Member
1967	50 annual (150 max)	100 (Medal of Service)	Nil
1968	*25** annual (150 max)	*50* (Medal of Service)	Nil
1972	*15* annual (150 max)	*40*	*80 (new level)*
1983	15 annual (150 max)	*46*	*92*
1994	15 annual (150 max)	*50*	*100*
1995	15 annual (*165 max*)	50	100
1997	Change in policy toward honorary appointments		
1998**	15 annual (165 max)	*52*	*106*
1999	15 annual (165 max)	*64*	*136*
2000	Increased membership in the Advisory Council to 5 additional members		

*Italics indicate a change in numbers of appointments.
**In 1998 the policy towards honorary appointments was again changed.

quite conservative in the number of honours it bestows per year. When it comes to bestowing honours, Canada is 'cheaper' by at least half than Australia, all EU countries (save Ireland), and many other countries.[16]

In March 2001, the size of the Advisory Council was increased. Since the early 1970s the council had included one or two additional members chosen from the ranks of the Order of Canada by the ex officio council members. These additional members have included such eminent Canadians as Pauline McGibbon and Roberta Bondar. To increase the breadth of representation on the Advisory Council, the number of additional members chosen from within the order was increased from two to five, each with a three-year term.[17] The change was enacted to 'broaden the representation on the Council as well as from other fields.'[18] With this change the council is now similar in size and composition to the Council of the Order of Australia, which makes appointments to that country's highest honour in the same fashion as the Advisory Council does in Canada. Lieutenant General James Gervais insisted that the signing of the Letters Patent be delayed so that the changes could be adopted in the fiftieth year of Queen Elizabeth's reign.[19] The Governor General signed the new Letters Patent on the evening of 20 March 2001.[20]

Without question, the various expansions have created an 'inflation of honour,'[21] with an ever increasing number of annual appointments. For the order to maintain any level of prestige, only a limited number of honours can be bestowed annually. At one time, France's *Légion d'honneur* was extensively bestowed on many French citizens, generally for long service. In 1963, in an effort to restore the prestige of the *Légion d'honneur*, the number of annual appointments was greatly reduced and a stringent selection process was put in place. In 1967 one out of every 307,000 Canadians could expect to receive the Order of Canada. Today, twice that number can expect to be honoured.[22]

Table 12.2
Ratio of Order of Canada Honours Appointments and Population of Canada, 1967–99

Year	Population (to the nearest million)	Number of honours bestowed	Honours/population ratio
1967*	20	65	1/307,000
1972	22	115	1/191,304
1995	30	165	1/181,818
1999	31	215	1/144,186

*Although 150 honours were bestowed in 1967, under the long-term plan for the two-level system there were to be a maximum of fifteen Companions appointed per year, and fifty Medals of Service. Calculations were made using the population statistics for 1967, 1972, 1995, and 1999.

In 1998 the Order of Precedence for Canadian Orders, Decorations, and Medals was revised at the direction of the Honours Policy Committee. The most significant change related to the order involved placing all three levels in one group. Thus, although the Victoria Cross and Cross of Valour remain at the top of the Canadian Order of Precedence, they are now followed by all three levels of the Order of Canada.[23] Previously, the various levels of the order had been ranked among other Canadian orders such as the Order of Military Merit and the Royal Victorian Order. This curious change means that Members of the Order of Canada now rank ahead of those who have been appointed a Commander of the Order of Military Merit or Commander of the Royal Victorian Order. Both of these latter distinctions are awarded for outstanding national service, whereas people are usually appointed Members of the Order of Canada for distinguished local service. This most unusual decision was first contemplated by the Working Group on Honours in the early 1970s, only to be discarded because it was illogical and contrary to tradition to lump all three levels of one order ahead of the nation's other orders and decorations.

Looking Back: The Origins of the Order of Canada

The development of the Order of Canada was a direct product of the Nickle debates of 1917 to 1919 and Canadian opposition to British Imperial honours. This opposition was rooted in a growing sense of nationalism in Canada. Key Canadians liberals such as Alexander Mackenzie and George Brown were disdainful of 'tawdry' titles. Further opposition to honours in Canada was manifested in the perception that they were tools of imperialism and thus were attempts to tie an autonomous Canada closer to London. That Canada endured half a century without honours before finally establishing an independent and national honours system is proof of the continuing potency of questions of honours in Canadian politics.

Support for the creation of a Canadian order came from two broad groups: senior members of the Canadian military, and equally senior Canadian public servants. The military's interest was rooted in the ancient connection between prowess on the battlefield and chivalry. Canadian public servants viewed honours as useful tools of the state, to reward loyal citizens – and servants of the state – and also as a method of demonstrating where the centre of power was located. Both these constituencies took up the matter of honours during and after the Second World War, when many proposals for a Canadian order were devised and submitted to Cabinet.

The order, like the Canadian flag and the Royal Commission on Bilingualism and Biculturalism, was created out of a sense of urgency and was intended to help unite the country and to smooth over the fissures that had been opened during the Quiet Revolution. Its birth also coincided with the broader realization that Canada was no longer a British Dominion, but had developed into an independent entity. The urgency of the situation is best demonstrated by the fact that the order was created in less than five months and was not part of any broader formal plan. Rather, it was just a tidy addition to the broader project of enchancing the Canadian character of the Crown.

The creation of the Order of Canada flowed out of the preparations for the Centennial celebrations. All involved in its creation were aware that they were involved in the 'invention of tradition,' and there was no attempt to cloak the new institution in a mock ancient ceremony or other such event. This lack of British or French tradition was necessary if the new institution was to gain support – or at the least not arouse opposition – from all corners of the country. There was almost an overt attempt *not* to emulate the traditions of any of Canada's founding peoples; this was best demonstrated in the bus ride that newly appointed members of the Order of Canada took following the inaugural investiture in November 1967 to bring them from the investiture at Rideau Hall to the banquet in the West Block of Parliament.

The connection between honour and citizenship has been solidified through the Order of Canada and its efforts to recognize exemplary citizenship. This focus on contributions to the broader community as the key to modern honour is fundamental. The transition from traditional honour to citizen-focused honour began with the honours lists compiled by R.B. Bennett between 1932 and 1935. His desire to recognize honours in a non-partisan manner, as a tool for the state to recognize community and volunteer service, has become a big part of our modern honours system. It was the first step toward reconciling honours with modern liberal democracy. To a lesser degree, this interest in non-partisan community contributions was continued during the Second World War through the creation of the Canada Medal.

The creation of a neutral advisory council – composed of senior Ottawa mandarins and friends of the federal state – was a key step in creating a modern honours system. Yet a politically neutral but well-connected honours board was not sufficient to alleviate many liberal concerns. To further democratize honours, a grassroots nomination process was developed, one that required nominations to come not from politicians or major state actors but rather from the general public. Giving the public a direct stake in the nomination process was an obvious product of the highly democratic idealism of the Centennial. The Pearsonian philosophy that honours should be available to all members of Canadian society, from the cleaning woman to the great scientist, is best demonstrated in the breadth of activities honoured through the order. That the Member level – which acknowledges local services – is the most widely awarded of the three levels fulfils Pearson's vision. The distribution of the order in a relatively even fashion across regions proves the role played by honours in tempering Canada's notoriously strong socio-economic and cultural divisions. No longer are honours used mainly to reward politicians and judges. Although a significant gender gap remains, there are continuing efforts to see women represented equally in the order's ranks. Nonetheless Canada remains the world leader in recognizing women with its national order.

The Order of Canada is a liberal-democratic honour used by the state to inculcate the values of good citizenship and thus further the aims and goals of the federal state. By involving the citizenry in the process, the state has given citizens a direct stake in the honours system and further connected them to the central government. Exemplary citizens serve as emissaries, ambassadors, and educators. In this way they help bind together people whose other forms of national attachment are often fleeting and shallow.

The Order of Canada Today

Since 1967 the Canadian honours system has grown and evolved to include a wide variety of awards. At the centre of this system is the Order of Canada, which served as the impetus for establishing the broader system we know today. Today Canada possesses one of the most well-rounded honours systems ever devised by a nation. This does not preclude revisions or additions, as perfection is an unachievable goal, but it does indicate that we are on the right course. Over the past decade, the number of annual appointments has nearly doubled, mainly to account for population growth. There is a risk, however, that if the number of annual appointments is tied directly to the size of the Canadian population, the value of the honours will be reduced. The solution to preserving the order's value can be found in preventing further rapid expansion and allowing for the broader distribution of the Meritorious Service Cross and Meritorious Service Medal. In the coming years, if demand for civil recognition warrants further awards, a separate order – perhaps an Order of the Legion of Service – junior to the Order of Canada, could easily fill this need. There remains room for cautious expansion of the Canadian honours system.

The transition to a complete honours system in Canada has signalled the development and expansion of a national institution that seeks to encourage national unity and Canadian nationalism in a way previously untested in Canada. The continued focus on citizen-based nominations and the persistent attempts of the Advisory Council to include previously unrecognized groups and endeavours was a direct outgrowth of the populism of the 1960s. The expansion of the order was a further attempt to encapsulate the Canadian identity – its meaning and its many facets – by selecting a group of exemplary citizens who had performed significant acts of service. The subdued but underlying importance of Canadian nationalism continues to play a role, with the expansion of the order to non-Canadians.

The ultimate expression of the order's legitimacy is the calibre of those who have received it. Canadians from every corner of our country and every walk of life have received the order by virtue of their outstanding contributions. We will not soon forget the likes of Charles Best, Sir Ernest MacMillan, Pauline McGibbon, Jean Drapeau, Cardinal Léger, Eugene Forsey, Yusuf Karsh, Evelyn Cudmore, or Terry Fox, all of whom have received the order. Their stories are but a single page out of the order's Register Book, yet they speak volumes about Canada's recent history. More than four thousand other Canadians have been appointed since 1967, and the number of nominations is growing. No society of honour is without controversy, but the Order of Canada has been fortunate to have had very few to date. It would be naive to suggest that every appointment has met with universal approval, and in retrospect one can discern a few ill-advised awards, yet this is open to interpretation.

One thing is certain: the society of honour established at the insistence of Lester B. Pearson and constructed by Vincent Massey, John Matheson, Esmond Butler, John Hodgson, and Michael Pitfield is the most equitable and fair yet devised. It is a system of which even the ever-cautious Mackenzie King would be proud. How far we have come from the age of W.F. Nickle, who is in many ways the father of our concept of what honours should embody. His disdain for partisan patronage, flunkeyism, and social gradation served as a catalyst for the nearly half-century-long project to create a Canadian order.

Perhaps there is, as Pierre Bourdieu argues, a larger game at play in the quest for symbolic capital. However, if this is true, why is there so seldom controversy associated with the vast majority of appointments to the order? Why, then, are people at the local level, who already have the respect and admiration of their fellow citizens, seeking to do the impossible and build upon that respect? The order accords recognition where honour, respect, and admiration already exist.

The members of the order have all in their own ways desired a better country, and they serve as a credit to all Canadians. Their display of exemplary citizenship and their devotion to humankind is a source of inspiration that can be drawn from by all.

Appendices

APPENDIX ONE: MEMBERS OF THE INTERDEPARTMENTAL COMMITTEE AND AWARDS COORDINATION COMMITTEE, 1942

Interdepartmental Committee

Dr Ephriam H. Coleman (chairman), Under-Secretary of State
J. François Delaute (secretary), Chief Clerk for the Department of the Secretary of State
Sir Shuldham Redfern, Secretary to the Governor General
John Erskine Read, Legal Advisor, Department of External Affairs
Frederick L.C. Pereira, Assistant Secretary to the Governor General
Robert Arthur Pennington, Paymaster Commander, RCN
O.M.M. Kay, Brigadier General
D.E. MacKell, Wing Commander, RCAF
C.T. Mee, Flight Lieutenant, RCAF
Reginald John Orde, Brigadier General, Judge Advocate General of the Army
Frank Llewellyn Houghton, Captain, RCN

First Members of the Awards Coordination Committee

Ephriam H. Coleman (Chairman), Under-Secretary of State
J. François Delaute (Secretary), Chief Clerk for the Department of the Secretary of State
Sir Shuldham Redfern, Secretary to the Governor General
John Erskine Read, Legal Advisor, Department of External Affairs
Frederick L.C. Pereira, Assistant Secretary to the Governor General
Charles Peter Edwards, Lieutenant Commander, Deputy Minister of Transport
H.F.G. Letson, Major General, Adjutant General
Duncan Kenneth MacTavish, Commander Deputy Judge Advocate General, RCNVR
J.A. Sully, Air Vice-Marshal, Air Member for Personnel, RCAF; Deputy Minister of Labour (circa 1943)
Robert Arthur Pennington, Captain, RCN
E. Rollo Mainguy, Captain, RCN
Gustave Lanctôt, Dominion Archivist

APPENDIX TWO: ROYAL WARRANT CREATING THE CANADA MEDAL, 1943

PREAMBLE

(a) From time to time, citizens of Canada, whether as civilians or as members of the Naval, Military and Air Forces and of the Merchant Navy, render valuable and meritorious service above and beyond their normal duties, which service is worthy of special recognition.

(b) There is at present no suitable award available for issue in recognition of such service.

(c) It is considered that such valuable and meritorious service should be recognized by the award of a suitable medal, which medal could also be awarded to citizens of other countries who render particularly valuable and meritorious service.

REGULATIONS

1 *Designation*   The medal shall be designated and styled 'THE CANADA MEDAL.'

2 *Description*   The medal shall be circular in form and in silver, it shall bear on the obverse the crowned Effigy of the Sovereign and on the reverse the Arms of Canada and the word 'CANADA.' The words 'MERIT' (or 'MERITE') will be inscribed on a bar attached to the mount of the medal.

3 *Ribbon*   The medal will be worn on the left breast, suspended by a ribbon one and a quarter inches in width of red, white and red equal stripes and will be worn immediately after the British Empire Medal and before War Medals.

4 *Miniatures*   Reproductions of the medal, known as a Miniature Medal which may be worn on certain occasions by those whom the medal is awarded shall be half the size.

5 *Precedence*   The award of the medal shall not confer any individual precedence but shall entitle the recipient to the addition, after his name, of the letters 'C.M.' in the case of English speaking recipients and (should they so desire) 'M du C' in the case of French speaking recipients.

6 *Eligibility*   Persons eligible to receive the medal shall be:
   (a) Citizens of Canada, whether civilians or members of the armed forces or the Merchant Navy.
   (b) Citizens of other countries who have rendered valuable and meritorious services of the nature set forth in the next succeeding paragraph.

7 *Service Required*   The medal may be awarded to persons named in the preceding paragraph for specially valuable and meritorious service of a high standard, faithful or zealous performance of ordinary duty not being sufficient in itself.

There must be either:

(a) special service of a high degree of merit, such as discharge of special duties superior to the person's ordinary work, or,

(b) highly meritorious performance of ordinary duties where these have entailed work of a specially trying character, or,

(c) display of a high degree of initiative and forethought.

8 *Limitations upon Award*   THE CANADA MEDAL will normally be awarded, in the case of members of the armed forces, up to and including the rank of Lieutenant-Commander or equivalent rank, but it may, in exceptional circumstance, be awarded to any rank.

9 *Publication and Registration*   The names of those upon whom the award is conferred shall be published in the *Canada Gazette* and kept in the REGISTER OF HONOURS AND AWARDS.

10 *Further Regulations*   The award shall be conferred under such regulations as to grant, forfeiture, restorations and other matters in amplification of these regulations as may be issued from time to time.

Source: LAC, RG 2, Vol. 9, File H-5, Order-in-Council establishing the Canada Medal, 14 October 1943.

APPENDIX THREE: PROPOSED ROYAL WARRANT CREATING THE
CANADIAN AWARD OF HONOUR AND CANADIAN DECORATION
OF HONOUR, 1943

Draft Arrangements for the Recognition of Exceptionally Distinguished Services by
Citizens of Canada

(This is based upon the assumption that it might be desirable to establish a senior
award which would not be an Order of Chivalry, but which would enable recognition
to be given for distinguished and meritorious services to persons whose services
cannot otherwise be appropriately recognized.)

PREAMBLE

It is considered that exceptionally distinguished service by citizens of Canada, whether
as civilians or as members of the Naval, Military and Air Forces and of the Merchant
Navy, should be recognized by the award of suitable decorations which could also be
given to citizens of other countries who may render distinguished service of the same
high order.

REGULATIONS

1 *Designation*   For the purpose of recognition of distinguished service there shall be
established THE CANADIAN AWARD OF HONOUR and THE CANADIAN DECORATION OF
HONOUR.

2 *Conditions*
   (a) Citizens of Canada, whose service to the State, whether in civil or in military
       capacity, has been outstanding will be eligible to receive the Canadian Award
       of Honour.

   (b) Citizens of Canada, whose service to the State, whether in civil or military
       capacity, has been distinguished and meritorious will be eligible to receive the
       Canadian Decoration of Honour.

   (c) Citizens of other countries who have rendered comparable service, whether in
       civil or in military capacity will be eligible to receive the Canadian Award of
       Honour or the Canadian Decoration of Honour.

3 *Description*
   The BADGE of the CANADIAN AWARD OF HONOUR is of silver and enamel, nonagonal,
   charged with three maple leaves conjoined on one stem, proper, superimposed on a
   laurel wreath seeded proper. And, underneath, the motto ACER GERENDO in raised
   letters enameled in red. The whole ensigned with the Royal Crown in gold.

   On the reverse, with an wreath of maple leaves proper, the Royal and Imperial
   Cypher enameled in red.

The BADGE is suspended from a riband 1¾ inches wide of watered silk in autumnal colours – red, yellow, green, purple and scarlet.

The BADGE of the CANADIAN DECORATION OF HONOUR is of the same design, in silver not enameled, with the crown in silver gilded. The riband is 1½ inches wide of watered silk as for the AWARD.

In ordinary full dress the BADGES are worn around the neck suspended by the riband so that the badge may hang ¾ outside and below the collar. By ladies the BADGES are worn on the left shoulder suspended by the riband tied in a bow.

4 *Precedence*
The recipient will not be entitled to any individual precedence but may use the letters after his name of C.A.H. or C.D.H. respectively.

5 *Publication and Registration*
The names of those upon whom the Canadian Award of Honour and the Canadian Decoration of Honour is conferred will be published in the *Canada Gazette*, and kept in a register established for that purpose.

6 *Regulations*
The award and the decoration will be conferred by His Majesty the King, upon the recommendation of the Prime Minister of Canada.

Source: LAC, RG 2, Vol. 9, File H-5, Draft proposal for the establishment of the Canadian Award of Honour and the Canadian Decoration of Honour, 3 May 1943

APPENDIX FOUR: LETTERS PATENT FOUNDING THE ORDER OF CANADA, 1967

CANADA

The Order of Canada	Elizabeth the Second By the Grace of God of the United Kingdom, Canada and Her other
Letters Patent	Realms and Territories Queen, Head of the Commonwealth, Defender Of the Faith.

TO ALL WHOM these Presents shall come or whom the same may in anywise concern.

GREETING

WHEREAS it is desirable and Our Privy Council for Canada has advised that Letters Patent do issue establishing a society of honour in Canada to be known as the Order of Canada, for the purpose of according recognition to Canadian citizens and other persons for merit.

NOW KNOW YE that by and with the advice of Our Privy Council for Canada, We by these Presents, do institute, erect, constitute and create a society of honour to be known by and have forever hereafter, the name, style and designation of the 'Order of Canada.'

AND WE DO Ordain, direct and appoint that the said Order shall consist of the Sovereign, the Governor General of Canada and such members together with such honorary members as We, Our heirs and successors or Our Governor General of Canada on Our behalf shall, in accordance with the constitution of the Order, from time to time appoint.

AND WE DO further ordain, direct and appoint that the said Order shall be governed by the Constitution of the Order of Canada set out in the Schedule hereto any by such ancillary Ordinances as may from time to time be established, made, amended and abrogated by Our Governor General of Canada.

AND to the end that the Ordinances of the said Order may be legally established, We do hereby authorize and command that a seal be immediately engraven, that the said Seal shall hereafter be the Seal of the Order, that the Ordinances of the Order shall be sealed by and with the said Seal after having received the signature of Our Governor General of Canada and that the Ordinances so signed and sealed shall be of the same validity and real and taken as if those Ordinances and every article of them had been recited verbatim in these Our Letters Patent passed under the Great Seal of Canada.

IN WITNESS &c ....

Source: LAC, MG 24, N4, vol. 1, Pearson Papers, Letters Patent for the Order of Canada.

The Order of Canada.

1 (1) The Order of Canada, hereinafter called 'the Order,' shall consist of the Sovereign, the Governor General of Canada and the members and honorary members of the Order.

(2) Every Canadian citizen appointed to be a Companion of the Order, every person to whom the Medal of Courage is awarded and every Canadian citizen to whom the Medal of Service is awards is a member of the Order.

(3) Every person appointed to be an honorary Companion of the Order and every person to whom the Medal of Service is awarded on an honorary basis is an honorary member of the Order.

Officers and Council of *the Order of Canada.*

2 The Governor General of Canada shall, by virtue of that Office, be the Chancellor of the Order and Principal Companion of the Order.

3 The Chancellor is charged with the administration of the Order.

4 There shall be an Advisory Council for the Order, hereinafter called 'the Council,' comprised of
   (a) the Chief Justice of Canada, who shall
       be the Chairman of the Council;
   (b) the Clerk of the Privy Council;
   (c) the Under Secretary of State;
   (d) the Chairman of the Canada Council;
   (e) the President of the Royal Society
       of Canada; and
   (f) the President of the Association of Universities and Colleges of Canada.

5 The Council shall
   (a) consider nominations of Canadian citizens
       of merit for
       (i) admission to the Order as Companions,
       or
       (ii) awards of the Medal of Service
       and compile lists of those nominees who,
       in the opinion of the Council, are the
       nominees of great merit;
   (b) consider nominations of persons, together
       with recommendations and supporting
       material, received from the Government
       of Canada Decorations Committee for
       awards of the Medals of Courage and compile
       lists of those nominees who,
       in the opinion of the Council, are nominees to whom a
       Medal of Courage may be awarded under
       section 17;

(c) forward to the Governor General each list
     compiled pursuant to paragraph (a) or (b); and
(d) advise the Governor General in respect of any other
     matters concerning the Order referred
     by the Governor General to the Council for
     consideration.

6 The Secretary to the Governor General shall be Secretary General of the Order and shall maintain the records of the Order and the Council, arrange for investitures and perform such other functions in respect of the Order as the Governor General may require him to perform.

7 The Governor General may appoint such other officials for the Order, as he, in his sole discretion considers advisable.

8 A person is not a member of the Order by reason only of his being a member of the Council or an official for the Order.

Appointments and Awards.

9 Appointments as Companions and honorary Companions of the Order and awards of the Medal of Courage and Medal of Service shall be made, with the approval of the Sovereign, by Instruments signed by the Governor General and sealed with the Seal of the Order and shall have effect from the date of the affixing of the Seal unless another effective date is specified in the Instrument.

10 Nothing in this Constitution limits the rights of the Governor General to exercise all powers and authorities of the Sovereign in respect of the Order.

Companions of the Order of Canada.

11 (1) Only Canadian citizens are eligible to be appointed as Companions of the Order.
    (2) Only persons other than Canadian citizens are eligible to be appointed as honorary Companions of the Order.

12 (1) Appointments as Companions and honorary Companions of the Order shall be made for merit, especially service to Canada or to humanity at large.
    (2)   Notwithstanding subsection (1) any distinguished citizen of a country other than Canada whom Canada desires to honour may be appointed as an honorary Companion of the Order.

13 (1) Any person or organization may submit to the Secretary General of the Order for consideration by the Council a nomination of a Canadian citizen for appointment to the Order as a Companion.
    (2) Appointments as honorary Companions of the Order shall be made with the advice of the Queen's Privy Council for Canada.

14 Subject to sections 15 and 16, the Governor General may appoint to be Companions of the Order of Canada, other than honorary Companion, a maximum of
   (a)   fifty persons in 1967; and
   (b)   twenty-five persons in any year thereafter.

15 Membership, other than honorary membership, in the Order is limited, in the case of Companions to one hundred and fifty Companions in addition to the Principal Companion.

16 When the maximum number of Companions of the Order have been appointed, a person may be appointed as a Companion of the Order only where a vacancy occurs.

The Medal of Courage.

17 (1) A Medal, to be known as the 'Medal of Courage,' may be awarded in connection with the Order to any person who, as a civilian or a member of an armed force or police force performs an act of conspicuous courage in circumstances of great danger.
   (2) The Medal of Courage may be awarded posthumously but the deceased recipient of the medal does not become a member of the Order.

18 Any person or organization may submit to the Secretary General of the Order for consideration by the Government of Canada Decorations Committee and the Council, a nomination of a person for an award of the Medal of Courage together with any descriptions, evidence and attestations in respect of the act of courage that are available.

The Medal of Service.

19 (1) A Medal, to be known as the 'Medal of Service,' may be awarded in connection with the Order to any person for merit, especially service to Canada or humanity at large.
   (2) Notwithstanding subsection (1), the Medal of Service may be awarded on an honorary basis to any distinguished citizen of a country other than Canada whom Canada desired to honour.

20 (1) Any person or organization may submit to the Secretary General of the Order for consideration by the Council, a nomination or a Canadian citizen for an award of the Medal of Service.
   (2) Awards of the Medal of Service to persons other than Canadian citizens shall be made by and with the advice of the Queen's Privy Council for Canada.

21 The Governor General may award the Medal of Service to a maximum of
   (a) one hundred persons in 1967; and
   (b) fifty persons in any year thereafter.

Termination of Membership in the Order.

22 A person ceases to be a member or honorary member of the Order upon
  (a) his death;
  (b) his resignation from the Order, which shall have effect from the date on which a resignation in writing is accepted by the Governor General; or
  (c) the termination of his appointment or revocation of his award by the Governor General.

Designations and Insignia.

23 (1) A Companion of the Order of Canada is entitled to
    (a) have the letters 'C.C.' placed after his name on all occasions when use of such letters is customary; and
    (b) wear as a decoration the insignia of the Order prescribed in the Ordinances of the Order.
  (2) A person whom a Medal of Courage is awarded is entitled to
    (a) have the letters 'C.M.' placed after his name on all occasions when use of such letters is customary; and
    (b) wear as a decoration the insignia prescribed for recipients of The Medal of Courage in the Ordinances of the Order.
  (3) A person whom a Medal of Service is awarded is entitled to
    (a) have the letters 'S.M.' placed after his name on all occasions when use of such letters is customary; and
    (b) wear as a decoration the insignia prescribed for recipients of The Medal of Service in the Ordinances of the Order.

24 (1) When worn in Canada by a Canadian citizen, the insignia of the Order shall be worn immediately after the Victoria Cross and the George Cross and in front of all other decorations.

  (2) When worn in Canada by a Canadian citizen, the Medal of Courage shall be worn immediately after the insignia of the Order and in front of all other decorations.

  (3) When worn in Canada by a Canadian citizen, the Medal of Service shall be worn immediately after the insignia of the Order and the Medal of Courage and in front of all other decorations.

25 Except as may otherwise be provided in the Ordinances, the insignia of the Order shall remain the property of the Order.

Ordinances of the Order.

26 The Governor General may make Ordinances, not inconsistent with this Constitution, respecting the establishment, government, investitures and insignia of the Order.

Motto.

27 The motto of the Order shall be *Desiderantes Meliorem Patriam.*

Seal.

28 (1) The Seal of the Order shall be confided to the custody of the Governor General.
   (2) No appointment, revocation or appointment, award or Ordinance has effect unless it has been sealed with the Seal of the Order.

Date of Institution.

2 Notwithstanding section 9, no appointment to the Order, other than an honorary appointment, shall have effect and no award of the Medal of Courage or Medal of Service, other than on an honorary basis, shall be deemed to be made before July 1, 1967, which date shall be deemed to be the date of institution of the Order.

Source: LAC, MG24, N4, vol. 1, Pearson Papers, Final Constitution of the Order of Canada 1967.

APPENDIX SIX: NOMINATION FORM FROM VINCENT MASSEY

NOTE: IF YOU DO NOT HAVE ALL THE INFORMATION REQUESTED BELOW, PLEASE GIVE AS MUCH AS AVAILABLE.

SURNAME OF NOMINEE	GIVEN NAMES	MARITAL STATUS	DATE OF BIRTH	SEX
ARTHUR,	Eric Ross	SINGLE ☐ MARRIED ☒	1 July 1898	☒ M ☐ F

ADDRESS	PLACE OF BIRTH	PRESENT CITIZENSHIP	TELEPHONE NUMBER

PRESENT OCCUPATION	OFFICIAL POSITION	NAME AND ADDRESS OF NOMINATOR
		The Rt.Hon.Vincent Massey

OTHER OFFICES NOW HELD — (INCLUDING SERVICE CLUBS, CIVIC GROUPS, PROFESSIONAL OR TRADE ORGANIZATIONS, ETC.)

Batterwood House,
Nr. Port Hope, Ontario.

CURRICULUM VITAE OR BIOGRAPHICAL SKETCH OF NOMINEE INCLUDING HONOURS AND DEGREES (CONTINUE ON REVERSE IF NECESSARY)

Professor of Architectural Design, University of Toronto (retired)
M.A., B.Arch., F.R.A.I.C., F.R.I.B.A., LL.D.

Educated: Otago Boys' High School, Dunedin, N.Z.
University of Liverpool

Served with New Zealand Rifle Brigade, 1917-18; in World War II
as Ordinary Seaman.

University of Alberta Gold Medal (1956) for national contribution
in the field of architecture.

Editorial Adviser to the Journal, Royal Architectural Institute of Canada.

Professional Adviser to the Corporation of the City of Toronto in
connection with the City Hall Competition, 1957-58

Founder of Vitruvian Society of Toronto; one of the founders of
the Architectural Conservancy of Ontario.

DETAILS OF SERVICES, TO CANADA OR TO HUMANITY AT LARGE, WHICH CAUSED YOU TO MAKE THIS NOMINATION (CONTINUE ON REVERSE IF NECESSARY)

Author of numerous brochures on early Canadian architecture,
including:

> "Small Houses of the late 18th and early 19th century
> in Ontario"
> "The Early Buildings of Ontario"
> "Moose Factory"
> "Early Forts in Upper Canada"
> "No Mean City" (an authoritative book on important
> buildings in our past and present)

Professor Arthur is probably the leading authority on
architectural history in Canada and has exercised a great influence
on public policy with regard to the preservation of old buildings
of importance and the design of new ones.

I feel certain that Professor Arthur is fully qualified for
admission to the Order of Canada, either as a Companion or as a
recipient of the Medal of Service.

APPENDIX SEVEN: DISTRIBUTION OF FIRST AWARDS OF THE ORDER OF CANADA, JULY 1967

Order of Canada Total

Total awards (CC and SM): 90
Average age of appointees: 64.5 years

Oldest appointed: R.S. McLaughlin, CC. (96 years old)
Youngest appointed: Marlene Streit, SM. (33 years old)
Number of women appointed: 13 (14 per cent)
Other awards: 24 (26 per cent) had other senior exemplary service or gallantry decorations prior to their appointment to the Order of Canada.

Provincial Distribution

	Place of birth	Place of residence
Ontario	27 (30%)	38 (42%)
Quebec	26 (29%)	29 (32%)
Nova Scotia	2 (2%)	1 (1%)
New Brunswick	6 (6%)	2 (2%)
Manitoba	2 (2%)	1 (1%)
P.E.I.	1 (1%)	2 (2%)
British Columbia	3 (3%)	8 (9%)
Alberta	2 (2%)	4 (4%)
Saskatchewan	1 (1%)	2 (2%)
Newfoundland	1 (1%)	1 (1%)
Northwest Territories	2 (2%)	2 (2%)
Born overseas	17 (19%)	

Companions of the Order of Canada

Awards: 35
Average age of appointees: 69 years
Oldest appointed: R.S. McLaughlin (96 years old)
Youngest appointed: Maureen Forrester (37 years old)
Number of women appointed: 3 (9 per cent)
Other awards: 11 had other senior exemplary service or gallantry decorations prior to their appointment to the Order of Canada.

Provincial Distribution

	Place of birth	Place of residence
Ontario	11 (31%)	18 (51%)
Quebec	9 (26%)	11 (31%)
Nova Scotia	2 (6%)	
New Brunswick	2 (6%)	1 (3%)
Manitoba	2 (6%)	1 (3%)
P.E.I.		
British Columbia	2 (6%)	3 (9%)
Alberta		
Saskatchewan	1 (3%)	1 (3%)
Newfoundland		
Northwest Territories		
Born overseas	6 (17%)	

Order of Canada Medal of Service

Awards: 55
Average age of appointees: 62 years
Oldest appointed: Dr Augustine MacDonald (93 years old)
Youngest appointed: Marlene Streit (33 years old)
Number of women appointed: 10 (18%)
Other awards: 13 had other senior exemplary service or gallantry decorations prior to their appointment to the Order of Canada.

Provincial Distribution

	Place of birth	Place of residence
Ontario	16 (29%)	20 (36%)
Quebec	17 (31%)	18 (32%)
Nova Scotia	1 (2%)	
New Brunswick	4 (7%)	1 (2%)
Manitoba		
P.E.I.	1 (2%)	2 (4%)
British Columbia	1 (2%)	5 (10%)
Alberta	2 (4%)	4 (8%)
Saskatchewan	1 (2%)	
Newfoundland	1 (2%)	1 (2%)
Northwest Territories	2 (4%)	2 (4%)
Born overseas	11 (20%)	

Companions

Edgar Spinney ARCHIBALD; agriculturalist and director of the Dominion Experimental Farms, 1919–50. United Nations liaison officer in Ethiopia. Born Yarmouth, NS, 1885.

Lieutenant Colonel Edwin Albert BAKER; helped to found and develop the Canadian National Institute for the Blind after losing his eyesight in the First World War. Former president to the World Council, Federation of the Blind. Born Ernestown, ON, 1898.

Marius BARBEAU; folklorist with the National Museum of Canada at Ottawa since 1911. Author of numerous works on Indian mythology, folk songs. Born Ste-Marie-de-Beauce, QC, 1883.

Lieutenant General Eedson Louis Millard BURNS, DSO, OBE, MC, CD; Canada's adviser on the Geneva disarmament talks. During the Second World War he served as chief of staff and other posts. Postwar director-general of veteran's rehabilitation, later deputy minister of Veterans Affairs. First Commander of the United Nations Emergency Force in the Middle East. Born Westmount, QC, 1897.

Dr Brock CHISHOLM, CBE; controversial psychiatrist and director general of the World Health Organization, 1948–1953. President of the World Federation of Mental Health since 1957. Served in the First World War and was director of Army Medical Services in the Second World War. Born in Oakville, ON, 1896.

The Honourable M.J. William COLDWELL, PC; retired political figure who helped found the CCF. Sat in Parliament 1935–58 and was CCF leader from 1942 to 1958. Now a member of the Royal Commission on Security. Born in Seaton, Devon, England, 1888.

Donald CREIGHTON; historian who has twice won the Governor General's Literary Award for academic non-fiction. Born in Toronto, ON, 1902.

Jean DRAPEAU, QC; dynamic Montreal mayor and a key figure in organizing EXPO '67. He modernized the city with a subway and a major arts centre. Born in Montreal, QC, 1916.

Maureen FORRESTER; world-renowned contralto and head of the Philadelphia Academy of Music's voice department; was a Montreal school dropout at 13. Born in Montreal, QC, 1930.

Raoul JOBIN; operatic tenor, sang with the Paris Opera Company, 1930–40 and 1947–55. Made Metropolitan Opera debut in 1940. Born in Quebec City, QC, 1906.

Walter C. KOERNER; Vancouver industrialist who came to Canada from Czechoslovakia in 1939. Chairman of Rayonier Canada Limited, director of Air Canada, CNR, and numerous corporations. Member of the Economic Council of Canada and Board of Governors of the University of British Columbia. Vice-president of the Canadian Welfare Council. Born in Czechoslovakia, 1898.

Arthur LISMER; member of the Group of Seven. Principal of the School of Art and Design, Montreal Museum of Fine Arts. Born in Sheffield, England, 1885.

John A. MacAULAY, QC; business executive, in 1960 accepted Nobel Peace Prize on behalf of the Red Cross, of which he was then international chairman. Has been president of the Canadian Bar Association and Canadian Red Cross Society. Born in Morden, MB, 1895.

Chalmers Jack MACKENZIE, CMG, MC; major figure in the Atomic Energy Control Board from its inception in 1946 until 1961. Chancellor of Carleton University since 1954. Former director of the Canadian Geographical Society. Born St Stephen, NB, 1888.

William A. MACKINTOSH, CMG; economist and retired director of the Bank of Canada and Empire Life Insurance Company. Principal and vice-chancellor of Queen's University, 1957–1961. Born in Madoc, ON, 1895.

Hugh MacLENNAN; honoured Montreal writer whose novel *Two Solitudes*, deftly depicts the gulf between Canada's two major cultures. Five-time winner of the Governor General's literary award. Lecturer at McGill University since 1952. Born in Glace Bay, NS, 1907.

Leo Edmond MARION; chemist and dean of science at the University of Ottawa. Editor-in-chief of the *Canadian Journal of Research*. Has held high government research posts since 1929. Born in Ottawa, ON, 1899.

The Right Honourable Vincent MASSEY, PC, CH, CD; Governor General of Canada, 1952–9, the first native-born Canadian to hold the post. Former chancellor of the University of Toronto, first Canadian minister to the United States, and High Commissioner to the United Kingdom. Born in Toronto, ON, 1897.

Colonel Robert Samuel McLAUGHLIN, ED, CD; pioneer auto manufacturer. President of General Motors Canada. He began working at the McLaughlin Carriage Co. in 1888, founding president of McLaughlin Motor Car Company in 1907. Born in Enniskillen, ON, 1871.

John B. McNAIR, QC; lieutenant-governor of New Brunswick since 1965. Was premier of New Brunswick from 1940 to 1952 and chief justice of New Brunswick from 1955 to 1964. Born in Andover, NB, 1899.

Dr Gordon MURRAY; Toronto surgeon who pioneered development of the artificial kidney, heart valve transplants and other breakthroughs. Senior surgeon at Toronto General Hospital. Born in Stratford, ON, 1894.

Monsignor Alphonse-Marie PARENT; chairman of the Royal Commission that produced a blueprint for education in Quebec. Now vice-rector of Laval University. Much-honoured member of many national and world education bodies. Born in St Chrysostome, QC, 1906.

Major General the Honourable George R. PEARKES, VC, PC, CB, DSO, MC, CD; Minister of Defence from 1957 to 1960 and lieutenant-governor of British Columbia since then. A Victoria Cross winner in the First World War, he commanded the 1st Canadian Division from 1940 to 1941 and later held the Pacific Command. Born in Watford, England, 1888.

Alfred PELLAN; a leader of the Montreal movement in painting. His work is internationally recognized. Born in Quebec City, QC, 1906.

Wilfrid PELLETIER, CMG; Quebec's director general of music teaching. Conductor of the Montreal and Quebec Symphony Orchestras. Has also been a regular conductor of the Metropolitan Opera Association's Sunday concerts. Born in Montreal, QC, 1896.

Colonel, Dr Wilder PENFIELD, OM, CMG; renowned neurosurgeon and director of the Montreal Neurological Institute, 1934–1960. Now president of the Vanier Institute for the Family. Born in Spokane, WA, 1891.

Norman ROBERTSON; career diplomat and public servant, now a Carleton University professor and senior advisor for the Department of External Affairs. He has held top Ottawa and foreign posts since 1929. Born in Vancouver, BC, 1904.

Gabrielle ROY; novelist who has won top Canadian and French literary awards. Born in St Boniface, MB, 1909.

The Right Honourable Louis St LAURENT, PC, QC; Liberal Prime Minister from 1948 to 1957. Left a successful law career in 1941 to enter the federal Cabinet. Born in Compton, QC, 1882.

Francis Reginald SCOTT, QC; prize-winning poet, editor, writer on politics and former dean of McGill University Law faculty. Eight years national CCF chairman. Helped organize the NDP. Born in Quebec City, QC, 1899.

Henry G. THODE, MBE; president and vice-chancellor of McMaster University. Conducted research in chemistry for the National Research Council and Defence Research Board. Born in Dundurn, SK, 1910.

W.P. THOMPSON; president emeritus of the University of Saskatchewan. Chaired committee that in 1962 prepared and recommended medical care insurance plan adopted by the Saskatchewan government. Born in DeCewsville, ON, 1889.

The Honourable Mrs Pauline VANIER, PC; widow of the former Governor General. Served with St John Ambulance in the First World War. Represented the Canadian Red Cross in France during the Second World War. Chancellor of the University of Ottawa. Born in Montreal, QC, 1898.

Leolyn Dana WILGRESS; former trade commissioner and top diplomat. First Canadian minister to the USSR in 1942 and ambassador in 1944. Attended United Nations founding conference for Canada. Was twice chairman of the General Agreement on Tariffs and Trade. Born in Vancouver, BC, 1892.

Healey WILLAN; world-renowned composer of more than 200 works. Long associated with the Toronto Conservatory of Music and the University of Toronto. For 46 years choirmaster at St Mary Magdalene Anglican Church, Toronto. Born in London, England, 1880.

Officers

Pierrette ALARIE; opera singer who has performed in Europe and the United States as well as Canada. Made her debut in 1943. Born in Montreal, QC, 1921.

Reverend David BAUER; adviser to Canada's national hockey team, a teacher, former player with Oshawa Generals and coach of the 1964 Olympic team. Born in Kitchener, ON, 1926.

James M. BENTLEY; president of the Canadian Federation of Agriculture and Edmonton and District Milk Producers Association. Born in Dawson City, YK, 1906.

Yvette BRIND'AMOUR; founder in 1948 of Montreal's Théâtre du Rideau Vert, which has performed at invitation in France and Russia. Born in Montreal, QC, 1930.

Thérèse CASGRAIN, OBE; president of the League of Human Rights, former president of the Voice of Women, founder of the Federation of Quebec Women. Born in Montreal, QC, 1896.

Floyd Sherman CHALMERS; chairman of Maclean-Hunter Publishing, started foundation to aid performing arts. Born in Chicago, IL, 1898.

Gregory CLARK, OBE, MC; associate editor of *Weekend Magazine*. Writer of feature articles and humour since 1911. Won Military Cross in First World War, served as a war correspondent in the Second. Winner of 1965 Stephen Leacock Memorial for Humour. Born in Toronto, ON, 1892.

Alexander COLVILLE; official war artist with the Canadian Army in the Second World War and former art teacher at Mount Allison University. Born in Toronto, ON, 1920.

Reverend Clement CROMIER, president of the University of Moncton, member of the Royal Commission on Bilingualism and Biculturalism. Born in Moncton, NB, 1910.

Air Marshal Wilfred Austin CURTIS, CB, CBE, DSC, ED, CD; retired Chief of Air Staff, vice-chairman of Hawker-Siddley of Canada. Joined the RFC in the First World War. Born in Havelock, ON, 1893.

Pauline DONALDA; opera singer, founder and president of the Opera Guild of Montreal. Born in Montreal, QC, 1882.

Philip S. FISHER, CBE, DSO, DSC; chairman of the board of Southam Company, past president of the Canadian Daily Newspaper Publishers Association. Born in Montreal, QC, 1896.

Robert MacLaren FOWLER; business and broadcasting executive who headed one Royal Commission. President of the Canadian Pulp and Paper Association. Born in Peterborough, ON, 1906.

Lawrence FREIMAN; president of A.J. Freiman, Ottawa Department Store, arts patron and chairman of trustees for the National Arts Centre. Born in Ottawa, ON, 1909.

Jean GASCON; actor, director, and founder of Montreal's Théâtre du Nouveau Monde, a founding director of the National Theatre School. Born in Montreal, QC, 1921.

Gratien GÉLINAS; actor, director, and playwright, founder of Comédie Canadienne. Born in St-Tite, QC, 1909.

Dr Gustave GINGRAS; pioneer in medical rehabilitation, executive director of Rehabilitation Institute of Montreal. International service includes planning in South Vietnam to help disabled children. Born in Montreal, QC, 1918.

Robert GLEN; agriculturalist, assistant deputy minister for research in the Federal Department of Agriculture. Born in Paisley, Scotland, 1885.

H. Carl GOLDENBERG, OBE, QC; lawyer and labour expert, federal mediator in the 1966 national railway strike and Royal Commissioner for a study on Metropolitan Toronto. Born in Montreal, QC, 1907.

John W. GOODALL; pioneer along Alberta's Athabaska Trail and early settler at Fort Simpson NWT. Representative on the Northwest Territories Council since 1954. Born in Staffordshire, England, 1890.

Leo GUINDON; teacher, president, and founder of the General Corporation of Catholic Teachers of Quebec. Born in Munsing, MI, 1908.

Raymond GUSHUE, CBE, QC; president and vice-chancellor of Memorial University. Former chairman of the Newfoundland Fisheries Board. Born in Whitborne, NF, 1900.

Henry Foss HALL; principal emeritus Sir George Williams University. Vice-president of Montreal's Theological College. Born in Cowansville, QC, 1897.

Eric L. HARVIE, QC; philanthropist, lawyer, and businessman. Chairman of the Glenbow Foundation, which collects items of historical interest to Western Canada. Born in Orillia, ON, 1892.

John HIRSCH; theatre director, associate director of the Stratford Festival and founding director of the Manitoba Theatre Centre. Born in Siofok, Hungary, 1928.

William Bruce HUTCHINSON; newspaper man, author, and historian. Editorial director of the *Vancouver Sun*. First winner of the Award for Distinguished Journalism in the Commonwealth. Born in Prescott, ON, 1901.

Claude JODOIN; president of the Canadian Labour Congress. Former Montreal city councillor and member of the Quebec legislature. Born in Montreal, QC, 1913.

Ashevak KENOJUAK; Inuit printmaker from Cape Dorset, subject of the award-winning motion picture by the National Film Board. Noted for her animal prints and drawings. Born in 1927.

David Arnold KEYS; physicist, retired vice-president of the Canadian atomic energy project at Chalk River. Author of many publications on geophysics. Born in Toronto, ON, 1890.

Gustave LANCTÔT, QC; author and history professor. Dominion Archivist from 1937 to 1948. Holder of the Royal Society of Canada's Gold Medal for history and a Governor General's Literary Award for non-fiction. Born in St-Constant, QC, 1883.

Lawrence LANDE; poet, author, and composer. Director of the Canadian Writers Foundation. His works include 'Old Lamp Aglow' and *The Third Duke of Richmond*. Born in Ottawa, ON, 1906.

Gilles LEFEBVRE; director of Jeunesses Musicales du Canada, which grew out of a summer camp he organized in 1951. Named president of the International Federation of Jeunesses Musicales in 1963. Born in Montreal, QC, 1922.

The Most Reverend Father Georges-Henri LÉVESQUE; founder of the Social Science School at Laval University, now president of the National University in Rwanda. Former superior at the Dominican College. Born in Roberval, QC, 1903.

Elizabeth Pauline MacCALLUM; Retired diplomat who served as Canada's first chargé d'affaires in Beirut, Lebanon. Born of Canadian missionary parents in Turkey, 1895.

Dr Augustine MacDONALD; general practitioner who served a rural area near Souris, PEI, for more than sixty years. With a farm kitchen for an operating room, he once successfully reattached the feet of a boy after they had been almost severed by a mower. Born near Souris, PEI, 1874.

Brian MACDONALD; choreographer, Royal Winnipeg Ballet. First Canadian choreographer to have his ballets presented in the USSR. Composer of 'Rose La Tulippe.' Born in Ontario, 1927.

Monseigneur Arthur MAHEUX, OBE; professor and author who taught at Laval University for more than thirty years. His books include *French Canada and Britain: A New Interpretation,* and *Problems of Canadian Unity*. Born in Ste-Julie-de-Megantic, QC, 1884.

Vernon Francis McADAM; national director of the Boys and Girls Clubs of Canada and for fifty years head of the Weredale House for homeless boys in Montreal. Born in St George, NB, 1899.

Reverend Mother Maura McGUIRE; superior-general of the Sisters of St Joseph, former administrative superintendent of St Michael's Hospital, Toronto. Born in Toronto, ON, 1900.

Leonard H. NICHOLSON, MBE; retired commissioner of the RCMP and former member of the Northwest Territories Council. He joined the force in 1923 and headed it from 1951 to 1958. Born in Mount Middleton, NB, 1904.

Jean PALARDY; painter, film director, and expert on early French-Canadian furniture. Currently working on restoring the fort at Louisbourg. Helped establish the National Film Board's French-language unit. Born of Canadian parents in Fitchburg, MA, 1905.

Harry Thomas PATTERSON; originator of the Stratford Shakespearean Festival and now its planning consultant and public relations director. Born in Stratford, ON, 1920.

Isaac C. PHILLS; steelworker who despite depression, strikes, and illness educated his six children to be a minister, doctor, a secretary, an industrial chemist, and a nurse. Born in St Vincent, West Indies, 1896.

Maurice RICHARD; star right wing with the Montreal Canadiens for eighteen seasons until 1960, during which he set sixteen NHL records which he still holds or shares. First player ever to score fifty goals in a season in fifty games. Born in Montreal, QC, 1921.

Paul-André RIVARD; social worker with the Quebec Justice Department, working with prisoners in Montreal. Previously worked with both juvenile and adult delinquents on parole. Born in Amos, QC, 1929.

Chester A. RONNING; retired diplomat. Taught in Edmonton and China before serving as an RCAF intelligence officer. Joined the foreign service and since his retirement has served as special Canadian envoy to Vietnam. Born in Fancheng, China, 1894.

Phyllis ROSS, CBE; economist with the Federal Tariff Board from 1934 to 1945. Her late husband was lieutenant-governor of British Columbia from 1955 to 1960. Mrs Ross served as the chancellor of the University of British Columbia. Born in Rossland, BC, ca. 1900.

Adelaide SINCLAIR, OBE; economist and deputy director of the United Nations Children's Fund. A wartime director of the Women's Royal Canadian Navy Service, she later joined the federal health department and held several posts with the UN. Born in Toronto, ON, 1900.

Ralph STEINHAUER; farmer, past president of the Alberta Federation of Indians and a board member of the Indian-Eskimo Association. Elected chief of the Saddle Lake Reserve in 1966. Born in Morley, AB, 1905.

Marlene Stewart STREIT; amateur golfer whose honours include the British and U.S. women's amateur titles. Elected to the Canadian Sports Hall of Fame in 1962. Born in Cereal, AB, 1934.

Kenneth W. TAYLOR, CBE; retired public servant. Joined the federal civil service in 1939 and retired as deputy finance minister in 1963. Taught at McMaster University and Queen's University. Born in Takutang, China, 1909.

The Honourable William Ferdinand Alphonse TURGEON, PC, QC; lawyer, judge, and diplomat. Saskatchewan attorney general from 1907 to 1921 and a justice on the provincial appeals court from 1921 to 1941, when he joined the Department of External Affairs. He served as a diplomat in Mexico, Argentina, Chile, Belgium, Ireland, and Portugal. Born in Petit Rocher, NB, 1877.

William Elgin van STEENBURGH, OBE, ED; biologist, retired deputy minister of mines and still an advisor to the resources department. Started as an insect control specialist with the federal Department of Agriculture in 1928. Born in Havelock, ON, 1899.

Dr. Alje VENNEMA; director of the Canadian Medical Air Service in Vietnam, who started an anti-tuberculosis clinic there and has flown many times to remote areas to bring medical service to the needy. Born in Holland, 1932.

Adam Hartley ZIMMERMAN, Sr, OBE; retired chairman of the Defence Research Board in Ottawa. A mining engineer before the war, he joined the Ministry of Munitions and Supply, directing small arms production and the production of communications equipment. Born in Hamilton, ON, 1902.

The Order of Canada.

1 (1) The Order of Canada, hereinafter called 'the Order,' shall consist of the Sovereign, the Governor General of Canada and the members and honorary members of the Order.

(2) Every Canadian citizen appointed to be a Companion of the Order, every person to whom the Medal of Courage is awarded and every Canadian citizen to whom the Medal of Service is awarded is a member of the Order.

(3) Every person appointed to be an honorary Companion of the Order and every person to whom the Medal of Service is awarded on an honorary basis is an honorary member of the Order.

Officers and Council of the Order of Canada.

2 The Governor General of Canada shall, by virtue of that Office, be the Chancellor of the Order and Principal Companion of the Order.

3 The Chancellor is charged with the administration of the Order.

4 (1) There shall be an Advisory Council for the Order, hereinafter called 'the Council,' comprised of
  (a) the Chief Justice of Canada, who shall
      be the Chairman of the Council;
  (b) the Clerk of the Privy Council;
  (c) the Under Secretary of State;
  (d) the Chairman of the Canada Council;
  (e) the President of the Royal Society of Canada; and
  (f) the President of the Association of Universities and Colleges of Canada.
  (g) where considered appropriate by the Governor General, not more than two other members to be appointed by the Governor General as provided in subsection (2).
  (2) Each member of the Advisory Council referred to in paragraph (1)(g)
      (a) shall be
          (i)   chosen from among members of the Order,
          (ii) nominated by the ex officio members of the Council, and
          (iii) appointed for a term not exceeding two years; and
      (b) is eligible for re-appointment to the council.

5 The Council shall
  (a) consider nominations of Canadian citizens
      of merit for
      (i)   admission to the Order as Companions,
      (ii) admission to the Order as Officers, or
      (iii) admission to the Order as Members;

(b) compile and submit to the Governor General lists of those nominees who, in the opinion of the Council, have the greatest merit in each category; and

(c) advise the Governor General on such other matters concerning the Order as he may refer to the Council for consideration.

6 The Secretary to the Governor General shall be Secretary General of the Order and shall maintain the records of the Order and the Council, arrange for investitures and perform such other functions in respect of the Order as the Governor General may require him to preform.

7 The Governor General may appoint such other officials for the Order, as he, in his sole discretion considers advisable.

8 A person is not a member of the Order by reason only of his being a member of the Council or an official for the Order.

Appointments and Awards.

9 Appointments as Companions and honorary Companions of the Order and awards of the Medal of Courage and Medal of Service shall be made, with the approval of the Sovereign, by Instruments signed by the Governor General and sealed with the Seal of the Order and shall have effect from the date of the affixing of the Seal unless another effective date is specified in the Instrument.

10 Nothing in this Constitution limits the rights of the Governor General to exercise all powers and authorities of the Sovereign in respect of the Order.

Eligibility for Appointment.

11 (1) Only Canadian citizens are eligible to be appointed as Companions, Officers or Members of the Order.

(2) Only persons other than Canadian citizens are eligible to be appointed as honorary Companions, Officers or Members of the Order.

Companions of the Order of Canada.

12 (1) Appointments as Companions and honorary Companions of the Order shall be made for outstanding achievement and merit of the highest degree, especially service to Canada or to humanity at large.

(2) Notwithstanding subsection (1), any distinguished person, who is not a Canadian citizen but whom the Government of Canada desires to honour, may be appointed as an honorary Companion of the Order.

13 (1) Where a Governor General ceases to hold that office, he shall, notwithstanding, section 11, continue by virtue of his having held that Office, be a Companion of the Order.

(2) Notwithstanding section 11, the spouse of a Governor General who serves

with the Governor General during any period when he holds that office shall be appointed to be a Companion of the Order and shall not cease to be a Companion by reason death or retirement.

14 Subject to sections 15 and 16, the Governor General may appoint to be Companions of the Order, other than honorary Companions, a maximum of fifteen persons in any year.

15 Membership, other than honorary membership, in the Order is limited, in the case of Companions to one hundred and fifty Companions in addition to the Principal Companion, his spouse and any former Governor General and his spouse or surviving spouse.

16 When the maximum number of Companions of the Order have been appointed, a person may be appointed a Companion of the Order only when a vacancy occurs.

Officers of the Order of Canada.

17 (1) Appointments as Officers and honorary Officers of the Order shall be made for achievement and merit of a high degree, especially service to Canada or to humanity at large.

(2) Notwithstanding subsection (1), any distinguished person who is not a Canadian citizen by whom the Government of Canada desires to honour, may be appointed as an honorary Officer of the Order.

18 The Governor General may appoint to be Officers of the Order, other than honorary Officers, a maximum of forty-six persons in any year.

Members of the Order of Canada.

19 (1) Appointments as Members and honorary Members of the Order shall be made for distinguished service in or to a particular locality, group or field of activity.

(2) Notwithstanding subsection (1), any distinguished person, who is not a Canadian citizen but whom the Government of Canada desires to honour, may be appointed as an honorary Member of the Order.

20 The Governor General may appoint to be Members of the Order, other than honorary Members, a maximum of ninety-two persons in any year.

Nominations and Advice.

21 (1) Any person or organization may submit to the Secretary General of the Order for consideration by the Council a nomination of a Canadian citizen for appointment to the Order as a Companion, Officer or Member.

(2) Appointments as honorary Companions, Officers and Members of the Order shall be made on the advice of The Queen's Privy Council for Canada.

Subsequent Appointments.

22 With his consent a Member of the Order may be appointed as an Officer or Companion, and an Officer of the Order may be appointed as a Companion, but no member shall
    (a) hold more than one appointment at any time; or
    (b) be entitled to place after his name or retain the insignia pertaining to the previous appointment.

Termination of Membership in the Order.

23 A person ceases to be a member or honorary member of the Order upon
    (a) his death;
    (b) his resignation for the Order, which shall have effect from the
date on which a resignation in writing is accepted by the Governor General; or
    (c) the termination of his appointment or revocation of his award by the Governor General.

Designations and Insignia.

24 (1) A Companion of the Order is entitled to
    (a) have the letters 'C.C.' placed after his name on all occasions when the use of such letters is customary; and
    (b) wear as a decoration the insignia prescribed in the Ordinances of the Order for Companions.
(2) An Officer of the Order is entitled to
    (a) have the letters 'O.C.' placed after his name on all occasions when the use of such letters is customary; and
    (b) wear as a decoration the insignia prescribed in the Ordinances of the Order for Officers.
(3) A Member of the Order is entitled to
    (a) have the letters 'C.M.' placed after his name on all occasions when the use of such letters is customary; and
    (b) wear as a decoration the insignia prescribed in the Ordinances of the Order for Members.

25 When worn in Canada by a Canadian citizen, the insignia of the Order should be worn in the sequence prescribed in the *Directive Respecting the Protocol for Wearing the Insignia of Canadian Orders and Decorations*, made by the Governor General on the Advice of the Queen's Privy Council for Canada.

26 (1) Except as may otherwise be provided in the Ordinances, the insignia of the Order shall remain the property of the Order.
    (2) When a person ceases, other than by death, to be a member of the Order, he shall forthwith return to the Secretary General of the Order the insignia of the Order that was presented upon his appointment to the Order.

Ordinances of the Order.

27 The Governor General may make Ordinances, not inconsistent with this Constitution, respecting the establishment, government, investitures and insignia of the Order.

Motto.

28 The motto of the Order shall be *Desiderantes Meliorem Patriam.*

Seal.

29 (1) The Seal of the Order shall be confided to the custody of the Governor General.

(2) No appointment, revocation or appointment, award or Ordinance has effect unless it has been sealed with the Seal of the Order.

Transitional.

30 Every person to whom the Medal of Service of the Order has been awarded is an Officer of the Order and entitled

(a) to have the letters 'O.C.' in lieu of the letters 'S.M.' placed after his name on all occasions when the use of such letters is customary; and

(b) upon returning to the Secretary General of the Order the insignia prescribed for recipients of the Medal of Service, to wear as a decoration the insignia prescribed in the Ordinances of the Order for Officers.

APPENDIX TEN: ORDER OF CANADA INSIGNIA MANUFACTURE,
1967–2004

Medal of Service of the Order of Canada

Made of .925 silver by Garrard & Company of London, unhallmarked
Manufactured 18 April 1967 until the award was abolished in 1972
The first issues of 1967 can be differentiated from later issues because the mounting
ring on the 1967 issue is of a thinner gauge of silver wire and not soldered shut.
Naming was on the lower arm of the reverse; initials and surname for men and full
given and surname for women.
325 insignia produced
189 melted

Medal of Courage of the Order of Canada

Made of gilded .925 silver by Garrard & Company of London, unhallmarked
Manufactured 18 April 1967 until the award was abolished in 1972.
The mounting ring on all issues is soldered shut and gilded.
Naming was to be on the lower arm of the reverse (same as Medal of Service); none
were issued.
24 insignia were produced
18 were melted

Companion of the Order of Canada

Garrard & Company
Made of 18 karat gold by Garrard & Company of London, unhallmarked
Order was placed for 14 karat but was never filled.
Manufactured 18 April 1967 to April 1982
Each insignia is numbered on the reverse starting with 001
There is also one special issue designated 'C' that is hung from the Chancellor's
Chain, and one other special issue with an unknown number that was presented to
Bruce Beatty in 1968 by the Governor General. Crown is set with actual jewels
(rectangular and diamond shaped).
Insignia numbered 001 to 260

Rideau Ltée
Made of 18 karat gold by Rideau Ltée of St Laurent, Quebec, hallmarked 18k RIDEAU
on the hanger, some hallmarks are also accompanied by a small snowflake similar to
the shape of the Order of Canada.
In 1985 the four small dots on the motto of the Order were changed to a quadrangle.
Crown is set with actual jewels (all round in shape).
Manufactured April 1985 to May 1996
Insignia 261–319

Insignia 320–339 were made of gold plated .925 silver (commencing in November 1993)

Birks & Son (Pressed Metal Products)
Made of .925 silver by Pressed Metal Products, hallmarked on the suspender 'BIRKS STERL'
In 2001 the thickness of the hanger was increased from 1.25mm to 1.75mm. Crown is set with actual jewels (all round in shape).
Manufactured 1996 to August 2004
Insignia 340 to 444

Rideau Ltée
Made of .925 silver by Rideau Ltée, hallmarked on the suspender accompanied by a small snowflake similar to the shape of the Order of Canada. Crown is set with actual jewels (all round in shape).
Manufactured September 2004 to present
Insignia 445–464

Officer of the Order of Canada

Garrard & Company of London
Made of gold-plated .925 silver by Garrard & Company of London, hallmarked on the reverse of the lower arm (Birmingham with date letters)
Manufactured January 1972 to 15 April 1983
Each insignia is numbered on the reverse starting with number 001
Insignia 001 to 700

Rideau Ltée
Made of gold-plated .925 silver by Rideau Ltée of St Laurent, Quebec, hallmarked on the reverse of the lower arm 'RIDEAU +R STER' some later issues also have a small snowflake
In mid 1984 the four small dots on the motto of the Order were changed to a quadrangle.
Manufactured 15 April 1983 to April 1996
Insignia 701 to 1154

Birks & Son (Pressed Metal Products)
Made of gold-plated .925 silver by Pressed Metal Products, hallmarked on the reverse of the lower arm 'BIRKS STERL'
Manufactured 1996 to August 2004
Insignia 1155 to 1680

Rideau Ltée
Made of gold-plated .925 silver by Rideau Ltée of St Laurent, Quebec, hallmarked on the reverse of the lower arm 'RIDEAU +R STER' also includes a small snowflake
Manufactured September 2004 to the present
Insignia 1681–1780

Member of the Order of Canada

Garrard & Company of London
Made of .925 silver by Garrard & Company of London, hallmarked on the reverse of the lower arm (Birmingham with date letters)
Manufactured January 1972 to 19 July 1982
Insignia 001 to 805

Rideau Ltée
Made of .925 silver by Rideau Ltée of St Laurent, Quebec, hallmarked on the reverse of the lower arm 'RIDEAU +R STER' some later issues also have a small snowflake
In mid 1984 the four small dots on the motto of the Order were changed to a quadrangle.
Manufactured 19 July 1982 to May 1996
Insignia 806 to 1952

Birks & Son (Pressed Metal Products)
Made of .925 silver by Pressed Metal Products, hallmarked on the reverse of the lower arm 'BIRKS STERL'
Manufactured 1998 to August 2004
Insignia 1953 to 3104

Rideau Ltée
Made of .925 silver by Rideau Ltée of St Laurent, Quebec, hallmarked on the reverse of the lower arm 'RIDEAU +R STER' with a small snowflake.
Manufactured September 2004 to the present
Insignia 3105–3334

APPENDIX ELEVEN: CHANCELLORS OF THE ORDER OF CANADA

The Right Honourable Daniel Roland Michener, PC, CC, CMM, CD, QC
1 July 1967 to 14 January 1974

The Right Honourable Jules Léger, PC, CC, CMM, CD
14 January 1974 to 22 January 1979

The Right Honourable Edward Schreyer, PC, CC, CMM, CD
22 January 1979 to 14 May 1984

The Right Honourable Jeanne Sauvé, PC, CC, CMM, CD
14 May 1984 to 29 January 1990

The Right Honourable Ramon John Hnatyshyn, PC, CC, CMM, CD, QC
29 January 1990 to 8 February 1995

The Right Honourable Roméo LeBlanc, PC, CC, CMM, CD
8 February 1995 to 7 October 1999

The Right Honourable Adrienne Clarkson, CC, CMM, COM, CD
7 October 1999 to the present

APPENDIX TWELVE: OFFICIALS OF THE ORDER OF CANADA

Secretary General of the Order of Canada

Esmond Unwin Butler, CVO, OC, 1 July 1967 to 3 November 1985

Léopold Henri Amyot, CVO, 4 November 1985 to 25 June 1988

Judith Anne Laroque, CVO, 26 June 1990 to 20 April 2000

Barbara Uteck, CVO, 21 April 2000 to Present

Registrar of the Order of Canada/Registrar of Honours (title changed 1 July 1972)

Kenneth Foster (Acting), 20 May 1967 to 31 October 1967

Roger De C.B. Nantel, CD, 1 November 1967 to 5 June 1983

Director of Honours

Carl Lochnan, 1 July 1972 to 1 July 1975

Roger De C.B. Nantel, LVO, CD, 1 July 1975 to 5 June 1983

David Johns, 6 June 1983 to 1988

Gordon Lewis, 1988 to 3 April 1996

Mary de Bellefeuille Percy, 4 April 1996 to 1 July 2004

Gabrielle Lappa (acting), 2 July 2004 to present

Director of the Chancellery of Canadian Orders and Decorations/Deputy Secretary and Herald Chancellor

Roger De C.B. Nantel, MVO, CD, June 1983 to 2 May 1988

Lieutenant General François Richard, CMM, CD, 2 May 1988 to 25 January 1993

Lieutenant General James Gervais, CMM, CD, 25 January 1993 to 30 June 2004

Mary de Bellefeuille Percy (acting), 2 July 2004 to present

APPENDIX THIRTEEN: MEMBERS OF THE ADVISORY COUNCIL OF THE ORDER OF CANADA*

Chairpersons (Chief Justice of the Supreme Court)

The Right Honourable Robert Taschereau, PC, CC, 13 June 1967** to 1 September 1967

The Right Honourable John R. Cartwright, PC, CC, MC, 1 September 1967 to 23 May 1970

The Right Honourable Joseph Honoré Gérald Fauteaux, PC, CC, 23 May 1970 to 23 December 1973

The Right Honourable Bora Laskin, PC, CC, 23 December 1973 to 26 March 1984

The Right Honourable Robert George Brian Dickson, PC, CC, CD, 18 April 1984 to 30 June 1990

The Right Honourable Antonio Lamer, PC, CC, CD, 1 June 1990 to 6 January 2000

The Right Honourable Beverley McLachlin, PC, 7 January 2000 to the present

Ex-Officio Members

Clerk of the Privy Council

The Honourable Gordon Robertson, PC, CC, 13 June 1967 to 15 January 1975

The Honourable Peter Michael Pitfield, PC, CVO, 16 January 1975 to 4 June 1979 and 11 March 1980 to 9 December 1982

The Honourable Marcel Massé, PC, OC, QC, 5 June 1979 to 10 March 1980

The Honourable Gordon Francis Joseph Osbaldeston, PC, CC, 10 December 1982 to 11 August 1985

The Honourable Paul M. Tellier, PC, CC, 12 August 1985 to 30 June 1992

Glen Scott Shortliffe, 1 July 1992 to 27 March 1994

The Honourable Joycelyne Bourgon, PC, OC, 28 March 1994 to 17 January 1999

Mel Cappe, 18 January 1999 to 12 May 2002

Alexander Himelfarb, 13 May 2002 to the present

*A complete list of the non–ex officio members of the Advisory Council is unavailable at this time.
**Although the Order of Canada did not officially come into existence until 1 July 1967, the first meeting of the Advisory Council took place on 13 June 1967, and thus this has been recognized as the first full day on which the Advisory Council began to discharge its duties. This has been chosen over 17 March 1967 – the day the Queen signed the Letters Patent – as the members of the Advisory Council were not informed of their new duties until mid-May 1967.

Under-Secretary of State/Deputy Minister of Canadian Heritage[†]

Granville G.E. Steele, 13 June 1967 to 14 November 1968

The Right Honourable Jules Léger, PC, CC, CMM, CD, 15 November 1968 to 2 March 1973

Jean Boucher, 3 March 1973 to 5 April 1975

(Vacant from 6 April 1975 to 23 November 1975)

André Fortier, 24 November 1975 to 14 February 1978

Pierre Juneau, 15 February 1978 to 27 August 1980

Huguette Labelle, 28 August 1980 to 7 January 1985

Robert Rabinovich, 8 January 1985 to 24 August 1986

Jean T. Fournier, 25 August 1986 to 8 September 1991

Marc Rochon, 8 September 1991 to 29 October 1992

Michèle Jean, 30 October 1992 to 24 June 1993

Marc Rochon, 25 June 1993 to 9 July 1995

Suzanne Hurtubise, 10 July 1995 to 30 May 1999

Alexander Himelfarb, 1 June 1999 to 12 May 2002

Judith A. LaRocque, CVO, 13 May 2002 to the present

Chair of the Canada Council for the Arts

Jean Martineau, CC, QC, 13 June 1967 to 17 May 1969

John G. Prentice, OC, 5 June 1969 to 4 June 1974

Gertrude Laing, OC, 23 December 1975 to 22 December 1978

Mavor Moore, OC, 15 February 1979 to 30 September 1983

Maureen Forrester, CC, 23 December 1983 to 22 December 1988

Allan Gotlieb, CC, 1 February 1989 to 31 January 1994

Donna Scott, OC, 31 May 1994 to 20 May 1998

Jean-Louis Roux, CC, CQ, 31 May 2000 to 13 September 2004

Karen Kain, CC, 14 September 2004 to present

President of the Royal Society of Canada

The Honourable Gerhard Hertzberg, PC, CC, 13 June 1967 to September 1967

James M. Harrison, CC, 1967–8

[†] In 1995 the position of Under-Secretary of State was replaced by that of Deputy Minister of Canadian Heritage.

Léon Lortie, OC, 1968

Claude E. Dolman, 1969–70

Roy Daniells, CC, 1970–1

Henry E. Duckworth, OC, 1971–2

John Tuzo Wilson, 1972–3

Guy Sylvestre, OC, 1973–4

Claude Fortier, CC, 1974–5

Samuel D. Clark, OC, 1975–6

J. Larkin Kerwin, CC, 1976–7

Robert E. Folinsbee, OC, 1977–8

Robert E. Bell, CC, 1978–81

Marc-Adélard Tremblay, OC, 1981–4

Alexander G. McKay, OC, 1984–7

Digby J. McLaren, 1987–90

The Honourable Jules Deschênes, CC, QC, 1990–2

John Meisel, CC, 1992–5

Robert Hall Haynes, OC, 1995–7

Jean-Pierre Wallot, OC, 1997–9

William Leiss, 1999–2001

Howard Alper, OC, 2001–2003

M. Gilles Paquet, CM, 2003–present

President and Chairs of the Association of Universities and Colleges of Canada‡

Walter H. Johns, OC, 13 June 1967 to September 1967

The Very Reverend Roger Guindon, CC, 1967

Colin B. Mackay, OC, QC, 1968

Roger Gaudry, OC, GOQ, 1969

Davidson Dunton, CC, 1970

Louis-Philippe Bonneau, OC, 1971

A.W.R. Carrothers, 1972

‡ The senior elected head of the AUCC was titled 'President' from 1911 to 1989. Since 1989 the title has been 'Chair.'

Catherine Wallace, OC, 1973

Larkin Kerwin, CC, OQ, 1974

Michael Oliver, OC, 1975

Henry E. Duckworth, OC, 1976

Moses Osborne Morgan, CC, CD, 1977

Paul Lacoste, OC, QC, 1978

Alan James Earp, OC, October 1979 to September 1981

Lloyd I. Barber, CC, SOM, October 1981 to September 1983

W.A. MacKay, October 1983 to September 1985

David Lloyd Johnston, CC, October 1985 to September 1987

Arnold Naimark, OC, October 1987 to September 1989

K. George Pedersen, OC, OOnt., October 1989 to September 1991

Kennneth L. Ozmon, OC, October 1991 to September 1993

Michael Gervais, OC, OQ, October 1993 to September 1995

Howard L. Tennant, October 1995 to September 1997

Paul Davenport, OC, October 1997 to September 1999

Ian D.C. Newbould, October 1999 to September 2001

Robert Lacroix, CM, OQ, October 2001 to September 2002

Peter MacKinnon, October 2002, to present

APPENDIX FOURTEEN: HONORARY RECIPIENTS OF THE
ORDER OF CANADA

Nelson Mandela, CC
Appointed to be a Companion 3 September 1998
Invested 24 September 1998
Citation: He is a universal symbol of triumph over oppression who has inspired people everywhere to work peacefully to end intolerance and injustice. A towering figure in the transition from apartheid to democracy in South Africa, he has emerged as one of this century's greatest statesmen and humanitarians, recognized the world over for his dignity, moral strength, and integrity. His lifelong struggle for freedom, justice, and equality guarantee his presence in the history books of generations to come.

Her Majesty Queen Elizabeth the Queen Mother, LG, LT, CI, GCVO, GBE, CC, CD
Appointed to be a Companion 1 August 2000
Invested 31 October 2000
Citation: Her dignity and grace have served as a source of strength and inspiration for generations of her admirers. She is greatly respected for her sense of duty and has repeatedly demonstrated perseverance in the face of adversity. During the Second World War, in particular, she was a symbol of steadfastness to the people of Britain and Canada. The 1939 visit of King George VI and Queen Elizabeth was the first visit to Canada by a reigning sovereign. The Queen Mother's warm and open nature was displayed at that time in the first royal walkabout which set the tone for all future visits. After the death of her husband, she visited Canada ten more times, covering most of the country. She also maintained strong ties, which have continued to this day, with charitable organizations and her regiments in Canada: the Black Watch, the Toronto Scottish, and the Canadian Forces Medical Service.

Frank Gehry, CC
Appointed to be a Companion 12 November 2002
Invested 16 June 2003
Citation: He is a creative genius who has emerged as one of the world's best architects. His journey to the pinnacle of his profession began in Toronto and led him to Los Angeles, where, since the early 1960s he has produced an innovative body of work. Known for his responsiveness to modern technologies and lifestyles, he has garnered international recognition for his avant-garde buildings which have transformed the urban landscape of major cities around the world. By pushing the envelope even further, he has made a major contribution to architecture, experimenting with and refining new construction materials and design techniques in his quest to synthesize art with function.

Vaclav Havel, CC
Appointed to be a Companion 5 August 2003 (effective 8 May 2003)
Invested 4 March 2004
Citation: A leading intellectual and respected figure in Eastern Europe, Vaclav Havel has exemplified the principles that Canadians hold in the highest regard. His unwa-

vering belief in democratic ideals has been conveyed in his plays and essays that attracted international attention to the Czechoslovakian struggle. In addition, his advocacy of peaceful resistance and his perseverance were inspirational. The first president of the independent Czech Republic, he oversaw the preparations made for his country's integration into both the European Union and the North Atlantic Treaty Organization (NATO). He also promoted respect for human rights and the importance of international dialogue on the world stage.

Boutros Boutros-Ghali, CC
Appointed to be a Companion 8 May 2003
Invested 7 May 2004
Citation: Whether as a jurist, diplomat, scholar or director of international institutions, Boutros Boutros-Ghali has been unrelenting in his efforts to promote peace. As Secretary-General of the United Nations, he carried out a major modernization of the UN machinery. He has also proven to be a staunch defender of human rights and of a more democratic and humane approach to globalization. This man, for whom culture is the great school of peace, is also the first secretary-general of la Francophonie. In order to promote the vitality of la Francoponie, he strongly supported interlinguistic and intercultural dialogue.

Honorary Officers

Charles Dutoit, OC
Appointed to be an Honorary Officer 23 October 1997
Invested 30 January 2002
Citation: For nearly 25 years, this energetic conductor has directed the Orchestre symphonique de Montréal with vigour. His enormous talent has enabled him to inspire each of the musicians in this great orchestra, which is now world renowned. Under his direction, the orchestra has achieved an international reputation and, as well as performing weekly for the Montréal public, it is invited regularly to appear on the most prominent stages in Europe, Asia and the Americas, notably in the United States, at Carnegie Hall in New York. With the OSM, Charles Dutoit has also recorded over 85 discs which have won numerous national and international prizes. In addition, the concerts played in the summer in parks give the whole population access to music which it would otherwise never have known.

John Kenneth Galbraith, OC
Appointed to be an Honorary Officer 17 April 1997
Invested 5 November 1997
Citation: One of the great liberal thinkers of our age, he is a world renowned economist and writer who has contributed much to the discussion of Western economics and politics for the last half of the twentieth century. While his economic theory has sparked debate, particularly among academics, his talent for communicating with the public has made him an influential commentator on the American and Canadian economic systems. He has been a trusted advisor to Heads of State, a respected scholar and a stimulating mentor to generations of students at Harvard University.

James Hillier, OC
Appointed to be an Honorary Officer 17 April 1997
Invested 5 November 1997
Citation: He is known internationally as the co-inventor of one of the scientific wonders of the modern world. The electron microscope has opened up the tiniest corners of the universe to the scrutiny of medical and space researchers, biologists, chemists, geologists and a multitude of others. Having dedicated his career to promoting its use in hospitals, universities and research centres, he also encourages young people to pursue careers in science and has contributed generously to a scholarship fund for students in his hometown of Brantford, Ontario.

Tanya Moiseiwitsch, OC
Appointed to be an Honorary Officer 10 October 2002
Died on 18 February 2003; a family member was presented with the insignia on 16 May 2003
Citation: She has had an enormous impact on arts in the 20th century. Throughout a long and illustrious career, this renowned theatre designer has set standards for innovation and excellence in her stage productions and design as well as costuming. Notably, in 1953, she collaborated in the founding of Ontario's Stratford Shakespearean Festival. Her creation of the Festival's thrust stage inspired theatre designers around the world and influenced playwriting itself. She has also generously shared her talent with younger artists, many who are now internationally recognized.

Honorary Members

Zena Khan Sheardown, CM
Appointed to be an Honorary Member 11 October 1981*
Invested 29 December 1986
Citation: Mrs Sheardown served with her husband, John Sheardown, a member of the Canadian Embassy in Tehran, during the Islamic Revolution. At serious risk but with courage and foresight, she sheltered a group of Americans in her home for over two months while plans were being made for their escape from the country. She thus contributed significantly to the success of the 'Canadian Caper.'

Lois Ada Lilienstein, CM
Appointed to be Honorary Member 1 May 2002
Invested 24 October 2003
Citation: Icons of children's entertainment they are best known as the trio Sharon, Louis & Bram. Since their musical debut in 1978, with One Elephant, Deux Éléphants, they have delighted fans of all ages and have contributed significantly to children's

---

*Mrs Sheardown's appointment was reviewed by the Advisory Council of the Order of Canada in 1986 and, because she had recently become a Canadian citizen, her appointment was changed to that of a Canadian citizen. Nevertheless, Mrs Sheardown was the first person appointed to the honorary division of the Order of Canada.

musical development. Reaching out to an every greater audience, by moving their act to educational television networks in Canada and the United States, they have inspired generations of children and parents alike. Also activists for children's causes, they have lent their voices and performed for numerous organizations, notably the musical education program 'Mariposa in the Schools' and UNICEF.

INTERPRETATION

1. The definitions in this section apply to this Constitution.

'Companion' means a Companion of the Order. *(companion)*

'Council' means the Advisory Council for the Order referred to in section 7. *(conseil)*

'Member' means a Member of the Order. *(membre)*

'Officer' means an Officer of the Order. *(officier)*

'Order' means the Order of Canada *(ordre)*

'Secretary General' means the Secretary General of the Order *(secrétaire général)*

THE ORDER OF CANADA

2. The Order of Canada shall consist of Her Majesty in right of Canada, the Governor General of Canada, the Governor General's spouse and the Companions, Officers and Members and honorary Companions, Officers and Members.

ADMINISTRATION

3. The Governor General of Canada shall be the Chancellor and Principal Companion of the Order, and the Governor General's spouse shall be a Companion.

4. The Chancellor is responsible for the administration of the Order.

5. The Secretary to the Governor General shall be the Secretary General of the Order, and shall be responsible for

(a) maintaining the records of the Order and of the Council;

(b) making the necessary arrangements for the conferment of insignia;

(c) accepting any nomination for appointments as Companion, Officer or Member;

(d) performing such other functions in respect to the Order as the Governor General may request.

6. The Governor General may appoint other officials for the Order as the Governor General considers advisable.

COUNCIL

7. (1) The Advisory Council for the Order shall consist of the following members:

(a) the Chief Justice of Canada, who shall act as Chairperson of the Council;

(b) the Clerk of the Privy Council;

(c) the Deputy Minister of the Department of Canadian Heritage;

(d) the Chairperson of the Canada Council;

(e) the President of the Royal Society of Canada;

(f) the Chairperson of the Board of Directors of the Association of Universities and Colleges of Canada; and

(g) not more than five additional members appointed pursuant to subsection (2).

(2) The Governor General may, on the recommendation of the members of the

Council referred to in paragraphs (1) *(a)* and *(f)*, appoint five persons belonging to the Order as members of the Council for a three-year term.

(3) The Governor General may, on the recommendation of the members of the Council referred to in paragraphs (1) *(a)* to *(f)*, extend the term of one or more of the members of the Council appointed pursuant to subsection (2) by two years.

(4) The Council shall invite the Deputy Minister of the Department of Foreign Affairs and International Trade to participate in the review of nominations for honorary Companions, Officers and Members.

8. The Council shall
(a) consider those nominations referred to in paragraph 5 (c) that the Secretary General has transmitted to it;
(b) compile and submit to the Governor General a list of those nominees in their categories of Companion, Officer and Member and honorary Companion, Officer and Member who have the greatest merit; and
(c) advise the Governor General on such matters as the Governor General may refer to the Council.

ELIGIBILITY
9. (1) Any Canadian citizen may be appointed as a Companions, an Officer or a Member.
(2) A person who is not a Canadian citizen may be appointed as a honorary Companion, Officer or Member.
(3) A person is not a member of the Order by reason only of being appointed as a member of the Council.

NOMINATIONS AND APPOINTMENTS
10 (1) Any person or organization may submit to the Secretary General for consideration by the Council a nomination of a Canadian citizen for appointment as a Companion, Officer or Member and a non-Canadian citizen for appointment as a honorary Companion, Officer or Member.
(2) The Governor General may appoint as honorary Companions, Officers and Members a maximum of five persons in any year.

COMPANIONS
11. Appointments of persons as Companions and honorary Companions shall be made in recognition of their outstanding achievement and merit of the highest degree, especially in service to Canada or to humanity at large.

12. (1) The Governor General shall cease to be Chancellor and Principal Companion at the end of the Governor General's term but shall continue to be a Companion.
(2) The Governor General's spouse shall continue to be a Companion of the Order after the retirement or death of the Governor General.

13. The number of Companions, other than honorary Companions, is limited to one hundred and sixty-five, in addition to Her Majesty the Queen, the Principal Companions and the Principal Companion's spouse, any former Governor General and that former Governor General's spouse.

14. Where the maximum number of Companions has been appointed, no other person may be appointed as a Companion until a vacancy occurs.

15. In the event of a vacancy, the Governor General may appoint a new Companion, and may fill a maximum of fifteen such vacancies in any year.

OFFICERS
16. Appointments of persons as Officers and honorary Officers shall be made for achievement and merit of a high degree, especially service to Canada or humanity at large.

17. The Governor General may appoint as Officers, other than honorary Officers, a maximum of sixty-four persons in any year.

MEMBERS
18. Appointments of persons as Members and honorary Members shall be made for distinguished service in or to a particular community, group or field of activity.

19. The Governor General may appoint as Members, other than honorary Members, a maximum of one hundred and thirty-six persons in any year.

INSTRUMENT OF APPOINTMENT
20. (1) Appointments to the Order shall be made by Instrument signed by the Governor General and sealed with the Seal of the Order.
(2) Unless otherwise provided in the Instrument of the appointment, an appointment shall take effect on the date on which the instrument of appointment is sealed.

DESIGNATIONS, INSIGNIA AND ARMORIAL BEARINGS

21 (1) Companions, Officers and Members are entitled to
(*a*) wear such insignia as the Governor General may, by Ordinance, prescribe;
(*b*) petition the Chief Herald of Canada to grant lawful armorial bearings, which in the case of Companions may include supporters;
(*c*) surround their shield of arms with the circle and motto of the Order and suspend therefrom the ribbon and badge of their rank; and
(*d*) place after their name the letters associated with their rank, namely,
    (i)   'C.C.,' in the case of a Companion
    (ii) 'O.C.,' in the case of an Officer; or
    (iii) 'C.M.,' in the case of a Member.
(2) Honorary Companions, Officers and Members are entitled to
(*a*) wear such insignia as the Governor General may, by Ordinance, prescribe; and
(*b*) place after their name the letters associated with their rank, as set out in paragraph (1) (d).

22. The insignia of the Order shall be worn in the sequence prescribed and in the manner described in publications issued by The Chancellery.

23. (1) Except as otherwise provided in an Ordinance, the insignia of the Order shall remain the property of the Order.

(2) Where a person who is a Companion, Officer or Member or an honorary Companion, Officer or Member, resigns from the Order or where a person's appointment to the Order is terminated by Ordinance, the person shall return the person's insignia to the Secretary General.

RANKS
24. (1) The Governor General may
(a) elevate any Member with the Member's consent, to the rank of Officer or Companion; or
(b) elevate any Officer, with the Officer's consent, to the rank of Companion.
(2) A person elevated to a higher rank is entitled to wear the insignia of that rank and to place the letters associated with that rank after the persons name.
(3) No person shall
(a) hold more than one appointment to the Order at any time; or
(b) place after the person's name the letters or retain the insignia, pertaining to the previous appointment to the Order.

TERMINATION
25. A person's membership in the Order ceases when
(a) the person dies;
(b) the Governor General accepts the person's resignation from the Order, which resignation shall have been made in writing and given to the Secretary General; or
(c) the Governor General makes an Ordinance terminating the person's appointment to the Order.

ORDINANCES
26. The Governor General may make Ordinances respecting the government and insignia of the Order and the termination of a person's appointment to the Order.

MOTTO
27. The Motto of the Order shall be:
DESIDERANTES MELIOREM PATRIAM.

SEAL
28. (1) The Seal of the Order, which is set out in the schedule, shall be committed to the custody of the Governor General.
(2) No appointment, termination of appointment award or Ordinance shall have effect unless it has been sealed with the Seal of the Order.

APPENDIX SIXTEEN: AMENDMENTS TO THE CONSTITUTION OF THE ORDER OF CANADA

1967   Constitution
      Order-in-Council 1967-389, 2 March 1967
      Letters Patent signed by Prime Minister Lester B. Pearson,
      Letters Patent signed by Governor General Roland Michener,
      Letters Patent signed by The Queen, 21 March 1967

1972   Order-in-Council 1972-809, 1 March 1972
      Letters Patent Signed by Prime Minister Pierre Elliott Trudeau,
      Letters Patent signed by Governor General Roland Michener,
      Letters Patent signed by The Queen, 10 May 1972

1983   Order-in-Council 1983-750
      Letters Patent signed by Prime Minister Pierre Elliott Trudeau,
      Letters Patent signed by Governor General Edward Schreyer, 17 March 1983

1994   Order-in-Council 1994-2026, 6 December 1994
      Letters Patent signed by Prime Minister Jean Chrétien, 16 January 1995
      Letters Patent signed by Governor General Ramon Hnatyshyn, 27 January

1995   Order-in-Council 1995-694, 26 April 1995
      Letters Patent signed by Prime Minister Jean Chrétien, 13 June 1995
      Letters Patent signed by Governor General Roméo LeBlanc, 30 June 1995

1997   Order-in-Council 1997-552, 15 April 1997
      Letters Patent signed by Prime Minister Jean Chrétien, 26 May 1997
      Letters Patent signed by Governor General Roméo LeBlanc, 26 May 1997

1998   Order-in-Council 1998-1373, 24 August 1998
      Letters Patent signed by Prime Minister Jean Chrétien,
      Letters Patent signed by Governor General Roméo LeBlanc, 10 September 1998

1999   Order-in-Council 1999-1743, 1 October 1999
      Letters Patent signed by Prime Minister Jean Chrétien, 1 October 1999
      Letters Patent signed by Governor General Roméo LeBlanc, 1 October 1999

2001   Order-in-Council 2001-203, 1 March 2001
      Letters Patent signed by Prime Minister Jean Chrétien, 12 March 2001
      Letters Patent signed by Governor General Adrienne Clarkson, 20 March 2001

Notes

Abbreviations

CHAN   Chancellery of Canadian Honours, Government House Working Files
COCS   Cabinet Office Ceremonial Secretariat (United Kingdom)
DND/DHH   Department of National Defence, Directorate of History and Heritage
NAC   National Archives of Canada
QUA   Queen's University Archives
UTA   University of Toronto Archives
WSRO   West Sussex County Records Office

CHAPTER ONE

1 Arthur Berriedale Keith, *The Sovereignty of the British Dominions* (London: Macmillan, 1929), 267.
2 The two states that currently lack a national order or national honours system are Ireland and Switzerland.
3 Nicholas Dirks, *The Hollow Crown: Ethnohistory of an Indian Kingdom* (Cambridge: Cambridge University Press, 1987), 129.
4 Sir Ivan De la Bere, *The Queen's Orders of Chivalry* (London: Spring Books, 1964), 13.
5 Pierre Bourdieu, *Outline of a Theory of Practice*, trans. R. Nice (Cambridge: Cambridge University Press, 1977), 14. 'The function of symbolic capital is to help sustain economic power by enabling it to present itself as something economically neutral' Derek Robbins, *The Work of Pierre Bourdieu* (Boulder and San Francisco: Westview, 1991), 116.
6 Maxwell Cohen, OC, 'A Round Table from Sea to Sea,' *The Register of Canadian Honours* (Toronto: Canadian Almanac and Directory, 1991), 17.
7 A.R.M. Lower, *Canadians in the Making* (Toronto: Longmans, 1958), 349.
8 See Harold Wilson, *The Imperial Policy of Sir Robert Borden* (Gainesville: University of Florida Press, 1966), 37.
9 Olive Dickason, *Canada's First Peoples* (Toronto: McClelland & Stewart, 1992), 111.
10 John C. Ewers, *Plains Indian History and Culture: Essays on Community and Change* (Norman: University of Oklahoma Press, 1998), 106.
11 Community Rules: Moraviantown, Munceytown, Grape Island, Regulations. '(11). None that has a Chief's or Captain's medal or silver.' Elizabeth Graham, *Medicine Man to Missionary* (Toronto: Peter Martin Associates, 1975), 105.

12 Peter Foote and David Wilson, *The Viking Achievement; The Society and Culture of Medieval Scandinavia* (London: Sidgwick & Jackson, 1970), 426.
13 Robert Werlich, *Orders and Decorations of All Nations* (Washington D.C.: Quaker, 1974), 140.
14 Ibid., 141.
15 This was usually only done when the King wished to bestow an honour on the Governor General himself. Also see Dale Miquelon, *New France, 1701–1744* (Toronto: McClelland & Stewart, 1987), 248.
16 *Dictionary of Canadian Biography*, vol. 2 (Toronto: University of Toronto Press, 1971), 401.
17 Miquelon, *New France*, 240.
18 Ægidius Fauteaux, *Les Chavaliers de Saint-Louis en Canada* (Montreal: Éditions des Dix, 1940), 12.
19 *Dictionary of Canadian Biography*, vol. 5 (Toronto: University of Toronto Press, 1971), 177.
20 Bruce Knox, 'Democracy Aristocracy and Empire: The Provision of Colonial Honours, 1818–1870,' *Australian Historical Studies* 25, no. 99 (October 1992), 249.
21 Only fifteen titular honours were awarded to ordinary residents of British North America (i.e., Canadians): Sir Narcisse Fortunat Belleau Kt, Speaker of the Legislative Assembly of Canada (1860); Sir James Carter Kt, Chief Justice of the Supreme Court of New Brunswick (1859); Sir Dominick Daly Kt, Lieutenant-Governor of Prince Edward Island; Sir Brenton Haliburton Kt, Chief Justice of Nova Scotia (1859); Sir Daniel Jones Kt, Colonel in Canadian Militia (1836); Sir Louis Hippolyte LaFontaine Bt, Chief Justice of Lower Canada; Sir William Edmund Logan Kt, Director of the Geological Survey of Canada (1856); Sir James B. Macaulay CB Kt, Chief Justice of the Court of Common Pleas for Canada West; Sir Allan Napier MacNab Bt Kt, Colonel of the Upper Canadian Militia (Bt awarded 1856); Sir James Monk, Chief Justice in Canada (1825); Sir John Beverley Robinson Bt, CB, Chief Justice of Upper Canada (1854); Sir John Stuart Bt, Chief Justice of Lower Canada; Sir Étienne Paschall Taché Bt, Colonel in the Canadian Militia; and Sir Henry Smith Kt, Solicitor-General for Upper Canada (1860). This list does not include Newfoundlanders or British officials who were knighted for services to Canada.
22 Sir George Fiddes, *The Dominions and Colonial Office* (London: Putnam's Son, 1926), 66.
23 The general public was neither encouraged nor discouraged from recommending people for honours. NAC, RG 7, Records of the Governor General, contains very few such recommendations, whereas the Laurier Papers and Borden Papers contain many letters requesting that awards be made. This suggests that many members of the public were aware of the key position the prime minister held with respect to honours.
24 Monck's official appointed office was 'Captain-General and Governor in Chief in and over our Province of Canada, in and over the Province of Nova Scotia and its dependencies and in and over the Province of New Brunswick and also our Governor-General of all our Provinces in North America and of the Island of Prince Edward.' John Cowan, *Canada's Governors-General: Lord Monck to General Vanier* (Toronto: York Publishing Company, 1966), 4.
25 Sir J.G. Bourniot, *How Canada Is Governed* (Toronto: Copp Clark, 1909), 77.
26 Elisabeth Batt, *Monck: Governor General, 1861–1868* (Toronto: McClelland & Stewart, 1976), 50. W.L. Morton, *The Critical Years: The Union of British North America, 1857–1973* (Toronto: McClelland & Stewart, 1964), 176.
27 C.P. Stacey, 'Lord Monck and the Canadian Nation,' *Dalhousie Review* 14 (1935): 180.
28 Ged Martin, *Britain and the Origins of Canadian Confederation, 1837–1867* (Vancouver: UBC Press, 1995), 234.

29 Stacey, 'Lord Monck and the Canadian Nation,' 179.
30 National Archives of Canada (NAC), MG 27 B 1, Monck, Sir Charles Stanley, fourth Viscount, Monck to Carnarvon, 7 September 1866.
31 Queen Victoria to Lord Canning, 18 May 1859. Michael Maclagan, *Clemency Canning: Charles John 1st Earl Canning, Governor-General and Viceroy of India, 1856–1862* (London: Macmillan, 1962), 258.
32 The Order of the Star of India and later the Order of the Indian Empire had no religious connotations, unlike all the other British orders of chivalry. That is, there was no patron saint of the order, no chapel for the order, and the top level was designated 'Knight Grand Commander,' not 'Knight Grand Cross,' to avoid any problems with members of the Order who were not of the Christian faith. Sir Ivan De la Bere, *The Queen's Orders of Chivalry* (London: William Kimber, 1961), 177. As Monck had chosen St Lawrence as the proposed honours designation, it is certain that it would have had an underlying Christian tone, with the top level being designated 'Knight Grand Cross.'
33 Statutes of the Most Exalted Order of the Star of India (London, 1866), 2.
34 Although the order is only mentioned as the 'Order of St. Lawrence,' it would have certainly been given a glowing adjectival designation – Illustrious, Honourable, Distinguished, or Eminent – as all other British orders. The prefix to these names have been added to suggest what the official name of the honour might have become.
35 NAC, MG 27 B 1, Monck, Sir Charles Stanley, fourth Viscount, Monck to Carnarvon, 7 September 1866.
36 John Buchan, *Lord Minto, a Memoir* (London: Thomas Nelson & Son, 1924), 121.
37 NAC, MG 27 B 1, Monck, Sir Charles Stanley, fourth Viscount, Monck to Carnarvon, 7 September 1866.
38 David Farr, *The Colonial Office and Canada, 1867–1887* (Toronto: University of Toronto Press, 1955), 53.
39 Stacey, 'Lord Monck and the Canadian Nation,' 186.
40 Peter Galloway, *The Order of St Michael and St George* (London: Millennium, 2000), 16.
41 Ibid., 65.
42 Royal Archives, R50/118, Duke of Buckingham and Chandos to Queen Victoria, 12 November 1868. The Duke of Buckingham and Chandos, 12 November 1868, cited in Galloway, *The Order of St Michael and St George*, 60.
43 Public Records Office (PRO), CO/732/2 Circular Dispatch, 8 December 1868.
44 Between 1867 and 1935, Canadians received 14 GCMGs, 74 KCMGs, and 382 CMGs.
45 Royal Archives, R50/118, Duke of Buckingham and Chandos to Queen Victoria, 12 November 1868. The Duke of Buckingham and Chandos, 12 November 1868, quoted in Galloway, *The Order of St Michael and St George*, 70.
46 R. MacGregor Dawson, *The Government of Canada* (Toronto: University of Toronto Press, 1964), 154.
47 Lady Susan Macdonald was raised to the peerage as Baroness Macdonald of Earnscliffe shortly after her husband's death.
48 Gwen Neuendorff, *Studies in the Evolution of Dominion Status* (London: Allen Unwin, 1942), 212.
49 Sir Joseph Pope, *The Correspondence of Sir John A. Macdonald* (Toronto: Oxford University Press, 1921), 305.
50 Queen's University Archives (QUA), Mackenzie Papers, p. 2134, Sir Richard Cartwright to Alexander Mackenzie, 8 October 1878. Mackenzie also offered Brown the post of

Lieutenant-Governor of Ontario; Brown turned down this offer as well. QUA, Mackenzie Papers, p. 814, Alexander Mackenzie to George Brown, 13 May 1875.

51 J.M.S. Careless, *Brown of the Globe* (Toronto: Macmillan, 1966), preface.

52 Order-in-Council 1868–598, 3 June 1868. Darrel Kennedy, 'The 1867 Confederation Medal: First Honour of the Dominion.' *Families: Ontario Genealogical Society Journal* 42, no. 3 (August 2003): 131.

53 Ibid.

54 Colin Cross, *The Fall of the British Empire* (London: Penguin, 1968), 153.

55 Seven peerages have been conferred on people born in Canada, but they were not Canadian residents at the time of their elevation. They are not included with the Canadian peerages as they were elevated in recognition of services rendered to the United Kingdom (or the British Empire in some cases). The first appointment occurred in 1898 when Sir Arthur Lawrence Haliburton became the First Baron Haliburton of Windsor in the Province of Nova Scotia in the Dominion of Canada. Haliburton served as Permanent Undersecretary of State for War. Sir William Pirrie, industrialist and head of the shipbuilding firm Harland and Wolff, was the second person born in Canada to be made a peer. Born in Quebec, Pirrie was made Baron Pirrie of Belfast in 1906 and later elevated to a Viscountcy. Sir Max Aitken was made First Baron Beaverbrook of Beaverbrook in the Province of New Brunswick in the Dominion of Canada and of Cherkley in the County of Surrey in 1917. The Rt Hon. Sir Edward Patrick Morris, PC, KCMG, Kt, Prime Minister of Newfoundland, was raised to the peerage as First Baron Morris of St John's in the Dominion of Newfoundland and of the City of Waterford in 1918. Morris served as Prime Minister of Newfoundland throughout the First World War. The Rt Hon. Richard Bedford Bennett was made Viscount Bennett of Mickleham, Calgary, and Hopewell in 1941. Roy Herbert Thomson, the newspaper and publishing magnate, was made Baron Thomson of Fleet, of Northbridge in the City of Edinburgh in 1964. Thomson was appointed to the peerage before the existence of dual citizenship and was forced to renounce his Canadian nationality. Most recently, in 2001, the Hon. Conrad Black, PC, OC, was raised to the peerage as Baron Black of Crossharbour. After a lengthy court battle Black was forced to renounce his citizenship in order to accept the peerage. Black is also the only Canadian-born holder of a life peerage.

56 I have included Sir Hugh Graham Lord Atholstan in this list because, technically, the Canadian prime minister and Governor General were consulted. Their advice was not followed.

57 Five peerages and one title have been conferred on people born in Canada with the consent of the Canadian government. These can be considered Canadian peerages as they were elevated in recognition of services rendered to Canada. Sir Hugh Graham, Kt, First Baron Atholstan of Huntingdon in the Province of Quebec in the Dominion of Canada and the City of Edinburgh (1917); [Lady] Susan Agnes Macdonald, Baroness Macdonald of Earnsciffe, in the Province of Ontario and Dominion of Canada (1891); Sir Thomas George Shaughnessy, Kt, KCVO, First Baron Shaughnessy of the City of Montreal in the Dominion of Canada and Ashford in the County of Limerick (1916); Sir George Donald Alexander Smith, GCMG, GCVO, First Baron Strathcona and Mount Royal (1900); Sir George Stephen BT, GCVO, First Baron Mount Stephen of Mount Stephen in the province of British Columbia and Dominion of Canada, and of Dufftown in the county of Banff, New Brunswick (1891), Charles le Moyne de Longueuil, Baron de Longueuil (1700).

58 Note the suggestion to this effect in David Cruise and Alison Griffiths, *Lords of the Line* (Markham, ON: Penguin, 1988), xv, citing a letter from Lord Shaughnessy, 8 May 1920.

59 This title still has issue.

60 He became the First Baron Shaughnessy of the City of Montreal in the Dominion of Canada and Ashford in the County of Limerick.

61 He became the first Baron Atholstan of Huntington in the Province of Quebec in the Dominion of Canada and the City of Edinburgh on 8 June 1917.

62 No less a figure than Joseph Chamberlain would hail Graham for conducting a campaign on behalf of Canadian involvement in the Anglo-Boer War 'that for vigour and effectiveness has seldom been surpassed in the history of journalism.' See John Saywell and Paul Stevens, eds., *Lord Minto's Canadian Papers*, vol. 2 (Toronto: Champlain Society, 1983), 193, citing Joseph Chamberlain to Lord Minto, 3 October 1903.

63 John English, *The Decline of Politics* (Toronto: University of Toronto Press, 1993), 136.

64 For this history, see especially John Reid, *Acadia, Maine, and New Scotland: Marginal Colonies in the Seventeenth Century* (Toronto: University of Toronto Press, 1981). It was interestingly invoked in Nickle's speech introducing his famous resolution: House of Commons, *Debates*, 8 April 1918, 477.

65 Sir Edward Mackenzie Mackenzie, 'The Baronets of Nova Scotia: Their Country and Cognizance,' *Transactions of the Royal Society of Canada*, 2nd ser., vol. 7 (May 1901), 88.

66 Until 1967, this would be the only instance of an order specifically designed for a Canadian purpose. In 1606, Champlain founded the Order of the Good Time (also known as the Order of Good Cheer) in Port Royal, although this organization was not an 'honour' but rather a male social organization devoted to 'good food and drink,' with the primary purpose of raising the morale of the outpost. William H. Craig, 'Order of the Good Time,' *Empire Digest* 4, no. 8 (June 1947): 41.

67 Their high status is visually indicated by a gold-and-enamel badge worn from around the neck and suspended from a ribbon.

68 House of Commons, *Debates*, 6 November 1867, 83.

69 Ibid., 21 April 1868, 524.

70 These include the Most Noble Order of the Garter (KG), founded in 1348 and one of the oldest Orders of Chivalry in Europe, whose ranks are (with a few exceptions) restricted to the Sovereign, the Prince of Wales, and twenty-four Knights; the Most Ancient and Most Noble Order of the Thistle (KT), founded in 1687, essentially Scotland's version of the Order of the Garter; and finally the Most Illustrious Order of St Patrick (KP), founded in 1783 and initially consisting of the Sovereign and fifteen Knights, enlarged to twenty-two in 1833, which foundered with the partitioning of Ireland in 1922 and became obsolete in 1974 with the death of the last holder. Also noteworthy were the Most Exalted Order of the Star of India (GCSI, KCSI, CSI), reserved for services rendered in British possessions on the Indian Subcontinent, which became obsolete with India's independence in 1948, and the Most Eminent Order of the Indian Empire (GCIE, KCIE, CIE), created in 1877 to mark the assumption of the title of Empress of India by Queen Victoria, the 'junior' level of the Star of India, and likewise obsolete in 1948.

71 See Ivan De la Bere, *The Queen's Order of Chivalry* (London: William Kimber, 1961), 99.

72 The Civil Division, which was created in 1815, continued to consist of a single class (Knight of the Bath), whereas the military division was divided into three classes: Knight

Grand Cross (GCB), Knight Commander (KCB), and Companion (CB). Not until 1847 was the Civil Division organized into three classes like its military counterpart.

73 Because the Garter, Thistle, and Order of St Patrick were not usually bestowed on commoners, the Knight Grand Cross of the Order of the Bath was the highest award available to the non-titled classes. The past fifty years have seen an increase in the number of non-Royal appointments to the Order of the Garter and Order of the Thistle.

74 General William D. Otter was awarded a KCB in 1913; Major General Henry Burnstall, General Arthur Currie, Major General Frederick Loomis, Major General Archibald Macdonnell, Major General Richard Turner, and Major General David Watson were also recognized for their service in the First World War. The last award of the Knight Commander of the Bath was made in 1935 to Major General James MacBrien, Commissioner of the RCMP.

75 On the occasion of Confederation, John A. Macdonald was made a KCB, while the other senior Fathers – Cartier, Galt, Howland, McDougall, Tilley, and Tupper – were made Companions of the Order of the Bath, civil division. All except McDougall went on to attain one or more knighthoods.

76 In 1868, the Statutes of the Order of St Michael and St George were altered to make it the principal order of all British overseas possessions. See C.P. Stacey, 'The Knighting of Sir Francis Hincks: Comments,' *Canadian Historical Review* 32 (1951): 301.

77 NAC, MG 26 H, Borden Papers, p. 3427. 'The Grant of Honours in Canada,' undated memorandum.

78 A KCMG was accompanied by an attractive neck badge and breast star made of silver gilt and enamels.

79 The last award was made in 1946.

80 As Deputy Minister of Labour, Mackenzie King was made a Companion of the Order of St Michael and St George in 1906, which was only one level below a knighthood. During his career as prime minister, while one can find photographs of him wearing the official court dress uniform, he never wore his CMG. Going by photographs, he wore his 1935 King George V Silver Jubilee and King George VI Coronation Medals during the 1939 Royal Visit, but never the CMG. Perhaps he was concerned that people would assume that it was a knighthood that he did not use. Mackenzie King was awarded the Order of Merit in 1947. Oddly enough, Mackenzie King was phobic only about British awards. Over the course of his career, he was made a Grand Cross of France's Order of the Legion of Honour, Grand Cross of the Crown of Oak of Luxembourg, Grand Cross of the Order of Leopold from Belgium, and Grand Cross of the Order of the Netherlands Lion from the Netherlands.

81 See Peter Galloway, David Stanley, and Stanley Martin, *Royal Service*, vol. 1 (London: Stephen Austin and Sons, 1996), 20.

82 Ibid., 106.

83 It would later be awarded to Vincent Massey on 22 July 1960 on his retirement as Governor General, and in similar circumstances to Roland Michener on 3 August 1973.

84 A total of 481 CBEs, 1,671 OBEs, 2,726 MBEs and 1,368 BEMs were awarded to Canadians. See Blatherwick, *Canadian Orders, Decorations and Medals* (Toronto: Unitrade Press, 1994), 143. One should also note the later significance of both the Order of Merit, established in 1902, and the Order of the Companions of Honour, established in 1917. The first is a non-titular order with only one class, consisting of the Sovereign and a maximum of twenty-

four members at any given time, and devoted to recognizing those who have made exceptional contributions to the arts, literature, or science. Three Canadians have received this award: Mackenzie King (in 1947) in recognition of his tenure as the longest-serving prime minister in the British Commonwealth; Wilder Penfield, the neurosurgeon (in 1953); and Lester Pearson (in 1971). This award remains open to Canadians. The second was intended as a junior version of the Order of Merit, confers no titles, is limited to the Sovereign and sixty-five members at any one time, and is intended to recognize those who have rendered 'exceptionally conspicuous service of national importance' in the fields of the arts, literature, science, politics, industry, and religion. Like the Order of Merit, it has been used in Canada as a means of rewarding those who, except for the reluctance to reinstitute knighthoods, might have been knighted. Eight Canadians have been so honoured: General A.G.L. McNaughton, General Henry Crerar, Vincent Massey, John Diefenbaker, Dr Charles Best, Arnold Smith, Pierre Trudeau, and General John de Chastelain. Like the Order of Merit, it is still open to Canadians.

85 Prior to 1929, Knight Bachelors received no insignia, but were simply permitted to use the prefix 'Sir' in front of their name and 'Kt' after their surname.

86 NAC, MG 26 H, Robert Borden Papers, 'The Grant of Civil Honours in Canada,' p. 3428.

87 Ibid.

88 All the orders of chivalry are accompanied by an insignia to denote the class and order to which the holder belongs. Holders of the Knight of the Order of the Garter, Knight of the Order of the Thistle, Knight of the Order of St Patrick, Knight Grand Crosses of the Order of the Bath, Order of St Michael and St George, Royal Victorian Order, Order of the British Empire, Knight Grand Companions of the Order of the Star of India and Order of the Indian Empire; Bailiff or Dame Grand Cross of the Order of St John – are all entitled to receive the sash, breast star, collar chain, and robes of their Order. Knights Commander of all the British orders and the Knight or Dame of Justice or Grace of the Order of St John receive a neck badge and breast star. Those who are made Companions or Commanders of the British orders of chivalry and the Order of St John receive a neck badge. The more junior levels, such as Officer, Lieutenant, and Member, receive a badge that is worn on the left breast from a short ribbon. In 1926, George V granted Knights Bachelor permission to purchase and wear an oval badge to denote their knighthood.

89 A common jest was that the post-nominal style of the Order of St Michael and St George was arranged to symbolize the God-like authority of the Colonial Office: CMG, Call Me God; KCMG, the King Calls Me God; GCMG, God Calls Me God. Anthony Sampson, in Cross, *The Fall of the British Empire* (London: Penguin, 1968), 134.

90 This was the case for Queen Victoria's Golden and Diamond Jubilee, Edward VII's Coronation, and George V's Coronation and Silver Jubilee.

91 Awards were not always listed in the *Canada Gazette*. Prior to 1905, few titular honours were listed. Senator Sir James Gowan was the first to have his knighthood gazetted. Even after 1905, the *Canada Gazette* failed to list some knighthoods awarded to Canadians. This became increasingly frequent in late 1917, when public scrutiny of titular honours was on the rise. All awards are listed in the *London Gazette*. There was often a three-week delay between publication of a notice in the London Gazette and its appearance in the *Canada Gazette*.

92 Ibid.

93 The principle is that the Sovereign cannot act other than on the advice of the minister responsible. In the case of honours, this meant the prime minister.

94 The Royal Victorian Order, the Order of the Garter, the Order of the Thistle, and the Order of Merit are the only Orders that the Sovereign can bestow without consulting the British prime minister. In the case of Canada, the Royal Victorian Order remains part of the honours system and the Governor General is consulted.

95 Arthur Berriedale Keith, *The Sovereignty of the British Dominions* (London: Macmillan 1929), 267. Sir Robert Walpole was largely responsible for the overt politicization of the honours system. Honours had always been used to reward royal favours and were in an indirect way also a political tool wielded by the Sovereign. Walpole secured effective control over awards of the Order of the Garter. See McMillan, *The Honours Game* (London: Frewin Press, 1969), 23.

96 Surprisingly, since 1967, Canadian politicians have had relatively little control over the flow of honours. Today the Order of Canada is approved by a special committee established under the auspices of the Governor General, with no political involvement. This committee submits a list of names to the Governor General (who acts on behalf of Her Majesty the Queen) twice a year. It is interesting to note that no ministerial responsibility is attached to awards made.

97 McMillan, *The Honours Game*, 23. Prior to Walpole, the Order of the Garter had been awarded at the discretion of the Sovereign without involvement of the prime minister.

98 While the British prime minister approved of all the awards, he was in fact rarely consulted about awards being made to those living in Canada. It was the Secretary of State for the Colonies who was primarily responsible. Sir Charles Jeffries, *The Colonial Office* (London: Allen and Unwin, 1956), 147.

99 This was only true of awards made in the Dominions and colonies. Awards of the Order of St Michael and St George made to members of the Foreign Service had to be approved by the Foreign Office and British prime minister. Not coincidentally, the Chancellor of the Order of St Michael and St George was the Secretary of State for the Colonies.

100 G. Neuendorff, *Studies in the Evolution of Dominion Status* (London: Allen and Unwin, 1942), 23.

101 The Royal Victorian Order, Order of the Garter, Order of the Thistle, and Order of Merit were the only awards over which the Sovereign had absolute control. This order was immune from the principal of ministerial responsibility because it was the 'personal' gift of the Sovereign. Only in 1946 did the Sovereign regain control over the bestowal of the Orders of the Garter and Thistle.

102 David Farr, *The Colonial Office and Canada, 1867–1887* (Toronto: University of Toronto Press, 1955), 53.

103 Saywell and Stevens, eds., *Lord Minto's Canadian Papers*, 2:42. Joseph Chamberlain to Lord Minto, 18 May 1901.

104 Ibid.

105 NAC, MG 26 G, Laurier Papers, pp. 131, 882–9, Alfred Deakin, Prime Minister of Australia to Lord Northcote, Governor General of Australia, 13 November 1907.

106 Laurier was nearly placed in the precarious position of refusing a peerage from Edward VII. Lord Strathcona worked to obtain a peerage for Laurier, who would have been made a peer at the 1902 coronation of Edward VII. Approval was not officially given by Chamberlain, but Edward VII wanted to 'offer Laurier peerage on occasion of Corona-

tion,' so Chamberlain's input was redundant. A peerage would have certainly been awarded, had Laurier approved. Laurier declined the offer, but if it had not been for the intervention of Lord Minto, the peerage would have been awarded. All cables to the Colonial Office of a sensitive nature were encoded in Canada and sent to London. The error of a Colonial Office cypher clerk distorted Laurier's refusal, and had the vigilant Lord Minto not taken a keen interest in the issue, Laurier might have returned from the 1902 coronation as the First Baron Laurier of St Lin! See Bodleian Library, Oxford, Monck-Bretton Papers, no.86, 2/5. Sir Montague Frederick Ommaney to Joseph Chamberlain, 3 May 1902; NAC, MG 25 II A2, Chamberlain Papers, p. 520, Joseph Chamberlain to Lord Minto, 10 June 1902; NAC, MG 25 II A2, Chamberlain Papers, p. 522, Lord Minto via Military Secretary to Joseph Chamberlain, 18 June 1902; Miller, *The Canadian Career*, 179, 182. Minto loved to surprise people, especially Laurier. In 1899, Queen Victoria approved the striking of the Canada General Service Medal for those who served to repel the Fenian Raids of 1866 and 1870 and the Red River Rebellion of 1870. Laurier had served as an ensign in the Athabaskaville Infantry Company from 23 July 1869 until the disbanding of the unit on 16 August 1878. Being a member of the Canadian Militia during the 1870 Fenian Raids, Laurier was entitled to the Canada General Service Medal with a 'Fenian Raid 1870' bar. Unbeknownst to Laurier, Minto applied for the medal and later presented it to the prime minister.

107 Smith's first knighthood was for his involvement with the CPR, and although he was made a peer while Canadian High Commissioner in London, it was precisely because of his prominence as a railway executive that he received the latter post.

108 Shaughnessy had gone to great trouble and expense to make the Duke and Duchess's stay in Canada pleasant. He had five custom rail cars built, and he placed the ship *The Empress of India* at their disposal. Carman Miller, *The Canadian Career of the Fourth Earl of Minto* (Waterloo, ON: Wilfrid Laurier University Press, 1980), 181.

109 The Colonial Office and Governor General wanted to recognize William Mulock and Frederick Borden for their services to the Empire. As defence minister, Borden had been most cooperative regarding Canada's involvement in the Anglo-Boer War. Mulock had developed the Imperial Penny Post, whereby one could send a letter to any part of the Empire for two cents Canadian. This was introduced in 1898 and was seen as a great advance for Imperial unity (it was also the world's first Christmas stamp). Laurier tacitly condoned these 'Imperial' achievements, but he did not want them dwelt upon. Thus he opposed knighthoods for Borden and Mulock. The Colonial Secretary, Joseph Chamberlain, and Lord Minto were adamant that they should be recognized, especially as their contributions pertained to the entire Empire. The fact that the awards were to recognize contributions to the entire Empire was seen as reason enough to overpower the prime minister's objections. But Chamberlain and Minto held off – an indication that the prime minister was informally involved in the process. The awards were originally to be made during the 1901 Royal Visit of the Duke and Duchess of Cornwall and York, but Laurier had them postponed. Borden received his KCMG on 26 January 1902, and Mulock was made a KCMG on 26 June 1902. Laurier was concerned that 'cabinet already possesses plenty of honours, and is afraid of jealousies.' Saywell and Stevens, eds., *Lord Minto's Canadian Papers*, 1:57, Lord Minto to Joseph Chamberlain, 18 April 1899.

110 Saywell and Stevens, eds., *Lord Minto's Canadian Papers*, 2: 66, Lord Minto to Joseph Chamberlain, 2 September 1901.

111 Ibid., 67, Lord Minto to Joseph Chamberlain, 2 September 1901.

112 Ibid., 69, Lord Minto to Sir Wilfrid Laurier, 3 September 1901.

113 Ibid., 70, Lord Minto to Sir Wilfrid Laurier, 5 September 1901.

114 On 10 September 1901, Lord Minto wrote to Laurier: 'Mercifully things seem to be going favourably with the President – but it shows how careful we must be.' Ibid., 73.

115 Miller, *Canadian Careers*, 182. Sir Wilfrid Laurier to Joseph Chamberlain, 17 September 1901.

116 Ibid.

117 During the 1901 Royal Visit of the Duke and Duchess of Cornwall and York a total of ten awards were made. Thomas Shaughnessy, president of the CPR, was awarded a Kt; Sir John Alexander Boyd, Chancellor of the High Court of Ontario, was awarded a KCMG only two years after being made a Kt; Louis Amable Jetté, Lieutenant-Governor of Quebec, was awarded a KCMG. Of the non-titular awards, six CMGs were awarded: George M. Grant, principal of Queen's University; Oliver A. Howland, mayor of Toronto; Oliver E. Mathieu, Reverend Principal of Laval University; Frederick S. Maude, military secretary to Lord Minto; William Peterson, principal of McGill University; and Joseph Pope, Undersecretary of State for External Affairs. During his visit the Duke of Cornwall and York received honorary degrees from the University of Toronto, McGill, Laval, and Queen's Universities. Only the president of the University of Toronto was unrecognized with an honour during the 1902 Royal Visit.

118 Saywell and Stevens, eds., *Lord Minto's Canadian Papers*, 2: 75, Lord Minto to Sir Wilfrid Laurier, 19 September 1901.

119 Ibid.

120 Ibid., 128.

121 *Toronto Star*, 26 September 1901.

122 Criticism came in two forms: some believed that Canada was not sending enough men and materials to fight the Boers, and some felt that Canada should remain uninvolved in all Imperial conflicts unless they directly attacked Canada. Miller, *Canadian Career*, 181.

123 NAC, MG 26 H, Borden Papers, 50,235, 'Report of the Committee of the Honourable Privy Council, Approved by His Excellency on 19 February, 1902.'

124 Ibid.

125 Ibid.

126 Ibid.

127 Arthur Berriedale Keith, *The Sovereignty of the British Dominions* (London: MacMillan, 1929), 267.

128 NAC, MG 26 G, Laurier Papers, 215,473, Joseph Chamberlain to Lord Minto, 23 April 1902.

129 Ibid.

130 NAC, MG 26 G, Laurier Papers, p. 131,882–9, Alfred Deakin, Prime Minister of Australia, to Lord Northcote, Governor-General of Australia, 13 November 1907.

131 NAC, MG 26 G, Laurier Papers, p. 142,827, Alfred Deakin to Sir Wilfrid Laurier, 20 July 1908. NA, MG 26 G, Laurier Papers, p. 142,828, Alfred Deakin to Lord Northcote, 1 September 1908.

132 NAC, MG 26 G, Laurier Papers, p. 216,002, Lord Elgin, the Colonial Secretary to Lord Grey, Governor General of Canada, 5 March 1908.

133 For an outstanding discussion, see H.B. Beatby, *Laurier and a Liberal Quebec: A Study in Political Management* (Toronto: McClelland & Stewart, 1973).

134 Saywell and Stevens, eds., *Lord Minto's Canadian Papers*, 1: xxx.

135 NAC, MG 26 G, Laurier Papers, p. 34,045, Sir James Gowan to Lord Minto, 31 May 1899.

136 Ibid.

137 We know Minto gave the letter to Laurier because it can be found in the Laurier papers.

138 NAC, MG 26 G, p. 51,788, David Mills to Sir Wilfrid Laurier, 22 December 1900. Senator Reesor resigned from the Senate in early January, and Andrew Wood was summoned on 21 January 1901. Dr George Landerkin was to follow, being summoned on 16 February 1901.

139 Ibid., Sir Wilfrid Laurier to David Mills, 24 December 1900.

140 Saywell and Stevens, eds., *Lord Minto's Canadian Papers*, 2:460, Lord Minto to Lyttelton, 19 May 1904.

141 Ibid., 2: 504, Lord Minto to Sir Wilfrid Laurier, 24 June 1904.

142 Ibid., 2: 505, Lord Minto to Sir Wilfrid Laurier, 25 June 1904.

143 NAC, MG 26 G, Laurier Papers, p. 20,334, Lord Grey to Sir Wilfrid Laurier, 8 November 1905.

CHAPTER TWO

1 A.R.M. Lower, *Colony to Nation* (Toronto: Longmans, 1946), 456.

2 The resolution passed at the 1917 Imperial War Conference affirmed the preservation of 'all existing powers of self-government and complete control of domestic affairs, that it must be based on a complete recognition of the Dominions as autonomous nations of an Imperial Commonwealth.' H. Wilson, *The Imperial Policy of Sir Robert Borden* (Gainesville: University of Florida Press, 1966), 44.

3 NAC, MG 26 H, Borden Papers, p. 1213, Sir Robert Borden to Prince Albert, Duke of Connaught, 8 December 1914. Here Borden discusses recommendations for knighthoods. Further evidence of his increasing involvement can be found in his correspondence with the Colonial Secretary, 15 May 1916: see NAC, MG 26 H, Borden Papers, p. 1219, Sir Robert Borden to the Colonial Office, 16 May 1916.

4 NAC, MG 26 H, Borden Papers, Borden's Private Diaries, 22 June 1914.

5 House of Commons, *Debates*, 5 February 1914, p. 479.

6 Ibid., p. 480.

7 NAC, MG 26 H, Borden Papers, p. 50,169, Sir Robert Borden to the Duke of Devonshire, 17 May 1918.

8 Arthur B. Keith, *The War Governments of the British Dominions* (Oxford: Clarendon, 1921), 281.

9 See John English, *The Decline of Politics* (Toronto: University of Toronto Press, 1993), 34.

10 NAC, MG 26 H, Borden Papers, p. 50,169, Sir Robert Borden to the Duke of Devonshire, 17 May 1918.

11 Beaverbrook paid J.C.C. Davidson, chairman of the British Conservative Party, £10,000 with the understanding that Andrew Holt would be knighted in the 1929 New Year's Honours List. However, no knighthood was awarded, and the money was returned to Beaverbrook. This is one of the few examples of honours purchasing where a trail of evidence was left. A.J.P. Taylor, *Beaverbrook* (London: Hamish Hamilton, 1972), 256. Tom Cullen, *Maudy Gregory, Purveyor of Honours* (London: Quality Books, 1975), 152.

12 For this history, see especially John Reid, *Acadia, Maine, and New Scotland: Marginal Colonies in the Seventeenth Century* (Toronto: University of Toronto Press, 1981).

13 Michael De-la-Noy, *The Honours System; Who Gets What and Why* (London: Virgin, 1992), 81.

14 Ibid., 99.

15 Ibid.

16 John McCusker, *Comparing the Purchasing Power of Money in Great Britain from 1264 to the Present*, Economic History Service, 2001, accessed 8 April 2002. www.eh.net/hmit/ppowerbp[.]

17 De-la-Noy, *The Honours System*, 97.

18 These included the *Toronto Evening Telegram, Toronto Globe, London Advertiser, Hamilton Herald, Guelph Mercury, Toronto News, Prince Albert Herald, Moose Jaw News, Newmarket Era, Sydney Record, Stirling Leader, Milton Champion, Ottawa Journal, Calgary Albertan, Winnipeg Tribune, Kenora Miner and News, Tweed News, St Thomas Journal, Brantford Expositor, Stratford Beacon, Guelph Herald, Peterborough Review, Lethbridge Herald, Guelph Herald, Brockville Recorder, Orangeville Sun, Edmonton Bulletin, Owen Sound Sun, Vancouver World, Victoria Times, Woodstock Sentinel-Review, Christian Guardian, Brantford Courier,* and *Hamilton Spectator*. A copy can be found in NAC, MG 26 H, Borden Papers, p. 42,054.

19 For example, Ernest Lapointe remarked that 'there is no place in public life in this country for hereditary leaders or rulers.' House of Commons, *Debates*, 8 April 1918, which is the same as the text in 'Titles in Canada' (1917), 12.

20 'Titles in Canada' in 1917, citing the *Brantford Expositor*.

21 'Titles in Canada' in 1917, citing the *Moose Jaw News*.

22 'Titles in Canada' in 1917, citing the *Calgary Albertan*.

23 *Toronto Globe*, 16 February 1917.

24 'Titles in Canada' in 1917, citing the *Calgary Herald*.

25 'Titles in Canada' in 1917, citing the *Belleville Intelligencer*.

26 'Titles in Canada' in 1917, citing the *Christian Guardian*.

27 J. Castell Hopkins in the *Canadian Annual Review of Public Affairs* (Toronto: Canadian Annual Review, 1918), 563.

28 J. Castell Hopkins noted that editorials attacking the new 'British Empire Order' had appeared in newspapers in Halifax, Toronto, and the West. *Canadian Annual Review*, 564.

29 NAC, MG 26 H, Borden Papers, p. 42,013, British Imperial Association to Sir Robert Borden, 5 April 1918.

30 NAC, MG 27 II D8, White Papers, p. 5026. Memorandum from Prime Minister Borden, March 1918.

31 Ibid., p. 5081, Sir Robert Borden to Sir Thomas White, 4 February 1919. The offer of a KBE – the second class in the order – to Borden is somewhat surprising, given that Borden was leader of the largest Dominion fighting in the Great War. A GBE would have been the more appropriate award.

32 See Christopher McCreery, 'Questions of Honour: Canadian Government Policy towards Titular Honours, 1867–1935,' MA thesis, Queen's University, 1999), esp. chapter 2, 'Canadian Honours: A Statistical Overview.'

33 Ibid.

34 On a number of occasions, Nickle had opposed his own party – most prominently in 1916, when he spoke against the creation of the Canadian National Railway, and in 1926 when as Ontario's attorney general he resigned over the easing of prohibition laws.

35 Robert Laird Borden, *Memoirs*, vol. 2 (Toronto: Macmillan, 1938), 792.

36 William Beeching and Phyllis Clarke, eds., *Yours in the Struggle: Reminiscences of Tim Buck* (Toronto: N.C. Press, 1977), 230.

37 Frederick Gibson, *Queen's University*, vol. 2, *1917–1961* (Kingston: McGill-Queen's University Press, 1983), 46.

38 Interview with Mr and Mrs A.G. Nickle, 24 February 2002.

39 The five were Peterson, Beatty, and Dawson from McGill, and Falconer and Wilson from the University of Toronto. Beatty had originally served as chancellor of Queen's University before moving on to McGill.

40 At some universities, the Lieutenant-Governor is an ex officio member of the board of governors. These appointments have not been included in this calculation.

41 This includes professors emeritus.

42 It is suggestive of McGill's perceived need for titled men that on the death of Peterson in 1919, it appointed the Right Honourable Sir Auckland Geddes as principal (who held the post for less than a year), and then replaced him with General Sir Arthur Currie.

43 The chancellor of the university in 1919 was Edward Beatty, president of the CPR; it was widely speculated that Beatty would be made a knight for his services as president of the CPR during the First World War. Sir Edward Peacock, knighted in 1934 for his services to the Royal Family, would be involved with the university until his death.

44 Note Saywell and Stevens, eds., *Lord Minto's Canadian Papers*, 2:99, Lord Minto to Joseph Chamberlain, 2 December 1901.

45 NAC, MG 26 G, Laurier Papers, p. 59,312, J.P. Sheraton to Sir Wilfrid Laurier, 14 October 1901.

46 NAC, MG 26 H, Borden Papers, pp. 1,866–7, Prince Arthur, Duke of Connaught to Borden, 1 November 1913.

47 The fourteen knighthoods handed out in 1915 would be eclipsed in 1917, when seventeen were awarded.

48 Out of the fourteen knighthoods made in 1915, five were KCMGs. Only two CMGs were awarded in 1915, one to Gordon, and one to G.J. Desbarats, deputy minister of the Naval Service.

49 The University of Toronto was not a factor here, because Sir Byron Edmund Walker had been knighted in 1910 and later became chairman of the University of Toronto. The chancellor, Sir William Meredith, had been knighted in 1896 and would serve in this position from 1900 to 1923. Sir Robert Falconer, president of the university, was knighted in 1917. The University of Toronto was, in 1918, very well titled in relation to its rival Canadian universities.

50 QUA, Gordon Papers, John Stewart to Daniel Miner Gordon, 15 June 1915.

51 He would retire as principal in May, 1916, after fourteen years of service.

52 Interview with Mr and Mrs A.G. Nickle, 24 February 2002.

53 Borden, *Memoirs*, 2: 792.

54 Report of the Committee of the Privy Council approved by His Excellency the Governor-General on the 25th day of March, 1918. NA, MG 26 H, Borden Papers, pp. 50,211–12. Canada, House of Commons, *Debates*, 8 April 1918, 495–6.

55 NAC, MG 26 H, Borden Papers, p. 1748, Duke of Devonshire to Sir Robert Borden, 13 March 1918; p. 1749, Sir Robert Borden to the Duke of Devonshire, 13 March 1918.

56 Ibid., p. 50,150, Sir Joseph Pope to Sir Robert Borden, 16 March 1918.

57 Ibid.

58 Ibid., p, 50,154. Duke of Devonshire to Walter H. Long, 28 March 1918.

59 Napoleon on the awarding of prizes and honours, as cited by Ernest Lapointe in the Nickle Debate: House of Commons, *Debates*, 8 April 1918, 505.

60 Gibson, *Queen's University*, 2:46.

61 NAC, MG 26 I, Meighen Papers, p. 67,269, R.H. Smith to Arthur Meighen, 6 November 1926.

62 Nickle was the son of a distiller, but perhaps because of his own family's difficulties with alcoholism, he was also a firm advocate of prohibition. See Peter Oliver, *G. Howard Ferguson: Ontario Tory* (Toronto: University of Toronto Press, 1977), 146. Touted by some as a possible successor to Ferguson as leader of the Conservatives, Nickle resigned over this issue.

63 By Ontario's Premier Howard Ferguson in the context of his difficulties with Nickle at the provincial level. See Oliver, *G. Howard Ferguson*, 146.

64 Interview with Mr and Mrs A.G. Nickle, 24 February 2002.

65 House of Commons, *Debates*, 8 April 1918 (W.F. Nickle), 469.

66 Ibid.

67 Ibid., 469–70.

68 Ibid., 472.

69 Ibid.

70 Ibid.

71 Ibid., 473.

72 Ibid.

73 Ibid., 475.

74 Ibid.

75 Nickle presented, in his own words, an aphorism that he attributed to Lloyd George: 'I could never see ... how we get to the position that all the quality is in the oldest pup in the litter.' Ibid.

76 Ibid., 485.

77 Ibid., 486.

78 Ibid., 487.

79 Ibid.

80 Ibid. (Laurier), 499.

81 Ibid. (Laurier), 500.

82 Ibid. (Lapointe), 505.

83 Ibid. (Lemieux), 508.

84 Ibid.

85 Ibid.

86 Ibid. (Hughes), 510. As R.C. Brown and Ramsay Cook point out, Sam Hughes was greatly concerned to 'stem the egalitarian tide.' *Canada, 1896–1921: A Nation Transformed* (Toronto: McClelland & Stewart, 1974), 273.

87 Ibid. (Hughes), 510–11.

88 Ibid. (Hughes), 511.

89 Ibid. (Hughes), 512.

90 Ibid. (Borden), 492.

91 Borden noted the exceptional circumstance of a person who had rendered a personal service to the Crown, either in attendance at the court, or in attendance on some tour made by a member of the Royal Family. Ibid. (Borden), 493.

92 Ibid.

93 Ibid.

94 Ibid., 496.

95 Because it is subject to an alternative interpretation, when the Report of the Special Committee on Honours and titles is examined, I will show that what is remembered as the 'Nickle Resolution' is more closely related to the contemporaneous Order-in-Council 1918-668 and to the report of the Special Committee on Honours and Titles.

96 Ibid. (Thomson), 507.

97 NAC, MG 26 I, Meighen Papers, p. 67,269, R.H. Smith to Arthur Meighen, 6 November 1926.

98 Nickle wrote to Borden on 18 April 1918 asking if he was 'attempting to draft a resolution.' Nickle was clearly worried that the prime minister was planning an amendment. Nickle's reputation as a rogue Tory had preceded him, and thus Borden did not solicit his assistance. NA, MG 26 H, Borden Papers, p. 46,241, 18 April 1918. William F. Nickle to Sir Robert Borden.

99 House of Commons, *Debates*, 21 May 1918, 2342 (Borden).

100 Ibid., 2365 (Borden).

101 Borden, *Memoirs*, 2:797.

102 This was technically Borden's amendment to Richardson's amendment to Nickle's Resolution.

103 NAC, MG 26 H, Borden Papers, p. 50,173. Walter H. Long to the Duke of Devonshire, 18 November 1918.

104 Ibid., p. 50,166. Walter H. Long to the Duke of Devonshire, 9 August 1918.

105 One of Borden's early proposals to the British government was that Canadians appointed to the House of Lords be made life peers. Britain rejected the proposal, until passage of the Life Peerages Act, 1958 (UK). House of Commons, *Debates*, 8 April 1918, 497.

106 NAC, MG 26 H, Borden Papers, p. 50,166a, Walter H. Long to the Duke of Devonshire, 9 August 1918.

107 Ibid., p. 1775, Sir Robert Borden to Sir Thomas White, 2 January 1919.

108 Ibid., p. 1779, Sir Robert Borden to Sir Thomas White, 17 January 1919.

109 Ibid.

110 The one award made well after the Nickle Resolution passed, and the only civilian award between the Nickle Resolution and Bennett's restoration of Canadian knighthoods in 1933, was to Hormisdas Laporte, Chairman of the War Purchasing Commission and president of La Banque Provinciale du Canada. Laporte's knighthood was gazetted on 2 August 1918, meaning that the recommendation would have been submitted in early July, two weeks after the Nickle Resolution was passed by Parliament.

111 James McMillan, *The Honours Game* (London: Ferwin, 1969), 106.

112 Ibid., 111.

113 Ibid., 112.

114 From the outbreak of the First World War in August 1914 until April 1919, a total of 61 peerages were created and 164 baronetcies. This does not include the number of knighthoods awarded, but with the creation of the Order of the British Empire, the numbers were staggering.

115 NAC, MG 26 H, Borden Papers, p. 50,194, Sir Thomas White to Sir Robert Borden, 14 May 1919.

116 House of Commons, *Debates*, 14 April 1919, 1441.

117 Ibid.

118 Ibid., 1443.

119 House of Commons, *Debates*, 22 May 1919, 2106.

120 Ibid., 14 April 1919, 1456.

121 Ibid., 1479.

122 Ibid., 22 May 1919, 2698.

123 Titles such as doctor for a physician, military ranks, and other designations such as professor, mayor, councillor.

124 House of Commons, *Debates*, 22 May 1919, 2702.

125 Ibid., 2723.

126 NAC, MG 26 H, Borden Papers, p. 50,197, Sir Robert Borden to Sir Thomas White, 18 May 1919.

127 English, *The Decline of Politics*, 221.

128 House of Commons, *Debates*, 22 May 1919, 2749.

129 NAC, MG 26 H, Borden Papers, p. 50,197, Sir Robert Borden to Sir Thomas White, 18 May 1919.

130 Ibid., pp. 1,285–6, Deputy Minister of Justice to the Minister of Justice, 15 September 1919.

131 *Royal Commission on Honours: Report* (London: HMSO, 1922).

132 Tom Cullen, *Maudy Gregory* (London: Quality Books, 1975), 125.

133 E.G.M. Alexander, *South African Orders, Decorations and Medals* (Cape Town: Huan and Rousseau, 1986), 130.

134 This ratio is calculated on a per capita basis.

135 A.B. Keith, *The Sovereignty of the British Dominions* (London: Macmillan, 1929), 265.

136 Ibid.

137 NAC, MG 26 J1, Mackenzie King Papers, p. 182,985, Lord Willingdon to Mackenzie King, 18 February 1935.

138 Bennett was first offered the GCMG by the British Secretary of State for the Dominions, although he declined it in the hope that Mackenzie King would accept it. After receiving the offer, Mackenzie King wrote in his diary: 'I might have had a GCMG ... might hope for any honours of the kind – but wish none of them – wish above all to be if I only could "a pillar in the temple of God."' The GCMG that both Bennett and Mackenzie King declined was awarded to Sir Thomas White, former deputy prime minister. NAC, MG 26 J5, Diaries of Mackenzie King, 26 May 1935.

139 Vincent Massey, *What's Past Is Prologue* (Toronto: Macmillan, 1963), 504.

140 Entry written by B.K. Sandwell in L.G. Wickhan Legg, ed., *Dictionary of National Biography, 1941–1950* (Oxford: Oxford University Press, 1959), 462.

141 NAC, MG 26 J, Mackenzie King Papers, p. 77,009. William Lyon King to Sir William Mulock, 15 January 1923.

142 Ibid., p. 62,728. William Lyon Mackenzie King to Peter Larkin, 25 November 1922.

143 Ibid., p. 86,686. William Lyon Mackenzie King to Peter Larkin, 25 January 1924.

144 There are many examples of Canadians living in the United Kingdom being allowed to receive an award from the British government for services rendered to the United Kingdom.

145 House of Commons, *Debates*, 12 February 1929, 74.

146 Ibid., 14 February 1929, 109.

147 John Herd Thompson and Allen Seager, *Canada, 1922–1939: Decades of Discord* (Toronto: McClelland & Stewart, 1985), 202.

148 Bruce Huchinson, *Mr. Prime Minister, 1867–1964* (Toronto: Longmans, 1964), 242.

149 See J.L. Granatstein and Norman Hillmer, *Prime Ministers: Ranking Canada's Leaders* (Toronto: HarperCollins, 1999).

150 Between 1931 and 1935, Bennett received 172 pieces of correspondence relating to the adoption of a new Canadian flag. Included with these were fifty-four separate designs. In 1935, Bennett sent forward his design for a new flag to George V. Although the proposal did reach the King's desk, it was never formally dealt with. Bennett's foray into the flag debate has only recently been uncovered. See Christopher McCreery, 'Bennett's New Canadian Flag, Part I,' *Heraldry in Canada L'héraldique au Canada* 37, no. 1 (Winter 2003): 11–17.

151 Bennett also believed that the reintroduction of honours into Canada would help enhance the weakening links between Canada and Britain.

152 Bessborough to George V, 14 December 1933.

153 The example of Senator Sir James Robert Gowan has already been examined, demonstrating the many uses of honours.

154 The list of Canadians knighted during this period is long: Sir Frederick Banting, codiscoverer of insulin; Sir Edward Beatty, Chancellor of McGill; Sir Thomas Chapais, historian; Sir Joseph Chisholm, Chief Justice of Nova Scotia; Sir Arthur Doughty, Dominion Archivist; Sir Lyman Poore Duff, Chief Justice of the Supreme Court of Canada; Sir Albert Gooderham, philanthropist; Sir Edmund Wyly Grier, president of the Royal Canadian Academy; Sir Charles Lindsay, philanthropist; Sir Herbert Marler, Envoy Extraordinary to Japan; Sir Ernest MacMillan, composer and conductor; Sir John McLennan, physicist; Sir George Perley, minister without portfolio and former acting prime minister; Sir Charles G.D. Roberts, poet and historian; Sir Charles Saunders, Dominion Cerealist; Sir Joseph Tellier, Chief Justice of Quebec; Sir Thomas White, former Minister of Finance.

155 NAC, MG 26 K, Bennett Papers, p. 237,550, Memorandum: Restoration of Honours, 1933.

156 This applied in most areas except amendments to the British North America Act and appeals to the Judicial Committee of the Privy Council.

157 A good example of this is the fact that each year, the House of Commons extends condolences or congratulations to other countries. It would be silly to assume that when the House of Commons passes a resolution extending birthday greetings to the Queen, Parliament is perpetually saying 'happy birthday.'

158 In 1935, Canada's allotment of honours was: 1 GCMG, 2 KCMGs, 1 GBE, 2 KBEs, 1 KCB military, and 4 Knights Bachelor. Bennett managed to acquire an extra KBE and Knight Bachelor for the 1935 Honours Lists. NAC, MG 26 K, Bennett papers, p. 236,126.

159 NAC, MG 26 K, Bennett Papers, p. 237,302, Clive Wigram, Memorandum from Buckingham Palace Re: Canadian Honours, 20 December 1933.

160 Awards of the Order of St Michael and St George were dealt with by the Secretary of State for the Dominions. Awards of the the Order of the Bath, Order of the British Empire, and Knights Bachelor were dealt with by the British prime minister.

161 COCS, Canadian Resumption of Recommendation for Imperial Honours Including Titles, 1933–1935, file C-35. H.G. Bushe to Sir Edward Horing, 8 December 1933.

162 COCS, Canadian Resumption of Recommendations for Imperial Honours Including Titles, 1933–1935, file C-35 Telephone conversation between Sir Clive Wigram and Lord Bessborough, 12 December 1933.

163 The *London Gazette* reported the award on 2 January 1933, thus demonstrating the time lag between when awards were listed in the *London Gazette* and *Canada Gazette*.

164 NAC, MG 26 K, Bennett Papers, p. 235,950, Canada House, London Dispatch to Prime Minister, 28 January 1933.

165 House of Commons, *Debates*, 14 March 1934, 1,474.

166 Ibid., 28 January 1935, 230.

167 See 'A Constitutional Question,' *Canadian Liberal Monthly* 4, no. 1 (January 1934). This short article reflects on the spirit of the Nickle Resolution and tacitly acknowledges the ambiguous status of the Nickle Resolution as a binding regulation.

168 NAC, MG 26 J5, Diary of William Lyon Mackenzie King, 13 May 1934.

169 Harold Nicholson, *King George V: His Life and Reign* (London: Constable, 1952), 514.

170 NAC, MG 26 K, Bennett Papers, p. 237,296. Allan Lascelles to Frederick L.C. Pereira, 23 March 1934. In the year prior to a Jubilee celebration a few extra awards are granted, the Jubilee serving as a reason to increase the number of awards made.

171 As of 2002, all of the British orders of chivalry now admit women to their ranks.

172 The gender balance of awards was quite weighted in favour of men, a result of the restrictive nature of British honours more than an unwillingness on Bennett's behalf to reward deserving women. Although an examination of the total number of awards shows that women were underrepresented, receiving only 77 (27 per cent) of the 207 awards, when one takes into account that women were only eligible to receive the various levels of the Order of the British Empire, a more balanced distribution of awards becomes apparent. In all, there were 165 awards of the various levels of the Order of the British Empire. The gender breakdown reveals a surprisingly representative dispersal of awards.

173 Bennett also consulted the Governor General, although he, along with the King, was so elated that Canada was re-entering the realm of imperial honours that he did not interfere with his recommendations. They only limited the number of awards. Bennett's personal secretary and the Under-Secretary of State played only a small role in compiling the names of worthy recipients; it was Bennett who ultimately decided who would receive recognition and who would have to wait.

174 This does not include awards made to women serving in the Canadian Army Medical Corps, as these were submitted by the Canadian Army and not the prime minister. Of the two hundred awards of the Commander of the Order of the British Empire CBE (the highest-level civilian honour available to Canadian civilians) made to Canadian civilians for services rendered during the Second World War, only ten were awarded to women. This ratio of 10:200 is in stark contrast to the 15:26 (28 CBEs were awarded during Bennett's premiership, of which two were to serving members of the military; thus, they have been excluded from this ratio).

175 Bennett was often said to look more like a Japanese diplomat than a Canadian politician. He was often seen wearing a tailcoat and morning pants with top hat.

176 Cartoon from the *Winnipeg Free Press*.

177 Michael Bliss, *Right Honourable Men* (Toronto: HarperCollins, 1995), 119.

CHAPTER THREE

1   NAC, MG 26J 1, Mackenzie King Papers, p. 406,381, W.R. Wright, Executive Assistant to the PM, to Squadron Leader D.D. Dall, 15 August 1949.

2   West Sussex County Record Office, Bessborough Papers, Bessborough to Sir Clive Wigram (Private Secretary to George V), 12 June 1934.

3   NAC, MG 26 J5, Mackenzie King Diary, 5 November 1935.

4   Lord Tweedsmuir to Sir Clive Wigram, November 1935. Carl Lochnan, 'History of Honours in Canada' (unpublished manuscript), chapter 4, page 3.

5   Chapter 4 examines Vincent Massey and his inability to accept a KG.

6   Massey befriended John Buchan in the early 1920s, and so close were the two men that Massey wrote 'when the Gov Gen and his lady came down the line of Cabinet Ministers and Generals etc, and passed me JB cried out "Vincent!" and I had to pull myself together to keep from saying "John!" University of Toronto, Vincent Massey Diary, 2 November 1935. Their close friendship is further mentioned in Massey's autobiography, *What's Past Is Prologue: The Memoirs of Vincent Massey* (Toronto: Macmillan 1963), 328.

7   Janet Adam Smith, *John Buchan* (London: Rupert Hart-Davis, 1965), 398.

8   NAC, MG 26 J5, Mackenzie King Diary, 5 November 1935.

9   Ibid.

10 Following passage of the Nickle Resolution and adoption of the Report of the Special Committee on Honours and Titles, 1919, Sir Robert Borden noted that it would be next to impossible for Parliament to abolish existing titles. Although the constitutional status of Canada had changed significantly since 1919, such a drastic measure would have only come about with great difficulty and extensive debate – both of which Mackenzie King sought to avoid. Clearly, the prime minister was going to the extreme merely to illustrate to the new Governor General his distaste for titles and honours.

11 NAC, MG 26 J5, Mackenzie King Diary, 5 November 1935.

12 Ibid.

13 Ibid.

14 In his biography of Lord Minto, Tweedsmuir mentioned that the Governor General was always in a precarious situation vis-à-vis his prime minister and the Sovereign.

15 NAC, MG 26 J5, Mackenzie King Diary, 15 June 1939.

16 When the Prince of Wales visited Canada in 1860, he knighted a number of Canadian politicians and judges on behalf of Queen Victoria. Similarly, during George VI's visit to Canada in 1939, the King knighted Sir Shuldham Redfern and Lord Tweedsmuir on the Royal Train.

17 Smith, *John Buchan*, 451; Andrew Lownie, *John Buchan: The Presbyterian Cavalier* (London: Constable, 1995), 281.

18 C.P. Stacey, *Official History of the Canadian Army in the Second World War*, Vol. 1 (Ottawa: Queen's Printer, 1955), 42.

19 NAC, MG 20 E 148, John E. Read Papers, vol. 9, file 61.

20 NAC, MG 26 J5, Mackenzie King Diary, 30 September 1943.

21 NAC, MG 26 J1, Mackenzie King Papers, p. 237,291, Sir Gerald Campbell to O.D. Skelton, 31 October 1939.

22   Ibid., p. 237,202. O.D. Skelton to Sir Gerald Campbell, 22 December 1939.

23   Ibid.

24   Stacey, *Official History*, 1: 72.

25   NAC, MG 30 E 148, vol. 8, Read Papers, Summary of Action Taken, Awards for Service in the Armed Forces, 6 February 1941.

26   The Interdepartmental Committee, or 'Special Committee on Honours and Awards,' should not be confused with what would become the House of Commons's 'Special Committee on Honours and Decorations.' For the sake of simplicity I will call the 'Special Committee on Honours and Awards' the 'Interdepartmental Committee,' as it is sometimes referred to in the minutes.

27   NAC, RG 6, vol. 377, file D-B, Minutes of the Special Committee on Honours and Awards, dated 2 April 1942, and 11 September 1942. Clearly, the body had been in existence prior to 2 April 1942 as the minutes of the committee indicate. However, only a few copies of the minutes remain, and I thus was unable to ascertain the exact date of founding.

28   John Erskine Read was awarded the Medal of Service of the Order of Canada, on 22 December 1967.

29   NAC, MG 30 E148, vol. 8, Read Papers, Summary of Action Taken, 6 February 1941.

30   From the time of the First World War until the creation of the Order of Canada in 1967, either the Under-Secretary of State or the Under-Secretary of State for External Affairs was responsible for administering the honours system. This was largely because quotas for honours came from the British government and were considered 'external' but not 'foreign.' Prior to the First World War, honours were administered through a combination of the Prime Minister's Office and the Governor General. During the Second World War, the task was largely split between E.H. Coleman, the Under-Secretary of State, and John E. Read, the legal adviser for the Department of External Affairs.

31   QUA, A.Arc. 2125a, Vol. 8a, file III, Norman Rogers Papers, Visit to the UK Diary.

32   Proof of this interest can be found in the fact that George VI personally designed both the George Cross and the George Medal. John W. Wheeler-Bennett, *King George VI, His Life and Reign* (London: Macmillan, 1958), 471–3.

33   *Proceedings of the Social Committee on Honours and Awards, 1942 Report No. 2*, 9 July 1942 (Ottawa: King's Printer, 1942). In the proceedings it is mentioned by Perry Ellis Wright that the idea for a Canadian Order was not his own, but rather that the Hon. C.H. Power, who had mentioned it as early as March 1941.

34   NAC, RG 2, 7C, Minutes of the War Committee of the Cabinet, 31 October 1940.

35   NAC, MG 30 E148, vol. 9, Read Papers, Establishment of a Special Canadian Award, 7 November 1940.

36   Debates occurred on 23 and 24 June 1942.

37   NAC, MG 26 J4, Mackenzie King Papers, Honours and Decorations Memorandum, 19 November 1940, p. C 277,978. The memorandum also goes on to explain that a Canadian would not be eligible for the Empire Gallantry Medal, British Empire Medal, Distinguished Service Order, George Cross, or George Medal. All of these policies would eventually be reversed. It demonstrates what a feeble grasp cabinet had on the issue of honours and awards.

38   The framework for the Special Committee on Honours and Decorations was developed by Read. NAC, MG 30 E 148 vol. 8, Read Papers, Heeney to C.G. Power (Minister of National Defence for Air), 14 October 1941.

39 NAC, MG 30 E148, John E. Read Papers, vol. 8, file 55, J.E. Read to A.D.P. Heeney, un-
    dated early October 1941.

40 NAC, MG E148, John E. Read Papers, vol. 8, file 55, A.D.P. Heeney to J.E. Read, 11 Octo-
    ber 1941.

41 House of Commons, *Debates*, 23 June 1942 (N. McLarty), 3643.

42 Ibid.

43 Ibid., 24 June 1942 (M.J. Coldwell), 3654.

44 Report of the Special Committee on Honours and Decorations, 1942 (Ottawa: King's
    Printer, 1942).

45 *Financial Post*, 12 June 1943.

46 F.R. Scott was appointed a Companion of the Order of Canada on 6 July 1967, and was
    one of the first twenty-five Companions.

47 The Hon. Cyrus Macmillan served as a Major and Commanding Officer of the 6th Battery
    Canadian Siege Artillery during the First World War. *The Canadian Directory of Parliament,
    1867–1967* (Ottawa: Queen's Printer, 1968), 431.

48 The Hon. Ernest Bertrand served in the Canadian Expeditionary Force, but never actually
    got to France, being injured during training. Thus only four had fought in the Great War:
    the Hon. Herbert Alexander Bruce, Inspector General of the Canadian Army Medical Corps,
    1916–17; the Hon. Cyrus Macmillan, Major in the Canada Field Artillery, 1915–18; James
    Gray Turgeon, Lieutenant in the CEF; and Perry Ellis Wright, Lieutenant in the Canadian
    Field Artillery, 1915–18. *The Canadian Directory of Parliament, 1867–1967*, various entries.

49 Ultimately it was realized that neither the George Cross nor the George Medal were
    orders of chivalry and could thus be awarded to Canadians. A total of ten Canadians
    would be awarded the GC, and seventy-seven would be awarded the George Medal.
    Prior to the creation of the Medal of Courage of the Order of Canada, the George Medal
    served as the primary bravery decoration for Canadian civilians. Canadians were made
    eligible for the George Cross and George Medal through Order-in-Council 3445 of 15 May
    1941. Later, on 28 October 1941, the award of foreign medals and decorations from for-
    eign governments was sanctioned through Order-in-Council 8317.

50 The witnesses called were John Read, legal adviser for the Department of External Af-
    fairs; Major General H.F.G. Letson, Department of National Defence; Lieutenant Com-
    mander R.A. Pennington, Department of National Defence; Wing Commander A.C.H.
    MacLean, RAF Administration Branch on exchange to the Department of National De-
    fence; Filip Konowal, employee of Parliament and recipient of the Victoria Cross; and
    Ephriam H. Coleman, Assistant Undersecretary of State.

51 *Proceedings of the Special Committee on Honours and Decorations, 1942, no. 4* (Ottawa: King's
    Printer, 1942).

52 *Proceedings of the Social Committee on Honours and Decorations, 1942, no. 5* (Ottawa: King's
    Printer, 1942).

53 The first report, published 2 July 1942, did not relate to honours; it was merely an order
    that five hundred English and three hundred French of the proceedings of the committee
    be printed. *Report of the Special Committee on Honours and Decorations, 1942, no. 1* (Ottawa:
    King's Printer, 1942), 2.

54 House of Commons, *Debates*, 31 July 1942 (Cyrus Macmillan), 5,041.

55 *Second Report of the Special Committee on Honours and Decorations, 1942* (Ottawa: King's
    Printer, 1942).

56 NAC, MG 30 E148, John Erskine Read Papers, vol. 8, file 54. Notes of points discussed in conference between J.E. Read, Brigadier Orde, and Flight Lieutenant Mee, with Robert Knox, in London, August 1942.

57 University of Toronto Archives (UTA), Massey Papers, Sir Alan Lascelles to Vincent Massey, 13 July 1950. Lascelles recounts the filed related to the 7 August meeting.

58 It was not until September 1942 that Order-in-Council 1430 was revoked. NAC, MG 30 E148, vol. 8, Read Papers, Draft Report to Council, 14 September 1942.

59 Ibid., 18 July 1942.

60 At some points the members of the meeting are referred to as the Interdepartmental Committee.

61 Minutes of a 'Meeting held on Friday 11th September, 1942 at 11 a.m., in the office of the Under-Secretary of State.' This meeting occurred to discuss Read's findings following his trip to Britain. Unfortunately, there is a copy of extracts from the minutes of the meetings (NAC, RG 6, vol. 377, file D) that refers to the Committee as the Awards Coordination Committee, when in fact the ACC did not yet exist. The 11 September meeting was not the first meeting of the ACC but rather an informal meeting of some key people who would become involved with the ACC. RG 6, vol. 377, file D-B.

62 NAC, RG 6, vol. 377, Interdepartmental Committee File, 11 September 1942.

63 NAC, MG 30 E148, Read Papers, Read to Massey, 14 September 1942.

64 NAC, MG 26 J4, Mackenzie King Papers, Memorandum, October 1942, p. C278,073. Unfortunately there is no precise date on this document.

65 Ibid., Memorandum, 28 October 1942, p. C2,777,876.

66 Ibid., Sir Shuldham Redfern to A.D.P. Heeney, 2 December 1942. Redfern first phoned Heeney to inform him the committee could be created, 1 December 1942. NAC, R 5759, vol. 11, file 19, Lochnan Papers.

67 The full mandate of the ACC was 'that the Awards Co-ordination Committee should be charged with responsibility for the maintenance of central records of all honours in war in Canada and with the maintenance of uniformity of standards as between Canadian civilian, navy, army and air force authorities, and as between Canadian and other au-thorities dealing with like matters in other parts of His Majesty's dominions. The recom-mendations and suggestions of the ACC touching questions of principle in regard to the award of honours and decorations should be placed before the Prime Minister of Canada for consideration and, if favourably considered will be submitted by the Prime Minister to His Majesty the King for approval. The recommendations of individuals suggested by Sub-Committees representing the different branches of the Armed Services and civilians (In accordance with principle approved on advice from the ACC) shall, when approved by the Prime Minister or other minister designated by him, be forwarded to His Excel-lency the Governor General for submission to His Majesty the King.'

68 See Appendix 1 for list of ACC members.

69 NAC, MG 26 J4, Mackenzie King Papers, E.H. Coleman to Mackenzie King, 4 November 1942, p. 278,064.

70 NAC, RG 24, vol. 4058, file NSS 1078-14-1, Minutes of the Awards Co-ordination Commit-tee, 2 December 1942.

71 NAC, MG 26 J4, Mackenzie King Papers, A.D.P. Heeney to Mackenzie King, 12 December 1942, p. C278,086. Also see E.H. Coleman to A.D.P. Heeney, Memorandum, 11 December 1942, pp. 278,087–90.

72 Ibid., p. C278,087A.

73 Ibid.

74 Ibid.

75 NAC, MG 30 E148 vol. 9, Read Papers, Memorandum on the Proposed Canadian Order of Chivalry, 2 December 1941.

76 'G's and 'K's refer to the top levels of the British Orders of Knighthood, Knight Grand Cross and Knight Commander. Letson felt that the proposed Royal Order of Canada was too restrictive as it did not provide for the bestowal of lower-grade decorations similar to the Officer of the Order of the British Empire and Member of the Order of the British Empire.

77 NAC, MG 20 E148, John E. Read Papers, vol. 10, file 61, Major General Letson to J.E. Read, 1 December 1942.

78 Ibid.

79 The Legion of Merit consists of four levels; Chief Commander, Commander, Officer, and Legionnaire. It was created to recognized both American and Allied citizens for service rendered in the Second World War. It continues to be awarded by the U.S. government in recognition of outstanding service to the United States or its allies.

80 Robert Werlich, *Orders and Decorations of All Nations* (Washington, D.C.: Quaker Press, 1974), 9.

81 NAC, MG 24, vol. 4058, file NSS 1078-14-2, Major General H.F.G. Letson to Ephriam Coleman, 16 January 1943.

82 Redfern to the Dominions Office, January 1943. Lochnan, 'History of Honours in Canada,' chap. 4, 10.

83 NAC, RG 2, vol. 9, file H-5.

84 UTA, Massey Papers, B87-0082, vol. 311, Massey Diary for 1943, 18 October 1943.

85 Cabinet Office Ceremonial Secretariat (UK) (COCS), Canadian Attitude towards Imperial Honours, 1942–1967, file C-135, E.G. Machtig (of the Dominions Office) to Sir Shuldham Redfern, 19 February 1943.

86 Major-General Harry F.G. Letson was quite familiar with the honours system. Having been awarded the Military Cross for gallantry in the First World War, during the Second World War he served at the Canadian Embassy in Washington. Later he would become Adjutant General of the Canadian Army. For his services in the Second World War he was made a CBE and a CB. An engineer by training, Letson headed one of the largest engineering firms in Western Canada. After the war he was appointed Secretary to Governor General, Field Marshal Lord Alexander, a post he held until 1952. Even after his retirement he continued to actively advise the military. Letson was nominated for the Order of Canada, but he died in 1989, before the appointment could be made.

87 NAC, RG 2 vol. 9, file H-5, Jan.–May 1943, Secret Memorandum to the Cabinet War Committee from A.D.P. Heeney, Clerk of the Privy Council. Ironically, Coleman's copy of this document had the registration number '13.' The proposal was not well received.

88 NAC, RG2, vol. 9, file H-5, E.H. Coleman to Vincent Massey, 25 February 1943.

89 Redfern to the Dominions Office, 26 February 1943, Lochnan, 'History of Honours,' chap. 4, p. 12.

90 COCS, The Order of the Companions of Honour, file H-59, Clement Attlee to Winston Churchill, 29 March 1943.

91 Ibid.

92 COCS, Canadian Attitude Towards Imperial Honours, to Sir Robert Knox, 20 January 1943.

93 NAC, MG 26 J4, Mackenzie King Papers, Notes for the Under-Secretary of State for External Affairs, 21 May 1943, p. C278,009.

94 Ibid.

95 COCS, The Companions of Honour, file H-59, Canadian Government to the Dominions Office, 6 July 1943 (to Sir Robert Knox).

96 Sir Ivan De la Bere, *The Queen's Orders of Chivalry* (London: Spring Books, 1964), 171.

97 See chapter 1, note 84 for a list of the Canadians who have received the Order of the Companions of Honour.

98 RG 2, vol. 377. First Statutes of the Canada Medal refer to the Canadian Meritorious Award which was crossed out and replaced with the Canada Medal.

99 NAC, MG 26 J4, Mackenzie King Papers, E.H. Coleman to Mackenzie King, 4 February 1943, C278,093.

100 Ibid., A.D.P. Heeney to Mackenzie King, 15 February 1943, p. C161,477.

101 Ibid., A.D.P. Heeney to Mackenzie King, 15 February 1943, p. C278,091.

102 NAC, RG 2, vol. 377, file H-5, E.H. Coleman to A.D.P. Heeney, 27 May 1943.

103 Ibid., Minutes of the Awards Co-ordination Committee 12 July 1943.

104 Ibid., Arrangements for the establishment of The Canada Medal, 1943. See Appendix 2 for the full document.

105 NAC, RG 2, vol. 377, Minutes of the Awards Co-ordination Committee, 23 July 1943.

106 Ibid., 16 August 1943.

107 Ibid., 2 November 1943. Although the subcommittee reported on 20 August 1943, it was not until 2 November 1943 that its findings were entered into the minutes of the ACC. It is likely that the first report of the subcommittee related solely to the quota, whereas the others issued (ii–iv) were added at a later meeting of the subcommittee.

108 Ibid., 27 August 1943.

109 John R. Matheson, *Canada's Flag: A Search for a Country* (Boston: G.K. Hall, 1980), 17.

110 NAC, RG 2, vol. 377, Minutes of the Awards Co-ordination Committee, 17 September 1943.

111 A total of 16,688 Canada General Service Medals were awarded, of which only 351 had the bar 'Red River, 1870.' Thus, the Canada General Service Medal could hardly be considered the 'Reil Rebellion Medal.' This was in fact the North West Canada Medal, 1885, of which only 5,650 were awarded. The ribbon for the North West Canada Medal was of gray-blue and crimson. F.J. Blatherwick, *Canadian Orders, Decorations and Medals* (Toronto: Unitrade, 1994), 192.

112 Arnold Heeney, Clerk of the Privy Council, wrote to McTavish to allay his concerns about the use of the Canada General Service Medal ribbon. NAC, RG2 vol. 9, A.D.P. Heeney to Commander McTavish, 15 September 1943.

113 NAC, MG 26 J1, Mackenzie King Papers, W.J. Turnbull to J.L. Ralston, 23 September 1943, 300,874.

114 NAC, RG 2, vol. 377, file C, Minutes of the Awards Co-ordination Committee, 17 September 1943.

115 NAC, RG 2, vol. 377, Minutes of the Awards Co-ordination Committee, 4 October 1943. Also see *Policy With Respect to Honours and Awards, Canadian Army Overseas, 1939–1944,* Report No. 112 of Army Historical Officer, dated 25 January 1944.

116 Press release on Canada Medal dated 23 September 1943, crossed and marked 'HOLD,' NAC, MG 26 J4, Mackenzie King Papers, Press Release, 23 September 1943, p. C161,484.

117 *Toronto Globe*, 18 October 1943.

118 NAC, RG 2, vol. 377, Minutes of the Awards Co-ordination Committee, 29 October 1943.

119 NAC, MG 26 J5, Mackenzie King Diary, 3 November 1943.

120 NAC, RG 2, vol. 9, file H-5, J.L. Ralston to A.D.P. Heeney, 11 November 1943, cypher no. 2833.

121 See Appendix 3.

122 The idea to create an award that was in everything but name an order of chivalry came from Arnold Heeney, Clerk of the Privy Council. He submitted a report to the ACC stating that 'the following plan might be considered. (a) The establishment of a senior award to be conferred by the King, upon recommendation of the Prime Minister of Canada. (b) The establishment of an award of a junior grade to be conferred under arrangements approved by the King, by the Governor General on recommendation of the appropriate Ministers.' NAC, RG 2, vol. 377, Heeney to ACC, 'Report of the Awards Co-ordination Committee,' 30 March 1943.

123 NAC, RG 2, vol. 9, file H-5, January–May 1943, Proposal for the Canadian Award and Canadian Decoration of Honour.

124 The motto, devised by Alan Beddoe, translates as 'a productive maple.'

125 NAC, RG 24, vol. 4059, Memo from Colonel A. Fortescue Duguid and Major-General H.F.G. Letson, 29 March 1943. Charles Comfort served as Canada's senior official war artist from 1943 to 1946. Following the war he became an assistant professor in the Department of Art and Archaeology at the University of Toronto. He would later serve as the director of the National Gallery of Canada from 1960 to 1965. A renowned painter, sculptor, and art administrator, Comfort was one of the first people to be appointed an Officer of the Order of Canada.

126 NAC, RG 2, vol. 377, file C, Minutes of the Awards Co-ordination Committee, 16 August 1943.

127 Ibid., file C, Minutes of the Awards Co-ordination Committee, 20 August 1943, Air Vice Marshall Sully and Captain Maingay to Letson.

128 The meeting took place on 8 October 1943.

129 NAC, MG 30 E148, John Read Papers, vol. 8, file 54, Cabinet War Committee Minutes, 10 November 1943.

130 NAC, RG 2, vol. 377, file C, Minutes of the Awards Co-ordination Committee, 8 October 1943.

131 UTA, Massey Papers, Prime Minister's Office Press Release, 30 December 1943.

132 The Order of the Bath has been purposely omitted from this list because it was awarded mainly to senior naval, military and air force officers. The last time a civilian award of the Order of the Bath was made in 1915, when Sir Sam Hughes was made a Knight Commander of the Civil Division of the Order. The only other civilian recipient of the Order of the Bath was Sir John A. Macdonald who was made a Knight Commander of the Order of the Bath on the event of Confederation and elevated to a Knight Grand Cross of the Order in 1884.

133 NAC, MG 30 E148, John E. Read Papers, vol. 8, file 54, Cabinet War Committee Minutes, 10 November 1943.

134 NAC, RG 2, vol. 377, Minutes of the Awards Co-ordination Committee, 14 April 1944.

135 Ibid., 12 July 1944.

136 Ibid., 17 May 1944.

137 Department of National Defence, Directorate of History and Heritage (DND/DHH) 75/601, file 25, Minutes of the Senior Sub Committee of the ACC, 1943–6, 30 March 1944.

138 Ibid., Army Suggested Arrangements for Recognition of Distinguished and Meritorious Service, 3 May 1944.

139 Ibid., RCAF Précis: Canadian Order of Honour, 3 May 1944.

140 Ibid., Proposal for Canadian Order, 25 May 1945.

141 NAC, RG 2, vol. 162, Memorandum from the Personnel Members Committee of the Department of National Defence, 8 August 1945, HCQ 54-27-94-38. From Major General A.E. Walford to E.H. Coleman.

142 NAC, RG 2, vol. 9, file H-5-F, Army Message from Canadian Join Staff Mission (Canadian Embassy) to Secretary Chiefs of Staff Committee, Secret JS40, 13 August 1945.

143 Ibid., Army message from Secretary Chiefs of Staff Committee to Canadian Joint Staff Mission, Restricted CSC-21, 18 August 1945.

144 NAC, RG 2, vol. 377, file C-C, Minutes of the Awards Co-ordination Committee, 20 August 1945.

145 NAC, RG 2, vol. 19, Commander D.K. McTavish (Secretary of the ACC) to Cabinet, 1 September 1945.

146 DND/DHH, 114/1 D68, Honours and Awards, Memorandum to the Defence Council, 27 June 1945.

147 NAC, RG 2, series 18, vol. 162, file H-5. Arrangements for the establishment of The Order of Canada, 10 October 1945.

148 NAC, RG 2, vol. 377, file C-C, Minutes of the Awards Co-ordination Committee, 10 October 1945.

149 NAC, RG 2, series 18, vol. 80, file H-5, E.H. Coleman to A.D.P. Heeney, 7 November 1945.

150 Ibid., A.D.P. Heeney to Mackenzie King, 11 December 1945.

151 NAC, MG 26 J4, Mackenzie King Papers, Cabinet Conclusions, 11 December 1945, p. C278,035.

152 UTA, Massey Papers, Massey to Mackenzie King, 11 December 1945, Despatch No. A. 621.

153 NAC, RG 2, vol. 80, file H-5, 1945, Memorandum to the Prime Minister, 11 December 1945, 'Important.'

154 Ibid.

155 Ibid.

156 Ibid.

157 Ibid.

158 NAC, RG 2, vol. 80, file H-5, 1945, Prime Minister's Office, 'Statement re Canadian civilian honours and awards,' 28 December 1945.

159 Whenever the Governor General retired and returned to the United Kingdom, there was a brief interim period during which the Chief Justice of the Supreme Court became Acting Governor General/Administrator of the Government of Canada. In 1941 and again in 1946, Frederick Pereira served as Deputy Governor General.

160 NAC, RG 2, series 18, vol. 162, C. Stein (Under-Secretary of State and Chairman of the ACC) to Norman A. Robertson (Clerk of the Privy Council), 14 October 1949.

161 NAC, MG 26 J4, Mackenzie King Papers, Cabinet Conclusions, 18 January 1946, C278,083.

162 NAC, MG 26 J1, Mackenzie King Papers, Mackenzie King to Vincent Massey, 9 June 1946, p. 369,423.

163 Ibid.

164 Ibid., Mackenzie King to Paul Martin, 1 June 1946.

165 NAC, MG 26 J1, Mackenzie King Papers, Mackenzie King to Louis St Laurent (Acting Secretary of State for External Affairs), 21 May 1946, p. 373,536.

166 Bissell, *The Imperial Canadian* (Toronto: University of Toronto Press, 1981), 174.

167 NAC, MG 26 J1, Mackenzie King Papers, Mackenzie King to Louis St Laurent, 22 May 1946, p. 373,534–5.

168 Ibid., St Laurent to Mackenzie King, 22 May 1946, p. 373,540.

169 Ibid., Mackenzie King to St Laurent, 22 May 1946, p. 373,542.

170 NAC, MG 26 J5, Mackenzie King Diary, 22 May 1946.

171 NAC, RG 2, vol. 80, file H-5, Memorandum for A.D.P. Heeney from the Privy Council, 13 March 1946.

172 Ibid., Paul Martin to E.H. Coleman 8 March 1946.

173 Ibid.

174 Paul Martin, *A Very Public Life* (Ottawa: Deneau, 1983), 435.

175 NAC, RG 2, vol. 377, Proposed Civilian Honours List, 1946, June 1946. The Breakdown of the 1,483 civilian awards is as follows: Companion of the Order of St Michael and St George, 40; Commander of the Order of the British Empire, 153; Officer of the Order of the British Empire, 479; Member of the Order of the British Empire, 597; British Empire Medal, 39; Imperial Service Order, 13; Polar Medal, 8; Bar to Polar Medal, 3; additional awards not individually listed in main 1946 list, 151.

176 Martin, *A Very Public Life*, 435.

177 UTA, Massey Papers, press statement from the Prime Minister's Office, 22 November 1946. Taken from file 'Papers Relating to Honours for Canadian Citizens, 1942–1946.'

178 De la Bere, *The Queen's Orders of Chivalry*, 168.

179 NAC, MG 26 J5, Mackenzie King Diary, 21 October 1947.

180 NAC, MG 26 J1, Mackenzie King Papers, p. 396,117, Lord Alexander to Mackenzie King, 24 March 1948.

181 NAC, MG 26 J1, Mackenzie King Papers, p. 396,120, Lord Alexander to Mackenzie King, 24 March 1948.

182 France's Légion d'honneur, founded in 1802 by Napoleon, consists of five grades: Grand Cross, Grand Officer, Commander, Officer, and Knight. The *Légion d'honneur* replaced the Orders of the Kingdom of France, which were abolished by a decree of 30 July 1791. The *Légion d'honneur* does not confer a title (such as 'Sir' or 'Chevalier') on the recipient. Jacques Blondel, *Guide pratique des décorations* (Paris: Lavauzelle, 1986), 25. Canadians would go on to receive the *Légion d'honneur* in the First and Second World Wars, and Sir Wilfrid Laurier was made a Grand Cross of the Order in 1896.

183 NAC, MG 26 J1, Mackenzie King Papers, p. 396,117, Lord Alexander to Mackenzie King, 24 March 1948.

184 Ibid., p. 396,119. In notes at the bottom of the document from Alexander to Mackenzie King, 24 March 1948, in Mackenzie King's handwriting, dated 26 March 1948, the prime minister explained to Lord Alexander that there was not going to be any Canadian Order in the near future, and also pointed out that the Canada Medal had not yet been awarded to a Canadian, let alone a foreign head of state.

185 Claxton and Letson served together in the Canadian Field Artillery during the First World War.
186 NAC, R 5769, vol. 12. Lochnan Papers, Brooke Claxton to H.F.G. Letson, 6 April 1948.
187 NAC, MG 26 J5, Diary of Mackenzie King, 6 March 1946.
188 Robert Wardhaugh in John English, Kenneth McLaughlin, and Whitney Lackenbauer, eds., *Mackenzie King: Citizenship and Community* (Toronto: Robin Brass Studio, 2002), 93.
189 See NAC, MG 26 J5, Mackenzie King Diary, 25 May 1935. The Governor General, Lord Willingdon – a good friend of the prime minister's – encouraged him to accept the GCMG, but Mackenzie King declined the honour.
190 R. MacGregor Dawson, *William Lyon Mackenzie King: A Political Biography*, 1874–1923 (Toronto: University of Toronto Press, 1958), 131.
191 Galloway, *Companions of Honour*, various entries.
192 De la Bere, *The Queen's Orders of Chivalry*, 168.
193 NAC, MG 26 J1, Mackenzie King to Louis St Laurent, 19 November 1947, p. 318,012. After receiving approval from Cabinet and the National Liberal Federation, Mackenzie King sent a telegram to Gordon Fogo, president of the National Liberal Federation: 'Am glad to know Royal Honour so cordially approved by the National Liberal Federation. Many thanks to all.' Mackenzie King, NAC, MG 26 J1, Mackenzie King Papers, p. 377, 606.
194 NAC, MG 26 J5, Mackenzie King Diary, 21 October 1947.
195 Ibid., 29 March 1950.

CHAPTER FOUR

1 'Honours,' *Canadiana Encyclopedia* (Ottawa: Grolier, 1960), 146.
2 David. E. Smith, *The Invisible Crown* (Toronto: University of Toronto Press, 1995), 45.
3 Ibid., 44.
4 J.W. Pickersgill, *My Years with Louis St. Laurent* (Toronto: University of Toronto Press, 1975), 112.
5 Ged Martin, *Britain and the Origins of Canadian Confederation, 1837–1867* (Vancouver: UBC Press, 1995), 282. Also see NAC MG 26 A, Macdonald Papers, Macdonald to Lord Knutsford, 18 July 1889.
6 Claude Bissell, *The Imperial Canadian* (Toronto: University of Toronto Press, 1986), 173.
7 Ibid., 176.
8 Ibid., 193.
9 Ibid., 176.
10 In 1949 the Personnel Members Committee of the Department of National Defence began working on the creation of a Canadian award for long service. It would replace the myriad of British awards for long service – the Efficiency Medal, the Efficiency Decoration, the Air Efficiency Award, the RCAF Long Service and Good Conduct Medal, the RCN Long Service and Good Conduct Medal, the RCN Reserve Decoration, and the RCNVR Reserve Decoration – and in 1951 would in turn be replaced by the Canadian Forces Decoration. This became the first decoration in the Canadian honours system, which for the time being remained integrated with the larger British system.
11 NAC, RG 2, series 18, vol. 162, W.B. Creery to C. Stein (Under-Secretary of State, and chairman of the ACC), 29 July 1949.

12 Marc Milner, *Canada's Navy: The First Century* (Toronto: University of Toronto Press, 1999), 242.

13 Latham Jenson, *Tin Hats, Oilskins, and Seaboots* (Toronto: Robin Brass, 2000), 274.

14 NAC, RG 2, series 18, vol. 162, W.B. Creery to C. Stein, 29 July 1949.

15 Ibid.

16 NAC, RG 2, series 18, vol. 162, C. Stein to Norman Robertson, 14 October 1949.

17 DND/DHH, 75/506, Norman Robertson to C. Stein, 22 November 1950.

18 Stein submitted the first proposal on 14 October 1949, and Robertson replied to his query on 22 November 1950. Robertson merely stated: 'I did not answer your letter of October 14th, 1949 at the time, as it was not feasible to have the matter given consideration then by the Cabinet.' DND/DHH, 75/506, Norman Robertson to C. Stein, 22 November 1950.

19 NAC, RG 2, series 18, vol. 162, J.W. Pickersgill to N.A. Robertson, 30 November 1949.

20 Bissell, *The Imperial Canadian*, 195.

21 NAC, RG 2, A-5a, Cabinet Conclusions, 18 March 1949. This decision was taken in response to a letter from the ACC dated 10 March 1949, regarding not only the question of a Canadian honour, but also foreign awards to Canadians.

22 NAC, RG 2, series 5A, Cabinet Conclusions, 25 April 1950.

23 Ibid., 28 June 1950.

24 Georges-Henri Lévesque would be awarded the Medal of Service of the Order of Canada in 1967 and be elevated to a Companion of the Order in 1979; Vincent Massey was appointed a Companion in 1967; N.A.M. Mackenzie, already made a Companion of the Order of St Michael and St George in 1946, and awarded the Military Medal and Bar for gallantry in the First World War, was made a Companion of the Order in 1969; Hilda Neatby was made a Companion of the Order of Canada in 1967; unfortunately, Arthur Surveyer died prior to the Order's founding.

25 Paul Litt, *The Muses, the Masses and the Massey Commission* (Toronto: University of Toronto Press, 1992), 17.

26 Ibid., 37.

27 UTA, Massey Papers, Sir Alan Lascelles to Vincent Massey, 13 July 1950.

28 Ibid.

29 Ibid.

30 Ibid., Lorne Pierce to the Royal Commission on behalf of the Royal Society of Canada, 'A Resolution Relating to Honours for Canadian Citizens,' 1950.

31 Ibid., Sir Michael Adeane to Vincent Massey, 26 March 1951.

32 Massey wrote Knox on 16 April 1951. UTA, Massey Papers, Vincent Massey to Sir Robert Knox, 16 April 1951.

33 Litt, *The Muses*, 194. Litt pays little attention to the honours issue and claims that there was division among members of the commission with regard to honours, yet there seems to be little evidence of this. The commission seemed to be more concerned about how the prime minister and press would react than about being accused of creating an elitist institution.

34 UTA, Massey Papers, Massey to St Laurent, 16 July 1951.

35 Ibid., St Laurent to Massey, 9 August, 1951.

36 Ibid., Sir Alan Lascelles to Vincent Massey, 20 April 1951. Massey posted a copy of the proposal in early April 1951. Not until 16 July did he present St Laurent with the same proposal.

37 Ibid., Massey to St Laurent, 1951. Excerpts from Confidential Report on Honours and Awards by Rt Hon. Vincent Massey and members of the Royal Commission on Arts, Letters and Sciences, 1951. III Recommendations.

38 One must assume that the inclusion of the Medal of the Order of St Lawrence meant that the Canada Medal was to be abolished, since it is not mentioned anywhere in the proposal.

39 NAC, R 5769, Lochnan Papers, Confidential Report on Honours and Awards, 1951.

40 Litt, *The Muses*, 35.

41 Ibid., 193.

42 NAC, MG 26 K, St Laurent Papers, St Laurent to George Drew, 6 September 1951.

43 NAC, R 5769, vol. 12, Lochnan Papers, Memorandum to Cabinet 216–51, 29 August 1951.

44 Pickersgill opposed honours and had little use for them. During debate in the House of Commons on 6 November 1963, when asked about the Canada Medal, he commented: 'As this question [about awarding the Canada Medal], has been outstanding for 20 years it does not seem to me to be urgent.' House of Commons, *Debates*, 22 July 1963 (Pickersgill), 2,458. In 1967, when the cabinet discussed creating the Order of Canada, Pickersgill opposed the whole project. Pickersgill would be made a Companion of the Order of Canada in 1970.

45 'The subject of honours is hydra-headed. It should be kept submerged from 1952 and all of 1953, and hopefully in that way it will be gotten rid of.' NAC, R 5769, vol. 12, Lochnan Papers, J.W. Pickersgill to Brooke Claxton, 30 September 1952.

46 UTA, Massey Papers, Sir Michael Adeane to Vincent Massey, 21 June 1954.

47 Ibid., Massey to Adeane to Massey, 30 June 1954.

48 Minister of National Defence at the Defence Council meeting, 27 May 1952. DND/DHH, 75/506, Paper for the Minister's Use: Concerning Honours and Awards in Canada, 7 November 1963.

49 DND/DHH, 75/506, Memorandum to Cabinet, Order of Canada and Canada Medal, September 1952.

50 There was no meeting of the ACC between 9 April 1947 and 28 February 1949. At the February 1949 meeting, only General Letson was well acquainted with the work of the ACC; the three armed services only sent alternate committee members, who had never been involved in the ACC.

51 A total of 3 CBEs, 21 OBEs and 59 MBEs were awarded.

52 This does not include gallantry decorations.

53 House of Commons, *Debates*, 16 June 1954 (George Nowlan), 6063.

54 Ibid., 12 January 1956, 36.

55 Ibid., 4 July 1959, 5644–63 (intermittent discussion).

56 The Canada Medal would be briefly discussed in the House on 5 July 1956, 14 August 1956, 5 February 1957, 7 March 1957, 11 March 1957, 15 March 1957, 27 January 1959, 8 September 1961, 22 July 1963, 6 November 1963, and 8 April 1965, and again in 1966 and 1967.

57 NAC, MG 26 N4, Pearson Papers, vol. 1, file 003-4, Cabinet Directive no. 30, 7 November 1956.

58 NAC, RG 2, A-5a, Cabinet Conclusions, 25 October 1956.

59 NAC, MG 26 N4, Pearson Papers, vol. 1, file 003-4, Cabinet Directive no. 31, 7 November 1956.

60 One final award was made in 1964. Brigadier General Jacques Dextraze was elevated from an Officer of the Order of the British Empire to become a Commander of the same Order for gallantry displayed during his service with the United Nations in the Congo. Dextraze would go on to be made a Companion of the Order of Canada and later a Commander of the Order of Military Merit.

61 NAC, R 5769, Lochnan Papers, Lionel Massey (Secretary to the Governor General) to Major General W.S.H. Macklin, Adjutant General, 29 July 1954.

62 Nine original members of the Royal Family received the Canadian Forces Decoration shortly after its establishment in 1951. Beyond that, only the Governor General and Sovereign receive the CD automatically. NAC, R 5769, Lochnan Papers, Lionel Massey (Secretary to the Governor General) to Major General W.S.H. Macklin, Adjutant General, 29 July 1954.

63 UTA, Massey Papers, Massey to Sir Michael Adeane, 22 October 1954.

64 Sir Ivan De la Bere, *The Queen's Orders of Chivalry* (London: Spring Books, 1964), 52.

65 The only orders the Queen can bestow in the United Kingdom without consulting her ministers are the Order of the Garter, Order of the Thistle, Royal Victorian Order, and Order of Merit. The Garter, like the Royal Victorian Order and Order of Merit, is a personal gift of recognition from the Sovereign and largely devoid of political pressures.

66 UTA, Massey Papers, Massey to Sir Michael Adeane, 22 October 1954.

67 Ibid.

68 Ibid., Massey to Sir Michael Adeane, 26 January 1955.

69 Ibid.

70 Ibid.

71 Ibid., Sir Michael Adeane to Vincent Massey, 1 February 1955. 'Thank you for your letter of the 26th January, which I have shown to the Queen and which, not unnaturally, caused Her Majesty some disappointment.'

72 Ibid., Sir Michael Adeane to Vincent Massey, 22 August 1957.

73 Ibid., Vincent Massey to Sir Michael Adeane, 8 September 1957.

74 Ibid., Massey to Sir Michael Adeane, 12 September 1958.

75 Ibid., Sir Michael Adeane to Vincent Massey, 21 September 1958.

76 Ibid., Massey to Sir Michael Adeane, 16 February 1959.

77 Norman Campbell, *Ottawa Citizen*, 24 January 1959.

78 Ibid.

79 *Canadian Institute of Public Opinion, Gallup Poll of Canada*, 2 May 1959. Gallup had undertaken a few polls on this subject, the first in 1942, shortly after Parliament released its report on honours, and again in 1953. Strangely, it seemed as though public opinion was swinging in favour of allowing Canadians to accept knighthoods and peerages. The question was 'There has been some argument about whether or not Canadians should be given titles (Sir, Lord, Viscount) for outstanding services to their country. What are your views?'

Total Polling Data 1942, 1953 and 1959

	1942	1953	1959
Favour Titles	32%	32%	38%
Oppose Titles	55%	53%	46%
Undecided	13%	15%	16%

Political affiliation made relatively little difference to one's support for or opposition to titles. The 1959 Gallup poll found that 41% of Liberals favoured the idea of titles while 45% opposed it. Conservatives were evenly split, with 42% in favour and an equal percentage opposed to titles.

80 House of Commons, *Debates*, 27 January 1959, 361.

81 Rather ironically, Pickersgill indirectly responded to a question from Mr D.M. Fisher (Port Arthur), who, after asking his initial question about Massey, asked about awarding the Canada Medal. Diefenbaker merely responded that the medal had become 'the finest and most sought after collector's item in this country,' to which Pickersgill retorted, 'No one has ever got one yet.' It should be remembered that Pickersgill blocked the award of the Canada Medal while he was Secretary of State from 1953 to 1957. House of Commons, *Debates*, 27 January 1959, 361.

82 UTA, Massey Papers, Massey to Sir Michael Adeane, 12 May 1959.

83 Ibid., Sir Michael Adeane to Massey, 6 July 1959.

84 Ibid., Sir Michael Adeane to Massey, 8 September 1959.

85 Ibid., Vincent Massey to Sir Michael Adeane, 30 August 1959.

86 Ibid., Queen Elizabeth to Massey, 9 September 1959.

87 *Saturday Night Magazine*, June 1986, 26–8.

88 UTA, Massey Papers, Vincent Massey to Sir Michael Adeane, 23 September 1959.

89 Ibid., Vincent Massey to Sir Michael Adeane, 26 November 1959.

90 Ibid., Sir Michael Adeane to Vincent Massey, 13 June 1960.

91 Peter Galloway, David Stanley, and Stanley Martin, *Royal Service*, Vol. 1 (London: Stephen Austin, 1996), 93.

92 In 1949, Sir Hugh Weir, GCVO, Physician to George VI, was the non-noble, non–head of state to receive the Royal Victorian Chain.

93 The three were Sir Hugh Weir (1949), Vincent Massey (1960), and Roland Michener (1973).

94 Bissell, *The Imperial Canadian*, 233.

CHAPTER FIVE

1 Other members of the Commonwealth who recognized the Queen as head of state continued to use the British honours system as their own.

2 Frank MacKinnon, *The Crown in Canada* (Toronto: McClelland & Stewart, 1976), 70; David E. Smith, *The Invisible Crown* (Toronto: University of Toronto Press, 1995), 25; Keith Roberts-Wray, *Commonwealth and Colonial Law* (London: Steven's Press, 1966), 12. The concept of the 'divisible Crown' seems to have originated with Sir William Blackstone, the eminent British legal scholar. He developed the idea of 'distinct Dominions,' or rather the theory that colonial possessions did not necessarily have to be a part of the Imperial metropol. This theory allowed for the granting of responsible government, autonomy, and eventually independence to Britain's Dominions and colonies. This is rather remarkable, when one realizes that Blackstone wrote about these things in the 1760s. Sir William Blackstone, *Commentaries on the Laws of England*, vol. 1 (Chicago: University of Chicago Press, 1979), 107.

3 DND/DHH, 71/389 Honours and Awards, Memorandum from F. Shrap, Chief of the Defence Staff, 30 October 1970.

4 Bill C-127, the National Centennial Act, was given Royal Assent on 29 September 1961.

5 Section 9(1), Bill C-127, the National Centennial Act (Ottawa: Queen's Printer, 1961).

6 House of Commons, *Debates*, 16 September 1961, 8465–83.

7 The bill was formally introduced on 18 September 1961 and would receive Royal Assent 11 days later, on 29 September. Such a speedy adoption of legislation is rare in Parliament, especially during peacetime. It usually takes months for legislation to be adopted. C.E.S. Franks, *The Parliament of Canada* (Toronto: University of Toronto Press, 1987), 129.

8 Gary R. Meidema, 'For Canada's Sake: The Revisioning of Canada and the Restructuring of Public Religion in the 1960s.' PhD thesis, Queen's University, 2000, 161.

9 Canadian Army Order 128.25, 1949, also Order-in-Council 6335, 15 December 1949. UTA, Sir Michael Adeane to Vincent Massey, 8 March 1950.

10 These submissions were usually received from the Inter-Service Awards Committee, a more junior body that was responsible for selecting the most worthy candidates for recognition.

11 DND/DHH, 75/601, The Order of Canada and Canada Medal, Confidential Memorandum to Personnel Member's Committee, 19 October 1959.

12 Ibid.

13 Ibid., Brief on the Order of Canada for Consideration of the Chiefs of Staff Committee, 26 February 1960.

14 Ibid., Memorandum to the Minister of National Defence from General Charles Foulkes, 17 February 1960.

15 NAC, MG 31 E80, vol. 7, Esmond Butler Papers, Memorandum from Butler to Vanier, 15 February 1961.

16 DND, DHH, 75/506, Centennial Medal. On 28 June 1962, the Personnel Members Committee (PMC) proposed the creation of a Centennial Medal 'to commemorate Canada's 100th anniversary.'

17 H. Taprell Dorling, *Ribbons and Medals* (London: George Phillip, 1963), 143–5.

18 NAC, RG 69, vol. 367, file 130-33, Decorations Committee Memorandum, Canadian Centennial Medal, 1967.

19 Halpenny served as a lieutenant colonel in the Royal Canadian Army Medical Corps from 1942 to 1945.

20 NAC, R 5769, vol. 12, file 16, Lochnan Papers.

21 Ibid.

22 Ibid., Centennial Commissioner to Lamontage, 10 March 1964.

23 J.L. Granatstein, *Canada, 1957–1967* (Toronto: McClelland & Stewart, 1986), 223.

24 *White Paper on Defence, 1964* (Ottawa: Queen's Printer, 1964).

25 Granatstein, *Canada*, 231.

26 Ibid., 235.

27 NAC, RG 2, Cabinet Submission From Paul Hellyer and Maurice Lamontage, 11 May 1965.

28 NAC, R 5769, vol. 12, file 16, Lochnan Papers, O.G. Stoner (Privy Council Office Staff) to Jean Miquelon (Chairman of the Decorations Committee), 30 September 1965.

29 Matheson spoke with Pearson about the matter in 1962. Matheson interview, 24 August 2001.

30 Lester B. Pearson, *Memoirs*, vol. 2 (Toronto: University of Toronto Press, 1975), 302.

31 Pearson received his OBE over the fence of a tennis court in 1935. Pearson, *Memoirs*, vol. 3, 302.

32 Pearson recalling his reaction to the 1943 honours list. Pearson, *Memoirs* 2: 302.
33 John English, *The Worldly Years* (Toronto: Vintage, 1993), 140.
34 West Sussex County Records Office, Bessborough Papers, Bessborough to George V, 18 December 1934.
35 Sir Conrad Swan, *Canada: Symbols of Sovereignty* (Toronto: University of Toronto Press, 1977), 64.
36 The Maple Leaf was used on the coins issued by New Brunswick, Nova Scotia, and the Province of Canada prior to Confederation, and used on the Dominion coinage issued between 1876 and 1936. *The Charlton Standard Catalogue of Canadian Coins* (Toronto: Charlton, 2001).
37 John R. Matheson, *Canada's Flag* (Boston: G.K. Hall, 1980), 122.
38 Ibid., 122.
39 Pearson, *Memoirs* 3: 274.
40 Ibid., 281.
41 House of Commons, *Debates*, 6 November 1963, 4449.
42 Bill C-92, House of Commons, 8 April 1965 (Ottawa: Queen's Printer, 1965).
43 Pearson, *Memoirs*, 3: 210.
44 UTA, Massey Papers, Vincent Massey to Lester Pearson, 3 February 1966.
45 Ibid.
46 Ibid., Lester Pearson to Vincent Massey 17 February 1966.
47 QUA, Matheson Papers, W.J. Lindall to Centennial Commission, 28 January 1966.
48 Ibid., Phillip Laundy to John Matheson, 10 February 1966.
49 UTA, Massey Papers, Vincent Massey to Lester Pearson, 2 March 1966.
50 Ibid., Vincent Massey to Lester Pearson, 9 March 1966.
51 Near Port Hope, Ontario.
52 UTA, Massey Papers, Vincent Massey to Esmond Butler, 14 March 1966.
53 Interview with John Matheson, 7 January 2000.
54 Massey set about drawing up a constitution for the Order. Although the first draft was not completed until 23 March, most of the details were agreed to during Matheson's visit of 16–17 March. UTA, Massey Papers, 23 March 1966, Proposal for a Canadian Order.
55 NAC, MG 26 J 4, series N4, vol. 1, file 001.4, Pearson Papers, John Matheson to Lester Pearson, 18 March 1966.
56 The meeting between Pearson and Vanier occurred on the evening of 17 March. UTA, Massey Papers, Esmond Butler to Vincent Massey, 18 March 1966.
57 NAC, MG 32 A2, vol. 24, file 9, Georges Vanier Papers, Esmond Butler to Vincent Massey 18 March 1966. The fact that this letter (also found in the Massey and Butler papers) is located in the Vanier Papers indicates that Vanier was aware of the project from the earliest stages. Unfortunately there is no record of his conversation with Pearson on 18 March 1966.
58 NAC, MG 26 J 4, series N4, vol. 1, file 001.4, Pearson Papers, Vincent Massey to Lester Pearson, 18 March 1966.
59 Ibid.
60 Ibid.
61 NAC, R 5769, vol. 112, Lochnan Papers, Historical Report, 1986.
62 UTA, Massey Papers, 'The Statutes of the Order of ...,' first draft, 23 March 1966.

63 QUA, Matheson Papers, series 2, file 227, A Proposal for the Establishment of 'The Order of Canada,' April 1966.

64 UTA, Massey papers, Vincent Massey to John Matheson, 29 March 1966.

65 QUA, Matheson Papers, file 295, Esmond Butler to John Matheson, 31 March 1966.

66 NAC, R 5769, Lochnan Papers, vol. 112, Pitfield to Matheson and Butler, 13 April 1966, also sent to Massey.

67 Ibid.

68 Ibid.

69 Ibid.

70 Ibid.

71 Although Pitfield did not outline that each of the three types of Canada Medals were to be different, it would only be logical that they were intended as such. This was further discussed by John Matheson and Conrad Swan on 25 April 1966, and can be found in QUA, Matheson Papers, file 295, John Matheson to Lester Pearson, 29 April 1966.

72 Ibid., 14 April 1966. Also see NAC, MG 26 N4, vol. 1, file 001-42.

73 NAC, MG 26 N4, vol. 1, file 001-42, John Matheson to Lester Pearson, 14 April 1966, notes in Pearson's handwriting on document not found on copy in Matheson Papers.

74 UTA, Massey Papers, Esmond Butler to Vincent Massey 25 July 1966.

75 NAC, MG 31 E80, vol. 7, file 8. Esmond Butler to Georges Vanier, 14 April 1966.

76 Massey was constantly sending letters and cables to Esmond Butler, awaiting news about the Order. So interested in the project was Massey that he contemplated postponing his month-long European trip so that he could remain in Canada to advise on the proposal. Massey departed for Europe, but not before leaving a comprehensive itinerary of where he could be reached at all times, on land and at sea. UTA, Massey Papers, Joyce Turpin (Massey's Secretary) to John Matheson, 21 April 1966.

77 NAC, MG 31 E80, vol. 7, file 8. Esmond Butler to Georges Vanier, 21 April 1966. 'Some time ago I left with you a copy of a memorandum which Michael Pitfield and I had prepared for the PM on honours and awards in Canada. You will remember that we put forward in it our proposals for a system of honours and awards with three grades to be known as the Order of Canada. I understand that the PM has now read the document and that, in general terms, he is pleased with it. I know that he wished to discuss it with you and in case he brings it up this evening I am attaching a copy of the memo.'

78 QUA, Matheson Papers, file 295. John Matheson to Lester Pearson, 29 April 1966.

79 NAC, MG 31 E80, vol. 7, file 8. Esmond Butler to Georges Vanier, 6 May 1966.

80 Butler's frustration and concern was most evident in a letter sent almost a month later to Vanier, which stated: 'I believe you wish to ask the PM what the situation is concerning this matter [honours and awards]. It would seem to me that unless action is taken almost immediately it would be quite impossible to set up the machinery for the selection of suitable candidates, to decide upon and strike the necessary insignia, etc. In time for the announcement of the awards or the holding of investiture in 1967.' NAC, MG 31 E80, vol. 7, file 8, Esmond Butler to Georges Vanier, 1 June 1966. Also see UTA, Massey Papers, Vincent Massey to Esmond Butler, 28 July 1966.

81 NAC, MG 32 A2, vol. 33, Vincent Massey to Georges Vanier, 12 July 1966.

82 NAC, MG 32 A2, Vanier Papers, Massey File, 1959–64, Esmond Butler to Vincent Massey, 25 July 1966.

83 Ibid., vol. 33, Georges Vanier to Vincent Massey, 29 July 1966.

84 UTA, Massey Papers, Esmond Butler to Vincent Massey, 26 August 1966.

85 NAC, MG 26 N4, vol. 1, file 001-4, Pearson Papers, Vincent Massey to Lester Pearson, 28 September 1966.

86 Ibid., Lester Pearson to Vincent Massey, 3 October 1966.

87 QUA, file 225, Matheson Papers, Philip Laundy (Chief of Research, Parliamentary Library) to John Matheson, 2 June 1966. Matheson had requested the research on 26 April 1966 so as best to attain full understanding of what attributes the Order would recognize and exemplify.

88 NAC, MG 26 N4 vol. 1, file 001-42, Pearson Papers, transcript of letter received from John Matheson, Park Lane Hotel, 14 July 1966.

89 QUA, file 296, Matheson Papers, John Matheson to Lester Pearson, 3 August 1966.

90 It is uncertain who the 'others' were, although we do know that E.C. Joslin was present. See NAC, MG 26 N4, vol. 1, file 001-42, Pearson Papers, J.S. Hodgson to D.F. Spink, 3 October 1966.

91 Ibid., Conrad Swan to Lester Pearson, 28 September 1966.

92 Ibid., Pearson Papers, J.S. Hodgson to Edith MacDonald, 4 October 1966. Regarding the statutes of the Order of the British Empire and Royal Victorian Order.

93 QUA, file 296, Matheson Papers, John Matheson to Mary Macdonald, September 1966.

94 Ibid., Conrad Swan to John Matheson, 31 October 1966.

95 Ibid. Matheson's first draft of a Constitution for the Order of Canada is dated 14 October 1966, with further revisions made on 19 October. In the second set of revisions, the title is changed from 'Constitution' to 'Statutes of the Order of Canada.' This was a short-lived change; by February 1967, it was decided to refer to the governing document of the Order as a constitution.

96 NAC, RG 2, vol. 6321, Cabinet Document 50–66, 5 May 1966.

97 Ibid., Cabinet Document 625-66, 7 November 1966.

98 In addition to privy councillors, lieutenant-governors and judges are afforded the appellation 'Honourable.'

99 Matheson interview, 7 January 2000. Paul Martin, Sr, was also absent from the meeting, but he made his views known to the prime minister shortly after receiving the 7 November memorandum. Also see Martin's autobiography, *A Very Public Life*, vol. 1 (Ottawa: Deneau, 1983), 434–5.

100 NAC, RG 2, Cabinet Document 625-66, 7 November 1966.

101 Hellyer had designs of his own on creating an honours system. Cabinet had sanctioned the creation of a committee to examine the institution of military decorations on 5 May 1966. The report was completed on 27 October, but it was held back until 10 December, as Hellyer did not want his proposal to end up in competition with the prime minister's Order of Canada. The Hellyer proposal contained many important suggestions, many of which would be used in the creation of the Canadian Bravery Decorations instituted in 1972, but the time was not yet right. Matheson was most alarmed with the impending race to create more honours. Writing to J.S. Hodgson, he commented: 'I am a little disturbed with some of these proposals, and I think they should be carefully considered.' QUA, file 296, Matheson Papers, John Matheson to J.S. Hodgson, 13 December 1966. Also Matheson interview, 7 January 2000.

102 Chancellery of Canadian Honours, Government House Working Files, Black Binder,

Secret Memorandum from Pitfield to Butler, Hodgson, and Matheson, 25 November 1966. Pitfield acknowledged that some change in the Advisory Council was necessary 'so that it would not be dominated by persons close to the federal government.'

103 NAC, RG 2, vol. 6321, Cabinet Conclusions No. 136–66, 29 November 1966.

104 Interview, Gordon Robertson, 6 December 2001.

105 NAC, R 5769, vol. 11, Chris Conliffe to Carl Lochnan, 20 November 1986.

106 NAC, RG 2, vol. 6324, file 118-67, Memorandum from the Prime Minister to Cabinet, 27 February 1967.

107 This was a revised version of the 19 October Constitution I have; see Matheson's notes on the actual document.

108 CHAN, Black Binder, Adeane to Butler, 10 January 1967. NAC, R 5769, Lochnan Papers, vol. 112.

109 NAC, MG 26 N4, vol. 1, file 001-42, Pearson Papers, Sir Michael Adeane to Esmond Butler, 9 January 1967.

110 Ibid.

111 Ibid., Esmond Butler to Sir Michael Adeane, 13 January 1967.

112 Ibid., Esmond Butler to J.S. Hodgson, 13 January 1967.

113 CHAN, Black Binder, Sir Martin Charteris to Esmond Butler, 18 January 1967. NAC, R 5769, Lochnan Papers, Vol 112.

114 Ibid., Esmond Butler to Sir Martin Charteris, 27 January 1967. NAC, R 5769, Lochnan Papers, vol. 112.

115 Other countries that utilize a red-white-red ribbon colour combination similar to the Order of Canada are Portugal, the Order of Agricultural and Industrial Merit; Bulgaria, the Order of the Red Flag of Work; Czechoslovakia, the Order of the White Lion (very similar, although there is a slight red border on each side); and Austria, the Decoration of Honour for Merit. This list encompasses only the European Orders; Chile, Japan, Fiji, and Vietnam provide other examples.

116 CHAN, Black Binder, Esmond Butler to Georges Vanier, 19 January 1967. NAC, R 5769, Lochnan Papers, vol. 112.

117 Butler and Hodgson were in London from 1 to 4 February. They met with Mr Summers at Garrard & Co.

118 NAC, R 5769, vol. 11, Lochnan Papers. Reference to Esmond Butler and John Hodgson's report to the prime minister on their deliberations in London, 9 February 1967.

119 CHAN, Black Binder, Memorandum Hodgson to Matheson, Butler, and Pitfield, 21 December 1966. NAC, R 5769, Lochnan Papers, vol. 112.

120 QUA, Matheson Papers, file 225, Constitution of the Order of Canada, February 1967.

121 Peter Galloway, *The Order of the British Empire* (London: Austin & Sons, 1996), 111.

122 CHAN, Black Binder, Esmond Butler to John Hodgson, 29 December 1966. NAC, R 5769, Lochnan Papers, vol. 112.

123 The only other people to serve longer terms on the Advisory Council were Esmond Butler (eighteen years) and the Right Hon. Bora Laskin (ten years).

124 CHAN, Black Binder, Esmond Butler to Georges Vanier, 17 February 1967. NAC, R, 5769, Lochnan Papers, vol. 112.

125 Constitution of the Order of Canada, 1967.

126 NAC, RG 2, vol. 6324, file 118-67, Memorandum to the Cabinet from the Prime Minister, 27 February 1967.

127 NAC, RG 2, vol. 6323, file 20-67, Cabinet Conclusions, 2 March 1967.
128 CHAN, Esmond Butler to Sir Michael Adeane, 24 February 1967. NAC, R 5769, Lochnan Papers, vol. 112.
129 CHAN, Black Binder, Sir Michael Adeane to Georges Vanier, 27 February 1967. NAC, R, 5769, Lochnan Papers, vol. 112.
130 Ibid., Sir Michael Adeane to Esmond Butler, 28 February 1967, NAC R 5769, vol. 112.
131 It is unclear whether the Canadian government planned on continuing to use the Victoria Cross and George Cross. However, since the Medal of Courage was to precede all other British gallantry decorations – and being that the Medal of Courage was still to rank after the VC and GC – it is safe to assume that the government planned to retain them. The Medal of Courage was to replace the Distinguished Service Cross, Military Cross, Distinguished Flying Cross, Air Force Cross, Distinguished Conduct Medal, George Medal, Conspicuous Gallantry Medal, Distinguished Service Medal, Military Medal, Distinguished Flying Medal, Air Force Medal and the Queen's Police/Fire Medal for Gallantry.
132 QUA, Matheson Papers, vol. 226, Draft Constitution of the Order of Canada, October 1966. Also see CHAN, Black Binder, Edith MacDonald to Hodgson, 19 October 1966; NAC, R 5769, Lochnan Papers, vol. 112.
133 CHAN, Black Binder, Edith MacDonald to John Hodgson, 19 October 1966; NAC R, 5769, Lochnan Papers, vol. 112.
134 QUA, Matheson Papers, vol. 226, Draft Constitution of the Order of Canada, early February 1967.
135 Ibid., late February 1967.
136 NAC, R 5967, Lochnan Papers , vol. 112, Gordon Robertson to Judy LaMarsh, 13 March 1967.
137 Ibid.
138 CHAN, Black Binder, Assistant Secretary to the Governor General to the Private Secretary to the Queen, 17 March 1967.
139 NAC, MG 26 N4, vol. 1, file 001-42, John Hodgson to Lester Pearson, 23 March 1967.
140 House of Commons, *Debates*, 17 April 1967, 14,968 (Pearson).
141 Ibid. (Diefenbaker).
142 Ibid., 14,969 (Diefenbaker).
143 Ibid. (David Lewis).
144 Lester B. Pearson, *Memoirs*, 3: 302.
145 QUA, Matheson Papers, file 227, Prime Minister's Office Press Release, 17 April 1967.
146 *Canada Gazette*, Part I, 29 April 1967, (Ottawa: Queen's Printer, 1967), 1249.
147 Miedema, *For Canada's Sake*, 146.
148 Galloway, *The Order of the British Empire*, 60.
149 NAC, RG 2, vol. 6323, file 20-67, Cabinet Conclusions, 2 March 1967. Cabinet approved and passed Order-in-Council 388, which revoked the order-in-council that founded the Canada Medal.
150 The most senior Soviet decoration was the 'Order of the Hero of the Soviet Union.' Awarded only five times, it was bestowed for great bravery. It is interesting to note that both the Order of Lenin and the Order of the Hero of the Soviet Union were made of precious metals (gold and platinum). In the case of the Order of the Hero, the insignia was encrusted with diamonds and rubies.

CHAPTER SIX

1 Esmond Butler's introductory address to the Advisory Council of the Order of Canada, 29 May 1967. Taken from Butler's speech for the special meeting of the Advisory Council of the Order of Canada, 17 January 1977, NAC, R 5769, vol. 10, file 22, Lochnan Papers.
2 Interview with the Gordon Robertson, 6 December 2001.
3 Peter Galloway, *The Order of the British Empire* (London: Stephen Austin, 1996), 38.
4 The Canadian Forces Decoration predated the Order of Canada and is considered an honour, but it was open only to members of the Canadian Armed Forces, not to all citizens. There is the additional component that the CD is awarded for long service.
5 House of Commons, *Debates*, 26 April 1967, p. 15,448. These comments were made by Ralph Bronson Cowan, Liberal member for York-Humber.
6 Ibid. (R.B. Cowan).
7 *Victoria Daily Colonist*, 19 April 1967.
8 *London Free Press*, 19 April 1967.
9 *Ottawa Citizen*, 19 April 1967.
10 *Ottawa Journal*, 19 April 1967.
11 *Toronto Telegram*, 19 April 1967.
12 *Le Soleil* (Montreal), 19 April 1967.
13 *Toronto Star*, 18 April 1967.
14 *Winnipeg Tribune*, 19 April 1967.
15 *Calgary Herald*, 21 April 1967.
16 *Fredericton Daily Gleaner*, 22 April 1967.
17 *Le Devoir* (Montreal), 21 April 1967.
18 *Montreal Star*, 18 April 1967.
19 *Saskatoon Star-Phoenix*, 19 April 1967.
20 *Halifax Chronicle-Herald*, 19 April 1967.
21 *Toronto Star*, 19 April 1967. Newman was actually accurate to the ratio of 38:50, as one person in his projected list was offered the Medal of Service but refused the nomination. Johnny Wayne and Frank Shuster were offered the Medal of Service in October 1968; both men turned down the award. In 1996, Frank Shuster was made an Officer of the Order. Had Johnny Wayne lived longer, he would have certainly received an OC as well.
22 *Toronto Globe and Mail*, 19 April 1967, by Scott Young.
23 *Ottawa Citizen*, 19 May 1967.
24 *Vancouver Sun*, 24 May 1967.
25 QUA, Matheson Papers, file 295, Esmond Butler to John Matheson, 19 May 1967.
26 Ibid.
27 Turpin later married and became Joyce Bryan. Having been awarded the British Empire Medal in 1945, she was made a Member of the Order of Canada in 1974, in recognition of her long and exemplary service to Government House.
28 QUA, Matheson Papers, file 296, Esmond Butler Circular on Order of Canada.
29 Gordon Robertson speaking to Esmond Butler, November 1967, as recalled by Butler on 17 January 1977, Meeting of the Advisory Council (10th Anniversary). NAC, R 5769, Lochnan Papers.
30 UTA, Massey Papers, vol. 363, Nomination Form for Eric Ross Arthur.

31 NAC, MG 30 E148, John Read Papers, vol. 9, Memorandum on the Proposed Canadian Order of Chivalry, from Vincent Massey to Ephriam Coleman, December 1942.

32 UTA, Massey Papers, vol. 363, file 7, Vincent Massey to Esmond Butler, 26 July 1966.

33 CHAN, 708-9, file 1, Esmond Butler, Working Paper Number 1, 26 May 1967.

34 NAC, MG 26 N4, vol. 1, file 001-42, Pearson Papers, Esmond Butler to G.G.E. Steele, 12 May 1967.

35 In terms of geographic origin, the balance titled towards Ontario and Quebec. Taschereau was from Quebec City; Robertson was from Davidson, Saskatchewan; Steele was from Windsor, Ontario; Martineau was from Montreal; Herzberg was from Hamburg, Germany; and Johns was from Exeter Ontario. Two members of the council were Roman Catholic, two United Church, and one Anglican; one (Herzberg) did not list his religion.

36 Interview with Gordon Robertson, 6 December 2001.

37 Esmond Butler's introductory address to the Advisory Council of the Order of Canada, 29 May 1967. Taken from Butler's speech for the special meeting of the Advisory Council of the Order of Canada, 17 January 1977. NAC, R 5769, vol. 10, file 22, Lochnan Papers.

38 NAC, R 5769, Lochnan Papers, vol. 11, Advisory Council Meeting 13 June 1967.

39 Ibid.

40 Ibid.

41 Recognition of the Medal of Service as a national and not primarily local award can be found in the fact that when the Order of Canada was restructured in 1972, recipients of the Medal of Service were made Officers of the Order of Canada. The Officer level has since been used as primarily a national award; the Member level has been employed to recognize provincial and local service.

42 Interview with Gordon Robertson, 6 December 2001.

43 This has been the standard method through which the Queen acknowledges and approves appointments to the Order of Canada. NAC, MG 26 A4, Michener Papers, vol. 36, Sir Michael Adeane to Roland Michener, 18 April 1969.

44 Since 1967, the tradition has been for the chancellor to hold a luncheon for the members of the Advisory Council whenever it is convened.

45 NAC, R 5769, Lochnan Papers, vol. 11, Advisory Council Meeting, 19 June 1967.

46 Interview with Gordon Robertson, 6 December 2001. Also see Gordon Robertson, *Memoirs of a Very Civil Servant* (Toronto: University of Toronto Press, 2000), 233. Also see NAC, R 5769, Lochnan Papers, vol. 11, Advisory Council Meeting, 19 June 1967.

47 A total of 24 (20 male and 4 female versions on bows) Medals of Courage were ordered from Garrard & Company at a cost of $30 each. CHAN, 708-3, file 1, Memorandum to the Prime Minister on the Order of Canada, 26 March 1969.

48 DND/DHH, 75/601, folder 20, Minutes of the Decorations Committee, February 1960.

49 NAC, MG 26, N4, vol. 1, file 001-42, Pearson Papers, John Hodgson to Lester Pearson, 4 August 1967.

50 The intention was that the Medal of Courage would replace not only the George Medal, but also the Distinguished Service Cross, Military Cross, Distinguished Flying Cross, Air Force Cross, Distinguished Conduct Medal, Distinguished Service Medal, Military Medal, Distinguished Flying Medal, and Air Force Medal, as well as the Queen's Police and Fire Medals. This was an unrealistic goal, considering that although each of these

awards recognize bravery, the degree varies depending on the specific award being made.

51 NAC, MG 26 N4, vol. 1, file 001-42, Pearson Papers, John Hodgson to Esmond Butler, 24 August 1967.

52 Ibid.

53 Ibid., Memorandum to the Prime Minister from John Hodgson, 12 May 1967.

54 CHAN, 708-1 file 1, Esmond Butler to Under-Secretary of State, 21 April 1967.

55 NAC, MG 26 N4, vol. 1, file 001-42, Pearson Papers, Gordon Robertson to Lester Pearson, 6 July 1967.

56 QUA, Matheson Papers, file 223, Government House Press Release, 6 July 1967.

57 NAC, MG 26 N4, vol. 1, file 001-42, Pearson Papers, Gordon Robertson to Lester Pearson, 6 July 1967.

58 Kenojuak, the noted Inuit artist, was the first.

59 Interview with Gordon Robertson, 6 December 2001.

60 This was in the form of the Medal of Service awarded to Air Marshal William Curtis.

61 *Ottawa Citizen*, 10 July 1967.

62 *Telegraph Journal*, 8 July 1967.

63 *Montreal Star*, 8 July 1967.

64 *Le Soleil*, 10 July 1967.

65 *Globe and Mail*, 8 July 1967.

66 Paul Martin, *A Very Public Life* (Ottawa: Deneau, 1983), 435.

67 NAC, MG 31 E80, vol. 31, Butler Papers, Esmond Butler's Day Book, 1967.

68 Twenty-nine Companions and forty-five Medal of Service recipients attended the first investiture. NAC, MG 32 B41 vol. 134, Mitchell Sharp Papers, investiture lists, 24 November 1967.

69 Manual of Official Procedure of the Government of Canada, Privy Council Office, 1968, vol. 2, 340.

70 Mrs Dody Evans took more than one hundred pages of notes during the first investiture, noting the dress of each individual. After the formal investiture recipients were also photographed with their guest.

71 The original seating plan listed Paul Martin, Sr, as the acting prime minister, but he too was indisposed and thus Sharp was appointed acting prime minister (on account of being the Minister of Finance, considered second only to the Minister for External Affairs). Sharp thought this most ironic, since at the time he was one of the few opponents in the Cabinet to the Order of Canada.

72 Mitchell Sharp, *Which Reminds Me: A Memoir* (Toronto: University of Toronto Press, 1994), 155.

73 Ibid., 155.

74 NAC, MG 32 B41, vol. 134, Mitchell Sharp Papers, Roland Michener to Mitchell Sharp, 14 December 1967.

75 Ibid.

76 Ibid.

77 Interview with Gordon Robertson, 6 December 2001.

78 UTA, Massey Papers, Vincent Massey to Esmond Butler, 22 June 1967.

79 Ibid., Vincent Massey to Mary Ryde, 21 July 1967.

CHAPTER SEVEN

1 NAC, MG 26 N4, vol. 1, file 001-42, Memorandum from John S. Hodgson to Lester Pearson, 8 January 1968.
2 Ibid., John S. Hodgson to G.G.E. Steele, 3 August 1967. 'No non-Canadians should be appointed honorary members of the Order until Canadian government policy is altered regarding the acceptance of foreign honours and awards by Canadian citizens.'
3 Ibid., file 003-4, Pearson Papers, G.G.E. Steele to John S. Hodgson, 7 June 1967.
4 This decision to re-examine Canadian policy towards accepting foreign decorations was also precipitated by questions of whether or not Canadians serving in the U.S. Army could accept American medals for service in the Vietnam War. NAC, MG 26 N4, file 003-4, Pearson papers, John S. Hodgson to Henry Hindley, 14 August 1967.
5 The only earlier response that could have been considered a refusal came from Claude Ryan, who was offered the Medal of Service in June 1967. Ryan declined the SM not because he desired a higher honour, but rather on account of his youth and involvement in the media and politics. Ryan would be made a Companion of the Order in 1995.
6 NAC, MG 26 N4, vol. 1, file 001-42, Memorandum from John Hodgson to Lester Pearson, 8 January 1968.
7 NAC, MG 32 A-3, vol. 49, file 8, Agenda, Special Meeting of the Advisory Council, 17 January 1977.
8 Callaghan was made a Companion in December 1982, fifteen years after having been offered the Medal of Service.
9 NAC, MG 26 N4, vol. 1, file 001-42, Memorandum from John Hodgson to Lester Pearson, 8 January 1968.
10 Ibid.
11 Ibid., Memorandum from John Hodgson to Lester Pearson, 3 October 1967.
12 CHAN, 708-3, file 1, Pierre Trudeau to Roland Michener, 13 May 1969.
13 Ibid., Memorandum to the Prime Minister on the Order of Canada, 26 March 1969. The memorandum was drafted jointly by Gordon Robertson and Michael Pitfield.
14 Ibid., Pierre Trudeau to Roland Michener, 13 August 1969.
15 NAC, MG 26 N4, vol. 1, file 003-4, Pearson Papers, Revision of Policy Concerning the Acceptance and Wearing by Canadians of British and Foreign Honours and Decorations, revised copy, 31 January 1968.
16 In terms of foreign honours, reform to the policy was also felt necessary as many Canadians were simply ignoring the 1956 directive prohibiting the acceptance of foreign honours. At a dinner held for the president of Iceland during the Centennial year, a number of Canadian officials wore Icelandic honours (the Order of the Falcon) even though the government had not given them permission to do so. Pearson, Butler, and Pitfield were all aware of this but felt that there would be little purpose in making examples of those who had – against a government directive – accepted and worn a foreign decoration. NAC, MG 26 N4, vol. 1, file 003-4, Pearson papers, Esmond Butler to Michael Pitfield, 20 February 1968.
17 Ibid., Revision of Policy Concerning the Acceptance and Wearing by Canadians of British and Foreign Honours and Decorations, revised copy 31 January 1968.
18 Ibid., Carl Lochnan to John S. Hodgson, 6 February 1968.
19 Ibid., Judy LaMarsh to Lester Pearson, 6 March 1968.

20 Ibid., John Hodgson to Prime Minister, recounted handwritten notes (by Hodgson), 19 March 1968.

21 It is not exactly clear what the government's policy towards military gallantry decorations such as the Distinguished Service Order, Distinguished Service Cross, Military Cross, Distinguished Flying Cross, and Air Force Cross was. The plan was likely to replace these awards with similar Canadian military awards, and in light of the unification of the Royal Canadian Navy, Canadian Army, and Royal Canadian Air Force into the Canadian Forces, it would not have made sense to continue on with 'service specific' gallantry awards. Just prior to Cabinet discussing the creation of the Order of Canada, the Department of National Defence had completed a report calling for the creation of new military gallantry awards, although this was shelved.

22 NAC, MG 26 N4 vol. 1, file 003-4, Pearson papers, John Hodgson to Pearson, recounted in handwritten notes (by Hodgson), 19 March 1968.

23 NAC, RG 2 series 5a, vol. 6338, Cabinet Conclusions, 17 April 1968.

24 Ibid., 10 April 1968.

25 On 30 October 1968, the Advisory Council looked at new levels.

26 Statistics taken from Robert Werlich, *Orders and Decorations of All Nations* (Washington: Quaker Press, 1990), various entries.

27 NAC, R 5769, vol. 11, Lochnan Papers, Carl Lochnan to the Under-Secretary of State, 29 October 1968.

28 Esmond Butler to the Special Meeting of the Advisory Council, 17 January 1977.

29 CHAN, 708-3, file 1, Memorandum from Esmond Butler to Roger Nantel, 13 March 1970.

30 CHAN, Minutes of the Special Meeting of the Advisory Council, 30 October 1968.

31 Ibid.

32 Ibid., 15 September 1972.

33 Ibid., 13 November 1970.

34 Ibid., Minutes of the Third Meeting of the Advisory Council, 19 and 20 October 1967.

35 Mrs Michener was nominated by five people in August and September 1967. CHAN, 708-9, file 1, Ordinance for Norah Michener, 29 March 1971. Also see Roland Michener to the Queen, NAC, MG 23 A4, vol. 36, Michener Papers, 8 April 1971. Although her contributions during the Centennial year were important, Mrs Michener would have been considered for the Medal of Service and not a Companionship in the Order had she not been the wife of the Governor General. There is much evidence to suggest that Mrs Michener was most anxious to be admitted into the Order.

36 CHAN, Minutes of the Fifth Meeting of the Advisory Council, 17 November 1968.

37 CHAN, Minutes of the Seventh Meeting of the Advisory Council, 29 and 30 October 1969.

38 Mrs Michener had a keen interest in jewellery, and although the Order of Canada is not actually jewellery, it certainly had all the attributes of a beautiful brooch. For more on Mrs Michener's interest in jewellery, see Peter Strusberg, *Roland Michener: The Last Viceroy* (Toronto: McGraw-Hill Ryerson, 1989), 189.

39 NAC, MG 32 A3, vol. 36, Michener Papers, Roland Michener to the Queen, 29 March 1971.

40 CHAN, Minutes of the Tenth Meeting of the Advisory Council, 1 and 2 April 1971.

41 CHAN, 708-9, file 1, Sir Michael Adeane to Roland Michener, 1 April 1971.

42 NAC, RG 2, vol. 6318, Cabinet Conclusions, 6 April 1971.

43 Initially, Michener was 'reluctant to support such a decision' that the Governor General

should be allowed to remain a Companion of the Order of Canada after his retirement. CHAN, 708-9, file 1, Kenneth Foster to Esmond Butler, 29 July 1967.

44 NAC, MG 32 A3, vol. 36, Michener Papers, Michener to the Queen, 8 April 1971.

45 Ibid.

46 NAC, R 5769, vol. 11, Lochnan Papers, Carl Lochnan to L.E. Levy, 19 October 1971.

47 NAC, RG 2, series A5a, vol. 6318, Cabinet Conclusions, 6 April 1971.

48 On 23 February 1984, the Royal Canadian Mint melted 189 of the returned Medals of Service. This leaves 105 in existence, plus a number of unnamed specimens.

49 Awards of the Queen's Bravery Commendations were to continue.

50 NAC, R5769, vol. 11, Lochnan Papers, Carl Lochnan to G.G.E. Steele, 26 October 1968.

51 In particular, Colonel N.A. Buckingham and Commissioner Stevenson of the RCMP felt that there should be separate awards not necessarily incorporated in the Order of Canada. Carl Lochnan at the Department of the Secretary of State seems to have been one of the first to suggest the creation of three separate awards.

52 NAC, R5769, vol. 11, Lochnan Papers, Carl Lochnan to G.G.E. Steele, 26 October 1968.

53 This proposal was first devised on 28 October 1968 at the meeting of the subcommittee of the Decorations Committee.

54 NAC, R5769, vol. 10, Lochnan Papers, Carl Lochnan to Director of Protocol, Province of Ontario, 9 May 1973.

55 QUA, Matheson Papers, file 296, Memorandum to Defence Council, 27 October 1966.

56 The proposal, dated 27 October 1966, was passed on to the prime minister in early November, although he had no desire to proceed with the recommendations of the Department of National Defence.

57 In March 1966, the idea of civilian and military divisions had been proposed by Vincent Massey.

58 NAC, R 5769, vol. 11, Lochnan Papers, Report of the Decorations Committee, 9 January 1970.

59 Ibid.

60 Harrold Gillingham, *French Orders and Decorations* (New York: American Numismatic Society, 1922), 20.

61 NAC, RG 2 series A5a, vol. 6338, Cabinet Conclusions, 19 December 1969.

62 When Australia established the Order of Australia in 1975, there was opposition from many quarters on the basis that the British system was still quite effective. Australia continued to make recommendations for British honours until October 1992; Michael Maton, *The National Honours and Awards of Australia* (Kenthurst: Kangaroo Press, 1995), 33.

63 NAC, RG 2, series A5a, vol. 6381, Cabinet Conclusions, 29 July 1971.

64 Ibid.

65 Ibid.

66 Ibid.

67 Ibid.

68 NAC, MG 32 A4, vol. 49, file 2, Léger Papers, order-in-council augmenting the Constitution of the Order of Canada.

69 CHAN, 708-3, file 2, Sir Martin Charteris to Esmond Butler, 10 May 1972.

70 COCS, C135, Canadian Attitude to Imperial Honours, 1943–1967, P.S. Milner-Barry to Sir Martin Chartiers, 27 April 1972.

71 House of Commons, *Debates*, 31 May 1972, 2713 (Trudeau).

72 Ibid.

73 Ibid.

74 The designation 'Chancellery' was not accepted until later. In Butler's estimation, 'The use of the word "Chancery" has some appeal, although it may have the drawback of sounding a little grand.' NAC, R 5769, vol. 9, Lochnan Papers, Esmond Butler to Carl Lochnan, 7 July 1972.

75 CHAN, 708-3, file 1, Pierre Trudeau to Roland Michener, 13 May 1969.

76 NAC, R 5769, vol. 9, Lochnan Papers, Esmond Butler's Memorandum to Roland Michener, 28 September 1971.

77 Ibid.

78 NAC, R 5769, vol. 8, Lochnan Papers, Suggested requirements for the New System of Honours and Awards to be Established at Government House, 16 December 1971, fourth draft, written by Roger Nantel.

79 Ibid., Esmond Butler's Memorandum to Roland Michener, 28 September 1971.

80 Ibid., Esmond Butler to A.E. Russell, Chief Executive Staffing Officer, Public Service Commission, 1 June 1972.

81 The Registrar of Honours was also charged with the task of arranging investitures and ensuring that a Register of Honours be maintained.

82 NAC, R 5769, vol. 9, Lochnan Papers, Carl Lochnan to Esmond Butler, 4 June 1972.

83 Ibid., Lochnan Papers, Esmond Butler to Carl Lochnan, 9 June 1972.

84 House of Commons, *Debates*, 4 December 1970 (Stanfield), 1752.

85 Peter Galloway, *The Order of St Michael and St George* (London: Third Millennium Group, 2000), 266.

86 CHAN, Meeting of the Advisory Council of the Order of Canada, 22 and 23 April 1970.

87 Ibid., 29 and 30 October 1970.

88 Ibid., Special Meeting of the Advisory Council of the Order of Canada, 13 November 1970.

89 Ibid.

90 NAC, MG 32 A4, vol. 71, Léger Papers, order-in-council, 1 June 1972.

91 Interview with Geoffrey Pearson, 14 November 2001.

92 Peter Galloway, David Stanley, and Stanley Martin, *Royal Service*, vol. 1 (London: Stephen Austin, 1996), 2.

93 NAC, MG 32 A3, vol. 36, Michener Papers, Sir Michael Adeane to Roland Michener, 11 October 1971.

94 COCS, C135B, Canadian Attitude to Imperial Honours, 1943–1967, A.L. Mayall to P.S. Milner-Barry, 4 August 1967.

95 Ibid.

96 COCS, C135, Canadian Attitude to Imperial Honours, 1943–1967, P.S. Milner-Barry to Sir Martin Charteris, 27 April 1972.

97 The Queen's Gallantry Medal was established on 29 June 1974.

98 Interview with Geoffrey Pearson, 14 November 2001.

CHAPTER EIGHT

 1 COCS, C135, Canadian Attitude to Imperial Honours, 1943–1967, P.S. Milner-Barry to Sir Martin Charteris, 27 April 1972.

 2 For reasons of confidentiality, the deliberations of the Advisory Council of the Order of Canada as they related to specific individuals are considered secret.

3 NAC, R 5769, vol. 9, Lochnan Papers, Roland Michener to Carl Lochnan, 10 November 1973.

4 Ibid.

5 NAC, MG 32 A4, vol. 74, Léger Papers, Esmond Butler to Jules Léger, 10 May 1978. The senior government official was neither Léger nor Butler.

6 NAC, R 5769, vol. 11, Lochnan Papers, Memorandum: Procedures Relative to Appoint ment of Nominees, 13 March 1975.

7 All living members of the Order of Canada; deceased members of the Order of Canada; living recipients by discipline; recipients of the Order of Canada with addresses; recipients of the Order of Canada by province; women recipients; a master list. All of these lists – except the women's list – were published twice yearly. In addition to this, a list of recipients of the Order of Military Merit and various bravery awards was also maintained and published twice yearly. NAC, R 5769, vol. 11, Lochnan Papers, Bureau of Management Consulting, Government of Canada, Honours List System, Government House, November 1973.

8 In 1971 more than 450 nominations were received for fewer than 65 possible awards; thus, the shortfall of total nominations was not serious and more closely related to a shortfall in sufficient nominations from outside Ontario and Quebec. NAC, R 5769, vol. 8, Lochnan Papers, Suggested requirements for the New System of Honours and Awards to be Established at Government House, 29 December 1971, fifth draft written by Roger Nantel.

9 QUA, Lower Papers, Order of Canada File, Roger Nantel to Arthur R.M. Lower, 20 May 1969.

10 Interview with Gordon Robertson, 6 December 2001.

11 Phills was a steelworker whose six children all went on to successful careers, despite the family's poverty. In 1995, Ernest Smith, one of Canada's last living holders of the Victoria Cross, was made a Member of the Order of Canada. Cecil Meritt, the other Canadian VC holder, refused the Order, citing that he had done nothing to warrant another award. Possibly the most famous case of an exemplar was Terry Fox, who was made a Companion of the Order of Canada shortly before his death. Although his 'Marathon of Hope' was a significant event at the time, it was not quite up to the level of national achievement for which the Companion level is normally awarded. Although the impact of the Terry Fox Run around the world has been great, that event that has only really taken hold since Fox's death. Such exemplar awards have been rare.

12 CHAN, Minutes of the 13th meeting of the Advisory Council, 10–11 April 1972.

13 Ibid.

14 'Je crois qu'il est hasardeux de demander aux membres de la Chambre des Communes des noms de candidats pour l'Ordre.' NAC, MG 32 A4, vol. 50, Léger Papers, May 1978.

15 Requests for nominations for the Order were not advertised greatly; instead, more detailed press releases about recent appointees to the Order were sent to all media outlets. CHAN, Minutes of the 6th meeting of the Advisory Council, 9–10 April 1969.

16 CHAN, Minutes of a Special Meeting of the Advisory Council, 20 February 1974.

17 NAC, R 5769, vol. 12, Lochnan Papers, References in Newspaper Clippings to Order of Canada Appointments in December 1973 and thus Invested in April 1974.

18 CHAN, Minutes of the Special Meeting of the Advisory Council of the Order of Canada, 13 November 1970.

19 Greta Chambers was made a Member of the Order of Canada in April 1994 and was promoted to Companion in April 2000.

20 (Gertrude Laing), Special Meeting of the Advisory Council of the Order of Canada, 17 January 1976.

21 CHAN, Minutes of the Meeting of the Lieutenant Governors at Government House, 6–7 November 1973.

22 CHAN, Meeting of the Advisory Council of the Order of Canada, 8 April 1976.

23 Confidential Memorandum; Power of the Provinces to Create Honours. NAC, R 5769, vol. 18, Lochnan Papers, 1973.

24 For instance, on 1 April 1987, the Lieutenant-Governor of Alberta invested Mrs Kathlene Ivey Taylor as a Member of the Order of Canada while Mrs Taylor was in hospital. Terminally ill, Mrs Taylor would die five days later, on 6 April.

25 This is of course in terms of the Commonwealth. Some members of the Commonwealth on becoming republics ended the practice of having their citizens knighted.

26 Michael Maton, *The National Honours and Awards of Australia* (Kenthurst: Kangaroo Press, 1995), 32.

27 NAC, R5769, vol. 10, Lochnan Papers, Points for Discussion with Mr Lochnan, March 1974.

28 Ibid., P.J. Lawler (Secretary to the Department of the Special Minister of State) to Carl Lochnan, 21 April 1975.

29 17 February 1975.

30 The Vice President of the Executive Council. The other members are the Chief Justice, Secretary of the Department of the Special Minister of State, Chief of the Defence Force, and not more than nine persons appointed by the Governor General, of whom not more than six are nominated by the states. The council has since been enlarged (in 1986 and again in 1988) to include people from the Australian Capital Territory and Northern Territory.

31 *Australia Gazette*, 19 February 1975.

32 Ibid., S92, 2 June 1976.

33 Ibid., S101, 11 March 1986.

34 Correspondence, Phillippe O'Shea to Christopher McCreery, 22 May 2002.

35 The New Zealand Royal Honours System, Te Punaha Tuku H nore a te Kuini M Aotearoa, Report of the Prime Minister's Honours Advisory Committee, September 1985.

36 NAC, MG 32 A3, vol. 49, Léger Papers, Summary of Yearly Output, 1977, 6 January 1978.

37 CHAN, Esmond Butler to the Special Meeting of the Advisory Council, 17 January 1977.

38 The Advisory Council did not agree to this until October 1977. This book was never completed, although a rough manuscript can be found in NAC, R 5769, vol. 9, Lochnan Papers.

39 Micheline Beauchemin was made an Officer of the Order of Canada in 1974.

40 This interest in social issues and in 'doing more for members of the Order' was in part sparked by the plight of one member of the Order. In 1974–5 there was an attempt to create a benevolent fund for destitute members of the Order. This sort of charity can be traced back to France's Order of St Louis. Unfortunately, a number of recipients, because of their great self-sacrifice and devotion to others, became unable to support themselves. The idea of having direct government involvement – though a cash gratuity – was rejected, but no barrier was created to prevent members of the Order from giving charity on

their own accord to another member. NAC, R 5769, vol. 9, Lochnan Papers, Gordon Robertson to Esmond Butler, 14 June 1974.

41 This investiture took place on 2 August 1973. Fifteen recipients of the Order of Canada, Fifteen recipients of the Order of Military Merit, and fifteen recipients of the bravery awards were invested. The Order of Canada investees were John Bradfield, CC; the Honourable Thane Campbell, CC; Jules Léger, CC; Laurent Beaudoin, OC; Arthur Irwin, OC; Florence Isabel Matheson, OC; Kathlene Richardson, OC; Sergeant-Major Henry Webb Stallworthy, OC; Jocelyn Bourassa, CM; George Clutesi, CM; Helen Beny Gibson, CM; Dorothy Macpherson, CM; Guy Mauffette, CM; Wilfred Notley, CM; and Reynond Pehkonen, CM. Aside from the various Governors General, so far these are the only people to have been invested with the Order of Canada by the Queen.

42 The party was held at Joyce Bryant's house at 102 Creighton Street in Ottawa, just a few blocks from Rideau Hall.

43 NAC, R 5769, vol. 13, Lochnan Papers.

44 NAC, MG 32 A3, vol. 49, Léger Papers, Minutes of the 25th Meeting of the Advisory Council, 19–20 October 1978.

45 The proposed insignia was to be composed of a collar of silver maple leaves, from which a Member's insignia would be hung.

46 CHAN, Minutes of the 22nd Meeting of the Advisory Council of the Order of Canada, 21–2 April 1977.

47 House of Commons, *Debates*, 29 November 1977, 1348.

48 Galloway, *The Companions of Honour* (London: Chancery Publications, 2002), 469.

49 Bill C-60, An Act to amend the Constitution of Canada, 1978.

50 David Smith, *The Invisible Crown* (Toronto: University of Toronto Press, 1995), 49.

51 NAC, MG 32 A3, vol. 49, Léger Papers, Sir Phillip Moore to Esmond Butler, 9 June 1978.

52 Ibid.

CHAPTER NINE

1 NAC, MG 30 E148, vol. 9, John E. Read Papers, Ephriam Coleman to John Read, 10 December 1942. Although the memorandum is from Coleman to Read, it was drafted by Vincent Massey. Coleman would later express his view that heraldry and the design were 'of trifling importance.' NAC, MG 26 J4, Mackenzie King Papers, Memorandum for the Prime Minister from Arnold Heeney and Ephriam Coleman, 12 December 1942, C268,089.

2 NAC, MG 30 E148, vol. 9, Read Papers, Ephriam Coleman to John Read, 10 December 1942.

3 QUA, Matheson Papers, file 226, Matheson Notes on Honours, March/April 1966.

4 Joyce Turpin, Vincent Massey's secretary, suggested that the name of the Order be the 'Order of the Cross of Canada.' UTA, Massey Papers, vol. 363, Notes for Mr. Massey from Joyce Turpin, 25 March 1966.

5 NAC, R 5769, vol. 11, Lochnan Papers, Memorandum from Michael Pitfield to Esmond Butler and John Matheson, 13 April 1966.

6 NAC, MG 26 N4, vol. 1, file 001-42, Conrad Swan to J.S. Hodgson, 28 September 1966.

7 NAC, RG 24, vol. 4059, file 1078-14-5, Memorandum from A. Fortescue Duguid to H.F.G. Letson, 29 March 1943.

8 QUA, Matheson Papers, file 295, Phillip Laundy to John Matheson, 10 February 1966.

9 Ibid., Herbert O'Driscoll, notes on speech to the Seminar on International Affairs, 1966.

10 Ibid.

11 Interview with John Matheson, 7 January 2000.

12 QUA, Matheson Papers, file 226, Rough Notes, March 1966. These notes contain the first reference to the motto 'desires a better country,' and comprise part of Matheson's early research. They date from roughly the same time that Matheson had commissioned the Parliamentary Library to research honours for him. Also see QUA, Matheson Papers, Philip Laundy to John Matheson, 10 February 1966. Matheson interview, 7 January 2000.

13 NAC, MG 26 N4, vol. 1, file 001-42, Pearson Papers, Phillip Laundy to Jack Hodgson, 3 October 1966.

14 QUA, Matheson Papers, file 296, Herbert O'Driscoll to John Matheson, 19 April 1967.

15 An early version of the Order's constitution is marked with the incorrect passage number 12:16. CHAN, 708-3, file 1.

16 *Toronto Daily Star*, 18 April 1967. Also see the *Globe and Mail*, 18 April 1967.

17 NAC, RG 2, vol. 80, H-5, Honours and Decorations 1945.

18 Ibid., 3 May 1943, proposal for the Canadian Decoration of Honour.

19 NAC, MG 26 J1, Mackenzie King Papers, Viscount Alexander to Mackenzie King, 24 March 1948, 396,120.

20 QUA, Matheson Papers, file 227, A Proposal for the Establishment of The Order of Canada, April 1966.

21 UTA, Massey Papers, vol. 363, Notes for Mr. Massey from Joyce Turpin, 25 March 1966.

22 Ibid., Statutes of the Order of ____ , First Draft, 23 March 1966.

23 Ibid., Statutes of the Order of ____ , 29 March 1966.

24 A remnant of this proposed sash can be found in the Massey Papers at the University of Toronto Archives.

25 QUA, Matheson Papers, file 295, John Matheson to Lester Pearson, 14 April 1966.

26 NAC, MG 26 N4, vol. 1, file 001-42, Pearson Papers, John Matheson to Lester Pearson, 14 July 1966.

27 Interview with Bruce Beatty, 3 September 2002.

28 NAC, MG 26 J4, Mackenzie King Papers, Memorandum for the Prime Minister from Arnold Heeney and Ephriam Coleman, 12 December 1942, C268,089.

29 NAC, RG 2, vol. 80, file H-5, 1943 and 1945, proposal for the Order of Canada.

30 Ibid., 3 May 1943, proposal for the Canadian Award of Honour and Canadian Decoration of Honour.

31 UTA, Massey Papers, vol. 363, Notes for Mr. Massey from Joyce Turpin, 25 March 1966.

32 Ibid., Constitution of the Order of ____ , 28 March 1966.

33 QUA, Matheson Papers, file 295, John Matheson to Lester Pearson, 14 April 1966.

34 NAC, MG 26 N4, vol. 1, file 001-42, Pearson Papers, D.F. Spink to John Matheson, 1 August 1966.

35 Interview with John R. Matheson, 7 January 2000. Also see QUA Matheson Papers, file 226, rough notes concerning trip to Britain 'Crown swivel, one red maple leaf on a white field.'

36 This was the only Friday in November when it snowed late in the afternoon. See Environment Canada Historical Statistics.

37 It should be noted that correspondence relating to the creation of the Order was usually marked 'Top Secret,' 'Secret or Confidential.'

38 QUA, Matheson Papers, file 314, John Matheson to Lester Pearson, 21 November 1966. Although Matheson makes no mention of his discussion with Halstead, this is the only occasion when the two men had contact with each other between November and December 1966, when the snowflake design was chosen as the basis for the Order of Canada.

39 Interview with John R. Matheson, 2 October 2001, Matheson quoting John Halstead. Also see NAC, R 974, vol. 21, Halstead Papers, Eulogy to Halstead by Jake Warren, 1998.

40 Ukichiro Nakaya, *Snow Crystals: Natural and Artificial* (Cambridge: Harvard University Press, 1954), 1.

41 Matheson interview, 7 January 2000. Matheson stated that it was diagram 2b; however, it is obvious he meant 1b, as the shape is nearly identical to the Order of Canada. The chart containing the various snow crystals can be found on page 80 of Nakaya's book *Snow Crystals*.

42 Nakaya, *Snow Crystals*, 80, 86.

43 The other two designs were not significantly different from the current insignia; the central devices of a snowflake, Maple Leaf and Crown were included in all three.

44 Although the three-digit number on the reverse of the Companion's insignia was originally intended merely as a method of inventory tracking (i.e., stock numbers), a register of the numbers has been maintained by the Chancellery. Today one can identify the recipient of a particular insignia (Companion, Officer, or Member) by looking up a particular number in the register. Companion's insignias started with number 001, as did those of Officers and Members.

45 NAC, MG 26 N4, vol. 1, file 001-42, John Hodgson to Lester Pearson, 23 March 1967.

46 Gordon Robertson, *A Very Civil Servant* (Toronto: University of Toronto Press, 2000), 232.

47 NAC, MG 32 A4, vol. 71, Léger Papers, Esmond Butler to Jules Léger, 13 January 1972.

48 Initially 160 Medals of Service were ordered from Garrard & Company at a cost of $4,700 including the dies. Only twenty-four Medals of Courage were ordered, at a cost of $700. There was no separate charge for the Medal of Courage dies, as the obverse dies were the same as those used for the Medal of Service. CHAN, 708-3, file 1, Memorandum to the Prime Minister on the Order of Canada, 13 March 1970.

49 NAC, R 5769, vol. 11, Lochnan Papers, Suggested Requirements for the New System of Honours to be Established at Government House, 10 February 1972. Prepared by Roger Nantel.

50 NAC, MG 26 N4, vol. 1, file 001-42, Pearson Papers, Conrad Swan to John Hodgson, 28 September 1966. Also discussed during Pearson's visit to London, September 1966.

51 NAC, R 5769, vol. 11, Lochnan Papers, Minutes of a Meeting with His Excellency the Governor General, 23 August 1967.

52 Each lapel badge cost $5. The first lot was manufactured by William Scully Limited of Montreal.

53 NAC, MG 32 A, vol. 49, Léger Papers, Memorandum to Carl Lochnan from Jules Léger, 14 May 1974.

54 Ibid., Bora Laskin to Jules Léger, 26 April 1977.

55 NAC, MG 26 N4, vol. 1, file 001-42, Major General C.H. Colquhoun to Esmond Butler, 6 February 1967.

56 The craftsman responsible for fabricating the Chancellor's Chain was Myron Cook, Chief Engraver at the Royal Canadian Mint. The Chancellor's Chain was made of 18-carat enamelling gold and inlaid enamel in the 'champlever' manner. The snowflake and the

Maple Leaf motto and design were modelled and reduced to the required size in the three-dimensional pantograph, while the Arms of Canada were cut directly into a steel die form by hand. The gold is struck into the dies to form work recesses, which are afterwards filled with enamel. These work recesses are then filled, and the parts are fired in an enamelling kiln. In this way the enamel is fused to the gold. The enamel is then ground to the desired chape and refired. When cooled, it is bright and shiny, and the excess gold is trimmed away. The snowflake, the Maple Leaf and motto design, and the Royal Arms of Canada are then polished and assembled with the chain links. Description courtesy of Bruce Beatty. Press Release, 23 December 1968. The Companion's insignia attached to the Chancellor's Chain is unnumbered (unlike other Companion's insignias) and is simply marked with '-C-' on the reverse where a number would normally be placed.

57 The Chancellor's chain was so heavy that the links of each small chain began to separate in early 1971. The chain was taken to Howard's Jewellers of Ottawa, and each link was soldered shut to prevent separation.

58 NAC, R5769, vol. 11, Lochnan Papers, Minutes of a meeting with His Excellency, 23 August 1967.

59 The post-nominals COOC, for Companions of the Order of Canada; OOC., for Officers of the Order of Canada, and MOC, for Members of the Order of Canada, were considered to be too long. Thus the shorter designations were chosen.

60 NAC, MG 26 N4, Pearson Papers, vol. 1, file 001-42, Esmond Butler to Carl Lochnan, 6 December 1967.

61 Ibid., Memorandum to the Prime Minister from J.S. Hodgson, 27 November 1967.

62 Ibid., L.M. Barker to R.A. Bell, 20 April 1967.

63 Ibid., Edith MacDonald to J.S. Hodgson, 12 June 1967.

64 Ibid., Esmond Butler to J.S. Hodgson, 18 July 1967.

65 Ibid., Memorandum from J.S. Hodgson to Lester Pearson, 20 July 1967.

66 UTA, Massey Papers, Vincent Massey to Mary Ryde, 21 July 1967.

67 Special Meeting of the Advisory Council, 13 November 1970.

68 NAC, MG 26 N4, vol. 1, file 001-42, Pearson Papers, John Matheson to Lester Pearson, 11 July 1966.

69 QUA, Matheson Papers, file 296, John Matheson to Lester Pearson, 3 August 1966.

70 The only British orders of chivalry not manufactured by Garrard's are the Order of Merit, Order of the Companions of Honour, Royal Victorian Order, Imperial Service Order and the Order of St John. These were manufactured by other British jewellers such as John Pinches, Collingwood & Son, Elkington & Company, and Spink and Son.

71 Garrard's was not as concerned about quoting on the Medal of Courage as it required much less work, not involving any enamelling. The Medal of Service had not yet been officially sanctioned, but since it was essentially a variation on the Medal of Courage, this was not of great concern. Dies for these medals could be engraved relatively quickly, whereas the more ornate and complex Companion insignia was a much more involved project.

72 NAC, MG 26 N4, vol. 1, file 001-42, Pearson Papers, W.H. Summers to Esmond Butler, 7 February 1967.

73 Ibid.

74 Ibid., J.S. Hodgson to Esmond Butler, 15 February 1966.

75 Interview with Bruce W. Beatty, 2 August 2002.

76 Garrard & Co Ltd Sale Ledgers, 1981. One gentlemen's Companion insignia was sold to the Canadian government at the cost of £2,200. The last delivery of the Order of Canada insignia from Garrard's was shipped via air freight on 28 June 1982; it was for 75 Officer's insignia priced at £150 each.

77 CHAN 703-3, file 2, Esmond Butler to Michael Pitfield, 16 June 1982.

78 Rideau Ltee began by making the miniatures for all levels of the Order of Canada. Once it had perfected that process, the government asked it to make some Members' insignia. Once it was ascertained that the quality was sufficient, Rideau was given the contract for making all Members' insignia. By 1984, Rideau was making all of the insignia for the Order of Canada.

79 Birks only finished the insignia. Most of the production was done by Pressed Metal Products of Vancouver.

80 House of Commons, *Debates*, 13 May 1981, 9531 (W. Kenneth Robinson).

81 Coldwell's CC sold for $7,900. The Officer's insignia awarded to Denise Pelletier-Zarov sold for $2,600. The Member's insignia awarded to Florence-Ferret Martel sold for $1,500. Torex Auction, 21–3 May 1981, Toronto, lots M-202, M-203, and M-204.

82 Eugene G. Ursual, Military Antiquarian, List No. 53, November 1984. W.D. John to Eugene Ursual.

83 The seal was designed by Bruce Beatty and engraved by the Royal Canadian Mint.

84 CHAN 708-3, file 1, Esmond Butler to Sir Michael Adeane, 19 May 1967.

85 NAC, R 5769, vol. 11, Lochnan Papers, Memorandum from Michael Pitfield to Esmond Butler and John Matheson, 13 April 1966.

86 This was Joyce Bryant (née Turpin).

87 CHAN 708-9, file 1, Memorandum on the Cameo Replica of the Order's Seal, 1967.

88 Charles Boutell, *English Heraldry* (London: Reves & Turner, 1907), 179.

89 NAC, R 5769, vol. 10, Lochnan Papers, Heraldry File, 1974.

90 Sauvé's arms were originally granted by the College of Arms in London, 19 November 1985.

91 David See-Chai-Lam's grant included the motto of the Order and Member's insignia (Lam was later promoted to an Officer of the Order); Public Register of Arms, Flags and Badges of Canada (PRA) I/26, 28 August 1989. General Jacques Dextraze was the first non-viceregal Companion of the Order to be granted arms with both the motto and insignia of the Order; PRA, II/44, 20 September 1990. Henry Pybus Bell-Irving was the first Officer of the Order to have the motto and insignia added to his arms, PRA, II/14, 11 April 1990.

92 Bruce M. Hicks, Hogtown Heraldry, 'The Campaign to Change the Royal Arms of Canada,' Vol. 12, No. 4, Winter 2000–1, 8.

93 The Canada 125th Anniversary of Confederation Medal was designed by Bruce Beatty.

94 House of Commons, *Debates*, 5 December 1995 (Deborah Gray), 17240.

95 Ibid. (Chuck Strahl), 17237.

96 Even members of the government managed for get their facts wrong, quoting the motto of the Order as 'To Build a Better Country,' not 'They Desire a Better Country.' See House of Commons, *Debates*, 5 December 1995 (Patrick Gagnon), 17232.

97 It was only in 2002 that the augmented Coat of Arms replaced the 1957 version on the

cover of Canadian passports. By 1997 most government departments and Parliament had switched to the augmented design.

98 Constitution of the Order of Canada, 1994.

99 James Risk, *The History of The Order of the Bath* (London: Robert Stockwell, 1972), 9.

100 QUA, Matheson Papers, file 296, John Matheson to Lester Pearson, 25 April 1967.

101 UTA, Massey Papers, vol. 363, Statutes of the Order of ____, first draft, 23 March 1966.

102 NAC, R 5769, vol. 11, Lochnan Papers, Memorandum from Michael Pitfield to Esmond Butler and John Matheson, 13 April 1966.

103 Ibid., Minutes of a Meeting with His Excellency, 23 August 1967.

104 QUA, Matheson Papers, file 296, Esmond Butler to John Matheson, 4 October 1967.

105 On 2 August 1973 the Queen invested fifteen people with the Order of Canada, fifteen with the Order of Military Merit, and fifteen with the Canadian bravery decorations.

106 This occurred during renovations to the ballroom at Government House.

107 On a few occasions, when the recipient is terminally ill, the Governor General has invested a recipient with the Order of Canada either in their home or in hospital.

108 A special investiture ceremony was held for R.S. McLaughlin, former president of General Motors Canada, on 18 September 1968. This included a banquet and public investiture ceremony held in Oshawa, Ontario.

109 Ezra Schabas, *Sir Ernest MacMillan: The Importance of Being Canadian* (Toronto: University of Toronto Press, 1994), 306.

110 CHAN 708-3, file 3, Minutes of the 54th meeting of the Advisory Council, 21–2 April 1993.

CHAPTER TEN

1 NAC, MG 23 A4, Michener Papers, vol. 36, 12 November 1970, Sir Michael Adeane to Roland Michener, 12 November 1970.

2 'The Order of Canada,' Nomination Pamphlet, 2001.

3 House of Commons, *Debates*, 8 April 1918, 507 (Richardson).

4 Some Canadians received multiple knighthoods. The most knighted Canadian was Sir Charles Tupper: initially made a Companion of the Order of the Bath following Confederation, Tupper was later made a Knight Commander of the Order of St Michael and St George and awarded a Baronetcy. Much later in life, he was made a Knight Grand Cross of the Order of St Michael and St George.

6 This chapter draws from statistics compiled using the membership register. 'Province' refers to the province in which a recipient of the Order of Canada was living at the time of his or her appointment. Thus a Companion such as Gordon Robertson, former Clerk of the Privy Council, who was born and raised in Saskatchewan, is listed under the Ontario section because that was his place of residence at the time his appointment was made. 'Discipline' is perhaps the most difficult term to define. Recipients of the Order of Canada are separated into twenty-five separate disciplines or categories. These disciplines are the area in which the honoured person performed his or her service. Thus, although former MP Serge Joyal was made an Officer of the Order of Canada in recognition of his contributions to Canadian heritage and art, he is listed under the Philanthropy section, not Heritage, Art, or Politics. In terms of the numbers used, I have

examined the gross number of appointments to the Order of Canada, not the number of individuals appointed. This is to account for elevations within the Order. On rare occasions, a person is appointed for contributions to one field and promoted for contributions to another. This takes into account such anomalies. 'Gender' is self-evident. The population statistics are taken from the 1996 Census. When comparisons are made between those awarded the Order of Canada in 1967 and the population of the country at that time, the 1966 Census has been employed. Unlike many countries, Canada keeps a detailed record of recipients of its national Order. Nevertheless, certain statistics are not included. Initially the religion of the recipient was recorded, but this practice ended in 1976, the Advisory Council having decided that the practice was no longer necessary. The socioeconomic status of citizens appointed to the Order is not recorded either, and would be exceedingly difficult to tabulate. When I was examining Canadians awarded knighthoods, such a calculation was relatively easy, because there were only 201 individuals, almost all of whom were listed in biographical directories such as *Who's Who* and the *Canadian Social Register*. These directories also tended to list the individual's religion, political affiliation, and education. Although many members of the Order of Canada are listed in *Who's Who*, religion and political affiliations are seldom mentioned. Merely being in *Who's Who* used to indicate membership in the country's elite, and this remains true. In the case of the Order of Canada, shortly after their appointment to the Order, recipients are often contacted by *Who's Who* and asked if they would like to submit an entry. Analysing the socioeconomic, religious, and political affiliation of every member of the Order of Canada falls beyond the scope of this history.

6 NAC, RG 2, vol. 377, Departmental Statistics, June 1946.

7 Architecture, Arts/Music, Arts/Stage, Arts/Visual, Arts/Writing, Aviation, Communications, Education, Engineering, Healthcare, Heritage, Industry/Commerce/Business, Labour Relations, Law, Philanthropy, Politics, Protective Services, Politics, Public Service, Religion, Science, Social Sciences, Social Services, Sports, Voluntary Service, and Other. 'Other' includes Antiquaries, Centennial Year Contributions, Chess, Dietician and Food Consultant, Good Citizenship, Heraldry, Philately and Numismatics, and Trucking.

8 CHAN, Meeting of the Advisory Council of the Order of Canada, April 1977.

9 All population statistics taken from Statistics Canada, 1996 Census.

10 Interview with Gordon Robertson, 2 December 2001.

11 The Soviet Union established the Order of the Glory of Motherhood (1st class to those who had nine children, 2nd class for eight children, 3rd class for seven children). The closest award that Canada had in this respect was the King's Bounty for Triplets, which was established by George V in 1919.

12 Peter Galloway, *The Order of the British Empire* (London: Stephen Austin & Son, 1996), 42.

13 Figures taken from Peter Galloway, *Order of the British Empire* (London: Chancellery Publications 1966), 38 and 60.

14 Galloway, *Order of the British Empire*, 60.

15 Letter from Claude Ryan to author, 15 August 2002.

16 Glenn Gould to Esmond Butler, 9 May 1970. Letter mentioned in NAC, R 5769, Lochnan Papers, vol. 10.

17 I have separated the reasons for refusal into six categories: modesty/age (that is, the prospective recipient did not feel worthy of the honour or felt that he/she was too

young); disagree with honours; Quebec nationalism; wanted a higher honour; did not know what the Order of Canada is; and other.

18 NAC, MG 32 A3, Léger Papers, vol. 49, Refusals File.

19 See *Globe and Mail*, 15 March 1974.

20 Ibid.

21 NAC, MG 32 A3, Léger Papers, vol. 49, Refusals File.

22 Ibid.

23 Ibid.

24 June Callwood, Hugh Clifford Chadderton, Joan Chalmers, H. Reuben Cohen, Jack Diamond, Reva Appleby Gerstein, Richard Macaulay Ivey, Phyllis Lambert, and Robert Landry.

25 Ivan De la Bere, *The Queen's Orders of Chivalry* (London: Spring Books, 1964), 78.

26 Ibid.

27 Peter Galloway, *The Order of St. Michael and St. George* (London: Third Millennium, 2000), 201.

28 Lieutenant Colonel Ludger Jules Oliver Daly-Gingras of the 22nd Canadian Infantry was awarded the Distinguished Service Order on 1 January 1917. His appointment was subsequently revoked on 11 February 1919. *Canada Gazette*, 3 May 1919, Supplement. NAC, RG 150, 1992–1993.66, box 2278, Lieutenant Colonel Daly-Gingras.

29 When a member of the Order dies, the membership is terminated, as only living people can be members of the Order. This is known as natural termination.

30 R. Alan Eagleson, personal letter to the author, 8 August 2001.

31 The termination date was set as 26 February 1998. The entire production of terminating Eagleson's membership was more for the benefit of the media, which had been quite insistent that he be 'kicked out of the Order.' In reality, Eagleson resigned from the Order under section 23(b) of the Order's constitution, and the Governor General accepted his resignation.

32 Ceaucescu's appointment as a Grand Cross of the Order of the Bath (GCB) was cancelled shortly after he was deposed.

33 The practice of automatic awards has a long history in Canada. From Confederation until 1918, all Canadian prime ministers, save Alexander Mackenzie, were knighted while in office.

34 Kim Campbell and Jean Chrétien have not yet been appointed to the order.

35 NAC, R 5769, vol. 9, Pierre Trudeau to Esmond Butler, 24 January 1973.

36 The Order's register boasts no fewer than four knights (Outerbridge, MacMillan, Stephenson, and Ondaatje), two recipients of the Order of Merit (Penfield and Pearson), five recipients of the Order of the Companions of Honour (Massey, Best, Smith, Trudeau, and de Chastelain), and many holders of the various levels of both the Order of the British Empire and the Royal Victorian Order. There is even one peer – Lord Black of Cross-harbour – among the Officers of the Order. The most decorated member of the Order of Canada was the Honourable George Pearkes, VC, PC, CC, CB, DSO, MC, KStJ, CD, war hero, former Cabinet minister and lieutenant-governor. Two other Victoria Cross holders received the Order of Canada: the Honourable Milton Gregg, VC, PC, OC, CBE, MC, and Ernest (Smokey) Smith, VC, CM, CD. Aside from the Queen and various Governors General, only one Canadian has been appointed as both a Companion of the Order

of Canada and a Commander of the Order of Military Merit: General J.A. Dextraze, CC, CMM, CBE, DSO*, CD. Five Nobel Laureates have received the Order: Lester Pearson, Gerhard Herzberg (a former member of the Advisory Council), John Polanyi, Bertram Brockhouse, and Michael Smith. Upwards of one hundred members of the Order have also received France's *Légion d'honneur* and other significant awards from abroad.

37 Namely, the Order of Military Merit and the Order of Merit of the Police Forces.

CHAPTER ELEVEN

1 British officials in particular were surprised by the separation of citizens and non-citizens, and initially considered such a differentiation as a sign that no awards were going to be made. They also felt that honorary awards would constitute a 'second-class' of membership within the Order. This, however, is clearly not the case. COCS, C135B, Canadian Attitude to Imperial Honours, 1943–1967, A.L. Mayall to P.S. Milner Barry, 15 November 1967.

2 Recipients of honorary knighthoods do not use the appellation 'Sir' or 'Dame'; they are entitled to use only the appropriate post-nominal initials.

3 Sir Ivan De la Bere, *The Queen's Orders of Chivalry* (London: Spring Books, 1964), 143.

4 NAC, MG 26 J4, Mackenzie King Papers, E.H. Coleman to A.D.P. Heeney, 11 December 1942, C278,087A.

5 Section 12(1) of the 1967 Constitution of the Order of Canada.

6 NAC, MG 26 N4, Pearson Papers, vol. 1, file 001-42, John S. Hodgson to G.G.E. Steele, 3 August 1967. 'No non-Canadians should be appointed honorary members of the Order until Canadian government policy is altered regarding the acceptance of foreign honours and awards by Canadian citizens.'

7 NAC, MG 26 N4, vol. 1, file 003-4, Pearson Papers, G.G.E. Steele to John S. Hodgson, 7 June 1967.

8 NAC, RG 2 Series 5a, vol. 6338, Cabinet Conclusions, 17 April 1968.

9 NAC, MG 26 N4, vol. 1, file 001-42, Pearson Papers, Roland Michener to Lester Pearson, 12 February 1968.

10 Ibid., file 001-43, John Hodgson to Michael Pitfield, 23 February 1968.

11 Ibid.

12 Ibid., Pearson Papers, Lester Pearson to Roland Michener, 29 February 1968. Also see memorandum from John Hodgson to Lester Pearson of the same date.

13 NAC, R 5769, vol. 11, Lochnan Papers, Esmond Butler to Carl Lochnan, 29 February 1972.

14 Ibid.

15 Ibid., Sydney Newman to Pierre Trudeau, 16 February 1972.

16 Ibid., Memorandum to the Under-Secretary of State, Carl Lochnan to Jules Léger, 18 February 1972.

17 Ibid., un-circulated memorandum to Cabinet, February 1972.

18 Ibid., Pierre Trudeau to Margaret Grierson, 21 February 1972.

19 Ibid.

20 Although the prime minister was endowed with this power, it was never exercised. When the only honorary member was appointed in 1981, Prime Minister Trudeau secured Cabinet's approval before proceeding.

21 NAC, R 5769, vol. 11, Lochnan Papers, Memorandum by Carl Lochnan to Jules Léger,

18 February 1972. Lochnan in particular was concerned that individual ministers would begin making honorary nominations, and insisted that all such recommendations emanate from the prime minister.

22 Originally, the project was to be dealt with by the Government Honours Policy Committee, although it had not yet convened. To speed up the process, it was given to the Working Group on Honours. NAC, R 5769, vol. 11, Lochnan Papers, Carl Lochnan to Jules Léger, 25 February 1972.

23 Ibid., Jules Léger to Gordon Robertson, 3 March 1972.

24 Ibid., Jules Léger to Mr. A.E. Ritchie, 2 March 1972.

25 NAC, R 5769, vol. 10, Lochnan Papers, Carl Lochnan to Esmond Butler, 14 March 1972.

26 Dextraze wrote Lochnan about honorary appointments to the Order of Military Merit in October 1973. NAC, R 5769, vol. 9, Lochnan Papers, General Jacques Dextraze to Carl Lochnan, 22 October 1973. In December 2003 the Constitution of the Order of Military Merit was amended to clarify the honorary appointment process.

27 NAC, R 5769, vol. 9, Lochnan Papers, Memorandum, 'Honorary Membership in the Order of Canada,' 4 December 1973.

28 Lochnan's revised version of the Memorandum on Honorary Membership in the Order of Canada, incorporating the changes agreed to by the Working Group on Honours on 4 December. NAC, R 5769, vol. 10, Lochnan Papers, Lochnan notes, 6 December 1973.

29 NAC, R 5769, vol. 11, Lochnan Papers, 17 February 1976.

30 Ibid., Draft Memorandum to Cabinet, April 1976.

31 The Government Honours Policy Committee consists of the Clerk of the Privy Council, Secretary to the Governor General, Under-Secretary of State, Under-Secretary of State for External Affairs, and Deputy Minister of National Defence. The Under-Secretary of State is now the Deputy Minister of Heritage, and the Under-Secretary of State for External Affairs is now the Deputy Minister of Foreign Affairs.

32 Edgar O'Ballance, *Islamic Fundamentalist Terrorism, 1979–1995* (London: Macmillan, 1997), 50.

33 Sheardown could have refused the award, although this was not explained to him. Officials at the Department of External Affairs were keen to see their employees recognized.

34 Sheardown Personal Papers, Flora MacDonald to Bora Laskin, 12 January 1981.

35 Ibid., Bora Laskin to Flora MacDonald, 19 January 1981.

36 House of Commons, Votes and Proceedings, 27 January 1981.

37 Sheardown Personal Papers, Pierre Trudeau to Zena Sheardown, 8 June 1981.

38 Order-in-Council 1981–1700.

39 Sheardown Personal Papers, Roger Nantel to Mrs Zena Sheardown, 7 January 1987.

40 NAC, R 5769, vol. 12, Lochnan Papers, Government Honours Policy Committee Study on the Establishment of an Order to Honour non-Canadians, 20 August 1986.

41 CHAN, 708-3, file 4, Government Honours Policy Committee Nineteenth Meeting, 24 November 1994.

42 This was approved at the 15 April 1997 meeting of the Advisory Council.

43 The Governor General and prime minister signed the amended Letters Patent on 26 May 1997.

44 Passed as an order-in-council on 24 August 1998 and signed by the Governor General on 10 September 1998.

45 It was also fitting in that one of the first non-Canadians originally intended to receive the Canada Medal was to be Jan Smuts, the last non-apartheid prime minister of South Africa.

46 The insignia was not pinned onto the Queen Mother, on account of the breach in protocol such an occasion would have created.

47 NAC, MG 26 N4, vol. 1, file 001-42, Pearson Papers, Roland Michener to Lester Pearson, 12 February 1968.

48 Ibid., John Hodgson to Lester Pearson, 23 February 1968.

49 David E. Smith, *The Republican Option in Canada, Past and Present* (Toronto: University of Toronto Press, 1999), 5.

50 Tom MacDonnell, *Daylight upon Magic: The Royal Tour of Canada, 1939* (Toronto: Macmillan, 1989), 67.

CHAPTER TWELVE

1 Unveiled on 19 March 2001, the Queen signed the Letters Patent creating the new Order in October 2000.

2 This political detente applies only to Canadian honours. The case of Lord Black of Crossharbour proves there remains resistance to British honours in some quarters.

3 CHAN, Minutes of the Thirty-Third Meeting of the Advisory Council, 1982.

4 The changes were approved by Cabinet with Order-in-Council 1983–750. The prime minister approved the changes on 6 July 1982. The Governor General verbally approved the changes on 29 December 1982 and signed the Letters Patent on 17 March 1983. The Queen was notified about the changes and expressed approval on 15 April 1982. CHAN 708-3, file 2, Roger Nantel to M.H. Pepper, 29 December 1982, and Bill Hesseltine to Roger Nantel, 15 April 1983.

5 CHAN, 708-3, file 2, Roger Nantel to Michael Pitfield, 14 April 1982.

6 Ibid., Esmond Butler to Michael Pitfield, 16 June 1982.

7 Also see chapter 11 and NAC, R 5769, vol. 12, Lochnan Papers, Government Honours Policy Committee Study on the establishment of an Order to honour non-Canadians, 20 August 1986.

8 CHAN, 708-3, file 3, Memorandum from the Government Honours Policy Committee, W.D. Johns to the Chancellery, April 1988. One other proposal was included, although it is not mentioned here to avoid embarrassment to the Canadian government. In the future edition, this proposed addition will be discussed.

9 See the Heraldry Section in chapter 9.

10 CHAN, Y.R. Gauntron to Maître Raymond Guay, 16 January 1991.

11 Order-in-Council 1994-2026 was passed on 6 December 1994. The prime minister signed the new Letters Patent on 16 January 1995, and the Governor General signed them on 27 January 1995.

12 The prime minister signed them on 13 June 1995.

13 Adopted through Letters Patent issued under Order-in-Council 1997-552, 15 April 1997.

14 Minutes of the 6 May 1998 meeting of the Advisory Council.

15 Adopted through Letters Patent issued under Order-in-Council 1999-1743, 1 October 1999.

16 Michael Jackson, 'The Development of Saskatchewan Honours' (unpublished research paper, 1990), 5.

17 Provisions were made to allow each additional member's term to be extended by two years if deemed appropriate by the Chancellor on the recommendation of the council.

18 CHAN, 708-3, file 4, General James Gervais to Mrs Rennie Marcoux, 1 February 2001.

19 Ibid., General James Gervais to Maître Raymond Guay, 12 December 2000.

20 It was later found that the ribbon which attaches each of the pages to the Great Seal of Canada had not been affixed correctly. The documents had to be carefully reattached.

21 Lawrence Stone, 'The Inflation of Honours,' *Past and Present* (1958): 45–70.

22 Michael Jackson, 'The Development of Saskatchewan Honours' (unpublished research paper, 1990), 5.

23 Order-in-Council, 1998-591, 2 April 1998.

Bibliography

Canadian Archives

Library and Archives Canada (formerly National Archives of Canada [NAC])
MG 26 Papers of the Prime Ministers
     A   Macdonald, Sir John Alexander
     C   Abbott, Sir John Joseph Caldwell
     D   Thompson, Sir John Sparrow David
     E   Bowell, Sir Mackenzie
     F   Tupper, Sir Charles
     G   Laurier, Sir Wilfrid
     H   Borden, Sir Robert Laird
     I   Meighen, Arthur
     J   King, William Lyon Mackenzie
     K   Bennett, Richard Bedford
     L   St Laurent, Louis
     M   Diefenbaker, John George
     O   Pearson, Lester Bowles
     P   Trudeau, Pierre Elliott

MG 27 I A-4   Kimberley, Sir John Woodhouse Kimberley, Earl of
MG 27 I B-1   Monck, Sir Charles Stanley, Viscount
MG 27 I B-2   Lisgar, Sir John Young, Lord
MG 27 I B-3   Dufferin and Ava, Sir Frederick Temple Hamilton-Temple-Blackwood,
                 Marquis of
MG 27 I B-4   Lorne, Sir John Douglas Sutherland Campbell, Marquess of
MG 27 I B-5   Aberdeen, Sir John Campbell Hamilton-Gordon, 7th Earl of
MG 27 I B-6   Lansdowne, Sir Henry Charles Keith Petty-Fitzmaurice, 5th Marquess of
MG 27 I B-7   Stanley, Sir Frederick Arthur, Baron
MG 27 II A-2   Chamberlain, Joseph
MG 27 II A-3   Milner, Sir Alfred, Lord
MG 27 II B-1   Minto, Sir Gilbert John Murray-Kynnynmond Elliot, Earl of
MG 27 II B-2   Grey, Sir Albert Henry George Grey, Earl
MG 27 II B-4   Devonshire, Sir Victor Christian William Cavendish, 9th Duke of
MG 27 II D-18   White, Sir Thomas

MG 29 A-5   Strathcona, Sir Donald Smith, Lord
MG 32 A 1   Massey Family Collection
MG 32 A 2   Vanier, Georges Phillias
MG 32 A 4   Michener, Roland
MG 32 A 3   Léger, Jules
MG 32 A 5   Schreyer, Edward
MG 32 A 6   Sauvé, Jeanne

MG 31 E-80   Butler, Esmond Unwin
MG 30 E-139   Coleman, Ephriam H.
MG 30 A-25   Forsey, Eugene
R 974   Halstead, John
MG 30 E-144   Heeney, A.D.P.
MG 31 E-76   Hubbard, R.H.
MG 32 B-8   LaMarsh, Judy
R 5769   Lochnan, Carl
MG 32 B-34   Pickersgill, Jack
MG 27 III B-11   Ralston, J.L.
MG 31 E-87   Robertson, Gordon
MG 27 III B-15   Rogers, Norman
MG 32–B41   Sharp, Mitchell
MG 31 D-78   Strusberg, Peter
MG 30 D-33   Skelton, Oscar Douglas
MG 30 E-78   Willis-O'Connor, Henry

Government Archives Division
RG 2   Privy Council Office
RG 6   Secretary of State
RG 7   Governor General's Office
RG 17   Supreme Court of Canada
RG 33   Royal Commissions
RG 69   Centennial Commission
RG 120   Royal Canadian Mint

Government House, Chancellery Records
CHAN 708–1 File 1
CHAN 708–3 File 1
CHAN 708–3 File 2
CHAN 708–3 File 3
CHAN 708–3 File 4
CHAN 708–3 File 5
CHAN, Black Binder

Department of National Defence, Heritage Directorate
DHH 75/505   Minutes of the Awards Co-ordination Committee
DHH 75/506   The Centennial Medal
DHH 75/601   Minutes of the Decorations Committee

Queen's University Archives

A.Arch 1023	Gordon, Daniel Miner
A.Arch 2361	Lower, A.R.M.
A.Arch 2112	Mackenzie, Alexander
A.Arch 1099.7	Matheson, John R.
A. Arch 1027	Nickle, William Folger
A. Arch 2125	Rogers, Norman
A. Arch 5021.7	Scott, F.R.
A. Arch 2110	Tweedsmuir, First Baron, Sir John Buchan

University of Toronto Archives
Massey Papers

Overseas Archives

Public Records Office, Great Britain
Dominion's Office Records 'Canada' 12/501
Foreign Office Records 'Canada' 09/728

Cabinet Office of the United Kingdom
Ceremonial Branch 'Honours in Confidence'

Garrard & Co, Crown Jewellers, Archives
Overseas Sale Ledgers

West Sussex Records Office
Bessborough Papers

Published Primary Sources

Borden, Sir Robert. *Robert Laird Borden: His Memoirs*. London: Macmillan & Company, 1938.
Canada: *Debates of the House of Commons*. Ottawa: King's/Queen's Printer.
– *Debates of the Senate*. Ottawa: King's/Queen's Printer.
– *Journals of the House of Commons*. Ottawa: King's/Queen's Printer.
Canadian Almanac and Directory, 1880 to 1996 editions. Toronto: Copp Clark.
Carnarvon, Earl of. *Speeches on Canadian Affairs*. London: John Murray Press, 1902.
Cook, Ramsay (ed.). *Dictionary of Canadian Biography*, vols 4 to 14. Toronto: University of Toronto Press, 1969–98.
Manual of Official Procedure of the Government of Canada. Privy Council Office, 1968 (Internal publication).
Ollivier, Maurice. *Colonial and Imperial Conferences*. Ottawa: Queen's Printer, 1954.
Pope, Sir Joseph (ed.). *The Correspondence of Sir John A. Macdonald*. Toronto: Oxford University Press, 1921.
Privy Council. *Minutes and Orders in Council*. Register and Index.
Saywell, John, and Paul Stevens (eds.). *Lord Minto's Canadian Papers*. Toronto: Champlain Society, 1983.

Smallwood, Joseph (ed.). *Encyclopedia of Newfoundland and Labrador*. St John's: Newfoundland Book Printers Ltd, 1981.

Wallace, Stewart (ed.). *Encyclopedia of Canada*. Toronto: University Associates of Canada, 1935 and 1966 editions.

Interviews and Extended Correspondence
Pierrette Alarie, CC
Bruce Beatty, CM, CD
Joyce Bryant, CM, BEM
Georgina Butler
Yves Chevrier, CM, RVM, CD
The Honourable Alex Colville, PC, CC
Lord Black of Crossharbour, PC, OC
Mrs Dody Evans
Ruth Gardiner, LVO, OBE
The Right Honourable Ramon Hnatyshyn, PC, GC, CMM, CD, QC
Sir Edwin Leather, KCMG, KCVO, Kt
The Honourable Flora MacDonald, PC, CC
Preston Manning
Melodie Massey
The Honourable John R. Matheson, OC, CD
Jacques Monet, sj
Mr A.G. Nickle
Mrs Betty Nickle
Phillippe O'Shea, LVO
Geoffrey Pearson, OC
Corinia Pike
The Honourable Gordon Robertson, PC, CC
The Honourable Claude Ryan, PC, CC
The Honourable Mitchell Sharp, PC, CC
John Sheardown, CM, CD
Zena Sheardown, CM
Sir Conrad Swan, KCVO
The Right Honourable John Turner, PC, CC, QC
Dr A. Vennema, OC

Biography

Batt, Elizabeth. *Monck: Governor General, 1861–1868*. Toronto: McClelland & Stewart, 1976.

Bissell, Claude. *The Imperial Canadian: Vincent Massey in Office*. Toronto: University of Toronto Press, 1986.

Borden, Sir Robert. *Letters to Limbo*. Toronto: University of Toronto Press, 1971.

Bourassa, Henri. *Great Britain and Canada: Topics of the Day*. Montreal: Beauchemin, 1902.

Brown, R.C. *Robert Laird Borden: A Biography*. Toronto: Macmillan, 1980.

Buchan, John. *Lord Minto, a Memoir*. London: Thomas Nelson & Son, 1924.

Careless, J.M.S. *Brown of the Globe*. Toronto: Macmillan, 1966.

Cowan, John. *Canada's Governors-General: Lord Monck to General Vanier*. Toronto: York, 1967.

Dawson, R. MacGregor. *Mackenzie King, 1874–1922*. Toronto: University of Toronto Press, 1972.

– *Mackenzie King, 1932–1939: The Prism of Unity*. Toronto: University of Toronto Press, 1963.

English, John. *Borden: His Life and World*. Toronto: McGraw Hill Ryerson, 1977.

– *The Worldly Years: The Life of Lester Pearson*. Toronto: Knopf, 1992.

Graham, H. *Old Man Ontario: Leslie M. Frost*. Toronto: University of Toronto Press, 1990.

Graham, Roger. *Arthur Meighen: A Biography*. Toronto: Clarke, Irwin, 1963.

Heeney, A.D.P. *The Things That Are Caesar's*. Toronto: University of Toronto Press, 1972.

LaMarsh, Judy. *Judy LaMarsh: Memoirs of a Bird in a Gilded Cage*. Toronto: McClelland & Stewart, 1970.

LaPierre, Laurier. *Sir Wilfrid Laurier and the Romance of Canada*. Toronto: Stoddart, 1996.

Levitt, Joseph. *Henri Bourassa on Imperialism and Bi-Culturalism, 1900–1919*. Toronto: Copp Clark, 1970.

Litt, Paul. *The Muses, the Masses and the Massey Commission*. Toronto: University of Toronto Press, 1992.

Maclagan, Michael. *Clemency Canning: Charles John 1st Earl Canning, Governor-General and Viceroy of India, 1856–1862*. London: Macmillan Press, 1962.

Margoshes, Dave. *Tommy Douglas: Building the New Society*. Lantzville: XYZ, 1999.

Martin, Paul. *A Very Public Life*. Ottawa: Deneau, 1983.

Massey, Vincent. *What's Past Is Prologue: The Memoirs of Vincent Massey*. Toronto: Macmillan, 1963.

Miller, Carman. *The Canadian Career of the Fourth Earl of Minto*. Waterloo: Wilfrid Laurier University Press, 1980.

Neatby, H. Blair. *Mackenzie King, 1924–1932: Lonely Heights*. Toronto: University of Toronto Press, 1963.

Nicholson, Harold. *King George the Fifth: His Life and Reign*. London: Constable, 1952.

Oliver, Peter. *G. Howard Ferguson*. Toronto: University of Toronto Press, 1977.

Pearson, Lester. *Mike: The Memoirs of the Rt. Hon. Lester B. Pearson*. Vol. 3. *1957–1968*. Ed. John A. Munro and Alex I. Inglis. Toronto: University of Toronto Press, 1975.

Pickersgill, J.W. *My Years with Louis St. Laurent*. Toronto: University of Toronto Press, 1975.

– *The Mackenzie King Record*. Toronto: University of Toronto Press, 1960.

Pope, Sir Joseph. *Memoirs of the Rt. Hon Sir John A. Macdonald*. Toronto: Oxford University Press, 1930.

Robertson, Barbara. *Wilfrid Laurier: The Great Conciliator*. Toronto: Oxford University Press, 1971.

Robertson, Gordon. *A Very Civil Servant*. Toronto: University of Toronto Press, 2000.

Rumilly, Robert. *Henri Bourassa: La vie publique d'un grand Canadien*. St Laurent: les editions Chanteleur, 1966.

Schabas, Ezra. *Sir Ernest MacMillan: The Importance of Being Canadian*. Toronto: University of Toronto Press, 1994.

Schull, Joseph. *Laurier: The First Canadian*. Toronto: Macmillan, 1965.

Sharp, Mitchell. *Which Reminds Me: A Memoir*. Toronto: University of Toronto Press, 1994.

Skelton, Oscar Douglas (ed.). *Life and Letters of Sir Wilfrid Laurier*. Toronto: Oxford University Press, 1921.

Smith, Dennis. *Rogue Tory: The Life and Legend of John G. Diefenbaker*. Toronto: Macfarlane Walter and Ross Press, 1995.

Smith, Janet Adam. *John Buchan*. London: Rupert Hart-Davis, 1966.

Strusberg, Peter. *Lester Pearson and the Dream of Unity*. Toronto: Doubleday, 1978.

Taylor, A.J.P. *Lord Beaverbrook*. London: Hamish Hamilton, 1972.

Thomson, Dale. *Louis St. Laurent: Canadian*. Toronto: Macmillan, 1967.

Trofimenkoff, Susan. *Stanley Knowles: The Man from Winnipeg North Centre*. Saskatoon: Prairie Books, 1982.

Williams, Jeffrey. *Byng of Vimy: General and Governor-General*. Toronto: University of Toronto Press, 1985.

Honours and Awards

Abbott, P.E., and J.M.A. Tamplin. *British Gallantry Awards*. New York: Doubleday, 1972.

Alexander, E.G.M. *South African Orders, Decorations and Medals*. Cape Town: Human & Rousseau, 1986.

Barber, Richard. *The Knight and Chivalry*. London, Longman, 1970.

Bere, Sir Ivan De la. *The Queen's Orders of Chivalry*. London: William Kimber, 1961.

Blatherwich, John F. *Canadian Orders, Decorations and Medals*. Toronto: Unitrade, 1994.

Blondel, Jacques. *Guide Pratique des Décorations*. Paris: Lavauzelle, 1986.

Boulton, D'Arcy Jonathan Dacre. *The Knights of the Crown; The Monarchical Orders of Knighthood in Later Medieval Europe, 1325–1520*. New York: St Martins Press, 1987.

Coddington, Deborah, and Alister Taylor. *Honoured by the Queen: New Zealand*. Auckland: Maxwell, 1994.

Cohen, Maxwell (ed.). *The Register of Canadian Honours*. Toronto: Macmillan, 1991.

Cullen, Tom. *Maundy Gregory: Purveyor of Honours*. London: Quality Book Club, 1975.

De-la-Noy, Michael. *The Honours System*. London: Allison & Busby, 1985.

Dorling, H. Taprell. *Ribbons and Medals*. London: George Phillip & Son, 1963.

Fauteaux, Ægidius. *Les Chevaliers de Saint-Louis en Canada*. Montreal: Éditions des Dix, 1940.

Ford, Frank. 'Titles of Honour in Canada.' *Queen's Quarterly* 10, no. 1, 1902.

Galloway, Peter. *The Order of the British Empire*. London: Austin and Son, 1996.

– *The Order of the Companions of Honour*. London: Chancery Publications, 2002.

– *The Order of St. Michael and St. George*. London: Third Millennium, 2000.

– *The Order of Saint Patrick*. Chichester: Phillmore, 1983.

Galloway, Peter, David Stanley, and Stanley Martin. *Royal Service: The Royal Victorian Order*. London: Victorian, 1996.

Galloway, Strome. *The White Cross in Canada, 1883–1983: A History of St. John Ambulance*. Ottawa: St John Ambulance, 1983.

Gillingham, Harold. *French Orders and Decorations*. New York: American Numismatic Society, 1922.

Guimaraes, Christophe. *Les Insignes et Medailles Commemoratives de L'Ordre de Saint-Louis, 1693–1830*. Paris: Symboles & Traditions, 2004.

Heywood, Valentine. *British Titles*. London: Adam & Charles Black, 1951.

Lochnan, Carl. 'History of Honours in Canada.' Unpublished manuscript, 1976.

Mackenzie, Sir Edward. 'The Baronets of Nova Scotia: Their Country and Cognizance.' *Proceedings and Transactions of the Royal Society of Canada*, 2nd ser., 7 (May, 1901): 87–137.

Macmillan, Gerald. *Honours for Sale: The Strange Story of Maundy Gregory*. London: Richards, 1954.

Matheson, John R. 'Badge of Order Recalls Kipling Poem.' *Heraldry in Canada* 20, 2 (June 1986): 13.
– 'Symbolism of the Order of Canada.' *Heraldry in Canada* 20, no. 3 (September 1986): 8–9.
Maton, Michael. *The National Honours and Awards of Australia*. Kenthurst: Kangaroo, 1995.
McCreery, Christopher. 'Questions of Honour: Canadian Government Policy towards British Titular Honours, 1867–1935.' MA thesis, Queen's University, 1999.
– 'Honour Nation and Citizenship in a Multicultural Policy: Federal Public Honours in Canada, 1917–1997.' PhD thesis, Queen's University, 2003.
McMillan, James. *The Honours Game*. London: Frewin, 1969.
O'Shea, Phillippe. *Honours, Titles, Styles and Precedence in New Zealand*. Wellington: Government Printer, 1977.
Palmer, Harry. *125 Companions of the Order of Canada*. Ottawa: Canadian Communications Group, 1992.
Patterson, Stephen. *Royal Insignia: British and Foreign Order of Chivalry from the Royal Collection*. London: Merrell Holberton, 1998.
Phillips, Sir Hayden. *Review of the Honours System*. London: British Cabinet Office, 2004.
Risk, James C. *The History of the Order of the Bath and Its Insignia*. London: Spink & Son, 1972.
Shell, Donald. *The House of Lords*. New York: Harvester, 1992.
Stacey, C.P. 'Lord Monck and the Canadian Nation.' *Dalhousie Review* 32, no. 13 (1935): 179–91.
Stone, Lawrence. 'The Inflation of Honours.' *Past and Present* 3 (1958): 45–70.
Thomas, Wendy. *The Register of Canadian Honours*. Toronto: T.H. Best, 1991.
Thomson, Donald Walter. 'The Fate of Titles in Canada.' *Canadian Historical Review* 10 (1929): 236–46.
Tozer, Charles. *The Insignia and Medals of the Grand Prior of the Most Venerable Order of the Hospital of St. John of Jerusalem*. London: Hayward and Sons, 1975.
Vickers, Hugo. *Royal Orders: The Honours and the Honoured*. London: Broadwall, 1996.
Walker, John. *The Queen Has Been Pleased: The British Honours System at Work*. London: Secker & Warburg, 1986.
Werlich, Robert. *Orders and Decorations of All Nations*. Washington, D.C.: Quaker, 1974.

General

Bliss, Michael. *Right Honourable Men*. Toronto: HarperCollins, 1995.
Bourdieu, Pierre. *Outline of a Theory of Practice*. Cambridge: Cambridge University Press, 1977.
Bourinot, Sir J.G. *How Canada Is Governed*. Toronto: Copp Clark, 1909.
Creighton, Donald. *Canada's First Century: 1867–1967*. Toronto: Macmillan, 1970.
– *The Forked Road, 1939–1957*. Toronto: McClelland & Stewart, 1972.
Cross, Colin. *The Fall of the British Empire*. London: Penguin, 1968.
Dawson, R. MacGregor. *Democratic Government in Canada*. Toronto: University of Toronto Press, 1957.
– *The Government of Canada*. Toronto: University of Toronto Press, 1964.
– *The Principle of Official Independence: With Particular Reference to the Political History of Canada*. Toronto: P.S. King and Son, 1922.
Dicey, A.V. *Introduction to the Study of the Law of the Constitution*. London: Macmillan, 1961.
Dickason, Olive. *Canada's First Peoples*. Toronto: McClelland & Stewart, 1992.

Dirks, Nicholas. *The Hollow Crown: Ethnohistory of an Indian Kingdom*. Cambridge: Cambridge University Press, 1987.

English, John. *The Decline of Politics*. Toronto: University of Toronto Press, 1993.

English, John. Kenneth McLaughin, and P. Whitney Lackenbauer, eds. *Mackenzie King: Citizenship and Community*. Toronto: Robin Brass Studio, 2002.

Evatt, Herbert. *The King and His Dominion Governors*. London: Oxford University Press, 1936.

Ewers, John C. *Plains Indian History and Culture: Essays on Community and Change*. Norman: University of Oklahoma Press, 1998.

Farr, David. *The Colonial Office and Canada, 1867–1887*. Toronto: University of Toronto Press, 1955.

Fiddes, Sir George. *The Dominions and Colonial Office*. London: Putman's Sons, 1926.

Foote, Peter, and David Wilson. *The Viking Achievement: The Society and Culture of Medieval Scandinavia*. London: Sidwick & Jackson, 1970.

Forsey, Eugene. *The Royal Power of Dissolution of Parliament in the British Commonwealth*. Toronto: Oxford University Press, 1968.

Gibson, Frederick W. *Queen's University*. Vol. 2. *1917–1961*. Kingston: McGill-Queen's University Press, 1983.

Graham, Elizabeth. *Medicine Man to Missionary*. Toronto: Peter Martin Associates, 1975.

Granatstein, J.L. *Canada 1957–1967: The Years of Uncertainty and Innovation*. Toronto: McClelland & Stewart, 1986.

– *The Generals: The Canadian Army's Senior Commanders in the Second World War*. Toronto: Stoddart, 1993.

Hutchinson, Bruce. *Mr. Prime Minister, 1867–1964*. Toronto: Longmans, 1964.

Jenson, Latham. *Tin Hats, Oilskins and Seaboots*. Toronto: Robin Brass Press, 2000.

Keith, Arthur Berridale. *The Dominions as Sovereign States*. London: Macmillan, 1928.

– *The Sovereignty of the British Dominions*. London: Macmillan, 1929.

– *The War Governments of the British Dominions*. Oxford: Clarendon, 1921.

Lower, Arthur. *Canadians in the Making*. Toronto: Longmans, 1958.

– *Colony to Nation*. Toronto: Longmans, 1946.

MacKinnon, Frank. *The Crown in Canada*. Calgary: McClelland & Stewart, 1976.

Marshall, Geoffrey. *Parliamentary Sovereignty and the Commonwealth*. Oxford: Clarendon, 1957.

Martin, Ged. *Britain and the Origins of Canadian Confederation, 1837–1867*. Vancouver: UBC Press, 1995.

Matheson, John. *Canada's Flag: A Search for a Country*. Boston: G.K. Hall, 1980.

Miedema, Gary R. 'For Canada's Sake: The Re-visioning of Canada and the Re-structuring of Public Religion in the 1960s.' Unpublished PhD thesis, Queen's University, 2000.

Miller, Marc. *Canada's Navy: The First Century*. Toronto: University of Toronto Press, 1999.

Miquelon, Dale. *New France, 1701–1744*. Toronto: McClelland & Stewart, 1987.

Monet, Jacques. *The Canadian Crown*. Toronto: Clarke Irwin, 1979.

Morton, W.L. *The Critical Years: The Union of British North America, 1857–1973*. Toronto: McClelland & Stewart, 1964.

Nakaya, Ukichiro. *Snow Crystals: Natural and Artificial*. Cambridge: Harvard University Press, 1954.

Neuendorff, Gwen. *Studies in the Evolution of Dominion Status*. London: Allen Unwin, 1942.

O'Ballance, Edgar. *Islamic Fundamentalist Terrorism, 1979–1995*. London: Macmillan, 1997.

Roberts-Wray, Sir Kenneth. *Commonwealth and Colonial Law*. London: Stevens and Son, 1966.

Smith, David E. *The Invisible Crown*. Toronto: University of Toronto Press, 1995.

Stacey, C.P. *Official History of the Canadian Army in the Second World War*. Ottawa: Queen's Printer, 1955.

Thompson, John Herd, and Allen Seager. *Canada, 1922–1939: Decades of Discord*. Toronto: McClelland & Stewart, 1985.

Wilson, Harold. *The Imperial Policy of Sir Robert Borden*. Gainesville: University of Florida Press, 1966.

Illustration Credits

Agnes Etherington Art Centre, Queen's University: William Folger Nickle (Artist: Francis J. Haxby)

Associated Press Photo: Queen Mother and Order of Canada (Photographer: Stefan Rousseau/WPA POOL)

Beatty Collection: Five-levelled Order of Canada, c. 1972 (Photographer: C. McCreery); Bruce Beatty

Canadian Press Photo: Queen Elizabeth II and Roland Michener (Photographer: Doug Ball); Terry Fox

Canada Post Corporation: 1977 tenth anniversary stamp; 1992 twenty-fifth anniversary stamps

Canadian Heraldic Authority: Royal Arms of Canada, 1957 (Artist: Lt. Cdr. Alan Beddoe); Royal Arms of Canada, 1994 (Artist: Cathy Bursey-Sabourin); Ramon Hnatyshyn's Coat of Arms (Register of Arms); Israel Asper's Arms (Register of Arms); Yves Chevrier's Arms (Register of Arms); Vera Roberts (Register of Arms)

Government of Canada: Queen Elizabeth II

Sgt. Eric Jolin: Canada Medal English obverse and reverse; Canada Medal French obverse; Reverse of the Chancellor's Insignia; Medal of Courage of the Order of Canada obverse and reverse; Medal of Service of the Order of Canada obverse and reverse; Bronze Order of Canada Seal Matrix paperweight; Order of Canada china plate

Office of the Secretary of the Governor General: Adrienne Clarkson (Photographer: Andrew MacNaughton); Leopold Amyot; Judith Anne Larocque; Barbara Uteck (Photographer: Sgt. Joanne Stoeckl)

Library and Archives of Canada (formerly National Archives of Canada, [NAC]): Parliament during the Nickle Resolution debates, PA 139684; Sir Robert Borden, C 22567; William

Lyon Mackenzie King, PA 126949; Lord Alexander of Tunis, PA 144173; Vincent Massey, PA 144172; Lester Pearson and Georges Vanier; Esmond Unwin Butler, C-000945223; The Canadian Decoration of Honour, C 150107 (Artist: Lt. Cdr. Alan Beddoe); The Canadian Award of Honour, C 150108 (Artist: Lt. Cdr. Alan Beddoe); The Order of Canada 'Cadillac LaSalle Design.' RG 2 (Artist : Dr. Charles Comfort); Order of Canada 1966 Navy Dept Design 1 and 2, C 149932 and C 149937 (Artist: unknown); **(All of the following illustrations are photographed by John Evans.)** Sovereign's Insignia, C000945229; The Chancellor's Chain, C000945219; Roland Michener wearing the Insignia, C 002107538; Companion of the Order of Canada obverse and reverse, C 002107539 and C 002107540; Companion on a Ladies Bow, C 002107545; Officer of the Order of Canada obverse and reverse, C 002107541 and C 002107542; Officer on a Ladies Bow, C 002107546; Member of the Order of Canada obverse and reverse, C 0020107543 and C 002017533; Member on a Ladies Bow, C 002107547; Lester B. Pearson's Award Scroll, C 149981; Honours Secretariat Celebration Photo, 1977, C 000945224; Oscar Peterson, C 002107535; Béliveau, Michener, Howe, and Filion, E 002505301; Robertson Davies, E 002505722; Roloff Beny, E 002505723; Sister Gervais, E 002505724; Gordon Robertson, E 002505296; Paul Martin Sr, E 002505295; Margaret Lawrence, E 002505299; Iran hostage heroes, E 002505289; George Stanley, E 002505725; David Suzuki, E 2505726; Chief Dan George, E 002505302; Solange Chaput Rolland, E 002505297; Joyce Bryant, E 002505293; Tommy Douglas, E 0029505298; Jane Mallett, E 002505298; Patricia Messner, E 002505290; Kenojuak, E 002505291; Blanka Gyulari, E 002505292

National Capital Commission: Roland Michener; Jules Léger; Edward Schreyer; Jeanne Sauvé; Ramon Hnatyshyn; Roméo LeBlanc

Office of the Secretary of the Governor General: Lapel Insignia for C.C. (OSSG Pamphlet); Lapel Insignia for O.C. (OSSG Pamphlet); Lapel Insignia for C.M. (OSSG Pamphlet); Royal Arms Window (Photographer: Sgt. Joanne Stoeckl); Vice Regal Window (Photographer: Sgt. Joanne Stoeckl); Rick Hansen, GGC88-891; Nelson Mandela, GGC98; Paul Desmarais, GGC87-474; Peter Lougheed, GGC87-475; Eugene Forsey, GGC89-1524; Sir Christopher Ondaatje, GGC93-215-22; John Matheson, GGC89-1234; Agnes Benidickson, GGC98-030-12; Karen Kain, GGC91-4302; Etuangat Aksayook, GGC95-873-01; Hugh Unungai, GGC88-3098; Ann Saddlemyer, GGC96-134-11; Frank Shuster, GGC97-158-15; Jean Goodwill, GGC92-1323; Brian Mulroney, GGC98-530-13; Maurice Richard, GGC98-530-19; Wayne Gretzky, GGC98-011-21A; Sue Johanson, GGC01-0483-2A; Edward Broadbent, GGC02-0827-14A; John Fraser, GG02-0982; Roméo Dallaire, GGC03-0246-29; Margaret Catley-Carlson, GGC03-0088-25A; Irène d'Entremont, GGC02-1106-26 D; Catherine Hennessey, GGC01-0482-18A; Richard Ivey, GGC01-0116-4A; Gilles Turcot, GGC01-1185-2A; Charles Dutoit, GGC02-0051-23A

University of Toronto Archives: The Royal Order of Canada 'Massey/Turpin Design,' Massey Papers (Photographer: C. McCreery)

Index